Patents as an Incentive for Innovation

Patents as an Incentive for Innovation

Edited by

Rafał Sikorski
Żaneta Zemła-Pacud

Wolters Kluwer

Published by:
Kluwer Law International B.V.
PO Box 316
2400 AH Alphen aan den Rijn
The Netherlands
E-mail: international-sales@wolterskluwer.com
Website: lrus.wolterskluwer.com

Sold and distributed by:
Wolters Kluwer Legal & Regulatory U.S.
7201 McKinney Circle
Frederick, MD 21704
United States of America
Email: customer.service@wolterskluwer.com

ISBN 978-94-035-2413-9

e-Book: ISBN 978-94-035-2414-6
web-PDF: ISBN 978-94-035-2415-3

Editors

Rafał Sikorski is a Professor of Law at the Adam Mickiewicz University in Poznań (Poland). He obtained his LLM from Central European University in Budapest, and his PhD in 2005 from the Faculty of Law of the Adam Mickiewicz University. His major research areas include patent remedies, the nexus between IP and competition law, standard essential patents, as well as various forms of private ordering in IP and particularly patent law. He has published on patent pools, access to standard essential patents, patent remedies, conflicts-of-law rules for IP contracts and IP infringement as well as copyright law. Results of his research appeared in books published by publishers such as Edward Elgar, Cambridge University Press, Wolters Kluwer and C.H. Beck. At the Law Faculty of Adam Mickiewicz University, he teaches various courses on IP, Civil Law, Private International Law and European Union Law. Rafał Sikorski is also an attorney-at-law at one of the leading Polish law firms where he advises clients in matters related to licensing and protection of IP.

Żaneta Zemła-Pacud is an Assistant Professor at the Institute of Law Studies of the Polish Academy of Sciences. She graduated from Adam Mickiewicz University in Poznań in both law and European Studies and in 2012 she obtained her PhD from the Jagielloniean University in Cracow. Żaneta Zemła-Pacud has published extensively on Intellectual Property IP protection in life sciences. She has also led and organized domestic and international research projects in the field. As an external expert she served in the joint WIPO/PPO project on IP in the health sector in Poland. In 2017 and 2018 she was awarded Max-Planck-scholarships at the MPI for Innovation and Competition in Munich, and in 2020 she was granted a research stay at CEIPI, Strasbourg. She has taught IP law, patent law and new technologies at prominent Polish institutions, including the Jagiellonian University and Polish Academy of Sciences. Her present research is centred on test data as subject matter of regulatory exclusivities and trade secrets protection. Żaneta Zemła-Pacud leads the practice group Life Science in one of Poland's most prominent law firms.

Contributors

Iga Bałos earned her PhD in Law in 2015. Her thesis concerned arbitration in patent disputes. She obtained First Prize for the best doctoral thesis in the field of IP law in the competition organized by the Patent Office of the Republic of Poland. She is an Assistant Professor at Andrzej Frycz Modrzewski University in Kraków (Poland), where she teaches Patent Law and Entertainment Law. She is also of counsel in one of the IP law firms in Krakow. Her current research focuses on different implications of AI for patent law, particularly the issue of patent quality. As a legal practitioner she specializes in IP rights related to filmmaking process. She is an author of several publications on IP rights and unfair competition.

Rochelle Cooper Dreyfuss is the Pauline Newman Professor of Law at New York University School of Law and co-Director of its Engelberg Center on Innovation Law and Policy. She holds a BA in Chemistry from Wellesley College, an MS in Chemistry from the University of California at Berkeley and a JD from Columbia Law School. She has visited Cambridge University (as the Arthur Goodhart Visiting Professor), Swinburne University, Oxford University, the National University of Singapore, the University of Washington School of Law, the University of Chicago School of Law, and the Max Planck Institute. She served as a law clerk for Chief Judge Wilfred Feinberg (United States Court of Appeals for the Second Circuit) and United States Supreme Court Chief Justice Warren E. Burger. She was a co-Reporter of the American Law Institute's Project on Intellectual Property: Principles Governing Jurisdiction, Choice of Law, and Judgments in Transnational Disputes and served on National Academies of Sciences Committees on Intellectual Property in Genomic and Protein Research; on Intellectual Property in the Knowledge Based Economy; and on Science, Technology and Law. She was also a member of the National Institute of Health Advisory Committee on Genetics, Health and Society. Her writings include *A Neofederalist Vision of Trips: Building a Resilient International Intellectual Property System* (Oxford University Press 2012) (with Graeme Dinwoodie) and *Balancing Wealth and Health: The Battle over Intellectual Property and Access to Medicines In Latin America* (Oxford University Press 2014) (with César Rodríguez-Garavito). With Justine Pila, she edited

The Oxford Handbook of Intellectual Property Law (Oxford University Press 2018). Her recent work focuses on patent law, private international law, and state-to-state and investor-state dispute settlement.

Susy Frankel is a Professor of Law, Chair in Intellectual Property and International Trade and the Director of the New Zealand Centre of International Economic Law at Victoria University of Wellington. She joined Victoria University's Faculty of Law as a lecturer in 1997 and in 2008 was the first woman promoted to full professor in the Faculty. From 2008 to 2020, Professor Frankel was Chair of the New Zealand Copyright Tribunal. She was the President of the International Association for the Advancement of Teaching and Research in Intellectual Property (ATRIP) from 2015-2017. She teaches copyright, trademarks, patents, international intellectual property and international trade law. She has taught in several law schools abroad, including in 2020 as a Global Professor at New York University, School of Law. She is a member of the editorial boards of the Journal of World Intellectual Property Law and the Queen Mary Journal of Intellectual Property. Her scholarship focuses on international intellectual property and its nexus with the protection of indigenous peoples' knowledge and innovation; and on the relationship between intellectual property and international trade. Susy Frankel was elected Fellow of the Royal Society of New Zealand in 2018 and appointed as a member of the Waitangi Tribunal in 2020.

Alfred Früh is a Professor for Private Law with Focus on Life Science Law and Intellectual Property Law at the University of Basel. He also co-heads the Center for Life Sciences Law (CLSL) at the Department of Law. After obtaining his PhD in 2011, he took the bar in Switzerland and worked as an attorney with a major Swiss law firm. From 2016 to 2020, he was the Managing Director of the Center for Information Technology, Society, and Law (ITSL) at the University of Zurich. In the past, Professor Früh was a Guest Researcher at the Max Planck Institute for Innovation and Competition in Munich and a Visiting Researcher at the Humboldt Institute for Internet and Society in Berlin. He is the Managing Director of the Swiss Forum for Communications Law (SF-FS) and a member of the OECD's Blockchain Expert Policy Advisory Board (BEPAB). His research focuses on the interaction of intellectual property rights and new technologies in the data economy.

Dietrich Kamlah is a Patent Litigator at Taylor Wessing in Munich, where he became partner in 2008. His work includes the representation of clients in national and international patent infringement litigation as well as advice on contractual matters involving patents and technical know-how, such as R&D cooperation agreements. He also works on antitrust related issues in IP cases such as the licensing of standard essential patents and litigation in this field. Before going into private practice, Dietrich Kamlah studied law at the University of Passau and King's College London. After taking the German bar exam in 2000 he worked as lecturer at the University of Erlangen-Nuremberg where he completed his PhD with a thesis on antitrust law in 2002. He publishes regularly in the field of patent law.

Amandine Léonard is an Early Career Fellow in IP law at the University of Edinburgh. Her research and teaching interests lie primarily in the area of patent law and, in particular, patent enforcement. She also conducts research on the rationales and objectives of IP law, the approach adopted by the US and European countries regarding limitations and exceptions in IP law, the interface between competition law and IP law, as well as issues of liability for patent infringement in the fourth industrial revolution (4IR). Prior to joining the University of Edinburgh, she was an Emile Noël Postdoctoral Fellow at the Jean Monnet Center of NYU School of Law (2019-2020). In May 2019, she obtained her PhD from the KU Leuven on the topic of *Abuse of rights in European Patent Law: Reconsidering the principle of the prohibition of abuse of rights as an internal correction mechanism against over-enforcement practices by right holders*. After her PhD, she remained an Affiliated Researcher at the Center for IT&IP Law (CiTiP) of the KU Leuven.

Justyna Ożegalska-Trybalska is an Associate Professor at the Intellectual Property Law Chair of the Jagiellonian University in Krakow (Poland). She serves as an arbitrator at the Domain Name Arbitration Court at the Polish Chamber of Informatics and Telecommunication and WIPO Arbitration and Mediation Centre and a senior expert on innumerous international IP projects, coordinator of the Joint Master's Degree Programme in Intellectual Property and New Technologies organized by the Jagiellonian University, WIPO and the Polish Patent Office. She conducted research at the Columbia University School of Law in New York and the Max Planck Institute for Innovation and Competition in Munich. Justyna Ożegalska-Trybalska is an author of over 50 national and foreign publications in the field of the IP, new technologies, IP management and commercialization, including two monographs *Limitations of patent protection and patent infringement* (Wolters Kluwer, 2019); *Domain Name – legal issues* (Zakamycze, 2003). As a co-author, she contributed to *Domain Name Law and Practice. An International Handbook* (Oxford University Press, 2015), *Patent Law* and *Industrial Property Law System* (CH Beck, 2018).

Peter R. Slowinski is a Junior Research Fellow at the Max Planck Institute for Innovation and Competition in Munich. He is admitted as attorney-at-law (Rechtsanwalt) in Germany. He studied law at the University of Passau, the Ludwig Maximilians University Munich, Cardiff University in Wales and Stanford Law School. At Stanford Law School he obtained Master in the Science of Law (J.S.M.) after researching on alternative dispute resolution and patent law as part of the Stanford Program in International Legal Studies (SPILS). He has given lectures at Stanford Law School and the Munich Intellectual Property Law Center (MIPLC). Until 2016, he practised as a patent litigator in infringement and nullity proceedings with a global law firm in Munich. In this capacity he represented clients in the Regional and Higher Regional Courts in Germany as well as the German Federal Patent Court and the Federal Supreme Court. His research focuses on patents and dispute resolution. He has published on copyright law and patent law. Mr Slowinski has conducted an empirical study on mediation proceedings in patent law at Stanford Law School and participated in the SPC Study of the Max Planck Institute for Innovation and Competition. He is a member of the research groups on data driven economies and artificial intelligence as well as life sciences at the Max Planck Institute.

Agnieszka Sztoldman lectures at the Faculty of Law of the University of Wrocław and Kozminski University in Warsaw. She received her PhD from the University of Warsaw in 2017. As an attorney she specializes in industrial property law with particular focus on patents and trademarks. She gained experience at international law firms in Poland and France. She is an author of numerous publications and papers on IP law, including an English language version of the monograph *The Experimental Use and Related Exemptions under Patent Law in the EU* (Kluwer Law International), articles for leading international IP law journals and a co-author of the commentary to the Polish Industrial Property Law and Pharmaceutical Law. Agnieszka Sztoldman was a visiting researcher at Max Planck Institute, Institute of Europe and Jagiellonian University. She is currently a Senior Associate at Taylor Wessing, where she leads the Life Sciences practice in Poland and advises on complex, multi-jurisdictional legal challenges faced by life sciences and FMCG companies. Agnieszka Sztoldman is a member of APRAM, INTA, AIPPI and MARQUES societies.

Marek Świerczyński is a Professor of Law at the Cardinal Stefan Wyszyński University in Warsaw. He is also a practicing attorney, who advises businesses and organizations on pharmaceutical law, reimbursement law, IP law and IT & AI law. He serves as a consultant to the Council of Europe on electronic evidence and digitization of the judiciary. He is the Chairman of the Artificial Intelligence Law team at the Virtual Chair of Law and Ethics. Marek Świerczyński is an author of numerous scientific publications, including first Polish legal manuals on artificial intelligence (C.H. Beck 2020), biological medicinal products (Wolters Kluwer 2016, 2019, 2020) and pharmaceutical law (Wolters Kluwer 2008, 2012 and 2020). He is also an active arbitrator at the Arbitration Court for Internet Domains. He worked in Switzerland as the Legal Director for Africa, South Africa and Israel in a multinational pharmaceutical corporation. He is a long-time associate and counsel at leading law firms such as Kieszkowska Rutkowska Kolasiński, Baker & McKenzie and Traple Konarski Podrecki.

Geertrui Van Overwalle is a Professor of Intellectual Property Law and a Professor of Methodology of Legal Science at the Faculty of Law, University of Leuven (Belgium). She is also a Visiting Professor at the School of Law, Sciences-Po, Paris (France). In her research, Geertrui Van Overwalle focuses on patents, genetics and their impact on access to health. The results of this research have been published in many internationally peer reviewed journals, such as *Nature* and *Science*, and in her books. She also works on this thread of research in the domain of agriculture. In her recent scholarly work, Geertrui Van Overwalle also started a new line of research on the legal architectures and the normative implications of open innovation initiatives. In doing so, she explores both firm-centred and community-centred open innovation models in a wide range of technologies, ranging from life sciences, over design to 3D-printing and the Internet of Things. Geertrui Van Overwalle was a member of the Economic and Scientific Advisory Board (ESAB) of the European Patent Office. She served as a president of the European Policy for Intellectual Property (EPIP) Research Association. She was a member of the Board of Appeal of the Community Plant Variety Office at Angers and a member of the National Belgian High Council for Intellectual Property. She often contributes as an expert to the European Parliament and the European Commission.

Juan Antonio Vives-Vallés is a Professor of Law at the Private Law Department of the University of the Balearic Islands in Palma (Spain) and a Researcher at the Department of Agro-food Production of the Agro-Environmental and Water Economics Institute in Palma. He is interested in agriculture and plant biotech law, IP protection of plants, with a particular focus on plant variety rights. He is a Guest Associate Editor within the section Plant Breeding in Frontiers in Plant Science, as well as an Expert of the Legal Expert Group of the European Union Intellectual Property Office. Dr Vives-Vallés earned two degrees in Agricultural Engineering and Law from the University of the Balearic Islands as well as several master's degrees, e.g., in Agricultural Engineering (Spanish Lic.) from the School of Agrifood and Forestry Science and Engineering of Lleida (Catalonia, Spain), in Business Administration from IE Business School (Madrid, Spain), and in IP and Competition Law from the MIPLC (Munich, Germany). He carried out his PhD in Law and Plant Biology at the University of the Balearic Islands. Dr Vives-Vallés was a Guest Research and Scholarship Holder of the Max Planck Institute for Innovation and Competition (Munich, Germany) from 2016 to 2018, and a Trainee at the CPVO (Angers, France). Since 2017, he has been coordinating the creation of an international research network focusing on basic and applied research on IP in agriculture.

Tomasz Zimny is an Assistant Professor at the Institute of Law Studies of the Polish Academy of Sciences. He specializes in industrial property law and relations between normative systems and the development of life sciences. He focuses on the IP aspects of this development as well as legislation and moral dimension of biosafety and risk regulation in modern biotechnology, spanning from stem cell research to the use of GMOs in agriculture. He often cooperates and publishes with researchers representing such fields as molecular biology, biochemistry, genetics or plant breeding. His recent research focused on the analysis of proposals for the reform of the current European Union GMO legislation and was conducted at the Department of Plant Breeding of the Swedish University of Agricultural Sciences. Dr Zimny was a faculty member of the Bioethics Programme for Central and Eastern Europe organized by the Mount Sinai School of Medicine and Vilnius University. He has taught IP Law and Biosafety at various graduate and postgraduate courses, including at the University of Warsaw, the Warsaw University of Technology, Warsaw University of Life Sciences and others. Tomasz Zimny is also an attorney-at-law, providing services facilitating protection and commercialization of research results in academic institutions.

Helena Żakowska-Henzler is a Professor of Law at the Institute of Law Studies of the Polish Academy of Sciences where she leads the Department of Polish and European Industrial Property Law. She specializes in industrial property law. Her research concentrates on patent law in the field of biological/medical sciences and in particular justification and ethical aspects of patent protection and its relationship with other values and interests (e.g., public health, indigenous peoples' knowledge). In 2003 as a scholarship holder, she conducted research at the Max Planck Institute for Innovation and Competition in Munich. She is an author of the numerous publications in the field of the industrial property law, including the monograph *Biotechnology Inventions – Subject of Patent Protection* (2006) and *European Union Internal Market and Intellectual Property Law* (2013). As co-author, she contributed to *Industrial Property Law System* (CH Beck, 2018).

Summary of Contents

Table of Contents

Foreword: The Complex Terrain of Intellectual Property Governance

Rochelle Cooper Dreyfuss

The concept for this book was formulated in 2018, long before the COVID-19 pandemic was on the horizon. However, it could not have been published at a more opportune moment. The intense global efforts underway to find diagnostics; treatments; vaccines; and technologies for analysing outbreaks, testing medications, and tracing infected individuals raise precisely the question explored in this volume: how can patent rights be deployed to incentivize investments in researching and developing socially critical innovations without sacrificing the public's interest in sharing the benefits that are produced?

The fascinating chapters included here examine this issue in four contexts, the life sciences, agriculture, artificial intelligence (AI) and information technology. Together, these contributions illustrate the many difficulties inherent in motivating invention while ensuring that its fruits are efficiently disseminated. Foremost among the problems are the many significant differences among innovations. Some, as Żaneta Zemła-Pacud describes, are revolutionary and fundamentally change the approach to particular technological problems; others represent modifications, improvements, or – as may be the case with many treatments for COVID-19 – the repositioning of existing technologies to meet new needs. Some advances have acceptable substitutes; others, such as antibiotics, are needed because existing technologies have failed or are floundering. Some inventions deal with crucial social problems, like nutrition; others are aimed at more attenuated concerns, such as computer gaming. Some technologies are clearly beneficial, whereas others, such as the human enhancement technologies described by Helena Żakowska-Henzler, are potentially dangerous or morally ambiguous.

Second, there are distinctions in how the period of exclusivity interacts with demand for a patented advance and its rivals. In some cases, the patentee can obtain benefits for the entire term of protection because the market is poised to immediately use the invention. But, as with pharmaceuticals, marketing may be delayed by the approval process or, as for computers and AI, it may take the public a long time to understand the value of the innovation and begin to purchase it. By the same token, there are innovations that rivals can make immediately available upon patent expiration, but in other cases, such as where competitors also need market approval, the patent term may be followed by a period of de facto exclusivity. Additionally, the markets for some innovations are inherently large. For example, the entire planet must be vaccinated against the coronavirus. However, some markets are naturally limited, either because the population that needs the invention is small or because few of the many who need it can afford to pay supra-competitive prices. Examples mentioned in the book include treatments for neglected diseases and plants bred for particular environments.

In addition, as Justyna Ożegalska-Trybalska's chapter points out, there are significant sectoral differences. In some fields, such as pharmaceuticals, innovation is risky and significant investments may be necessary. In those areas, inventors require a long period of protection from free-riding competitors to capture an adequate return. In other sectors, the argument for patent protection is weaker. For example, in computer technology, where upfront costs are lower, innovation entails less risk. Moreover, there are mechanisms such as network effects, licensing and servicing possibilities, or in-app purchases that prolong lead time or provide sufficient compensation in other ways. There are also fields where user-innovation (innovations developed by users for their own needs) is common and therefore external rewards are less important. Thus, as Juan Antonio Vives-Vallés notes, farmers are also breeders; they can often benefit directly from their inventions.[1] There are also subject areas where inventions may be found in Pasteur's Quadrant, that is, where an advance is simultaneously a fundamental scientific discovery (e.g., the discovery of the genetic cause of a disease) as well as a technological application (the diagnostic for the disease).[2] Although the discovery may be one innovator's output, for which it seeks a financial return, for other researchers, it is a necessary input. Geertrui Van Overwalle's contribution illustrates how this duality can affect progress in the agricultural sector. As the contributions of Dieter Kamlah and Rafał Sikorski suggest, an analogous dynamic operates in the ICT sector, where concerns about interoperability can require that rivals use one another's patented technologies.

These differences – among advances, in the relationship between demand and the period of protection, and among technological sectors – clash with the trans-substantive nature of patent legislation. These laws are drafted abstractly in order to ensure that they readily apply to every conceivable technical advance. As a result, they do not generally make any of these critical distinctions. Thus, one of this book's key contributions lies in exploring the mechanisms for dealing with the friction between generalized application and specialized concerns.

1. For an extended discussion of user innovation, *see* Eric von Hippel, *Sources of Innovation* (Oxford University Press 1988).
2. *See, e.g.*, Donald E. Stokes, *Pasteur's Quadrant: Basic Science and Technological Innovation* (Brookings Institution Press 1996).

One approach is to craft defences to infringement liability that respond to specific issues. For example, Agnieszka Sztoldman's chapter addresses the effort to shorten the delay between the expiration of pharmaceutical patents and generic entry though the so-called regulatory review exception, which permits generic pharmaceutical firms to use the patent period to generate the data they need to obtain market clearance. In addition, she notes, many countries recognize a general experimental use defence to facilitate basic research involving necessary patented inputs. These exceptions, which are geared to specific public concerns, can be helpful. However, striking the balance in this way relies heavily on judicial interpretation of the relevant exception. As Sztoldman shows, courts can easily miss the mark and narrow or expand exceptions in ways that do not fulfil the original intent of the legislature.

That said, interpretation itself offers a mechanism for dealing with particular problems, for with careful statutory construction, judges can tailor general provisions to specific fields. In their well-known book, *The Patent Crisis and How the Courts Can Solve It*, Mark Lemley and Dan Burk give the example of the height of the inventive step. Because it is measured by the knowledge of those with ordinary skill in the art, the authors argue that it can be used to adjust this criterion of patentability to the level of sophistication in the technological field to which the invention pertains.[3] An analogous approach is discussed here by Alfred Früh, who considers how patent law's disclosure requirement should be adapted for inventions involving AI. But even with judges highly attuned to legislative intent, interpretive approaches are limited, for without an appropriate statutory hook, it is not possible to deal with every distinctions identified in this volume.

A third idea is to address these differences from 'the outside' – through laws and policies external to the framework of exclusive rights. For example, Tomasz Zimny's empirical study of patenting in the agricultural sector demonstrates the significant influence of legislation regarding genetically modified foods, an area in the 'potentially harmful' category of advances. Similarly, in Amandine Léonard's examination of the opportunistic behaviour of patent assertion entities, she considers tackling the problem not only from the inside, through the remedial provisions of patent law, but also through procedural approaches, such as limitations on standing, as well as the application of substantive competition law. More generally, Vives-Vallés illustrates the effect of the EU's Common Agricultural Policy on exclusive rights aimed at innovations regarding plants. But as these authors show, governance from outside the exclusive rights system is not a perfect solution. Indeed, laws and policies aimed, in part, at issues other than innovation can work at cross purposes with regimes that are focused on promoting invention and ensuring public access.

An intermediate approach is therefore attractive and several of the contributions to this volume discuss such a mechanism: a series of exclusive right regimes layered on top of general patent law, each directed at specific problems. Thus Zemła-Pacud describes the use of Supplementary Protection Certificates (SPCs) to compensate originator pharmaceutical companies for regulatory delay. She also mentions orphan

3. Dan L. Burk and Mark A. Lemley, *The Patent Crisis and How the Courts Can Solve It* (University of Chicago Press 2009).

drug and paediatric exclusivities to improve incentives to find treatments for diseases that afflict small or poor populations. Similarly, the EU's Biotech Directive is layered over the European Patent Convention (EPC) in order to clarify certain of the difficult issues raised by biotechnology, such as the protectability and morality of according private rights over material derived from the human body. So too for plants, where the EU relies on the EPC, the Biotech Directive, and the Community Plant Variety Rights System to adjust the balance between innovators, breeders, and consumers. In many cases, patent holders can also avail themselves of trade secrecy protection. For instance, the training data used to perfect patented innovations in the AI sector are arguably trade secrets in that they often remain, as Früh notes, undisclosed in patents. Similarly, innovators in the pharmaceutical and agricultural chemical industries can rely on data exclusivity regimes to protect the information they must generate to acquire market approval for their patented products.

While layering offers interesting opportunities to overcome the generality of trans-substantive basic laws within an exclusivity framework, this approach has problems of its own. Each layer requires interpretation, which, as with patent rights themselves, can be more or less in line with legislative intent. They also come with their own set of exceptions, such as the SPC export exemption discussed by Ożegalska-Trybalska, which preserves EU generic manufacturers' competitive position outside the EU. Moreover, the multiplicity of layers raises concerns about overlap. In particular, innovators can sometimes fit their advances into several focused regimes and thereby acquire more exclusivity than was intended by the legislature. And the public may receive less than expected because the exceptions provided to safeguard its interests in one system may not carry over to other relevant legislation.

To some extent, these problems may be avoided through private ordering. This approach, discussed in the chapters by Kamlah and Sikorski, is particularly prevalent in the ICT sector. Because interoperability is a key concern, rivals join standard setting organizations to choose particular technologies for common use and agree that patents essential to the standard will be licensed on fair, reasonable, and non-discriminatory (FRAND) terms. Ostensibly, this approach solves the input/output problem and protects consumers' interest in ensuring that their purchases have broad applicability and enduring utility. However, courts have had particularly difficult interpretive problems in connection with this practice. Private agreements can raise hard questions about what the parties meant, such as whether they intended to preclude injunctive relief or how they expected the royalty rate to be calculated. Moreover, private ordering relies on voluntary action by right holders. As a consequence, it has less potential than state action to protect public concerns. Indeed, private ordering can work in reverse and destroy the balance states have struck. Private agreements lend themselves to anticompetitive practices, such as collusive standard setting agreements and as Leonard documents, in certain fields, right holders can adopt litigation strategies that enable them to extract royalties that far exceed the value of the intellectual contributions represented by their patents.

Finally, there is the matter of international law. As Susy Frankel observes, the desire to be part of a global trading system can lead countries to agree in multinational, regional, and bilateral settings to obligations that are stronger than what they might see as the optimal domestic balance. Moreover, the objectives of public regarding national legislation can be obscured through dispute resolution in international tribunals, such as the World Trade Organization's Dispute Settlement Body (DSB).

What emerges is a complex terrain of governance regimes, comprising national laws (e.g., Polish law), regional laws (such as EU law), supraregional law (the EPC), and international law (the UPOV Convention, the TRIPS Agreement, the Paris Convention). Laws are applied and interpreted by local administrative agencies (such as domestic patent offices); by regional administrative agencies (such as the European Patent Office); by local and regional courts, some specialized (e.g., the United States Court of Appeal for the Federal Circuit) and some general (such as the Court of Justice of the European Union); and by international tribunals (the WTO's DSB and Tribunals established under the authority of the International Center for the Settlement of Investment Disputes (ICSID) or the UN Conference on Trade and Development (UNCTAD)).

What should we make of this fragmented picture? To some extent, fragmentation is inevitable. After all, a law designed to encourage advances beyond the abilities of the ordinary artisan is sure to produce advances beyond the imagination of the ordinary legislator. Thus, it must be expected that not every breakthrough will fit comfortably into existing legislative frameworks. For example, as Marek Świerczyński notes, biopharmaceuticals are medicines, but they are nothing like the medicines that existed when most patent acts were drafted. Coping with the differences between small and large molecules requires rethinking many issues, including determinations of infringement, identifying acceptable generic substitutes, and developing methodologies for ensuring safety. Similarly it has only recently become evident that AI would reach a point where a machine might, as Peter R. Slowinski claims, be an inventor. It is not insignificant that the identical pattern is found in the copyright sector, where a succession of new technologies have spawned a multiplicity of national laws, regional legislation – in the EU, numerous directives – and international instruments (the Berne Convention; TRIPS; the WIPO Copyright Treaty; the WIPO Performances and Phonograms Treaty; and the Marrakesh Treaty to Facilitate Access to Published Works for Persons Who Are Blind, Visually Impaired or Otherwise Print Disabled).

Fragmentation is also advantageous. To paraphrase U.S. Supreme Court Justice Louis Brandies, as new technologies emerge, states and regions can serve as laboratories and try novel experiments without risk to the rest of the world.[4] Once a novel way to deal with the problems posed by a new technology proves successful, other countries will adopt it; when a degree of convergence is achieved, the solution can be 'uploaded' to the international system.[5] The novel approach might prove useful in connection with other emerging developments. The COVID-19 pandemic may turn out to furnish a good example. Never has the need to strike the right balance between innovation and access been clearer and countries are, in fact, experimenting with

4. *New State Ice Co. v. Liebmann*, 285 U.S. 262, 272 (1932).
5. For further discussion, *see* Graeme B. Dinwoodie and Rochelle C. Dreyfuss, *A Neofederalist Vision of TRIPS: The Resilience of the International Intellectual Property Regime* (Oxford University Press 2012).

multiple responses: government funding, crown use, compulsory licensing schemes, encouraging private ordering such as pooling and private-public partnerships, and claiming ownership interest in inventions produced in government laboratories. Surely, much will be learned by observing how these variations play out. Once it is understood how to strike the balance that best facilitates global cooperation at both the research and dissemination stages, international, regional, and domestic laws and institutions will hopefully adapt and the world will be better prepared the next time a pandemic strikes.

To be sure, fragmentation also has significant costs. Current work on COVID-19 illustrates how transnational collaborations and transactions are more difficult when there are multiple regimes, with different levels of deference to right holder concerns and with different ideas about where distributional priorities lie. Some actions will likely lead to lawsuits and international dispute resolution, conducted before multiple adjudicators. These possibilities reduce legal certainty and can result in inconsistent judgments and over- or under-deterrence. And those problems can, in turn, affect the power of the law to promote investments in innovation. There are, however, several efforts to reduce incoherence. Transnational administrative networks, such as fiveI-Poffices, a coalition of national patent offices, identify regulations, laws, and legal interpretations that are causing a high degree of friction and bring them to the attention of legislators.[6] Multinational disputes can sometimes be resolved through private arbitration.[7] Some courts have consolidated global disputes, and have not only brought peace to the parties in a single forum, but also harmonized the interpretation of disparate national laws.[8] The Vienna Convention on the Law of Treaties deals with fragmentation at the international level, as does the work of Martii Koskenniemi for a Study Group of the International Law Commission of the United Nations.[9] Of course, at the end of the day, it may be necessary to rethink the entire system, as Iga Bałos suggests in the AI context. Which approach is best is a difficult question to answer. Fortunately, books like this one can help us understand the problems and think through the options.

---

6. Anne-Marie Slaughter, A New World Order (Princeton University Press 2004); Kal Raustiala, *The Architecture of International Cooperation: Transgovernmental Networks and the Future of International Law*, 43 Va. J. Int'l L. 1 (2002); FiveIPOffices, https://www.fiveipoffices.org/index.
7. *See, e.g.*, Trevor Cook and Alejandro I. Garcia. *International Intellectual Property Arbitration* (Kluwer Law International 2010).
8. *See, e.g., Actavis UK Ltd v. Eli Lilly and Company* [2017] UKSC 48; *Unwired Planet International Ltd v. Huawei Technologies (UK) Co Ltd.*, [2020] UKSC 37.
9. *See* Vienna Convention on the Law of Treaties, opened for signature 23 May 1969 (entered into force 27 January 1980), 1155 U.N.T.S. 331; Rep. of the Study Grp. of the Int'l Law Comm'n, Fragmentation of International Law: Difficulties Arising from the Diversification and Expansion of International Law, 58th Sess., 1 May - 9 June, 3 July - 11 Aug. 2006, U.N. Doc. A/CN.4/L.682 (13 April 2006), as corrected, U.N. Doc. A/CN.4/L.682/Corr.1 (11 August 2006) (finalized by Martti Koskenniemi).

Introduction

Rafał Sikorski & Żaneta Zemła-Pacud

Innovation has always affected the way we live. It has led to tremendous progress in areas such as medicine or agriculture. It has transformed the way we communicate with each other. Thanks to human inventiveness, we can work, study and have access to entertainment in the digital environment. However, innovation has also posed numerous challenges to values, such as human dignity, privacy or integrity of the human body.

Encouraging innovation is certainly desirable. One of the tools used to provide incentives for innovation is granting legal protection for human creation. Technical innovation is specifically incentivized by means of patent systems, with patents being a reward for human inventiveness.

A well-functioning patent system needs, however, to balance various interests, that is, provide incentives for valuable innovation, safeguard dynamic competition and protect the public interest.

The relationship between innovation and its legal protection via intellectual property rights in general, and patents in particular, is a very complex issue. It needs to be considered on various levels and from multiple perspectives. This book deals mostly with patent law but is not limited to it—it also covers other intellectual property (IP) regimes of protection for technical innovation, such as plant variety protection, supplementary protection certificates, and regulatory data protection. Protectability criteria, the length and scope of the granted protection, exemptions, exclusions, and limitations of IP rights, and eventually, enforcement of rights are the perspectives taken into consideration by the authors. These aspects are analyzed on the domestic, international, and global levels.

An intrinsic feature of technological development is its acceleration over centuries and decades. Hence, IP systems need continuous rethinking and recalibrating. This is especially the case in the highly sensitive sectors we chose for consideration by the authors, namely healthcare, plants, Information and Communication Technologies (ICT) and Artificial Intelligence (AI).

Part I of the book is devoted to legal protection of pharmaceuticals. This sector, one of the greatest beneficiaries of the patent system, has always been subject to tensions among its stakeholders. Nowadays, the need for both plausible innovation and sustainable access to it is more significant than ever. The chapters presented here provide reflections on balanced legal framework of IP protection for pharmaceuticals from various perspectives. This part begins with a consideration of the fundamental paradigms of international IP law and innovation policy. Three further texts deal with the subject matter of protection. They cover a general analysis of the threshold of protected—and incentivized—innovation and, subsequently, capture the irregularities of supporting two specific kinds of inventions: human enhancement technologies and biologic medicines. Finally, with chapters dedicated to the regulatory testing exemption and the supplementary protection certificate (SPC) manufacturing waiver, this part explores the correlations between innovation and limitations of IP rights.

Part I begins with Susy Frankel's chapter, which focuses on the connections between intellectual property rights and trade in the context of innovation. She reaches to the very essence of both trade and patents, searching for their value for modern societies and the economic and social rationales underlying their domestic and international legal constructs. While depicting the global landscape of patent protection in the post-TRIPS era, she points to an increasing number of deficiencies of the status quo, which undermine the primary goal of patents, i.e., to incentivize innovation. Frankel analyzes a handful of very recent developments, such as intensification of protectionist tendencies, a break down in the multilateral system of dispute settlement, or the implications of the European Union (EU) having changed its approach to Trade-Related Aspects of Intellectual Property Rights (TRIPS) flexibilities. Frankel concludes with evidence that when it comes to incentivizing innovation, informed multilateralism is preferable to Free Trade Agreements (FTAs).

Żaneta Zemła-Pacud's chapter presents the role of patents, SPC, and data exclusivity in stimulating primary and secondary innovation in the pharmaceutical area. The author discusses what threshold of pharmaceutical innovation renders it eligible for IP protection. She presents recent developments within the SPC system in this regard, depicts the specific targets of regulatory incentives, and shows the shortages of the European patent system in stimulating valuable pharmaceutical innovation. Zemła-Pacud names several postulates concerning the interpretation of the examined protectability criteria to secure their better correspondence with stimulating non-trivial innovation, to achieve a higher degree of legal certainty, and to provide a more balanced competitive environment in the pharmaceutical field.

Helena Żakowska-Henzler discusses the patentability of human enhancement technologies (HET), i.e., innovations aiming at improving physical, intellectual, and psychological skills and abilities. The author outlines the controversies about the possible consequences of HET and examines their consistency with the values underlying modern social and legal orders. Against this background, Żakowska-Henzler deals with the patentability criteria of the HET subject matter, taken as a decisive factor of legal control over HET, and discusses the appropriate scope of patent monopoly over HET. Considering the early stage of HET and uncertainty about their further developments, she underlines the need for careful assessment of current cases, which should in effect lead to the creation of well-weighted instruments for limiting patent rights over HET. Another controversial subject matter of patent protection and the subject of Marek Świerczyński's chapter is biological medicines. Referring to their growing importance in the health sector and both technical and functional specifics, which clearly distinguish them from other medicinal products, the author argues for their legal separation as a subject of legal protection. In the view of the author, there is a need for strong patent protection incentivizing innovation of biopharmaceuticals, which are characterized by higher costs and longer time of clinical trials. Special attention and an adjusted legal framework should also be given to biosimilars—medicines following up innovative biologic drugs.

Agnieszka Sztoldman thoroughly considers the limitations of IP rights in pharma. First, she discusses the regulatory testing exemption. Though not impacting innovation directly, it significantly influences the balance of rights in the pharmaceutical market by preventing unduly prolonged patent and SPC monopolies and by stimulating competitive activity and follow-up generic production. Sztoldman observes a shift in the interpretation of the regulatory testing exemption in recent years in the EU and examines whether this shift fits the purpose of the exemption. In conclusion, the author opts for giving it a broad scope of application as corresponding to its social and economic importance.

Justyna Ożegalska-Trybalska, in turn, focuses on supplementary protection certificates and their limitation by means of an SPC manufacturing waiver—a derogation from SPC rights allowing for manufacture and stockpiling of generic medicines for export. The author presents this exemption in a twofold narration: as an incentive for the generic industry to develop their production capacity and as a disincentive for innovators, discouraging them from conducting R&D works in Europe. Ożegalska-Trybalska locates the exemption as a part of a broader EU policy towards the limitation of exclusive IP rights for the sake of better-balanced interests of patent holders and third parties and poses a set of questions for future, more evidence-based considerations.

Part II of the book is dedicated to IP protection for plants. The rules for the protection of plants, although typically not seen as being as controversial as those for pharmaceuticals, do indicate great complexity. Due to their economic and social importance for nutrition and as environmental safeguards, here again, the values of innovation and access need to be reflected in the relevant legislation in a harmonized way. Interestingly, the three following chapters show the interrelations between various legal orders in the context of enhancing plant innovation, namely, between patents and breeders' rights, between patents and regulatory frameworks, and eventually, between patents and the common agricultural policy of the EU. These chapters prove that no part of the IP regime can be considered in separation from its broader legal, economic, and social background.

Part II begins with Geertrui Van Overwalle's chapter in which she searches for a legal framework optimal for follow-up plant innovation, inherent for breeding activity and necessary for fulfilling viable social interests. The author revisits the very foundations of IP protection for plants and examines the exclusivity/access balance in this field through the lens of the type/token ontology. Her thorough analysis of both the patent regime and the system of plant variety protection concludes with recommendations of how public and private ordering mechanisms can assist in rebalancing the exclusion/access in the plant area. Finally, van Overwalle leaves open the question of deploying type/token ontology into IP theory and suggests further research areas to be explored.

In the next chapter, Tomasz Zimny takes a closer look at patent law, EU laws on the usage of genetically modified organisms (GMO), and patent data in order to see if the patentability of plants in Europe plays the role of a driving force for innovation. He proves that the development of plant biotechnology, in particular in agriculture, is to a large extent independent from the possibility of patenting plants or their groups warranted by modern patent law. In conclusion, he highlights other factors not connected with patent law as having a bigger impact on the development and widespread adoption of the products of modern agricultural biotechnology.

Juan Antonio Vives-Vallés focuses on an exemption fundamental for the breeder's rights system, namely the farm-saved seed exemption (FSS). The author analyzes its grounds and scope under the Community Plant Variety Rights (CVPR) system and the adjustment to the FSS under the UPOV system. He concludes that the scope of the FSS provisions at the EU level and in some EU Member States appears to be beyond the limits set in EU primary and secondary legislation. To address these issues, Vives-Valles proposes an amendment of the list of species covered by the exemption. By recouping for breeders, the incentives partially lost in the current configuration of the FSS, the proposed modification is supposed to have a positive effect on plant innovation.

Part III of the book is concerned with the challenges that AI poses to patent law. The three chapters that can be found in this section deal with the most fundamental concepts of patent law. These chapters also provide basic, though highly relevant information on what AI actually is and how AI systems function. Concepts such as AI-related invention, patent eligibility, novelty, inventive step as well the requirement of sufficient disclosure are analyzed in the context of the growing importance of AI.

Iga Bałos deals with the question of patent eligibility of AI-related inventions. Her chapter is divided into three sections, which are followed by the final section, where possible future scenarios related to AI patents are discussed and concluding remarks are presented. In the first part, the author presents the current state of discussions on the eligibility of AI-related patents from the US and European perspectives. It also gives an overview of the existing practice of the EPO and the USTPO. The second part attempts to answer the question of whether patent protection for AI-related inventions is justified from the perspective of stimulating innovation. The author draws on the experience with software patents to show that the availability of patent protection may stifle innovation. The third part discusses public interest concerns in the context of AI-related patents.

Alfred Früh's chapter deals with the disclosure requirement in patent law and how it is challenged by AI. The author perceives the disclosure requirement as central to patent law as the disclosure justifies granting exclusive right to practice the disclosed invention. Früh realizes that if the disclosure was fundamentally challenged by AI, the patent system would run the risk of losing its legitimacy. The author suggests that the use of AI may lead to new disclosure deficits as some AI-related patents may be considered insufficiently disclosed and lacking reproducibility. However, Früh points to the fact that AI could also remedy imbalances in the disclosure requirement. The author recognizes the need for rebalancing the quid pro quo bargain of patent law's contract theory and suggests two types of solutions. First, he suggests changes to substantive patent law and proposes that patentees should be required to disclose the best mode of working their invention. Secondly, he proposes that changes to the substantive patent law should be paired with technical remedies such as a better (AI-powered) use of the patent register to the benefit of the public.

Peter R. Slowinski believes that the rise of AI provides an excellent opportunity to examine the foundations, key concepts and the functioning of the patent system. He provides valuable insights into the most widely used AI technologies and looks at how the use of AI influences the application of patentability criteria such as novelty and inventive step. The author is fully aware of AI's limitations and observes, for example, that AI systems are not able to recognize the need for a new invention on their own. AI still needs humans in order to be fed with the required data and to be equipped with proper models and algorithms. However, the author points out, as AI systems evolve and become more widely used, their application should make the process of innovation easier, faster, and cheaper. Consequently, lower costs of innovation will undermine the justification for charging monopoly prices to recoup the costs of innovation. He also suggests that in some areas, the need for patents as incentives for innovation may disappear and that other justifications for the patent system as making new knowledge available through the patent register or the possibility to trade intangible goods will become more important.

Part IV of the book deals with selected aspects of patent enforcement. The authors examine whether the enforcement mechanisms in place allow balancing the rights of patent holders and those using and implementing patented technologies. With more and more cases of excessive enforcement of patents, it has now become clear that enforcement, when excessive, allows the patent holders to stifle a lot of valuable follow-on innovation. The first article deals with abusive practices adopted by non-practicing entities and particularly patent assertion entities. The second is a review of the jurisprudence of the German courts concerning disputes related to standard essential patents. The final chapter deals with the dilemma currently faced by litigants in numerous courts in various jurisdictions around the world, whether holders of standard essential patents are free to decide whether to license makers of component parts or the manufacturers of final products. All three chapters show that the way we structure patent law enforcement mechanisms may have a significant effect on how patents impact innovation.

Amandine Léonard deals with abusive practices by non-practicing entities, particularly by a particular subset of such entities, namely patent assertion entities. Though traditionally such entities have been active in the United States, many reports and studies show that more and more cases are initiated by such entities in Europe. Leonard analyzes the case law from leading European courts and looks at whether national courts have taken into account the status of patent litigants in deciding in patent infringement cases. The author also looks at the mechanisms that the courts use to deal with such excessive patent enforcement. Having analyzed the case law, Leonard sees the mechanisms capable of countering excessive enforcement in EU competition law and the negotiating framework resulting from CJEU's decision in *ZTE v. Huawei*. She also points to the possibility of using rules of unfair competition as well as general principles prohibiting abuse of rights or requiring right holders, including IP right holders, to act in good faith. The author also notices the reluctance of the courts to refer more broadly to the principle of proportionality in the application of remedies, even though the Enforcement Directive explicitly refers to that principle.

In his chapter, Dieter Kamlah deals with access to standard essential patents under German law. Germany has traditionally been one of the leading jurisdictions for patent litigation. It is no different with the litigation concerning standard essential patents. Kamlah, before analyzing the application of the *Huawei v. ZTE* framework by courts in Germany, explains the legal consequences and nature of the FRAND commitments made by standard essential patent holders. He stresses that the FRAND commitments result in obligations under contract and competition law. The main part of the chapter contains an analysis of the most crucial and recent case law concerning access to standard essential patents. Kamlah draws interesting conclusions and shows, among others, that the negotiation process must be transparent. This means that holders of standard essential patents when making their offers, must make other, prior licensing contracts available to potential licensees. He also notices quite a significant degree of flexibility with which the German courts assess the behavior of the parties during licensing negotiations. Finally, the author also realizes that certain issues concerning SEP licensing still remain unresolved by the courts.

Finally, in the last chapter, Rafał Sikorski analyzes whether standard essential patent holders, who committed during the standard-setting process to license their patents on FRAND terms, are free to decide whether to license makers of components (such as chips that enable connectivity with communication networks) or producers of final products (such as smartphones or cars). The author analyzes how refusals to license component makers should be assessed under competition law. Sikorski discusses US court decisions in *FTC v. Qualcomm*. He is critical of the approach taken by the Court of Appeals for the 9th Circuit, which reversed the decision reached by Judge Lucy Koh of the District Court in California and sees it as extremely formalistic in the way in which it approached the competition consequences of the practices and licensing policies adopted by those who refuse to license their SEPs to component makers. Sikorski also analyzes the recent developments in the EU. He considers the most recent developments in the German courts, particularly the questions referred to the CJEU in *Nokia v. Daimler*.

The COVID-19 pandemic does not make the reflection on patents as incentives to innovation easier. On the contrary, it clearly shows the urgent need to rethink the balance between exclusivity and access. It also fosters thinking about private ordering mechanisms that could be deployed without prejudice for innovation and with great benefit to efficient exploitation of patented solutions. In short, it reveals how many recalibrations need to be done within patent law and in other IP systems protecting technology. We do hope this book will contribute to a better understanding of many phenomena causing tensions between innovation— and IP protection.

Part I Patents and the Health Sector

CHAPTER 1

TRIPS and Post-TRIPS Trade Agreements and Their Impact on Innovation

Susy Frankel

1 INTRODUCTION

The nexus between intellectual property law and trade is not new, but it has evolved in ways that challenge whether international intellectual property law really supports innovation. The cross-border activities of those producing and those seeking new inventions and access to new technology, new works of art and literature spurred the creation of the earliest multilateral international intellectual property agreements. An example was the development of protection for when inventions were exhibited internationally.[1] There was concern that such exhibiting was an important way of knowledge sharing, but that it should not be used to create opportunities for misappropriation by others or for patentability to be destroyed because exhibition could undermine novelty.[2] So, the Paris Convention for the Protection of Industrial Property included protection both to encourage such exhibition and to retain the possibility of patenting the invention.[3] The free use of books in places where they were traded, without there being copyright protection, gave rise to much controversy. Indeed, in the

1. Paris Convention for the Protection of Industrial Property (as amended on 28 September 1979), (Paris Convention), Art. 11 provides, '(1) The countries of the Union shall, in conformity with their domestic legislation, grant temporary protection to patentable inventions, utility models, industrial designs, and trademarks, in respect of goods exhibited at official or officially recognized international exhibitions held in the territory of any of them.'
2. Novelty or newness was a requirement for patentability in most jurisdictions. Now international law requires that inventions must be novel to be patentable, *see* Agreement on Trade-Related Aspects of Intellectual Property Rights (opened for signature 15 April 1994, entered into force 1 January 1996) 1869 UNTS 299 (TRIPS Agreement), Art. 27.1.
3. Paris Convention, Art. 11. For a discussion of the history of patents and the great exhibitions, *see* Megan Richardson, *Patents and Exhibitions*, (2009) 12 Journal of World Intellectual Property 402.

United Kingdom, a Royal Commission (an independent inquiry of the highest order) was established to address not only the protection of literary property but also its effects on trade.[4] As Lauriat has said:[5]

> The doctrine of free trade dominated Victorian political discourse for decades, including debates about copyright law. But professed free trade advocates could and did disagree profoundly on the question of copyright. Some saw it as an illegitimate restriction on trade, while others viewed it as a mode of enforcing a natural property right.

A few years earlier, a Royal Commission inquired about the value and scope of patents in the face of growing free trade.[6]

The purpose of patent protection is often and simply described as to encourage innovation. In other words, patents are innovation incentives. Patent laws in national regimes of the common law tradition have historically been described as being based on a 'social contract'.[7] The essence of this social contract is that in exchange for the exclusivity of a patent (a reward), society ultimately benefits from the disclosure of the invention in order for the exclusive right to be granted (disclosure in the form of a patent that enables the invention to be made by a person skilled in the relevant art).[8] The disclosure part of this rationale is reflected in modern trade agreements. The Agreement on Trade-Related Aspects of Intellectual Property Rights (TRIPS Agreement) provides that national systems must require that patents disclose the best way of making the invention.[9] There are many difficulties with the social contract or bargain concept not being fit for purpose, particularly as it explains some aspects of patent law but not all.[10] Also, patentees exclusive rights are growing in scope and flexibility, and disclosure is not always what it should be.[11] These issues point to the need for better

4. *See* Barbara Lauriat, *Revisiting the Royal Commission on Copyright*, (2013) Journal of World Intellectual Property 47.
5. Barbara Lauriat *Free Trade in Books – The 1878 Royal Commission on Copyright*, (2013) 61(4) Journal of the Copyright Society of the USA 1.
6. *See* generally, Barbara Lauriat, *Intellectual Property and Victorian Inquiry: The Royal Commissions on Patent (1864) and Copyright (1878)* (Hart Publishing, 2021).
7. Peter Drahos, *The Global Governance of Knowledge: Patent Offices and Their Clients* (Cambridge University Press, 2010), at pp. 27-32 and Hector L. MacQueen, Charlotte Waelde and Graeme T. Laurie, *Contemporary Intellectual Property: Law and Policy* (Oxford University Press 2008), at paras 10.15-10.16.
8. Importantly, the disclosure is before the right is granted, *see* Rebecca S. Eisenberg, *Patents and the Progress of Science: Exclusive Rights and Experimental Use*, (1989) 56 The University of Chicago Law Review 1017 at 1022.
9. TRIPS Agreement, Art. 29.1 provides, 'Members shall require that an applicant for a patent shall disclose the invention in a manner sufficiently clear and complete for the invention to be carried out by a person skilled in the art and may require the applicant to indicate the best mode for carrying out the invention known to the inventor at the filing date or, where priority is claimed, at the priority date of the application.'
10. *See*, for example, Shubha Ghosh, *Patents and the Regulatory State: Rethinking the Patent Bargain Metaphor after Eldred*, (2004) 19 Berkeley Technology Law Journal 1315 suggests that the 'bargain metaphor' in patent law rests on an outdated notion that is inconsistent with regulatory goals of patent law.
11. For a discussion of how patent disclosure 'under performs', *see* Jeanne Fromer, *Patent Disclosure*, (2008-2009) 94 Iowa Law Review 539.

evidence and more detailed rationales than either the reward for disclosure bargain or social contract if patent law is to retain its credibility.

Rationales for patent law and the property rights it enables must be explicable because patents are a wholly legal construct; meaning that they do not exist without the law. Patents in effect regulate many aspects of uses of inventions. The law creates the property device of a patent that has an independent existence from the invention it regulates. All property is regulated to some extent and in different ways depending on the society and its political choices, but there is no society in which patents exist without regulation, whereas land, buildings and pianos do so exist, for example. Recognising that patents are regulated property is not simply a matter of legal semantics but underscores why the exclusive rights that arise from patents must be justified. The most common justification is that patents reward innovation and thus incentivize it.

The pharmaceutical industry repeatedly uses this reward for innovation rationale in its lobbying, at both national and international level, for more extensive protection, whatever kind of protection is sought. Whether that protection is extension of patent term, requiring new uses of various sorts to be patentable, increases on data exclusivity in the regulatory process or any other matter the same claim is made. That claim is that new and extended protection is needed for innovation. The frequent assertions that more protection is needed for innovation is equally as often not supported by any evidence which shows why one particular development in patent law would incentivize more innovation than the existing rules do. Much patent law is devoid of a grounding in evidence-based policy,[12] although in some jurisdictions that has started to change, even if imperfectly, as the examples of emerging patent exceptions in section 2 of this chapter show.

Although, as noted above, the trade and intellectual property relationship is long-standing, the TRIPS Agreement, as part of the World Trade Organization (WTO), integrated the trade and intellectual property relationship more intensively and in more detail than the Paris Convention or any other intellectual property-related treaty. Not only did the TRIPS Agreement result in multilateral standards to protect intellectual property obligations as part of the international trade regime, those standards also became enforceable.[13] As of 2020, the enforceability of multilateral disputes is in jeopardy because the standing Appellate Body of the WTO is no longer able to function as replacement members have not been appointed, owing to the United States' refusal

12. For a discussion of what evidence-based policy might require *see* Susy Frankel, *Intellectual Property as a Regulator of Behaviour*, in Susy Frankel and Daniel Gervais (eds), *Intellectual Property and the Regulation of the Internet* (Victoria University Press 2017) pp. 193-211 and *see* Jeremy de Beer, *Evidence-Based Intellectual Property Policymaking: An Integrated Review of Methods and Conclusion*, (2016) 19 Journal of World Intellectual Property 150.
13. As part of the WTO disputes about the TRIPS Agreement may be heard by the panels of the dispute settlement system, TRIPS Agreement, Art. 64.

to agree to any appointments.[14] As of this writing, an interim appeal process of the dispute settlement system is in place for some WTO members that have agreed to it.[15]

Subsequent to the formation of the WTO, bilateral and some plurilateral free trade agreements (FTAs) have flourished and have extended intellectual property protection standards well beyond the minimum standards that are included in the TRIPS Agreement. The TRIPS Agreement provided the framework for intellectual property chapters in FTAs to expand protection, as it provides that Members may provide more extensive protection. Importantly, extensive protection must be consistent with the rest of the Agreement.[16] On the face of it, increased standards are consistent with the TRIPS Agreement because of the articulated permission to provide more extensive protection.[17] The one-way ratchet of increased protection, however, cuts across the objectives and principles of the TRIPS Agreement and is consequently not entirely consistent with the rest of the Agreement.[18] After all, the objective and principles require that the TRIPS Agreement is for the mutual advantage of producers and users,[19] and increased protection mostly speaks to the producers' side of that objective. The domestic law rationales of innovation incentives are not as one-sided.

When rationales for national patent laws are utilized in the international legal regime, the notion of innovation incentives, which can drive domestic patent law, changes. In essence, international protection, while preventing imitation, also serves to increase the profits of patent owners. Patent owners' needs for innovation incentives are to at least recoup the cost of research and development (R&D). It has often been said that the costs of R&D are recouped in the home market, and international sales are on top of that. Some have also suggested that innovation in the pharmaceutical market is already too high and that resources might be better used in other fields, such as education.[20]

Market size may increase profits, but that does not mean that the profit made in foreign markets is needed to recoup the investment in the place of innovation or to

14. *See* Tetyana Payosova, Gary Clyde Hufbauer and Jeffrey J. Schott, *The Dispute Settlement Crisis in the World Trade Organization: Causes and Cures*, Petersen Institute for International Economics (March 2018), https://www.piie.com/publications/policy-briefs/dispute-settlement-crisis-world-trade-organization-causes-and-cures.
15. European Commission, *Interim appeal arrangement for WTO disputes becomes effective*, 30 April 2020, at https://trade.ec.europa.eu/doclib/press/index.cfm?id=2143.
16. TRIPS Agreement, Art. 1.1. states, 'Members shall give effect to the provisions of this Agreement. Members may, but shall not be obliged to, implement in their law more extensive protection than is required by this Agreement, provided that such protection does not contravene the provisions of this Agreement.'
17. *Ibid.*
18. Susy Frankel, *Challenging TRIPS – Plus FTAs – The Potential Utility of Non-Violation Complaints*, (2009) 12(4) Journal of International Economic Law 1023.
19. TRIPS Agreement, Art. 7 provides, 'The protection and enforcement of intellectual property rights should contribute to the promotion of technological innovation and to the transfer and dissemination of technology, *to the mutual advantage of producers and users* of technological knowledge and in a manner conducive to social and economic welfare, and to a balance of rights and obligations' [emphasis added].
20. Richard Frank and Paul B. Ginsburg, *Pharmaceutical Industry Profits and Research and development*, USC-Brookings Schaeffer on Health Policy (17 November 2017), at https://www.brookings.edu/blog/usc-brookings-schaeffer-on-health-policy/2017/11/17/pharmaceutical-industry-profits-and-research-and-development/.

prevent any unfair competition. The rationales for having a baseline of protection (the minimum standards of the TRIPS Agreement) abroad is to prevent free-riding and imitation,[21] but the rationale of increasing protection to levels above that baseline, in other countries, is predominantly to maintain profits abroad. So while lobbyists may convince their own governments that more protection is needed in order to improve innovation at home, those states negotiating on the international stage have a different task to convince foreign governments that they also need to protect foreign innovation, which also likely means purchasing it at a high price. Since the TRIPS Agreement has been in force there has been an air of inevitability that countries accept a certain level of protection which is out of step with their needs and level of development and this pattern has continued in FTA negotiations. In post-TRIPS bilateral FTA negotiations, the power imbalance between large economies and smaller ones or developing countries has mostly meant that patent standards of the large developed countries (which are more extensive than the minimum standards of the TRIPS Agreement) prevail in exchange for other parts of the FTA (such as market access for goods) or for just having an agreement.[22] The effects of increased protection are many, including decreases in innovation incentives for some incumbents, making a market entry for newcomers or competitors more difficult[23] and progressively shifting the baseline of global protection away from the TRIPS Agreement minimums.[24]

Once international patent rules are in place, any disputes about compliance with those rules will not focus on whether the rules are, in fact, operating as innovation incentives or otherwise. Rather, the disputes are about whether the standard of protection provided for in the international agreement is complied with domestic law. When patent rules are globalized, the assumptions about the need for the standards are rarely revisited. After all, once the treaty is finalized, the job for policymakers and decision makers is to interpret the treaty. While negotiations for additional articles and amendments can take place, the ongoing role of dispute settlement is not to renegotiate the treaty, to rewrite it or to fill in any gaps.[25] Consequently, the focus is on enforcing the rules.

---

21. Before the TRIPS Agreement, this was disputed. It remains a matter of dispute, although for those seeking greater protection, TRIPS was never enough, *see* Susan Sell, *TRIPS Was Never Enough: Vertical Forum Shifting, FTAs, ACTA, and TPP*, (2011) 18 Journal of Intellectual Property Law 447. However, the twenty-first century supporters of the TRIPS Agreement were some of its twentieth-century opponents.
22. Peter Drahos argues that this imbalance of power can also be present in multilateral negotiations, *see* Peter Drahos, *When the Weak Bargain with the Strong: Negotiations in the World Trade Organization*, (2003) 8 International Negotiation 79-109.
23. *See* discussion below in s. 3 regarding the EU manufacturing and stockpiling waivers.
24. Susy Frankel, *The Legitimacy and Purpose of Intellectual Property Chapters in FTAs*, in Ross Buckley, Vai Io Lo and Laurence Boulle (eds), *Challenges to Multilateral Trade the Impact of Bilateral, Preferential and Regional Agreements* (1st ed., Wolters Kluwer, 2008) at 185.
25. The WTO Understanding on Rules and Procedures Governing the Settlement of Disputes (opened for signature 15 April 1994, Marrakesh Agreement Establishing the World Trade Organization, Annex 2 (1994) 1869 UNTS 401 (DSU), Art. 3.2 states:

> The dispute settlement system of the WTO is a central element in providing security and predictability to the multilateral trading system. The Members recognize that it

To a certain extent, the role of Articles 7 and 8, the principles and objectives of the TRIPS Agreement as interpretative tools[26] can bring the notion of innovation into the treaty interpretation process. Particularly in the patent context, the WTO has not effectively done this to date. Further, interpretation is by its nature a limited lever for discussion of innovation incentives, as such. Rather the relevant discussion would be about the interpretation of existing obligations and that discussion would tend to treat those obligations as if they are based on justifiable rationales. There is considerable potential to use the principles and objectives of the TRIP Agreement to support competition and innovation enhancing exceptions.[27] To be most effective any discussion about innovation needs to take place at the negotiating stage and in the bilateral environment. The demandeurs have not shown any willingness to do this in a substantive evidence-based way. Plurilateral agreements that include developing countries and small developed countries have been more successful than bilateral FTAs at partially curbing excessive demands.[28]

The increase of cross-border patent standards since the formation of the TRIPS Agreement has been exclusively by means of FTAs and not by multilateral agreement. That indicates that the appetite for more extensive protection multilaterally does not exist among enough countries to justify altering the multilateral platform of minimum standards. Indeed, the WIPO Patent Law Treaty that aimed to increase harmonisation of patentability criteria (among other goals) has not been successful beyond harmonising procedural norms.[29] In contrast, the only multilateral change to patent law was an amendment to the TRIPS Agreement, which allows for pharmaceuticals that are made under compulsory license to be exported to countries in need of those pharmaceuticals in a national emergency, and where those importing countries are unable to utilize

> serves to preserve the rights and obligations of Members under the covered agreements, and to clarify the existing provisions of those agreements in accordance with customary rules of interpretation of public international law. *Recommendations and rulings of the DSB cannot add to or diminish the rights and obligations provided in the covered agreements.* [emphasis added].

This principle is reiterated in Art. 19.2. One of the reasons for the current criticisms of the Appellate Body is that it has intruded into matters more appropriate for negotiation than dispute settlement.

26. The Doha Declaration on the TRIPS Agreement and Public Health, World Trade Organization, 20 November 2001, WT/MIN(01)/DEC/2, Art. 5 (a) (2001), para. 5 (a) provides, 'in applying the customary rules of interpretation of public international law, each provision of the TRIPS Agreement shall be read in the light of the object and purpose of the Agreement as expressed, in particular, in its objectives and principles'. *See also* Susy Frankel, *WTO Application of 'the Customary Rules of Interpretation of Public International Law' to Intellectual Property*, 46 Virginia Journal of International Law 365, (2006); and Rochelle Dreyfuss and Susy Frankel, *From Incentive to Commodity to Asset: How International Law Is Reconceptualizing Intellectual Property*, (2015) 36 Michigan Journal of International Law 557, at 593-595, discussing how WTO panels could better use interpretative principles.
27. *See* discussion section 3 below.
28. *See* discussion of the suspension of certain patent terms in the TPP below in section 2.
29. WIPO, Patent Law Treaty (done at Geneva on 1 June 2000). *See also* Jerome H. Reichman and Rochelle Cooper Dreyfuss, *Harmonization Without Consensus: Critical Reflections on Drafting a Substantive Patent Law Treaty*, (2007) 57 Duke Law Journal 85-130.

compulsory licenses to manufacture pharmaceuticals for themselves.[30] In this chapter, section 2 discusses the ways in which the post-TRIPS Agreement FTAs have extended patent protection. Section 3 then looks at moves to make patent rules more flexible in relation to pharmaceuticals, including the introduction of Article 31bis of the TRIPS Agreement and the EU waiver for manufacturing and stockpiling of generic chemical medicines and of biosimilars, before the expiry of extended patent term, destined for export from the European Union.[31] Section 4 concludes with some observations as to why the multilateral approach is preferable to the bilateral and plurilateral approaches if patents are to act mostly as innovation incentives.

2 TRADE AS A LEVER FOR MORE EXTENSIVE PROTECTION BEYOND THE TRIPS BASELINE

For those who are interested in the patent system living up to its rationale of creating innovation incentives for more than just a few dominant developed country players, multilateral agreements are mostly preferable to plurilateral and bilateral agreements in the field of patent law. This is because a multilateral agreement is much more likely to have provisions that enable a variety of approaches to patent law, which reflect differing economic goals and different stages of development. While the TRIPS Agreement was primarily an instrument to enhance the position of developed countries seeking protection in export markets for their inventions, particularly pharmaceutical products and processes, the Agreement does reflect some developing country concerns. It provides for a delayed period for compliance for developing countries and even longer for least developed countries. The Agreement allows for some flexibility around patent criteria (there is no definition of inventive step, for example)[32] and some exceptions to patent rights.[33] Also, the TRIPS Agreement includes objectives and principles that recognize the needs of producers and users of intellectual property and the need for technology transfer.[34] None of these flexibilities, however, have proved to be enough to enhance innovation in many parts of the world and, at most, they have acted as a partial and fragile buffer against excessive rent-seeking of patent owners in offshore markets.

The position of non-patent owning nations may become even worse when the multilateral system dispute settlement breaks down because rules-based systems can assist the weak against the strong.[35] The global situation is also one where protectionism of domestic industry has been increasing during 2020 and from 2021 will likely

30. TRIPS Agreement, Art. 31bis.
31. EC Regulation 2019/933: *Concerning the Supplementary Protection Certificate for Medicinal Products*.
32. Article 27 of the TRIPS Agreement requires that inventions must be novel, involve an inventive step and be capable of industrial application, but the Agreement does not define these terms and leaves it to each member to do so.
33. Exceptions can be found in Arts 27.2, 27.3, 30 and 31 of the TRIPS Agreement.
34. TRIPS Agreement, Art. 7, above (n. 19).
35. For example, the success that developing countries have had in using the cross-retaliation provisions of the WTO DSU (n. 25), to enforce cases where they have won against developed countries, but those developed countries have not complied with the rulings of a WTO panel and

continue to do so, at least for a while. In protectionist circumstances, the risk of less availability and higher prices for pharmaceuticals is even more extreme. One might return to the question of why these ever-increasing standards are systematically supported by the international trade regime when they are not necessarily conducive to welfare, particularly in the area of access to medicines, and where increasing costs has even caused large developed countries to question the patent system.

The simple economic purpose of trade is to increase overall welfare.[36] The international protection of intellectual property emerged at the multilateral level in the late nineteenth century through the organization that later became the World Intellectual Property Organization (WIPO).[37] Agreement to minimum standards for intellectual property protection did not formally join the international trade regime until the WTO was formed in the late twentieth century. This is a pathway that is different from other trade issues. If one accepts *ad arguendo* that some degree of intellectual property protection is necessary for a trade regime, then the challenge is how to ensure that intellectual property protection can act as an innovation incentive and how to prevent that protection from becoming the reverse of an innovation incentive. Ensuring that patent law functions to incentivize innovation – and does not only function to improve the position of existing patent-dominant nations – is particularly difficult because the framework of the TRIPS Agreement enables increases in intellectual property protection to proceed apace with no real opportunity either for any international legal challenge or for flexibilities and exceptions to act as an effective counterbalance to those increases. Part of the difficulty is that the TRIPS Agreement gives definition to the obligations, but it does not define the exceptions to the same degree, rather the Agreement provides a framework that the exceptions must meet.[38] Consequently, what has unfolded is that obligations are not contested, but flexibilities became subject to international challenge for not meeting the framework test, even though that test was designed to allow a degree of national autonomy.

In the one dispute, before a WTO panel, that directly discussed patent flexibilities, the scope of those flexibilities was not generously interpreted in a way that reflected policy rationales. The European Communities (EC), as the EU then was, brought a complaint against Canada alleging that two of its patent exceptions violated the TRIPS Agreement.[39] The resolution of the dispute required interpretation of the

---

Appellate Body, *see* Susy Frankel, *The TRIPS Agreement and Cross-Retaliation*, in Susy Frankel and Meredith Kolsky Lewis (eds), *Trade Agreements at the Crossroads* (Routledge, 2013) 208-225.

36. For an introduction to the economic theories of trade, *see* Michael J. Trebilcock and Joel Trachtman, *Advanced Introduction to International Trade* (2nd ed., Edward Elgar Publishing, 2020).
37. For a history of WIPO and the development of its agreements, *see* generally Sam Ricketson (ed.), *Research Handbook on the World Intellectual Property Organization: The First 50 Years and Beyond* (Edward Elgar Publishing, 2020).
38. The test is known as the three-step test. It has its origins in the Berne Convention for the Protection of Literary and Artistic Works (opened for signature 9 September 1886, entered into force 5 December 1887) 1161 UNTS 31 (Revised 1971) (Berne), Art. 9.2, which is included in TRIPS and has been adapted to provide a framework for exceptions in that Agreement.
39. WTO Panel Report, *Canada-Patent Protection of Pharmaceutical Products*, WT/DS114/R (17 March 2000) (*Canada Pharmaceuticals*).

three-step test (the framework for patent exceptions).[40] The Canadian measures that the EC challenged were for making and using the patented pharmaceutical products in order to obtain regulatory approval for sale (known as regulatory review) and to stockpile the same patented products so that when the relevant patents expired the market (both home and overseas) could immediately be supplied with the relevant pharmaceuticals. Without the ability for others to stockpile patented products, before the patent expires, the owner of a patent had a period of de facto exclusivity beyond the term of the patent because it takes time to manufacture pharmaceuticals. The regulatory review and stockpiling exceptions were designed in combination to truncate this post-patent exclusive time as much as possible. The WTO dispute settlement panel found that the regulatory review exception complied with the TRIPS Agreement three-step test, but that the stockpiling exception did not.[41] The main reason was that stockpiling did not meet the first step of the test, as it was not limited sufficiently because it implicated more than one exclusive right (making and using) and had insufficient limits on the abrogation of those rights.[42] Several commentators have disagreed with the reasoning of the panel for a variety of reasons. One such reason is the failure of the panel to effectively use the Vienna Convention rules on treaty interpretation[43] and particularly the part of those rules that requires a full analysis of the treaty's object and purpose.[44] The panel claimed it took into account Articles 7 and 8 of the TRIPS Agreement (which contain objectives and principles that are relevant to object and purpose) in its interpretation, but the panel was not explicit about how it took those articles into account.[45]

Finding the balance between implementing obligations for the protection of rights and effectively using exceptions is something the international framework anticipates, but the framework is such that protection is easier to implement than are the flexibilities. Flexibilities usually must meet a test or rely on support for the interpretative principles found in the objectives and principles, whereas rights are expressly articulated in the TRIPS Agreement.[46] The framework of the TRIPS Agreement also does not support flexibilities operating across borders and, consequently, it does not reflect the global nature of some patent dependent industries. The global nature of some patent-related industries, however, is in part reflected in arguments that were made at the WTO in connection with Canada's patent flexibilities for regulatory review and stockpiling. As part of its overall argument before the WTO panel, Canada

40. For patents, the relevant three-step test is found in TRIPS Agreement, Art. 30, which provides, 'Members may provide limited exceptions to the exclusive rights conferred by a patent, provided that such exceptions do not unreasonably conflict with a normal exploitation of the patent and do not unreasonably prejudice the legitimate interests of the patent owner, taking account of the legitimate interests of third parties.'
41. This was even though under the relevant legislation the stockpiling exception could not be used unless the generic company had also applied for regulatory review.
42. *Canada Pharmaceuticals*, above (n. 39) at para. 7.34.
43. These rules are found in Vienna Convention on the Law of Treaties, 23 May 1969, 1115 UNTS 331 (entered into force 27 January 1980), Arts 31-32.
44. Frankel, above (n. 26).
45. *Ibid.*
46. For each area of intellectual property, the agreement set out the rights of the owners. For patents, these are found in TRIPS Agreement, Art. 28.

explained the global nature of the generic pharmaceutical market and why the reality of the global market supported the flexibilities it had enacted in its law. Canada stated:[47]

> Both the brand name and generic pharmaceutical industries were global in nature. Very few countries had fully integrated brand name or generic drug industries within their borders. Even in large countries, generic producers frequently had to obtain ingredients such as fine chemicals from producers in other countries. Many countries had no generic industries at all and had to obtain generic (as well as brand name) products from other countries. Smaller countries that did have generic industries did not have domestic markets sufficiently large to enable those industries to operate on an economic scale. Those industries had to export in order to be able to manufacture in sufficient quantities to achieve economies of scale, so that domestic consumers could receive the benefits of cost-effective generic products.

The international framework has meant that the industries that depend on exceptions are much less able to operate globally than those that depend only on the rights side of the equation. The reality of trade and how innovation frameworks operate is somewhat different from the traditional way in which patents are 'based on concepts of discrete innovation, linear technical progress and exclusive distribution control'.[48] This mismatch of how innovation works and how patents are globalized is one facet of the innovation system that overprotection can exacerbate.

The problems with overprotection of intellectual property are simple to describe but can be difficult to regulate globally. Intellectual property rules are designed in a framework where they facilitate the economic reward of innovators and creators after invention and creation takes place and are thus *ex post* incentives. In contrast, subsidies that are payments for production are *ex ante* and are regarded as inefficient by those seeking to liberalize trade. The reason that liberalized trade disfavours subsidies is that they distort comparative advantage and consequently also markets. In simple terms, subsidies can enable inefficient producers to keep producing and selling. Subsidies make products that would be more expensive to produce, cheaper to buy and can mean that products which would have otherwise been cheaper and which are not subsidized become more expensive and cannot be sold.[49] Some suggest that the current trade subsidy rules are no longer fit for purpose because they do not take into account the reality of global value chains.[50]

47. *Canada Pharmaceuticals*, above (n. 39), at para. 4.38. The United States, as a third party, agreed with this point but pointed out it was a large enough nation to deal with this issue within its borders. *See also* discussion in, Susy Frankel, *Test Tubes for Global Intellectual Property Issues: Small Market Economies* (Cambridge University Press, 2015), at 103-105.
48. Keith Maskus, *Private Rights and Public Problems: The Global Economics of Intellectual in the 21st Century* (Petersen Institute for International Economics, 2012), at 17.
49. When Brazil was able to cross-retaliate under the TRIPS Agreement, *see* above (n. 35) and DSU above (n. 25), Art. 22.3. it was because the United States had violated other WTO agreements by giving its farmers subsidies for growing cotton. *See also* Allison L. Whiteman, *Cross Retaliation under the TRIPS Agreement: An Analysis of the Policy Options for Brazil*, 6 North Carolina Journal of International Law & Commercial Regulation 187 (2010-2011).
50. Bernard M. Hoekman and Douglas Nelson, *Rethinking international subsidy rules*, Working Paper, EUI RSCAS, 2020/20, at https://cadmus.eui.eu/handle/1814/66586.

In the traditional subsidy model the subsidized producer lacks any incentive to be competitive because they are rewarded by the subsidy and not by a competitive price. Excessive intellectual property can have a similar effect.[51] Consider, for example, the owner of a pharmaceutical product patent, that owner knowing that extensions and related new use patents are available with very few third-party exceptions may have a diminished incentive to innovate.[52] The reward can be anticipated meaning that even if it the granting of the legal right is *ex post* the effect is analogous to an *ex ante* subsidy. This may be especially so where the right is granted after the initial grant of the patent, such as for term extension. One can view innovation and subsidies at the opposite ends of a continuum and effective intellectual property should be towards the innovation end of that continuum, rather than creeping nearer and nearer to the subsidy end. More extensive protection, than the TRIPS Agreement minimum standards, that is found in FTAs overall support this subsidising effect.

The TRIPS Agreement set up minimum standards for patentable subject matter and rights. It did not define how all those standards should be implemented but left that to members to do in accordance with their own legal systems and practices.[53] The TRIPS Agreement also includes exceptions. The push for more definition in those standards, less flexibility in their implementation and for fewer exceptions has continued post-TRIPS. Multilateral attempts at such negotiations have not succeeded, but a similar effect is progressively being achieved through multiple bilateral and a growing number of plurilateral FTAs. Most FTAs, including EU partnership agreements, increase patent protection and in doing so also move it towards the subsidy end of the continuum making some patents and, therefore, the overall system function less as innovation incentives. For example, the EU negotiations with Indonesia show that the EU is pressuring Indonesia to allow for the extension of patent term and the patenting of new uses, but the EU is not suggesting that Indonesia adopt any flexibilities that would be suitable to Indonesia and its development needs.[54]

A well-publicized plurilateral trade agreement was the Trans-Pacific Partnership[55] (TPP), which is not in force as first agreed with the United States but is partly in force as the Comprehensive and Progressive Trans-Pacific Partnership (CPTPP) without the United States.[56] The version that included the United States had substantial increases in patent protection. Those provisions have been suspended in the CPTPP.[57]

51. *See Test Tubes for Global Intellectual Property Issues*, above (n. 47), at pp. 81-89.
52. Third parties may also be less likely to innovate if they know an existing patentee can easily prevent new uses of known substances.
53. TRIPS Agreement, Art. 1.1.
54. The proposed text is under negotiation, *see* https://trade.ec.europa.eu/doclib/docs/2020/january/tradoc_158573.pdf.
55. *Trans-Pacific Partnership Agreement*, Office of the United States Trade Representative, at https://ustr.gov/trade-agreements/free-trade-agreements/trans-pacific-partnership (entered into 4 February 2016, not in force) (TPP).
56. *Comprehensive and Progressive Trans-Pacific Partnership*, New Zealand Foreign Affairs and Trade (2018), at https://www.mfat.govt.nz/assets/CPTPP/Comprehensive-and-Progressive-Agreement-for-Trans-Pacific-Partnership-CPTPP-English.pdf (CPTPP).
57. For an explanation of what provisions are suspended, *see* CPTPP v. TPP, Ministry of Foreign Affairs and Trade, https://www.mfat.govt.nz/en/trade/free-trade-agreements/free-trade-agreements-in-force/cptpp/understanding-cptpp/tpp-and-cptpp-the-differences-explained.

Suspended means that the provisions are not in force but are there for negotiation should any state (particularly the United States) wish to negotiate to join the CPTPP.

Those suspended provisions include requirements relating to patentable subject matter, including that patents are available for at least one of 'new uses of a known product, new methods of using a known product, or new processes of using a known product'[58] and that patents are available for inventions that are derived from plants.[59] Patent term extension for unreasonable delay in either the patent office registration process or the regulatory/marketing approval process has also been suspended.[60] The suspended provisions also include those relating to regulatory data exclusivity and marketing approval that provided substantially more detail than the obligation found in the TRIPS Agreement.[61] The relevant TRIPS Agreement obligation only applies to new chemical entities (not biologics) and it does not set out a time frame for 'protecting data from unfair commercial use'. [62] This leaves countries to determine what time frame is required to prevent the unfairness and what activities amount to 'unfair commercial use'. The lack of definition around 'unfair commercial use' enables countries to define what is unfair according to their standards and common practice.[63] While some countries consider that data exclusivity must exist to satisfy unfairness, other countries take the approach that the regulatory agency can use the data to assess the safety and efficacy of generic medicines but cannot reveal that data to the generic medicine applicant.[64] This involves keeping the data confidential but not necessarily exclusive. Seen from this perspective, requiring data exclusivity is more extensive protection than TRIPS requires.

The TPP and other FTAs extend the data exclusivity obligation to biologics and provide time frames for such exclusivity. After some reputedly controversial negotiation, the relevant articles in the TPP set five years of data exclusivity for new chemical and small molecule medicines[65] and eight years for biologics.[66] The TPP text, including the now-suspended provisions (with even longer time periods), became the basis for the United States' position in negotiations for the new North American Free Trade

58. TPP, above (n. 55), Art. 18.37.2.
59. TPP, above (n. 55), Art. 18.37.4.
60. TPP, above (n. 55), Arts 18.46. and 18.48.
61. TPP, above (n. 55), Arts 18.50.-18.54.
62. TRIPS Agreement, Art. 39.3 provides: 'Members, when requiring, as a condition of approving the marketing of pharmaceutical or of agricultural chemical products which utilize new chemical entities, the submission of undisclosed test or other data, the origination of which involves a considerable effort, shall protect such data against unfair commercial use. In addition, Members shall protect such data against disclosure, except where necessary to protect the public, or unless steps are taken to ensure that the data are protected against unfair commercial use.'
63. This is how the minimum standards nature of the TRIPS Agreement and FTAs that build on TRIPS operate to cause difference rather than complete harmonization.
64. Manthan D. Janodia, Ajay Chauhan, Shuaib M. Hakak, D. Sreedhar, V.S. Ligade and N. Udupa, *Data Exclusivity Provisions in India: Impact on Public Health*, (2008) 13 Journal of Intellectual Property Rights 442.
65. TPP, above (n. 55), Art. 18.50.1(a).
66. TPP, above (n. 55), Art. 18.51.1(a).

Agreement (NAFTA), the United States, Mexico, Canada Agreement (USMCA).[67] Interestingly, in the final stages of the United States implementation of the USMCA, the requirements for regulatory data exclusivity, beyond those already in US law, were rejected.[68]

The TPP also included patent linkage measures relating to the marketing of pharmaceuticals that would have required the patent holder to be notified if a third party requests marketing approval.[69] Somewhat differently, the Canada EU Trade Agreement (CETA) provides that if a party relies on 'patent linkage' mechanisms when marketing approval for generic pharmaceutical products is provided, that party 'shall ensure that all litigants are afforded equivalent and effective rights of appeal'.[70]

The TPP text also found new life in the Regional Comprehensive Economic Partnership (RCEP), a plurilateral negotiation, which includes the Association of Southeast Asian countries (ASEAN), plus six other nations (China, India, Japan, South Korea, Australia, New Zealand). Japan is reputed to have introduced the intellectual property text from TPP text as a negotiating draft.[71] India is reported as having said, categorically, 'no way' to the TPP patent style protections and has left the RCEP negotiations.[72] This is hardly surprising given India's negotiations against certain provisions in the TRIPS Agreement and its use of that Agreement's flexibilities to provide some of the lowest levels of pharmaceutical patent protection possible within the framework of the TRIPS Agreement.[73] The RCEP negotiations were concluded in late 2021.

---

67. United States- Mexico- Canada Agreement, Office of the United States Trade Representative (30 November 2018), https://ustr.gov/trade-agreements/free-trade-agreements/united-states-mexico-canada-agreement (USMCA).
68. *Ibid.* The final text entirely deletes the former Art. 20.49. of the earlier draft of the USMCA, which required that parties 'provide effective market protection [...], for a period of at least ten years from the date of first marketing approval of that product in that Party'. Thanks to Gabriel Ferrante, NYU LAW School, JD student whose research detailed this point, *see* Gabriel Ferrante, *Luck & Labor: A Brief History of the U.S.M.C.A. & How It Got That Way* May 2020, (unpublished on file with author).
69. TPP, above (n. 55), Art. 18.53.
70. Comprehensive Economic and Trade Agreement (CETA) Between Canada and the European Union, http://ec.europa.eu/trade/policy/in-focus/ceta/ceta-chapter-by-chapter/ (CETA), Art. 20.8.
71. Japan has a system of post-marketing surveillance that bars generic entry to the market. *See Does Japan Have 'Data Exclusivity' System? What is PMS (Post Marketing Surveillance Period?*, Tokyo Acti (26 September 2015), https://tokyo-acti.com/2015/09/26/does-japan-have-data-exclusivity-system-what-is-pms-post-marketing-surveillance-period/.
72. Suhasini Haidar, *India opposes rejoining RCEP over China concerns*, The Hindu, 16 May 2020, at https://www.thehindu.com/news/national/india-opposes-rejoining-rcep-over-china-concerns/article31602985.ece.
73. Section 3(d) of India's Patents Act, for example, excludes patents on pharmaceutical substances that do not demonstrate a significantly enhanced efficacy over and above prior known substances, *see* Shamnad Basheer, *Trumping TRIPS: Indian Patent Proficiency and the Evolution of an Evergreening Enigma*, (2018) 18(1) Oxford University Commonwealth Law Journal 16.

There are other examples of FTAs increasing patent standards, such as the United States FTAs with Korea[74] and Australia[75] and the EU agreements with Singapore[76] and Vietnam.[77] Each FTA increases patent protection standards to different degrees and, in some instances, in slightly different ways. The above examples of increased protection are illustrative of the types of measures found in these various agreements. The overall picture is one of increased measures and decreases in concomitant flexibility. Although the EU-Vietnam agreement indicates a recognition of the importance of the Doha Declaration on Public Health.[78] Notably, however, it does not specify what that importance means in terms of the practical implementation of patent flexibilities and exceptions.

3 POST-TRIPS FLEXIBILITIES IN PATENT LAW

Since the TRIPS Agreement came into force, there have been many increases in patent protection standards that have been achieved through a web of FTAs. Several countries have agreed to these increases making them more than simply bilateral in nature, even if they are not fully multilateral. In contrast, there have been relatively few flexibilities agreed to in FTAs and some restrictions on flexibilities in those FTAs. Furthermore, some countries struggle to fully utilize existing flexibilities. At the multilateral level, however, flexibility was introduced to allow some limited parallel importation of pharmaceuticals made under compulsory licence. The EU has also introduced a manufacturing waiver for generic chemical and biosimilar pharmaceuticals made for export. Each of these flexibilities is discussed here.

3.1. Parallel Importing and TRIPS

Under the TRIPS Agreement, countries can choose whether or not they allow parallel imports.[79] Parallel imports of pharmaceuticals are something that the United States and the European Union have discouraged in their trade agreements but have not entirely discouraged at home.[80] I have elsewhere discussed how Singapore, Israel and New

---

74. Free Trade Agreement between the United States of America and the Republic of Korea, 21 February 2012, https://ustr.gov/trade-agreements/free-trade-agreements/korus-fta/final-text (KORUS).
75. The Australia-United States Free Trade Agreement, U.S.-Austl., 18 May 2004, 43 I.L.M. 1248 (AUSFTA).
76. EU-Singapore Trade and Investment Protection Agreement (signed 19 October 2018, entered into force on 21 November 2019).
77. EU-Vietnam Trade and Investment Protection Agreement (signed on 30 June 2019, pending ratification).
78. Doha Declaration, above (n. 26).
79. TRIPS Agreement, Art. 6. For a full discussion of the international rules around parallel importing, *see* Susy Frankel and Daniel Gervais, *International Intellectual Property Rules and Parallel Imports*, in Irene Calboli and Edward Lee (eds), *Research Handbook on Intellectual Property Exhaustion and Parallel Imports* (Edward Elgar Publishing, 2016), 85-105.
80. *See*, for example, AUSFTA, above (n. 75), Art. 17.2.2., where the parties agree to limit parallel importing. In 2017, the Supreme Court of the United States ruled in *Impression Products, Inc. v. Lexmark International, Inc.* 137 S.Ct. 1523 (2017) that patented products could be parallel

Zealand illustrate the different approaches to parallel importation of pharmaceuticals driven by their trade interests. These countries are small market economies, and because they have interests in common with both developed and developing countries, they are like 'test tubes' used for experiments and provide useful examples of how global intellectual property issues can be balanced.[81] New Zealand does not allow any parallel imports of patented products even though it allows parallel imports of copyright and trade-marked products. This limitation on the parallel imports of patented pharmaceuticals was the result of a compromise with the trading partners, particularly the United States.[82] Singapore allows parallel importing of pharmaceuticals, but only after the patent owner has a window of opportunity to supply the Singapore market. This compromise was a change from allowing all parallel importing and was a result of the Singapore-US FTA.[83] This kind of policy choice, however, is not possible for many countries and particularly not for those that have no manufacturing capacity to make pharmaceuticals and no purchasing power to import them at developed country prices.

The TRIPS Agreement was, in part, designed to limit the number of suppliers of pharmaceutical products. It did so by requiring that patents be available for not only processes relating to pharmaceuticals but also products.[84] Prior to the advent of the TRIPS Agreement India, for example, did not protect product patents in the field of pharmaceuticals but only processes.[85] This enabled more production of generic pharmaceuticals. This sort of flexibility is not possible under TRIPS because it requires that patents are available for all inventions, whether products or processes.[86] Another restriction under the TRIPS Agreement is compulsory licensing of pharmaceutical patents, which is limited to a few situations including to address national emergencies.[87] Such licences can only be issued under certain conditions. One such condition was that the pharmaceuticals produced under the licence must be predominantly for the supply of the domestic market.[88] However, least developed countries in need of pharmaceuticals for national emergencies could not utilize this provision because they lack the capacity to manufacture pharmaceuticals. Rather, such countries need to import pharmaceuticals at an affordable price, but they could not do this because pharmaceuticals manufactured elsewhere, under a compulsory licence, must only be

imported into the United States because the patent owner exhausted its rights wherever the product is put on sale. On the facts of Lexmark, the owner of the patent in the United States was the same as the overseas patent owner and, in effect, had authorized the sale. It is possible that a future court might rule differently if the owners were different and there had been no consent to the overseas sale by the objecting patent owner.

81. *See* above (n. 49).
82. For a discussion of the parallel importing rules of New Zealand and Singapore, *see* above (n. 49), at pp. 174-179.
83. United States-Singapore FTA (entered into force 1 January 2004), Art. 16.7.2.
84. TRIPS Agreements, Art. 27.1.
85. *See* Jayashree Watal, *Patents: An Indian Perspective*, Jayashree Watal and Antony Taubman (eds), *The Making of the TRIPS Agreement: Personal insights from the Uruguay Round Negotiations* (World Trade Organization, 2015).
86. TRIPS Agreements, Art. 27.1.
87. TRIPS Agreement, Art. 31.
88. TRIPS Agreement, Art. 31(f).

for supply of the domestic market and so could not be exported to other countries in need.[89] The reluctance to allow for the export of products made under compulsory licensing stands in contrast to the fact that compulsory licenses in least developed countries would not be likely to undermine potential gains from innovation anyway, especially as the full-priced products could never be bought in least developed countries.[90]

The position of least developed countries being unable to access medicines that they need eventually led to the amendment of the TRIPS Agreement so that it now allows for two countries (and in some circumstances a regional group) to be part of the same compulsory licensing arrangement that would allow both the export and import of pharmaceuticals in national emergencies, under certain conditions.[91] This change initially took the form of a temporary solution emerging from the Doha Declaration on Public Health in 2001.[92] An amendment to the TRIPS Agreement eventually came into force in 2017.[93] The end result requires countries to qualify as eligible importers and eligible exporters. Eligible importers are mostly least developed countries without any relevant manufacturing capacity.[94] Many developed countries and some developing countries with manufacturing capacity have declared that they are able to act as eligible exporters.[95] In spite of these changes, few countries have, in fact, utilized the system.[96] The administrative and packaging requirements to use the flexibility may very well be regarded as too burdensome to make it worthwhile. Indeed, a Canadian company obtained a compulsory licence to manufacture and export pharmaceuticals to Rwanda

89. Even if the medicines are available without compulsory licence, they are often unaffordable; *see* J. Kuanpoth, *Compulsory Licence: Law and Practice in Thailand*, in Reto Hilty and Kung-Chung Liu KC (eds), *Compulsory Licensing: Practical Experiences and Ways Forward* (Springer, 2015).
90. The claims of the pharmaceutical industry that compulsory licensing will hurt them is discussed in Jerome H. Reichman, *Compulsory Licensing of Patented Pharmaceutical Inventions: Evaluating the Options*, (2009) 37(2) Journal of Law Medicine Ethics 247, at 263.
91. TRIPS Agreement, Art. 31bis.
92. Doha Declaration above (n. 65).
93. TRIPS Agreement, Art. 31bis.
94. *See* WTO Analytical Index, TRIPS Agreement – Art. 31bis (Practice), Annex to the TRIPS Agreement, Art. 1(b) fn. 3, at https://www.wto.org/english/res_e/publications_e/ai17_e/trips_art31_bis_oth.pdf, states:

> 'eligible importing Member' means any least-developed country Member, and any other Member that has made a notification to the Council for TRIPS of its intention to use the system set out in Article 31bis and this Annex ('system') as an importer, it being understood that a Member may notify at any time that it will use the system in whole or in a limited way, for example only in the case of a national emergency or other circumstances of extreme urgency or in cases of public non-commercial use [...] and that some other Members have stated that, if they use the system, it would be in no more than situations of national emergency or other circumstances of extreme urgency.

95. WTO, Notifications by exporting WTO members, at https://www.wto.org/english/tratop_e/trips_e/public_health_notif_export_e.htm.
96. *See* World Health Organization, Country experiences in using TRIPS safeguards: Part I', at https://apps.who.int/iris/rest/bitstreams/1140143/retrieve.

and eventually dropped the plan as the whole matter became too cumbersome and unaffordable.[97]

Many developed countries declared that they would not attempt to use the system as eligible importers. Their experience under COVID-19 has caused some of them to revisit this status.[98] The pandemic sheds light on just how restrictive the compulsory licensing system is. The system is designed to address national emergencies and create bilateral and sometimes regional compulsory licensing arrangements.[99] One might ask whether the system can be used for more global compulsory licensing arrangements. A correct interpretation of the TRIPS Agreement arguably supports such an approach.[100]

The amendment of the TRIPS Agreement to incorporate a limited extension to compulsory licensing is in some ways remarkable as it was one of the only successful multilateral negotiations to amend the text of any WTO covered agreement. It is also a significant political victory for least developed countries. In other ways it is very unremarkable because it changes little at a practical level, as access to medicines remains problematic.

3.2. The EU Manufacturing Waiver

The EU as well as seeking increases to patent standards around the globe, as discussed above, has increased flexibilities for the EU in the form of a manufacturing and stockpiling waiver for generic chemical and biosimilar pharmaceuticals, provided that they are made for export.[101] This exception is not available during the twenty-year patent term but can only be used during the period of a supplementary protection certificate (SPC)[102] – a form of patent term extension. The EU Parliament stated the purpose of the law change was to solve the problem of the [103]

> unintended consequence of preventing makers of generics and biosimilars established in the Union from making in the Union, even for the purpose of exporting to third country markets in which protection does not exist or has expired. Likewise,

97. Holger Hestermeyer *Canadian-Made Drugs for Rwanda: The First Application of the WTO Waiver on Patents and Medicines*, (2007) 11 (28) The American Society of International Law Insights, at https://www.asil.org/insights/volume/11/issue/28/canadian-made-drugs-rwanda-first-application-wto-waiver-patents-and.
98. Above (n. 94), para. 1(b) indicates members can change their opt out status at any time.
99. The purpose of a regional arrangement is for 'harnessing economies of scale for the purposes of enhancing purchasing power for, and facilitating the local production of, pharmaceutical products: where a developing or least developed country WTO Member is a party to a regional trade agreement', *see* TRIPS Agreement, Art. 31bis.3.
100. For a full analysis of this interpretation, *see* Susy Frankel, *International Intellectual Property and COVID-19* (forthcoming).
101. Commission Regulation 2019/933, 2019 J.O. (L 153) 1 (EC).
102. For a discussion of the details of the supplementary protection certificate system, *see* Żaneta Pacud, *Patents, SPC and Data Exclusivity at the Service of Legal Protection for Pharmaceuticals*, in Susy Frankel (ed.), *The Object and Purpose of Intellectual Property* (Edward Elgar Publishing, 2019).
103. *See* Annex to a Proposal Commission Regulation 2019/933, above (n. 101), at (4).

> they are prevented from making for the purpose of storing for a limited period before the expiry of the certificate.

The introduction of this law, even if it is framed as mending unintended consequences, shows a change of policy on the part of the EU compared to the restrictive approach it took, before the WTO dispute settlement panel, to flexibilities and the interpretation of the three-step test for patent exceptions.[104] Furthermore, this is a change in internal policy only, as the EU has not encouraged the adoption of this flexibility, or other flexibilities, in its FTAs. The regulation creating SPC exceptions refers to the necessity of SPCs for innovation.[105] Addressing the 'unintended consequences' is, in some ways, also about innovation, but innovation in the generic and biosimilar industries rather than the originator industry which usually lays claim to being the innovative part of the pharmaceutical industry. The Regulation also refers to other goals which are less directly about innovation and have more of an air of development, such as increasing job opportunities.[106]

The EU Regulation allows for making and stockpiling pharmaceuticals during the SPC period, the making of which would otherwise infringe the supplementary protection. Any pharmaceuticals made under the exception must be intended for export. The exceptions allow EU generic pharmaceuticals and biosimilars to compete in the United States and other foreign markets even before they can compete in the EU market. The delay of EU generic competition entering export markets was precisely the 'unintended consequence' that the law is supposed to remedy. From an international viewpoint this raises the question as to whether the EU's law is TRIPS Agreement compliant. The first step, therefore, is to ask whether and how the rules of the TRIPS Agreement applies.

Some commentators have proceeded as if the SPC system is sui generis to the TRIPS Agreement and claim that the TRIPS Agreement does not apply.[107] This argument is ill-conceived. A correct analysis proceeds as follows. The SPC system is a separate and very detailed regime from what is required in the TRIPS Agreement, but that does not make it sui generis from the TRIPS Agreement obligations. The SPC system is a form of regulated patent term extension beyond the minimum period of 20 years that the TRIPS Agreement requires.[108] The SPC regime is a form of patent term extension for some patents and is, therefore, more extensive protection than the 20-year minimum period required under the TRIPS Agreement.[109] As the TRIPS Agreement covers patent term, the extension of that minimum term requirement will be caught under the subject matter of the Agreement which includes 'patent rights' and, therefore, the provisions of the Agreement will apply to SPCs and any related

104. *Canada Pharmaceuticals*, above (n. 39) para. 7.34.
105. Commission Regulation 2019/933, above (n. 101), at (2).
106. *Ibid.*, at (8).
107. Xavier Seuba, *The Export and Stockpiling Waivers: New Exceptions for Supplementary Protection Certificates*, (2019) 14 Journal of Intellectual Property Law and Practice 876, 880-882.
108. TRIPS Agreement, Art. 33.
109. SPCs are a more extensive form of protection than the minimum requirement of patent term under the TRIPS Agreement, Art. 33. Extension is, therefore, permitted under TRIPS Agreement, Art. 1.1., but is within the scope of the TRIPS Agreement and so its provisions apply. *See also* Max Planck Institute, *Study on the Legal Aspects of Supplementary Protection Certificates in the EU, Final Report* (European Union, 2013), 3.2.

exceptions. Article 1.1 permits more extensive protection, but it does not exempt any more extensive protection from the other parts of the agreement.

It may be useful to consider that the purpose of the claim of sui generis status. Presumably such a claim would be to avoid national treatment obligations and when it comes to the manufacturing and stockpiling waiver to avoid compliance with Article 30 of the TRIPS Agreement. Patent term extension differs from matters that are wholly outside of the TRIPS Agreement, which may for that reason be sui generis. An example is the sui generis system for plant varieties, which is expressly labelled as sui generis in the wording of TRIPS.[110] To argue that the SPC regime is outside the national treatment provisions of TRIPS is inconsistent not only with that provision but also with the meaning of Article 1.1. of TRIPS, which permits more extensive protection.

The EU itself acknowledges that SPCs give patent type protection that is the same as the patent grant.[111] The sui generis claim is also inconsistent with the EU's own approach before the WTO panel, where it argued that as a consequence of certain rights under Article 28 of TRIPS, any de facto extensions to patent term were part of the TRIPS Agreement.[112] It would be illogical to suggest that de facto extension is part of the Agreement but not legal extension.

Because the subject of patent term is covered by the TRIPS Agreement and more extensive protection is permitted, the other provisions of the TRIPS Agreement are relevant to the interpretation of whether the SPC regime and its exceptions comply with TRIPS. Most relevantly, the regime should comply with national treatment[113] and the three-step test.[114] The three-step test was discussed in the patent context in the *Canada Pharmaceuticals* dispute. That panel created a restrictive approach to the test and found that the stockpiling exception was not limited enough to meet the first limb of the test.[115] Perhaps ironically, the restrictive interpretation of that test is a result of the EU's own policy pursued at the WTO through dispute settlement.[116] In assessing whether the manufacturing and export exception is compliant with the Article 30 three-step test, the EU seems to rely on the Max Planck report commissioned to assess the implications of the review. The Max Planck report argues that the application of Article 30 would have a different result than what occurred at the WTO. The report appears to disagree with the WTO panel, even though that panel was found in favour of the EU's argument. The Max Planck report states:[117]

> The [WTO] Panel expressly abstained from considering the legal objectives on which the exception is based. That approach contradicts the Doha Declaration,

110. TRIPS Agreement, Art. 27.3. provides '[...] Members shall provide for the protection of plant varieties either by patents or by an effective sui generis system or by any combination thereof [...]'.
111. Commission Regulation 469/2009, 2009 J.O. (L 152) 1 (EC), Art. 5; Commission Regulation 2019/933, above (n. 101), Art. 1(2) both provide, 'the certificate shall confer the same rights as conferred by the basic patent and shall be subject to the same limitations and same objections'.
112. *Canada Pharmaceuticals*, above (n. 40).
113. TRIPS Agreement, Art. 3.
114. TRIPS Agreement, Art. 30.
115. *Canada Pharmaceuticals*, above (n. 40) at paras 7.33-7.37.
116. *Ibid.*
117. Max Planck Report, above (n. 109), at 309-310.

> which confirmed that the principles and objectives of TRIPS must always guide the interpretation of rights and obligations, thus disallowing an assessment which is decidedly policy-blind.
>
> Thus, in the case considered here, account must be taken of the policy objective of manufacturing waivers, namely to correct or at least mitigate imbalances resulting from the fact that generic companies in the EU are hindered from competing on a level playing field with companies based in non-PTE countries.

It is not the purpose of this chapter to fully discuss if the EU waivers meet the three-step test. Notably, however, while flexibility can allow for appropriate adjustments to intellectual property law and policy, it can be complex to prove the legitimacy of a particular flexibility within the international regime.

The uses of flexibilities can also result in incoherence. One might say the EU has changed its mind over time and has recalibrated its more extensive protection regime according to its regional needs. But this is not persuasive. The EU approach in the WTO dispute was a direct attack on Canada's use of patent law to make generic pharmaceuticals available earlier, especially in developing country destinations because it enabled Canada to compete in the relevant markets ahead of the EU. The EU policy is, from an intellectual property perspective, somewhat contradictory. While protection of its own generic pharmaceutical industries explains the change, the changes to the EU approach reflect protectionism rather than a desire to enhance the availability of pharmaceuticals in markets in most need of generic competition. There is no evidence that the EU would encourage this sort of waiver in its FTAs. However, should countries wish to adopt a similar waiver, the EU would not easily be able to oppose such adoption without jeopardizing its own law. For countries that would not be able to manufacture the relevant generics, such a waiver would not be very useful in any event. Such countries may, however, wish to adopt other flexibilities. It remains to be seen whether in doing so they would be challenged as non-compliant with the TRIPS Agreement. Further, many countries are concerned to follow the approach set out in *Canada Pharmaceuticals* that was advocated for by the EU. The EU, as a norm maker, has changed the application of that norm for itself but not necessarily in a way that would help other nations innovate.

In addition, when considering the enactment of the waiver, the Max Planck Institute concluded that the EU would not be in violation of existing FTA provisions, which require among other things patent term extension.[118] This conclusion is also debatable. In any event, such an approach would allow other parties to those FTAs to have similar exceptions and not face a challenge from the EU that they are in breach of any FTA. The United States may, however, disagree as regards its FTAs that impose similar more extensive protection.

118. Max Planck Report, above (n. 109), at para. 15.3.2.4.

4 MOUNTING EVIDENCE THAT MULTILATERALISM IS PREFERABLE TO FTAS FOR INNOVATION

> In isolation, many of these developments are incremental changes. However, the net effect is a difference not merely in degree, but in kind. In total, the changes create new norms regarding the appropriate level of protection and excludability and an unravelling of the incentive-based rationale for protection. Together, the new agreements re-conceptualize the nature of IP. [119]

FTAs are changing the standards for patent protection, although the progression is not linear and is scattered among agreements in different ways. There have also been roadblocks to increased protection, such as the suspended provisions of the TPP. The TRIPS Agreement, as part of the WTO, is unlikely to be expanded to provide greater protection or flexibilities in the near future given the difficulties the WTO presently faces. Attempts to increase protection through negotiations at WIPO have also not succeeded. At a certain point, the negative effects of increases are not only felt in countries that have not sought those increases but may also be felt in some of the countries from which those increases have originated. Those originator countries may then wish to reverse their laws. The EU manufacturing and stockpiling waiver is an illustration of this phenomenon. We may well see the demanders of greater protection seeking even more flexibility as their economies strain in the current challenging times.[120] Flexibilities have been uneven in their development and are not globally uniform or necessarily innovation-enhancing in all countries, in any event.

When patents do not work to achieve the kind of protection that some innovators see as necessary, as has been the case for some biologics, the role of data exclusivity becomes more important. FTAs are being used to increase requirements for data exclusivity. Yet these increases are neither necessarily innovation-enhancing nor indeed assisting with much-needed access to medicines. Trade rules have the potential to support innovation if patent rules are devised predominantly as innovation incentives rather than protectionist measures. This requires patent lawmakers to consider not just the claims that more protection is needed for innovation, but rather what is rational for patent law to contribute effectively to innovation incentives and the public good, including access to much-needed patented products, especially medicines. This sort of analysis requires evidence, not assertion. At the international level assertion could be tempered by informed multilateralism as such negotiations involve many actors and, therefore, have a better chance of balancing the needs of economies of different sizes and at stages of development. This could lead to an approach where patent law incentivizes innovation overall and not only for a few.

---

119. Rochelle Dreyfuss and Susy Frankel, *From Incentive to Commodity to Asset: How International Law Is Reconceptualizing Intellectual Property*, (2015) 36 *Michigan Journal* of International Law 557, at 570.
120. *See also*, Susy Frankel, *It's Raining Carrots: The Trajectory of Increased Intellectual Property Protection*, in Gustavo Ghidini, Hanns Ullrich and Peter Drahos (eds), *Kritika: Essays on Intellectual Property* (vol. 2, Edward Elgar Publishing, 2016).

CHAPTER 2

In Between Breakthrough and Incremental Innovation: Rethinking Pharmaceuticals' Eligibility for IP Protection*

Żaneta Zemła-Pacud

1 INTRODUCTION

The necessity of enhancing innovation in the pharma sector is widely recognized. The importance of an innovative health sector is reinforced by ageing societies, uncontrolled disease transmission, and the increasing resistance of viruses and bacteria to existing drugs. Pharmaceutical innovations are necessary to prolong and improve the quality of life of patients. Developing innovative medicines means that there is a greater choice of medicinal products, and new products, satisfying hitherto unmet needs, will become available. All these facts acquire unprecedented importance in light of the COVID-19 pandemic.

Conducting complicated and lengthy research and development work on pharmaceutical products is time-consuming, extraordinarily expensive, and burdened with a high risk of failure. In contrast, imitation of final products through reverse engineering is easy in principle. Therefore, patents[1] and other instruments of intellectual

* This chapter is based on the studies conducted within the research project 'Protection of Regulatory Data in European Intellectual Property Law' financed by the National Center for Research (Polish: Narodowe Centrum Nauki) on the basis of the agreement: UMO-2019/33/B/HS5/02198.

1. Patent law in the EU is only partially unified: the grant of European patents is governed by the Convention on the grant of European Patent of 1973, as amended in 2000, whereas the legal effects of European patents are governed by the domestic laws of EU Member States. EU legislation on unitary patents, comprising EU Regulation No 1257/2012 (OJ EPO 2013, 111) and EU Regulation No 1260/2012 (OJ EPO 2013, 132), entered into force on 20 January 2013. The

property protection, in Europe specifically, supplementary protection certificates[2] as well as regulatory exclusivities and rewards,[3] are seen as necessary to incentivize pharmaceutical innovation.

However, granting IP-based protection for pharmaceutical innovations directly impacts the prices of medicinal products and their accessibility; as such, it affects the public health interest. It also influences the play of market forces and competition in the market of pharmaceuticals. Thus, pro-innovation IP-based legal instruments that create costs for societies and burden competition should be deployed only if they compensate for the said costs by a corresponding increase in welfare – i.e., when they generate net benefits.[4] Measuring the ratio between the social costs of IP-based incentives to innovation and the benefits generated from it is difficult. There is, however, one invariable assumption: the costs paid by society due to a temporary market monopoly should not be the same regardless of the level of the innovation embodied in a certain good. In other words, IP systems should grant protection with its scope corresponding to the level of innovation.[5]

All three legal systems – patents, supplementary protection certificates, and regulatory data protection – are aimed at incentivizing pharmaceutical innovation. However, in the EU – as elsewhere in the world[6] – only partial discussions have taken place about what exactly is meant by pharmaceutical innovation, and what kind and level of it deserves protection and incentives via intellectual property instruments. Innovation in the pharmaceutical sector may have many faces – from new and revolutionary products and technologies to minor improvements or refinements of existing pharmaceuticals and manufacturing processes.

This chapter discusses what the threshold of pharmaceutical innovation protected and incentivized by each of the three legal regimes is. It presents the most recent developments within the SPC systems in this regard, depicts specific targets of regulatory incentives and shows the shortcomings of the European patent system in stimulating valuable pharmaceutical innovation. It presents the role of patents, SPC, and data exclusivity in stimulating primary and secondary innovation in pharmacy. In the conclusions, it names several postulates for achieving a higher degree of legal certainty and a greater coherency among the three regimes in the contexts of their pro-innovative function.

---

unitary patent system is, however, not in operation yet and it will only apply from the date of entry into force of the Agreement on the Unitary Patent Court (UPC Agreement).

2. Regulation (EC) No 469/2009 of the European Parliament and of the Council of 6 May 2009 concerning the supplementary protection certificate for medicinal products (OJ 2009, L 152/1).
3. Data exclusivity for reference medicinal products is regulated in Art. 10(1) of the Directive 2001/83/EC of the European Parliament and of the Council of 6 November 2001 on the Community code relating to medicinal products for human use (OJ L 311, 28.11.2001, p. 67).
4. Pedro Henrique D. Batista, Dennis Byrski, Matthias Lamping & Roberto Romandini, *IP-Based Incentives Against Antimicrobial Crisis: A European Perspective*, 50 IIC 30-76, p. 67 (2019).
5. *See*, e.g., Graham Dutfield, *Healthcare Innovation and Patent Law's 'Pharmaceutical Privilege': Is There a Pharmaceutical Privilege? And If So, Should We Remove It?*, 12 Health Economics, Policy and Law 453-470 (2017).
6. Susy Frankel, Jessica C. Lai, *Patent Paw and Policy*, p. 5 (2016).

2 SPECIFICS OF PHARMACEUTICAL INNOVATION

2.1 Pharmaceutical Innovation in the EU Regulatory Legislation

The EU pharmaceutical regulatory regime provides certain guidelines on delineating innovative medicinal products. Regulation 1394/2007 on advanced therapy medicinal products[7] encompasses products used in gene therapy, somatic cell therapy, or derived from tissue engineering. Further, Regulation 726/2004, laying down the centralized marketing authorization procedure, indicates products that, due to their high level of innovation, complication, and significance, must be authorized via this route. These are products of certain biotechnological processes,[8] products consisting of new chemical entities for several significant therapeutic indications[9] and orphan drugs.[10] Optionally, the procedure may be used for other products based on a new active substance,[11] or for medicinal products which are based on known active substances and nevertheless constitute a significant therapeutic, scientific or technical innovation.

To determine whether a medicinal product constitutes a significant therapeutic, scientific or technical innovation, it is examined whether the medicinal product provides a new alternative for patients in treating, preventing or diagnosing a disease, or, if the medicinal product development is based on significant new scientific knowledge, the application of new scientific knowledge, or new technology or a new application of technology is used for the development or the manufacture of the medicinal product.[12] These criteria, however, are not precise, and they leave much of

---

7. Regulation (EC) No 1394/2007 of the European Parliament and of the Council of 13 November 2007 on advanced therapy medicinal products and amending Directive 2001/83/EC and Regulation (EC) No 726/2004 (OJ L 324, 10.12.2007, pp. 121-137).
8. The biotechnological processes mentioned here are: (a) recombinant DNA technology, (b) controlled expression of genes coding for biologically active proteins in prokaryotes and eukaryotes including transformed mammalian cells and (c) hybridoma and monoclonal antibody methods.
9. These are: (a) acquired immune deficiency syndrome, (b) cancer, (c) neurodegenerative disorder, (d) diabetes, (e) auto-immune diseases and other auto-immune dysfunctions, and (f) viral diseases.
10. Regulation (EC) No 726/2004 of the European Parliament and of the Council of 31 March 2004 laying down Community procedures for the authorization and supervision of medicinal products for human and veterinary use and establishing a European Medicines Agency (OJ L 136, 30.4.2004, pp. 1-33). *See also* Recitals 8 and 9 of the Regulation.
11. A new chemical, biological or radiopharmaceutical active substance, as defined in Annex III to Chapter 1 of the Notice to Applicants, includes: (a) a chemical, biological or radiopharmaceutical substance not previously authorized as a medicinal product in the European Union, (b) an isomer, mixture of isomers, a complex or derivative or salt of a chemical substance previously authorized as a medicinal product in the European Union but differing in properties with regard to safety and efficacy from that chemical substance previously authorized, (c) a biological substance previously authorized as a medicinal product in the European Union, but differing in molecular structure, nature of source material or manufacturing process, (d) a radiopharmaceutical substance which is a radionuclide, or a ligand not previously authorized as a medicinal product in the European Union, or the coupling mechanism to link the molecule and the radionuclide has not been authorized previously the European Union.
12. European Medicines Agency, *Pre-authorisation guidance of the EMA, Steps prior to submitting the application, 2.1.1.2. Optional Scope (Article 3(2))*, https://www.ema.europa.eu/en/human-regulatory/marketing-authorisation/pre-authorisation-guidance (last updated 18 May 2020).

the assessment up to the discretion of evaluation committees, rendering this assessment rather casuistic. In the EMA glossary directed to the general public, an innovative medicine is defined simply as a 'medicine that contains an active substance or combination of active substances that have not been authorized before'.[13]

To summarize, the indicated EU regulatory legislation refers to pharmaceutical innovation in one of three ways: either pointing to the diseases, where innovative treatment is most needed (e.g., rare diseases, AIDS, cancer), or naming certain chemical features of the products (advanced biotechnology products and processes, new chemical molecules), or, lastly, pointing to products beyond the first two categories, but constituting meaningful therapeutic indications. The innovation of the two first types is unquestioned and relatively easy to distinguish through objective criteria. What becomes problematic, however, is qualifying medicinal products as innovative when it comes to medicines consisting of known substances, but constituting alternative treatments to those already known, or contributing other scientific or technological advancements of various significance.

2.2 Rationales for Incentivizing Primary and Secondary Innovation

The actual scope of marketed pharmaceutical innovation may be systematized from various perspectives. One may differentiate between innovative medicinal products for specific therapeutic indications – certain illnesses, or certain groups of patients: e.g., paediatric or orphan medicines, pharmaceuticals combating tropical diseases, viral or microbial infections. As regards chemical structure, there are innovations based on small molecules, those being traditional chemical medicines, and biological drugs – so-called large molecule medicines. Biotechnological solutions and personalized medicine based on genetic testing may be differentiated on the grounds of the specific genetic tools that are used. Each of these exemplary types of innovative products responds more or less to the specific needs of public health and may become equally important to it at a certain time. Across all these divisions, there is a general one, based on the threshold of involved therapeutic advancement, which allows for differentiating between primary and secondary innovation.

Various levels of innovatory character are an intrinsic feature of innovating processes. According to the Organization for Economic Cooperation and Development Manual,[14] the notion of innovation denotes the implementation of a new or significantly improved product (good or service) or process, a new marketing method, or a new organizational method in business practices, workplace organization or external relations.[15]

In the pharmaceutical area, primary innovation can be characterized by a substantial, revolutionary advancement in therapy, or an entirely new approach to

13. European Medicines Agency, *Glossary*, https://www.ema.europa.eu/en/about-us/about-website/glossary/name_az/I (last visited 20 August 2020).
14. ECD/Eurostat, *Oslo Manual: Guidelines for Collecting and Interpreting Innovation Data*, The Measurement of Scientific and Technological Activities (3d ed., 2005).
15. *Ibid.*, para. 146.

prevention, treatment, or diagnosis. Primary pharmaceutical innovations are usually based on the development of a new chemical entity as the active ingredient of a medicinal product.

Secondary innovation is constituted of a modified or improved version of a previously known product or method used in prophylaxis, treatment or diagnosis. It usually involves the modification or application of a known active substance or a new combination of active substances.

Some examples of secondary innovations are:

- a new pharmaceutical form, e.g., new polymorphic or new isomeric form of a known substance;
- new therapeutic indications, e.g., use of a known active substance for the treatment of a different illness or treatment of a new patient group;
- a new dose or new dosage regime of a known substance;
- a new method of administration of a known medicinal product;
- improved manufacturing technology of a known medicinal product.

Secondary innovations may contribute to various advancements in treatment. New therapeutic indications may play a significant role in medicinal progress, especially if they concern the use of a known active substance in the treatment of an illness not related to one previously targeted. Polymorphic forms of a drug may have different physical properties such as melting point, solubility, or mechanical properties. These properties can influence the formulation, stability, or bioavailability of the active substance. New dosages or new methods of administration may have an impact on patient compliance and convenience.

Despite their unquestioned usefulness in medicine, there is a long-lasting dispute over whether granting IP protection for secondary pharmaceutical innovations is justified, and if so, to what extent – where should the threshold of innovation eligible for protection be?

For public health policy, primary innovations are more valuable than the improvement ones. They significantly push the boundaries of knowledge and provide a real advance in treatment. Referring to the well-known mining metaphor,[16] one could say that developing a new active substance resembles the discovery of a promising new mining terrain, to be explored and exploited, whereas most of the improvement inventions are akin to finding that there are better ways to exploit a known terrain. Primary innovations are thus a condition *sine qua non* for secondary innovations.

Beyond this general superiority of primary innovation over secondary, there are areas where new active substances are necessary, and cannot be replaced by the refinement of the known ones. This is the case for antibiotics. Moreover, due to increasing resistance to existing medicines, there is a strong need not only for new but

16. *See* Cornish referring to concept of Kitch, William Cornish, *Intellectual Property: Omnipresent, Distracting, Irrelevant?*, p. 14 (2004).

also a need for qualified novelty - namely for chemical entities not belonging to existing classes.[17]

From the economic perspective, setting a well-weighted threshold of protection is necessary for achieving an optimal relationship between the social costs of patent systems and the social welfare associated with them. Economic literature concerning an optimal system of IP protection for pharmaceuticals is extensive.[18] As rightly observed by Daria Kim, there is no 'ready-made' formula for how to optimize multiple welfare effects of various incentive instruments applicable to drugs.[19] One commonly known economic paradigm is that, if the threshold of protection is set too low, there is a risk of underutilization of innovations; if it is set too high - there is a risk of their underproduction. The desired equilibrium lies in assigning IP rights to inventions which actually stimulate technical progress and avoiding misallocation of rights at trivial solutions.[20] If there are lesser incentives for protecting trivial solutions or none at all, their monopolization gains are smaller, which in turn makes the number of IP rights decline and renders the IP systems more manageable. Setting the threshold of protection for secondary pharmaceutical innovation too low, combined with a high market entry barrier for primary innovation, results in decreased innovation incentives for incumbents, and weakens the competitive position of newcomers.

Over the last decades, there has been much criticism over the expanding IPR framework and many proposals for how to change it. The most revolutionary ones postulate abolishing the system of IP rights, claiming that they often can be unnecessary.[21] Some others see the need to optimize the IPR systems by introducing new exceptions or limitations.[22] Others want to restructure certain parts of the system, remarkably the IP in the pharmaceutical area.[23] The more sophisticated the proposals are, the more 'computationally complex' they appear.[24] However, as Rochelle Dreyfuss points out, it is necessary to return to incentive-based assumptions and justifications of

17. Batista et al., *supra* n. 4. At this point, it is worth noting that not all new antimicrobial agents would be able to promote real advances against the antimicrobial crisis. New antimicrobials belonging to existing classes would be more susceptible to rapid cross-resistance. For this reason, the literature indicates that qualified innovation is needed such as new agents that are able to attack new targets or offer new mechanisms of action in microbial cells.
18. For example, S.Y. Wu, Michael A. Riddiough & Ronald Hansen, *Pharmaceutical Innovation, Product Imitation, and Public Policy* (in:) *Drugs and Health: Economic Issues and Policy Objectives* (Robert B. Helms ed., 1981), Frederic M. Scherer, *Pricing, Profits, and Technological Progress in the Pharmaceutical Industry*, 7(3) The Journal of Economic Perspectives (1993); Daniel J. Gifford, *How Do the Social Benefits and Costs of the Patent System Stack Up in Pharmaceuticals?*, 12 Journal of Intellectual Property p. 75 (2004).
19. Daria Kim, *Rationalising Innovation Incentives under Drug Approval Regulation: National Policy Perspective* (in:) *Contemporary Issues in Pharmaceutical Patent Law: Setting the Framework and Exploring Policy Options* (Bryan Mercurio & Daria Kim eds, 2017), p. 224.
20. *See* Oliver Baldus, *The 'One Size Fits All' Problem of Patent Systems*, JIPLP, 5, 10 (2010), p. 728.
21. *See* Kal Raustala & Ch. J. Springman, *The Knockoff Economy: How Imitation Sparks Innovation* (2012).
22. *See*, e.g., Geertrui Van Overwalle, *Fair use: A Workable Concept in European Patent Law?* (in:) *Compulsory Patent Licencing* (Reto Hilty & Kung-Chung Liu, eds, 2014) 421-435.
23. *See* Baldus, *supra* n. 21, who proposed patents of three different classes, to be termed S, M and L.
24. *See* Robert P. Merges, *Justifying Intellectual Property* (2011).

IP law.[25] What can be done without a revolution, is considering modifications that are relatively easier to introduce, by virtue of certain policy of the European Patent Office (EPO), or in the jurisprudence of the domestic courts and in the Court of Justice of the European Union (CJEU), both directed to an incentive-based recalibration of the IP systems.

This chapter focuses on the threshold of eligible protection as the key factor of what type and level of innovation are incentivized. The following sections analyse where the threshold of protection for primary and secondary pharmaceutical innovations within patents, SPC, and regulatory exclusivities is, and what could be changed to make the systems better tailored to the complex aim of incentivizing valuable pharmaceutical innovation.

3 PATENTS

The role of patent law is, in general, to stimulate inventiveness within the entire area of technique and technology.[26] There is as yet no harmonized patent law across the European Union (EU).[27] However, for almost half a century, the European patent system, based on the European Patent Convention (EPC), has been common for all EU Member States.[28] This Convention provides for uniform rules of granting European patents.

According to Article 54(1) of the EPC, European patents are granted for any inventions, in all fields of technology, provided that they are new, involve an inventive step, and are capable of industrial application. This general provision enables obtaining patent protection for pharmaceutical innovation in the form of processes or products as such, i.e., for chemical entities, substances, or compositions. As regards pharmaceutical invention, the EPC provides special provisions for patentability of first and second medical uses.

First medical use is a category of inventions directed to an already known substance when used for the first time in a medical method.[29]

The patentability of first medical uses raised controversy as contrary to the commonly accepted requirement of absolute novelty. It was, however, justified as necessary in order to answer the needs of the European pharmaceutical industry,

25. Rochelle C. Dreyfuss, *In Praise of an Incentive-Based Theory of Intellectual Property Protection* (in:) *Framiong Intellectual Property Law in the 21st Century: Integrating Incentives, Trade, Development, Culture, and Human Rights* (Rochelle Cooper Dreyfuss & Elisabeth Siew-Kuan Ng eds, 2018).
26. Availability of patent protection in all fields of technology is required in Art. 27 of the TRIPS Agreement. *See* Agreement on Trade-Related Aspects of Intellectual Property Rights, constituting Annex 1C to the General Agreement on Tariffs and Trade of 1994.
27. The so-called Unitary Patent package, consisting of EU Regulation No 1257/2012, EU Regulation No 1260/2012 and Agreement on a Unified Patent Court, all three documents adopted in December 2012, is still not yet in force.
28. Convention on the grant of European Patent of 1973, amended in 2000. The original version of the Convention is quoted as EPC 1973, and the amended version – as EPC.
29. According to Art. 54(4), the novelty requirement shall not exclude the patentability of any substance or composition, comprised in the state of the art, for use in a medical method, as referred to in Art. 53(c), provided that its use for any of such method is new.

which was experiencing increasing difficulties in the synthesis of new compositions and searching for new drugs among already known chemical substances.[30] From the point of view of the character of innovation, products patented as first medical use may be assessed as primary innovations. Discovering any therapeutic effects of a chemical substance for the first time may be as significant as the synthesis of a new active substance. First medical use inventions are granted strong and broad protection covering the active substance in the whole area of medical methods.

A second (and further) medical use is a claim directed to a substance or composition known in medicine for a so far unknown therapeutic indication. Theoretically, a second medical use patent may be used for protecting both primary and secondary innovation. The first, rather rare case, is possible if the second medical use consists of discovering a therapeutic indication fairly far from the hitherto known one, e.g., use of the known compound to cure a disease not related to the previously cured one. Typically, however, a further medical use embodies secondary innovation. In the well-established case law of the EPO, a broad range of types of further medical uses are permitted as potential inventions.[31] They include the use of a known active substance for the treatment of a different disease, as well as its use in treating the same disease, differing only in the dosage, administration regime, group of subjects, or route of administration.[32] As a rule, such inventions represent secondary innovations and usually constitute so-called extension line developments made within the limits of patent protection obtained for the corresponding primary innovations.

Most trivial pharmaceutical improvements are not eligible for patent protection. This includes new forms of ready preparations or patient compliance features of a medicinal product. Examples of such secondary innovations are different additives or preservatives in the composition of a medicament, a refined tablet coating for easy swallowing, a certain shape or colour of tablets, like pink heart-shaped tablets in cardiological treatment. These off-patent improvements may come from technical solutions that are not novel, obvious in light of patent law or both.

Examples of primary innovations among process inventions are new processes of synthesis of a chemical substance or new methods of transporting the drug molecules into the body, like using nanoparticles. Secondary innovations usually involve improved, less costly, or less time-consuming manufacturing processes or particular phases thereof. Their importance is differentiated, starting from methods of confectioning and ending up with producing the active substance with lesser impurities. Whereas primary process innovations easily get patent protection, secondary ones may gain it only when they indicate nonobviousness. Secondary process innovations show

30. Lionel Bentley & Brad Sherman, *Intellectual Property Law*, p. 546 (4th ed. 2014). On average of about 80% of R&D expenditure was spent on examining known substances, with only 16%-20% spent for synthesis of new moieties. Cf. Gerhard Klöpsch, *Patentability of Pharmaceuticals According to the European Patent Convention (EPC)*, 13 IIC 461 (1982).
31. The decisions, which are most important for the patentability of further medical uses, do not deal at all with the issue of incentivizing innovation through European patents. *See* decisions G 5/83 of 5 December 1984 (OJ 1985, 64), T 1020/03 of 29 October 2004 (OJ EPO, 204), G 2/08 of 19 February 2010 (OJ EPO 2010, 456).
32. *See* reasoning of decision G 2/08 of 19 February 2010 (OJ EPO 2010/10, p. 456).

yet another inclination. As they are not prone to reverse engineering, they are often purposely kept beyond the patent protection regime, benefitting from trade secrets protection instead.[33]

The requirements of patentability are the same for new active substances, first and further medical uses or new technologies. The threshold of protected innovation has not been the subject of consideration in any of the important decisions of the EPO, which have substantially changed the framework of patent protection for pharmaceuticals.[34] The EPC patent system is a one-size-fits-all system, where both types - primary and secondary innovation - are equally protected and incentivized. This is one of the main points of critique of the patent protection regime for pharmaceuticals - that it offers the same protection for both breakthrough discoveries and relatively trivial findings such as a better-suited dosage regime.

It is important to note here that the extent of patent protection for pharmaceutical inventions is differentiated - product patents and first medical use patents benefit from absolute protection within the medical area; second medical uses are granted narrow protection, limited to the patented use. This is, however, not a deliberate adjustment of patent law - such differentiated scopes of protection correspond to various types of subject matter protected. Hence, it does not change the general opinion that the patent system is blind when it comes to the assessment of how groundbreaking an invention may be, or what technological or utilitarian progress it represents.[35]

Patent law indicates its weakness in this one-size-fits-all character. It is difficult to accept that a full 20-year period of patent protection is granted for a newly developed active substance on the one hand, and on the other hand, the same period for its new polymorphic form. The ease of patenting incremental inventions discourages more valuable innovation.

What rationale should the EPO take when granting patents for further medical uses? After the amendment of 2000,[36] the patentability of second medical uses became codified in law. But the criteria of their patentability are subject to dynamic interpretation by the Technical Boards of Appeals and the Enlarged Board of Appeal. It is the role of the EPO to interpret the provisions of the EPC in light of the rationale underlying

33. In Europe, it is harmonized on the grounds of Directive (EU) 2016/943 of the European Parliament and of the Council of 8 June 2016 on the protection of undisclosed know-how and business information (trade secrets) against their unlawful acquisition, use and disclosure (OJ L 157, 15.6.2016, pp. 1-18). According to Art. 2(1) of this directive, a trade secret is information that (a) is secret in the sense that it is not, as a body or in the precise configuration and assembly of its components, generally known among or readily accessible to persons within the circles that normally deal with the kind of information in question, (b) it has commercial value because it is secret, and (c) it has been subject to reasonable steps under the circumstances, by the person lawfully in control of the information, to keep it secret.
34. These decisions include G 5/83 on patentability of second medical use, T-1020/03 concerning legal effects of second medical use claims, G 2/08 on dosage regimes.
35. Dutfield, *supra* n. 5, at 453-454.
36. Act revising the European Patent Convention of 29 November 2000 (Revision Act 2000) and the decision of the Administrative Council of 28 June adopting the new text of the European Patent Convention (OJ EPO Special editions No. 4/2001, pp. 56 et seq.; No. 1/2003, pp. 3 et seq.; No. 1/2007, pp. 1 to 88).

patent system: the system should incentivize innovation, not innovation no matter what, but innovation at a certain level.

Whereas an all-or-nothing approach is not necessary here, modifications in the realm of the secondary medical use patents are certainly recommended. The problem of trivial inventions concerning new dosage regimes or new modes of administration should be approached by setting clear guidelines on the inventive step. The guidelines should be based on the common knowledge and experience that the use of the same active substance to treat the same illness in the same group of patients is obvious unless it authentically meets the criteria of an inventive step.

Further, taking into account the problem-solution approach applied routinely by the EPO to assess the nonobviousness of an invention, it should refer to a physician practising the hitherto known medical application as a person skilled in the art. State of the art, in turn, should comprise not only the hitherto known therapeutic methods themselves but also concrete experiences and observations about the effects of said treatment from such a physician while applying this method. The understanding of a person skilled in the art and the state of the art resembles the professional reality of applying secondary medical use inventions and developing further medical uses – identifying better ways of treatment by therapy, diagnosis or surgery. It is unreasonable to conduct an assessment of the inventive step of further medical use *in abstracto,* i.e., in separation from the factual application of the known methods and their practical results.

Lastly, for the sake of transparency, the guidelines should present positive and negative indicators of nonobviousness, embracing specialist knowledge derived from the regulatory framework. Examples of such indicators could be:

- If a secondary medical use is a new mode of administration, it should be based on a different technical effect of the active substance. For example, a change from a nasal aerosol to under-tongue drops is not non-obvious as both methods operate on the mucous membrane.
- Introducing supplementary technical or functional features, not changing the hitherto known technical effect, does not render the use non-obvious.

4 SUPPLEMENTARY PROTECTION CERTIFICATES

4.1 Purposes of the SPC System

Supplementary protection certificates, governed by Regulation 469/2009, are legal instruments aiming at extending patent protection for certain medicinal products.[37]

37. Regulation (EC) No 469/2009 of the European Parliament and of the Council of 6 May 2009 concerning the supplementary protection certificate for medicinal products (Codified version) (OJ L 152, 16.6.2009, pp. 1-10), cited later as SPC Regulation.

Before the establishment of the SPC system,[38] the period that elapsed between filing a patent application for a pharmaceutical invention and obtaining marketing authorization for the final medicinal product resulted in the length of the effective patent protection being insufficient to cover the investment put into the research and to incentivize further research in the EU.[39]

The function of an SPC is to enable the holder of a patent covering a medicinal product to enjoy an overall maximum of 15 years of exclusivity from the time the medicinal product in question first obtains authorization to be placed on the market in the EU.[40] For the sake of public interest, the certificates are granted for a period not exceeding five years, and the protection granted is strictly confined to the product which obtained authorization.[41]

The specific purposes of the SPC legislation may be found both in the Preamble and in the *travaux préparatoires*.[42] Both indicate that the original aim of the SPC system was to incentivize research into new active ingredients, i.e., substances with a therapeutic effect, that have never been authorized before in the EU. Such substances require full preclinical and clinical testing, resulting in huge costs and shortening the period of an effective patent monopoly. The *Explanatory Memorandum* of the European Commission states clearly that 'the proposal for a Regulation, therefore, concerns only new medicinal products. It does not involve granting a certificate for all medicinal products that are authorized to be placed on the market. Only one certificate may be granted for any one product, a product being understood to mean an active substance in the strict sense'.[43]

---

38. SPCs were introduced on the grounds of Council Regulation (EEC) No 1768/92 of 18 June 1992 concerning the creation of a supplementary protection certificate for medicinal products (OJ L 182, 2.07.1992, pp. 0001-0005), subsequently cancelled by specified recodified Regulation (EC) No 469/2009 of the European Parliament and of the Council of 6 May 2009 concerning the supplementary protection certificate for medicinal products (OJ L 152, 16.6.2009, pp. 1–10). Supplementary protection certificates are available also for plant protection products as provided in Regulation (EC) No 1610/96 of the European Parliament and of the Council of 23 July 1996 concerning the creation of a supplementary protection certificate for plant protection products (OJ L 198, 8.8.1996, pp. 0030-0035). They are not however subject to analysis within this chapter.
39. Recital 4 of the SPC Regulation. The Explanatory Memorandum indicated that an average period of 12 years between the discovery of a new medical product, at which time the patent application is filed, and its being made available to patients is currently necessary, the effect of which is to reduce the exclusive exploitation period under the patent to only 8 years. *See* European Commission, Explanatory Memorandum to the Proposal for a Council Regulation (EEC), of 11 April 1990, concerning the creation of a supplementary protection certificate for medicinal products (COM(90) 101 final - SYN255), para. 2.
40. Recital 9 of the SPC Regulation.
41. Recital 10 of the SPC Regulation.
42. European Commission, Explanatory Memorandum, *supra* n. 39, para. 3.
43. *Ibid.*, para. 11. An analogous view was presented in the Opinion of the Economic and Social Committee on the proposal for a Council Regulation (EEC) concerning the creation of supplementary protection certificate for medicinal products of 1991 (OJ C 69/22). It was stated there that the certificate is designed to encourage research into new medicinal products so that the duration of protection it affords, together with the effective duration of protection by patent, is sufficient to enable the investments made in the research to be recovered. Further it added that an SPC shall be restricted to 'pharmaceutical discoveries that genuinely involve a basic innovation'.

The SPC system was thus not intended to reward and incentivize all possible research in the pharmaceutical area but was addressed towards fostering the development of medicines based on new chemical molecules.[44] Such a conclusion is confirmed by a literal reading of the provisions concerning SPC eligibility. According to Article 3(d) of the SPC regulation, an SPC may be granted only when based on the first marketing authorization (MA) in the state concerned, and according to Article 3(c), only one SPC may be granted for this product. The combined effect of these provisions is that an SPC was meant to be granted only for substances that were authorized for the first time as a medicinal product.[45]

4.2 SPC Eligibility

According to Article 3 of the SPC Regulation, an SPC may be granted if: (a) a product, understood as an active ingredient, is protected by a basic patent in force; (b) a valid authorization to place the product on the market as a medicinal product has been granted in accordance with Directive 2001/83/EC or Directive 2001/82/EC, as appropriate; (c) the product has not already been the subject of a certificate; and (d) the authorization referred to in point (b) is the first authorization to place the product on the market as a medicinal product (Article 3 of the SPC Regulation). A basic patent denotes a patent that protects a product as such, a process to obtain a product or an application of a product, and which is designated by its holder for the purpose of the procedure for grant of a certificate.[46]

While there is no doubt that SPC protection is available for new active substances, the premises of SPC eligibility have been subject to increasing controversies as regards the protection of further medical uses. From the point of interest of this article, the core problem lies in determining where the borderline is between innovations that deserve additional protection via SPC and those that do not, and what is the criterion of differentiation between them. This issue lay behind subsequent references for preliminary rulings to the CJEU in cases *Neurim*, *Abraxis* and *Santen*. These cases will serve as an illustration of the problem.

As far as further medical uses are concerned, according to the strict, literal interpretation of the requirements of Article 3, an SPC may be granted only when a basic patent covers an active substance authorized for the market as a medicinal product for the first time. *A contrario,* an SPC may not be granted for a medicinal product whose active substance was authorized for the market earlier than the marketing authorization designated by the patent holder in the SPC application. Such

44. For a detailed analysis of the legislative objectives of the SPC regulation, *see* Max Planck Institute for Innovation and Competition, *Study on the Legal Aspects of SPC – Final Report*, Publications Office of the European Union, p. 15 (2018).
45. As underlined in the Study on the Legal Aspects, if the product had already been authorized in the past, and the applicant identified new uses or a new formulation of the product and obtained a more recent MA, an SPC was meant to be excluded due to either Art. 3(d) or Art. 7 Reg. *See ibid.*, p. 15.
46. *See* Art. 1 (c) of the SPC Regulation.

an interpretation would result in granting SPCs solely for active substances that were not present on the market as medicinal products before.

In *Neurim*, the referring court looked for an answer as to whether an SPC indeed may only be granted for an active substance that has not been already subject to any MA. It asked whether the first MA in the meaning of Article 3b must be the first MA of the active substance at all or a first MA of the active substance as is subject to the basic patent in question. If the latter was going to be the case, i.e., an SPC could be granted for a substance protected by a further medical use patent and authorized on the grounds of a further MA, the court queried what circumstances could be important for assessing the further MA as fulfilling the requirement of being the first MA within the meaning of Article 3b. It referred to three aspects: (1) the notion of a first MA, whether to be interpreted as dependent on the limits of the basic patent or independently; (2) a change of indication from veterinary use to a human medicinal product; and (3) the achievement of an MA in a full data procedure (full application). In fact, the referring court asked the CJEU to identify the threshold of pharmaceutical innovation, or of therapeutic significance, which deserves protection via SPC.

In its judgment C-130/11 *Neurim*,[47] the CJEU adjudicated that:

> if a patent protects a therapeutic application of a known active ingredient which has already been marketed as a medicinal product, for veterinary or human use, for other therapeutic indications, whether or not protected by an earlier patent, the placement on the market of a new medicinal product commercially exploiting the new therapeutic application of the same active ingredient, as protected by the new patent, may enable its proprietor to obtain an SPC the scope of which, in any event, could cover, not the active ingredient, but only the new use of that product.[48]

In other words, the Court allowed for granting an SPC for an active substance patented for a new therapeutic indication and authorized for the first time for this new therapeutic indication, even if the marketing authorization relevant for the SPC procedure was not the first MA of this active substance.

Having allowed for granting an SPC in the case of a further MA of the same active substance, the Court triggered further questions about the relation of that MA to the relevant basic patent. Here, in the opinion of the Court, only the MA of the first medicinal product, comprising the product and authorized for a therapeutic use corresponding to that protected by the patent relied upon, may be considered to be the first MA of 'that product' as a medicinal product exploiting that new use within the

47. Judgment of the European Court of Justice in case C-130/11 *Neurim Pharmaceuticals (1991) Ltd v. Comptroller-General of Patents*, EU:C:2012:489 (19 July 2012).
48. *Ibid.*, point 25 of the Reasoning/Judgment. In its argumentation line, the CJEU referred to para. 29 of the Explanatory Memorandum to the proposal for a Council Regulation (EEC) of 11 April 1990, concerning the creation of a supplementary protection certificate for medicinal products (COM(90) 101 final). In the opinion of the CJEU it is apparent from this paragraph that, like a patent protecting a 'product' or a patent protecting a process by which a 'product' is obtained, a patent protecting a new application of a new or known product may, in accordance with Art. 2 of the SPC Regulation, enable an SPC to be granted, with the scope of protection limited to the new use of that product.

meaning of Article 3(d) of the SPC Regulation.[49] The criterion of the first MA was, in fact, to be read as the first MA within the limits of the basic patent protection. It meant that subsequent MAs comprising the same active substance and authorized for new therapeutic use as protected by the same basic patent could not be relevant for the sake of the obtaining of an SPC. But, these subsequent MAs could be relevant if they were protected by other patents. A far-reaching ramification of this setup was the potential existence of many SPCs for different applications of the same active substance, provided each of these applications was protected by another patent and subject to another MA.

Neurim changed the formerly strict approach to SPC eligibility and raised at least three big topics for further considerations. First, whether any further new therapeutic application, by analogy to second medical use inventions, was SPC eligible. Second, whether an SPC could be granted for a new use of a known substance if this substance as such had already been granted another SPC. And lastly, if a new formulation or composition of known active substances could be relevant for obtaining an SPC.

Chronologically, the issue of new formulation came up first. In its judgment in the case C-443/17 *Abraxis*,[50] the Court adjudicated that an MA for a new formulation of a known active ingredient, the latter being subject to an earlier MA, cannot be regarded as the first marketing authorization in the meaning of Article 3(d). The judgment followed well-established CJEU case law, according to which, an addition of a substance without its own therapeutic effect does not render this set a new product or a new composition.[51] It explicitly referred to the intentions of the EU legislature, to protect 'not all pharmaceutical research giving rise to the grant of a patent and the marketing of a new medicinal product, but to protect research leading to the first placing on the market of an active ingredient or a combination of active ingredients as a medicinal product'.[52]

The issue of SPC eligibility for new therapeutic applications, triggered by *Neurim*, became subject to considerations in the case C-673/18 *Santen*.[53] The prejudicial questions concerned whether a new therapeutic application eligible for an SPC must be understood as falling within a new therapeutic field, in the sense of a new medical application, as compared to the previous MA, or may merely differ in the different mode of action of the active substance. In more general terms, the Court asked what,

49. Other circumstances mentioned in the preliminary questions – full data MA application and ownership of particular rights – were deemed not relevant for grant of SPC. As regards the importance of full data procedure for the SPC, the CJEU found this issue related to procedural aspects only and as such not relevant to substantive law requirements (point 33 of the Judgment). Likewise, it was deemed irrelevant who is the holder of successive patents, authorizations or SPC applications.
50. Judgment of the Court of Justice of the EU in case C-443/17 *Abraxis Bioscience LLC v. Comptroller-General of Patents*, ECLI:EU:C:2019:238 (21 March 2019).
51. *See*, e.g., Judgment of the European Court of Justice in case C-210/13 *GlaxoSmithKline Biologicals SA and GlaxoSmithKline Biologicals, Niederlassung der Smithkline Beecham Pharma GmbH & Co. KG v. Comptroller-General of Patents, Designs and Trade Marks*, ECLI:EU:C:2013:762 (14 November 2013), point 44.
52. Judgment in case Abraxis, *see supra* n. 50, Reasons, para. 37.
53. Case C-673/18 *Santen SAS v. Director General of the National Institute of Intellectual Property*.

in light of the objectives of the SPC, should be the criteria of SPC eligibility and whether they need to be stricter than the criteria of patentability for further medical uses.

The Advocate General, in his comprehensive opinion,[54] criticized *Neurim* for standing in clear conflict with the wording of Article 3(d) of the SPC regulation and with former case law, in particular with decisions in C-31/03 *Pharmacia*,[55] C-202/05 *Yissum*,[56] and C-431/04 *MIT*.[57] Moreover, he found the *Neurim* interpretation incompatible with the *ratio legis* of SPC regulation, aiming at awarding protection for new active substances and not for new therapeutic indications thereof.

Following this opinion, in its judgment of 20 July 2020,[58] the CJEU overturned the *Neurim* approach, adjudicating on three important issues.

First, the Court confirmed the strict interpretation of the term 'product' as required in *Abraxis*.

Second, it stated that a new therapeutic application does not render an MA of an active ingredient its first MA, regardless of how far from the known use this new therapeutic application lies.

This approach deals with the critical problem of SPCs for new therapeutic applications in an uncompromised way. Considering that breakthrough, pharmaceutical innovations patented as second medical uses may occur, such a policy might be regarded as too simplistic. However, even if not perfect, it still is better tailored for the SPC purposes, and more sustainable than setting a vague threshold of SPC eligibility by reference to particular types of therapeutic applications. As mentioned earlier, patents claim an invention, describing its technical or functional features in terms of specific patent law requirements. An MA is granted for a certain active substance for a certain therapeutic indication, described in a detailed way as regards its form, way of administration, and dosage. There are very few limits to applying for numerous patents and numerous MAs concerning the same or similar active substances, in their various compositions, formulations, and therapeutic indications. However, the experience with second medical use patents shows that any adopted policy would be subject to constant challenges by the pharmaceutical lobby, and most probably it ends up with relatively lenient standards of eligibility.

The last important issue adjudicated in *Santen* is the interpretation of the notion of a first MA, as required in Article 1(b) of the SPC Regulation. According to the Court, it cannot be understood as the first MA within the limits of basic patent protection, but as the first MA in general. In this respect, the Court came back to the early policy of the

54. Opinion of the Advocate General in case C-673/18 *Santen SAS v. Director General of the National Institute of Intellectual Property*, ECLI:EU:C:2020:34 (23 January 2020).
55. Judgment of the European Court of Justice in case C-31/03 *Pharmacia Italia SpA*, ECLI: EU:C:2004:641 (19 October 2004).
56. Judgment of the European Court of Justice in case C-202/05 *Yissum Research and Development Company of the Hebrew University of Jerusalem v. Comptroller-General of Patents*, ECLI: EU:C:2007:214 (17 April 2007).
57. Judgment of the European Court of Justice in case C-431/04 *Massachusetts Institute of Technology*, ECLI:EU:C:2006:291 (4 May 2006).
58. Judgment of the Court of Justice of the European Union (Grand Chamber) of 9 July 2020, in case C-673/18 *Santen SAS v. Director General of the National Institute of Intellectual Property*.

CJEU: one SPC per one product per patent, which means that any representations of an invention covered by one patent may be subject only to one SPC.

The decision is of great importance for the legal protection of pharmaceuticals. It means that an SPC may be granted only for a new active substance, understood as an active substance not authorized before in the Member State where the protection is sought.

In the view of the Court, such an approach enables a fair balance to be struck between, on the one hand, the objective of the SPC regime, of compensating for the inadequacy of protection conferred by a patent for the purpose of covering the investment put into research concerning new active ingredients or combinations of active ingredients, and therefore, of encouraging such research, and on the other hand, the EU legislature's intention, to achieve that objective in a manner that takes into account all the interests at stake, including those of public health, in a sector as complex and sensitive as the pharmaceutical sector.[59]

The third of the before mentioned cases, C-354/19 *Novartis*, concerns the issue of an SPC for an active substance that has been subject to an earlier SPC. The referring court asks if, in such a situation, it is possible to grant an SPC to the same applicant, for a different therapeutic application which is specifically protected by a new basic patent.

Should the answer be positive, it would still leave room for clarifications as regards numerous basic patents and numerous SPC applications for various therapeutic uses of the same active substance. Should the answer be in the negative, it would be followed by applications for annulment of earlier SPC's and prejudicial questions about its legality.[60]

In light of *Santen* and *Abraxis*, the preliminary questions are not likely to be answered in the positive. If an SPC has been deemed not possible for a new therapeutic application of an earlier authorized, active substance, then, *a fortiori*, it is not supposed to be allowed for the new therapeutic application of an active substance already protected by an earlier SPC. This, in turn, deprives importance of the potentially upcoming issue of invalidating an already granted SPC to make the active substance SPC eligible again.

To conclude, the SPC system was drafted with the intention of stimulating primary innovation. In the course of the interpretative activity of the CJEU, the criteria of SPC eligibility have been subject to differing approaches.[61] From the perspective of time, *Neurim* seems to be a step out from the prevailing line of strict SPC eligibility

59. *See Abraxis Bioscience*, C-443/17, para. 36, and *Santen*, C-673/18, para. 57.
60. First judgments of European domestic courts deemed the practice legal. *See* judgment of the German Federal Patent Court of 7 December 2016 (trifloxystrobin), 15 W (pat) 22/14, http://juris.bundespatentgericht.de/cgi-bin/rechtsprechung/document.py?Gericht=bpatg&Art=en&sid=73d9f34319145314b0392b8bcb8aa696&nr=31492&pos=0&anz=1&Blank=1.pdf; judgment of the French Supreme Court of 5 April 2018 (RG no. 18/02118), http://patentblog.kluweriplaw.com/wp-content/uploads/sites/52/2018/12/Novartis_SPC_FR_3.pdf.
61. Apart from the interpretation of the first MA criterion, crucial for the subject of this chapter, there are other issues, still leaving room for doubts, e.g., notion of the basic patent.

standards indicated in several decisions of the CJEU.[62] Such standards correspond well with the aim of the SPC system – to incentivize innovations based on new chemical molecules.

5 REGULATORY EXCLUSIVITIES

5.1 Pharmaceutical Regulatory Framework in the EU

Placing a product on the pharmaceutical market in the EU encounters the barrier of a highly specific regulatory framework. Directive 2001/83,[63] constituting the EU pharmaceutical code, requires that each medicinal product that is introduced to the market must undergo a marketing authorization procedure and prove the fulfilment of certain safety and efficacy requirements.[64] These requirements are verified on the basis of the results of (a) pharmaceutical tests, i.e., physicochemical, biological or microbiological tests; (b) preclinical tests, i.e., toxicological and pharmacological tests; and (c) clinical trials.[65] A medicinal product authorized on the grounds of full data, encompassing the above-mentioned tests and trials, is called a reference medicinal product.[66]

By way of derogation from this rule, applicants are not required to provide the results of preclinical tests and clinical trials if they can demonstrate that a medicinal product is a generic of a reference medicinal product that has been authorized in the EU and the period of data exclusivity has elapsed.[67] A generic medicinal product is defined as a medicinal product which has the same qualitative and quantitative composition in active substances and the same pharmaceutical form as the reference medicinal product, and whose bioequivalence to the reference medicinal product has been demonstrated by appropriate bioavailability studies. The different salts, esters, ethers, isomers, mixtures of isomers, complexes or derivatives of an active substance are considered to be the same active substance unless they differ significantly in properties with regard to safety and/or efficacy.[68]

In certain situations, when the definition of a 'generic medicinal product' is not met strictly, or where the bioavailability studies cannot be used to demonstrate

62. *See* especially Judgment of the European Court of Justice in case C-322/10 *Medeva BV v. Comptroller-General of Patents, Designs and Trade Marks*, ECLI:EU:C:2011:773 (24 November 2011); judgment of CJEU in case C-484/12 *Georgetown University v. Octrooicentrum Nederland*, OJ UE 2014/C 52/33 (12 December 2013); judgment of CJEU in Case C-577/13 *Actavis Group PTC EHF, Actavis UK Ltd v. Boehringer Ingelheim Pharma GmbH & Co. KG*, OJ EU 2015/C 146/04 (12 March 2015); judgment of CJEU in case C-493/12 *Eli Lilly and Company Ltd v. Human Genome Sciences Inc.*, OJ EU 2014/C 45/24 (12 December 2013); judgment of CJEU in case C-130/11 *Neurim Pharmaceuticals (1991) Ltd v. Comptroller-General of Patents*, OJ EU 2012, C 295 (19 July 2012).
63. Directive 2001/83/EC of the European Parliament and of the Council of 6 November 2001 on the Community code relating to medicinal products for human use (OJ EU 2004, L 136/34) with subsequent changes.
64. *Ibid.*, Art. 6(1).
65. *Ibid.*, Art. 8 3).
66. *Ibid.*, Art. 10(2)(a).
67. *Ibid.*, Art. 10(1). Rules of data exclusivity for reference drugs are described below.
68. *Ibid.*, Art. 10(2)(b).

bioequivalence, or, where there are changes in the active substance(s), therapeutic indications, strength, pharmaceutical form or route of administration of the generic product compared to the reference medicinal product, then a hybrid procedure applies. Hybrid applications rely in part on the results of preclinical tests and clinical trials for a reference product and in part on new data. They are a form of generic application.

Based on the rules presented for marketing authorization of reference and generic drugs, one could be tempted to see a simple dichotomy: reference drugs are the innovative products, commonly called original drugs, i.e., the desired pharmaceutical innovations, whereas the generic drugs are mere copies, imitations of the reference drugs, and thus are not innovative. The situation is, however, far from obvious.

First, the notion of a reference product is broader than that resulting from a literal reading of Article 10(2)(a) and covers not only medicines authorized for the first time on the basis of a full registration dossier but also products authorized based on so-called well-established medicinal use. This way of interpreting the concept of reference medicinal products was confirmed by the CJEU in its judgment in case C-104/13.[69] It is stated there that the notion of a reference medicinal product also encompasses a medicinal product for which the marketing authorization was granted on the grounds of Article 10a of the directive. This article provides that the applicant shall not be required to provide the results of preclinical tests or clinical trials if they can demonstrate that the active substances of the medicinal product have been in well-established medicinal use within the Community for at least ten years, with recognized efficacy and an acceptable level of safety.

Therefore, not all reference products are innovations. What's more, sometimes important innovations may also take the form of secondary improvements to known medicines, authorized for the market in a hybrid procedure. Therefore, not only reference products can be innovative.

5.2 Data and Market Protection for Reference Medicinal Products

Pharmaceutical legislation in the EU provides specific forms of protection for regulatory data in regards to chosen medicinal products to incentivize their development and commercialization. There are three separate regulations concerning the protection of regulatory data: data and market exclusivity for new reference drugs, orphan exclusivity, as well as the system of paediatric exclusivity and rewards.

The system of data and market exclusivity for reference medicinal products is regulated in Directive 2001/83. According to Article 10(1), the regulatory data of a new reference product, consisting mostly of the results of clinical trials and preclinical tests, and provided by the first entrant, are protected against their re-use for the sake of generic entry for the period of eight years from the date of the marketing authorization. After this period of data exclusivity, the relevant data are not disclosed – they may, however, be relied on in order to launch the so-called abridged marketing procedure of

69. Judgment of the European Court of Justice in case C-104/13 *Olainfarm* (23 October 2014) OJ 2014 C 439.

a generic medicinal product. An already authorized generic medicinal product may not be placed on the market until ten years have elapsed from the authorization of the reference product.[70] This period of an additional two years constitutes so-called market exclusivity, guaranteeing a ten-year period of access to the market which is undistorted by the generic competition. Theoretically, during the whole period of the ten-year exclusivity period, another entity could obtain a marketing authorization on the grounds of its own full documentation. Therefore, this is not a *de lege* but de facto exclusivity. In practice, however, alternative full documentation of a medicinal product identical to an already authorized one happens extremely rarely.

The 10-year period of market exclusivity may be extended, by one year, if during the first eight years, the marketing authorization holder obtains authorization for one or more new therapeutic indications which are assessed as bringing a significant clinical benefit in comparison with existing therapies.[71] Such an extension may be obtained only once; subsequent improvements or developments of an authorized innovative medicine do not enjoy any additional periods of data and market exclusivity. Following the rule of global marketing authorization, 'a marketing authorization for a new product includes all its additional strengths, pharmaceutical forms, administration routes, presentations as well as any variations and extensions which are authorized later'.[72]

This rule is, in fact, an interpretative clause of what level of pharmaceutical innovation is protected by data and market exclusivity for reference drugs. Before its normative regulation, it was established by the CJEU case law, in judgment *Generics*.[73] This decision was one of the very few CJEU rulings in pharmaceutical cases in which the court directly addressed the issue of protection for innovation.

The referring court asked, among other points, if the provision in question, underlying an abridged procedure at that time and not providing for extended protection for subsequently authorized indications of an active substance,[74] is invalid as contrary to the principles of protection of innovation, non-discrimination, proportionality and respect for property.[75] According to the Court, however, none of the rules was infringed by the provision at issue, as interpreted in this judgment. To the contrary, in the opinion of the Court, it was an appropriate and reasonable means of reconciling its aims: providing the necessary extent of protection for innovation, and securing public interest by avoiding the repetition of tests on humans or animals.[76]

70. *Supra* n. 64, Art. 10(1), second section.
71. *Supra* n. 64, Art. 10(1) in fine.
72. *Supra* n. 64, Art. 6(1) in fine. *See* also judgment of the European Court of Justice in case C-368/96 *Generics UK v. Glaxo-BMS*, ECLI:EU:C:1998:583 (3 December 1998), which introduced this rule, without a clear legal basis at that time, as well as other judgments following it: C-36/03 *The Queen on the application of Approved Prescription Services Ltd v. Licensing Authority*, ECR I-11606 (9 December 2004).
73. *Ibid.*, Judgment of the CJEU in case C-368/96.
74. It was Art. 4.8(a)(iii) of Council Directive 65/65/EEC of 26 January 1965 on the approximation of provisions laid down by Law, Regulation or Administrative Action relating to proprietary medicinal products (OJ 22, 9.2.1965, pp. 369-373).
75. *See supra* n. 72, *Generics*, preliminary question no. 5.
76. *Supra* n. 72, *Generics*, paras 60-86.

The CJEU gave this ruling while being aware that such an interpretation could undermine protection for secondary, but nevertheless major, therapeutic innovations.[77] In the course of the proceeding, the European Commission expressed the view that therapeutic indications representing a major therapeutic innovation requiring full new pharmacological or toxicological tests or clinical trials should be given independent protection. The proposed criteria for a 'major therapeutic innovation' were that the innovation was patented or that it corresponded to a list of significant therapeutic interests indicated in Regulation 2309/93.[78] The CJEU found such criteria not sufficiently precise and possibly harmful to the principle of legal certainty, stating simultaneously that separate legal measures would have to be adapted if the pharmaceutical innovative undertakings were to be protected.[79]

An additional year of market exclusivity for new therapeutic indications with a significant clinical benefit, as indicated above, is clearly such a measure, adapted in the amending Directive 2004/27. This notion of significant clinical benefit, however, has no legal definition.

In the Guidelines of the European Commission,[80] it is accepted that a new indication would normally include the following:

- a new target disease;
- different stages or severity of disease;
- an extended target population for the same disease, e.g., based on a different age range or other intrinsic (e.g., renal impairment) or extrinsic (e.g., concomitant product) factors;
- a change from the first-line treatment to second-line treatment (or second-line to first-line treatment), or from combination therapy to monotherapy, or from one combination therapy (e.g., in the area of cancer) to another combination;
- a change from treatment to prevention or diagnosis of a disease;
- a change from treatment to prevention of progression of a disease or the prevention of relapses of a disease;
- a change from short-term treatment to long-term maintenance therapy in chronic disease.

77. 'According to the MCA, Article 4.8(a)(iii) of Directive 65/65, as amended, must be interpreted as meaning that where the applicant shows that the composition of the product for which he is seeking marketing authorization is essentially similar to that of the original product, he may, under the abridged procedure, obtain a marketing authorization for both the original indications, dosage schedules, doses or dosage forms and any addition or change to the indications, dosage schedules, doses or dosage forms for which the original product was authorized, whether or not during the last 10 years, *save where those additions or changes constitute major therapeutic innovations* (emphasis added).' *See supra* n. 72, *Generics*, para. 17.

78. *See* Part B of the Annex to Council Regulation (EEC) No 2309/93 of 22 July 1993 laying down Community procedures for the authorization and supervision of medicinal products for human and veterinary use and establishing a European Agency for the Evaluation of Medicinal Products (OJ 1993 L 214, p. 1).

79. *See supra* n. 72, *Generics*, para. 52.

80. European Commission, *Guidance on elements required to support the significant clinical benefit in comparison with existing therapies of a new therapeutic indication in order to benefit from an extended (11-year) marketing protection period*, para. 3.1 (November 2007), https://ec.europa.eu/health//sites/health/files/files/eudralex/vol-2/c/guideline_14-11-2007_en.pdf.

The clinical benefit of a new indication is assessed not only in comparison to the relevant reference medicine, being subject to 10-year regulatory exclusivities, but also to all existing therapies and all medicine products authorized for the market, which makes this assessment more objective. On the other hand, the evaluation itself is very discretionary. As is indicated in the Guidelines, a new treatment could generally be of significant clinical benefit if it provides a clinically relevant advantage or a major contribution to patient care. In general, demonstration of greater efficacy, an improved safety profile, and/or more favourable pharmacokinetic properties resulting in demonstrable clinical advantages compared to existing methods may support the notion of significant clinical benefit.[81] The Guidelines do not provide for any objective qualitative or quantitative criteria – all terms used are descriptive and are considered on a case-by-case basis. This difficulty in setting objective criteria of significant clinical benefit within the harmonized pharmaceutical regulatory framework may serve as a good explanation of the problem of setting a relevant threshold of innovation within the so much more complicated legal framework of patents and SPC.

To sum up, the threshold of innovation protected and incentivized by data and market exclusivity for reference medicines covers new active substances, i.e., authorized for the first time for the market in the EU, and new indications with significant clinical benefit. The first type is granted a 10-year protection period, the latter – an additional year. Primary innovation is the main aim of this exclusivity system. Secondary innovation is incentivized to a much lesser extent, and only when it has a significant meaning for existing therapies.

What is interesting is that there is no analogical exclusivity – and thus no incentive at all – for data provided in the hybrid procedure. The results of new tests and trials, possibly leading to meaningful secondary innovations, are not covered by any form of exclusivity.[82] On the one hand, it prevents extending the data exclusivity period for new indications on the grounds of subsequent hybrid applications. On the other – it discourages third parties from authorizing new indications of active substances via the route of the hybrid procedure.

5.3 Orphan Exclusivity

Market exclusivity for orphan medicines was established on the grounds of Regulation 141/2000[83] and aims at incentivizing R&D on orphan medicines, i.e., medicinal products used for the treatment of rare diseases, as a rule occurring in the Community in less than five in 10,000 persons. Due to such rareness, orphan diseases have no economic impact to constitute an incentive for research works under normal market conditions.

81. *Ibid.*, para. 3.3.
82. *See* the judgment of High Court of Justice in Napp Pharmaceuticals [2016] EWHC 1982, (29 July 2016) http://www.bailii.org/ew/cases/EWHC/Admin/2016/1982.html.
83. Regulation (EC) No 141/2000 of the European Parliament and the Council and of Council of 16 December 1999 on orphan medicinal products (OJ L 18/1, 22 January 2000).

Orphan exclusivity is not connected to the market authorization procedure and as such, is independent of data exclusivity. Instead, it is related to a specific designation of a medicinal product as an orphan and lasts 10 years from a marketing authorization of such a product.[84]

Orphan designation is granted for a medicinal product fulfilling two requirements: (a) that it is intended for the diagnosis, prevention or treatment of a rare disease or another a life-threatening, seriously debilitating or serious and chronic condition that is unlikely to generate sufficient return to justify the necessary investment; and (b) that there exists no satisfactory method of diagnosis, prevention or treatment of the condition in question that has been authorized in the Community, or if such a method exists, that the medicinal product will be of significant benefit to those affected by that condition.[85] The application for orphan designation is to be done at any stage of the development of the medicinal product before the application for marketing authorization.[86] This latter requirement means that, on the one hand, orphan exclusivity was supposed to be an incentive to carry out R&D works for potential orphan medicines, at the early stage of their development, i.e., for new active substances and not the development of already existing medicines.[87] On the other hand, according to the implementing rules provided in EC Regulation 847/2000, an application for orphan designation may be submitted for a new therapeutic indication for an already authorized medicinal product. In this case, however, the marketing authorization holder shall apply for a separate marketing authorization which will cover only the orphan indication(s).[88] According to the general rule, such an indication must be of significant benefit in comparison to the existing ones.

In an early case law of the CJEU, the Court clarified that the criteria for a finding of a significant benefit are strict and the development of a medicinal product which is of significant benefit in comparison with the medicinal product already authorized to treat the same condition involves investment in research and development of this potentially improved medicinal product. Further, the Court concluded that an undertaking cannot thus merely develop a similar medicinal product to obtain its designation as an orphan medicinal product.[89]

84. Regulation 141/2000 provides also for several secondary incentives: a centralized marketing authorization, fee redundancy, scientific consultation and possibility of conditional marketing authorization.
85. Art. 3(1) of the Regulation 141/2000.
86. Art. 5(10) of the Regulation 141/2000.
87. In the judgment of the General Court of 9 September 2010 in case T-264/07 it was stated that this provision of Art. 5(1) tends to confirm that the application of the incentives laid down by regulation 141/2000 is not justified for a medicinal product which has already been authorized in the European Union.
88. Art. 2(4) of the Commission Regulation (EC) No 847/2000 of 27 April 2000 laying down the provisions for implementation of the criteria for designation of a medicinal product as an orphan medicinal product and definitions of the concepts 'similar medicinal product' and 'clinical superiority' (OJ L 103, 28.4.2000, pp. 0005-0008), amended by Commission Regulation (EU) 2018/781 of 29 May 2018 (L 132 1 30.5.2018).
89. Judgment of the General Court in case T-264/07 *CSL Behring GmbH v. European Commission and European Medicines Agency (EMA)*, ECLI:EU:T:2010:371 (9 September 2010).

In the recent case *Shire v. EMA*, the CJEU admitted that the essential question for the legislature is whether a medicinal product represents a development in comparison with the treatment for which an application for marketing authorization has already been made, or which has already been authorized. The Court interpreted the relevant provisions in a way that allows for orphan application for the same indication as already authorized, differing only in excipients and mode of administration.[90] By rulings in *Teva* and *Shire*, the CJEU admitted orphan designations of the same active substance, contrary to the global authorization rule provided for reference medicines.

As regards the scope of protection, orphan exclusivity provides much stronger protection than the regime of exclusivities for reference medicinal products: any application concerning a similar product for the same indication may be submitted only after the expiry of the 10-year exclusivity, which prolongs the period of monopoly by the several months necessary for a generic authorization. Within these 10 years, it is not possible to apply for authorization either in an abridged or full data procedure; any application is precluded even if the second entrants could deliver their own preclinical tests and clinical trials. Hence, the market exclusivity for an orphan drug provides an absolute monopoly for the holder of a marketing authorization for an orphan medicine and as such is a *de lege*, not de facto, exclusivity.

The scope of orphan exclusivity covers not only the same medicinal product but also a similar one for the same therapeutic indication. Definitions of a similar medicinal product and similar active substance are provided in Commission Regulation 847/2000.[91] Using very detailed instructions of what shall be understood as a similar active substance, this Regulation provides for a sui generis rule of equivalence, analogous to the patent realm, in this way providing a substantial extent of legal certainty for both the orphan exclusivity holders and the generic industry.[92]

Such strong protection was supposed to be balanced by derogation mechanisms triggered by an insufficient supply of the orphan medicine,[93] and by the clinical superiority of a similar medicinal product.[94] In the case of the latter, marketing

90. Judgment of the European Court of Justice in case C-359/18 P *European Medicines Agency v. Shire Pharmaceuticals Ireland Ltd*, ECLI:EU:C:2019:639 (29 July 2019).
91. *Supra* n. 88, EC Regulation 847/2000.
92. *See* Art. 3(3)b of the EC Regulation 847/2000 which defines 'similar medicinal product' as a medicinal product containing a similar active substance or substances as contained in a currently authorized orphan medicinal product, and which is intended for the same therapeutic indication. Art. 3(3)c defines 'similar active substance' as an identical active substance, or an active substance with the same principal molecular structural features (but not necessarily all of the same molecular structural features) and which acts via the same mechanism. However, in the case of advanced therapy medicinal products, for which the principal molecular structural features cannot be fully defined, the similarity between two active substances shall be assessed on the basis of the biological and functional characteristics. Specific guidelines on the similarity are given as regards chemical, biological, radiopharmaceutical medicinal products and advanced therapy medicinal products.
93. *See* Art. 8(3)(b) of the Regulation 141/2000.
94. These two derogation mechanisms serve factual access to a possible best treatment of rare diseases. What is interesting, whereas the issue of similarity of products is addressed in a highly precise definition, the criterion of clinical superiority is again left to the discretion of health authorities. Limited guidelines on this criterion are presented in Communication from the Commission. Guidelines on aspects of the application of Art. 8(1) and (3) of Regulation (EC) No

authorization may be granted, for the same therapeutic indication, to a similar medicinal product if the second applicant can establish in the application that the second medicinal product, although similar to the orphan medicinal product already authorized, is safer, more effective or otherwise clinically superior. The second orphan product, similar to the first one but indicating clinical superiority over it, is granted its own 10-year period of orphan exclusivity.[95] Theoretically, this provision constitutes an incentive for third parties to improve the known orphan drug. In fact, it works mostly to the benefit of the hitherto orphan designation holder. Other innovative producers are not able to overcome the barrier of patent protection, and generic producers are additionally constrained by the data exclusivity period. The fact that there is no 'global designation' rule and that each subsequent, clinically superior, orphan indication of the same substance is granted a full period of exclusivity, together with the rule of protection for similar medicinal products, enables the holder of both designations to extend the protection for the product authorized first by the time of protection granted for the second product. As a result, the protection of the first orphan product may last long after the original 10 years of exclusivity.[96] To avoid this unplanned and unjustified extension of the orphan exclusivity period, a mechanism of skinny labelling could be introduced here, allowing for a generic authorization while carving out the orphan indication under exclusivity.[97]

Apart from this incentive for secondary innovation, with its depicted weaknesses, orphan exclusivity is aimed at incentivizing R&D works on orphan indications, regardless of whether related to new or known active substances. Currently, there is no difference in this regime as regards the threshold of innovation needed. It seems, however, that the original intention of the legislature was not to generally promote medicinal products to treat orphan diseases but to stimulate the development and marketing of potential orphan medicinal products by the use of the incentives.[98] In fact, it appears that new orphan indications may become crucial to benefit from the system,

141/2000: Assessing similarity of medicinal products versus authorized orphan medicinal products benefiting from market exclusivity and applying derogations from that market exclusivity, (19 September 2008) https://ec.europa.eu/health/sites/health/files/files/orphanmp/doc/c_2008_4077_en.pdf.

95. *See* judgment of the European Court of Justice in case C-138/15 P *Teva Pharma BV and Teva Pharmaceuticals Europe BV v. European Medicines Agency (EMA)*, ECLI:EU:C:2016:136 (3 March 2016).
96. *See ibid.* the cited judgment in case in case C-138/15 P and the arguments of the appellant stating that this system 'creates "perverse" incentives for undertakings to develop a series of slightly different, but nevertheless similar, orphan products, thereby benefiting from a prolongation of the period of market exclusivity, which is normally limited to 10 years', para. 36. The interpretative line of CJEU in case C-138/15 P was upheld in its recent judgment, as of 29 July 2019, in case C-359/18 P (*see supra* n. 90).
97. *See* Art. 11 in fine of the Directive 2001/83.
98. *See supra* n. 89, the judgment in case T-264/07, para. 51. In light of the analysis of *travaux préparatoires* made there, the Court concluded that the main objective of the legislature is to enable patients suffering from rare conditions to benefit from the same quality of treatment as other patients. The legislature, therefore, implicitly, but certainly, considered that incentives were not at all necessary for medicinal products which had already been developed and authorized. *Ibid.*, para. 53.

especially after judgments in cases *Teva* and *Shire*, giving an option to the extension of original orphan exclusivity by developing and protecting similar orphan indications.

5.4 Paediatric Rewards

The last regulatory regime is related to paediatric products and paediatric indications. Regulation 1901/2006 establishes the requirement to carry out tests and trials of medicinal products entering the market in the context of their safety and efficacy for children and youth at the age below 18 years.[99] As a compensation for the costs invested in carrying out the so-called paediatric investigation plan, and irrespective of its outcomes, the Regulation provides specific rewards: extension of the SPC period by six months, or extension of orphan exclusivity by two years.[100] Those extensions do not apply when an applicant has already secured a one-year extension for a new therapeutic indication with a significant clinical benefit. According to the European Commission Inventory of 2015, only two orphan medicinal products, for which a paediatric investigation plan was completed, enjoyed an extended 12-year market exclusivity by that year.[101] Several orphan designations were however withdrawn in order to apply for the SPC extension.[102] This means that the latter option, although much shorter, is more beneficial than the orphan extension, most likely because it comes into play later in the life cycle of a medicinal product. The orphan exclusivity extension is granted for the eleventh and twelfth year of the market exclusivity, whereas an SPC extension can come into play up to 16 years from marketing authorization. Obviously, if an extended SPC period ends before the expiry of an extended orphan exclusivity, the latter would be chosen. This can only be the case if over 15 years elapse between relevant patent application and marketing authorization of the orphan drug.

This Regulation aims to facilitate the development of medicinal products for use in the paediatric population. The foreseen incentives variously influence innovation. On the one hand, rewards for conducting paediatric tests and trials do not have a direct connection with innovation. They are intended at generating data confirming the safety and efficacy of medicines used for children and are granted regardless of whether they lead to a paediatric indication or not.[103] But, indirectly, they may support secondary innovation and result in developing valuable paediatric indications.

---

99. Regulation (EC) No 1901/2006 of the European Parliament and of the Council of 12 December 2006 on medicinal products for paediatric use and amending Regulation (EEC) No 1768/92, Directive 2001/20/EC, Directive 2001/83/EC and Regulation (EC) No 726/2004 (OJ L 378/1, 27 December 2006).
100. According to European Commission *Inventory of Union and Member State incentives to support research into, and the development and availability of, orphan medicinal products. State of play 2015* (22 February 2016), https://ec.europa.eu/health/sites/health/files/files/orphanmp/doc/orphan_inv_report_20160126.pdf, only two orphan medicinal products for which a paediatric investigation plan was completed enjoyed extended 12-year market exclusivity.
101. *Ibid.*
102. An example is Glivec, an anti-cancer medicine, for which orphan status has been unilaterally withdrawn by the designation holder for the sake of extension of the SPC by six months.
103. According to Art. 36 of Regulation 1901/2006, the rewards apply where completion of the agreed paediatric investigation plan fails to lead to the authorization of a paediatric indication,

5.5 Paediatric Data and Market Exclusivity

In order to establish incentives for paediatric products no longer covered by intellectual property rights, a new type of marketing authorization was established, the Paediatric Use Marketing Authorization (PUMA).[104] Medicinal products, based on already authorized active substances, developed exclusively for use in the paediatric population, may be subject to data and market exclusivity, with the same periods of protection as in the case of reference medicines, i.e., eight years of data exclusivity and two or three years of market exclusivity.[105]

Paediatric exclusivity aims to stimulate research into existing products and to help transform known off-label use into authorized use that is safer and better circumscribed. So far, however, only single PUMA authorizations were granted,[106] and their concept is assessed as not well-thought-out, mostly because even after a PUMA is granted, medicinal products with the same active ingredient are available at a cheaper price and continue to be used off-label for children. This makes the incentive ineffective in practice.[107]

6 CONCLUSIONS

The threshold of innovation protected via patents, SPC, and regulatory data protection is not uniform within the three systems. This is no surprise, as the specific purposes and subjects of protection of the particular regimes differ, too. Each of the rights rewards a specific achievement and is granted at a different phase in the life cycle of a medicinal product.

Patents grant a market opportunity. SPCs give the promise to extend the term of patent protection if the basic works to develop a marketable drug will be continued. Regulatory exclusivities have a character of rewards – they compensate for the costs of commercialization of a final medicinal product, either being a stand-alone form of protection or extending other rights.

---

but the results of the studies conducted are reflected in the summary of product characteristics and, if appropriate, in the package leaflet of the medicinal product concerned.

104. *See supra* n. 99, Recital 19 of the Regulation 1901/2006.
105. They may also benefit from additional incentives: partial fee exemption, optional access to EU centralized procedure.
106. *Data exclusivity, market protection, orphan and paediatric rewards* presented at the SME info day: Regulatory toolbox for medicines and combined devices developers by Sonia Ribeiro, (26 October 2018), https://www.ema.europa.eu/en/documents/presentation/presentation-data-exclusivity-market-protection-orphan-paediatric-rewards-s-ribeiro_en.pdf.
107. Con. Available reports and studies: *Study on the economic impact of the Paediatric Regulation, including its rewards and incentives Final Report*, (Dec. 2016), SANTE/2015/D5/023, https://ec.europa.eu/health/sites/health/files/files/paediatrics/docs/paediatrics_10_years_economic_study.pdf; Max Planck Institute for Innovation and Competition, *Study on the Legal Aspects of SPC – Final Report*, Publications Office of the European Union (11 September 2018), https://op.europa.eu/en/publication-detail/-/publication/8ffeb206-b65c-11e8-99ee-01aa75ed71a1/language-en/format-PDF; *European Union Review of Pharmaceutical Incentives: Suggestions for Change*, Medicines Law & Policy (3 June 2019), https://medicineslawandpolicy.org/2019/06/eu-review-of-pharmaceutical-incentives-recommendations-for-change/.

However, it is common across all three systems that the relevant criteria for protection ability are challenged by the pharmaceutical industry in order to achieve their gradual mitigation by means of administrative or judicial decisions. As a result of fast technological development and lack of corresponding normative response, the threshold of innovation protected by particular IP regimes is indicated by various bodies, but not by the actual legislator: by the EPO's boards of appeal interpreting criteria of patentability; the CJEU construing and redefining the criteria of SPC eligibility, and deciding on the extent of the regulatory data protection; domestic patent offices granting SPCs, and domestic courts and patent offices invalidating patents or SPCs. It depends very much on the current decisions of these institutions how the IP regimes do and will fulfil their aim of incentivizing valuable pharmaceutical innovation.

In patent law, the threshold for protection of pharmaceutical innovations has been set very low, making trivial, very low-innovation solutions patentable. In the current practice of the EPO, an inventive step of a further medical use may be minimal, corresponding to a potential secondary innovation of a new mode of use of a known active substance in a known therapeutic indication. The patent system is one-size-fits-all, granting the same exclusivity for all inventions, regardless if trivial or substantial. Thus, it is postulated in this chapter to rethink and establish clearer criteria for the inventive step of further medical uses, based on higher requirements than a mere nominal change to a mode of use of a known active substance. These requirements should be envisaged in the problem-solution approach, referring to a practising physician as the person skilled in the art and comprising their potential experience of applying known treatment in the state of the art. The EPO guidelines should present positive and negative indicators of nonobviousness, possibly embracing specialist knowledge derived from the regulatory legislation.

Data protection for reference medicinal products is principally granted for primary innovation at a very high level – for medicinal products based on a new active substance that required the conducting of preclinical and clinical tests. The 10-year period of data and market exclusivity is granted for medicinal products authorized in the full data procedure. It may be extended only once, by one year, for one or more new therapeutic indications which are assessed as bringing a significant clinical benefit in comparison with existing therapies (the so-called global MA rule).

There is no one-year period of analogical exclusivity for data provided by third parties in the hybrid procedure. Such exclusivity should be introduced to provide a balanced incentive for both the MA holders and other entities, to authorize newly developed therapeutic indications of known medicines.

The 10-year orphan exclusivity is granted for medicinal products used in the treatment of rare diseases. The scope of orphan exclusivity covers not only the original medicinal product but also a similar one for the same therapeutic indication. Such strong protection was supposed to be balanced by derogation mechanisms, triggered by the clinical superiority of a similar medicinal product. The fact that there is no 'global designation' rule, and that each subsequent, clinically superior, orphan indication of the same substance is granted a full period of exclusivity, together with the rule of protection for similar medicinal products, enables the holder of both designations to extend the protection for the first product authorized by the time of protection granted for the second product. To avoid this unplanned and unjustified extension of the orphan exclusivity period, a mechanism of skinny labelling could be introduced here, allowing for a generic authorization while carving out the orphan indication still under exclusivity.

In the SPC system, the very recent decision in *Santen* plays a crucial role. Together with an earlier judgment in *Abraxis*, they both are a clear return to the initial policy of granting SPC in respect of primary innovations only: for active substances not having been authorized before. Such an approach corrects the undesired results of a too lenient policy concerning the patentability of further medical uses. Currently, it is fair to say that SPC extends patent protection for and, by the same token - incentivizes, breakthrough innovations only. By setting the SPC eligibility threshold at the level of a new active substance, CJEU chose an objective criterion, prone to dilution and corresponding to the SPC aims. Any lower threshold of protection would be inconsistent with the SPC *ratio legis*. Last but not least, this decision renders the two systems - regulatory data protection and SPC - consistent with each other.

In thinking about setting a threshold of IP protectable innovation, there is yet another aspect to be taken into account - that this threshold will make it possible for the European industry to efficiently compete on the global scene. European policymakers tend to see the problem in a rather simplistic way - the protection must be at least as strong as elsewhere, strong protection being understood as wide availability thereof. Analysis of this issue exceeds the limits of this paper, but it is worth mentioning that 20 years ago, a report prepared for the European Commission[108] already indicated that, at that time, the European pharmaceutical industry had been losing competitiveness in comparison with the USA, both because it was found to be less specialized in R&D activities and had a much larger presence of companies specializing in low value-added activities.[109]

Setting a lower and lower threshold of protection for pharmaceutical innovation seems to be an easy mechanism allowing for broader availability of IP rights and giving the right holders a stronger position. Such adjustments diminish the value of IP rights for groundbreaking innovation. Due to many specific needs in the realm of pharmaceutical innovation, its support demands various legal and economic push and pull

108. Alfonso Gambardella, Luigi Orsenigo & Fabio Pammolli, *Global Competitiveness in Pharmaceuticals: A European Perspective*, Enterprise Papers (November 2000), https://ec.europa.eu/docsroom/documents/2957/attachments/1/translations/en/renditions/pdf.
109. Proposal for a Regulation of the European Parliament and of the Council laying down Community procedures for the authorization and supervision of medicinal products for human and veterinary use and establishing a European Agency for the Evaluation of Medicinal Products Proposal for a Directive of the European Parliament and of the Council amending Directive 2001/83/EC on the Community code relating to medicinal products for human use Proposal for a Directive of the European Parliament and of the Council amending Directive 2001/82/EC on the Community code relating to veterinary medicinal products (OJ 075 E, 26 March 2002, pp. 0189-0215).

mechanisms. However, the variety of IP-based instruments serving substantially the same general aims and offering multiple ways of combining the possible protective titles makes the system non-transparent and prone to misuse. An imprecise, lowerable threshold of protection enhances this tendency to the disadvantage of public health interest.

CHAPTER 3

Human Enhancement and Patent Law

Helena Żakowska-Henzler

1 INTRODUCTION

In recent decades, the development of science and technology has made possible the technical enhancement of various human skills and abilities - physical, intellectual, psychological, and even moral. For such purposes, different methods and techniques are used, e.g., pharmaceuticals, neurostimulation, genetic engineering, implants. All of these means - even the most revolutionary - are widely accepted if they are intended to help people whose ability and skills had been weakened because of an illness or disabilities (handicaps). The approach to technical ways of strengthening the capacity and abilities of healthy people is much more differentiated, as the measures, called human enhancement (HE), go beyond what is necessary for curative purposes, i.e., to sustain health or repair the body.[1]

According to some authors, interventions that are not dictated by therapeutic needs - especially, but not only, those that aim to exceed the capabilities and abilities inherent in the human species, endanger the existence of a human being, and endanger the world as we know it, in particular, because they risk drastically altering relationships between people, the system of values now recognized as the cornerstone of the social and legal order of democratic states, and may even interfere with the natural process of evolution.[2] The potential anticipated outcome of such practices is described as a 'post-human era'. On the other hand, there is a belief that such actions are

1. In 2003, a report 'Beyond Therapy' was published by the US President's Council on Bioethics (PCB 2003); Policy Engagement - a debate on the ethics of body enhancement technologies and regeneration By Monique Frize, P. Eng., OC, FIEEE.
2. Jürgen Habermas, *The Future of Human Nature: On the Way to a Liberal Eugenics?*, Cambridge UK, Polity Press 2003. A.W. Torrance, *Patenting Human Evolution*, Kansas Law Review, volume 56, 2008.

absolutely positive because they bring the mankind closer to the 'Human plus era', i.e., to the era of a perfect human being – superior to the current version of *homo sapiens*.[3]

These divergent approaches and the resulting controversies are based primarily on differences of belief regarding the core of humanity, the core which should be protected and inviolable; so, the defining borders that, if exceeded, will ruin humanity. Consequently, the answers to the question of whether, and to what extent, the creation and the use of technologies that enable the improvement of human beings, i.e., Human Enhancement Technologies (HETs) should or may be acceptable are also differentiated.[4] According to some, work on and use of HET should at least be closely monitored if not banned or rigorously limited. Others think, however, that the green light should be given to any measures that serve to support HE. They have a definite positive opinion of all HE projects as facilitating people's lives in the modern world, and in particular meeting the challenges resulting from the transformed social and technical environments. HETs are indicated as the only way to reduce the gap between the cognitive and physical abilities of Artificial Intelligence (AI) and humans,[5] and in consequence, as a vital means which allow the human species to control the development of AI.[6] In addition, it is emphasized that the history of mankind has not given grounds for considering that *homo sapiens* is a species that has already reached physical, intellectual or psychological perfection. Therefore, the rationale for the demands of the absolute protection of human nature is questioned. However, regardless of these disputes and controversies, HETs are created and applied. In these circumstances, it seems to be reasonable to consider the issues of the influence of such technologies and their deployment on social and human relations at a micro and macro scale. In particular, the question arises as to whether there is a need to introduce specific regulations for HET, i.e., controlling the development, use, and dissemination of such technologies, including access to them.

These discussions, though of great importance for everyone, go beyond the subject of the present chapter which concerns only HETs in the context of patent law. Generally, I would like to answer the question of whether the emergence of these technologies should be reflected in the rules of patent protection. In other words, whether the patent law is suited to the specificity of HET inventions, or maybe some changes are needed in this respect. The chapter focuses on two issues. The first one concerns the suitability of the prerequisites for patentability as provided for in the corpus of contemporary patent law to assess the patentability of HET. The question is

3. N. Agar, *Liberal Eugenics: In Defence of Human Enhancement*, Wiley 2004; J. Savulescu, B. Foddy, *To Gattaca and Beyond*, The Age, 29 April 2007; S. Chan, J. Harris, *In Support of Human Enhancement*, Studies in Ethics, Law, and Technology, volume 1, Issue 1, 2007, Art. 10.
4. Some of the issues and controversies have been raised by, among others, L.Y. Cabrera, *Rethinking Human Enhancement: Social Enhancement and Emergent Technologies*, Palgrave McMillan 2015, 201 pp.; T. Żuradzki, *The New Liberal Eugenics: A Critical Review of Arguments Against Biomedical Enhancement of Human Physical or Mental Capabilities* (in Polish)', Diametros, no. 42, pp. 204-226, Dec. 2014.
5. J. Savulescu, B. Foddy, *To Gattaca and Beyond*, above.
6. M. Cavazza, *A Motivational Model of BCI-Controlled Heuristic Search*, Brain Sciences, volume 8, issue 9(2018), p. 166. N. Boström, *Superintelligence: Paths, Dangers, Strategies*, Oxford University Press 2014.

whether those prerequisites are suitable to distinguish objectively and predictably between HETs which are patentable and those whose patentability is prohibited. The second issue is of a different nature. It concerns the scope of exclusivity that *should result* from the patent on HET – the question of whether the scope of exclusivity should be the same as for patents on other inventions, or whether specific rules should apply only to HET.

It is worth noting that it would not be extraordinary to introduce changes to patent law because of the emergence of HET. The phenomenon of adapting patent law to new types of inventions arising as a result of scientific and technological developments is nothing new. As one example, we can mention the evolution of patent law caused by the development of the chemical industry at the beginning of the twentieth century. The emergence of new chemical products made their patentability widely accepted, although such a change had previously raised many objections and controversies. However, the most significant change so far was caused by the development of modern biotechnology, as well as computer science. Its impact was, among others, a change in the content of some essential concepts of patent law, including fundamental notions for this area, such as the concept of an invention. The concept of an invention was broadened by shifting a pre-established and undisputed borderline between inventions as patentable items and discoveries for which patents cannot be granted, and by including in the category of inventions abstract solutions which had not been previously included in that category.

The considerations on the first issue, i.e., the adequacy of rules established in modern patent law to assess the patentability of HET inventions is based on patent law applicable within the territory of the EU. Despite the advanced process of globalization of patent law, which can be seen mainly in the Trade-Related Aspects of Intellectual Property Rights (TRIPS) Agreement,[7] there are still differences in the method of interpretation, even of uniform legal texts. They are clearly visible in particular in the context of the premises for patentability. Therefore, considerations concerning the first issue are based on a certain legal system – the rules of patent protection that apply in the territory of the EU. These rules are largely determined by the European Patent Convention (EPC)[8] and the European Union (EU) legal acts, as well as by the case law of the Court of Justice of the European Union and the policy of the European Patent Office (EPO).[9] From a different perspective, the second issue is considered because the question is not about what the law is, but what the law should be. Therefore, these considerations are not based on a specific legal system – they are of a general nature.

7. The Agreement on Trade-Related Aspects of Intellectual Property Rights (TRIPS) is annex to the agreement on the establishment of the World Trade Organization (1994).
8. The Convention on the Grant of European Patents (European Patent Convention) – signed in 1973, revised by the Act revising Art. 63 EPC of 17 Dec. 1991 and the Act revising the EPC of 29 Nov. 2000.
9. European Patent Office is an organ of the European Patent Organization. EPO grants patents for the contracting states to the European Patent Convention.

2 THE CONCEPT OF HE AND HET

According to the Oxford Dictionary, 'enhancement' means 'an increase or improvement in quality, value, or extent'.[10] In such a general understanding, HE has been an inseparable and intrinsic component of the history of mankind since its very beginning, and of every human being since the moment of birth. As a species, we have been expanding our capabilities, for instance, thanks to a variety of inventions such as the invention of literacy, as well as the invention of different tools and instruments (glasses, electric motors, planes, microscopes, computers, the Internet). As individuals, we enhance ourselves by learning to write, read, practising sports or training to control one's emotions, and gaining the skills to use the above-mentioned tools and instruments. Since time immemorial, in order to strengthen our personal capabilities (physical fitness, resistance to fatigue, sleepiness, hunger) or to achieve a desired emotional state, beyond physical, intellectual or mental training, various substances have been used – initially obtained from nature, later also manufactured from different substances.

In recent decades, the possibilities and methods of HE have been significantly changed due to the development of science and technology. The possibilities of technical influence on the functioning of the human organism have been extended, and therefore, the duration and predictability of its results are greater than ever before.[11] They are substantially different from those available and used in the past.[12] This change has made the issue of HE an object of interest and fuelled the controversy mentioned above.[13] As a result, the term 'human enhancement' has got a new narrower meaning. It refers mainly to activities that directly intervene in the functioning of the human body through technical means and are aimed at improving individual human performance. However, it should be noted that even on the basis of such a meaning of HE, in different publications and statements on HE and HET, including discussions on their ethical aspects, different content is attributed to these terms. It depends on the purpose of identifying and defining such interventions and on the context in which the statement is made.[14] On one point, there seems to be a broad

10. Oxford Dictionary – https://en.oxforddictionaries.com/definition/enhancement (retrieved on 17 Sep. 2019).
    Likewise: Cambridge dictionary – *a change, or a process of change, that improves something or increases its value* – https://dictionary.cambridge.org/dictionary/english/en hancement (retrieved on 17 Sep. 2019)
11. G. Wolbring, *The Unenhanced Underclass*, p. 122. https://www.researchgate.net/publication/259219749_(retrieved on 17 September 2019).
12. On these differences, *see*, e.g., G. Wolbring, *Obsolescence and Body Technologies*, Dilemata, International Journal of Applied Ethics, no. 4 (2010), pp. 67-83.
13. In the context of genetics in particular, e.g., A. Buchanan, D.W. Brock, N. Daniels, D. Wikler, *From Chance to Choice*, Cambridge University Press 2000.
14. For two decades, many alternative definitions of human enhancement have been proposed and discussed (E. Parens, *Is Better Always Good?*, A Special Supplement to the Hastings Centre Report January-February 1998, The Enhancement Project; N. Agar, 2008, *Liberal Eugenics. Supra*; N. Bostrom, R. Roache, *Ethical Issues in Human Enhancement in:* J. Ryberg, T.S. Petersen, C. Wolf; Moore (eds), New Waves in Applied Ethics, Palgrave Macmillan, 2008, pp. 120-153; A. Nordberg, *Defining Human Enhancement: Towards a Foundational Conceptual Tool for Enhancement Law*, Journal of Law, Information & Science, volume 25, issue 3, 2016.

consensus, i.e., that the term HE refers only to changes that are perceived as being positive from a cultural and social perspective. In the broadest sense of the concept of HE, this term refers to any of the modifications aimed at improving individual human performance and brought about by technology-based interventions in the human body.[15] HET understood in this way includes very different kinds of influences on the human body: technologies (methods) aimed at the elimination or correction of symptoms or effects of a disease, as well as at the strengthening, i.e., enhancing the ability or efficiency of a healthy person, thus intervening beyond therapy. The HETs defined in such a way also contain both activities that lead to human performance or ability beyond the limits of the *homo sapiens* species, and those that fall within their limits. In some publications, the term HE refers only to these interventions which are beyond therapy, for instances, as interventions intended to improve human function or characteristics beyond which it is necessary to sustain health or repair the body.[16] But some even narrow down the content of this concept by referring only to those whose effects exceed features specific to the human species.[17] The way of defining HE and consequently, HET obviously has a significant impact on how such activities are perceived and assessed.

Since, in this chapter, the considerations on the patentability of HET are based on European law, in which therapy methods are subject to specific rules different from those applied to other types of methods of influencing the human body, the term HET refers not only to intervention beyond therapy but to all interventions, regardless of the scale and character of their result. The effects of HET can be either long term or even

N. Bostrom, J. Savulescu, *Human Enhancement Ethics: The State of the Debate 2009;* L. Cabrera, *supra* 2017), M. Frize, *A Debate on the Ethics of Body Enhancement Technologies and Regeneration,* Engineering Dimension January/February 2013, pp. 52-55; A. Eckhardt, A. Bachmann, M. Marti, B. Rütsche, H. Telser, *Human Enhancement,* TA-Swiss 56/2011 (further 'TA-Swiss56/211), pp. 5-9; C. Cinel, D. Valeriani, R. Poli, *Neurotechnologies for Human Cognitive Augmentation: Current State of the Art and Future Prospects,* Frontiers in Human Neuroscience vol. 13, issue 13, 2019, https://www.ncbi.nlm.nih.gov/pmc/articles/PMC6365771/ (retrieved on 17 September 2019).

15. Such character is not attributed to activities aimed at equipping a person with tools which may be used to increase his or her performance or ability, insofar as such tools are external to the human body and can easily be used and laid aside in a simple manner (e.g., walking stick, glasses, hearing aid, computer). *See,* e.g., Human Enhancement Study (2007) – further referred to as 'STOA'; the study prepared within the scope of the activities of the European Parliament – Science and Technology Options Assessment (IP/A/STOA/FWC/2005-28/SC35, 41 & 45): pp. 15-16 – it was stated that HE 'should be meaningfully limited and therefore exclude such practices as the ordinary use of body-external technological devices, education, physical exercise, mnemonic training, and the consumption of "natural" drugs, such as coca leaves, and food (although these practices can contribute to an enhancement of performance)'.
16. Beyond therapy is understood as the directed use of biotechnical power to alter, by direct intervention, not disease processes but the 'normal' workings of the human body and psyche, to augment or improve their native capacities and performances – instead of many *see*: President's Council on Bioethics (2003) *Beyond therapy: biotechnology and the pursuit of happiness* (Washington DC: President's Council on Bioethics); similar M. Frize, *A Debate on the Ethics,* above.
17. *Inter alia:* A. Nordberg, *Defining Human Enhancement,* above.

permanent (as in the case of genetic enhancements), or temporary (such as improved concentration levels brought about by drugs). The aim of HET may be to improve human's natural abilities (e.g., by making an individual stronger or feeling happier) or to give people characteristics or abilities that no human being has ever possessed before, such as full night vision, or even extra senses.

A detailed and comprehensive analysis of the substance of the various HETs would require knowledge beyond the author's competence. Therefore, the chapter focuses only on examples of such HETs and their features that give rise to the question of their patentability and the scope of patent exclusivity. HETs can be classified according to various criteria, such as the purpose of the intervention, i.e., the functions to be strengthened or changed (e.g., cognitive,[18] physical, emotional, moral), or the methods or means of influence (pharmaceutical, neurotechnology, neurostimulation by technical methods, genetic modification, prosthesis and prosthetic implants) as well as the processes whose courses are modified. These different methods can serve different purposes. It should be noted that most, if not all, of the HETs that are used today, have been developed as methods of treatment for various types of diagnosed diseases. For example, Ritalin and Modafinil, which were developed to treat people suffering from Attention Deficit Hyperactivity Disorder (ADHD) or narcolepsy, are used by healthy people to increase their ability respectively to concentrate and to reduce the need for sleep and the same to alleviate cognitive difficulties resulting from its deficiency.[19] Identifying in human DNA areas that impact on human cognitive functions[20] as well as emotional responses,[21] combined with the development of DNA sequence manipulation techniques (e.g., CRISPR), creates new possibilities to control and influence cognitive functions, or at least raises new hopes in this regard. An almost direct influence on brain functioning, and consequently on various human capacities and performance (including cognitive, physical, emotional) is possible thanks to neurostimulation methods, both non-invasive and invasive ones. The example of the first of these is methods of brain stimulation with the use of magnetic or electrical energy produced outside the skull of the treated person (e.g., transcranial electrical

18. Cognitive enhancement is referred to, *inter alia*, as the amplification or extension of core capacities of the mind through improvement or augmentation of internal or external information processing systems – N. Bostrom, A. Sandberg, *Cognitive Enhancement: Methods, Ethics, Regulatory Challenges, Science and Engineering Ethics*, volume 15, issue 3, 2009, pp. 311-341.
19. An online poll by the journal Nature found that of 1,400 respondents from 60 countries, one in five said they had used drugs for non-medical reasons as a cognitive enhancer – B. Maher, Poll Results: Look Who's Doping, *Nature* volume 452, 2008, pp. 674–675. And as has been pointed out in STOA, the demand for and the use of such cognitive enhancers is already widespread, as well as the proposals for a wide legislation of such uses – STOA, p. 99.
20. Research and very promising achievements in this area are reviewed, *inter alia*, by Bostrom and Sandberg, *Cognitive enhancement*, above (pp. 319-320), and STOA, p. 30 and next. For instance, genetic experiments with rodents have raised expectations that memory and learning skills could significantly do by adding (even an adult being) extra copies of a receptor (STOA, p. 30).
21. STOA p. 30.

stimulation (TES[22]).[23,24] For their non-invasive character, such methods are sometimes called 'Botox for the brain'.[25]

The methods of invasive neurostimulation, including Deep Brain Stimulation (DBS), are very different from Transcranial Magnetic Stimulation because they involve implanting a stimulator into a specific part of the brain.[26] Although research on the use of DBS in therapy is widely accepted (e.g., Parkinson's disease, treatment of intrinsic tremor[27]), the major risk is associated with such methods, and work on the use of DBS beyond therapy, i.e., for the purpose of HE, is much narrower. Huge expectations concerning both therapy and HE are also related to the Brain Computer Interface (BCI[28]). Such interfaces 'consist of hardware and software for direct communication between the brain and external devices'.[29] They enable passing information 'from the brain to an external device, for example to enable control of a computer or robot arm with thought nerve signals'[30] or in the opposite direction, such as from an artificial eye to the brain.[31] Thanks to BCI systems, paralysed people can, for example, use a computer to directly control impulses from the brain, and the operation of prostheses

22. More information about expectations and prospects as well as possible threats and doubts related to the application of such methods: *inter alia* C. Cinel, D. Valeriani, R. Poli, *Neurotechnologies for Human Cognitive*, above.
23. M. Hallet, *Transcranial Magnetic Stimulation and the Human Brain*, Nature, volume 406, 13 July 2000, www.nature.com.
24. E.M. Wassermann, T. Zimmermann, *Transcranial Magnetic Brain Stimulation: Therapeutic Promises and Scientific Gaps*, - https://www.ncbi.nlm.nih.gov/pmc/articles/PMC3241868/ (retrieved on 17 September 2019).
25. TMS devices are available in shops including online, many companies that offer TMS sets offer one-day training on their use.
26. More information, *see Deep Brain Stimulation for Enhancement of Learning and Memory* Nanthia Suthana, Ph.D.1,2 and Itzhak Fried, Neuroimage. 15 January 2014; 85 (03): 996–1002: https://www.ncbi.nlm.nih.gov/pmc/articles/PMC4445933/ (retrieved on 17 September 2019).
27. Therefore, the latter tests are performed mainly in situations where the pacemaker was implanted for therapeutically justified reasons. In some cases, with the reservation that the information is only of an anecdotal nature, it is signalled emergence of such side effects of the therapeutic action, which are of an enhancement nature. For instance, 'a graphic designer, who received DBS surgery for a severe Tourettes disorder, found that stimulation through one specific electrode could actually make her more creative' - M.N. Gasson, E. Kosta, D.M. Bowman (eds), *Human ICT Implants: Technical, Legal and Ethical Considerations*, p. 23.
28. More about these different systems - *see inter alia* R. Tadeusiewicz, P. Rotter, *From Cochlear Implants to Brain Computer Interfaces*, Bio-Algorithms and Med-Systems volume 8, issue 3, 2012, pp. 267-286; E. Mikołajewska, D. Mikołajewski, *Interfejsy mózg-komputer jako rozwiązania dla osób niepełnosprawnych z uszkodzeniami układu nerwowego*, Niepełnosprawność - zagadnienia, problemy, rozwiązania. Issue III/2012 (4).
29. R. Tadeusiewicz, P. Rotter, above.
30. R. Tadeusiewicz, P. Rotte, above; M.N. Gasson, E. Kosta, D.M. Bowman (eds), *Human ICT*, above; P. Kucharski, A.J. Rybicki, M. Kopaczyńska, *Połączenie Mózg-Komputer Jako Metoda Komunikacji Z Niereagującymi Pacjentami* - Przegląd Literatury, s. 14-15; *Human ICT Implants: Technical, Legal and Ethical Considerations* s. 15; zob. także: P. Kucharski, A. Jan Rybicki, M. Kopaczyńska, *Połączenie Mózg-Komputer Jako Metoda Komunikacji Z Niereagującymi Pacjentami*- Przegląd Literatury, Acta Bio-Optica et Informatica Medica Inżynieria Biomedyczna, volume 21, issue 3, 2015, pp. 148-157.
31. Examples of the use of such interventions for HE purposes and their impact on the human body are presented, i.e., in European Group on Ethics in Science and New Technologies (EGE) Opinion n° 20 - 16/03/2005 - *Ethical aspects of ICT Implants in the Human Body*; M. Hazes, BCI and BMI: *Therapeutic Treatment or Human Enhancement?* A comparative study on the above, p. 13.

replacing or supporting damaged organs (e.g., limbs) or their components, e.g., hearing or vision, is becoming more and more effective.[32] A person can see in the dark, receive acoustic signals at frequencies inaccessible to human senses,[33] as well as receive and convert signals enabling them to determine the distance without using any instruments.[34] These systems can also be used for the transfer of information from the brain of one person to the brain of another via a computer. Depending *inter alia* on the area of the human body in which the elements of the BCI system are implanted, these systems are also divided into invasive (directly into the grey matter of the brain), partially invasive (in the skull but outside the brain) and non-invasive BCIs.[35] As in the case of neurostimulation, the level of public acceptance of such 'invasive' measures depends on whether they are dictated by curative therapy or HE demands. This does not mean, however, that the use of invasive BCI systems is not foreseen for HE. Although it is undisputed that a significant part of today's existing or theoretical HET has its origins in therapeutic methods, there are more and more research works directed specifically at the creation of HET, i.e., technologies enabling interventions beyond therapy.

3 PATENTABILITY OF HET

Even such a brief review of HET reveals the diversity of the methods referred to under this term, and particularly the diversity of the way they affect the human body and their results. The only things common to all methods referred to as HET are the object of their influence (the human body) and the aim of such influence. From the perspective of patent law, the diversity of technologies is irrelevant. Under the rules commonly respected under modern patent law, the type of technology does not affect the legal patent qualification of an invention.[36] However, the object of the invention, the nature and purpose of its use, are relevant in many jurisdictions, which means they carry implications for its patentability. This is the case, for instance, in legal systems which contain prohibitions, permitted by TRIPS, on the patenting of: (a) inventions whose use (including their purpose) is considered contrary to public policy or morality;[37] and

32. More about the operation of such implants, *see*, e.g., D.B. Shire et al. 'Development and Implantation of a Minimally Invasive Wireless Subretinal Neurostimulator', Biomedical Engineering, IEEE Transactions volume 56, issue 10 (2009): 2502-2511.
33. E. Mikołajewska, D. Mikołajewski, *Interfejsy mózg-komputer,* above.
34. R. Tadeusiewicz, above; T. Macaulay, *Meet Captain Cyborg: the Man That Biohacked His Own Body*, Techworld, 24 May 2017: https://www.techworld.com/apps-wearables/professor-cyborg-reveals-secrets-of-cybernetic-communication-3659400/ (retrieved on 17 September 2019).
35. Gasson et al., *supra.*
36. According to Art. 27(1), The Agreement on Trade-Related Aspects of Intellectual Property Rights ('TRIPS') patents are granted for inventions, i.e., technical solutions from all fields of technology, provided that the following conditions are met (common in modern patent law): novelty, inventive level (not obvious – the USA), industrial applicability (utility).
37. TRIPS Art. 27 s. 2 Members may exclude from patentability inventions, the prevention within their territory of the commercial exploitation of which is necessary to protect order public or

(b) certain methods of influencing the human body.[38] Such rules are reflected, *inter alia*, in the EPC. In accordance with Article 52(1) of the EPC, European patents are granted for any inventions, in all fields of technology, provided that they are new, involve an inventive step and are susceptible of industrial application; but with the exception of inventions, the commercial exploitation of which would be contrary to 'ordre public' or morality (Article 53(a) EPC) and of *methods for treatment* of the human or animal body by surgery or therapy (Article 53c EPC).[39] Such bans also exist in the national patent laws of EPC Member States, including all the countries of the EU. It should be noted, however, that EU law does not oblige the Member States to exclude the patentability of such inventions. Only in respect of biotechnological inventions, Directive 98/44 clearly and strictly prohibits the patentability of inventions whose commercial exploitation would be contrary to ordre public or morality.[40] However, no EU legislation regulates the patentability of therapeutic or surgery methods, which is left to the competence of the EU countries.[41]

In light of the controversies regarding technical methods of HE, its creation and use, it is obvious that the examination of patentability of HET through the terms of bans such as that contained in Article 53(a) of the EPC may lead to substantially different conclusions. And since the perception of HET, in terms of its compliance with morality and public order, is largely determined by the viewpoint of the world, there is little chance of reaching common agreement on this issue. Bearing in mind the way in which controversies of this kind concerning biotechnological inventions were dealt with in EU patent law, we cannot exclude the possibility that in the future, for reasons of legal certainty, a normative catalogue will be created of those HETs whose patenting is prohibited or, on the contrary, those whose patenting is permitted. However, as far as I know, patent authorities have not yet had the opportunity to adopt a position on the impact of a ban such as Article 53(a) of the EPC on the patentability of HET. This issue deserves to be analysed separately and, therefore, remains beyond the scope of this chapter, which concerns only the issue of the patentability of HET in light of the second of the above-mentioned prohibitions – the ban on the patentability of therapeutic and surgical methods (Article 53(c) EPC).

The ban on patenting under Article 53(c) of the EPC, and under national laws modelled on that provision, applies to inventions that involve a specific influence on

morality, including to protect human, animal or plant life or health or to avoid serious prejudice to the environment, provided that such exclusion is not made merely because the exploitation is prohibited by their law.

38. Members may also exclude from patentability diagnostic, therapeutic and surgical methods for the treatment of humans or animals (Art. 27(3)(a) TRIPS). The bans on patents may also apply to inventions concerning plants and animals (Art. 27(3)(b) TRIPS, but due to the subject matter of the article, they are not included in it.
39. The prohibition of Art. 53(c) EPC also covers diagnostic methods, but they are not relevant in the context of the article topic.
40. Art. 6 of the Directive 98/44/EC of the European Parliament and of the Council of 6 July 1998 on the legal protection of biotechnological inventions, OJ L 213, 30.7.1998, pp. 13-21 ('Directive 98/44').
41. Recital 35 of Directive 98/44.

the human body, including therapeutic, surgical methods.[42] Therefore, when addressing the first question - concerning the legal patent qualification of HET - it is essential to determine whether the technologies referred to by that term can be considered as therapeutic or surgical methods under patent law.

The patentability of HE technology in light of the ban on the patentability of therapeutic methods

Prima facie, based on the presumption that the term HET refers to such methods of influencing the human body that are beyond therapy, there should be no problem with the patentability of HET in light of the ban on patenting of therapy methods (Article 53(c) EPC). But such a conclusion will turn out to be incorrect if we have analysed how the patent authorities, including the EPO, understand the object of this ban.

In the EPC, the content of the word 'therapy' is not defined or otherwise specified. It is left to the patent authorities and courts to describe the content of that concept. In such a situation, according to the Vienna Convention,[43] the ordinary meaning of the term applies. However, in colloquial language, there is no universally respected ordinary meaning of the word therapy. In fact, the term 'therapy' has many meanings also in legal language. They are very different from one another as they are set for different purposes, e.g., definitions drawn up for insurers or health systems, or for determining the scope of responsibilities and authorizations of doctors. The EPO has clarified the meaning of the word 'therapy' used in Article 53(c) of the EPC in several decisions. From these decisions, as well as from the EPO Guidelines, it is clear that under European patent law, the term 'therapy' in Article 53(c) EPC is not restricted to curing disease and removing its consequences. It consists of activities (methods) that can be classified into three groups: (a) *curative methods of treating disease*, e.g., the *curing* of a disease or malfunction of the body and *alleviation of the symptoms of pain, suffering, malfunctions, discomfort caused by disease;*[44] (b) methods of alleviation of the symptoms of pain, suffering and malfunctions, discomfort or incapacity irrespective of its origin (not caused by disease);[45] and (c) *prophylactic treatment.*[46] All of these methods of therapy cannot be patented due to the ban contained in Article 53(c) EPC.

The difference between the content of the concept of therapy under European patent law and that attributed to it in statements presented in other contexts, particularly in debates on HE, seems to be evident. In the latter, the word 'therapy' refers mainly to actions aimed at the elimination of diseases (curing), and elimination or alleviation of their symptoms or effects, thus HE is opposed to therapy.[47] The

42. Due to the nature of HET and the topic of the chapter - it only covers the ban on patenting methods of therapy and surgical methods, leaving out the issues related to patenting diagnostic methods.
43. Art. 31(1) The Vienna Convention on the Law of Treaties (concluded in Vienna on 23 May 1969).
44. In decision T 188/83, the EPO clarified for the first time the content of the term 'therapy' for the purposes of patent law.
45. In this way *inter alia* in the decisions T 81/84, T 24/91, T 144/83.
46. For instance: immunization against a certain disease (*see* T 24/91, T 19/86) and the removal of plaque (*see* T 290/86); T 780/89 - 1991r. G 1/04; Enlarged Board Decision G 1/07.
47. Unless there is a distinction within HE between therapeutic HE and HE which is beyond therapy.

consequence of this assumption is the distinction (separation) between the methods of therapy and HET. On the other hand, under patent law, the content of the term 'therapy' is broader since, in addition, it includes interventions aimed at alleviating ailments, discomfort or disability resulting from causes other than diseases[48] (b) and those of a preventive nature (c). The above juxtaposition raises the question about the impact of such a broad understanding of therapy on the patentability of HET, and in particular on the criteria for its examination. As the article deals with HETs understood as interventions aimed at purposes other than the cure for diseases and the alleviation of their symptoms and effects (beyond therapy), the considerations concern only these two types of methods listed under (b) and (c) above.

Many of the measures aimed at elimination or alleviation of disability, malfunctions resulting from causes other than diseases, as well as some preventive measures are consistent with the concept of HET as adopted in this article (e.g., improved memory, increased fatigue resistance, enhanced ability to concentrate weakened due to age or meteorological conditions and strengthening resistance to pathogens such as viruses and bacteria). The analysis of the policy of the patent authorities, and in particular that of the EPO, leads to the conclusion that, with regard to this kind of method, the borderline between the patentable and the non-patentable ones is far from clear and unambiguous. On the one hand, there are several EPO decisions which explicitly state that *the cause* of the pain, discomfort or incapacity does not affect the legal qualification of a method of removing or alleviating that condition.[49] Thus, irrespective of the origin of incapacity or malfunctions, its relief, by the administration of an appropriate agent is treated on the basis of patent law as 'therapy' or 'therapeutic use'. That means that methods of enhancing cognitive, emotional or physical abilities and skills weakened due to, e.g., age, fatigue, weather conditions, or pregnancy, are unpatentable (as therapy methods within the meaning of Article 53(c) EPC). However, in view of the fact that the ban on patenting therapies covers all methods of eliminating not only pain but also discomfort or malfunction irrespective of their cause, in the context of the HET patentability analysis, it is essential to determine the content of the terms 'discomfort' and 'malfunction' and to indicate the objective criteria on the basis of which existence of those premises should be determined.

However, on the other hand, there are also some EPO decisions which, equally clearly, stated that the legal status of the intervention was dependent on whether it was to counteract ailments or malfunctions resulting from physiological or pathological causes. And only the latter were considered to be covered by the patent ban as therapy.[50] The former (not patentable) are only methods aimed at restoring the organism from a pathological condition, or at preventing pathology. The second approach *may* lead to different conclusions as to the patentability of HETs than those resulting from the previous position, but it undoubtedly requires a different way of examining their patentability. This is because, unlike the first approach, it is not

48. Decisions: T 0036/83 Thenoyl peroxide / ROUSSEL-UCLAF (1985) and T 0144/83 Appetite Suppressant (1986).
49. The decisions T 81/84, T 24/91.
50. The decisions T 469/94, T 774/89; 385/09.

enough to identify an undesirable state (malfunction, discomfort), but it is necessary to find its cause and specify its nature. Only on this basis is it possible to answer the question as to the patentability of the method. Therapeutic nature is attributed only to the methods whose purpose is to remove or correct a state considered as a disruption to the normal functioning of a healthy organism or preventing a pathological state.[51] Whereas a non-therapeutic improvement of performance begins in a state in which there is no disease (normal healthy state) and in such a state, it ends as well. Therefore, any method aimed at strengthening or improving a healthy human being should be considered as technologies which are outside the scope of the ban of Article 53(c) ECP, as not having a therapeutic character.[52]

It should be stressed, however, that despite the categorical and seemingly clear indication of the differences between those interventions, the EPO decisions of this second kind do not establish objective criteria enabling a real and predictable distinction to be made between patentable and non-patentable methods of influencing the human body.[53] Such a role is not fulfilled by the distinction made by the EPO between the interventions concerning a healthy person, i.e., a person in a normal state, and a person in a pathological state.[54] The concepts of normality and health have never been fully clear or uniformly defined, and what is more, their ambiguity has been further increased recently. It is a result of both cultural and social changes, as well as scientific development and technological advancement. In particular, not long ago, the fact that with age, some physical and intellectual functions become imperfect was perceived as a normal phenomenon. The same applies to other limitations resulting either from the nature of *homo sapiens* or from characteristics of an individual. However, with time, alongside the understanding of phenomena and processes within the human body, the ability (or at least the vision of the ability) to counteract or even overcome many of those limitations has occurred. Consequently, what was perceived as a 'normal' and 'healthy' state (even if it were not perfect) in the past, nowadays begins to be perceived as a malfunction and as a state which should be eliminated or corrected. It is so-called medicalization[55] – the process by which some aspects of human life start to be

51. Decision T 774/89.
52. Decision T 385/09.
53. For example, Decision T 469/94 specifies the characteristics of a condition whose removal or alleviation is not considered a therapy (normality, temporality, spontaneous waiver). However, the same features can be attributed to the discomfort caused by menstruation – and a method of alleviating that discomfort was considered unpatented as a therapy.
54. Decision T 469/94.
55. Until the 1970s, the shamefulness was considered a positive feature of women. Nowadays, since 1990, this feature, formerly called natural shame, as a pathological shame is listed, e.g., in WHO 'Diagnostic and Statistical Manual of Mental Disorders'; and is treated as a disease requiring therapy – *Tailor-made for better performance. Improving the person with Human Enhancement* Abridged version of the TA-SWISS study. (Human Enhancement), Zentrum für Technologiefolgen-Abschtzung (Hrsg.). vdf Hochschulverlag AG der ETH Zürich, 2011. p. 30: *https://www.ta-swiss.ch/2011_TA_56A_KF_Human_Enhancement.pdf* (retrieved on 17 September 2019).

considered as medical problems, whereas before they were not considered pathological. It is one of many reasons why the boundaries between health and disease, and normal and pathological states are becoming less and less clear.[56]

The lack of clarity of these concepts in patent law has been more evident also because, according to more and more commonly accepted views, the state of health is determined not only by physiological but also psychological condition.[57] Since the co-dependency of mental and physical condition, and in particular the influence of the psyche on physical condition, are commonly known, the question arises whether and to what extent the psychological suffering of a particular person caused by their level of ability, skills or performance may affect the patent qualification of methods for its enhancement. For example, can someone's psychological suffering, caused by their limited career options because their **Intelligence Quotient** (IQ) level is lower than 100 (which is considered to be the average), justify considering the method of cognitive enhancement to be therapeutic and, therefore, unpatentable (because it alleviates mental suffering)? These doubts may be further exacerbated if the use of patented HET enables the achievement of such a level of ability or efficiency, which is considered by society as 'normal'. In my opinion, the answer to this question should be negative. It is because the word 'normality' is very ambiguous; for instance, the level of skills considered as normal (standard), may be species-determined, but the term 'normal' may also be used to describe the average level in a given community obtained as a result of the widespread use of HET. Thus, an affirmative answer to the question posed would lead to the situation in which development and diffusion of HET may reduce the possibility to get patent on such technologies as they would become increasingly necessary to achieve 'normality'. Moreover, it is worth noting that the 'normality' understood in this way would be not only variable in time but also difficult to establish, due to the diversity of standards (understanding of normality) in different communities. In my opinion, there is no justification for accepting the legal uncertainty, which would result from that approach.

Some commentators note the difficulties and doubts resulting from the above-mentioned approach to methods of influencing the human body. Namely, according to them, its patentability, in the case when states and feelings causing discomfort and are not caused by illness, should depend on whether they are induced beyond man's control and whether man can avoid them. The juxtaposition of Decisions T 81/84 and Decision T 469/94 seems to indicate that they are based on just such an approach as presented in this proposal. However, none of them explicitly mentioned the inevitability and voluntariness aspects. In the first one, it was decided that a method for

56. An illustration of the variability of what is considered normal is the average growth of women and men in the USA and Europe in the 1950s and today. 'Only during the last 35 years, the average growth of Polish men has increased by 7 centimeters' says Professor Janusz Piontek, an anthropologist from the Adam Mickiewicz University in Poznań. – a statement from 2006 – https://nauka.wiara.pl/doc/469229.Rosniemy-jak-na-drozdzach (retrieved on 17 September 2019).
57. 'Health is a state of complete physical, mental and social well-being and not merely the absence of disease or infirmity.' Preamble to the Constitution of the World Health Organization, opened for signature on 22 July 1946 (entered into force on 7 April 1948).

relieving women's discomfort connected with menstruation (although it is a physiological and not a pathological state) is considered therapeutic and thus unpatentable. On the other hand, in the second decision (T 469, 94), the therapeutic character was denied in the case of the method of reducing the perception of fatigue in a person about to participate in a major exercise or having completed a major exercise. EPO said that this method *was not even comparable* with the relief of pain, discomfort, and incapacity, which was recognized as a therapy method and, therefore, can be patented. It was mentioned that the non-therapeutic character of the method is also reflected in the fact that the condition of fatigue induced by the performance of exercises was a transitory physiological condition caused by natural circumstances and removable by a simple rest period.

Nevertheless, the usefulness of such a criterion based on the concepts of voluntariness and the inevitability of the state in question seems doubtful, or at least very limited. The consequence of their approval and application would be the necessity to clarify further vague concepts and terms, and in particular, to answer the question what it means that a given state can be avoided and how to understand 'voluntariness'. Doubts concerning the difference between patentable and non-patented methods are also not removed by the additional guidance provided in that decision. The characteristics specified in decision T 469/94 as justifying the non-therapeutic character of the method of relieving the feeling of fatigue (a transitory physiological condition caused by natural circumstances and removable without any medical intervention) can also describe the ailments accompanying menstruation, the relieving of which was considered a therapeutic method (T 81/84).

Less doubt arises in relation to the understanding of the third type of methods classified under European patent law as a therapy (point (c) above), i.e., preventive methods. 'Preventive' methods ('prophylaxis') from the medical perspective include various ways of strengthening immunity (lifestyle, diet, vaccination) and diagnostic methods enabling early detection of diseases or predispositions to them. Since, in Article 53(c) of the EPC, diagnostic methods are listed alongside therapies, it is indisputable that methods of prevention, whose patentability is prohibited because they are treated as therapy, do not include methods of diagnosis. These are predominantly methods of strengthening immunity through different types of vaccination.[58] Recently, however, new measures have been developed to achieve this result. As an illustration, experiments on the use of genetic modification for this purpose can be mentioned. In 2018, an article was published that claimed human embryos had been modified to be HIV resistant.[59] This experiment has caused a great wave of criticism in the scientific community for several different reasons. Namely, it should be taken into account that this would be repeated, and with time may eventually even gain wider acceptance, especially, if it turns out to be effective and safe. Nowadays, in Europe,

58. S. Rauch, E. Jasny, K.E. Schmidt, B. Petsch, *New Vaccine Technologies to Combat Outbreak Situations*, Frontiers in Immunology volume 9, 1963. 19 September 2018; D. Hobernik, M. Bros, *DNA Vaccines – How Far From Clinical Use?*, International Journal of Molecular Sciences volume 19, issue 11. 2018, 3605.
59. Instead of many D. Normile, *CRISPR Bombshell: Chinese Researcher Claims to Have Created Gene-Edited Twin*, Science volume 26 (November 2018).

attempts to obtain a patent for such a solution would be unsuccessful, in particular, because of the clear ban on the patenting of human embryonic genetic modification. However, if there were no such obstacle (and it is also controversial), the possibility of obtaining a patent would depend on whether this method would be considered therapeutic under Article 53(c) EPC.[60]

With regard to the above, many HETs are, in fact, methods that have been developed for therapy and only over time did the possibility of their application as HE emerge. Eventually, there come to be many methods which have dual uses, i.e., the same method can be used both for therapeutic purposes and beyond therapy. In accordance with the policy established in the EPO, in such cases, the patentability of this kind of methods depends on whether a clear distinction can be made between therapeutic and non-therapeutic use. The prohibition of patenting applies only to the first one. If, however, it is not possible to separate therapeutic and non-therapeutic use, then no patent can be granted. Such rules have been applied in EPO for a long time in respect of methods that can have dual uses: cosmetic (patentable) ones and therapeutic (unpatented) ones.

In light of the above, it could be concluded that the rules for examining the patentability of such inventions (dual use) are established, however in the context of HET, the question arises of whether these rules are justified. In other words, whether there is a *ratio legis* to differentiate, on the one hand, the unpatentable status of the methods aimed at restoring efficiency or abilities *weakened* by diseases or physiological or external processes, and on the other hand, methods aimed at strengthening the ability or efficiency inherent to a given person (genetically and culturally determined) being patentable. This doubt relates especially to cases where the initial state of the organisms to be treated by the method is the same, but it is caused by different factors. For example, two boys have the potential to achieve a maximum height perceived by society as very low. In one case, the cause of it is a disease, while in the other, it is determined genetically by the low height of his parents. What is the reason for providing the sick boy with access to the height correction methods more easily rather than the healthy one? In both cases, the aim of said methods is to facilitate social relations by eliminating or minimizing differences in appearance from the properties that are typical (average) in society. A similar situation may be observed in the context of intellectual skills. For example, the IQ level is considered normal if it is higher than 70, and an average level is 100. Therefore, a method of increasing IQ levels lower than 70 will be treated as a therapy (unpatentable) whereas an increase from a higher level will be treated as a non-therapeutic enhancement and, therefore, patentable. However, according to the prevailing views, lower IQ, although within the norm, may cause difficulties, including serious discomfort in everyday life.[61]

---

60. A separate issue is the patentability of such an invention in the light of other prerequisites and bans under European patent law. But this is beyond the scope of the article.
61. Such an example in the context of considerations regarding the distinction between therapy and HE is given by J. Savulescu in an interview carried out by M. Winsby, *Should Human Enhancement Be a Moral Imperative?* An interview with Julian Savulescu, Science and Society, 16 Apr. 2018.

In light of the above, it appears justified to conclude that it has not yet been possible to point out clear and objective criteria for examining patentability of HET from the view of a ban on patenting therapies. It is mainly because the doubts and controversies that for many years have been associated with the distinction between therapeutic (i.e., unpatentable), and other (i.e., patentable) methods of influencing the functioning of the human body, are particularly evident and even deeper in the context of HET. Given the social and also commercial importance of HET, it is to be expected that disputes over their patent status will be further intensified.

Additionally, it is worth noting here that the above rules for examining the patentability of inventions concerning the method of influencing the human body and the doubts arising from them are the effect of the EPO's interpretation of Article 53(c) of the EPC, and especially the content attributed to the word 'therapy'. This term is defined neither in the EPC nor in other patent acts. Therefore, in order to change them, and simultaneously to change the status of such inventions, there is no need to alter the provisions of the law - it would be enough to modify their interpretation. During recent years, significant changes, including modification of the fundamental concepts of patent law, have been introduced to European patent law in this way.[62] Thus, aside from the doubts and uncertainties mentioned above, the issue of the stability of the concepts and interpretations currently dominant in European patent law arises, especially in EPO policy.

The justification for these questions is also supported by the fact that, for a long time now, proposals have been submitted to abandon the ban on patenting methods of therapy (and diagnostics), or at least to narrow down their scope. History provides many illustrations of the fact that the postulates to increase the availability of patent protection, *inter alia*, by eliminating patent bans, were intensified with the emergence of new types of achievements, and recent decades are the time when completely new possibilities of influencing the functioning of the human body have appeared.

The patentability of HE technology in light of the prohibition of patentability of surgical methods (method for treatment by surgery)

The ban on patentability contained in Article 53(c) of the EPC covers not only therapeutic but also - separately - surgical methods. Since the term 'surgical procedures' is also not clarified in the EPC, in order to answer the question as to what extent that prohibition applies to HET, it is crucial to determine the type of intervention considered to be surgical under European patent law.

For many years, EPO decisions have expressed the view that the ban of patenting of surgical methods applies to *any intervention* that results in irreversible damage or

62. The nature and significance of these changes, according to some, justifies the thesis that the EPO is acting as if it were entitled to legislate, e.g., changing the concept of an invention by including solutions previously considered as discoveries, i.e., a non-patentable category, as well as including abstract solutions in the concept of an invention; narrowing the ban on patenting therapeutic methods by allowing the so-called Swiss claims formula. For more on the legal and political circumstances enabling the EUP to fulfil such a role, *see* A. Plomber, *The EPO as Patent Law-Maker in Europe*, European Law Journal, volume 25, 57-74.

destruction of living cells or living tissue of an organism, regardless of the intervention type (mechanical, electrical, thermal or chemical).[63] Recently, however, the justification for attributing such context to the concept of surgical methods was questioned by the Enlarged Board of Appeal in Decision G 1/07,[64] which described it as too broad in relation to the purpose of the ban on patenting surgical methods. The purpose of this ban is to minimize the risks associated with such interference with the human body, which requires the destruction or damage of living cells or tissues. This risk shall be minimized by the freedom to choose the optimal method to be used in certain circumstances. According to the view expressed in Decision G 1/07, the above-mentioned characteristics of surgical methods had been shaped in the past and suited to the circumstances of that time, when such interventions were almost always associated with a risk to health or even life. The situation has changed due to the technical progress and, therefore, the unmodified definition now includes also interventions which do not involve such risks, making it too broad. Thus, although Decision G 1/07 does not define surgical methods within the meaning of Article 53(c) of the EPC, it stated that the interpretation of that term must exclude interventions of minor importance and without significant risk to the health of the person treated from the scope of the ban.

This decision also addresses an issue that has been the subject of controversy for many years, namely whether the purpose of surgical intervention affects its patentability. It also expressly states that the ban on patenting covers surgical methods irrespective of their purpose.[65] It means that it embraces not only surgical methods with a therapeutic purpose but also those with other aims, e.g., cosmetic ones.[66] It is worth noting that such a view is not new in EPO policy, but also was not the only one.

Many types of HET require the destruction or damage to living cells or tissue. In particular, this is the case for the methods associated with the placement of implants in the human body. It follows from the rules set out in Decision G 1/07 that the patent status of such HETs depends on the significance and risk of the intervention. On this basis, for instance, it can be almost definitely stated that the ban contained in Article 53(c) of the EPC applies to methods of placing implants in the brain (e.g., for the needs of invasive methods of neurostimulation, including Deep Brain Stimulation or invasive BCIs). Less obvious is the patent status of methods of placing implants in other parts of the body. It will be dependent on the patent authority's assessment of the risk and the significance of each surgery intervention. Such criteria for examining patentability introduce an element of uncertainty and unpredictability of decisions.

63. Decisions: T 182/90 and T 35/99.
64. Decision Enlarged Board of Appeal G1/07 of 5.12.2010 – Method for treatment by surgery.
65. In decision T 182/90, and then in decision T 35/99, the \EPO stated that concept of therapy 'comprise particular treatments which were not directed to restoring or maintaining the health of the human or animal body'; similar in the Guidelines for Examination in the European Patent Office (June 2005); differently, however, in decision T 383/03, and later in decisions: T 1102/02, T 9/04 and also in the decision of Enlarged Board of Appeal – G 1/04 – however as an obiter dictum.
66. Decision G 1/07 also correctly pointed out that, if there was a different understanding of surgical methods, it would be pointless to list them in Art. 53(c) as a separate category of non-patentable interventions, distinct from therapy.

Also, in the context of such HETs, which are associated with the destruction of cells or tissues, a question arises about the stability of the rules of their legal patent qualifications. The content of the term 'surgical methods', like the content of the term 'therapy', does not derive from the text of the EPC, but from the EPO's interpretation of Article 53(c) of the EPC. Therefore, also the interpretation of the ban on patenting surgical methods may be altered, for instance, by returning to the idea that the prohibition of patenting surgical methods applies *only* to those interventions causing damage to cells or tissues that have a *therapeutic purpose* within the meaning of patent law. As a consequence of such an approach, also in the context of this HET group, the above-mentioned doubts related to the distinction between therapy methods and other types of impact on the human body would appear.

4 SHOULD HET BE CONSIDERED AN 'ORDINARY' INVENTION?

The above comments applied only to inventions concerning methods of HE. This part focuses on all types of HE inventions (i.e., methods, products) but mainly on these whose results go beyond the biologically determined capabilities of *homo sapiens* or at least far beyond the average level. So, it only concerns such HETs that lead to skills and abilities which, without such interventions, do not occur in human beings (e.g., seeing in the dark, having an extremely wide viewing angle, receiving sounds of a frequency beyond human hearing) or whose occurrence is not common (e.g., exceptional speed of acquiring knowledge and remembering information, or physical endurance, low sleep demand). Whether the rules of patent protection of HET should be the same as those applicable to other inventions or maybe different rules should be laid down.

This point derives from the specific nature of the impact that HET has on the human body and, consequently, from the potential social implications of limited access to such technologies. The ongoing development of different HETs raises hope and even a vision that in the future people will be equipped with skills and abilities that open completely new possibilities for them in their professional and social lives. The difference between the effect of HET and the effect of inventions that were created in the past and led to revolutionary changes in the life of individuals and societies (e.g., washing machine, plane, computer, the Internet) resides in the fact that HET is the first technology that is not aimed at changing the world around the human being, but at changing the human being, and those changes are not aimed at curing diseases or eliminating their consequences.

As a result of the application of HET, there may appear two groups of people with different skills and abilities: the enhanced and the non-enhanced.[67] Their physical or intellectual abilities may differ so significantly that they will determine their life prospects, including their professional, economic, and social position. For instance, people with enhanced cognitive abilities, with reduced needs for sleep, with direct

67. G. Wolbring, *The Unenhanced Underclass* (in:) J.M.P Wilsdon (ed.) *Better Humans? The Politics of Human Enhancement: The Politics of Human Enhancement and Life Extension*, Demos Institute 2006, pp. 122-129.

'connection' with computers or other external devices may *inter alia* - in some areas - push out non-enhanced people from the labour market.

Although it is too early to predict when and which HETs will be developed, which will be the most appreciated and which will be the most desired, and on what scale, it is very likely that those that induce the most desired changes will be expensive and therefore accessible only to a limited group of people.[68] It means that existing social inequalities might be exacerbated by adding to the advantages of elites. Thus, access to HET may become one of the significant determinants of social position. It should be stressed, however, that it is not just the differences between people and the inequalities in social status and life chances that are the main source of concern. Even very significant differences between the skills and capabilities of people are nothing new. But the differentiation of social status that could be the result of limited access to HET would be substantially different from the one that has traditional causes because only the former would be a direct consequence of human decisions and actions, both by technology providers (owners) and individuals being enhanced. Even if such a way of creating differentiation between people has some advantages over a 'random', i.e., 'natural' distribution of abilities, it gives rise to several new doubts and questions. The basic question is whether it will be possible to preserve and respect the principle of equality as one of the basic foundations of modern society if enhanced and unenhanced human beings exist side by side. The fear is expressed that with time people who have been subject of HE may be regarded as 'better human beings', and even 'more human beings' than those who remain unenhanced.[69]

Due to the topic of the chapter, issues related to individual decisions about the use of HET in order to obtain certain abilities or skills are outside the scope of consideration. It covers only questions and doubts stemming from the fact that the possibility of using HET, and thus of obtaining features requiring the use of HET, will be dependent on the decision of a third party. Such a situation is of particular concern where the third party will be able to block access to HET and thus block access to higher social status.

In the discussions on HET, despite differences of opinion, there is a broad consensus among adversaries on one issue. Almost all of them share the view that it is necessary to create systems that at least minimize the risk of exacerbating social inequalities which could result from the application of HET. This postulate is based on the belief that even if HET has the potential to provide benefits to both individuals and society, such benefits are not possible if HET is not fairly distributed.[70] For instance, the European Group on Ethics in Science and New Technologies in its opinion concerned one of the types of invention aimed at HE, i.e., Information and Communication Technologies implants, stressed that efforts should be made to ensure that this

68. F. Swindells, *Economic Inequality and Human Enhancement Technology*, Humana Mente 7 (26) (2014).
69. Francis Fukuyama, *Our Posthuman Future: Consequences of the Biotechnology Revolution*, 1st ed., Farrar, Straus and Giroux 2002, pp. 9-10.
70. F. Swindells, *Economic Inequality and Human Enhancement Technology*, above.

technology is not used to create a two-class society or to increase the gap between industrialized countries and the rest of the world.[71]

Therefore, the question arises as to what kind of HET distribution method, or rather what kind of rules of access to HET are to be considered fair, i.e., those rules that prevent the risk of creating two classes of people.

Societies have always been internally diverse, and this diversity has always had many different causes. The social status of individuals is determined to a great extent by their material situation, which is decisive for the possibility of gaining access to various goods and services, and also for the possibility of professional and personal development of individuals and their perception by others. From a historical perspective, however, a change can be seen in the perception of certain needs, the importance that is attached to their fulfilment, and the importance which is attached to their fulfilment, both from the point of view of an individual and from public interest. The fulfilment of certain needs is considered as an implementation of fundamental rights. As a result of these changes, the scope and directions of state interventions aimed at decreasing the disparities in access to certain goods have been gradually extended, and state systems have even been set up to enable everyone to have access to certain goods (health and education).

Against this background, the question arises as to what differences between people resulting from the limited access to HET will be accepted in a democratic society, and what differences would be considered contradictory to its fundamental axiological assumptions. The answer to the above question is necessary as a starting point for identifying those HETs to which everyone should have access, and in particular, this access should not depend on the decision of any other person. The importance of this issue is obvious in the context of considerations on the patent protection of HET.

One of the main instruments of limiting access to a HET may be the price policy of the HET's provider – i.e., imposing high prices of access to HET since there are already various proposals to prevent undesirable social consequences from such behaviour on the part of HET owners.[72] However, the question arises whether mere patenting of HET can have socially undesirable effects and if that question is answered in the affirmative, what would those effects be?

It is known that the patent holder may not only demand a very high licence fee but may also refuse to grant a licence, thereby excluding some entities or whole groups of people from access to patented inventions. The social importance of such a situation depends on the type of features (skills, abilities) enhanced by a given HET and its potential impact on the social and professional position of individual persons. Because of the diversity of technologies covered by the concept of HET, there is (and will be) a deep differentiation in both the social impact of their use and the social impact of the limited access to them. Thus, at first, it would be unreasonable to conclude that the limitation of access to each of these technologies leads to socially undesirable and

71. Ethical aspects of ICT implants in the human body – Opinion N° 20 – 2005, https://ec.europa.eu/commission/presscorner/detail/en/MEMO_05_97.
72. F. Swindells, *Economic Inequality and Human Enhancement Technology*, above.

consequently unacceptable consequences. Therefore, a general ban on the patenting of HET (like a ban on the patenting of therapeutic methods) would not be justified. For the same reason (i.e., differentiation of HET), it seems impossible, or at least premature, to create limitations on HET patents like those provided, for example, for research tools in some jurisdictions.

At the same time, since it is indisputable that blocking access to certain HETs may, in certain circumstances, produce harmful implications for the public interest, it seems necessary to have legal possibilities to counteract the limits. Under the contemporary patent law, such purposes, i.e., adjusting the general rules of patent law to the specific nature of the particular invention and circumstances, can be achieved by the so-called compulsory licence. Noting the widespread presence of compulsory licences in modern patent law, it should be mentioned, however, that the premises and scope of their application are differentiated. As a rule, the prerequisites for the compulsory licence are set out in the law: the types of inventions that may be affected, the circumstances (e.g., not meeting market demands), the goal: e.g., for reasons of public interest or the need to protect competition. The question arises whether, in a situation where the patent holder refuses to grant a licence, a compulsory licence may be issued on such a basis that the use of this invention is necessary for human beings to acquire features which determine their higher social status. The answer to such a question requires an analysis based on the particular legal systems, i.e., their legislation and jurisprudence. However, even taking into account the differences in the legal regime for compulsory licensing across different jurisdictions, it seems justified to conclude that the possibility of obtaining a compulsory licence on those grounds is at least highly uncertain, if not impossible. This finding appears to be justified regardless of the impact that the limitation of access to the HET posed by the patent holder may have on the social structure because the use of a compulsory licence in almost all jurisdictions and throughout the whole history of this legal instrument has been very limited and prudent. It has been rightly thought that a contrary approach would destroy the system of patent protection – its economic importance. The compulsory licence, by its very nature, affects the essence of the patent as a right of exclusivity. In recent years, however, there has been an increasing tendency to change the approach to compulsory licences – in the direction of extending its use. This is a reaction to the expansion of patent law, and in particular, to the granting of patent protection to goods that meet the needs of particular importance to individuals and the public interest. This new approach is reflected, among other things, in the introduction of provisions in patent laws to clarify or even broaden the list of circumstances justifying the granting of a compulsory licence. This concerns, first of all, inventions related to health care in the broad sense of the term since the patent exclusivity of such inventions and its consequences provoke particularly heated controversies.

However, it seems to be in line with this trend, and at the same time axiologically justified, to ensure the existence of legal possibilities to grant a compulsory licence for HET where the manner in which the patentee exercises his right generates threats that are typical for limiting the availability of just such inventions. It is a situation in which the patent holder has the possibility to influence the process of creating new social groups/classes (enhanced; non-enhanced) and to influence the assignment of individual persons or communities to each of these classes; whereas obtaining features determining belonging to the 'better' class is possible only through the use of HET.

5 CONCLUSIONS

To answer briefly and concisely the first question raised in the introduction, it can be concluded that under European patent law (it means EPC and national patent acts containing provisions modelled on Article 53(c) of the EPC) there are no clear, fully objective criteria for examining the patentability of HET, i.e., interventions not aimed at treating a disease or eliminating its symptoms and effects. Such a categorical statement is justified in view of the clear lack of stability in the approach presented in the EPO decisions and especially because of vagueness criteria indicated in them in order to distinguish therapy and surgery methods as interventions whose patentability is prohibited.

It should be emphasized that this situation results mainly from the ambiguity of the way in which inventions whose patenting is prohibited (therapy and surgery methods) are defined in the regulations, and not from difficulties in determining whether the particular invention belongs to these categories – i.e., whether it fulfils the requirements for being included in them. Consequently, the patent status of many types of HETs as methods of influence on the human body is unpredictable.

Also, the reference to the purpose or function of the ban on patenting contained in Article 53(c) EPC and in the provisions modelled on it, does not make it possible to eliminate the uncertainty as to its subject matter. The analysis of the EPO's approach to such inventions, from a historical perspective, as well as the changes introduced to the EPC 2000, makes it difficult to identify unambiguously the purpose and, consequently, the framework of the prohibition in Article 53(c) of the EPC. In the above-mentioned changes in the legal text and in the EPO's approach to methods of influencing the functioning of the human body, the dominance of the tendency to narrow the scope of the patent ban is clearly visible. However, there is no reason to conclude from this that such a tendency will be continued, or at least that the current interpretation of this ban will not be changed by broadening its scope. Therefore, it is difficult to predict, both for the near and long future, to which HET European patent will be available and to which ones patent protection will be refused on the basis of the ban of Article 53(c) EPC.

Such uncertainty is clearly undesirable from the point of view of both patent applicants and third parties, and – which deserves particular attention – from the perspective of the public interest. However, as mentioned above, uncertainty about the subject matter of the ban contained in Article 53(c) EPC did not arise only with the emergence of HET. Doubts and controversies have accompanied the application of this ban for many years. But it is undeniable that the emergence of HET – the new goals of technical interventions on the human body – gave an additional impulse to these discussions (added fuel to the fire). This was mainly because the spectrum of inventions which may be affected by the ban has been broadened.

Although it is undisputed that the postulate to eliminate the state of uncertainty is justified, it is equally obvious that it is extremely difficult to formulate proposals for such changes in the law that would make this goal achievable. This requires, first of all, agreement and definition of the purpose of the ban on patenting contained in Article 53(c) of the EPC and in the provisions of national laws modelled on it. Only on this basis would it be possible to specify its subject matter and thus eliminate doubts in this area. This will also be the background to the answer for the question of whether this ban can apply to HET and, if so, to which ones.

As a side-note, it is worth noting that in view of the growing controversy over the rationale for maintaining the ban on patenting therapies and surgical methods, it seems desirable to reopen a discussion on this topic. However, regardless of views on this question and the arguments invoked to defend each of the positions presented in this discussion, it seems indisputable that the prohibition of Article 53(c) EPC in its current form does not meet the expectations of any party to the dispute.

The analysis of the second of the issues covered by this article did not allow for the formulation of direct conclusions *de lege ferenda* either. As HETs are still technologies at the early stages of development, it is difficult, if not impossible, to accurately predict the impact of both dissemination and patenting of such technologies on individuals and societies. With the necessary caution, it can be said that the use of HET can reduce or even eliminate some of the differences between people in their intellectual, cognitive and physical abilities. HET also gives the possibility to equip people with qualities, abilities, and skills that go beyond these inherent to the *homo sapiens*. Regardless of whether HE is perceived as a positive, negative or even as a dangerous phenomenon for humanity, it is undisputed that, depending on the rules of HET distribution, these technologies may facilitate the equality and life chances of people and entire communities, or, on the contrary, may lead to the deepening of existing differences and divisions. One of the factors that substantially limits access to HET is the patentability of such technologies. The patent owner deciding to whom and under what conditions to grant a HET licence and to whom this consent is refused, may significantly or sometimes even decisively influence the formation of social structures and the status of individuals – their affiliation to particular classes or groups. Such an obviously undesirable effect may, of course, result from a patent policy concerning not all but only certain types of HET, and only in particular economic, political and social context.

In light of the above-mentioned, it seems reasonable to conclude that the counteraction to such undesirable phenomena and situations should be preceded with their identification *in concreto* rather than *in abstracto*, which means that it should be established whether they actually occur in the given circumstances. As a rule, the procedure of granting a compulsory licence, which is common in modern patent law, allows for the determination of the consequences of certain behaviour of the patent holder (exercise of patent rights) in certain circumstances. Such findings shall be the basis for the decision to grant or refuse a compulsory licence. The possibility of using a compulsory licence to counteract the undesirable effects of limiting access to patented HET depends on whether such effects or the practices leading to them are included in the list of prerequisites for granting the compulsory licence. It appears that it is already worthwhile to analyse these prerequisites in terms of their usefulness for this purpose and, if necessary, to make the necessary amendments.

This is not a proposal to create casuistic regulations, especially since it is impossible to predict which specific situations and phenomena would be harmful and even dangerous to the values that are nowadays considered fundamental. To the contrary, it is a matter of formulating the prerequisites for a compulsory licence in such a way that they also encompass the negative impact that the way in which patents are enforced could have on the social structure and, in particular, on human equality in a certain situation. Generally speaking, it can be said that the emergence of HET is one of the numerous factors that induce, and perhaps even force the analysis of the purpose and function of the system of patent protection. Without this, however, one can expect growing controversy, ambiguity, and legal uncertainty, and as a result, there may be a risk that the rules of patent law will not be governed by the accepted values and goals but rather be created under the pressure of the stronger party.

CHAPTER 4

Do We Need Patent Protection for Biopharmaceuticals?

Marek Świerczyński

1 INTRODUCTION

Biological medicinal products (biopharmaceuticals) have been increasingly used in almost all areas of medicine and have become one of the most effective ways of clinical treatment for a wide range of diseases, such as cancer or metabolic disorders. These are medicinal products containing one or more active substances derived from biological material.[1] Biological medicines currently include preparations containing a traditionally derived active substance, as well as those whose substances are manufactured using biotechnological techniques.[2]

Directive 2003/63/EC[3] defines a biological medicine as a product whose active substance is a biological substance. A biological substance is a substance that is produced or extracted from a biological source. Biological sources include microorganisms, organs and tissues of plant or animal origin, cells or fluids (including blood or plasma) of human or animal origin and biotechnological cell constructs using cellular substrates. In contrast, US law does not provide a single definition for

1. C. Mund, *Patenting Biosimilars* (in:) *Research handbook on Intellectual Property and the Life Sciences* (ed. D. Matthews, H. Zech), Cheltenham 2017, p. 4; H.H. Shih, P. Miller, D.C. Harnish, *An Overview of Discovery and Development Process For Biologics* (in:) *Biological Drug Products: Development and Strategies*, (ed. W. Wang, M. Singh), Wiley 2013, p. 3 and f.
2. M. Sanzo, *The Promise and Problem of Biologics*, Santa Clara High Technology Law Journal 2017, vol. 34, issue 1, p. 80: K. Buchholz, J. Collins, *Concepts in Biotechnology. History, Science and Business*, Weinheim 2010, pp. 380-381.
3. Commission Directive 2003/63/EC of 25 June 2003 amending Directive 2001/83/EC of the European Parliament and of the Council on the Community code relating to medicinal products for human use (OJ 2003 L 159, p. 46, as amended).

biological drugs. The Food and Drug Administration (FDA) treats biological products as 'complex products that are not easily identifiable or characterised'.[4]

Biopharmaceuticals become the most important group of medicines in the world.[5] They have dominated virtually every field of medicine, improving the effectiveness of and safety of therapy, and sometimes radically changing the prognosis in some diseases. Their application concerns cancer, rheumatoid, dermatological, gastrointestinal, neurological and respiratory diseases as well as metabolic disorders.[6] They make it possible to treat patients for whom therapy with traditional chemical drugs was ineffective. These products belong to the fastest-growing segments of the prescription medicinal products market.[7] Most clinical trials are now focused on biotechnology.[8] It is estimated that around 40% of the 6,000 products in clinical trials in the world are already biologically active.[9] Of all the medical products currently available, it is estimated that biopharmaceuticals already account for more than 20%. The share of these drugs is expected to increase, which is also a result of the observation of the US market, where 207 drugs containing a new molecule (chemical or biological) have been registered in the last four years, of which as much as 47% were innovative biological drugs manufactured using biotechnological techniques.[10]

These products also bring significant profits for their Intellectual Property (IP) rights owners.[11] As the significance of biopharmaceuticals and their share among available pharmaceuticals increases, it also becomes more important to create a complete regulatory framework thereof.[12] Maturation of the biopharmaceuticals market made legal debate aimed at their regulation come to the surface. Every country needs now to carefully consider and balance its own socio-economic needs, cultural and ethical norms, intellectual property laws, and international obligations on protection and access to new biopharmaceuticals.[13]

As it has been already said, the bio-medicine market is one of the fastest-growing segments of the pharmaceutical industry. Dynamic development of the market for biopharmaceuticals in recent years is related to the expiration of the IP exclusive rights (including patents, Statistical Process Controls (SPCs), data and market exclusivity) on original (patented, reference) – innovative biological medicinal products. This results in the introduction to the market of follow-on products. We call them biosimilars.

4. FDA, https://www.fda.gov/ForConsumers/ConsumerUpdates/ucm048341.htm.
5. S.K. Niazi, *Biosimilars and Interchangeable Biologics. Strategic Elements*, Boca Raton 2016, pp. 1 and f.
6. C. Mund, *Patenting...*, p. 6.
7. W. Smith, A. Cohen (in:) *Pharmaceutical and Medical Device Law. Regulation of Research, Development and Marketing* (red. M. Clark), Cumulative Supplement, Arlington 2017, pp. 9-16.
8. K. Rajan, *The Experimental Machinery of Global Clinical Trials: Case Studies from India* (in:) *The Pharmaceutical Studies Reader* (ed. S. Sismondo, J. Greene), Oxford 2015, p. 223.
9. G. Walsh, *Biopharmaceutical...*, pp. 1136-1145.
10. D.J. Craik, D.P. Fairlie, S. Liras, D. Price, *The Future of Peptide-Based Drugs*, Chemical Biology & Drug Design 2013/81/1, pp. 136–147.
11. *Ibid.*
12. Y. Helled, *Biologics, Biosimilars and Other Idiosyncrasies* (in:) *Contemporary Issues in Pharmaceutical Patent Law: Setting the Framework and Exploring Policy Options* (ed. B. Mercurio, D. Kim), Abingdon 2017, p. 66.
13. *Ibid.*, p. 67.

Biosimilars need to be distinguished now in the legal debate, due to their legal, social, ethical and commercial importance. The scale and significance of this process are unprecedented. In this respect, the 'patent cliff' metaphor is being used.[14] Examples of biologics for which patents have expired are human insulin, interferons and growth hormones.[15] In view of the fact that the patent protection period of several important biological medicines has expired or will soon expire: Herceptin in 2014, Enbrel in 2015, Lucentis in 2016, Humira in 2018 and Avastin in 2019, more biosimilars are about to be registered. It is estimated that 50 biosimilars are currently under research in the European Union (EU) and/or the US.[16] The research and development of biopharmaceuticals are expensive and time-consuming. High prices of these products make their reimbursement under national health care systems difficult.[17] But when IP exclusive rights for original biological medicinal product expire, cheaper follow – on biosimilars may be introduced into the market and may become subject to the reimbursement by the public payer.[18] In result, biosimilars increase patients' access to biological therapy. Biosimilars start to compete with original products in an increasing number of therapeutic areas. They provide public payers, physicians and patients with the opportunity to use a wider range of therapeutic options.[19]

One of the greatest challenges is the change of law to ensure a balance between the market development of biosimilars and access of patients to biological therapy.[20] It seems obvious that discussion on the improvement (rethinking) of the patent law in the context of biopharmaceuticals needs to be aimed at the improvement of the patients' access to new biological therapies. In my opinion, the model of protection provided by the patent law should not be separated from the regulatory pharmaceutical and reimbursement framework existing in the national healthcare system. Ultimately, access to new biological therapies for patients is to be considered a decisive factor for the scope of patent protection. The often indicated reason for limited use of biological therapies is their high price. As a rule, patients cannot afford to finance the purchase of biological drugs on their own; hence, the only possibility to access them is the reimbursement system, which depends on the state budget constraints. It is worth

14. H. Yu, *Achieving Proof of Concept in Drug Discovery and Development*, Cheltenham 2017, pp. 39-40; B. Calo-Fernández, J. Martínez-Hurtado, *Biosimilars...*, p. 1393-1408.
15. M. Pavlovic, J.-L. Prugnaud, *From the Biosimilar Concept to the Marketing Authorisation* (in:) *Biosimilars: A New Generation of Biologics* (ed. J.-L. Prugnaud, J.-H. Trouvin), Paris 2012, pp. 23-36.
16. *Winning with biosimilars. Opportunities in global markets*, https://www2.deloitte.com/content /dam/Deloitte/us/Documents/life-sciences-health-care/us-lshc-biosimilars-whitepaper-final. pdf.
17. M. Minn, *Patenting Practices in the Competitive European Pharmaceutical Market: A Thin Line Between Patents, Innovation and Strategy*, EIPR 2018, issue 1 (40), p. 16.
18. H.H. Shih, P. Miller, D.C. Harnish, *An Overview...*, pp. 3 and f.
19. T. Pieńkowski (in:) *Leki biologiczne biopodobne w praktyce klinicznej*, Puls Medycyny Raport 2017, Warszawa 2017, p. 33.
20. 'Today's pharmaceutical innovation system is firmly rooted in the patent system' – E. Hoen, *Private Patents and Public Health: Changing Intellectual Property Rules for Access to Medicines*, Diemen 2016, p. 128.

noting, however, that the problem of high prices of biological drugs does not concern only EU but is a global problem.[21]

It seems obvious that the holistic approach to public health-related IP is needed.[22] The patent system should be designed to balance the interests of inventors with those of the public, including patients. Excessive protection of investors' rights has a negative effect on public health.[23] On the other hand, the existing IP system does not protect biopharmaceutical innovators in an effective way either.[24] The existing patent system is difficult to be applied in the field of the biotechnology industry. It is expensive and slow for biotechnology development.[25] It should be adapted to the needs of biopharmaceuticals.[26]

There are fundamental questions that should be asked in the context of patent law:

(1) Are we allowed to claim that biopharmaceuticals are the result of nature and should be treated as a common good (part of the public domain)?
(2) Should we enact new exemptions to the scope of the patent law focused on the biosimilars (e.g., similar to the Bolar exemption[27]?). Is there a difference between generics and biosimilars? Or should there be? Why does it matter for biosimilars?

The above questions concern the very essence of the patent system, which consists in the fact that a patented invention cannot be used in a specific territory by persons other than the patent holder (owner) unless he agrees to such use, e.g., by

21. J. Borrás-Blasco, E. Casterá, X. Cortes, J. Martín-Alonso, J.D. Rosique-Robles, F.J. Abad, *Dealing with the High Cost of Biological Therapies: Developing and Implementing a Biological Therapy Prioritization Protocol for Ankylosing Spondylitis Patients in a Tertiary Hospital*, International Journal of Clinical Pharmacology and Therapeutics 2015, vol. 53, issue 12, pp. 997-1004; M. Manova, A. Savova, M. Vasileva, S. Terezova, M. Kamusheva, D. Grekova, V. Petkova, G. Petrova, *Comparative Price Analysis of Biological Products for Treatment of Rheumatoid Arthritis*, Frontiers in Pharmacology 2018, https://www.frontiersin.org/articles/10.3389/fphar.2018.01070/full.
22. V. Vadi, *Investment Disputes, Pharmaceutical Patents and Health-$elated Goods* (in:) *The New Intellectual Property of Health: Beyond Plain Packaging* (ed. A. Alemanno, E. Bonadio), Cheltenham 2016, p. 254.
23. *Ibid.*
24. *Ibid.*
25. Ch. Holman, *Intellectual Property in the Age of Personal Genomics and Synthetic Biology*, Biotechnology Law Report 2012, vol. 31, issue 1.
26. Comp. S. Melethi, *Landscape and Consideration of Intellectual Property for Development of Biosimilars* (in:) *Biological Drug Products: Development and Strategies* (ed. W. Wang, M. Singh), Wiley 2013, pp. 111-132.
27. The Bolar exemption in EU is governed by Directive 2001/83 (as amended by Directive 2004/27). Art. 10(6) provides that: '[c]onducting the necessary studies and trials with a view to the application of paragraphs 1 to 4 [i.e. bioequivalents and biosimilars] and the consequential practical requirements shall not be regarded as contrary to patent rights or to supplementary protection certificates for medicinal products'. The exact language, scope and interpretation of Bolar exemption vary across EU.

concluding an appropriate licence agreement. There is also a growing diversity in the area of patent law, in particular, the fact that pharmaceutical patents have little in common with patents obtained in 'classical' technical fields. Biotechnology distinguishes the subject matter of the process, i.e., living matter, from other technologies, which results in exceptional difficulties in their legal protection. The challenges associated with patenting biotechnology also arise from the complexity of the invention, which translates into a complication of the process of determining whether the biotechnology patent has been infringed. Usually, when a dispute arises, the first step is to determine whether the patent is valid at all.

2 WHY DO BIOPHARMACEUTICALS NEED TO BE LEGALLY SEPARATED FROM CHEMICAL (SMALL MOLECULE) MEDICINAL PRODUCTS?

The introduction of biopharmaceuticals turned out to be a breakthrough in the treatment of millions of patients affected by diseases for which previously used chemical medicinal products were ineffective.[28] First biopharmaceuticals were approved already in the 1980s.[29] In the following decades, many other such medicines have been developed and marketed. Biopharmaceuticals have been used in patients suffering from serious diseases, often previously incurable, such as cancer and chronic inflammatory diseases. Examples of biopharmaceuticals are insulins,[30] growth hormones[31] and monoclonal antibodies used in the treatment of autoimmune diseases or cancer.[32]

The very first proposal should be to legally separate biopharmaceuticals from traditional medicinal products based on active chemical substances.[33] Existing EU legal pharmaceutical regime for medicinal products was created and is focused on chemical products. It disrespects biopharmaceuticals although they have a much more complex structure.[34] Particular series of the same biopharmaceutical product may differ from each other, and any changes in the starting biological materials and method of production affect the safety of products.[35] This results in significant differences in the

28. Y. Helled, *Biologics...*, p. 48.
29. K. Buchholz, J. Collins, *Concepts...*, pp. 95-97.
30. *Ibid.*, pp. 399-400.
31. M. Szalecki (in:) *Leki biologiczne biopodobne w praktyce klinicznej*, Puls Medycyny Raport 2017, Warszawa 2017, pp. 23-25; K. Buchholz, J. Collins, *Concepts...*, pp. 400-401.
32. T. Pieńkowski (in:) *Leki biologiczne...*, pp. 31-33; K. Buchholz, J. Collins, *Concepts...*, p. 401.
33. *See Guide to Biological Medicines. A Focus on Biosimiliar Medicines*, https://www.scribd.com/document/212444737/Guide-to-Biological-Medicines-a-Focus-on-Biosimilar-Medicines.
34. M. Marklowska-Dzierżak (in:) *Leki biologiczne biopodobne w praktyce klinicznej*, Puls Medycyny Raport 2017, Warszawa 2017, p. 7.
35. Y. Helled, *Biologics...*, p. 64.

process of their manufacturing, marketing authorization,[36] pharmacovigilance,[37] and interchangeability (substitution).[38]

Biological medicines differ from chemical medicines in every respect. The difference between the two groups of drugs includes the source of the active ingredient, the product itself, equivalence, structure, manufacturing methods, composition, formulation, dosage, as well as intellectual property, regulation and marketing.

Specific differences are as follows: (1) biopharmaceuticals are characterized by greater variability; (2) due to their complex structure, they present a greater risk of immunogenic reactions[39]; (3) they are administered by injections or infusions; and (4) these products usually require dedicated transport and storage conditions, as it may affect their quality, effectiveness and safety. That is why the traceability of a specific series of biopharmaceuticals is so important.[40]

Setting up the legal framework for biopharmaceuticals is difficult, as the long-term effects of their use are not yet fully known. Despite the studies that present a relatively high safety profile, each decision to initiate treatment with these products should be carefully considered. Therefore, the priority is to monitor their potential adverse effects (*pharmacovigilance*).[41] In the marketing authorization procedure, the category of biopharmaceuticals also needs to be separated.[42]

3 CATEGORIES OF BIOPHARMACEUTICALS

A clear distinction between different categories of the biopharmaceuticals under the law. Biological medicinal products are first to be distinguished depending on the active substance. This is of particular importance for the IP law. Initially, biological drugs were produced using traditional methods, such as extracting therapeutic proteins from human organs, taken from deceased people, animal organs or separated fractions of human blood. A large part of biological medicines, which were originally produced using traditional methods, are now produced using biotechnological techniques.

First category of biopharmaceuticals includes products based on naturally occurring substances in nature (e.g., pig or beef insulin, pig heparin, alpha and beta interferons from human lymphocytes, erythropoietin). These active substances are

36. *See* EMA guidelines: The European Medicines Agency (EMA) has a dedicated webpage on biosimilar medicines which can be accessed here: http://www.ema.europa.eu/ema/index.jsp?curl=pages/special_topics/document_listing/document_listing_000318.jsp. An overview of all relevant scientific guidelines for biosimilar medicines can also be found on the EMA website and are directly accessible here: http://www.ema.europa.eu/ema/index.jsp?curl=pages/regulation/general/general_content_000408.jsp&mid=WC0b01ac058002958c .
37. Cf. Guideline on good pharmacovigilance practices (GVP) Product- or Population-Specific Considerations II: Biological medicinal products, 4 August 2016, EMA/168402/2014.
38. This important problem is analysed in detail in the monograph *Biologiczne produkty lecznicze* (ed. M. Świerczyński), Warszawa 2016.
39. EMA, Guideline on good pharmacovigilance practices (GVP). Product-or Population-Specific Considerations II: Biological medicinal products, 4 August 2016, p. 5.
40. *Ibid.*, p. 7.
41. M. Nowicki, J. Zimmer-Nowicka, *Biofarmaceutyki...*, p. 125.
42. *See* point 17 preamble of the regulation 1235/2010 and point 10 preamble of the directive 2010/84.

derived from non-genetically engineered living organisms (animals, plants, microbes) or from human blood. In such a case, patent protection must be limited and may concern only the manufacturing method a given product and not the active substance itself.[43] Such substances are not patentable even as second medical uses.

Second group of substances includes those specially designed to affect various underlying mechanisms of disease (e.g., low molecular weight heparins, recombinant proteins, monoclonal antibodies, interleukin antagonists).[44] Those are active substances obtained by means of cells or organisms into which foreign genes have been introduced (transgenes).[45] In this case, not only the method of their manufacturing but also the active substances themselves can be subject to patent (exclusivity) protection. This division may also influence other IP rights, such as market exclusivity.

Another division of biopharmaceuticals refers to its development and marketing order. First, innovative, original products are being developed and launched on the market. We call them reference medicinal products under pharmaceutical law.[46] Once exclusivity granted by patent and SPC expires, the biosimilars, as follow-on substitutes, start to be marketed.[47] The first is approved for marketing on the basis of full regulatory documentation (dossier), while the marketing authorization of the latter is based on simplified documentation (dossier), similar to generics (chemical products). However, this simplified documentation, in contrast to generics (chemical products), must also include studies confirming the biological similarity of biosimilars to the reference products.[48] The possibility of the market launch of a biosimilar is closely related to both

43. The case law of the EPO Boards of Appeal and Enlarged Boards of Appeal has provided guidance to take adequate account of technological developments involving biological material. Cf. also US Myriad case: *Association for Molecular Pathology v. Myriad Genetics*, Inc., 569 U.S. 576 (2013).
44. W.-H. Boehncke, H.H. Radeke, *Introduction: Definition…*, p. 1.
45. *Ibid.*
46. The reference medicinal product is a medicinal product which has been granted a marketing authorization by a Member State or by the Commission on the basis of a complete dossier, i.e., with the submission of quality, pre-clinical and clinical data in accordance with Arts 8(3), 10a, 10b or 10c of Directive 2001/83/EC and to which the application for marketing authorization for a generic/hybrid medicinal product refers, by demonstration of bioequivalence, usually through the submission of the appropriate bioavailability studies.
47. S. Ruiz, G. Calvo, *Similar Biological Medicinal Products: Lessons Learned and Challenges Ahead*, Journal of Generic Medicines: The Business Journal for the Generic Medicines Sector January 2011, issue 8, pp. 4-13.
48. The legal requirements and the procedures for making an application for a marketing authorization are set out in Directive 2001/83/EC and in Regulation (EC) No 726/2004. For similar biological applications, the legal basis can be found in Art. 6 of Regulation (EC) 726/2004 and Art. 10(4) of Directive 2001/83/EC. According to Art. 10(4) of Directive 2001/83/EC, where a biological medicinal product which is similar to a reference biological medicinal product does not meet the conditions in the definition of generic medicinal products, owing to, in particular, differences relating to raw materials or differences in manufacturing processes of the biological medicinal product and the reference biological medicinal product, the results of appropriate pre-clinical tests or clinical trials relating to these conditions must be provided. The type and quantity of supplementary data to be provided must comply with the relevant criteria stated in Annex I and the related detailed guidelines. Regulation (EC) No 726/2004 creates a centralized procedure for the authorization of medicinal products, for which there is a single application, a single evaluation and a single authorization, allowing direct access to the single European Union market. The types of products, which fall within the scope of the Regulation, are set out in Art. 3 and the Annex to that Regulation and includes biological products. For similar biological

the expiration of the patent (including SPC), as well as other exclusivity rights to the reference product, as the data or market exclusivity.[49]

A generic is a substitute for an original medicine that contains the same active substance. The name is used to refer to chemical substitutes. For these medicines, due to their characteristics, obtaining a preparation containing an accurate copy of the active pharmaceutical ingredient is relatively fast, simple and inexpensive.[50]

If an equivalent biological medicine is obtained and authorized after the expiry of the patent for a reference biological medicine, the term 'generic' is not used, as it is not identical to its reference medicine. The EMA considered that the term 'biosimilars' should be introduced to describe biological medicinal products containing a version of the active substance contained in a previously registered original biological medicinal product, the so-called reference medicinal product.

In non-EU countries, it has also been pointed out that biosimilars may act differently from the original ones, which has been reflected in the separation and naming of this product group. Canada has now introduced the name biosimilar biologic drug or biosimilar drug (biosimilar biologic drug), replacing the original name Subsequent Entry Biologic (SEB). The US Drug Registration Agency also noted that this group of drugs was distinct and introduced the name biosimilar or follow-on biologic. These differences are mainly due to the differences in the production systems, manufacturing and purification processes used, which are unique to each manufacturer of biological drugs.

The fact that biosimilars are not generics affects their registration procedure. Registration requirements for biosimilars are much higher than for generics but still lower than for innovative medicines. Biosimilars are registered on the basis of a demonstrated biosimilarity with the corresponding previously registered innovative medicine. These medicines may be registered upon presentation of the required comparative documentation for the reference medicine or upon presentation of the complete documentation, i.e., that is required for the innovative medicine.

Another important aspect needs to be underlined here. It refers to the proper terminology of biopharmaceutical follow-on products. It is still being discussed. Unfortunately, neither EU law nor Polish law contains the legal definitions yet. Only EMA Guidelines refer to similar biological medicinal products, also called biosimilars.[51]

---

medicinal products, also known as 'Biosimilars', eligibility can be granted to the Centralized Procedure in Art. 3(1) of Regulation (EC) No 726/2004. According to this article, medicinal products developed by means of biotechnological processes as described in the Annex (point 1) of Regulation (EC) No 726/2004 should be authorized by the EU. *See* for details K. Ho, J.-H. Trouvin, *Biologicals' Characteristics...*, p. 2.

49. M. Pavlovic, J.-L. Prugnaud, *From the Biosimilar...*, pp. 23-36.
50. K. Klein, M.L. De Bruin, A.W. Broekmans, P. Stolk, *Classification of Recombinant Biologics in the EU: Divergence between National Pharmacovigilance Centers*, BioDrugs2015/29, pp. 373-379.
51. *See*, e.g., Questions and answers for patients – Biosimilar medicines explained (http://ec.europa.eu/DocsRoom/documents/26643) or European Medicines Agency procedural advice for users of the centralized procedure for similar biological medicinal products applications (https://www.ema.europa.eu/en/documents/regulatory-procedural-guideline/european-medicines-agency-procedural-advice-users-centralised-procedure-similar-biological-medicinal_en-0.pdf).

For example, in Polish language 'biosimilar' name ('biopodobny' in Polish) may suggest a product of inferior nature ('like a product'). That is why other names are proposed, such as 'bio-equivalent' ('biorównoważny' in Polish). Other examples are: *follow-on biologic*[52] or *subsequent entry biologic,*[53] *similar biological medicinal product, biosubstitute, biocomparative, follow–on-protein, generic biopharmaceutical, biological near similar, SEBs, similar Biotherapeutic Products (SBP).* As we see, there is terminological uncertainty. I am of the opinion that we should continue to use the 'biosimilar' indication as it is the most popular term used abroad.[54]

Some biosimilars are also being called 'bio-better' products.[55] It is true that in a clinically relevant application, a biosimilar may stand out in comparison to the original reference product. The reasons may be a better safety profile; it can be more effective; it may have lower immunogenicity, longer duration of action, or a dose reduction is possible. In general, I am of the opinion that biosimilars are more innovative than generics.[56] That is why some incentives for the development of biosimilars are needed.[57]

Biosimilar medicinal products are most often covered by the reimbursement system, due to their lower price in comparison with reference medicinal products. It should be noted, however, that the price reduction is not as significant as in the case of generic medicinal products based on chemical substances. Typically, the price of a biosimilar medicine is 65-85% of the reference medicine's price.[58] The reason is the higher costs of generation and registration than in the case of generic medicinal products based on chemical substances.[59] On the other hand, this explains why the generic industry is so eager to manufacture biosimilars as it ensures much more profits than in the case of generics.

4 WHY DO WE NEED PATENT PROTECTION FOR BIOPHARMACEUTICALS?

It is obvious that the postulate of total abandonment of the IP protection for biopharmaceutical inventions is unrealistic. The mere fact that these products are based on biological material (created by nature) is not sufficient for the deprivation of IP protection. I have the same negative opinion on the proposal to exclude or limit IP

52. C. Mund, *Patenting...*, p. 5.
53. S.K. Niazi, *Biosimilars...*, p. 2.
54. P. Nambisan, *An Introduction to Ethical, Safety and Intellectual Property Rights Issues in Biotechnology*, London 2017, p. 331.
55. P. Nambisan, *An Introduction...*, pp. 333-334.
56. M. Sanzo, *The Promise...*, p. 107.
57. *Ibid.*, p. 108.
58. B. Calo-Fernández, J. Martínez-Hurtado, *Biosimilars...*, pp. 1393-1408.
59. R. Dolinar, M. Reilly, *The Future of Biological Therapy a Pathway Forward for Biosimilars*, Generics and Biosimilars Initiative Journal 2013, vol. 2, issue 1, pp. 36-40.

protection due to its alleged collision with so-called subjective patients right to health protection.[60]

There is no doubt that patent law plays a key role as an incentive for innovation in the biotechnology industry.[61] It should also be reminded that one of the significant goals of the EU is to support innovation (Article 173(1) TFEU). The patent system is one of the important instruments of economic policy. Patents (and other exclusivity rights) encourage inventiveness and innovation. The need for such an incentive is based on the opinion that in the market economy, the level of innovation (knowledge production) is not optimal.[62] It is rightly pointed out in the literature that innovative pharmaceutical companies would not be willing to spend an average of USD 1.2 billion and wait an average of 98 months for the marketing authorization for biopharmaceuticals, risking that the substance is immediately copied and sold by biosimilars manufacturers, who spend significantly lesser funds on research and development activities.[63] In fact, the biopharmaceutical market exists thanks to patents. We see that regulatory pharmaceutical requirements and costs incurred to the safety and efficacy of medicines are constantly increasing. In this regard, patents are not a problem, but a solution to it because they reward biomedical innovators for the development of the intellectual property while allowing the market to specify how big a (financial) reward should be granted for such innovation.

In light of patent law, there is no doubt about the admissibility of patenting biotechnological inventions, both in terms of their manufacturing or use of biological material. The functioning of European and national regulations for many years,[64] as well as the long-standing practice of patenting biological material in the category of 'product', means that proposals to exclude such protections are completely unrealistic.

The development of biopharmaceutical inventions constituting new (breakthrough) technology closely cooperates with the patent system.[65] High research costs and low copying costs (imitations) make patent protection particularly important.[66]

60. D. Delcourt, *Recherches sur l'évolution du droit international des brevets de médicaments: vers l'insertion du 'modèle européen' de droit pharmaceutique dans le système commercial multilatéral*, Aix-Marseille 2010, p. 181.
61. Ż. Pacud, *Ochrona patentowa produktów leczniczych*, Warsaw 2013, p. 263.
62. P. Demaret, *Patents, Territorial Restrictions, and EEC Law: A Legal and Economic Analysis*, IIC Studies, New York 1978, p. 3.
63. J. Hay, *Prices, Regulation and Innovation in Pharmaceuticals and Biotechnology* (in:) *The Value of Innovation: Impact on Health, Life Quality, Safety, and Regulatory Research* (ed. I. Farquhar, K. Summers, A. Sorkin), Bingley 2008, p. 90.
64. The literature on this subject is extensive; *see* e.g. T. Cook, *Pharmaceuticals, Biotechnology and the Law*, London 2016; *Life Sciences: A Global Guide from Practical Law* (ed. S. Fellows), London 2016; in Polish doctrine *see* e.g. *Prawo farmaceutyczne. Komentarz* (ed. W.L. Olszewski), Warsaw 2016; *Prawo farmaceutyczne. Komentarz* (ed. L. Ogiegło), Warsaw 2015 and 2018; *Prawo farmaceutyczne. Komentarz* (ed. M. Kondrat), Warsaw 2015; *Biologiczne produkty lecznicze* (ed. M. Świerczyński), Warsaw 2016; *Instytucje rynku farmaceutycznego* (ed. R. Stankiewicz), Warszawa 2016.
65. Cf. E. Waszkiewicz, *Patenty na 'produkty natury'*, Ochrona Własności Przemysłowej. Publikacje Urzędu Patentowego RP, vol. 78, pp. 3-4.
66. R.J.R. Peritz, *Patents and Progress: The Economics of Patent Monopoly and Free Access* (in:) *The Structure of Intellectual Property Law. Can One Size Fit All?* (ed. A. Kur, V. Mizaras), Cheltenham 2011, p. 43.

Biotechnology is an extremely expensive field, and the use of its medical applications is associated with high risk. Therefore, the search for strong legal protection by the biopharmaceutical industry is not surprising. It is even argued that without proper protection for investors, there would be no progress in many areas of biotechnology.[67] In the field of biotechnology, patents have played a key role in the development of the knowledge-based industry. The transition to a knowledge-oriented economy is also closely related to the existence of the patent system.[68] It should be underlined that IP rights in the biopharmaceutical sector are crucial for promoting innovation due to the very long time of product development. It is exactly the area in which patents make sense. With a patent, the biopharmaceutical company can act with greater certainty that its investments are not wrong.[69]

Empirical studies show that patenting is also in the interest of small companies (start-ups), whereas in an innovative biotechnology industry such a statement is simply obvious and difficult to argue with. Uniform standards for patent protection and other intellectual property rights are at the heart of the General Agreement on Tariffs and Trade and World Health Organization agendas. Even J. Straus, a well-known expert on biotechnological inventions, who is critical of the patent system, welcomes the new economic governance introduced by Trade-Related Aspects of Intellectual Property Rights (TRIPS), pointing out that the costs and benefits of an increased level of intellectual property protection should be considered in relation to the overall macroeconomic impact of global economic governance.[70] Meanwhile, the Polish literature is dominated by criticism of the adoption of uniform standards of industrial property protection, with particular emphasis on TRIPS or pharmaceutical product patenting.

On the other hand, it seems too optimistic to say, as some authors do,[71] that patent law remains fresh and alive as never before. The continuity of patent system and its stability, despite the ongoing technological changes, results not only from the flexible general principles contained in it but also from the actions of lawyers and judges who should creatively read and apply patent law, reinterpreting it for the needs of current times.[72]

The basic source of law in the EU is the directive on biotechnological inventions and the European Patent Convention. Its aims are to promote research and development in the field of genetic engineering in the EU and to harmonize the laws of the

67. Y. Flaningan, A. Ramachandran, *Intellectual Property...*, p. 53.
68. U. Peterson, *Patents and Open Access in the Knowledge Economy* (in:) *The Structure of Intellectual Property Law: Can One Size Fit All?* (ed. A. Kur, V. Mizaras), Cheltenham 2011, pp. 94-95.
69. J. Barnett, *Do Patents Matter? Empirical Evidence on the Incentive Thesis* (in:) *Handbook on Law, Innovation and Growth* (ed. R. Litan), Cheltenham 2011, pp. 196-197.
70. J. Straus, *The Impact of the New World Order on Economic Development: The Role of Intellectual property Right System*, John Marshall Review of Intellectual Property Law 2006, vol. 6, p. 7.
71. J. Scott-Miller, *Introduction* (in:) *Patents: Critical Concepts in Intellectual Property Law* (ed. J. Scott Miller), Cheltenham 2010, p. xi.
72. *Ibid.*

Member States in the field of patenting biological material, distinguishing biotechnological inventions and discoveries, non-patentable exceptions and patent protection of biotechnological inventions.[73]

Access to biological medicines is not only affected by patent law. Legal exclusivity is also provided by other similar legal institutions, such as data exclusivity (regulatory data protection) for the authorization of biological medicinal products. This implies the rule that biological medicinal products based on the same active substance as the previously registered product (i.e., biosimilars) may be authorized without the need to present all the test results. Indeed, the applicant may refer to the results of studies submitted for the first registration of a biological medicinal product (the so-called reference medicinal product). Data exclusivity means that the manufacturer of a biosimilar drug may not refer to the registration dossier of the original biological medicinal product for a specified period of time. It leads to the impossibility of using the results of pre-clinical and clinical trials included in the application for marketing authorization of the original medicine during the period of data exclusivity. It has been assumed that this exclusivity exists independently of any possible patent protection for the active substance concerned. The data exclusivity period runs from the grant of the authorization and may run concurrently with the remaining patent protection period for the biological medicine. Data exclusivity is generally not linked to the existence of patent protection for medicine but arises by operation of the law alone if certain conditions are met, including the absence of patent protection for any reason. In practice, data exclusivity can be a substitute for patent protection.

There is a need for strong patent protection of biopharmaceuticals.[74] Without it, biopharmaceutical innovators may not survive as independent companies.[75] In the case of biological medicinal products, the product development period can take up to 15 years. It is more than in any other industry. In result, the important part of the protection time is lost before it comes to market entry. Much of the cost associated with medicinal product discovery and development is related to the high risk of failure in translating innovations into safe and effective products, demonstrating how challenging it is to move a molecule from discovery to commercialization.[76] Patenting process in the biopharmaceutical sector is now similar to playing a lottery because there is often uncertainty surrounding the outcome of clinical trials and the eventual economic value of patents to the proprietor. It differs from small molecule medicines due to significantly higher costs of innovation and its commercialization. Therefore, cumulative patenting practices are partly inevitable because the patentee, at least initially, cannot predict the (economic) value of all patents within the portfolio. In only one industry, medicinal products, product patents are regarded as more effective than other means of appropriation and pharmaceuticals are described as one of the few industries in which patents really do seem to matter.[77]

73. T. Aplin, J. Davis, *Intellectual...*, pp. 556-557.
74. P. Nambisan, *An Introduction...*, pp. 334-335.
75. N. Lee, J. Drexl, *Introduction* (in:) *Pharmaceutical Innovation, Competition and Patent Law: A Trilateral Perspective* (ed. J. Drexl, N. Lee), Cheltenham 2013, p. 1.
76. H. Yu, *Achieving...*, p. 7.
77. M. Minn, *Patenting...*, p. 17.

The aim is to balance the interests of the manufacturers of innovative biological medicines in terms of their investments and the public interest in accessing cheaper biosimilars. This assessment should not be simplified by confronting these interests, as it is also in the public interest for manufacturers of biological reference medicines to bring innovation to the market. The phenomenon of conflicting interests permeating or even blurring is particularly evident in the case of biosimilars since their introduction is also being carried out by global pharmaceutical corporations (Big Pharma). It is not true that global pharmaceutical corporations (Big Pharma) want to keep the patent system unchanged at all costs. They also see the need for rational changes. The current patent system is difficult to apply in a biotechnology industry dominated by products based on complex systems of many elements of genetic recombination.

5 CONCLUSIONS

The critical contribution of the biopharmaceutical industry to the development of new medicines is undeniable. Over the decades, the research and development efforts of the biopharmaceutical industry have led to new treatments for a wide range of diseases, saving lives and improving the health and well-being of millions of patients.[78] To the benefit of individuals and society, medical innovations and technologies have the ability to lead to better healthcare, improve quality of life, and increase longevity.[79]

The holistic approach to public health-related IP is needed.[80] The relationships between health, innovation and the law are dynamic and arguably changing faster now than ever before. The factors are internationalization, complexification, personalization, digitalization and fragmentation.[81]

The following conclusions follow from this chapter:

(1) Both in the EU and national pharmaceutical regulation (such as Directive 2001/83/WE) biopharmaceuticals should be legally separated from traditional medicinal products based on active chemical substances.
(2) Clear distinction of biosimilars should be made under the legal regime.
(3) We should continue to call follow – on biopharmaceuticals 'biosimilars' ('leki biopodobne' in Polish).
(4) Biopharmaceuticals are not to be treated as a common good (part of the public domain) resulting in deprivation of IP exclusivity rights. Quite the opposite, the patent law should be adapted to the needs of the biopharmaceutical industry.

78. A. Chowdhury, A. Gaigl, *The Economics of Competition Law and of Pharmaceutical Patents* (in:) *Competition and Patent Law in the Pharmaceutical Sector: An International Perspective* (ed. G. Pitruzzella, G. Muscolo), Alphen aan den Rijn 2016, p. 5.
79. H. Yu, *Achieving...*, p. 3.
80. V. Vadi, *Investment...*, s. 254.
81. G. Dutfield, *Healthcare Innovation, Personalization and the Patent System, Where Is the Public Interest?* (in:) *Intellectual Property Issues in Biotechnology* (ed. H. Singh, A. Jha, C. Keswani), Oxfordshire 2016, p. 165.

CHAPTER 5

Changing Approach to the Regulatory Testing Exemption in Patent Law: The European Union Perspective*

*Agnieszka Sztoldman***

1 INTRODUCTION

This chapter discusses the recent legislative changes and case law developments in major patent jurisdictions in the European Union ('EU') concerning the so-called regulatory testing exemption in patent law. The registration procedure of a generic medicinal product involves an entry into the patent exclusivity covering the original product.[1] Regulatory testing exemptions in the EU Member States allow testing and studying patented substances to register the corresponding generic medicinal product[2] in the EU or in its Member States. The active substances contained in medicinal products can be protected by many patents.[3] This means that even if one patent ceases

* This article is based on the studies conducted within the research project: '*Freedom of research and patent exclusivity (research exception)*' financed by the National Center for Research (Polish: Narodowe Centrum Nauki) on the basis of the agreement number: 2013/11/N/HS5/03999 (PRELUDIUM 6).

** Polish academic identification number: 0000-0001-7202-2338.

1. Interestingly, in Polish law, the regulatory testing exemption is not limited only to inventions on the pharmaceutical market. On the contrary, in the majority of EU legislations, the regulatory testing exemption is directly limited only to registration of a medicinal product.
2. According to Art. 1(2) of Directive 2001/83, a medicinal product is 'any substance or combination of substances intended to treat or prevent disease in human beings or any substance or combination of substances which may be administered to human beings with a view to making a medical diagnosis or to restoring, correcting or modifying physiological functions in human beings'. The concept of medicinal product is clarified by European Union case law.
3. A patent may be granted on: (1) a product, i.e., an active substance or a new combination of active substances (having a combined effect different from that of each active substance alone), as well as the finished form of the medicinal product; (2) a method of manufacture of a medicinal

to exist, the same combination of active substances can be protected under another family patent. Alternatively, once an active substance patent has lapsed, combinations of active substances can be protected by way of a patent for its first or subsequent medical use or even dosage. In each case, the prohibition rights under the patent will prevent a competitor from using the protected active substance to develop and register its own medicine.

The legal basis for the regulatory testing exemptions for medicines for human use in the EU is Article 10(6) of Directive 2001/83 on the Community code relating to medicinal products for human use.[4] It provides that '*conducting the necessary studies and trials with a view to the application of paragraphs 1, 2, 3 and 4 and the consequential practical requirements shall not be regarded as contrary to patent rights or to supplementary protection certificates for medicinal products*'. Paragraphs 1, 2, 3, 4 refer to generic, hybrid, biosimilar registration of medicinal products in the EU.[5] Pursuant to Article 10(6) of Directive 2001/83, as amended by Directive 2004/27, the EU regulatory test review also applies to the use of inventions protected under supplementary protection rights ('SPC'). The equivalent of Article 10(6) of the Directive 2001/83/EC includes Article 13(6) of Directive 2001/82/EC on veterinary medicinal products.[6] According to Article 5 of Regulation 469/2009,[7] the holder of the SPC right has the same rights as under the patent. Furthermore, the supplementary protection right is subject to the same restrictions as the basic patent, the expiry of which gives rise to supplementary protection.[8]

Also, medical devices and biocide products are subject to regulatory delays caused by marketing authorization and thereby, their launch without delay may facilitate public health.[9] Therefore, in some countries, e.g., Poland, the regulatory

product (e.g., synthesis of a molecule) which extends to the product directly obtained by that method; (3) a new medical use of a known active substance; (4) new poliformic forms – *see* A. Denoon, D. Royle, A. Christopher, *The Law: Intellectual Property,* [in:] The law and regulation of medicines, ed. P. Feldschreiber, Oxford 2008, p. 387.

4. Directive 2001/83/EC of the European Parliament and of the Council of 6 December 2001 on the Community code relating to medicinal products for human use (OJ L 311, p. 67), hereinafter 'Directive 2001/83'.
5. In this chapter, the terms generic, hybrid, biosimilar are defined collectively: follow-up medicines or follow-up applications.
6. Directive 2001/82/EC of the European Parliament and of the Council of 6 November 2001 on the Community code relating to veterinary medicinal products (OJ L 311, 28 December 2001, pp. 1-66), hereinafter 'Directive 2001/82'.
7. Regulation (EC) No 469/2009 of the European Parliament and of the Council of 6 May 2009 concerning the supplementary protection certificate for medicinal products (OJ L 152, 16 June 2009, pp. 1-10).
8. The scope of use allowed for registration of an invention protected under the supplementary protection right may be wider than for patent protection of the invention. This is because the legal protection resulting from the grant of the supplementary right of protection extends only to the subject matter of the invention as defined in the marketing authorization for the medicinal product. *See* M. Stief, D. Bühler [in:] *Supplementary Protection Certificate (SPC). A handbook*, ed. M. Stief, D. Bühler, Munich 2016, p. 17; P. Kostański, *Die Schutzwirkung des Patents nach polnischem Recht*, Baden-Baden 2010, p. 409.
9. The issue of extending the regulatory testing exemption on the other categories of product requires in-depth analysis and thereby due to limits and subject of this chapter, this might have been only mentioned.

testing exemption due to the lack of restriction to use a protected invention in the registration of a medicinal product, the invention may also be used to register other products. Furthermore, in the United Kingdom (UK), the experimental use applies to all subject matter, including medicines, medical devices and agrochemicals. The UK legislation goes beyond the strict wording of Article 10(6) of Directive 2001/83/EC and Article 13(6) of Directive 2001/82/EC, which only concern medicinal products. In fact, many EU countries limit the scope of the regulatory review exemption to the use of a patented invention solely for the registration of medicinal products and not for other products, e.g., UK, France, Spain, Switzerland.

The purpose of 'regulatory review' exemption was to address the uncertainty over the scope of application of the experimental use exemption to patent or SPC (if existing) infringement. The uncertainty relates to whether applicants for generic marketing authorizations under the abridged procedure could be liable for patent infringement if they conduct the necessary bioequivalence and stability studies for registration purposes of a given medicinal product. The regulatory review exemption is a limitation to patent exclusivity. It was introduced into domestic laws of all EU countries based on the transposition of Article 10(6) of the Directive 2001/83/EC (as amended). Regulatory testing exemption represents a balance between the interest of the patent holder in the exclusive use of a protected invention and legitimate social and economic rationale and the public interest in accessing a protected technical solution to prepare a medicinal product for placing on the market at the time of termination of patent protection. The regulatory testing exemption has an impact on the patent system. It consists in the fact that, on the one hand, the scope of the regulatory review exemption affects innovation and, on the other hand, stimulates the dissemination of the technical solution as soon as it enters the public domain, preventing the excessive extension of the patent monopoly.

One may note that both the terms regulatory review exemption and regulatory testing exemption can be found. This chapter uses the term regulatory review and regulatory testing exemption alternately. The 'regulatory review' exemption or the regulatory testing exemption, better known as the 'Bolar exemption' after a judgment giving rise[10] to a similar provision in the United States (US) law[11] and US court law,[12]

10. The 'Bolar exemption' has been adopted in the Hatch-Waxman Act, which was introduced following the decision of the Court of Appeals of the *Federal Circuit in Roche Products v. Bolar Pharmaceuticals Company*, 733 F2d 858 (FedCir).
11. Regulatory testing exception/exemption is the term commonly used in Poland and most EU countries, however, in the EU literature, one may also find the expression the 'Bolar exemption' which refers actually to the US provision. In this chapter, I will use the names interchangeably: 'Regulatory testing exemption', 'the 'regulatory review' exemption' and 'the 'Bolar exemption' or 'Safe Harbour'.
12. It should also be noted that the scope of the Bolar exemption is being discussed in US law, as confirmed by the growing number of recent case law. On the basis of publicly available resources, I identified 97 cases under US law related to the Bolar provision, including most recent ones, for example, judgment of United States Wisconsin Eastern District Court of 25 April 2018, in *Acantha LLC v. Depuy Orthopaedics Inc.*, no. 15C-1257 (state level); judgment of United States California Northern District Court of 11 October 2017, in *Blackbird Tech LLC v. Cloudflare Inc.*, no. 17-283.

first came into force in the EU in October 2005.[13] The term regulatory testing exemption reflects that the provisions, resulting from the transposition into national law of Article 10(6) of Directive 2001/83, constitute restrictions of patent exclusivity and not merely a procedural measure in the framework of a strategy against infringement claims.[14]

Although national legislation of the various EU Member States (including the UK[15]), therewith mostly overlap, the scope of these exceptions is interpreted differently. This directive is intended to harmonize legislation across the Member States of the EU, and, as a directive, it must be implemented by the national laws of each country concerned – it does not have a direct effect. Nowadays we may observe a shift in understanding and interpretation of the regulatory testing exemption in recent years in the entire EU due to the major changes in national patent laws (i.e., in the UK, Poland, Belgium and Spain) and its domestic jurisprudence, both resulting in extending the original scope of the regulatory testing exemption under the Directive 2001/83/EC significantly.[16] Therefore, this chapter discusses the question: *does the observed shift in the understanding of the regulatory testing exemption in the EU fit its purpose?* To answer this question, we need to examine the original provision introducing the regulatory testing in the national laws of the EU members states (i.e., Article 10(6) of the Directive 2001/83/EC). To this end, this chapter discusses national case law in the EU that interprets the regulatory review exemption and describes recent changes in the legislation of selected EU countries. The final remarks consider whether Article 10(6) of the Directive 2001/83/EC, as transposed into national laws, fits its EU legislative purpose.

2 RATIONALE FOR THE REGULATORY TESTING EXEMPTION: HOW DOES IT IMPACT INNOVATION?

Patents, and the limited term of exclusivity that they provide, enable innovators such as pharmaceutical companies to adopt the costs and take risks inherent in pharmaceutical research and development, to invest in clinical studies, which demonstrate the safety and efficacy of their new medicinal products. After all, that exclusive right

13. The deadline for transposition into national laws formally expired on 30 October 2005.
14. Please note that the theoretical classification of the regulatory review exemption should be discussed separately due to the dispute over the legal character of this provision in the EU law, i.e., whether the regulatory review exemption in the EU law provides for the limitation to patent exclusivity or patent limits (in the meaning of the patent scope) – *see more* on the theoretical background in international doctrine: Ch. Geiger, *Effectivité et flexibilité: deux impératifs de l'adaptation du droit des 'exceptions'*, RLDI 2013/6, p. 3144; H. Holzapfel, G. Werner, *Interpreting exceptions in intellectual property law,* [in:] Patents and technological progress in a globalized world, ed. W. Prinz zu Waldeck und Pyrmont, M.J. Adelman, R. Brauneis, J. Drexl, R. Nack, Heidelberg 2009, p. 99 and pp.; A. Sztoldman, *Korzystanie z chronionego wynalazku w celu rejestracji produktu leczniczego*, Warszawa 2018, pp. 93-102.
15. Due to the withdrawal of the UK from the EU, the UK is no longer since 31 January 2020 a member of the EU. Nevertheless, the UK regulatory testing exemption was shaped under the EU case law and in accordance with the relevant EU directive 2001/83.
16. Also, the directive 2001/82 for veterinary products provides for the same regulatory testing provision. All references in this chapter made to the regulatory review exemption under the directive 2001/83 automatically apply to the relevant provision under the directive 2001/82.

represents the essential means of asserting their intellectual property.[17] While patents encourage investment and innovation by guaranteeing the right for the owner to exploit any resulting invention, in the pharmaceutical industry, it also has the potential to stifle new research if scientists risk infringing a medicine patent when conducting clinical trials.[18] An exclusive right which stems from the patent may prevent access to medicinal products when a new medicine is developed. This is, for example, if the price is too high or if the demand exceeds the production capabilities of the patentee. Patent law may thereby restrict the use of patented (medicinal) products or devices in the search for a vaccine or cure, even in the extreme case of an epidemiological threat, if it were without limitations of patent exclusivity.[19]

To ensure the incentives for further innovations and follow-up products, as well as stimulating the competition in the market and lowering prices of medical products for patients, patents should be used responsibly. Once the patent (or SPC) term expires, the patent holder should not unduly delay the use of the protected inventions by others, in particular in the pharmaceutical industry in order not to delay entering follow-up products. Follow-up medicinal products are important for national healthcare and patient safety policy in the EU. The costs of public health care are also reduced.[20] Manufacturers of follow-up medicines are thus able to obtain authorization to place their less costly and competitive medicines on the market. At the same time, the process of securing regulatory authorization to market a follow-up medicine takes time. A follow-up medicinal product must demonstrate 'bio-equivalence' by comparative studies to the patented medicine that the follow-up medicinal product seeks to substitute, as a copy or a modified product. The said comparative studies and related activities enter the patent monopoly, which prohibits any third party from exploiting the patented invention for commercial or industrial purposes, without the prior consent of the patent owner. Such activities would normally constitute a patent infringement if not exempt by the legal provision in the given statutory laws. Furthermore, comparative studies and activities related to testing for registering a follow-up medicine could only begin after the expiry of the patent, leading to delays in the launch of follow-up medicines. The regulatory testing exemption, under the Article 10(6) of the Directive 2001/83/EC (as transposed to national laws), makes it easier for competing manufacturers to use a protected invention without the consent of the right

17. According to settled case law, the essential objective of a patent is to ensure, in order to reward the creative effort of the inventor, that the owner of the patent has the exclusive right to use an invention with a view to manufacturing industrial products and selling them, either directly, or by granting licences to third parties, as well as the right to oppose infringements. Cf. CJEU 31 October 1974 (*Centrafarm v. Sterling*), 15/74, ECLI:EU:C:1974:114, para. 9 and CJEU 4 October 2011 (*Football Association Premier League Ltd and Others*), C-403/08, ECLI:EU:C:2011:631, para. 107. *Also see* the Opinion of AG Wathelet of 20 November 2014 (*Huawei v ZTE*), C-170/13, ECLI:EU:C:2014:2391, para. 61.
18. S. Shorthose, s. 3.12: *Clinical Trials and Patent Legislation: The Bolar and Research Exceptions*, in: Guide to EU Pharmaceutical Regulatory Law, ed. S. Shorthose, London 2017.
19. D. Mulder, P. England, Ch. Dekoninck, A. Lunze, P. Boháček, A. Sztoldman, *Pharmaceutical patent law in times of crisis: a comparative study Part I – The experimental use exemption, related exemptions and compulsory licensing*, 'European Intellectual Property Review', forthcoming.
20. P. Li, *Health technologies and international intellectual property: A precautionary approach*, New York 2014, pp. 6-9.

holder. This exemption prevents the blocking of competitive activity and the de facto extension of the patent monopoly by delaying, on the one hand, the market entry of competing products and, on the other hand, access to protected goods as soon as patent protection is terminated.[21] Stimulating competitive activity, in turn, promotes the pursuit of the public interest in such a way that, as competition in the market for medicinal products increases, their price falls, and the medicinal product is accessible to more patients.

3 THE REGULATORY TESTING EXEMPTION IN THE EU: AN OVERVIEW

3.1 Article 10(6) of the Directive 2001/83/EC

The EU Commission supported a formal exemption from patent infringement for activities concerning the patented invention, which are undertaken as part of the regulatory testing process. To date, there is no EU legislation governing the exclusive rights granted by a patent and their limitations (apart from the fragmented Directive on Biotechnological Inventions[22]). Article 10(6) of the Directive 2001/83 was added to the directive in 2004 by amending the Directive 2004/27.[23] Prior to Article 10(6) of the Directive 2001/83/EC, the regulatory testing exemption was first introduced into the federal US patent law in 1986 following the famous judgment in the *Roche v. Bolar* case of 1985.[24] The exemption was primarily intended to introduce harmonization and certainty.

The limit is the achievement of the result set out in the pharmaceutical directives - Directive 2001/83/EC and Directive 2001/82/EC, based on Article 288 of the Treaty on the Functioning of the European Union (TFEU).[25] The Directive 2001/83/EC has the effect of minimum harmonization in the EU with respect to human medicinal products. Member States may determine on their own the legal framework of the regulatory review exemption and extend it to the use of the invention to register the medicinal product abroad outside the EU. This means that the EU Member States may introduce a regulatory review exemption with a broader scope to facilitate the placing on the market of follow-up medicinal products as soon as the patent protection is terminated (and under SPC law, as appropriate).

21. *See also* J. Pila, P. Torremans, *European Intellectual Property Law...*, pp. 214-215.
22. Directive 98/44/EC of the European Parliament and of the Council of 6 July 1998 on the legal protection of biotechnological inventions, Official Journal of the European Communities, L 213/13.
23. Directive 2004/27/EC of the European Parliament and of the Council of 31 March 2004 amending Directive 2001/83/EC on the Community code relating to medicinal products for human use (OJ L 136, p. 34), hereinafter: 'Directive 2004/27'. The deadline for transposition into national systems expired on 30 October 2005.
24. Judgment of 13 October 1983, *Roche Products Inc. v. Bolar Pharmaceutical Co., Inc.*, 733 F.2d 858 (Fed. Cir. 1984).
25. *See* C. Barnard, *The substantive law of the EU: The four freedoms*, Oxford 2013, pp. 662-667.

3.2 An Overview of the EU Bolar Exemption under the Current National Legislations

The regulatory testing exemption is regulated in the EU countries, with minor differences among them. For example, in (i) Poland (Article 69 paragraph 1 point 4 of the Polish Act on the Industrial Property Law[26]), (ii) Germany (Article 11 paragraph 2b of German Patent Law[27]), (iii) France (Article 613-5 d) of Intellectual Property Code[28]), (iv) Spain (Article 52 (1)(b) of the Spanish Patent Act),[29] (v) Italy (Article 68(1)(a)) of Industrial Property Code[30] or (vi) the UK (Article 60 paragraph 6E of the Patent Act) and (vii) Belgium (Article XI.34 (1)(b) of the Code of Economic Law[31]). The 'regulatory review' exemption was also recently amended in Switzerland[32] (Article 9 paragraph 1 lit. c of Federal law on patents for inventions[33]). Due to the lack of harmonized judicial guidelines on how to apply the regulatory testing exemption in practice, some countries decided to amend its local provisions (*see* section 4 of this chapter).

Recently, the new legislation was enacted into the Polish law, and its purpose is to clarify all doubts resulting from unclear wording and the judgment of the Polish Supreme Court of 2013. The wording, revised in 2019, of the regulatory testing exemption under Polish law is:

> the use of the invention which consists of the manufacture, use, storage, offering, placing on the market, exporting or importing in order to perform activities which are required by law to obtain, also by a third party, registration or authorization as a condition for admission to the marketing of certain products due to their

26. Art. 69 para. 1 point 4 reads as follows: '[...] use of the invention consisting in the manufacture, use, storage, storage, offering, placing on the market, exporting or importing in order to perform activities that are required by law to obtain, also by a third party, registration or authorization as a condition of admission for the marketing of certain products because of their intended use, in particular medicinal products on the territory of the European Economic Area or another country' – Art. 69, para. 1, point 4 as amended by Art. 1, point 12(a), first indent of the Act of 16 October 2019. (OJ 2019.2309) amending this Act as of 27 February 2020.
27. Section 11 no. 2 b GPA reads as follows: 'The effects of the patent shall not extend to studies and trials and the resulting practical requirements necessary for obtaining a marketing authorization to place a medicinal product on the market in the European Union or marketing authorization for a medicinal product in the Member States of the European Union or in third countries.'
28. Art. 613-5 d) of Intellectual Property Code provides that 'studies and trials required in view of obtaining a marketing authorisation for a drug, as well as acts necessary to the performance thereof and to the obtaining of the authorisation'.
29. Ley 24/2015, de 24 de Julio, de Patentes – Boletín Oficial del Estado of 25 July 2015.
30. Art. 68(1)(a)) of Industrial Property Code provides that 'acts performed privately and for non-commercial purposes, or for commercial purposes, even if aimed at obtaining an authorisation to market a medicinal product in any country, and subsequent practical requirements, including the preparation and the use of the active pharmaceutical ingredients if they are absolutely necessary'.
31. Law of 19 April 2014, on the Insertion of Book XI 'Intellectual Property' to the Code of Economic Law, and Specific Provisions to the Book XI in Books I, XV and XVII of the Code (updated on 30 October 2015).
32. Switzerland is neither an EU nor European Economic Area member but is part of the single market.
33. Art. 9 para. 1(c) reads as follows: 'The effects of the patent do not extend to: [...] acts necessary for obtaining marketing authorisation for a medicinal product in Switzerland or in countries with equivalent medicinal product control.'

intended use, in particular medicinal products on the territory of the European Economic Area or another country.[34]

The new provision is a result of a long-standing industry battle over the ambiguous scope of the regulatory testing exemption provision, and it is directly connected with the judgment of the Polish Supreme Court of 23 October 2013 in the German and Polish case *Astellas Pharma v. Polpharma*. It was the result of a complex litigation in Poland and Germany regarding the infringement of the Astellas' substance patent for *Solifenacin* by a Polish manufacturer of active ingredients. The decision of the Polish Supreme Court on 23 October 2013 confirmed a narrow scope of the original regulatory review exemption. The new exemption came into being because of concerns that Poland was losing out on opportunities to conduct work in support of obtaining marketing authorization, such as trials, because of the limited Poland regulatory testing exemption.

Under German law, the current relatively broad scope of the regulatory testing exemption resulted from an extended interpretation of the research exemption (section 11 no. 2 German Patent Act), which was regulated earlier than the regulatory testing exemption. In particular, the two cases 'Clinical Trials I' and 'Clinical Trials II', decided by the Federal Court of Justice (BGH) in the late 1990s, had a decisive influence on the understanding of the exemption. In the decision Clinical Trials I, it was stated that the German Patent Act allows all trials which serve to obtain information and thus to realize the scientific purpose, including those which serve to discover the effects of a substance or possibly new, previously unknown uses. It should be irrelevant whether the experiments serve to verify the statements made in the patent or to obtain further more recent research results. In particular, the Federal Supreme Court held that it is irrelevant that the tests are carried out for the purpose of obtaining marketing authorization.[35] In the decision Clinical Trials II, the Federal Supreme Court decided that the experimental privilege of section 11 no. 2 German Patent Act should also apply if and to the extent that the trials serve the purpose of researching the subject matter of the invention which is actually protected by a patent. The exemption from an otherwise applicable patent law provision applies irrespective of any additional motives and purposes which the results might serve; they may range from purely scientific experiments to specific commercially indicated experiments.[36] Currently, the regulatory testing exemption provides in section 11 no. 2b German Patent Act in 2005 that the effect of a patent does not extend to studies and tests and the resulting practical requirements which are necessary to obtain marketing authorization for medicinal products in the EU or a marketing authorization for medicinal products in the Member States of the EU or in third countries. This wording is relatively broad and does not distinguish, for example, whether the authorization should be granted to generic or innovative medicines. The provision also covers studies and trials necessary to obtain marketing authorization in the EU and in third countries.

34. *See* Art. 69 point 1(4) of the Polish Act on Industrial Property Law (Dz.U.2020.286 of 21 February 2020).
35. Judgment of the Federal Supreme (BGH) of 11 July 1995, file no. X ZR 99/92.
36. Judgment of the Federal Supreme Court (BGH) of 17 April 1997, file no. X ZR 68/94.

The regulatory testing exemption was also significantly extended in the UK through changing the provision on 'the experimental use exemption'. The original experimental use exemption in the UK was set out in section 60(5)(b) Patents Act 1977. The UK implementation of the regulatory testing exemption set out in Article 10(6) Directive 2001/83/EC was linked by explicit reference to the abridged application procedures for marketing authorizations in this directive. Although there was no case law on the precise scope of the exemption, the UK Intellectual Property Office (UKIPO) and the Medicines and Healthcare Products Regulatory Agency (MHRA) published a practice note to explain their understanding that UK regulatory review exemption is exempt from patent infringement activities conducted only for the purpose of obtaining an abridged marketing authorization application by a generic and no more.[37] The new regulatory testing provision came into force on 1 October 2014, by way of an addition to the original wording of section 60(5)(b) Patents Act 1977. A medicinal product assessment is defined as '*any testing, course of testing or other activity undertaken with a view to providing data for purposes*'. In addition to the activities covered by the regulatory testing exemption, the preparation and running of clinical trials on innovative medicinal products for marketing authorization are also exempt. Work undertaken in the UK in support of a regulatory filing in a country outside of the EU is also now covered.

Similar changes relating to regulatory testing exemption were made in Spanish patent law which came into force on 1 April 2017. The regulatory testing exemption featured in the new Spanish patent law includes two main changes: (i) it has been separated from the exemption relating to acts carried out for experimental purposes; and (ii) it was extended to actions relating to registration of all types of medicinal products and irrespective of the procedure.[38]

Furthermore, Belgium's patent law was also revised in this regard, but the changes were significantly narrower.[39] The Belgian legislator adopted a narrow approach when implementing Article 10(6) of the Directive 2001/83/EC, and thereby the regulatory testing provision limited the exemption to the necessary studies, tests, and trials undertaken by generic applicants seeking to avail themselves of the abridged, hybrid procedures, or the biosimilar application. The new Belgium laws explicitly excluded the use of patented research tools and instruments out of the scope of the regulatory testing exemption. Conversely, the new provision stated that preparatory acts to register biosimilar or generic medicinal products are allowed. Belgium law also makes reference between the regulatory testing exemption and experimental use

---

37. *See* document named: 'The Bolar Exemption – Activities covered by the exemption' available on-line: https://webarchive.nationalarchives.gov.uk/20140603113939/http://www.ipo.gov.uk/pro-types/pro-patent/p-policy/p-policy-pharmaceutical/p-policy-pharmaceutical-activities.htm.
38. L. Fernández-Novoa Valladares, *The new Spanish Patent Act, Journal of Intellectual Property Law & Practice,* Volume 13, Issue 12, December 2018, pp. 975-979.
39. *See*: the Belgian Official Gazette of 28 December 2017 with the title 'Act amending various provisions on patents in relation to the implementation of the unitary patent and the unified patent jurisdiction.'

exemption. Thus, actions which refer to innovative medicines should be caught under the experimental use exemption and not the Belgian regulatory testing provision.

3.3 An Overview of National Case Law

The regulatory testing exemption becomes more and more important, which is reflected in the growing number of patent disputes between producers of medicinal products or active substances and court settlements based on these disputes. Since 2005, in the EU, at least 40 local cases were judged, which involved the studies and trials necessary to obtain pharmaceutical marketing authorization.[40] One may identify 11 judgments in Spain,[41] 10 judgments in France,[42] 2 in both Germany[43] and Italy[44], 1 judgment in the Netherlands[45], 1 in Poland[46] as well as 1 in the

40. The number is based on the author's independent search in publicly available jurisprudence databases comprising case law of all of the EU countries.
41. This means the following judgments: Judgment of Juzgada de lo Mercantil Barcelona of 1 August 2011, in *H. Lundbeck et alia v. Galenicum Health et alia*, no. 65/2010; judgment of Tribunal Supremo of 30 June 2010, in *Laboratorios Cinfa v. Pfizer*, no. 424/2010; judgment of Audiencia Provincial Pamplona of 19 May 2006, in *Laboratorios Cinfa v. Pfizer*, no. 59/2006; judgment of Juzgado Mercantil Barcelona of 19 October 2009, in *Laboratories Almirall v. Alter Farmacia*, no. 286/09; judgment of Audiencia Provincial of 16 September 2008, in *Almirall-Prodesfarma v. Alter Genericos*, no. 430/2007; judgment of Juzgado de lo Mercantil of 13 March 2007, in *Almirall-Prodesfarma v. Alter Genericos*, no. 160/2007; judgment of Juzgado de lo Mercantil Barcelona of 31 July 2008, in *Pfizer v. Bexal Farmaceutica*, no. 765/2005; judgment Juzgado de lo Mercantil Barcelona of 28 July 2007, in *Janssen Pharmaceutica v. Teva Genericos*, no. 382/2008; judgment of Audiencia Provincial Barcelona of 17 May 2006, in *Goedecke Pfizer v. Laboratorios Rubio* no. 696/2004; judgment of Audienica Provincial Madrid of 5 May 2006, in *Merck Sharp v. Bexal Farmaceutica*, no. 89/2006; judgment of Audiencia Provincial Barcelona of 4 January 2006, in *Pfizer v. Laboratorios Davur*, no. 3/2006.
42. This means the following judgments: judgment of Tribunal de Grande Instance de Paris of 15 March 2016 in *Ono Pharmaceutical Bristol-Myers Squibb v. Msd France Schering-Plough*, RG. 16/51152; judgment of Tribunal de Grande Instance de Paris of 15 December 2014 in *Sanofi-Aventis Deutschland v. Lilly France*, RG. 14/58023; judgment of Tribunal de Grande Instance de Paris of 7 October 2014 in *Lilly France v. Sanofi-Aventis Deutschland*, RG. 14/12276; judgment of Tribunal de Grande Instance de Paris of 10 August 2012 in *Sanofi-Aventis France v. Mylan*, RG. 12/55804; judgment of Tribunal de Grande Instance de Paris of 10 August 2012 in *Sanofi-Aventis France v. Arrow Generics*, RG. 12/55805; judgment of Tribunal de Grande Instance de Paris of 10 August 2012 in *Sanofi-Aventis France v. Sandoz*, RG. 12/55806; judgment of Tribunal de Grande Instance de Paris of 10 August 2012 in *Sanofi-Aventis France v. Sandoz*, RG. 12/55806; judgment of Tribunal de Grande Instance de Paris of 5 April 2011, in *Novartis Pharma v. Eg Labo-Laboratoires Eurogenerics*, RG. 11/52706; judgment of Tribunal de Grande Instance de Paris of 15 March 2011 in *Laboratoires Merck Sharp & Dohme-Chibret v. Mylan*, RG. 10/03075; judgment of Tribunal de Grande Instance de Paris of 19 August 2010 in *Sanofi-Aventis France v. Teva Sante*, RG. 10/56889; judgment of Cour d'Appel Aix-en-Provence of 1 July 2010 in *Bioagency v. Innate Pharma*, RG. 10/00886.
43. Judgment of Oberlandesgericht Düsseldorf of 5 December 2013, in *Astellas Pharma v. Polpharma Pharmaceutical Works*, 2U 68/12; judgment of Landgericht Düsseldorf of 26 July 2012, in *Astellas Pharma v. Polpharma Pharmaceutical Works*, 4a 0 282/10; Judgment of Oberlandesgericht Düsseldorf of 19 May 2005, in *Merck & Co. v. Stada Arzneimittel*, 2U 74/04.
44. Judgement of Tribunale di Milano of 2 April 2009, in *Eli Lily and Company v. Ratiopharm et alia*, n. 582425.07; judgement of Tribunale di Roma of 23 October 2006, in *Pronova Biocare AS v. Chiesi Farmaceutici* (preliminary proceedings), Rom-20061023.
45. Judgment of Rechtbank's-Gravenhage of 7 April 2008, in *Eli Lilly v. Ratiopharm*, KG ZA 08-63.
46. Judgment of 23 October 2013, in *Astellas Pharmac v. Polpharma*, IV CSK 92/13.

UK.[47] So far there was only one resolved case concerning the regulatory testing exemption under Article 10(6) of the Directive 2001/83/EC pending before the Court of Justice of the EU. The matter was discontinued before handing down the judgment (C-661/13).[48] The proper formation of the regulatory review exemption is one of the most important issues of modern patent law and requires critical analysis.

On a practical note, the regulatory review exemption triggers controversy. Article 10(6) of the Directive 2001/83/EC does not clearly identify the scope of this exemption but indicates the criteria for using the invention. Consequently, even if in domestic EU Member States statutory laws, the regulatory testing exemption is well-defined, questions remain regarding the scope of this exemption, and, more generally, regarding the types of activities and products which should benefit from the exemption. Whilst provision of Article 10(6) Directive 2001/83/EC refers to the abridged application procedure for marketing authorizations available to applicants for generic medicines, it does not clarify issues such as: (1) what do 'trials' mean? (2) should a third party which assists a primary party in carrying out preparatory work for regulatory authorization (e.g., by contract manufacturing) benefit from the regulatory testing exemption? (3) does the regulatory testing exemption apply to all qualifying activities, regardless of whether those activities relate to marketing authorization of a generic or biosimilar medicine or a new innovative medicine? (4) is the regulatory testing exemption limited to those activities which occur prior to regulatory authorization, including the storage of test batches covered by the regulatory testing and are clinical trials to investigate market potential covered by the exemption? Furthermore, since Directive 2001/83/EC offers leeway in locally implementing the exemption, it seems that there are no obstacles under Article 10(6) of the Directive 2001/83/EC to prevent each Member State from extending this exemption for all actions related to regulatory review, i.e., registering medicines in full or hybrid procedures (combination innovative medicines or biosimilars), as well as medical devices or biocide products.

4 KEY TENDENCIES IN THE APPROACH TO THE REGULATORY TESTING EXEMPTION IN THE EU

4.1 The Regulatory Review Exemption Is Not Only Limited to the Abridged or Hybrid Procedure

According to Article 6 of Directive 2001/83/EC, no medicinal product may be placed on the market of a Member State without marketing authorization issued by the competent authorities of that State. In pharmaceutical law, there are three registration procedures: full, abridged and hybrid. In view of the explicit reference in Article 10(6) of Directive 2001/83/EC, it has so far been clear that the regulatory testing exemption covers the use of a protected invention to register a medicinal product in an abridged or hybrid registration procedure. The procedure for registration of similar biological

47. Judgement of High Court of Justice (Patents Court) of 15 May 2014, in *Actavis UK et alia v. Eli Lilly Company*, [2014] EWHC 1511 (Pat) (HC12E02962).
48. Order of 7 May 2014 in *Astellas Pharma Inc.*, ECLI:EU:C:2014:588.

medicinal products (so-called biosimilar medicinal products) under Article 10(4) of Directive 2001/83/EC is somewhat abridged. The hybrid procedure concerns medicinal products which do not meet the criteria for a reference product equivalent to but follows on from innovative products, pursuant to Article 10(3) of Directive 2001/83/EC.[49]

An abridged or hybrid EU registration procedure covers generic medicinal products[50] and biosimilar medicinal products, respectively. Therefore, *a dispute has arisen under Article 10(6) of Directive 2001/83/EC whether the regulatory testing exemption also covers the use of a protected invention for the registration of a medicinal product under the full registration procedure*. Doubts arise from the original aim of the EU regulatory testing exemption. This was to support the development of the market of generic and biosimilar follow-up medicinal products. Conversely, innovative medicines and those which consist of a mixture of known active substances in a hitherto unknown fixed combination shall be registered in the full procedure in accordance with Article 10b of Directive 2001/83/EC. The traditional approach to the development of a medicinal product involves carrying out tests and trials that compare the composition and properties of the competing medicinal products, in particular those protected under a patent, and compare them with others of potentially similar utility.[51] The full procedure for registration of a medicinal product shall include qualitative tests: physicochemical, biological, microbiological, preclinical tests: efficacy, pharmacological and toxicological, an assessment of the risk-benefit/safety balance, as well as clinical trials, including an assessment of the safety profile of the medicine, with a view to preparing the summary of product characteristics.[52] Thus, the development of an innovative medicinal product (including a combination) may involve the use of a patented invention. Currently, the importance of this issue has increased due to the development of the market for biological medicines, produced by biotechnological methods using genetic engineering and due to the patent protection of biotechnological inventions. The subject matter of potential activities of innovative medicine manufacturers relating to the use of someone else's invention may include the use of the invention: (1) in order to check a known application or manner of operation of the protected invention; (2) in order to discover new information or new use; (3) to improve or create a new invention; and (4) to compare properties in preclinical or clinical trials and pharmaceutical or biological laboratory tests.

49. It may refer to a procedure during the duration of data exclusivity (performed by the holder) or after the cessation of data exclusivity (performed by a competitor) – *see* C-106/01, *Novartis Pharmaceuticals UK Ltd v. The Licensing Authority*, ECLI:EU:C:2004:245, para. 47.
50. It should be noted that Art. 10(a) of Directive 2001/83 provides that medicinal products which have a well-established medicinal use may also be registered under the abridged registration procedure. The results of non-clinical studies or clinical trials are replaced by the relevant scientific literature. The active substances of medicinal products have been in well-established medicinal use in the EU for at least 10 years, with recognised efficacy and an acceptable level of safety.
51. T. Cook, *A European perspective as to the extent to which experimental use, and certain other, defences to patent infringement, apply to differing types of research*, A report for the Intellectual Property Institute 2006, p. 161.
52. T. Cook, *Pharmaceuticals, biotechnology and the law*, London 2009, p. 286; *see* Art. 13-16 and Art.16a of the Directive 2001/83.

Can such use fall under the regulatory testing exemption? For example, Article 69, paragraph 1, point 4 of Polish Industrial Property Law Act before the 2019 amendment, did not limit the regulatory testing exemption exclusively to the registration of a medicinal product under the hybrid or abridged procedure. Also, the current wording of the regulatory review exemption under German law does not distinguish, whether the exemption only applies to generic medicinal products or also innovative (new) medicines. In line with Article 10(6) of the Directive 2001/83/EC, the regulatory review exemption may cover the studies and clinical trials necessary to obtain marketing authorization, and also the acts necessary to carry them out and to obtain authorization.[53] The usage of the patented invention must be necessary for registration purposes of a given medicinal product, which means it is covered by practical requirements under the Directive 2001/83/UE. This means that the regulatory review exemption does not extend to forms of use of the invention in the framework of initial research aimed at developing an innovative medicinal product. It is questionable as to whether the regulatory review exemption under Article 10(6) of Directive 2001/83/EC could cover tests and trials performed by innovative drug manufacturers at a later stage aimed at developing the results of tests required in the full registration procedure for a medicinal product. This could concern the stage of development of the finished form of the medicinal product or clinical trials in which the innovative medicine would be compared to those to which patent protection relates.

Article 10(6) of Directive 2001/83/EC does not expressly limit the legal institution of the regulatory review exemption to the use of an invention for registration in the abridged procedure. The reference in Article 10(6) of Directive 2001/83/EC to paragraph 3 indicates that the regulatory review exemption concerns also preclinical and clinical trials, that is to say, those carried out in principle by manufacturers of innovative medicines, as well as in situations where a medicinal product does not meet the definition of a generic medicinal product.[54] One notes that under the Article 10(1) and (2) of Directive 2001/83/EC the regulatory review exemption in the EU law also applies to the registration of a medicinal product in the full and hybrid procedure. It should also be recalled that paragraphs 1 to 4 of this provision of Directive 2001/83/EC concern the authorization of three categories of products: generic medicinal products; medicinal products which cannot be qualified as generic (as defined in Article 2(b)); biological medicinal products which are similar to reference products but which are not generic. The EU Member States may implement a regulation which extends the regulatory testing exemption to the use of a protected invention to register an innovative medicinal product.[55]

Manufacturers of innovative medicines can primarily exploit a protected invention in trials under the research exemption. They can use someone else's invention to

53. *See* for instance the interpretation of the Art. 10(6) od the directive 2001/83 in the French case law: 'Les actes ainsi définis ne concernent pas que les études et essais cliniques nécessaires à l'obtention de l'AMM mais également les actes nécessaires à leur réalisation et à l'obtention de l'autorisation et ce sans en dresser de liste limitative' – judgment of Tribunal de Grande Instance de Paris (preliminary proceedings) of 15 March 2016, case no. 16/51152.
54. U. Gassner, *Unterlagenschutz im Europäischen Arzneimittelrecht*, GRUR Int. 2004/12, p. 993.
55. T. Cook, *EU Intellectual property law...*, p. 556.

check a known application or mode of operation of the patented invention. It is also possible to research a biotechnological invention or an active substance to check how such inventions work (German: *Funktionsprüfung*). Studies or experiments relating to the development of innovative medicinal products may include the use of a protected invention to discover new information or a new (further) use of an active substance or combination of active substances.[56] Finally, innovative medicinal product manufacturers, or those acting on their behalf, may use a protected invention in studies or experiments to develop an improvement or an invention.[57]

Considering the above, the activities of innovative medicines manufacturers or those acting on their behalf at the stage of initial testing, go beyond the regulatory testing exemption. Those activities are rather covered by the research exemption. For instance, this is the approach taken by the revision of Belgian patent law. Pursuant to Article XI. 34.1/1 all actions taken to assess a medicinal product are experiments relating to the subject matter of the patented invention.

The prevailing trend in the other EU Member States is, however, to extend the regulatory testing exemption to the use of an invention for the registration of any type of medicinal product, including innovative medicines. See for examples in French legislation (Article L. 613-Swiss (Article 9(1)(c BundesPatG), English (Article 60(6E) Patent Act) and Polish (Article 69 paragraph 1 point 4 Industrial Property Law). In my view, a regulatory testing exemption may include studies and trials relating to an innovative medicine at the later stage of research under certain factual circumstances, including clinical or preclinical trials of a specific medicinal 5(d c.p.i.), product. The regulatory testing exemption may extend to Phase I of clinical trials, relating to the testing of a new medicinal product on a narrow group of subjects, during which its safety, safe dosage is assessed, and side effects are identified; Phase II of clinical trials to verify its efficacy and assess its safety, as well as to check the relationship between the medicinal product and its therapeutic effects; Phase III, in which the medicine is administered to a wider group to confirm its efficacy, analyse side effects, compare it with available treatments and obtain information which will allow its safe use.

Expanding the limits of the regulatory test exemption beyond the regulatory purpose of Article 10(6) of Directive 2001/83/EC is, however, not acceptable. In light of Article 10(6) of Directive 2001/83/EC, for the use of a patented invention to fall within the regulatory test exemption, the following conditions should be met. These are, first, whether the use of the invention in the trials and experiments is necessary to meet the requirements of the registration procedure (the information thus obtained is necessary to be presented in the test results for registration) and, second, whether the user of the protected invention has actually acted for the purposes of registration and

56. J. Pitz, A. Kawada, J.A. Schwab, *Patent Litigation in Germany, Japan and the United States. A Practitioner's Guide*, Munich 2015, p. 71.

57. P. Chrocziel, *Benutzung zu Versuchszwecken als Einwand gegenüber einem Anspruch wegen Patentverletzung (Q 105)*, GRUR Int. 1992/3, p. 206; P. Chrocziel, *Die Benutzung patentierter Erfindungen zu Versuchs – und Forschungszwecken*, München 1986, p. 178; W. Vomhof, *Die Forschung ist frei!*, GRUR 1967/6, p. 280; V. Tetzner, *Patentverletzung durch Forschung*, GRUR 1966/11, p. 604.

not ostensibly. It must be established whether it is apparent from objective circumstances that a manufacturer of an innovative medicine, or one acting on its behalf at the time of entering a patent monopoly, intends to register a particular innovative medicine. It would certainly be desirable for the future legislative work of the European Commission (EC) to draw clearer boundaries between the research exemption and the regulatory testing exemption.

4.2 Extending the Regulatory Review Exemption to Registering Medicinal Products Abroad

The regulatory review exemption covers only activities, which are linked for registration purposes of the given medicinal product. Thus, to satisfy the administrative requirements, one must obtain the marketing authorization in the given market.[58] The question of *whether the export of a protected product (active substance or trial drug series) to register a medicinal product abroad falls under the regulatory testing exemption or infringes a patent* is linked to the territorial aspect of the regulatory testing exemption. In other words, does the regulatory review exemption only cover the use of a protected invention to register a medicinal product in the national territory concerned, or in other EU countries, as well as in a third country (e.g., the US)?

Article 10(6) of Directive 2001/83/EC does not deal with this issue. Similarly, the legislative history of the regulatory review provision in EU law does not explain this issue. Some of the legislation in the most recent wording of the regulatory testing exemption, e.g., German, French, Swiss, Italian and English, explicitly states that the regulatory testing exemption covers the use of a protected invention for registration in that legislation and abroad, either within the EU or in a third country. According to § 11(2b) of German Patent Law, the patent law does not cover the conduct of tests or experiments and practical requirements necessary to obtain marketing authorization for a medicinal product in the EU or in any EU Member State or a third country.[59] According to Article L. 613-5(d) of French Intellectual Property Code, the regulatory review exemption covers the studies and experiments necessary to obtain marketing authorization for a medicinal product in any Member State of the EU or the EEA, as well as any operation to perform them. Under Article 9(1)(c) of the BundesPatG, the effects of a patent do not extend to acts required to obtain marketing authorization for a medicinal product in Switzerland or in another country with a comparable system for

58. *See*: U. Scharen [in:] *Patentgesetz*, ed. G. Benkard, München 2006, commentary to § 11, point 10; T. Kühnen [in:] *Patentgesetz mit Europäischem Patentübereinkommen. Kommentar auf der Grundlage der deutschen und europäischen Rechtsprechung*, ed. R. Schulte, Köln 2014, commentary to § 11, point 17; T. Kühnen, *Handbuch der Patentverletzung*, München 2011, Nb 1642; J. Ensthaler [in:] *Patentrechtskommentar*, ed. U. Fitzner, R. Lutz, T. Bodewig, München 2012, commentary to § 11, pkt 16, p. 218; P. Chrocziel, F.E. Hufnagel, *Versuchsprivileg und Unterstützungshandlungen – Abgrenzungsfragen im 'Bermuda-Dreieck'* der § 9, 10 und 11 Nr. 2/2 b PatG [in:] Festschrift für Peter Mes zum 65. Geburtstag, ed. M. Bergermann, München 2009, p. 59, 61; U. Worm, O. Guski, *Analoge Anwendung des Zulassungsprivilegs auf Medizinprodukte? Zu den Grenzen von Versuchshandlungen an und mit patentierten Medizinprodukten*, Mitt. 2011/6, p. 265 and ss.
59. J. Pitz, A. Kawada, J. A. Schwab, *Patent Litigation...*, p. 72.

the control of medicinal products. According to Article 68(1)(b) of the Italian Industrial Property Code, trials and experiments to obtain marketing authorization for a medicinal product, including abroad, do not constitute a patent infringement. In turn, under Article 60(6E) of the UK Patent Act, the evaluation of a medicinal product means tests and experiments or other activities undertaken with a view to obtaining information for the following purposes: (1) to obtain or vary marketing authorization for a medicinal product, both within the UK and abroad; (2) to comply with the requirements of the regulatory procedure, both within the UK and abroad; and (3) to assess the benefits and costs of a medicinal product or treatment in comparison with the available alternatives (so-called health technology assessments – HTA), both within the UK and abroad. Similarly, Spanish legislation, in force since 1 April 2017, where, pursuant to Article 61(c) of the new Spanish Patent Law on the basis of a patent, does not extend to the performance of tests and trials necessary to obtain authorization to place medicines on the market in Spain or abroad and the practical requirements arising therefrom, including the preparation, obtaining and use of the active substance for those purposes. Finally, according to revised Article 69, paragraph 1, point 4 of Polish Industrial Property Law, the regulatory testing exemption covers the use of an invention in order to perform activities which, under the provisions of law, are required to obtain, also by a third party, registration or permission, which are a condition for allowing certain products to be marketed due to their intended use, in particular, medicinal products on the territory of the EEA or another country.

The question arises as to *whether such broad coverage of the territorial scope of the use of a protected invention under the regulatory testing exemption is consistent with the original purpose of Article 10(6) of Directive 2001/83/EC*. It should first be considered if the wording or aim of Article 10(6) of Directive 2001/83/EC allows the specific purpose of the regulatory testing exemption to be achieved abroad, This should be read in the context of the EU regulation of regulatory testing exemption, which refers to harmonized rules on the registration of medicinal products.[60] It is worth mentioning that the historical drafts of Article 10(6) of Directive 2001/83/EC provided for an explicit mention of the regulatory review exemption of exporting the protected product for the purpose of registering the medicine abroad – only within the EU. Then, the removal of this provision from the wording of Article 10(6) of Directive 2001/83/EC was justified by the negative effects of covering the regulatory review exemption of such exports to third countries, i.e., outside the EU. Notwithstanding the historical legislative objective of Article 10(6) of Directive 2001/83/EC, it can be pointed out that restricting the territorial scope of the regulatory testing exemption to the use of the invention to register the medicine in a given country is contrary to the EU principle of free movement of goods (Articles 34 and 36 TFEU). The requirement that the active substance be manufactured by an applicant for registration of a medicine in a country

60. Proposal for a Directive of the European Parliament and of the Council amending Directive 2001/83/EC on the Community code relating to medicinal products for human use (COM(2001) 404 final), 26 November 2001, p. 85 – the document states that the purpose of the regulatory review exemption is to allow generic medicinal products to enter the market immediately after the expiry of patent protection, irrespective of the restrictions imposed by industrial property law.

is not specifically justified in the wording of the patent and would, therefore, be contrary to the free movement of goods.[61] In the French study of J.-Ch. Galloux states that the regulatory testing exemption covers the export of a protected product for registration of a medicinal product abroad, within the EU Member States. In his opinion, the author argues in favour of such a view of harmonizing pharmaceutical law within the EU legal order and justifying the regulatory testing exemption in the EU legislation, as well as the free movement of internal market goods.[62] The regulatory review exemption covers the use of a protected invention by a third party if a valid application for registration of the medicinal product concerned is sought. If the use of the invention is undertaken for the purpose of registering the medicinal product in question in a procedure carried out by a foreign regulatory body, it should be for the national law of that body to determine what action was necessary and had a functional connection to the registration of the medicinal product in question. J. Straus rightly points out that the assessment of the condition of 'use to the extent necessary' is based on the national law of the country in which the medicinal product is registered.[63] Therefore, it might be appropriate to link the focus of the question as to whether exporting for the purpose of registering a medicinal product abroad falls within the scope of the regulatory testing exemption with the type of procedure for registering the medicinal product - EU or domestic. The reasons for consistency between the regulatory review exemption in Article 10(6) of Directive 2001/83/EC and the principle of free movement of goods and services - in my view - sufficiently justifies the extension of the regulatory review exemption to exports of protected products for registration outside the national territory in the EU registration procedure.

4.3 The Regulatory Testing Exemption Covers Third-Party Actions under the 'Practical Requirements'

Under Article 10(6) of Directive 2001/83/EC, it does not infringe the patent (or supplementary protection certificate) to carry out the necessary examinations and tests in connection with the registration procedure and the practical requirements resulting therefrom. Article 10(6) of the Directive 2001/83/EC sets the boundaries of the regulatory testing exemption in light of the 'practical requirements', however, it does not provide any further clarifications. T. Kühnen states that the concept of the practical requirements means any form of use of a protected invention necessary to undertake the required examinations or experiments in the registration of a medicinal product. Practical requirements include preparatory steps for studies or experiments, including

61. M. Krekora, M. Świerczyński, E. Traple, *Prawo farmaceutyczne*, Warszawa 2012, p. 250.
62. In particular, J.-Ch. Galloux points out that since the entry into force of Council Directive 65/65 of 26 January 1965 on the approximation of provisions laid down by law, regulation or administrative action relating to medicinal products (OJ 1965 L 22, p. 369), procedures relating to the commercialization of medicinal products within the EU have gradually been harmonized - *see* J.-Ch. Galloux, *L'exception 'Bolar'*, RTD Com 2015, p. 93.
63. J. Straus, *The Bolar exemption and the supply of patented active pharmaceutical ingredients to generic drug producers: an attempt to interpret Article 10(6) of Directive 2004/27*, JIPL&P 2014/11, p. 903.

the manufacture or import of a patented product or the preparation of samples required by the regulatory procedure.[64] J. Bukow argues that 'practical requirements' include all forms of use of a protected invention necessary to conduct research or experiments, including, for example, the manufacture of a medicinal product to the extent that it is necessary to conduct research or experiments and for the purpose of conducting bioequivalence studies regarding the generic medicinal product.[65] Furthermore, according to F.E. Hufnagel's practical requirements, allowed are all forms of use of the invention in order to carry out research or experiments, e.g., the manufacture of a medicinal product to carry out bioequivalence studies.[66] Similarly, J. Straus argues that the practical requirements also cover acts of usage of the patented invention that have been taken before the conduct of tests or studies (e.g., manufacturing and supplying of the patented active ingredient).[67] A wide interpretation of the 'practical requirements' requirements under Article 10(6) of the Directive 2001/83/EC and its local versions is confirmed by the domestic EU Member States court decisions. On 15 December 2014, in *Sanofi-Aventis v. Lilly France* Tribunal de Grande Instance de Paris, the scope of the exemption in Article L.613-5 d) French Code of Intellectual Property Code allows third parties to carry out the acts necessary to obtain marketing authorization (including the manufacture and possession of infringing products).[68] On 7 October 2014, in a simultaneous case *Lilly France against Sanofi-Aventis*, the court ruled that the regulatory review exemption also covers the acts necessary to carry out the studies and clinical trials necessary to obtain marketing authorization and to obtain authorization without drawing up an exhaustive list.[69]

'Practical requirements' are all activities necessary to obtain marketing authorization. They relate to the necessary use of the invention in the context of testing of a reference medicine substance or in developing a finished product form (bioequivalence study or safety and efficacy study). 'Practical requirements' also cover other forms of exploitation of the protected invention than applying in the studies or trials, which are linked for registration purposes of the given medicinal product. This means satisfying the administrative requirements in order to obtain marketing authorization in the given market.[70] Also, manufacturing (including the production of samples) or offering,

64. T. Kühnen, *Patent litigation proceedings in Germany*, Munich 2015, p. 536.
65. J. Bukow, *Patent law. A handbook on European and German patent law*, ed. M. Haedicke, H. Timmann, Munich 2014, p. 801.
66. F.E. Hufnagel, *Ausweitung des Versuchsprivilegs in Europa und den USA – Verschiebung der Grenzen zwischen Patentschutz und Versuchfreiheit bei Arzneimitteln*, PharmaR 2006/5, p. 209, 211.
67. J. Straus, *The Bolar exemption and the supply of patented active pharmaceutical ingredients to generic drug producers: an attempt to interpret Art. 10(6) of Directive 2004/27*, JIPL&P 2014/11, p. 903-904.
68. Judgment of the Tribunal de Grande Instance de Paris of 15 December 2014, case no. 14/58023.
69. Judgment of the Tribunal de Grande Instance de Paris of 7 October 2014, case no. 14/12276.
70. *See*: U. Scharen [in:] *Patentgesetz*, ed. G. Benkard, München 2006, commentary to § 11, point 10; T. Kühnen [in:] *Patentgesetz mit Europäischem Patentübereinkommen. Kommentar auf der Grundlage der deutschen und europäischen Rechtsprechung*, ed. R. Schulte, Köln 2014, commentary to § 11, point 17; T. Kühnen, *Handbuch der Patentverletzung*, München 2011, Nb 1642; J. Ensthaler [in:] *Patentrechtskommentar*, ed. U. Fitzner, R. Lutz, T. Bodewig, München 2012, commentary to § 11, point 16, p. 218; P. Chrocziel, F.E. Hufnagel, *Versuchsprivileg und Unterstützungshandlungen – Abgrenzungsfragen im 'Bermuda-Dreieck' der § 9, 10 und 11*, Nr.

importing and delivery by a third party of the buyer are allowed if they are associated with the purpose of registration, i.e., purpose to be used for testing and trials.[71] Said forms of using the protected invention may constitute preparatory activities for the performance of research or experiments. In practice, they may constitute a necessary premise for any research and analysis on the invention[72] and thereby are allowed under the regulatory testing in the EU. Practical requirements include forms of using the invention which are necessary and directly related to achieving the purpose of registration in the abridged procedure of a medicinal product.[73] Beyond the scope of 'practical requirements' are actions, which are not necessary for the application of Article 10 paragraphs 1-4 of Directive 2001/83/EC. This is a significant difference regarding the regulatory testing exemption in the legislation of EU Member States compared to the Bolar exemption in US Patent Law.[74]

The already mentioned German and Polish dispute in the famous *Astellas Pharma v. Polpharma* case showed how difficult it is to evidence the functional link between third parties' activities and registration purposes covered by the regulatory review exemption. The assessment as to whether third-party activities, such as production or exporting, are exempt under the regulatory review exemption is based on the objective criteria. The objective criteria may be demonstrated through contractual arrangements between the producer of the patented active ingredient and the medicinal products' manufacturer interested in the registration of the given medicinal products. In the French doctrine, J.-Ch. Galloux states that the regulatory testing exemption covers the export of a protected product for registration of a medicinal product abroad, within the territory of EU Member States. In his opinion, the author argues in favour of such a view of harmonizing pharmaceutical law within the EU legal system and justifying the regulatory testing exemption in the EU legislation, as well as the free movement of internal market goods.[75]

The key question related to understanding the regulatory testing exemption under the EU law is who may benefit from this exemption and thereby, who would not infringe patent rights. In the above-mentioned German-Polish case *Astellas Pharma v. Polpharma*, the courts assessed if the marketing authorization holder, who exploited

2/2 b PatG [in:] *Festschrift für Peter Mes zum 65. Geburtstag*, ed. M. Bergermann, München 2009, p. 59, 61; U. Worm, O. Guski, *Analoge Anwendung des Zulassungsprivilegs auf Medizinprodukte? Zu den Grenzen von Versuchshandlungen an und mit patentierten Medizinprodukten*, Mitt. 2011/6, p. 265.

71. A. Sztoldman, *Krąg upoważnionych do działania w ramach wyjątku Bolara – glosa do wyroku Sądu Najwyższego z 23 października 2013 r. (IV CSK 92/13)*, 'Glosa' 2014/2, p. 91.
72. *See*: M. Fähndrich, W. Tilmann, *Patentnutzende Bereitstellungshandlungen bei Versuchen*, GRUR 2001/10–11 p. 903, D. Gilat, *Experimental use and patents*, Weinheim 1995, p. 85.
73. T. Kühnen, *Patent litigation proceedings in Germany*, Munich 2015, p. 537; H. Holzapfel, *Die patentrechtliche Zulässigkeit der Benutzung von Forschungswerkzeugen*, GRUR 2006/10, p. 10, 16; U. Gassner., *Unterlagenschutz im Europäischen Arzneimittelrecht*, GRUR Int. 2004/12, p. 988, 991.
74. The judgment of the US Supreme Court in *Merck v. Integra* found that to cover the use of a protected invention with the exception of Bolar, it is sufficient that the action is reasonably related to the purpose of registration and not directly. *See* Judgment of 2005, *Merck KGaA v. Integra Lifesciences I Ltd.*, 545 US 193.
75. J.-Ch. Galloux, *L'exception 'Bolar'*, RTD Com 2015, p. 93.

the patented invention to register the medicinal product for its behalf, shall benefit from the German and Polish regulatory testing exemption. On a practical note, in the pharmaceutical market, it is very common that the process of developing a medicinal product involves many parties. Apart from the marketing authorization holder, the process may involve a third-party manufacturer of the patented active ingredient or a third-party trial organization. Unfortunately, the Court of Justice of the EU had no opportunity to examine and discuss the status of third parties under the Article 10(6) of the Directive 2001/83/EC since the respective prejudicial questions in the German-Polish case *Astellas Pharma v. Polpharma*, referred by the German court, were at the end withdrawn by Astellas. The Regional Court in Dusseldorf and the Higher Regional Court in Gdansk ruled in June and July 2012 that the regulatory testing exemption and the experimental use exemption only apply to the testing entity and that a third party's manufacturing and selling to the testing entity is not exempt.[76] Both the Regional Court in Dusseldorf and the Higher Regional Court in Gdansk clarified that a supplier cannot rely on the exemptions only because its customer uses the purchased item exclusively for experimental or regulatory testing purposes as this would lead to free trade with protected substances. Furthermore, according to a judgment of the Higher Regional Court of Düsseldorf, even the import of an active ingredient manufactured in a third country without patent protection into the domestic market where protection exists could fall under the German regulatory review exemption if such import occurs for the purpose of carrying out trials to obtain a marketing authorization.[77] This reasoning was reproduced by the Polish Supreme Court, which in its ruling stated that the regulatory testing exemption is only limited to those persons who perform experimental activities in order to obtain marketing authorization for the product for their own needs.[78] It has also recently been discussed in French case law; does the regulatory test exemption only cover the use of a protected invention 'for oneself' or whether another entity in each group of companies can register a medicinal product? In two decisions of 7 October 2014 and 15 December 2014, the French court held that the regulatory testing exemption under French law covers the use of a protected invention for the registration of a medicinal product where the various stages of use of the invention are carried out by different companies in the group (manufacture, storage, registration).[79]

What is the status of third parties under the European regulatory review exemption and are acts such as commission studies or trials, delivery and manufacturing allowed or do they infringe a patent?

First, Article 10(6) of the Directive 2001/83/EC does not limit who is authorized to act under the regulatory review exemption, including that it does not limit this scope to

76. Judgment of 26 July 2012, case no. 4a O 282/10; judgment of 26 June 2012 case no. IX GC 76/11.
77. Higher Regional Court Düsseldorf (*Oberlandesgericht Düsseldorf*) 5 December 2013, Case No. I-2 U 68/12.
78. Judgment of the Polish Supreme Court of 23 October 2013, case no. IV CSK 92/13.
79. Order of the TGI de Paris of 7 October 2014, RG No 14/12274, *Lilly France v. Sanofi-Aventis Deutschland*; order of the TGI de Paris of 15 December 2014, RG 14/58023, *Sanofi-Aventis Deutschland v. Lilly France.*

persons who carry out research or experimental activities to obtain marketing authorization for their own needs. Article 10(6) of Directive 2001/83/EC is formulated in general and does not specify the detailed conditions to apply this EU regulation. The EU lawmaker does not specify the 'practical requirements', which may indicate the intention to expand the catalogue of permitted activities and include activities other than examinations and tests. On the contrary, it may suggest that a wide range of 'practical requirements' also include the use of a protected invention which consist of the preparation of an active substance for use in research and trials or its purchase from a third party for this purpose.

Second, not all manufacturers of medicinal products have the necessary technical infrastructure to manufacture active substances or carry out the necessary examinations and tests to register a medicinal product.[80] The restrictive approach leads to the unjustifiable consequences that facilitating the marketing of a medicinal product immediately after termination of protection only applies to a small group of entities on the pharmaceutical market. This approach is contrary to the economic reality based on the specialization of the activity.

Third, limiting the regulatory testing exemption only to producers of generic medicinal products does not seem to be compatible with its function (*see* point 3 above). As already mentioned, it aims at allowing research or experiments to be conducted during the period of exclusive protection in a specific aim, which is the registration of a medicinal product. If only an intermediary of the entity that registers the medicinal products has a direct link - at the point of manufacturing or offering (and so on) with the aim of registration of the given medicinal product - this intermediary does not infringe an intellectual property right. The regulatory exemption allows a complex (indirect) functional relationship between an intermediary and the patent/SPC holder. Also, the functional link between the intermediary and the patent/SPC holder does not have to be direct or consistent of two steps. This means that in the registration process of a specific medicinal product referred to in Article 10(6) of the Directive 2001/83/EC, many entities may be involved in the process of execution of individual stages necessary to meet the regulatory requirements of submitting the application for marketing authorization for a medicinal product. It is possible to act for registering a medicinal product (using the invention to submit an application for registration on one's own behalf) or acting for someone else's purpose of registration (using the invention to submit an application for registration by another entity). The privileged status of the third party depends on whether the manufacturer of generics supplied indeed uses the provided active substance in privileged studies or trials within the meaning of Article 10(6) of Directive 2001/83/EC.

Under Article 10(6) of the Directive 2001/83/EC, however, it does not fall within the scope of the regulatory review exemption to store a protected product for the purpose of enabling studies or trials to be conducted in the future, beyond the temporal link with the purpose of registration of the medicinal product. The premise for action for the purpose of registration is fulfilled if, at the time of the patent monopoly, there

80. F.E. Hufnagel, *Ausweitung des Versuchsprivilegs in Europa und den USA – Verschiebung der Grenzen zwischen Patentschutz und Versuchfreiheit bei Arzneimitteln*, PharmaR 2006/5, p. 146.

was a functional relationship between the action of a third party and the registration of the medicinal product. Thus, a third party who does not register a medicinal product operates under the regulatory review exemption if they co-organize registration activities and the registrant has control over a particular use of the invention. It is sufficient that this functional relationship is demonstrated by ensuring that there is a contract between the manufacturer and the registrant containing at least the buyer's statements that the order to manufacture the protected active substance is for the purpose of registering the medicinal product. Companies within the capital group may divide tasks necessary for the registration of a medicinal product because of contracts for the provision of services or other cooperation agreements, which perform separate activities necessary to obtain registration.

4.4 The Regulatory Testing Exemption Includes Storage

The use of a protected invention under the regulatory testing exemption must correspond to the studies or trials required for registration, as well as 'practical requirements'. Therefore, the question *is: in light of Article 10(6) Directive 2001/83, are storage for clinical trials and stockpiling allowed?*

Most EU countries do not allow stockpiling of commercial batches which exceed the registering purpose under Article 10(6) Directive 2001/83/EC. Stockpiling is a commercial activity, which is not directly connected with obtaining market authorization for a given medicinal product and should not be covered by the exemption due to a lack of a functional link with the registration purposes. Commercial activities are not directly connected to obtaining marketing authorization. The regulatory review exemption includes such storage, which is determined by the necessity resulting from the type and extent of studies and trials conducted to register a particular medicinal product. In the case of Canada – Patent Protection of Pharmaceutical Products, a World Trade Organization (WTO) panel stressed that the limitation of a patent, which consists of the permitted production according to a patented invention in order to store the final product before the patent protection ceases, does not constitute a minor limitation of the patent monopoly. Consequently, such patent limitation does not fulfil the first condition of the three-step test and is, therefore, not compatible with Article 30 and Article 28(1) of the Trade-Related Aspects of Intellectual Property Rights (TRIPS) Agreement.[81] However, the ruling in Canada – Patent Protection of Pharmaceutical Products does not mean that it is, in any event, contrary to Article 30 of the TRIPS Agreement to restrict a patent by allowing the protected invention to be used to produce and stockpile medicine for the purpose of placing it on the market immediately after the patent has expired.[82] In particular, the regulatory review exemption allows for the storage of protected products for the development of another reproducible medicinal product (e.g., another form of administration), provided that the third party

81. WTO Panel Decision of 18 August 2000 in Canada – Patent Protection of Pharmaceutical Products, WT/DS114/R.
82. A. Kur, *Limitations and exceptions under the three-step test...*, pp. 240-241.

concerned can demonstrate the rationale for the regulatory testing exemption under the circumstances (functional link with the registration and necessity of storage).

However, commercial stockpiling is not covered by the regulatory review exemption under Article 10(6) of the directive 2001/83/EC. A functional link with the registering purpose means that the regulatory testing exemption is limited to activities which were taken before registering the given medicinal product. Activities which occur after a given medicinal product is approved should not be principally exempted. The regulatory testing exemption does not exempt actions which exceed this limited purpose. Other actions interfere with core patent rights and undermine the innovation incentives that patents were designed to provide.

5. FINAL REMARKS

There is no single model of the transposition of the regulatory review exemption into the EU national laws. Member States implement the regulatory testing exemption' in different ways. On the one hand, some Member States do not allow the supply of active pharmaceutical ingredients (APIs) to EU-based generic manufacturers for the purpose of seeking marketing authorization. On the other hand, in a number of Member States, it is not certain whether testing in the EU by originators and biosimilars can benefit from these exemptions when seeking marketing authorization in the EU and in non-EU countries, or for meeting emerging regulatory requirements such as those related to health technology assessment. Local differences open stand for issues, which may be clarified by the Court of Justice of the EU in its case law.

Notwithstanding the above, there is a trend in the legislation of the selected most important countries in the EU economy to extend the scope of the regulatory testing exemption beyond the original wording of Article 10(6) of Directive 2001/83/EC. Key changes in approach to the regulatory testing exemption in major patent jurisdictions in the EU include extending the regulatory testing exemption to: (1) registering the medicinal product in the full procedure, including innovative medicinal products (combinations); (2) registering the medicinal product abroad; (3) including within the exemption third party actions, including offering and manufacturing; and (4) storage of clinical batches of medicinal products for registering purposes.

It appears that in the next year, we may see the increasing harmonization of regulatory review exemption in the European national case law. The development of the EU pharmaceutical sector requires a tailored and unified approach that boosts the competitiveness of the EU pharmaceutical market. The regulatory review exemption is a measure to balance the interests of different stakeholders interested in gaining access to the patented invention for the purpose of research and development. Although the regulatory review exemption has commercial purposes and is functionally linked with introducing a pharmaceutical product on the market, it seems that the courts should not interpret this exemption in a manner that exceeds the link with a registration of a given medicinal product. Consequently, rethinking the regulatory testing exemption by courts and stakeholders requires that all acts subject to exemption are really necessary and functionally linked to register a product and are not associated with its further commercialization, which infringes patents or SPC rights. One may observe that recent legislative changes in the UK, Belgium, Spain and Poland significantly extended the regulatory review exemption, in a way that they did not explicitly address to key boundaries of the regulatory review exemption under the Article 10(6) of the 2001/83/EC, i.e., the practical requirements and the functional link. Taking all this into account, there is some way to go before the regulatory review exemption is applied equally in all EU countries and is really fit for purposes which are securing the public health, without stifling innovation unduly.

The key challenge for the EU patent system may be indeed how to rethink the regulatory review exemption in a way that it balances colliding interests of patent holders and manufacturers of follow-up medicinal products. This should take into consideration the aim of the patent monopoly which is economic exclusivity within the patent term and the strict legislative purpose of the regulatory testing provision. The balance of interest requires facilitation of the imminent entry of the follow-up medicinal product shortly after the patent or SPC elapses. The regulatory review exemption expresses a compromise between the interest of the patent holder in the exclusive use of the protected invention and the legitimate social and economic reasons and the public interest in accessing the protected technical solution in order to launch follow-up medicines. The regulatory review exemption also has an important social value, which enables competitive generic or biosimilar or combination products to be entered into the market resulting in the reduction of prices of medicinal products in the market. My view is that the social value of the regulatory review exemption demands for a reasonably wide interpretation of the local transpositions in EU Member States of Article 10(6) of the Directive 2001/83/EC. Some unanswered questions resulting from the unitary patent system (if any) and its relationship to domestic laws providing for regulatory resting exemption is also far from clear – making it another possible ground for rethinking this part of the EU and the national patent law.

CHAPTER 6

Rethinking SPC Protection: Manufacturing Waiver as an Incentive for the Generic Sector or a Disincentive to Innovators?

Justyna Ożegalska-Trybalska

1 INTRODUCTION

Effective patent protection has always been considered to be an engine of innovation, the reward for contributing to technological progress and the legal tool ensuring the recovery of investments in R&D activities. This, in particular, is the case for patent protection in the pharmaceutical sector, characterized by the long and costly: line of development for innovative medicinal products, preclinical and clinical trials ensuring theirs safety, the procedure of obtaining patent protection and authorization for the circulation of such products within the market.[1]

The value of pharmaceutical patents and incentives for innovation in the sector is driven by costs and revenues and is determined significantly by the scope and time

1. Negative consequences of a long authorization procedure are reduced in the EU through a special regulatory patent exemption (the so-called Bolar exemption) adopted through Directive 2004/27/EC of the European Parliament and the Council of 31 March 2004 (OJ L 136 of 30 April 2004, p. 34), amending Directive 2001/83/EC of 6 November 2001 on the Community code relating to medicinal products for human use OJ L 311 of 28 November 2001, p. 67. It enables generic competitors of innovative companies owning patents for medical products to conduct necessary studies and trial required for authorization and to file an application for marketing approval of the competing generic product(s) as soon as possible, after the expiry date of the patent. According to Art. 10 s. 6 of Directive 2001/83/EC 'conducting the necessary studies and trials with a view to the application of paras 1, 2, 3 and 4 and the consequential practical requirements shall not be regarded as contrary to patent rights or to supplementary protection certificates'. It exempts from patent infringement studies and trials undertaken in view of abridged applications, hybrid applications, and biosimilar applications (applications for bioequivalents and biosimilars).

of market exclusivity.[2] As recent econometric results confirm, there is a positive relationship between the effective protection period for medicinal products and R&D activities undertaken within the pharmaceutical sector. More specifically, such relation can be found between (Intellectual Property) IP protection in the markets where medicinal products are sold, and the level of R&D expenditures invested by companies.[3] Although the debate over the positive or negative impact on IP system on innovation is still open and the relationship between IP rights and innovation has not been clearly determined, recent economic studies confirm the close link between the effective IP protection and the incentive for innovation in the pharmaceutical sector.[4]

Considering the above circumstances, for many years, the pharmaceutical sector and medical products have been given special attention under European patent law, with both the specific limitations of pharmaceutical patents known as a Bolar exemption and the preferable extension of patent protection in the form of a supplementary patent certificate (SPC), allowing for additional (patent-like) protection for pharmaceutical products subject to market authorization up to five years after patent expiry.

The European Union (EU) legislator has recently rethought the SPC protection for medicinal products by introducing a new form of derogation (limitation of patent rights) – called 'SPC manufacturing waiver' or 'SPC export exemption' under Regulation (EU) 2019/933 of the European Parliament and of the Council of 20 May 2019 amending Regulation (EC) 469/2009 of 6 May 2009 concerning the Supplementary Protection Certificate – SPC, referred to as Regulation (EU) 2019/933).[5]

According to the justification for the adoption of the amendment, during the SPC period of protection in the EU, generic companies cannot manufacture equivalents of protected products for any purpose, including export outside of the EU, where such protection has expired or does not exist. Meanwhile, manufacturers based in those non-EU markets can freely do so, and that puts them in a more competitive position. As argued, having the possibility to manufacture SPC-protected product for markets outside of Europe, should stop forcing generic and biosimilar medicines to relocate production to those non-EU countries where no similar protection is in place.[6]

2. *See* Fabian Gaessler, Stefan Wagner, *Patents, Data Exclusivity, and the Development of New Drugs*, Discussion Paper No. 176 5 August 2019, pp. 8-9; https://rationality-and-competition.de /wp-content/uploads/discussion_paper/176.pdf (accessed 20 August 2020).
3. *See* Study on the economic impact of supplementary protection certificates, pharmaceutical incentives and rewards in Europe Final Report prepared for EC by Copenhagen Economics, 277 (2018); https://ec.europa.eu/docsroom/documents/29521 (accessed 28 June 2019).
4. *See A critical incentive – not a barrier! How IP incentives spur biopharmaceutical innovation and the creation of new health technologies*; study prepared by Pugatch Consilium, 2017; https://www .pugatch-consilium.com/reports/A_CuITICAL_INCENTIVE_%E2%80%93_NOT_A_BARRIER!. pdf (accessed 24 November 2019), pp. 7-9.
5. O.J.L 153/1 of 11 June 2019.
6. *See* Recital 3 and 4 of the Regulation (EU) 2019/933. As explained, the EU-based generic producers, in contrast to producers located in third countries where protection does not exist or has expired, cannot enter the Union market immediately after the expiry of the certificate, given that they are not in a position to build up production capacity for the purpose of export or for the purpose of entering the market of a Member State until the protection provided by that certificate has expired.

EU-based companies also cannot easily prepare production facility (capacity) until the protection provided by the SPC certificate has expired. Again, generic companies located in non-EU countries are free to do so and can benefit from being first on EU-SPC free markets. As argued, it is more difficult for EU manufacturers to enter the EU market immediately after the SPC protection of the original product has expired, which negatively impacts the possibility to build a competitive position within the newly opened market. As studies have shown, there is the 'first mover' advantage and only the very first biosimilars to reach the market capture over 70% of the market share.[7] Thus, a quick entrance and sales on the market after SPC protection expires is of crucial importance from the point of view of being successful with a generic equivalent of an innovative drug.

As explained, the main purpose of amending the SPC regulation is to eliminate the disadvantage vis-à-vis those manufacturers located outside the EU, who are not limited by the SPC protection, by allowing EU-based companies to manufacture a generic or biosimilar version of an SPC-protected medicine during the term of the certificate for the sole purpose of exporting it to a non-EU market where protection has expired or simply never existed, or for stockpiling during the final six months of an SPC ahead of entry into the EU market. According to the EC, the revision of SPC 'is a well-calibrated adjustment to the current regime striking a balance between ensuring the attractiveness of Europe for innovative pharmaceutical companies and allowing EU-based generics and biosimilar to compete on the global market'.[8]

Additionally to the characteristics of the manufacturing waiver, this chapter aims to analyse whether this direction of rethinking SPC protection standards truly ensures the balance declared by the amended SPC regulation and whether an SPC manufacturing waiver should be considered as an incentive for the generic sector or quite the reverse – a disincentive to innovation in the EU pharmaceutical sector.

2 TOWARDS EXTENDING PATENT PROTECTION BY SPC AND LIMITING IT BY MANUFACTURING WAIVER

In 1992, a new sui generis right was introduced by Regulation 1768/92 concerning the creation of a SPC for medicinal products which entered into force on 2 January 1993. It was replaced by the mentioned Regulation 469/2009 EC with effect from 6 May 2009, which did not make any changes to the merit compared to the original version . The binding SPC Regulation aims at strengthening patent protection for those medicinal products entering the market that are the result of long, costly research and time-consuming regulatory authorization. SPC extends the monopoly period for a 'product' (active ingredient or a combination of active ingredients) that is protected by a patent

7. *See* Commission Staff Working Document Impact Assessment Accompanying the document Proposal for a Regulation of the European Parliament and of the Council amending Regulation (EC) No 469/2009 concerning the supplementary protection certificate for medicinal products {COM(2018) 317 final} – [SEC(2018) 246 final] – [SWD(2018) 241 final] – [SWD(2018) 242 fin, Brussels, 28 May 2018 SWD(2018) 240 final], pp. 17-18. As indicated, second and third entrants captured respectively 30-40% and 5-22% market share.
8. O.J.L 153/1 of 11 June 2019.

and thus compensates pharmaceutical innovative companies for the time needed to comply with market authorization (and thus 'lost' for market exploitation of such products) and covers the investment put into the research and development of the product. As decided, the duration of the protection granted by the certificate should not be given for a period exceeding five years and should allow patent holders for medicinal products to enjoy a maximum overall period of 15 years of exclusivity from the time the medicinal product in question first obtains authorization to be placed on the market within the EU. The initial version of SPC Regulation 1768/92 clearly explains that the additional protection should reduce the risk of the research centres of pharmaceuticals innovative companies situated in the Member States being relocated to countries that offer greater (longer) protection. Moreover, it should ensure investments in developing new innovative drugs and support innovative EU pharmaceutical companies. Paradoxically, almost 30 years later, quite similar arguments for avoiding the relocation of generic EU business and supporting the competitiveness of generic companies are raised as justification for a limitation of SPC by an export exemption.

Discussion on the consequences of reducing the exclusivity rights of the innovators had already been initiated in the EU in 2002 in the proposal of modification of Directive 2001/83 on the Community code relating to medicinal products for human use considering an export clause in a Bolar-type exemption from patent infringement of patented pharmaceutical products.[9] In 2015, the Commission considered for the first time the introduction of a manufacturing waiver within the Single Market Strategy as a part of a possible 'recalibration' and reform of the SPC system.[10] Later, the initiative was the subject of a series of studies, as well as of public consultation and impact assessment in 2017. The EC announced the possible legislative and non-legislative initiatives in this regard, as well as investigated the economic consequences, both benefits and drawbacks from the point of view of the EU pharmaceutical sectors and patients themselves.[11] In opposite to the Commission's proposal of 2018 including an

9. According to Art. 10(4) included in the version of the directive proposed by the European Parliament, exempted activities covered 'conducting the necessary tests and trials with a view to application of paras 1, 3 and 4 as well as for export, the submission of an application, the submission of samples in accordance with Art. 19, as well as the granting of a marketing authorization.' *See* Position of the European Parliament adopted at first reading on 23 October 2002 with a view to the adoption of European Parliament and Council Directive 2002/.../EC amending Directive 2001/83/EC on the Community code relating to medicinal products for human use, P5_TC1-COD (2001) 0253, OJ, C 300 E/C 300 E/, p. 361. This provision has been deleted as a result of the Council's position. *See* Common Position (EC) no 61/2003 adopted by the Council on 29 September 2003 with a view to the adoption of a Directive 2003/. . ./EC of the European Parliament and of the Council of . . . amending Council Directive 2001/83/EC on the Community code relating to medicinal products for human use (2003/C 297 E/02), OJ, 9 December 2003, C 297 E/41.

   See Proposal for a Directive of the European Parliament and the Council amending Directive 2001/83/EC, document COM (2001) 440 final 2001/0253 (COD), OJ C 75E, 216-233.

10. EC communication 'Upgrading the Single Market: more opportunities for people and business'. COM (2015) 550, followed by the study 'Assessing the economic impacts of changing exemption provision during patent and SPC protection in Europe.' https://publications.europa.eu/en/publication-detail/-/publication/6e4ce9f8-aa41-11e7-837e-01aa75ed71a1/language-en (accessed 26 June 2019).

11. Study 'Impact Assessment to evaluate options for optimising the legal framework concerning SPCs and patent research exemptions for sectors whose products are subject to regulated market

exemption for export purposes only, the compromise text of the Regulation (EU) 2019/933 introduces it not only for generics or biosimilars produced for export to third countries where protection of the original medicine does not exist but also for their production for stockpiling purposes (including a day-one launch after a patent for the original products expires).[12]

3 DEROGATION FROM EXCLUSIVITY: A CHARACTERISTIC OF THE MANUFACTURING WAIVER

The amended SPC regulation confirms the effects of the certificate as conferring the same rights as are conferred by the basic patent and being subject to the same limitations and the same obligations.[13] By way of derogation from this rule, Article 5 section 2 of the Regulation 469/2009, as amended by Article 1 of the Regulation (EU) 2019/933, allows, without the consent of the SPC holder, for the making of SPC-protected active ingredients and corresponding medicinal products for two kinds of purposes: (1) export to third countries outside the EU where SPC protection does not exist or has expired; and (2) stockpiling for day-one entry to the EU market immediately after SPC expiry.[14] Under this article, the expression 'making' should be

---

authorisations' followed by public consultations. https://ec.europa.eu/smart-egulation/roadmaps/docs/2017_grow_051_supplementary_protection_certificates_en.pdf (accessed 24 July 2019).

12. *See* the report of 28 January 2019 on amendments of the Parliament to the Commission proposal, explaining that the 'amendments do not go beyond the scope of the Commission's proposal, but aim at making its implementation more streamlined and transparent, while keeping the proposal targeted, proportionate and balanced and taking into account the interests of the various stakeholders.' http://www.europarl.europa.eu/doceo/document/A-8-2019-0039_EN.html?redirect (accessed 12 June 2019).
13. According to Art. 1(c) of the Regulation (EC) 469/2009, basic patent means 'a patent which protects a product as such, a process to obtain a product or an application of a product, and which is designated by its holder for the purpose of the procedure for grant of a certificate'.
14. The amended Article reads as follows:

    1. Subject to the provisions of Article 4, the certificate shall confer the same rights as conferred by the basic patent and shall be subject to the same limitations and the same obligations.
    2. By way of derogation from paragraph 1, the certificate referred to in paragraph 1 shall not confer protection against certain acts which would otherwise require the consent of the holder of the certificate ('the certificate holder'), if the following conditions are met:
       (a) the acts comprise:
          (i) the making of a product, or a medicinal product containing that product, for the purpose of export to third countries; or
          (ii) any related act that is strictly necessary for the making, in the Union, referred to in point (i), or for the actual export; or
          (iii) the making, no earlier than six months before the expiry of the certificate, of a product, or a medicinal product containing that product, for the purpose of storing it in the Member State of making, in order to place that product, or a medicinal product containing that product, on the market of Member States after the expiry of the corresponding certificate; or
          (iv) any related act that is strictly necessary for the making, in the Union, referred to in point (iii), or for the actual storing, provided that such related act is carried out no earlier than six months before the expiry of the certificate.

understood as one of the acts falling within the scope of a patent (SPC) exclusivity, aiming at manufacturing an SPC-protected product.[15]

The derogation also extends to any related act that is strictly necessary for the manufacturing in the EU or for the actual export, as well as to any related act that is strictly necessary for the manufacturing in the Union for the actual storing, provided that such a related act is carried out no earlier than six months before the expiry of the certificate. The Regulation does not specify 'related acts', but they could cover activities such as, for example, transportation, weighing, packing, labelling, sorting, transport, warehousing, advertising, within the EU, provided that it is necessary for the distribution of goods in third countries.[16]

As briefly described, the material, territorial and temporal scope of a manufacturing waiver is characterized and limited by:

(1) a defined form of permitted acts, which are only the making of a product, or a medicinal product containing that product and acts necessary for performing the allowed use;
(2) a purpose of performed acts covering only export and storing (only with a view to entering into the Union market) and other associated acts, but only strictly necessary for such production and such storing or for the actual export or the actual storing;
(3) the territory covered by the permitted production for export, which is limited only to countries outside the EU;

(b) the maker, through appropriate and documented means, notifies the authority referred to in Article 9(1) in the Member State in which that making is to take place, and informs the certificate holder, of the information listed in paragraph 5 of this Article no later than three months before the start date of the making in that Member State, or no later than three months before the first related act, prior to that making, that would otherwise be prohibited by the protection conferred by a certificate, whichever is the earlier;
(c) if the information listed in paragraph 5 of this Article changes, the maker notifies the authority referred to in Article 9(1) and informs the certificate holder, before those changes take effect;
(d) in the case of products, or medicinal products containing those products, made for the purpose of export to third countries, the maker ensures that a logo, in the form set out in Annex I, is affixed to the outer packaging of the product, or the medicinal product containing that product, referred to in point (a)(i) of this paragraph, and, where feasible, to its immediate packaging;
(e) the maker complies with paragraph 9 of this Article and, if applicable, with Article 12(2).

15. Making as a form of exploitation of IP protected subjects is listed in many international, regional and national regulations. For example, in regard to patents, making as a form of a patent exploitation is indicated by: Art. 28(1) of the TRIPS, Art. 25 of the Agreement on the Unified Patent Court, § 9 s. 1 of German Patentgesetz. From the practical point of view, 'manufacturing' is close in the meaning to term to 'making'.
16. *See* Adrian Niewęgłowski, *SPC manufacturing waiver, czyli przywilej wcześniejszej produkcji generycznej*, Dziennik Gazeta Prawna, E1-E4, n. 137 (2018) https://edgp.gazetaprawna.pl/wydanie/55583,17-lipca-2018/65250,Polpharma/2 (accessed 20 July 2019).

(4) the time framework of allowed stockpiling limited to the last six months of an SPC life (only with a view to entering the Union market upon protection expiry).

So, under a manufacturing waiver, making products for export is permitted throughout the entire SPC lifetime, but only for non-EU markets, whereas the manufacturing and stockpiling for day-one marketing in the EU are allowed, but only during the last six months before SPC expiry.

What is potentially important from the point of view of parties entitled to benefit from the derogation, but surprisingly hardly noticed whatsoever in the comments on the new standards, is that the derogation covers not only directly involved parties but also those indirectly involved in allowed activities. The amended Regulation adds a new point (f) to Article 1 with a broad definition of a 'maker' being described as 'the person, established in the Union, on whose behalf the making of a product, or a medicinal product containing that product, for the purpose of export to third countries or for the purpose of storing, is carried out'. As provided, this definition is not limited only to the generics or biosimilars producers and thus does not formally exclude other innovative companies, so direct competitors of SPC holders.[17]

In order to avoid any doubts, both the wording of Article 5 section 3 of the amended Regulation 469/2009 and the Preamble of the Regulation (EU) 2019/933 confirm that the following should not be covered by the exemption and thus considered as an SPC infringement: (1) placing a product, or a medicinal product made for the purposes determined above, on the market of a Member State or re-importation into the market of a Member State where a certificate is in force, either directly or indirectly after export; (2) act or activity carried out for the purpose of import of products into the

17. The discussion about the personal scope of another exemption that applies to SPC and patented medicinal products, namely the Bolar exemption, has been over recent years on the EU agenda, further to concerns in this regard raised by the court decisions in Poland and Germany, followed by relevant preliminary questions to ECJ on the interpretation of Art. 10(6) of the Directive 2001/83/EC of 6 November 2001 on the Community code relating to medicinal products for human use (OJ L 311 of 28 November 2001, p. 67). The questions were withdrawn by the German court from the CJEU register in July 2014 and the case was closed, thus the issue was not clarified by CJJEU. The questions were raised in the disputes between *Astellas Pharma Inc. v. Polfarma SA Pharmaceutical Works*, where the mentioned national courts dealt with the problem whether the Bolar exemption applies to third parties not directly involved in the process of obtaining marketing authorization, or only to manufacturing and supplying APIs for such purposes. In the decision of 23 October 2013 the Polish Supreme Court (IV CSK 92/13), OSP 2014/7-8, pp. 1008–1028), in line with the decision of the lower courts (Appeal Court in Gdańsk from 26 June 2013, I Ca320/12), LEX 1220452), ruled that the exemption provided by Art. 69 s. 1 item 4 of the Polish Industrial Property Law is only available to the testing entity itself, which has a direct interest in obtaining market approval for the generic drug. It is not extended to any third party that does not intend to apply for marketing authorization for the generic drug or conduct the necessary tests and trials for this purpose, but who merely manufactures the product according to the protected invention with the sole purpose of offering and selling it. The important issue of the beneficiaries of Bolar exemption has been recently clarified by the Polish legislator, who in the Law amending the Industrial Property Act of October 16, 2019 (O.J. 2309, 2019) decided to amend Art. 69 s. 1 item 4 by providing Bolar rule, by extending the scope of exempted activities also for 'third parties'.

Union merely for the purposes of repackaging and re-exporting; (3) storing for any purposes other than those set out in Regulation (EU) 2019/933.

To ensure the protection of the rights of certificate holders, the new SPC exemption is accompanied by a special safeguarding regime involving various 'proportionate, and transparency' measures, such as information obligation and due diligence requirements for 'makers', as a condition for benefiting from the exemption.[18]

First, the legality of the exempted acts is subject to fulfilling double notification obligations addressed to the SPC holder and the patent office in the Member State in which that making is to take place, which should ensure the transparency of permitted activities. According to amended Article 5 section 2 (b) and (c) of Regulation 469/2009, the maker is obliged to submit to the parties, through appropriate and documented means, a number of information items including, among others, the name and address of the producer, the purpose of production (export, storing or both), the Member State where production or storage takes place, the number and other details relating to the relevant SPC.[19] In the case of multiple locations for production activities, notification is required for each location (each Member State). The list of information items includes information which is supposed to help the SPC holder to monitor and verify whether the planned activities are performed in the allowed form and that they meet the requirements of Regulation (EU) 2019/933, and if necessary, the initiating of legal proceedings for non-compliance. The information provided should be used solely for this purpose but not involve the collection of confidential or commercially sensitive information.

The notification should take place within the required, alternative time limits: no later than three months before the start date of production in that Member State, or no later than three months before the first related act, prior to such production whichever is the earlier. The notification obligation of the maker is followed by the obligation of the competent authority to publish the notified information. As opposed to the Commission Proposal of the Regulation of 2015 with a short 14-day deadline for publication, the new Article 11 section 4 of Regulation (EU) 2019/933, does not determine a fixed time for publications, but nonetheless requires the publication of notified information 'as soon as possible' together with the date of notification of that

18. *See* Recital 20 of the Preamble the Regulation (EU) 2019/933.
19. A standard form for notification is provided in Annex 1-a of the Regulation. According to Art. 5 s. 5, the full list of required information being subject to notification includes:
    (a) the name and address of the maker;
    (b) an indication of whether the making is for the purpose of export, for the purpose of storing, or for the purpose of both export and storing;
    (c) the Member State in which the making and, if applicable, also the storing is to take place, and the Member State in which the first related act, if any, prior to that making is to take place;
    (d) the number of the certificate granted in the Member State of making, and the number of the certificate granted in the Member State of the first related act, if any, prior to that making; and
    (e) for medicinal products to be exported to third countries, the reference number of the marketing authorization, or the equivalent of such authorization, in each third country of export, as soon as it is publicly available.

information.[20] The national patent offices will be allowed to charge a fee for such notifications. The notification is aimed at disclosing information about exempted activities to third parties so that the SPC holder and the competitors will know the maker's intentions. It ensures better transparency of the exempted activities and reduces the risk of any illicit diversion of manufactured products onto the Union market during the term of the certificate. In practice, however, due to a short notice period involved, it will not significantly influence the business decisions of parties having access to this information.

Second, in order to ensure identification of products manufactured under an SPC exemption for export, Article 5 section 2 (d) of Regulation (EU) 2019/933 imposes labelling obligations on the 'maker' in the form of the requirement to use a special EU export logo affixed to the outer packaging of the product and, where feasible, to its immediate packaging, in the form provided for in the Regulation. The labelling obligation provided by the regulation should be without prejudice to the labelling requirements in force in third countries to which such labelled products are exported. The concept of mandatory labelling has practical value since this requirement provides a presumption that every product, including the logo, was produced according to the required standards and thus falls outside the SPC protection.

Third, manufacturers of SPC-protected products are subject to due diligence requirements as a condition for using the exemption. The obligation of information established in the Regulation 469/2009 is aimed at informing parties within the supply chain of the maker or in the downstream, that the act of making particular products is subject to activities allowed under the Regulation, namely exporting and storing and that any other acts, such as placing on the market, the import or re-import of the product performed during the life of the SPC could be considered as an infringement. The scope of this obligation extends to those having a contractual relationship with the maker, but only those objectively having the capacity to perform acts, such as placing on the market, importing, re-importing, here mainly distributors. As it has been correctly observed, the obligation should not extend in practice to subcontractors for such intermediaries who are merely involved in associated activities and providing technical support, such as packaging, transporting products manufactured under the control of the maker and his direct contractors under the exemption.[21]

The Regulation specifies the required form of meeting the obligation of informing contractors as by 'appropriate and documented means', in particular, contractual arrangements (written agreements). As with other safeguarding measures, this diligence requirement is an important condition for producers since failure to comply with them excludes the act of making and related acts performed by a third party from a safe harbour and allows the holders of an SPC to enforce their rights under general rules

20. The obligation applies accordingly to publication of the changed (updated) information.
21. *See* Miguel Vidal-Quadras Trias de Bes, *Analysis of the proposal for a Regulation of a manufacturing exception related to the SPC and aimed to make the European Industry Competitive*, 18 (2018) https://www.medicinesforeurope.com/wp-content/uploads/2018/09/Legal-opinion-on-proposal-of-EU-Regulation-on-SPC-manufacturing-exception-180913-2.pdf (accessed 12 July 2019).

provided in national regulations harmonized as regards to the available legal enforcement tools.

Finally, as highlighted in Recitals, the Regulation provides special safeguarding measures for SPC holders by rules regarding the applicability of manufacturing exemption depending on the granting status of SPC. The exemption will cover any SPC applied for on or after 1 July 2019 and 'to safeguard the rights of certificate holders' it will not apply to certificates that took effect before that date. The Regulation also applies, for a certain period, to SPCs that were applied for before the date of entry into force of this Regulation but have not taken effect before that date. To these SPCs, new rules will apply from 2 July 2022. This special regime supposes to ensure 'a progressive applicability', depending on the date on which it takes effect and, on its duration, and was introduced 'in order to ensure that the rights of certificate holders are not excessively restricted'. As explained in Recital 27 of the Preamble of the Regulation, such application of the exemption would allow the holder of a certificate that has been granted, but that has not yet taken effect by the date of the entry into force of this Regulation, a reasonable period of transition to adapt to the changed legal context, while at the same time ensuring that makers of generics and biosimilars can benefit effectively, without excessive delay, from the exemption.

The above-mentioned explanations setting out a timetable for the applicability of the manufacturing waiver do not seem to be fully consistent with the explanations contained in the same Preamble, declaring that the exemption does not affect the normal use of SPCs and does not interfere with the interests of SPC beneficiaries.

Apart from the obvious argument of non-retroactivity, it is also not entirely clear why the impact of the exemption to interests of existing and future SPC holders is justified differently, if the scope of the SPCs and the scope of a manufacturing exemption are the same for all medicinal products, regardless of when they obtain protection. The reason for not applying the exemption to existing SPCs is safeguarding of SPC holders' rights. The different reason for not unduly restricting such rights is given as the justification for the concept of a 'certain period of time' for SPCs that were applied for before the date of entry into force of the Regulation, but which have not yet taken effect before that date. One might also wonder why SPC holders need to adapt to the changed legal context and what relevant changes there are supposed to occur if the exemption is not intended to come into conflict with the normal exploitation of the product in the country in which the SPC is granted.

4 DEROGATION FROM EXCLUSIVITY OR EXEMPTION FROM CONFERRED RIGHTS?

A manufacturing waiver has become a part of the EU patent system, and most arguments raised during the proposal phase about its incompatibility with international standards have lost their validity, leaving ongoing discussions on its economic consequences and the future impact of the new SPC regime for the pharmaceutical market within the EU. However, it is still interesting to make some comments to Regulation (EC) 933/2019 from the legal point of view, as the construction of a manufacturing waiver is not fully obvious, and its legal nature may be important for the overall assessment of this institution.

Contrary to the 2018 Commission proposal of Article 4 which included a reference to 'exemption to rights conferred', the approved version of Article 5 section 2 of Regulation (EC) 933/2019 confirms the scope of the exclusivity defined by the SPC and provides 'a derogation' from SPC exclusivity. This wording differs from the traditional provisions introducing exemptions from IP rights, which usually refers to 'exemptions (limitations) from conferred rights'.[22] Even though the dictionary meaning of 'derogation' and 'exemption' is similar, and regards a special permission not to obey a rule, law, etc., a change from 'exemption' to 'derogation' during a legislative procedure for adopting a manufacturing waiver seems far from accidental.[23]

On the one hand, this softening of the wording could be interpreted as confirmation of a declared EC intention of 'recalibrating' and 'reconsidering' the scope of SPC exclusivity to eliminate the 'unintended consequence' of Regulation (EC) No 469/2009, rather than limiting it.[24] This kind of approach was supported by some commentators who argue that the provision introducing a manufacturing waiver constitutes a 'clarification of the protection granted by an SPC with only declaratory meaning', not the limitation of an exclusive right.[25] According to this view, SPC protection should be limited only to the protected substance as such, while its scope - determined by its purpose - should be limited only to the use of a protected product on a protected territory and only for the purposes covered by the market authorization.[26] This approach clarifies, however, only doubts regarding the legal qualification of acts involved the preparation of the substance for the same medical use authorized in the country granting the SPC and would not justify export as activity possibly infringing the SPC.[27] On the other hand, Article 5 section 2 of Regulation (EC) 933/2019 clearly limits the rights conferred by an SPC providing the list of activities which 'would otherwise require the consent of the SPC holder'. The legal consequence of the adoption of the provision so drafted is the same as of traditional patent exemption, namely ineffective enforcement of a legal exclusivity against excepted activities.

The qualification of manufacturing waiver as a traditional exemption of an IP right provokes another question about its assessment in light of the EU trade agreements and international standards dealing with exemptions.[28] From the beginning of

22. *See*, e.g., Art. 30 of TRIPS, Art. 27 of the UPC Agreement.
23. *See* report from 28 January 2019 on the amendments of the Parliament to the Commission proposal.
24. As is declared in Recital 30 of the Preamble, it is appropriate to introduce that exemption in order to increase the competitive position of makers of generics and biosimilars is established in the Union in third countries whose markets are in any event open to competition, 'whilst leaving the scope of the protection granted by the certificate in the Union untouched'.
25. *See* Study on the Legal Aspects of Supplementary Protection Certificates in the EU, Final Report, ed. Reto Hilty, Max Planck Institute for Innovation and Competition, 77, https://ec.europa.eu/docsroom/documents/29524 (accessed 19 June 2019 and quoted there CJEU, C-322/10 Medeva [2011] ECLI:EU:C:2011:773, Opinion of AG Trstenjak, para. 107.
26. Study on the Legal Aspects of Supplementary Protection Certificates in the EU, *supra* n. 25, at 77.
27. Study on the Legal Aspects of Supplementary Protection Certificates in the EU, *supra* n. 25, at 77.
28. *See* as an analysis of the incompatibility of a manufacturing waiver with bilateral and regional the EU trade agreement, White paper: legal analysis on how the 'manufacturing waiver' impacts

the legislative process, some commentators have argued that as a form of a patent exemption potentially negatively affecting the legitimate interests of SPC holders, any new SPC provision should be questioned as not compatible with the three-step provided by Article 30 of Trade-Related Aspects of Intellectual Property Rights (TRIPS).[29] As others argue, the TRIPS Agreement does not extend to SPCs as patent restoration.[30] According to a more balanced approach, obligations provided in Article 30 of TRIPS must be evaluated carefully and not applied directly to an SPC, due to the special (hybrid) character of the right.[31] The view as to the specific legal nature of SPC is supported by other authors who does not consider acts covered by an SPC manufacturing waiver as being in conflict with the normal exploitation of SPC-protected products because of no impact of such activities for a monopoly of SPC holders over putting protected products on the market (considered as a main form of use ensuring market monopoly and generating revenues).[32]

Indeed, there are no legitimate interests of SPC right holders in keeping competitors out of putting products on the EU market following the expiration of an SPC, as well as on markets of countries not covered by SPC protection. But it could be argued that from the economic perspective, a normal exploitation of SPC also covers manufacturing products for sales outside the EU after SPC expiry. Under the new regulation, SPC holders should compete on those markets with generic companies selling competitive products manufactured under SPC export waiver. The same economic argument is relevant for putting medicinal products on the EU markets after an SPC expires and competing with generic companies ready for market expansion with stockpiled production.

Despite these concerns, the EC took a clear position regarding the compatibility of export and stockpiling waivers with a normal exploitation of SPC. As explained in the amending Regulation (EC) 933/2019, it is ensured by limiting the scope of the exemption to making for the purpose of export outside the Union or to making for the purpose of storing, and to acts strictly necessary for such making and, not interfering with the core exclusive right of the certificate holder to making that product for the purpose of placing it on the Union market during the term of the certificate.[33]

The reference to a normal exploitation test as well as balancing the interests of right holders, competitors and patients included in the Preamble of Regulation (EC) 933/2019 could confirm that the new exemption was verified by the TRIPS three-step

the European patent extension mechanism, EFPIA report, https://www.efpia.eu/media/288698/white-paper-the-impact-of-the-manufacturing-waiver-on-the-european-patent-extension-mechanism.pdf (accessed 21 June 2019).

29. Miquel Montañá, *Would the proposed 'manufacturing waiver really pass the TRIPS test?*, 30 May 2018, Kluwer Patent Blog, http://patentblog.kluweriplaw.com/2018/05/30/proposed-manufacturing-waiver-really-pass-trips-test-2/.
30. As suggested, SPCs are not the object of regulation in the TRIPS Agreement, thus they are not subject to the TRIPS Agreement, including Art. 30. *See* Miguel Vidal-Quadras, Analysis of EU Regulation 2019/933 on the SPC Manufacturing Waiver Exception, IIC 8 (2019), pp. 981-984.
31. *See* Study on the Legal Aspects of Supplementary Protection Certificates in the EU, *supra* n. 25, at 623.
32. *See* Niewęgłowski, *supra* n. 16.
33. *See* Recital 12.

test scrutiny.[34] So, it might be argued that the exemption was accepted in the adopted form rather because it met the requirements of the three-step test and not because Article 30 of TRIPS did not apply to it at all.

In this context, the above-mentioned arguments that TRIPS would apply to patents but not to SPCs could be considered less convincing in light of the following arguments. First, since Article 5 section 1 of the Regulation equates patent and SPC in terms of legal effects, both in terms of the same scope of rights covered as well as of the same limitations, SPC can be considered as a patent-like form of protection covered by TRIPS. Second, as far as there are no doubts that traditional patent exemptions like a research exemption or Bolar exemption apply to SPCs and the TRIPS test applies to them with no exclusions for SPCs, it could be questionable why TRIPS should not apply to the new SPC exemption, such as the manufacturing waiver.[35] Also, a different approach can be mentioned, confirming the compatibility of the amended SPC Regulation with the conditions of Article 30, although the TRIPS Agreement is not applicable to SPCs.[36]

5 REVIEWING ARGUMENTS: A CHANCE OF INCREASING COMPETITIVENESS OR RISK OF AFFECTING INNOVATION?

The pharmaceutical industry, as the most competitive sector in the EU and as a leader in R&D, plays an important role in the development of an innovative EU economy.[37] Innovation in the pharmaceutical sector understood as an application of better solutions that meet new market and consumers' requirements and needs is a broad concept. It covers incentives and disincentives to undertake innovative research, including IP protection, innovative business models implemented by the market players, level of employment in the sector, innovative healthcare system ensuring access of patients to the most advanced, latest medicines and treatments. As far as R&D and innovation are sources of competitive advantages on the EU pharmaceutical market, the competitiveness of pharmaceutical companies is also directly linked with innovation.[38] Thus, an analysis of the possible (positive or negative) impact of changes in the sector's regulatory framework such as the discussed manufacturing waiver,

34. For detailed analysis of each three-step test condition in case of SPC manufacturing waiver, *see*: Xavier Seuba,Mariano Genovesi, Pedro Roffe, A Manufacturing for Export Exception in B. Mercurio and D. Kim (eds), *Contemporary Issues in Pharmaceutical Patent Law: Setting the Framework and Exploring Policy Options*, Routledge, 2017, pp. 173-181.
35. As a point of reference for a discussion on a similar export waiver for patents, *see* the comments on the Doha declaration with export waiver, Hiroko Yamane, Interpreting TRIPS. Globalization of Intellectual Property Rights and Access to Medicines, 315 (2011).
36. *See* Miguel Vidal-Quadras, *supra* n. 30, at 982-984.
37. As estimations confirm, pharmaceuticals and biotechnology sector keeps the first position in the R&D ranking with the total R&D investment of 17.7% of total R&D spending among other technology-based sectors, *see* EU Industrial R&D Investment Scoreboard, European Commission, 2012, p. 43.
38. *See* Alfonso Gambardella, Luigi Orsenigo, Fabio Pammolli, *Global competitiveness in pharmaceuticals. A European perspective*, the European Commission, Luxembourg (2000), pp. 36-57.

should involve different perspectives covering all the above-mentioned components influencing the EU innovation system.

According to the EC position, the manufacturing exemption 'intends to restore the level playing field between EU-based generics and biosimilars manufacturers and non-EU-based ones, which would be beneficial for the competitiveness of the former and the European economy as a whole, while maintaining the current high level of IP protection in the EU'.[39]

It aims at promoting the competitiveness of the Union, thereby 'enhancing growth and job creation in the internal market and contributing to a wider supply of products under uniform conditions'. As estimated, the expected benefits envisaged by the EC also include EUR 1 billion net additional sales per year and up to 25,000 new jobs over 10 years.[40] According to the EC view, the new regulation should be beneficial not only for generic and biosimilar companies but also for patients (due to speedier access upon SPC expiry to more affordable medicines) and for health systems.[41] As the regulation declares, all the above benefits should be achieved 'while bearing in mind that intellectual property rights remain one of the cornerstones of innovation, competitiveness and growth in the internal market'.[42]

Next to an optimistic assumption on the positive impact of a manufacturing waiver on competitiveness and no distortion for innovation and justifications for a new SPC regulation, there are arguments and evidence from inside of the sector against this reform.

The adopted version of the amending SPC regulation, offering a broader scope of a manufacturing waiver including not only export but also stockpiling exemption is welcome to the generic sector.[43] Generic companies could, however, still lobby for the removal of anti-diversion measures, considered as anti-competitive, unjustified and unnecessary forcing generic/biosimilar companies to cover additional costs.

Not surprisingly, the reaction from innovators for the final scope of the Regulation proposal is proportionally unwelcoming. As the results of public consultations prove, the majority of originators are against the introduction of the SPC manufacturing

39. Recital 9 of the Preamble of Regulation (EC) 933/2019.
40. *See* Raphaël De Coninck, Elina Koustoumpardi, Roman Fischer, Guillaume Débarbat, *Study Assessing the economic impacts of changing exemption provisions during patent and SPC protection in Europe*, 2 (2017), https://publications.europa.eu/en/publication-detail/-/publication/6e4ce9f8-aa41-11e7-837e-01aa75ed71a1/language-en (accessed 29 July 2019).
41. Recital 7 of the Preamble of Regulation (EC) 933/2019. *See also* EXECUTIVE SUMMARY OF THE IMPACT ASSESSMENT Accompanying the document Proposal for a Regulation of the European Parliament and of the Council amending Regulation (EC) 469/2009 concerning the supplementary protection certificate for medicinal products [COM(2018) 317 final] – [SEC(2018) 246 final] – [SWD(2018) 240 final] – [SWD(2018) 242 Brussels, 28 May 2018 SWD(2018) 241 final], Commission Staff Working document, https://eur-lex.europa.eu/legal-content/EN/TXT/PDF/?uri=CELEX:52018SC0241&from=EN (accessed 21 June 2019).
42. Recitals 7 and 8 of the Preamble of Regulation (EC) 933/2019.
43. As argued during the discussion of the draft EC proposal for amending Regulation of 2018 by the organization representing such companies (e.g., Medicines for Europe), in the initially proposed form, an SPC manufacturing waiver would be practically useless and would not produce the expected benefits for the producers of generics/biosimilars or patients, thus the sector called for an extension of exempted activities for stockpiling (introduction of the 'EU day-1 launch'), as well as the immediate applicability of the SPC manufacturing waiver.

waiver in the EU with the view that the current SPC framework does not put EU-based generics/biosimilars manufacturers at a particular disadvantage when compared with foreign-based manufacturers, both in the case of exporting generics/biosimilars outside the Union, as well as placing generics/biosimilars on the EU market after SPC protection expires.[44] Studies commissioned by originators also question the correctness of the estimations declared by the EC, proving that the economic results of introducing a manufacturing waiver in terms of an increase in revenues or job places are much lower than declared, if any at all.[45]

The amended SPC regulation is also criticized as having a negative impact on patients and their access to the most innovative medicines and – what is important – the innovation in the sector.

As argued, the analysed modification of SPC standards by introducing the manufacturing waiver weakens the commitment to IP on the part of innovative companies and causes erosion of the IPR system, which would disincentivize originators and innovation in Europe.[46] According to the studies and reports representing the interest of innovators, the new privilege sends out a negative message to innovators and investors, impacts on legal certainty. It also increases the risk of not generating envisaged returns from highly costly investments in the development of new drugs and thus decreases the incentives for R&D investment and innovation in the pharmaceutical sector within the EU. As the European Federation of Pharmaceutical Industries and Associations (EFPIA) insists, allowing the stockpiling of generic medicines while the innovator medicine is still under SPC protection will make Europe a less attractive destination for life science investment.[47] As indicated, new exemptions put investments in new medical products at risk and will kill off small biotech companies that depend upon strong IP portfolios to attract investors, reduce sales of innovators outside the EU and jeopardize patients' access to innovative treatment. For all the above reasons, the reform is considered by innovators as detrimental to future innovation.

Undoubtedly, the message behind introducing SPC sui generis protection for medicinal products was strengthening the patent exclusivity by a possibility for prolongation of the effective life of the pharmaceutical patent, considered as an

44. *See* Summary of the replies to the public consultation on Supplementary Protection Certificates and patent research exemption for sectors whose products are subject to regulated market authorizations, accompanying the document Proposal for a Regulation of the European Parliament and of the Council amending Regulation (EC) 469/2009 concerning the supplementary protection certificate for medicinal products, Brussels, 28 May 2018 SWD(2018) 242 final Commission Staff Working document, https://eur-lex.europa.eu/legal-content/EN/TXT/PDF/?uri=CELEX:52018SC0242&from=EN, (accessed 31 June 2019).
45. Meir Pugatch, David Torstensson, Ma'ayan Laufer, *Unintended Consequences: How Introducing a Manufacturing and Export Exemption to Supplementary Protection Certificates Would Weaken Global Standards of IP Protection and Result in Direct Losses to Europe's Research-Based Biopharmaceutical Industry*, 5-12 (2017), https://papers.ssrn.com/sol3/papers.cfm?abstract_id=3051545 (accessed 31 June 2019).
46. *See* Mathias Bauer, *Unintended and Unattended Consequences: The Opportunity Costs of Reducing Exclusivity Rights for Intellectual Property*, ECIPE Policy Brief, 7 (2017).
47. Jorge Mestre-Ferrandiz, Mikel Berdud and Adrian Towse, Review of CRA's Report *Assessing the economic impacts of changing exemption provisions during patent and SPC protection in Europe*, Consulting Report for EFPIA, 2018, https://www.efpia.eu/media/361669/ohe-consulting-report-cra-review-final.pdf (accessed 5 Jun. 2019).

incentive for further investments in timely and costly R&D and patent protection. Based on such assumption, it may be argued that a reduction of exclusivity of SPCs by activities involving protected products during the SPC protection period can have the opposite effect, namely act as a disincentive for engaging in innovative research.

However, two issues need to be distinguished: the length of protection as an incentive to innovation and, more generally, the scope of such protection not only determined by a term of IP right duration.

As regards to a duration of protection of the medicinal product, it is very difficult to determine whether SPCs correct the distortion of research incentives associated with fixed 20 years' patent protection, considered as too short to generate profits enough for covering high costs of research on innovative drugs.[48] As recent studies suggest, the exact length of exclusivity period and the interaction with other incentives in the context of stimulating innovation is unclear and depend on a number of factors, such as the IP incentives and frameworks in place in each jurisdiction.[49] According to the findings, the potential for stimulating significant R&D would have a clearly defined statutory market exclusivity period.[50]

With the view for this approach, it could be relevant to discuss on how to ensure the legal certainty of protection of SPC holders within limits introduced by the exemption for avoiding abuse of a manufacturing waiver and reducing the risk of infringement of their SPCs in the Union. Next to legal measures such as labelling and notification, further preclusion measures may be developed as a market standard, e.g., differentiation of drugs manufactured for export from those produced for the SPC protection market. (e.g., the colour of the drug itself should be different from that sold in the EU), inspection rights to monitor the quantity of the drugs being produced for export, implementation of a 'track and trace' system for exported products.

While analysing the relation between the scope of SPC protection as an incentive for innovative research and developing innovative pharmaceutical products, as well as the possible negative impact of limiting it through the manufacturing waiver, a patent-induced-theory can be noted as a reference. It identifies a link between the level of innovativeness of an invention, patent protection as an incentive for developing such invention and the justified scope of the protection for the invention. According to this theory, revolutionary inventions with large but unpredictable commercialization potential need a strong incentive to create them, without which they would not ever be created. This incentive requires broad protection, compensating uncertainty as regards to the future market opportunities for the commercialization of such an invention.[51] The theory is surely relevant to innovative pharmaceutical products with often breakthrough application.

48. *See* Margaret Kyle, *Economic Analysis of Supplementary Protection Certificates in Europe*, 31-32 (2017) https://ec.europa.eu/info/publications/economic-analysis-supplementary-protection-certificates-europe_el (accessed 27 June 2019).
49. *Supra* n. 3, at 57.
50. *Supra* n. 3, at 57.
51. *See* Matthew Fisher, *Fundamentals of patent law: Interpretation and scope of protection*, (2007), pp. 139-141.

Also, the traditional J. Schumpeter theory of economic development is relevant to be mentioned here, as dealing with 'creative destruction' as a force for development and innovation. It adopts the approach of the primacy of innovation over inventiveness and the assumption that even if the economic potential of an invention does not result from the possibility of its protection within the patent system, the functioning of such a system is justified because the investment related to the creation of an invention and offering it to society would not be undertaken without it because of the risk of free use of an innovative product by other entities.[52]

Even, there are no standardized economic tools and models helping to verify the optimal protection period and the most effective incentive to innovate, the conclusions of some authors suggest that optimal protection can only be achieved if a balance is struck between the incentive to innovate and the safeguarding benefits of society in terms of subsequent access to innovation.[53] Exemptions from exclusive rights such as manufacturing waiver are essential to ensure such a balance and benefits of society. From that point of view, adoption of the SPC manufacturing waiver is in line with current trends in the EU to extend exemptions in the area of patent law (as the most relevant for SPC protection), for better balancing the interests of patent holders and third parties. In this context, new forms of limitations of patent rights provided by the Agreement on a Unified Patent Court should be mentioned, including the exemption for interoperability (Article 27(k)), the research privilege of the breeder (Article 27(c)), exceptions in favour of agricultural production of agricultural products (Article 27(j) and (j)).[54] Discussions within the EU on a further reduction in protection concern, in particular, the pharmaceutical sector and its key Bolar rule.[55] The trend towards specific patent law arrangements applicable to this sector is also visible at the national level, as evidenced by the new regulation on the use of patented inventions for the purpose of health technology assessment (HTA).[56] This issue is also on the EU agenda.[57]

52. *More* Iurii Bazhal, *The Theory of Economic Development of J.A. Schumpeter: Key Features*, https://mpra.ub.uni-muenchen.de/69883/ (accessed, 30 October 2019), pp. 1-14.
53. *See* Vincenzo Denicolò, *Patent Race and the Optimal Patent Breadth and Length*, Journal of Industrial Economics, 44 (1996), pp. 249-265.
54. OJ. 2013/C 175/01. Even the UPC Agreement is not in force yet, some countries have already decided to include exemptions in national patent regulation, e.g., UK, Belgium.
55. Summary of the replies to the public consultation on Supplementary Protection Certificates and patent research exemption for sectors whose products are subject to regulated market authorizations. Accompanying the document Proposal for a Regulation of the European Parliament and of the Council amending Regulation (EC) 469/2009 concerning the supplementary protection certificate for medicinal product, Brussels, 28 May 2018 SWD(2018) 242 final, https://eur-lex.europa.eu/legal-content/EN/TXT/PDF/?uri=CELEX:52018SC0242&from=EN (accessed 30 June 2019).
56. Art. 60(5) (d) UK Patent Act.
57. Proposal for a Regulation of the European Parliament and the Council on health technology assessment and amending Directive 2011/24/EU (Text with EEA relevance) [SWD(2018) 41 final] - [SWD(2018) 42 final]; Brussels, 31 January 2018 COM(2018) 51 final 2018/0018 (COD);. *Impact Assessment to evaluate options for optimising the legal framework concerning Supplementary Protection Certificates (SPCs) and patent research exemptions for sectors whose products are subject to regulated market authorizations*, 2 (2017) http://ec.europa.eu/smart-regulation/roadmaps/docs/2017_grow_051_supplementary_protection_certificates_en.pdf (accessed 30 Jun. 2019).

However, as an example of these trends, the manufacturing waiver deserves special attention. In contrast to the existing and proposed exemption limiting a patent as an exclusive right, justified by values such as freedom of research, health protection, including access to cheaper medicines, protection of investments of bona fide use before filing a patent application by another party, the rationale for an SPC exemption is quite different. It strongly emphasizes the protection of the competitiveness of the EU generic sector and the protection of jobs and the implementation of employment policies in the EU. These are not strictly the individual objectives of the IP system, but rather elements of the EU's general economic policy.

Optimization of employment in the pharmaceutical sector can be considered as an element of broadly understood innovation of the sector, but a *ratio legis* of restricting exclusive rights to increase competitiveness and level of employment still may be subject of further discussion. The assessment is also relevant to the point of view of the possible impact of the manufacturing waiver for EU health system and patients. Under Denicolò's theory of balancing the incentive to innovate by the safeguarding benefits of society, relevant could be the discussion on the impact of the SPC manufacturing waiver for the access of patients to innovative medicinal products. Although there is undoubtedly room for a further exchange of legal arguments about the legal status, construction and admissibility of manufacturing waiver, the entry into force of the new regulation makes further debate pointless, at least until a review of the application of the new provisions by the Commission has taken place.[58] What remains unclear is the question of the future impact and consequences of the new exemption for the future operation of the EU's pharmaceutical sector. In light of the different approaches supported by conflicting legal arguments, economic data and estimations, until the amended Regulation is in operation, it is difficult to make binding conclusions and assessment on the actual positives or negatives of SPC manufacturing waiver for both innovative and generic companies, patients and the EU market as such.

To make a binding assessment on the effect of the manufacturing waiver, more evidence-based on future market data is required to prove that introducing the manufacturing waiver will truly impact the amount of exported medicinal products of EU-based companies, both in regard to the increase of export of generic drugs and the possible decrease of export of innovative drugs. For the moment, the decrease in export

58. According to Art. 21a of the amended Regulation (EU)No 469/2009, no later than five years after the date referred to in Art. 5(10), and every five years thereafter, the Commission shall carry out an evaluation of Art. 5(2) to (9) and Art. 11 in order to assess whether the objectives of those provisions have been achieved, and present a report on the main findings to the European Parliament, the Council and the European Economic and Social Committee. The evaluation should pay special attention to the effects of making for the purpose of storing in order to place that product and verify whether the period provided for the making of generics and biosimilars for the purpose of storing is sufficient to achieve the objective of the EU day-one entry, including its effects on public health. According to Recital 28 of the Preamble of the Regulation as a part of evaluation, the EC should 'study an impact of the exemption on research and production of innovative medicines in the Union by certificate holders and consider the balance between the different interests at stake, in particular as regards public health, public expenditure and, in this context, access to medicines within the Union'. 'It should also study whether the period provided for as regards the making of generics and biosimilars for the purpose of storing is sufficient to achieve the objective of EU day-one entry, including its effects on public health.'

of innovative drugs is identified as having negative consequences for innovators and innovation.

Success in the export strategy of EU-based companies depends upon various factors: on the situation in the export countries regarding the earlier expiration date of existing SPC protection there, distribution and marketing opportunities, price level, local patient preferences, and incentives for local producers. As research confirms, also additional conditions impact on the EU exports of pharmaceuticals, including the economic size of the partner country, the distance between the EU and the importing countries, size of the healthcare sector of the partner country.[59] What is especially relevant for the discussion is that the level of IP protection of the receiving country, not the country of export, is identified as having a positive effect on the EU exports.[60]

The same is true for stockpiling. As indicated in recent studies, this activity is one among a number of determinants of the timing of generic entry, alongside other factors including ones possibly associated with obtaining market authorization for medicinal products to be put on the market, pricing and reimbursement negotiations; demand- and supply-side incentive policies, the size of the market pre-protection expiry (the higher the probability of generic entry, the speedier generic entry is), the level of competitiveness on the market (the more competitive a market is, the lower the likelihood of generic entry).[61]

From an economic point of view, future market data can objectively confirm whether a new institution is truly neutral or will cause a decrease in the export of original products outside the EU as a result of competition for market share with generic and biosimilar products manufactured for export in the EU during the period of SPC protection.[62]

However, existing economic analyses try to prove that the manufacturing waiver will push manufactures of originator drugs and innovative biosimilars to develop and adopt new business models and strategies, and new opportunity risk assessment, possibly by containing R&D activities or increasing revenues by increasing drug prices during the time of market exclusivity. This is considered as one of the unexpected side-effects of introducing changes in the SPC regime.[63] More pessimistic estimations on unintended consequences of amended SPC regulation predicts the detrimental effect of SPC exemption in the loss of jobs and investments in R&D within Europe and aggravation of international standards of IP protection.[64]

59. *See* Ludivine Blanc, *The European Pharmaceutical Industry in a Global Economy: what drives EU exports of pharmaceuticals?*, Bruges European Economic Research Papers 31 (2015), pp. 26-27.
60. *Ibid.*, pp. 26-27.
61. Jorge Mestre-Ferrandiz & Mikel Berdud and Adrian Towse, Review of CRA's Report, *Assessing the economic impacts of changing exemption provisions during patent and SPC protection in Europe*, Consulting Report for EFPIA, 78-79 (2018) https://www.efpia.eu/media/361669/ohe-consulting-report-cra-review-final.pdf (accessed 26 June 2019).
62. *See* Ramya Logendra, Per Troein, *Assessing the impact of proposals for a Supplementary Protection Certificate (SPC) Manufacturing Exemption in the EU*, https://www.efpia.eu/media/288516/efpia-spc-report_120917_v3_10217-002.pdf (accessed 26 June 2019).
63. *See* Mathias Bauer, *Unintended and Unattendent Consequences: The Opportunity Costs of Reducing Exclusivity Rights for Intellectual Property*, ECIPE Policy Brief, 7 (2017), pp. 12-13.
64. *See* Meir Pugatch, David Torstensson, Ma'ayan Laufer, Unintended Consequences: *How Introducing a Manufacturing and Export Exemption to Supplementary Protection Certificates Would*

For the time being, the question as to whether the amended SPC regulation is a mechanism for increasing the competitiveness of generic companies or rather a legal tool detrimental to innovation in the pharmaceutical sector in the EU remains unanswered. Without a doubt, the adopted new legal tool requires further investigation and verification once it becomes fully operational.

Weaken Global Standards of IP Protection and Result in Direct Losses to Europe's Research-Based Biopharmaceutical Industry, 5-12 (2017), https://papers.ssrn.com/sol3/papers.cfm?abstract_id=3051545 (accessed 31 June 2019).

PART II Patents and Plants

CHAPTER 7

Rethinking IP Protection for Plants? Revisiting the Exclusivity-Access Balance Through the Type-Token Ontology

Geertrui Van Overwalle

1 INTRODUCTION

Intellectual property (IP) theory is based on the balancing of exclusivity and access.[1] Exclusivity is conceived as an instrument to foster innovation, whereas access is contemplated as an instrument to enable others to further improve innovation. Over the past years, concern has been expressed that the balance of exclusivity and access is tilting over to exclusivity in the plant area.[2] It has been argued that part of the root of this phenomenon is the expansion of the patent system, both in terms of patentable subject matter and the number of patents granted.[3] On the other hand, it is claimed that

1. Kur, A. & Schovsbo, J., 'Expropriation or Fair Game for All? The Gradual Dismantling of the IP Exclusivity Paradigm', in Kur, A. & Levin, M. (eds), *Intellectual Property Rights in a Fair World Trade System*, Edward Elgar, 2011, 408; Osenga, K., 'Get the Balance Right!: Squaring Access with Patent Protection', 35 *Global Business & Development Law Journal*, 2012, 309; Peukert, A., 'Intellectual Property as an End in Itself?', 33 *EIPR*, 2011, 67-71.
2. *See* Louwaars, N., Dons, H., Van Overwalle, G., Raven, H., Arundel, A., Eaton, D. & Nelis, A., *Breeding Business: The Future of Plant Breeding in the Light of Developments in Patent Rights and Plant Breeder's Rights*, Wageningen, Centre for Genetic Resources, 2009, 61 (CGN Rapport 2009-14 EN) (study available at http://ssrn.com/abstract=1720088, last visited 30 July 2019); P.H. Feindt and the Advisory Board on Biodiversity and Genetic Resources at the Federal Ministry of Food, Agriculture and Consumer Protection (BMLEV), *Biopatents – A Threat to the Use and Conservation of Agrobiodiversity?* Position Paper of the Advisory Board on Biodiversity and Genetic Resources at the Federal Ministry of Food, Agriculture and Consumer Protection (translation of German original paper) 26 May 2010.
3. Van Overwalle G. & van Zimmeren, E., 'Functions and Limits of Patent Law', in Claes, E., Devroe, W. & Keirsbilck, B. (eds), *Facing the Limits of the Law*, Springer, 2009, 415-442, and the references cited there.

guaranteed access to variation and IP-protected plant material, is essential for the development of new plants and food security in the long run.[4]

The present chapter aims to understand the exclusivity/access balance in the particular field of plant breeding through the lens of the prevailing type/token ontology in IP law. Furthermore, the chapter aims to assess how public and private ordering mechanisms can assist in re-balancing the exclusion/access in the plant area.

The chapter is structured as follows. First, we will examine the different forms of plant breeding to assist the novice in the prevailing technologies applied in this area (section 2). Next, we will provide a brief overview of the characteristics of the two proponent IP regimes at stake – plant breeder's rights law and patent law – in terms of eligible subject matter, protectability requirements and scope of rights (section 3). Then we will address the core of the present chapter, and analyse the effect of differing exclusivity/access regimes in plant breeder's rights law and patent law through the lens of the type/token ontology, and examine what the impact is of different gradations of exclusivity on further breeding (section 4). Last but not least, we will examine how legal architectures can craft more openness within and beyond patent law (section 5). We wind up with some concluding thoughts (section 6).

A multitude of concepts and definitions will come to the fore in the present chapter. 'Access' refers to access to *and* use of IP-protected technology. The terms 'access' and 'openness' are used alternately. 'Universal access' is defined in relation to *scope*, where access and use are awarded to an indefinite number of users and where nobody can be excluded. Universal openness can be established in the patent realm by licenses of right or patent pledges.[5] On the other hand, 'sustainable access' is defined in relation to *continuity, virality, infectiousness, or perpetuity*, where openness is passed on from one inventor/improver to another, thus establishing a chain of openness which can be endorsed amongst follow-on improvers. Procedural contamination can be infused by copyleft in the copyright field or grant-back mechanisms in the patent area.[6]

2 PLANT BREEDING TECHNIQUES

In the area of plant breeding, a common distinction is made between 'traditional' and 'modern' breeding techniques. Quite recently, 'new breeding techniques' (NBTs) have entered the stage.

---

4. *See* Louwaars, N., Dons, H., Van Overwalle, G., Raven, H., Arundel, A., Eaton, D. & Nelis, A., *Breeding Business: The Future of Plant Breeding in the Light of Developments in Patent Rights and Plant Breeder's Rights*, Wageningen, Centre for Genetic Resources, 2009, 61 and the references cited there (CGN Rapport 2009-14 EN) (study available at http://ssrn.com/abstract=1720088, last visited 30 July 2019).
5. *See* Van Overwalle, G., 'Inventing Inclusive Patents. From Old to New Open Innovation', in P. Drahos, G. Ghidini and H. Ullrich (eds), 1 *Kritika: Essays on Intellectual Property*, Edward Elgar, 2015, 206-277.
6. *See* Van Overwalle, G., 'Inventing Inclusive Patents. From Old to New Open Innovation', in P. Drahos, G. Ghidini and H. Ullrich (eds), 1 *Kritika: Essays on Intellectual Property*, Edward Elgar, 2015, 206-277.

Traditional or conventional plant breeding is based on controlled pollination and selection. The plant breeder artificially crosses different selected plants, and from the progeny of the cross he picks out plants with the best combinations of desirable characteristics, and which he then breeds in to obtain a pure line that breeds true. Conventional methods of plant breeding have been remarkably successful in generating improved varieties of many of the major world crops. Most of the improvement has been in yield and has occurred through the breeding of lines which are resistant to pests and diseases, which can tolerate stressful environments and which are larger or have heavier croppers, apart from improvements in the intrinsic quality of the crop, such as taste, protein content, etc.[7]

Modern plant breeding applies molecular techniques, including recombinant Deoxyribonucleic Acid (DNA) technology (r-DNA-t), to introduce new hereditary characteristics into plant cells, which are then grown into full-bodied plants.[8] Recombinant DNA technology is a technique to move genetic material from one organism to another; in other words, a technique that 'recombines' specific DNA fragments from different organisms.[9] Most often, exogenous DNA is directly transferred into the plant cell by use of cloning vectors derived from bacterial plasmids (notably those derived from the Ti-plasmid of the plant pathogen *Agrobacterium tumefaciens*). This definition sets the scene for the basic steps of a recombinant DNA experiment. First of all, the DNA to be inserted (called foreign DNA) and a suitable vehicle for transmission (called vector DNA) are joined, resulting in a composite recombinant DNA molecule. The second step is to introduce the composite recombinant DNA molecule into a suitable plant cell, after which the foreign DNA integrates with the plant DNA.

Today, new plant breeding techniques (NBTs) have been added to the technical toolbox of breeders.[10] Commonly accepted NBTs of major importance include agro-infiltration, cisgenesis, grafting, meganuclease, oligonucleotide-directed mutagenesis,

7. There is a vast literature on this topic – the reader might care to consult the following books and articles Khush, G.S., 'Green Revolution: The Way Forward', 2 *Nature Reviews Genetics*, 2001, 815-822; Tester, M. & Langridge, P., 'Breeding Technologies to Increase Crop Production in a Changing World', 327 *Science*, 2010, 818-822.
8. There is a vast literature on this subject – the jurist might care to consult the following books and articles: Primrose, S.B., *Modern Biotechnology*, Oxford, Blackwell Scientific Publications, 1987, 137-162; Watson, J.D., Tooze, J. & Kurtz, D.T., *Recombinant DNA. A Short Course.* Freeman & Company, 1983, 164-175.
9. *See* Watson, J.D., Tooze, J. & Kurtz, D.T., *Recombinant DNA. A Short Course*, in *Scientific American Books*, Freeman & Company, 1983, 243; Winnacker, E.-L., *From Genes to Clones. Introduction to Gene Technology*, VCH Verlagsgesellschaft, 1987, 1.
10. *See* Lusser, M. & Rodríguez Cerezo, E., *Comparative Regulatory Approaches for New Plant Breeding Techniques Workshop Proceedings*, European Commission JRC Institute for Prospective Technological Studies, 2012, 31 p. *Also see* Lusser, M. et al., *New Plant Breeding Techniques: State-of-the-Art and Prospects for Commercial Development*, European Commission JRC Institute for Prospective Technological Studies (IPTS) in cooperation with the JRC Institute for Health and Consumer Protection, 2011, 109-112 (and the references cited there). *Also see New Techniques in Agricultural Biotechnology*, European Commission Directorate-General for Research and Innovation Unit RTD.01 – Scientific Advice Mechanism (SAM), 2017, 56-70 (available at https://ec.europa.eu/research/sam/pdf/topics/explanatory_note_new_techniques_agricultural_biotechnology.pdf#view=fit&pagemode=none, last visited October 15 2018).The New Breeding Techniques (NBT) Platform is a coalition of SMEs, large industry and prominent academic and research institutes, striving to achieve regulatory clarity on whether or not such

reverse breeding, RNA-directed DNA Methylation, and ZINC finger nuclease techniques.

The long-range objectives of traditional breeding, modern plant breeding and NBTs are exactly the same: the creation of new plants with increased vigour and yield, the incorporation of value-added traits, and the development of disease, herbicide and pesticide-resistant crops. However, the major advantage of recombinant methods, as compared to conventional breeding, is that in this way characteristics can be introduced more quickly and that totally new characteristics, which do not exist in any member of the same plant family, or even in any plant, can be inserted.

3 IP PROTECTION REGIMES

At present, plant-breeding achievements can be protected with plant breeder's rights or with patents, depending on the subject matter under consideration. Plant breeder's rights mainly protect plant *varieties*, whereas patents provide protection for *plants*.

3.1 Plant Breeder's Rights[11]

The Trade-Related Aspects of Intellectual Property Rights (TRIPS) Agreement[12] prescribes that Members shall provide for the protection of plant varieties either by patents or by an effective sui generis system or by any combination thereof (Article 27 (3) (b)). In the context of TRIPS, it was usually understood that the reference in Article 27 (3) (b) to a sui generis system pertained to the system of plant breeder's rights, based on the International Convention for the Protection of New Varieties of Plants of 1961,[13] which created a Union for the Protection of New Varieties of Plants, which is commonly known under its French abbreviation UPOV (*Union pour la Protection des Obtentions Végétales*).[14] The UPOV Convention was drastically revised in 1991.

NBTs are to be defined as resulting in genetically modified organisms (GMO) (*see* http://www.nbtplatform.org/, last visited, 15 October 2018).

11. This section only provides a brief introduction to plant breeder's rights law. The interested reader might care to consult the following monographs for a more in-depth analysis: Janis, M.D., Jervis, H.H. & Peet, R., *Intellectual Property Law of Plants*, OUP, 2014; Llewelyn, M. & Adcock, M., *European Plant Intellectual Property*, Hart Publishing, 2006, 578 p.; Metzger, A. & Zech, H., *Sortenschutzrecht*, Verlag C.H. Beck, 2016, 988 p.; van der Kooij, P., *Introduction to the EC Regulation on Plant Variety Protection*, Kluwer Law International, 1997, 248 p.; Würtenberger, G., Van der Kooij, P., Kiewiet, B. & Ekvad, M., *European Union Plant Variety Protection*, OUP, 2016, 368 p.
12. Agreement on Trade-Related Aspects of Intellectual Property Rights (TRIPS Agreement), included as an Annex to the WTO Agreement, 15 April 1994 (*see* https://www.wto.org/english/docs_e/legal_e/27-trips.pdf, last visited 29 April 2020).
13. *See* Gervais, D., *The TRIPS Agreement: Drafting History and Analysis*, Sweet & Maxwell, 2003, 227-234, especially last paragraph on p. 229.
14. For a detailed historic (1940 up to today) and comparative (EU versus US) account of plant breeder's rights protection, the interested reader might wish to consult Van Overwalle, G., 'Patent Protection for Plants: a Comparison of American and European Approaches', 39 *IDEA-Journal of Law and Technology* (USA), 1999, 143-194 and the references cited there; Van Overwalle, G., *The Legal Protection of Biotechnological Inventions in Europe and in the United States: Current Framework and Future Developments*, in *Leuven Law Series*, University Press,

The UPOV Convention formed the basis for a system of European plant breeder's rights. The EC Regulation on Community Plant Variety Rights (PVR) of July 27 1994[15] (PVR Regulation) introduces a community PVR. The community PVR offers the opportunity to a breeder to get an exclusionary right valid throughout the Community, through submission of only one application. The UPOV Convention was also the basis of the introduction of a system of national plant breeder's rights in many countries all over the world. In the present chapter, the focus of events will lie on the international and European level.

3.1.1 Eligible Subject Matter: Plant Varieties

The UPOV Convention offers protection for plant *varieties*. A plant variety is defined as 'a plant grouping within a single botanical taxon of the lowest known rank which grouping can be defined by features characterizing a given genotype or combination of genotypes, and is distinguished from any other plant grouping by the expression of at least one of the said characteristics' (Article 2 (i) 1991 UPOV Convention). (For more details on the distinction between plant variety and plant, *see* further).

In the same line, the PVR Regulation offers protection for plant varieties (Article 5 (1) PVR Regulation), applying a definition of plant variety which matches the one of the 1991 UPOV Convention:

> 'Variety' shall be taken to mean a plant grouping within a single botanical taxon of the lowest rank, which grouping, irrespective of whether the conditions for the grant of a PVR are fully met, can be defined by the expression of the characteristics that results from a given genotype or combination of genotypes, distinguished from any other plant grouping by the expression of at least one of the said characteristics, and considered as a unit with regard to its suitability for being propagated unchanged (Article 5 (2) PVR Regulation).

3.1.2 Substantive Protection Criteria

Under the UPOV Convention, a plant variety shall receive plant breeder's right protection if the variety is distinct, uniform, stable and (commercially) novel (Article 5 (1) 1991 UPOV Convention).

Distinctness – A variety shall be deemed to be distinct if it is clearly distinguishable from any other variety whose existence is a matter of common knowledge at the time of the filing of the application (Article 7 1991 UPOV Convention). Morphological characteristics include such aspects as leaf shape, flower colour, or general form.

1997, p. 78; Van Overwalle, G., *Octrooieerbaarheid van plantenbiotechnologische uitvindingen. Een rechtsvergelijkend onderzoek naar een rechtvaardiging van een uitbreiding van het octrooirecht tot planten.* [Patentability of Plant Biotechnological Inventions. A Comparative Study towards a Justification of Extending Patent Law to Plants (Substantive Summary)], Brussels, Bruylant, 1996, p. 739

15. *Official Journal EC,* 1 September 1994, L 227/1.

Physiological characteristics could include disease resistance, winter hardiness and the like.

Uniformity – A variety shall be deemed to be uniform if, subject to the variation that may be expected from the particular features of its propagation, it is sufficiently uniform in its relevant characteristics (Article 8 1991 UPOV Convention). With asexually propagated species like the potato, or with species like the garden pea that are fully self-fertilized, uniformity poses no great problem. But with wholly or partly cross-pollinated species, plants of the variety will exhibit diversity in character. The requirement of sufficient uniformity limits the divergences.

Stability – A variety shall be deemed to be stable if its relevant characteristics remain unchanged after repeated propagation or, in the case of a particular cycle of propagation, at the end of each such cycle (Article 9 1991 UPOV Convention). Stability can be particularly difficult to achieve with sexually reproduced varieties, where cross-pollination can lead to a shift in type with loss of the important characteristic(s). Nevertheless, a variety must remain sufficiently true to its description when multiplied through such numbers of generations as is necessary to produce the quantities of seed required by commerce.

Novelty – A variety shall be deemed to be new if, at the date of filing of the application for a breeder's right, propagating or harvested material of the variety has not been sold or otherwise disposed of to others, by or with the consent of the breeder, for purposes of exploitation of the variety (i) in the territory of the Contracting Party in which the application has been filed earlier than one year before that date, and (ii) in a territory other than that of the Contracting Party in which the application has been filed earlier than four years or, in the case of trees or of vines, earlier than six years before the said date (Article 6 1991 UPOV Convention). The meaning of 'novelty' in the plant breeder's rights regime is, in fact, 'commercial novelty': a variety lacks commercial novelty if it was commercialized by the breeder prior to the filing date.

The PVR Regulation largely adopts the UPOV conditions for protection (*see* arts. 6, 7, 8, 9 and 10 PVR Regulation).

3.1.3 Scope of Rights

Generally speaking, a plant breeder's right awards the holder the exclusive right to produce reproductive material of his plant variety for the purpose of sale and to sell this material within a particular territory and for a given period. The basic exclusive right of the breeder implies that any person must obtain, from the breeder, the authorization for the performance of the following acts, in respect of the *propagating material* of the protected variety: '(i) production or reproduction (multiplication), (ii) conditioning for the purpose of propagation, (iii) offering for sale, (iv) selling or other marketing, (v) exporting, (vi) importing, (vii) stocking for any of the purposes mentioned in (i) to (vi)' (Article 14 (1) (a)1991 UPOV Convention).

The breeder's right shall not extend to acts done privately and for non-commercial purposes, (Article 15 (1) (i) 1991 UPOV Convention), in other words, to acts of reproduction or propagation of the variety for pleasure, as many private gardeners might do. Nor shall the breeder's right extend acts done for experimental purposes (Article 15 (1) (ii) 1991 UPOV Convention).

The breeder's right contains two additional limitations, which are quite unique. First and foremost, the so-called breeder's exemption. The breeder's exemption entails that the breeder's right shall not extend to acts done for the purpose of breeding other varieties (Article 15 (1) (iii) 1991 UPOV Convention – mandatory exception), meaning that a protected variety may be used by other breeders in a breeding program and subsequent commercialization without the consent of the plant breeder's right holder. For example, if a protected flower variety has red and white flowers, a competitor using purchased seed, can improve the strain that produces only white flowers, receive a certificate for a new variety developed from that strain, and put it on the market without the consent of the plant breeder's rights holder of the white flower. In addition, there is the so-called farmer's exemption (also called farmer's privilege), restricting the breeder's right to permit farmers save seed for planting on their own holdings (Article 15 (2) 1991 UPOV Convention – optional exception).

European breeder's rights law (*see* Article 13 PVR Regulation) provides an exclusive right comparable to the 1991 UPOV protection. The conventional exceptions (private and non-commercial use; experimental use – Article 15 (a) (b) PVR Regulation), and the more typical exemptions (breeder's exemption – Article 15 (c) PVR Regulation; farmer's exemption – Article 14 PVR Regulation) to that exclusive right have all been built into the European framework.

3.2 Patents

The TRIPS Agreement contains an optional provision which is highly relevant for patent protection for plants. Article 27 (3) (b) states in its first sentence that Members may exclude from patentability plants and animals other than microorganisms, and essentially biological processes for the production of plants or animals other than non-biological and microbiological processes. The optional nature of that provision has led to a variety of approaches to the patent protection of plants and animals worldwide. More, in particular, Europe did not opt for the implementation of the exclusionary TRIPS provision in the European Patent Convention (EPC).[16]

3.2.1 Eligible Subject Matter: Plants

In principle, a European patent shall be granted for any invention (Article 52 (1) EPC). The case law of the European Patent Office (EPO) confirmed that subcellular fragments (like DNA sequences, genes, plasmids and vectors), microorganisms, plant cells and

16. European Patent Convention of 5 October 1973 (*see* https://www.epo.org/law-practice/legal-texts/html/epc/1973/e/ma1.html, last visited 29 April 2020).

plants per se[17] could be the subject of patent protection. This approach was strengthened by the European Parliament in 1998, with the adoption of a Directive on the legal protection of biotechnological inventions[18] (the so-called Biotechnology Directive) and the incorporation of this Directive into the EPC in 1999,[19] thus providing more detailed guidelines with regard to the patenting of biotechnological inventions and plants for the EPO.[20]

On the other hand, the EPC excludes certain inventions from its field of application of direct interest here, namely the exclusion of 'plant or animal varieties or essentially biological processes for the production of plants or animals' (Article 53 (b) EPC).

As to the exclusion of plant varieties, the Biotechnology Directive aligns itself with the case law of EPO, setting forth that plant varieties are not patentable (Article 4 (1) (a) Biotechnology Directive). A reason for the exclusion of plant varieties from patent protection is that several European countries introduced a UPOV-based sui generis protection for plant varieties. However, the Biotechnology Directive only prohibits the patenting of plants in the form of a plant *variety* but does not exclude inventions which concern plants or animals if the technical feasibility of the invention is not confined to a particular plant or animal variety (Article 4 (2) Biotechnology Directive), in other words, plants per se.

The differentiation between plant *varieties* and plants per se as deployed in the Biotechnology Directive is based on the modern biological taxonomy founded by Carl Linnaeus (1707 - 1778). On the basis of flower structure, the plant kingdom is subdivided into families, genera and species, whereby each 'higher' taxon subsumes all 'lower' taxa. An example might clarify the current taxonomy of the plant kingdom. Let us take the potato (*see* Table 7.1):

Table 7.1 Example of the Taxonomy of the Plant Kingdom: The Potato

Kingdom	Plantae
Division	Tracheophyta
Class	Angiospermae

17. Technical Board of Appeal, 13 October 1997 (T 1054/96 – Novartis), Official Journal EPO, 1998, 511 (*see* http://legal.european-patent-office.org/dg3/biblio/t961054ep1.htm); Enlarged Board of Appeal, 20 December 1999 (G 1/98 – Novartis), Official Journal EPO, 2000, 111-141; Technical Board of Appeal, 6 December 2000 (T 1054/96 – Novartis) (*see* http://legal.european-patent-office.org/dg3/biblio/t961054eu1.htm).
18. Directive 98/44/EC of 6 July 1998 of the European Parliament and of the Council on the legal protection of biotechnological inventions (Official Journal L 213, 30/07/1998 p. 0013) (*see* http://europa.eu.int).
19. Notably by a decision of the Administrative Council of 16 June 1999, inserting what is now Chapter V. Biotechnological Inventions (Rule 26 – Rule 34) in the Implementing Regulations of the EPC.
20. For more details, Van Overwalle, G., 'Biotechnology and Patents: Global Standards, European Approaches and National Accents', in *Genetic Engineering and the World Trade System*, Wüger, D. & Cottier, T. (eds), Cambridge University Press, first published 2008, 77-108; first paperback edition 2012, 77-108.

Order	Dicotyledonae
Family	Solanaceae (Nightshades)
Genus	*Solanum* (Nightshade)
Species	*Solanum tuberosum* (potato)
Variety	Bintje, Charlotte, ...

In terms of the EPC and the Biotechnology Directive, no patent protection is possible for the Charlotte *variety* of potato, but it is possible to acquire patent protection at the level of the (transgenic) *potato* (*Solanum tuberosum* L.). It has been argued that this way of viewing the matter is acceptable given the observation that, with the help of modern modification techniques, induced characteristics can be introduced not only to one particular plant variety but also to a range of plant varieties.

As to the exclusion of essentially biological processes for the production of plants, the interpretation of the wording of that exclusion has recently been the subject of EPO case law. In *Broccoli/Tomato I*,[21] the Enlarged Board of Appeal of the EPO decided that a non-microbiological process for the production of plants which contains or consists of the steps of sexually crossing the whole genomes of plants and of subsequently selecting plants is, in principle, excluded from patentability as being 'essentially biological', and that such a process does not escape the exclusion merely because it contains a step of a technical nature which serves to enable or assist the performance of the steps of sexually crossing the whole genomes of plants or of subsequently selecting plants. In *Broccoli/Tomato II*,[22] the Enlarged Board of Appeal of the EPO held that for plants resulting from such (excluded) essentially biological processes patent protection was available. The European Commission fiercely opposed the latter interpretation and issued a notice.[23] In response to the notice, initially, the EPO gave in: the EPO Administrative Council amended Rule 28 (2) of the EPC Implementing Regulations,[24] saying that '[u]nder Article 53 (b) EPC, European patents shall not be granted in respect of plants or animals exclusively obtained by means of an essentially biological process'.[25] Later on, the EPO distanced itself from this approach: the EPO Board of Appeal decided that plants resulting from essentially biological processes are

21. EPO Enlarged Board of Appeal G1/08 (*Tomatoes I*) and G2/07 (*Broccoli I*), 9 December 2010, *Official Journal EPO*, 2012, 130 (available at https://www.epo.org/law-practice/case-law-appeals/eba.html, last visited 15 October 2018).
22. EPO Enlarged Board of Appeal G2/12 (*Tomatoes II*) and G2/13 (*Broccoli II*), 25 March 2015, *Official Journal EPO*, 17 (available at https://www.epo.org/law-practice/case-law-appeals/eba .html, last visited 15 October 2018).
23. Commission Notice on certain articles of Directive 98/44/EC of the European Parliament and of the Council on the legal protection of biotechnological inventions (2016/C 411/03), *Official Journal EU C* 411/3, 8 November 2016 (available at https://eur-lex.europa.eu, last visited 15 October 2018).
24. Decision of the Administrative Council CA/D 6/17 of 29 June 2017 (*EPO Official Journal*, 2017, A56), entered into force on 1 July 2017.
25. For a detailed analysis, *see* C. Godt, 'Technology, Patents and Markets: The Implied Lessons of the EU Commission's Intervention in the *Broccoli/Tomatoes* case of 2016 for Modern (Plant) Genome Editing', 49 IIC, 2018, 512-535.

considered patentable after all,[26] thus following the earlier decision of the Enlarged Board of Appeal in *Broccoli/Tomato II*. Most recently, the Enlarged Board of Appeal abandoned its earlier interpretation. Based on a dynamic rather than on a classical interpretation of Article 53 (b) EPC, the Enlarged Board decided that plants and animals exclusively obtained by essentially biological processes should be excluded from patentability after all.[27]

3.2.2 *Substantive Protection Criteria*

As is well known, a European patent shall be granted for any invention which meets the criteria of novelty, inventive step, industrial application (Article 52 (1) EPC) and enabling disclosure (Article 83 EPC). These requirements do not seem to constitute particular insurmountable hurdles for the patenting of plant-related inventions.[28]

3.2.3 *Scope of Rights*

A patent right shall confer on its owner the exclusive right, where the subject matter of a patent is a product, to prevent third parties not having the owner's consent from the acts of making, using, offering for sale, selling, or importing for these purposes that *product* (Article 28 (a) TRIPS Agreement).

As is widely known, many TRIPS Member States have included an exception for acts done privately and for non-commercial purposes and acts done for experimental purposes.

4 LOOKING AT THE EXCLUSIVITY/ACCESS BALANCE THROUGH THE TYPE/TOKEN LENS

A comparison between the scope of exclusivity in both the plant breeder's rights and the patent regime (sections 3.1.3 and 3.2.3) brings us to the core of the present chapter. Both plant breeder's rights and patents are similar regarding their exclusionary *nature*: in both regimes, the right has been defined as a right to exclude third parties from conducting certain acts without the consent of the right holder. A plant breeder's right and a patent right differ, however, regarding the protected *subject matter* on which that right can be exercised. The difference invites us to reflect on the type/token ontology

26. EPO Board of Appeal, 5 December 2018 (T 1063/18) (available at https://www.epo.org/law-practice/case-law-appeals/advanced-search.html, last visited 29 July 2019).
27. EPO Enlarged Board of Appeal G3/19 (*Pepper*), 14 May 2020, not yet published in the *Official Journal EPO* (available at https://www.epo.org/law-practice/case-law-appeals/eba.html, last visited 27 August 2020).
28. For more details, Van Overwalle, G., 'Biotechnology and Patents: Global Standards, European Approaches and National Accents', in *Genetic Engineering and the World Trade System*, Wüger, D. & Cottier, T. (eds), Cambridge University Press, first published 2008, 77-108; first paperback edition 2012, 77-108.

in IP law. Furthermore, the difference has far-reaching consequences for the exclusion/access balance.

4.1 Plant Breeder's Rights Law

In plant breeder's rights law, the exclusive right is not exercised through warranting exclusivity on the subject matter of protection, *in casu* the plant variety, but on providing exclusivity on the *propagating material* of the protected subject matter, namely seeds (generatively propagating material) and tubers, bulbs, etc. (vegetatively propagating material). In doing so, plant breeder's rights law crafts a distinction between the *abstract* subject matter of the right, namely the plant variety, and the *concrete* subject matter of the right, namely the propagating material, the latter being the subject of the exercise of the right. Put differently: the exclusive right is not exercised on the *abstract* level of the subject matter (the variety) but on the *concrete* incarnation of the subject matter (propagating material). The plant breeder's rights holder owns the right to the intangible, abstract object (plant variety) allowing him to stop anyone else from producing the concrete object (propagating material) without this consent (*see* Figure 7.1).

This approach fits within the prevailing type/token ontology in IP law, suggesting that exclusive IP rights pertain to intangible goods, which are conceived of as *abstract* objects ('types'), which are strictly distinguished from their *concrete* embodiments ('tokens').[29] An invention (abstract object) is embodied in a product or process (concrete object), a work (abstract) is embodied by fixing/expressing it in a copy (concrete), a sign (abstract) is embodied by affixing it to a good or to a packaging (concrete), a plant variety (abstract) is embodied in reproducing it in propagating material (concrete).

Let us now revisit this analysis, taking into account the breeder's exemption. The in-built breeder's exemption implies that a plant breeder can stop others not having his consent from reproducing propagating material from the protected plant variety, but he cannot stop others from using the protected variety for further breeding *and* commercialization. In doing so, plant breeder's rights law establishes a chain of *independence*, where each and every breeder can exploit his improved variety without having to ask the consent from the initial rights holder. He can stand on the shoulders of previous breeders, without being indebted to any prior breeder (*see* Figure 7.1).

29. Peukert, A., 'Rethinking the Ontology of IP', Working paper on file with the author, 2016. Also *see* Wilson, J., 'Ontology and the Regulation of Intellectual Property', 93 *The Monist*, No. 3, Intellectual Property, 2010, 450-463.

Figure 7.1 Differing Objects to Exercise the Exclusionary Right in Patent Law and Plant Breeder's Rights Law

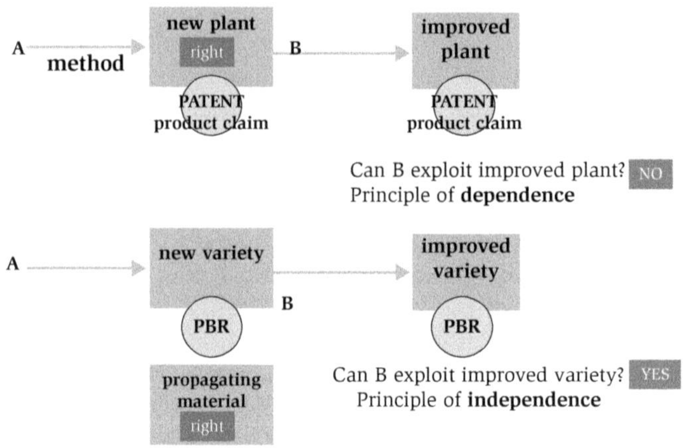

In terms of the exclusivity/access balance, it follows that the subject matter of a plant breeder's right *always* remains open: anyone can use and improve the subject matter *and* commercialize the newly developed subject matter without the consent of the initial plant breeder. Put differently: universal openness is structurally woven into the architecture of plant breeder's rights law.

This unique architecture of plant breeder's rights automatically turns the property rule into a liability rule, crafting guaranteed access, in the sense that licenses have not to be bargained and negotiations cannot result in a veto to access the protected technology.[30] The plant breeder's rights regime creates a fully codified, government-determined liability regime, providing immunity to breeders making use of protected plant varieties during research, development *and* commercialization.[31]

In terms of the type/token ontology, both the *abstract* object of a plant breeder's right (the variety) *and* the *concrete* object (the propagating material) are always open for anyone to use, improve *and* commercialize. I am curious to learn to what extent far-reaching exemptions, such as the breeder's exemption, modify the traditional and well-accepted type/token ontology. Is the type/token ontology an adequate lens to understand the exact scope of plant breeder's right regime with a breeder's exemption and universal openness woven into its DNA? How would that work out?

30. For more details, *see* Van Overwalle, G., 'Creating Universal and Sustainable Access to Plants and Seeds: The Role of Clearinghouses, Open Source Licenses and Inclusive Patents', in *The Commons, Plant Breeding and Agricultural Research: Challenges for Food Security and Agrobiodiversity*, Girard, F. & Frison, C. (eds), Routledge, 2018, 88-106 and the references cited there.
31. Van Overwalle, G., 'Inventing Inclusive Patents. From Old to New Open Innovation', in P. Drahos, G. Ghidini and H. Ullrich (eds), 1 *Kritika: Essays on Intellectual Property*, Edward Elgar, 2015, 206-277.

4.2 Patent Law

In patent law, the exclusive right of the patent holder is exercised through creating exclusivity on the subject matter of protection, *in casu* the invention. This entails that a patent holder can stop anyone not having his consent from using the invention for improvement going beyond experimentation (*see* Figure 7.1).

In view of the exclusivity/access analysis, it is clear that the subject matter of a patent does, in principle, *not* remain open to third parties to be used with commercial intent. Patent law thus establishes a chain of *dependence*, where each and every inventor who improves on the invention, needs the consent from the initial inventor and remains indebted to the prior inventor on whose shoulders he stands. (Universal) openness is structurally *not* woven into the architecture of patent law. Looking at patent law from the property/liability rule perspective suggests that the default exploitation regime for patents is the property rule regime (*see* Figure 7.2), resulting in no or restricted access (*see* Figure 7.1).

Figure 7.2 Turning the Property/Exclusivity Rule into a Liability Rule Regime in Patent Law[32]

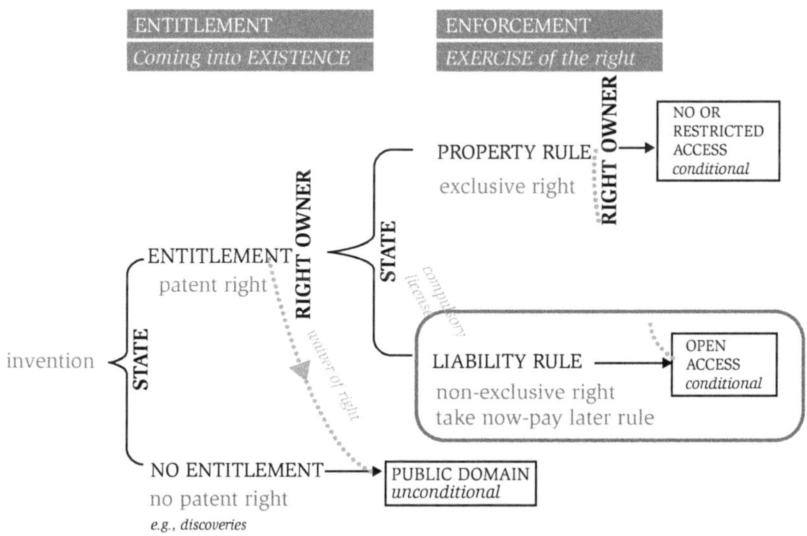

Looking at the specifics of patent law through the type/token lens, it is clear that the right to an invention (abstract object) is embodied in a product or process (concrete object). The owner of an invention exploits his right by stopping others from producing the invention.

32. *Source*: Van Overwalle, G., 'Exclusive Property Versus Open Commons. The Case of Gene Patents', 4(2) *The WIPO Journal: Analysis and Debate of Intellectual Property Issues*, 2013, 139-158.

5 RE-ASSESSING THE EXCLUSIVITY/ACCESS BALANCE

Various approaches have been contemplated to temper the right to exclude in patent law and to foster access to plants and seeds. The first series of initiatives figures *within* the patent regime and aims at tuning down the exclusionary character of patents via the creation of patent clearinghouses and platforms, or by weaving in the breeder's exemption into patent law. The second series of measures consciously steps *outside* the patent discourse and seeks to facilitate the access by dedicating plants and seeds to the public domain, or by crafting open source licenses.[33]

We will briefly reflect here on the introduction of a breeder's exemption in patent law. At present, some governments are considering infusing a breeder's exception into patent law.[34] Such initiatives indicate the legislature's willingness to embed more sharing norms into patent law and rethink the exclusion/access balance. Two main scenarios have been set forth. In a first scenario, the introduction of a *full* breeder's exemption is contemplated: an exemption of the use in plant breeding of genetic material falling under the scope of the patent, and *also* of the commercialization of the new varieties – plant propagation material originating from such breeding. Introducing a codified full breeder's exemption into the patent regime with a statutory in-built user's/improver's exemption for research, development *and* commercialization. In the second line of thought, the introduction of a *restricted* breeder's exemption is considered: an exemption of the use of genetic material for plant breeding, but *not* of the commercialization of the varieties originating from this activity when these varieties carry this patented trait. A restricted type of exemption has been introduced in France, Germany and Switzerland.[35]

Both scenarios have major advantages over patent clearinghouse initiatives in the sense that they provide greater legal certainty and greater robustness. Public ordering by the state can stabilize access in a way that private ordering can never achieve.[36] It remains to be seen which of both scenarios – the full or the restricted breeder's exemption – will be most fit to safeguard incentives to innovate for inventors and

33. For an in-depth analysis of the other measures, the interested reader may consult the following publications: Van Overwalle, G., 'Creating Universal and Sustainable Access to Plants and Seeds: The Role of Clearinghouses, Open Source Licenses and Inclusive Patents', in *The Commons, Plant Breeding and Agricultural Research. Challenges for Food Security and Agrobiodiversity*, Girard, F. & Frison, C. (eds), Routledge, 2018, 88-106; Van Overwalle, G., 'Patent Pools and Clearinghouses in the Life Sciences: Back to the Future', in *Research Handbook on Intellectual Property and the Life Sciences*, Matthews, D. & Zech, H. (eds), Edward Elgar, 2017, 304-334.
34. *See* van der Kooij, P., 'Towards a Breeder's Exemption in Patent Law?', 32(11) *European Intellectual Property Review*, 2010, 545-552. *Also see* Louwaars, N., Dons, H., Van Overwalle, G., Raven, H., Arundel, A., Eaton, D. & Nelis, A., *Breeding Business. The Future of Plant Breeding in the Light of Developments in Patent Rights and Plant Breeder's Rights*, Wageningen, Centre for Genetic Resources, 2009, 61 (CGN Rapport 2009-14 EN) (study available at http://ssrn.com/abstract=1720088, last visited 30 July 2019).
35. *See* § 11. no. 2a of the German Patentgesetz, Art. L 613-5-3 of the French Code de la Propriété Intellectuelle and Art. 9(e) of the Swiss Bundesgesetz über die Erfindungspatente.
36. For more details, *see* Van Overwalle, G., 'Inventing Inclusive Patents. From Old to New Open Innovation', in P. Drahos, G. Ghidini and H. Ullrich (eds), 1 *Kritika: Essays on Intellectual Property*, Edward Elgar, 2015, 206-277.

improvers. That is an economic and/or ideological assessment which goes beyond the current chapter.

Looking at both scenarios from the type/token ontology, I wonder whether and how the type/token dichotomy can capture the fundamental difference between plant breeder's rights law (with its in-built broad breeder's exemption), traditional patent law, and modified patent law (with an in-built full or restricted breeder's exemption).

6 CONCLUDING THOUGHTS

With the introduction of new and disruptive technology - such as software, 3D printing, or artificial intelligence - academic IP discourse is always concerned about the shift in the exclusivity/access balance. With the upsurge of new technologies in the plant area - such as recombinant DNA technology, CRISPrCas9 or NBT's - scholarly research has equally been worried about the exclusivity/access paradigm in plant breeder's rights law and in patent law, in particular.

As is well known, the exclusivity/access balance is codified much more access-friendly in the plant breeder's rights regime, as compared to the patent regime, thanks to the existence of the codified breeder's exemption. In the search for a clear and coherent theoretical understanding of the fundamental legal architecture in plant breeder's rights law (reconciling exclusivity with *broad* access as a default enforcement regime) and patent law (mixing exclusivity with *restricted* access as a default regime), the present chapter turned to the type/token ontology. A conscientious analysis of the multi-layered nature of the subject matter of the exclusionary right, and the abstract (type) and concrete (token) subject matter in both regimes leaves me somewhat puzzled. Can the type/token ontology provide a clear explanation for the impact of an in-built breeder's exemption in plant breeder's rights law and the introduction of a full or restricted breeder's exemption in patent law? Or is the type/token concept an invidious and deficient theory inadequate to clarify the differences between different IP regimes? When rethinking IP protection in the plant area, IP scholarship should scrutinously revisit the type/token notion. Recent scholarly IP teachings might provide a fruitful perspective to deepen our understanding of this academic journey in the plant field.[37]

37. Peukert, A., *Kritik der Ontologie des Immaterialgüterrechts*, Mohr Siebeck, 2018. The translation of this study is soon to be expected under the title *A Critique of the Ontology of Intellectual Property Law* (Personal communication from the author).

CHAPTER 8

Non-patent Legal Factors of Marketability in Plant Biotechnology in Europe

Tomasz Zimny

1 INTRODUCTION

Plants have been, and still remain, the staple of human nutrition, but they are also used as a source of materials, fuels and for other means. Plants for human consumption are mostly produced by the agricultural industry, and the developments of that industry allow humanity to keep up with the increasing growth of the population. These developments occur through advancements not only in mechanics, chemistry but also in agricultural biotechnology,[1] including plant breeding. For thousands of years, people have been performing activities devoted to the production of novel plants that would allow for an increase in productivity, tolerance of abiotic stresses (e.g., drought), pest resistance and improvement of other features. These activities, for the most part, involved crossing prospective organisms and subsequently selecting their promising offspring. This type of innovative activity is usually called 'conventional breeding'[2] as opposed to modern breeding techniques, involving, e.g., genetic modifications, genome editing and other techniques that can also be employed in order to obtain new plant varieties.

Most of the accomplishments in improving the biological potential of plants were achieved through the application of methods of conventional breeding, whose pinnacle was probably the development of high yielding wheat and rice in the 1960s by the team of Norman Borlaug, which contributed strongly to keeping production levels in line

1. Anjan Sen, *IPR in Agriculture and their prospects*, in *The Role of Intellectual Property Rights in Agriculture and Allied Sciences*, 2-63, 3 (Chandan Roy ed., 2018).
2. Maria Lusser & Howard V. Davies, *Comparative regulatory approaches for groups of new plant breeding techniques*, 30 New Biotechnol. 437-446, 442 (2013).

with population growth.[3] Nevertheless, in recent years, the growth of yields in some staple species, such as wheat, seems to have stagnated, which causes scientists to turn to more advanced methods of increasing the genetic potential of plants.[4]

New varieties in the European Union (EU) are mostly protected through plant variety rights based on the International Convention for the Protection of New Varieties of Plants (UPOV),[5] or more specifically *Regulation 2100/94/EC on Community plant variety rights*[6] and domestic laws. Advancements in plant breeding and agricultural biotechnology can also be protected by patents. This also applies to groups of plants, if the protected invention is not limited to a particular variety (since, according to Article 53b of the European Patent Convention (EPC),[7] varieties as such cannot be patented). This clarification was introduced in the 98/44/EC *Directive on the protection of biotechnological inventions* (hereinafter 'Biotech Directive'),[8] in order to foster development in the field of plant biotechnology, by allowing for patent protection of its products (*see* further - part 3).

In this chapter, I will look at patent law, the EU laws on the usage of genetically modified organisms (GMO), and patent data (publications of the European Patent Office) in order to see if the ability to patent plants in Europe is a 'driving force for innovation'. It seems that the development of plant biotechnology, in particular in agriculture, is to a large extent independent from the possibility of patenting plants or their groups warranted by modern patent law. Rather, it seems that other factors, not connected with patent law per se, constitute obstacles to the development and widespread adoption of the products of modern agricultural biotechnology, in particular in the EU.

Biotechnology is a term introduced in the early twentieth century and refers to activities where 'products are produced from raw materials with the aid of living organisms', or more recently, to techniques 'that use living organisms (or parts of organisms) to make or modify products, to improve plants or animals or to develop microorganisms for specific uses'. [9] Both these definitions are rather broad; there are,

3. Dulce E. de Oliveira & Marc Van Montagu, *Plants for the Future, in Challenges for Agricultural Research* 209-219, 210 (OECD ed., 2011), https://www.oecd-ilibrary.org/agriculture-and-food/challenges-for-agricultural-research_9789264090101-en (last visited 26 March 2019).
4. Gustavo A. Slafer, *Challenges and Opportunities for Further Improvements in Wheat Yield* in: *Challenges for Agricultural Research* 153-164, 154-155 (OECD ed., 2011), https://www.oecd-ilibrary.org/agriculture-and-food/challenges-for-agricultural-research_9789264090101-en (last visited 26 March 2019).
5. International Convention for the Protection of New Varieties of Plants, adopted on 2 December 1961, came into force on 10 August 1968, having been ratified by the United Kingdom, the Netherlands and Germany. The UPOV Convention has been revised on 10 November 1972, on 23 October 1978, and on 19 March 1991.
6. Council Regulation (EC) No 2100/94 of 27 July 1994 on Community plant variety rights, OJ L 227, 01 September 1994 pp. 1-30.
7. Convention on the Grant of European Patents (European Patent Convention), of 5 October 1973 as revised by the Act revising Art. 63 EPC of 17 December 1991 and the Act revising the EPC of 29 November 2000.
8. Directive 98/44/EC of the European Parliament and of the Council, of 6 July 1998, on the legal protection of biotechnological inventions, OJ L 213, 30 July 1998, pp. 13-21.
9. *See further* Graham Dutfield, *Intellectual Property Rights and the Life Science Industries: a twentieth century history*, 135-137 (2016).

however, more specific terms used in literature that pertain to the topic of this paper, namely 'agricultural biotechnology' and 'plant biotechnology'.[10] The terms 'agricultural biotechnology' and 'plant biotechnology' are not synonymous, but their meanings overlap. The first one indicates the employment of biotechnology for all purposes connected with agriculture, while the other indicates the use of biotechnology for the development of new types of plants, regardless of purpose. In this chapter, I use them to denote the application of modern methods such as genetic modification or new plant breeding techniques for the development of new plants, mostly for the purposes of agriculture.

2 THE GOAL OF PATENT PROTECTION

The debate about the reasons for which the patent system exists is still not over, yet it has resulted in the development of several approaches to the problem. According to some proponents, enabling the protection of inventions is a result of a natural right of humans to the fruits of their work. According to a different approach, a patent granted to the first inventor is a form of a prize for their efforts in developing the technology. Also, the monopoly granted by a patent creates a potential for future income, thus enabling the investor to recover investments made into the development of an invention. There is also a theory according to which the patent is granted in return for the disclosure of an invention. It thus provides an incentive to share the solution and facilitate the transfer of technology.[11] Each of these approaches can be criticised for different reasons, as not providing the full rationale for the existence of the patent system. They differ from each other as to the indicated mechanisms or values that supposedly justify the existence of such a system. What they have in common is the view that this system provides some kind of incentive for contributing to the state of the art.

In a situation where a system for patent protection of inventions already exists, the question of why it exists can be presented as a set of narrower questions, concerning the reasons for the protection of certain groups or types of inventions. In particular: why do we protect biotechnological/medical/chemical/other inventions? These specific questions can be answered generally: that there is a belief that the development of a certain area of human activity is beneficial for the public. If this is so, incentives should be created for investments in this particular area. This approach was also taken in the European Union (EU), when the Biotech Directive was drafted, which is clearly visible in its recitals.

According to recital one 'biotechnology and genetic engineering are playing an increasingly important role in a broad range of industries and the protection of biotechnological inventions will certainly be of fundamental importance for the

10. For example, Jim M. Dunwell, *Review: intellectual property aspects of plant transformation*, 3 Plant Biotechnology Journal 371-384 (2005).
11. S.J.R. Bostyn, *Enabling Biotechnological Inventions in Europe and the United States: A Study of the Patentability of Proteins and DNA Sequences with Special Emphasis on the Disclosure Requirement*, 33-37 (2001), https://books.google.pl/books?id=mY9QAQAAIAAJ.

Community's industrial development', while (recital 2) 'in particular in the field of genetic engineering, research and development require a considerable amount of high-risk investment and therefore only adequate legal protection can make them profitable'. Furthermore, 'effective and harmonised protection throughout the Member States is essential in order to maintain and encourage investment in the field of biotechnology' (recital 3). In addition, according to recital 10, 'regard should be had to the potential of the development of biotechnology for the environment and in particular to the utility of this technology for the development of methods of cultivation which are less polluting and more economical in their use of ground' and furthermore, 'the patent system should be used to encourage research into, and the application of, such processes'. Echoes of the aforementioned approaches to the justification of the existence of a patent system and protection of particular solutions can clearly be identified in the quoted fragments and were also voiced at the outset of the works on the Biotech Directive – in the White Paper on the Completing of the Internal Market.[12] It was the lack of harmonisation in the protection of *inter alia* biotechnological inventions that was seen as a barrier to investment in the area and furthermore a barrier to its development. This barrier has, to a large extent, been removed with the adoption of the Biotech Directive and its subsequent implementation into the legal systems of the Member States, but maybe more importantly, into the system of the EPC. A conviction that a harmonised system of patent protection would allow augmenting the development of biotechnology was at the basis of adoption of the Biotech Directive. Since this conviction applies to all kinds of biotechnological inventions, it applies to plant biotechnology as well.

3 PATENT PROTECTION OF PLANTS IN EUROPE

According to Article 27 paragraph 3(b) of the TRIPS Agreement,[13] 'Members shall provide for the protection of plant varieties either by patents or by an effective sui generis system or by any combination thereof.' The system of intellectual property protection in plant biology adopted in the European Union consists of a combination of both of the mentioned systems. Prima facie it would seem that since the patentability of plant varieties is expressly excluded both in the EPC (Article 53(b)) and in the Biotech Directive (Article 4 paragraph 1(a)), both systems are separate. Indeed, the protection of plant varieties is *expressis verbis* provided by the 2100/94/EC Regulation on Community plant variety rights, or by domestic laws on plant variety protection, which create a sui generis system of protection, introducing plant variety rights – industrial property rights designed specifically in order to protect plant varieties.

12. European Commission, *White Paper from the Commission to the European Council on the Completing of the Internal Market*, 145-149 (1985), http://aei.pitt.edu/1113/ (last visited 27 February 2019).
13. Agreement on Trade-Related Aspects of Intellectual Property Rights (TRIPS), Annex 1C of the Marrakesh Agreement Establishing the World Trade Organisation, signed in Marrakesh, Morocco on 15 April 1994.

Nevertheless, both the sui generis and the patent systems coexist and overlap to some extent, due to the way exceptions from patentability are drafted and interpreted.

As it has been previously mentioned, the EPC exceptions to patentability encompass plant varieties in particular. The notion of a plant variety is defined in laws introducing the sui generis system, in particular in the 2100/94/EC Regulation, to which the Biotech Directive refers in Article 2 paragraph 3. According to Article 5 paragraph 2 of the said regulation, 'variety' means:

> 'A plant grouping within a single botanical taxon of the lowest known rank, which grouping, irrespective of whether the conditions for the grant of a plant variety right are fully met, can be defined by the expression of the characteristics that results from a given genotype or combination of genotypes, distinguished from any other plant grouping by the expression of at least one of the said characteristics, and considered as a unit with regard to its suitability for being propagated unchanged.'

Hence, an invention concerning plants, whose application is not technically confined to a single variety is not covered by the exception (*see* Recital 29 of the Biotech Directive). Furthermore, as it is expressed in Recital 31, if a plant grouping is characterised by a particular gene and not by its whole genome, it does not constitute a variety and thus shall also not be covered by the patenting exception.[14] Similar provisions were introduced into the Implementing Regulations to the EPC, where rule 26(4) defines a plant variety in the same way as the Biotech Directive, while currently, rule 27(b) states that biotechnological inventions concern plants or animals if the technical feasibility of the invention is not confined to a particular plant or animal variety (without prejudice to rule 28(2), which prohibits patenting of plants or animals developed exclusively through essentially biological processes – *see further*). According to the reasoning presented in the European Patent Office (EPO) Enlarged Board of Appeal (EBA) decision in the case G 1/98, if a claim is directed to a plant grouping distinguishable by a particular feature, such claim is generally valid even if such group may encompass several plant varieties. [15] The EBA argued, among other points, that patents protect development activity of a different kind than plant breeding, and inventors in the field of genetic engineering would be deprived of the ability to protect their innovation if the exception was to be interpreted in such a way that a claim to a group of plants that may contain varieties is inadmissible due to the exclusion of plant varieties from patentability.

The patentability of plants is also limited through the exclusion of essentially biological processes for the production of plants or animals. According to Article 4 paragraph 1(b) of the Biotech Directive, such processes are not patentable. The patentability of essentially biological processes is also excluded on the basis of Article 53(b) of the EPC. According to Article 2 paragraph 2 of the Biotech Directive, 'a process

14. Bernard Le Buanec & Agnès Ricroch, *Intellectual Property Protection of Plant Innovation*, in *Plant Biotechnology*, 64 (Agnès Ricroch, Surinder Chopra, & Shelby J. Fleischer eds, 2014), http://link.springer.com/10.1007/978-3-319-06892-3.
15. G 1/98, EBA, G 0001/98 (Transgenic plant/NOVARTIS II) of 20 December 1999, ECLI:EP:BA:1999:G000198.19991220, para. 3.8.

for the production of plants or animals is essentially biological if it consists entirely of natural phenomena such as crossing or selection'. This definition was also incorporated in the Implementing Regulations to the EPC (rule 26(5)). The exclusion of essentially biological processes does not apply to microbiological processes and their products (Article 4 paragraph 3 of the Biotech Directive, Article 53(b) of EPC). A microbiological process is understood as any process involving or performed upon or resulting in microbiological material (Article 2 paragraph 1(b) of the Biotech Directive).

A biological process needs to entail at least one step of a technical nature in order not to be deemed essentially biological. As follows from the EBA decisions in the Broccoli/Tomato I cases, a 'non-microbiological process for the production of plants which contains or consists of the steps of sexually crossing the whole genomes of plants and of subsequently selecting plants is in principle excluded from patentability as being 'essentially biological' within the meaning of Article 53(b) EPC'. Furthermore, an addition of a technical step that does not merely serve to assist the processes of sexual crossing and selection of organisms does not allow the process to escape the exclusion.[16] The steps of a technical nature should constitute part of the patented process and not be a mere addition used in order to circumvent the exception. 'Additional technical steps which are performed either before or after the process of crossing and selection should, therefore, be ignored when determining whether or not the process is excluded from patentability under Article 53(b) EPC'.[17] In both of the mentioned cases, the applicants argued that an addition of a technical step after the breeding process (in order to select prospective plants) renders the whole process not essentially biological. The 'Tomato and Broccoli I' decisions were followed by decisions in cases 'Tomato and Broccoli II' (G 2/12 and G 2/13), where the EBA decided that 'the exclusion of essentially biological processes for the production of plants in Article 53(b) EPC does not have a negative effect on the allowability of a product claim directed to plants or plant material such as plant parts' and furthermore allowed for product-by-process claims where the product was an effect of an essentially biological process.[18] [19] The practical effect of these decisions was that although conventional breeding processes were excluded from patentability, their products were not, as long as they didn't constitute varieties. While in accordance with a general rule that exceptions in law should be interpreted narrowly (the exception clearly mentions processes), the mentioned EBA decisions caused a lot of criticism that resulted in the European Commission issuing a statement that 'EU legislator's intention when adopting Directive 98/44/EC was to exclude from patentability products (plants/animals and plant/animal parts) that are obtained by means of essentially biological processes'.[20]

16. G 2/07, EBA, G 0002/07 (Broccoli/PLANT BIOSCIENCE) of 9 December 2010, ECLI:EP:BA:2010:G000207.20101209; G 1/08, EBA, G 0001/08 (Tomatoes/STATE OF ISRAEL) of 9 December 2010 (2010), ECLI:EP:BA:2010:G000108.20101209.
17. G 1/08, EBA, *supra* n. 16.
18. G 2/12, EBA, G 0002/12 of 25 March 2015, ECLI:EP:BA:2015:G000212.20150325.
19. G 2/13, EBA, G 0002/13 () of 25 March 2015, ECLI:EP:BA:2015:G000213.20150325.
20. European Commission, *Commission Notice on certain articles of Directive 98/44/EC of the European Parliament and of the Council on the legal protection of biotechnological inventions* 1.3 (2016), https://eur-lex.europa.eu/legal-content/EN/TXT/?uri=CELEX%3A52016XC1108%2801%29 (last visited 1 March 2019).

This was followed by a decision of the Administrative Council of EPO, of 29 June 2017 (CA/D 6/17), taken on the basis of Article 33(1)(c) EPC. In this decision, a new paragraph 2 was added to rule 28 of the Implementing Regulations to EPC, stating that 'under Article 53(b), European patents shall not be granted in respect of plants or animals exclusively obtained by means of an essentially biological process'. This decision seemingly ended the discussion about the patentability of products of essentially biological processes, in particular – plants. However, the Technical Board of Appeal of the European Patent Office (TBA), in the case T 1063/18, went another way. In a reasoning concerning more an analysis of the Administrative Council's power to amend the EPC than the patentability itself, the TBA reasoned that Article 53(b) of the EPC was interpreted by the EBA in the Tomato/Broccoli cases. While the Administrative Council is competent to amend Implementing Regulations, it is not competent to amend the EPC itself, and its decisions cannot be interpreted as a subsequent agreement between the parties that shall be taken into account for the interpretation of the convention.[21] Nevertheless, following a referral of the President of the European Patent Organisation, the EBA of the EPO has abandoned the interpretation of Article 53(b) given in decision G 2/12 and, in light of Rule 28(2) EPC. Currently, the term 'essentially biological processes for the production of plants or animals' in Article 53(b) EPC 'is to be understood and applied as extending to products exclusively obtained by means of an essentially biological process or if the claimed process feature defines an essentially biological process'.[22] The cited decision has already been subject to criticisms, due to apparent loopholes it creates (the ban could apparently be avoided by the applicant showing how the effect could have been achieved in a technical fashion) and its undermining of the Article 164 EPC, specifying that the articles of the EPC prevail over the rules, in case of a conflict of norms.[23]

Regardless of the confusions as to the scope of Article 53(b) of the EPC, processes involving a technical step, such as genetic modification of a plant's genome, are not to be considered essentially biological and thus not to be excluded from patentability. According to the EPO Guidelines for Examination (Part G Chapter II, 5.4), transgenic plants and technically induced mutants are patentable. This applies both to genome editing techniques and their products (such as CRISPR/Cas9) and random mutagenesis.[24] The European patent system allows for a rather broad range of protection for plants and processes of their modification. This applies, in particular, to situations where the application of the invention is not limited to one variety. Hence, when it comes to plants developed through genetic modification or some new plant breeding

21. T 1063/18, TBA, T 1063/18 (Extreme dark green, blocky peppers/SYNGENTA) of 5 December 2018, ECLI:EP:BA:2018:T106318.20181205.
22. G 3/19, EBA, (Pepper (follow-up to Tomatoes II and Broccoli II)) of 14 May 2020, Enlarged Board of Appeal 2020 ECLI:EP:BA:2020:G000319.20200514.
23. Julian Cockbain & Sigrid Sterckx, *Quis custodet custodes? Referral G-3/19 before the EPO Enlarged Board of Appeal and the imperative of challenging the board's interpretation of Art. 53(b) EPC*, J World Intellectual Property 2020;1-33, first published: 26 August 2020, https://doi.org/10.1111/jwip.12168.
24. Guidelines for Examination, *Guidelines for Examination in the European Patent Office November 2018 edition*, G.II.5.4 (2018), https://www.epo.org/law-practice/legal-texts/guidelines.html (last visited 1 March 2019).

techniques, the legislation is rather patentee friendly. A look at the recitals to the Biotech Directive shows that the goal of the drafters of the law was to boost investments in this area of research through the creation of opportunities to protect newly developed inventions. A glance at patent activity in the last two decades does not seem to show a particular boost, especially in comparison to other areas of biotechnology.

4 PLANT PATENTS IN EUROPE

The numbers of European patent documents published for angiosperm plants were analysed for each year between 2000 and 2018 and compared to overall numbers of biotechnological patents in this same territory for this same period. This was done in order to compare the overall volume as well as trends in patents claiming plants (as products) to patents whose subject are biotechnological inventions in general.

4.1 Method

An internet database and search tool lens.org was used in order to search for patent documents. The search string for patents for plants was as indicated in the footnote.[25] It is based on the CPC classification. The search encompassed applications that claimed 'plant*'. Angiosperm plants were chosen due to the fact that they are the most important plants in agriculture (A01H5* or A01H6*). Other inventions from the A (Human necessities) section were excluded in order to limit the search to product patents claiming plants. In particular, class A61K* was excluded in order to eliminate medical inventions. The results were filtered by publication date (2000-2018) and restricted to filings with the European Patent Office only.

The search for biotechnological inventions was based on classes indicated by OECD as a representative for the group[26] with some amendments to reflect recent changes in classification. Class A61K* was also removed from the search to avoid overlapping. The search string is included in the footnote.[27] The results were filtered by

25. Claims: (plant*) AND (classification_cpc: (A01H5*) OR classification_cpc: (A01H6*)) NOT classification_cpc: (A61K*) NOT classification_cpc: (A01B OR A01C OR A01D OR A01F OR A01G OR A01N OR A01P).
26. OECD, *OECD Patent Databases. Identifying Technology Areas for Patents* (2008), http://www.oecd.org/sti/inno/40807441.pdf (last visited 7 March 2019).
27. Search string: classification_ipcr:(A01H1/00*) OR classification_ipcr:(A01H4/00*) OR classi fication_ipcr:(A01H5/00*) OR classification_ipcr:(A01H7/00*) OR classification_ipcr:(C07G11/00*) OR classification_ipcr:(C07G13/00*) OR classification_ipcr:(C07G15/00*) OR classification_ipcr:(C07K4/00*) OR classification_ipcr:(C07K14/00*) OR classification_ipcr:(C07K16/00*) OR classification_ipcr:(C07K17/00*) OR classification_ipcr:(C07K19/00*) OR classification_ipcr:(C12M*) OR classification_ipcr:(C12N*) OR classification_ipcr:(C12P*) OR classification_ipcr:(C12Q*) OR classification_ipcr:(C12R*) OR classification_ipcr:(G01N33/48*) NOT classification_ipcr:(A61K*).

publication date (2000-2018) and restricted to filings with the European Patent Office only.[28]

4.2 Results

Figure 8.1. Number of 'Biotech' and 'Plant' patent documents published 2000-2018 by the EPO

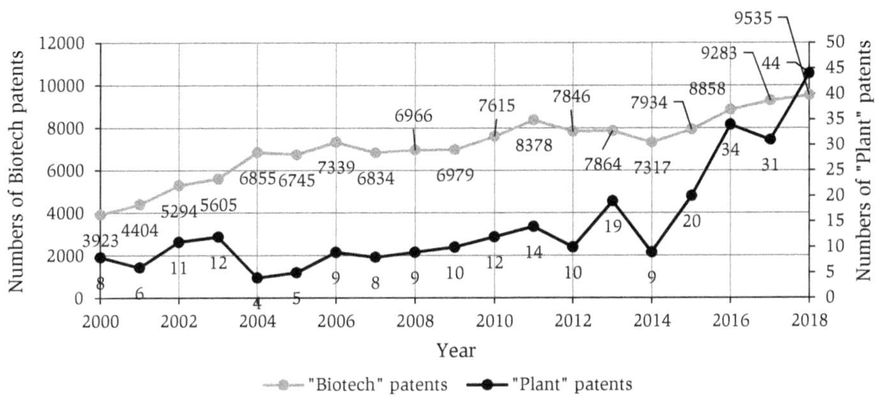

In the researched period, a total number of 135,574 patent documents were published for the 'biotech' inventions and a total number of 275 for the flowering (angiosperm) plants. As the data indicate (*see* Figure 8.1), patents for plants constitute only a small proportion of the patents for biotechnological inventions overall (three orders of magnitude lower). As the number of patents for biotechnological inventions indicates, there is a general growing trend in the last two decades, with their numbers nearly tripling. On the other hand, the numbers of patents for plants as such stayed in the vicinity of 10 for the first decade, with a rapid growth between 2014 and 2018. It is beyond the scope of this chapter to analyse the reasons for this growth; it may also be connected with developments in the field of new plant breeding techniques (*see* 5.2) or an outcome of EPO decisions regarding the patentability of essentially biological processes for the production of plants and their products (*see* 3). The behaviour of

28. Different authors propose different classifications for inventions in the field of biotechnology. For instance, Ulrich Schmoch, *Concept of a Technology Classification for Country Comparisons* 5 (2008), http://www.wipo.int/edocs/mdocs/classifications/en/ipc_ce_41/ (last visited 7 March 2019) proposes the 8th IPC edition classes C07G; C12M, N, P, Q, R, S for inventions in this field. The search using those classes, with A61K* excluded, returns a smaller total number of patent documents (126 225 instead of 135 574) but it does not change the order of magnitude. Search string for the alternative search: classification_ipcr:(C07G*) OR classification_ipcr:(C12M*) OR classification_ipcr:(C12N*) OR classification_ipcr:(C12P*) OR classification_ipcr:(C12Q*) OR classification_ipcr:(C12R*) NOT classification_ipcr: (A61K*).

applicants and the EPO in subsequent years may shed some light on that issue, as well as qualitative analysis of particular patent documents.

Regardless of the reasons for the apparent boost in the numbers of 'plant' patents, it can be seen that they constitute only a small proportion of the patents for biotechnological inventions in general. This could indicate an apparent lack of research and development investments in this area; however, other data show that this might not be the case. In particular, the acreage of genetically modified (GM) plants has constantly been growing worldwide since their commercialisation in 1996 and has reached 189.8 million hectares in 2017, but at this same time, the acreage and number of countries where they are grown in the EU have dropped to a little over 130,000 hectares (in Spain and Portugal).[29] This indicates a broad adoption of plant biotechnology products outside Europe.

Most of the 'plant' patents were applied for by large seed companies (including affiliates): Monsanto - 26, Syngenta - 18, DuPont - 17, Bayer - 16, Dow Agroscience - 10. These are correlated with companies applying for authorisation of GM plants for the EU market, yet this does not indicate that there is a causal link between the two activities (patenting and applying for authorisation).

5 GMO LEGISLATION IN THE EU[30]

5.1 Overview of the GMO Legislation

As it follows on from the analysis of the principles for patent protection of plants, the patent law focuses on allowing for patents on plants that were altered in other ways than are characteristic for conventional breeding. This is exemplified not only by the explicit ban on the patentability of plant varieties and essentially biological processes but also by explanations given in the recitals to the Biotech Directive or, for instance, in the EPO Guidelines for Examination.[31] They indicate that according to the drafters, patent law was seen as a tool for protecting such innovations that essentially differ from the results of conventional breeding and as such are difficult to protect through the plant variety protection system. The dispute about the scope of the essentially biological processes exception does not change this situation significantly. Even if it were to be decided eventually that products of essentially biological processes are patentable, it wouldn't change the general aim and reading of the Biotech Directive or the Implementing Regulations to the EPC, where the patentability of groups of plants **not developed** through essentially biological processes is undisputable.

29. ISAAA, *Global Status of Commercialised Biotech/GM Crops in 2017: Biotech Crop Adoption Surges as Economic Benefits Accumulate in 22 Years* (2018), http://www.isaaa.org/resources/publications/briefs/53/executivesummary/default.asp (last visited 19 September 2018).
30. A more in-depth analysis of the GMO legislation and the GMO definitions has been published in: Tomasz Zimny et al., *Certain new plant breeding techniques and their marketability in the context of EU GMO legislation – recent developments*, 51 New Biotechnology 49-56 (2019). The part here is meant to present only a general overview of the legal situation.
31. Guidelines for Examination, *supra* n. 24, G.II.5.4.

If we look at the numbers of patents where plants were claimed, applied for yearly at the EPO for the last 20 years, we notice that there does not seem to be a significant increase (in terms of orders of magnitude) in their numbers. Such an increase could be interpreted as an indicator of progress or at least increased investment in that area.[32] Since patent law seems to be encouraging when it comes to the protection of innovations in the field of plant biotechnology, there might be other factors that limit or slow down progress in that area. Since a patent in and of itself does not grant positive rights to exploit an invention, such exploitation being often subject to different laws, one may raise a hypothesis that legal or bureaucratic thresholds may contribute to the low adoption of technology (aside from different factors, such as social opposition), even if the patenting policy is fundamentally inventor-friendly.

A GMO is 'an organism, with the exception of human beings, in which the genetic material has been altered in a way that does not occur naturally by mating and/or natural recombination', as it was defined in the 2001/18/EC *Directive on the deliberate release into the environment of genetically modified organisms and repealing Council Directive 90/220/EEC*. Research and marketing of GMOs have been regulated in several acts of EU law, the most important of which, from the point of view of this chapter are the aforementioned 2001/18/EC Directive and the 1829/2003/EC *Regulation on genetically modified food and feed*. The first one regulates the rules for the authorisation of an experimental deliberate release of GMOs into the environment (part B) and marketing for purposes other than food and feed, which includes authorisation of sowing material for the purposes of cultivation (part C). The second one introduces procedures for authorisation and supervision (including post-market monitoring) of GM food and feed on the common market. It also introduces provisions for labelling of GM food and feed marketed in the EU. Both of the mentioned acts are built on the precautionary principle that mandates undertaking precautionary measures when scientific data about the outcomes of a decision is incomplete, unreliable or inconclusive, while prima facie such activity can be risky (*see* Article 1 of Directive 2001/18/EC and recital 43 of Regulation 1829/2003/EC). The main objectives of those acts are connected with the protection of human and animal health, as well as protection of the environment (Article 1 of Directive 2001/18/EC, Article 1 of Regulation 1829/2003/EC). These objectives are achieved through three main instruments:

(1) mandatory authorisation of all GM products that are to enter the market, preceded by risk assessment (Article 13 and next of Directive 2001/18/EC, Article 4 and 16 of Regulation 1829/2003/EC);
(2) mandatory labelling of GM food and feed present on the market (Article 21 of Directive 2001/18/EC, Articles 12 and 24 of Regulation 1829/2003/EC);
(3) supervision of GM products (Article 20 of Directive 2001/18/EC Articles 9, 17, and 21 of Regulation 1829/2003/EC).

32. OECD, *A Framework for Biotechnology Statistics* 14 (2005), http://www.oecd.org/sti/sci-tech/34935605.pdf (last visited 3 March 2019).

All GM products that are to be placed on the EU market have to be authorised. The authorisation for food and feed is granted by the European Commission, after a positive opinion of the European Food Safety Authority (EFSA), in the comitology procedure. Sowing material for cultivation has to be authorised on the basis of the 2001/18/EC Directive. Such authorisation is by default granted by a competent body of a Member State; however, it can also be granted 'alongside' the authorisation of food and feed, under certain conditions. In order to receive a positive opinion from the EFSA, the applicant has to perform a risk assessment (i.e., gather scientific evidence) and prove that the product complies with the requirements of the directive or the Regulation. As research by Smart et al. showed, the time needed to receive authorisation for food or feed is currently about five years after the risk assessment.[33] Delays in GMO authorisation times were, in some cases, deemed by the European Ombudsman to be examples of maladministration on the side of the European Commission.[34]

GM products are mostly used as animal feed in the EU, and tens of millions of tonnes of GM soybean, but also rapeseed and maize are imported into the EU every year.[35] While there are numerous GM food and feed products registered for the EU market, so far only the MON 810 maize has been successfully placed on the market for the purposes of cultivation and was recently cultivated in two Member States only – Portugal and Spain.[36] As of the adoption of the 2015/412/EC *Directive amending Directive 2001/18/EC as regards the possibility for the Member States to restrict or prohibit the cultivation of genetically modified organisms (GMOs) in their territory*, the EU Member States can easily restrict the cultivation of GMOs on their territories, regardless of safety or environmental issues and 19 states or regions decided to do so.[37]

The abovementioned situation creates a high entry barrier for entrepreneurs, who would like to market their products in the EU. They have to comply with very high safety standards and bear the cost of extensive testing, and even if such research returns satisfactory results, the outcome of the authorisation procedures is not only uncertain but also strongly delayed. Already 10 years ago, it was estimated that the cost of preparing a risk assessment dossier oscillates between EUR 7 and 10 million per one transformation event (modification).[38] This means that only larger companies can bear

33. Richard D. Smart, Matthias Blum & Justus Wesseler, *Trends in Approval Times for Genetically Engineered Crops in the United States and the European Union*, 68 Journal of Agricultural Economics 182-198 (2017).
34. *See*, e.g., European Ombudsman, *Decision of the European Ombudsman closing the inquiry into complaint 1582/2014/PHP on the European Commission's handling of authorisation applications for genetically modified food and feed* (2016), https://www.ombudsman.europa.eu/en/decision/en/63025#_ftnref6 (last visited 16 September 2018).
35. European Commission, *Genetically modified commodities in the EU* 27 (2016), https://ec.europa.eu/transparency/regdoc/rep/10102/2016/EN/10102-2016-61-EN-F1-1.PDF (last visited 18 September 2018).
36. ISAAA, *supra* n. 29.
37. European Commission, *Restrictions of geographical scope of GMO applications/authorisations: EU countries demands and outcomes*, Food Safety – European Commission (2016), https://ec.europa.eu/food/plant/gmo/authorisation/cultivation/geographical_scope_en (last visited 4 March 2019).
38. COGEM, *Should EU Legislation Be Updated? Scientific developments throw new light on the process and product approaches* 10 (2009), https://www.cogem.net/showdownload.cfm?

the cost of complying with the formal requirements for applying for the authorisation, let alone cope with the procedures and delays. This is confirmed by the list of applicants who obtained authorisation. Out of 61 authorisations for food or feed valid in 2018 in the EU, 30 were obtained by Monsanto, 13 by Bayer, 7 by Pioneer and 6 by Syngenta.[39] This list correlates strongly with the list of applicants obtaining patents for plants. Commercially available products are offered exclusively by large companies. Also, the number of registered events is not very high if one considers that there are currently 229 transformation events registered worldwide for maize alone.[40]

GM products are not popular in the EU, partly due to strong public opposition towards them. As surveys show, many members of the general public consider them unsafe or harmful to the environment.[41] The strictness of regulations correlated with an apparent timid reaction towards the technology indicates distrust towards the existing legislation or mechanisms for ensuring biosafety in the EU. This situation is, to some extent, similar to reactions towards nuclear energy.[42]

5.2 New Plant Breeding Techniques and the Legal Status of Their Products

The very concept of a GMO (as it was defined in the law) gives rise to debates about its designation. According to Article 2(2) of the 2001/18/EC Directive, a GMO is 'an organism, with the exception of human beings, in which the genetic material has been altered in a way that does not occur naturally by mating and/or natural recombination'. This article further refers to Annex I A part 1 of the directive that contains an exemplary list of techniques, which according to the drafters, result in the creation of a GMO.[43] Annex I A part 2 contains a list of techniques considered not to result in genetic modification 'on condition that they do not involve the use of recombinant

objectId = FFFE884E-1517-64D9-CC44F68B25E8231F&objectType = mark.apps.cogem.contentobjects.publication.download.pdf (last visited 4 March 2019).

39. EU GMO Registry, *Genetically Modified Organisms* (2019), https://webgate.ec.europa.eu/dyna/gm_register/index_en.cfm (last visited 14 January 2019).
40. ISAAA, *GM Approval Database | ISAAA.org GM Maize* (2019), http://www.isaaa.org/gmapprovaldatabase/advsearch/default.asp?CropID = 6&TraitTypeID = Any&DeveloperID = Any&CountryID = Any&ApprovalTypeID = Any (last visited 5 March 2019).
41. Eurobarometer, *Special Eurobarometer 341: Biotechnology* (2010), http://ec.europa.eu/public_opinion/archives/eb_special_359_340_en.htm#341.
42. Jaesun Wang & Seoyong Kim, *Comparative Analysis of Public Attitudes toward Nuclear Power Energy across 27 European Countries by Applying the Multilevel Model*, 10 Sustainability 1518, 8 (2018).
43. Techniques of genetic modification referred to in Art. 2(2)(a) are *inter alia*:
    (1) recombinant nucleic acid techniques involving the formation of new combinations of genetic material by the insertion of nucleic acid molecules produced by whatever means outside an organism, into any virus, bacterial plasmid or other vector system and their incorporation into a host organism in which they do not naturally occur but in which they are capable of continued propagation;
    (2) techniques involving the direct introduction into an organism of heritable material prepared outside the organism including micro-injection, macro-injection and micro-encapsulation;

nucleic acid molecules or genetically modified organisms made by techniques/methods other than those excluded by Annex I B'.[44] The latter Annex contains a list of organisms considered to be created by techniques of genetic modification that are exempted from the scope of the directive (Article 3 paragraph 1).[45] This list is, in turn, exhaustive. There are generally three groups of organisms being products of various breeding techniques: GMOs regulated by the directive (and other acts on GMO), organisms created through techniques listed in Annex I A part 2 that are not considered GMOs and organisms created through techniques listed in Annex I B that are considered GMOs but not covered by the scope of the directive. The reason that the last group was listed seems to be indicated in recital 17 to the directive, reading: 'this Directive should not apply to organisms obtained through certain techniques of genetic modification which have conventionally been used in a number of applications and have a long safety record'. This may mean, e.g., techniques of random mutagenesis, i.e., random alteration of plants genome through nuclear or chemical mutagens and subsequent selection of the desired offspring.

The trigger for the GMO authorisation process in the EU is strongly process-based in this case – it is not necessarily the features of the product that decide whether an organism is regulated, but the process by which an organism was created. The definition of a GMO contains a condition that in order to be a GMO, an organism should be altered in a way that does not occur naturally by mating or natural recombination. Yet the further clarification present in Article 2(2a) seems to indicate that it is the technique used that is decisive here, not the nature of the change. If we accept this approach, it may lead to the outcome that a plant that had part of its genome removed by the usage of one of the techniques mentioned in Annex I A part 1, and then had this same fragment reinserted at this same locus, should be treated as a GMO – although it is indistinguishable from its unmodified counterpart. The definition of a GMO along with its exceptions is a source of controversies regarding the legal status of products of newly developed plant breeding techniques called the new plant breeding techniques (NBTs).

---

(3) cell fusion (including protoplast fusion) or hybridisation techniques where live cells with new combinations of heritable genetic material are formed through the fusion of two or more cells by means of methods that do not occur naturally.

44. Techniques referred to in Art. 2(2)(b) which are not considered to result in genetic modification, on condition that they do not involve the use of recombinant nucleic acid molecules or genetically modified organisms made by techniques/methods other than those excluded by Annex I B:

(1) in vitro fertilisation;
(2) natural processes such as: conjugation, transduction, transformation;
(3) polyploidy induction.

45. Techniques/methods of genetic modification yielding organisms to be excluded from the directive, on the condition that they do not involve the use of recombinant nucleic acid molecules or genetically modified organisms other than those produced by one or more of the techniques/methods listed below are:

(1) mutagenesis;
(2) cell fusion (including protoplast fusion) of plant cells of organisms which can exchange genetic material through traditional breeding methods.

New breeding techniques are not a uniform group. The term 'NBT' is usually understood to encompass such techniques as cisgenesis, where a fragment of DNA from the same species is introduced into the plant genome,[46] genome editing through site-directed nucleases (SDN), where an enzyme (nuclease) is used in order to induce precise breaks and other changes in the DNA strand,[47] or oligonucleotide-directed mutagenesis (ODM) – a technique where short fragments of nucleic acids are used to induce precise mutations in the genome.[48] Recently, the development of the CRISPR (Clustered Regularly Interspaced Short Palindromic Repeats) technology was seen as a breakthrough in genome editing and thus, also a very useful tool in plant breeding. The technology usually utilises a Cas9 nuclease and a fragment of synthetic ribonucleic acid (RNA) in order to cause breaks in the DNA of the receptor plant at precisely selected sites that are later repaired by the cell repair mechanism.[49]

The methods listed above can be used to introduce small changes in the DNA (single mutations), and some of them can be also utilised to introduce large fragments of foreign DNA into the edited genome. The small changes are not different from naturally occurring mutations, and often it is impossible to distinguish such an edited plant from a plant where the mutation occurred spontaneously.[50]

In view of the definition of the GMO (as quoted above) and the list of exceptions to the 2001/18/EC Directive, a question arose as to whether products of some of those new breeding methods should be regulated by the GMO legislation or not. On the one hand, according to Annex I B to the directive, products of mutagenesis are exempted from the GMO legislation, despite being considered to be GM. On the other hand, according to recital 17 of the 2001/18/EC Directive, some techniques were exempted from the directive because they have 'conventionally been used in a number of applications and have a long safety record'. Some of the newer gene editing techniques, in particular, CRISPR do not have such a long usage record since they have been developed or widely used fairly recently (e.g., CRISPR was first revealed in 2011).[51] Some countries, including those that export large amounts of food and feed products into the EU, decided not to regulate products of certain NBTs in the same way GMOs

46. EFSA Panel on Genetically Modified Organisms (GMO), *Scientific opinion addressing the safety assessment of plants developed through cisgenesis and intragenesis: Plants developed through cisgenesis and intragenesis*, 10 European Food Safety Authority Journal 2561 (2012).
47. EFSA Panel on Genetically Modified Organisms (GMO), *Scientific opinion addressing the safety assessment of plants developed using Zinc Finger Nuclease 3 and other Site-Directed Nucleases with similar function: Plants developed by ZFN-3*, 10 European Food Safety Authority Journal 2943 (2012).
48. Noel J. Sauer et al., *Oligonucleotide-directed mutagenesis for precision gene editing*, 14 Plant Biotechnology Journal. 496-502 (2016).
49. Magdy M. Mahfouz, Agnieszka Piatek & Charles Neal Stewart, *Genome engineering via TALENs and CRISPR/Cas9 systems: challenges and perspectives*, 12 Plant Biotechnology Journal 1006-1014 (2014); M. McNutt, *Breakthrough to genome editing*, 350 Science 1445-1445 (2015).
50. Group of Chief Scientific Advisors, A Scientific Perspective on the Regulatory Status of Products Derived from Gene Editing and the Implications for the GMO Directive 5 (2018), https://ec.europa.eu/info/sites/info/files/2018_11_gcsa_statement_gene_editing_2.pdf (last visited 6 March 2019).
51. M. Jinek et al., *A Programmable Dual-RNA-Guided DNA Endonuclease in Adaptive Bacterial Immunity*, 337 Science 816-821 (2012).

are regulated, notably Argentina and the USA.[52] This more lax regulation (or lack thereof) was introduced due to the nature of the changes of the genome editing when no foreign DNA fragments are inserted into the plant genomes (as in case of genetic modification) and also due to the number of changes caused by those methods (precise point mutations versus random changes in a multitude of places in the case of random mutagenesis, which is anyway not regulated as strictly as GMOs).[53]

The dispute about the scope of the mutagenesis exemption in Annex I B to the 2001/18/EC Directive (whether the exemption applies only to traditional random mutagenesis or if it also applies to the modern, precise methods) was subject to an ECJ preliminary ruling last year. In the case C-528/16, the French Conseil d'Etat asked *inter alia* if organisms obtained by mutagenesis constitute genetically modified organisms within the meaning of Article 2 of Directive [2001/18], although they are exempt under Article 3 of and Annex I B to the directive from the obligations laid down for release and placing on the market of genetically modified organisms. In particular, may mutagenesis techniques, in particular new directed mutagenesis techniques implementing genetic engineering processes, be regarded as techniques listed in Annex I A, to which Article 2 refers? Consequently, must Articles 2 and 3 of and Annexes I A and I B to Directive [2001/18] be interpreted as meaning that they exempt from precautionary, impact assessment and traceability measures all organisms and seeds obtained by mutagenesis, or only organisms obtained by conventional random mutagenesis methods by ionising radiation or exposure to mutagenic chemical agents existing before those measures were adopted?[54]

The question was first answered by Advocate General Bobek, who argued that the directive did not make distinctions between 'new' and 'old' methods and that the drafters of the directive were aware of scientific progress hence the directive should not be statically interpreted. Besides, it would be impractical to apply the criterion of methods that were routinely used in 2001. It would raise even more questions, such as to how to qualify methods that were used routinely but were improved later or were used routinely but only in a laboratory, etc.[55] The advocate argued further that the

52. Agustina I Whelan & Martin A Lema, *Regulatory framework for gene editing and other new breeding techniques (NBTs) in Argentina*, 6 GM Crops Food 253-265 (2015); USDA, *Secretary Perdue Issues USDA Statement on Plant Breeding Innovation*, USDA Animal and Plant Health Inspection Service (2018), https://content.govdelivery.com/accounts/USDAAPHIS/bulletins/1e599ff (last visited 19 Oct. 2018).
53. Group of Chief Scientific Advisors, *supra* n. 50.
54. CJEU C-528/16, Judgment of CJEU in the case C-528/16 Confédération paysanne and others *v.* Premier ministre de l'agriculture, de l'agroalimentaire et de la forêt, ECLI:EU:C:2018:583 (2018), http://curia.europa.eu/juris/document/document.jsf?text=&docid=204387&pageIndex=0&doclang=EN&mode=lst&dir=&occ=first&part=1&cid=756053 (last visited 20 September 2018).
55. Michal Bobek, Opinion of Advocate General Bobek, Case C-528/16, *Confédération paysanne and others v. Premier ministre de l'agriculture, de l'agroalimentaire et de la forêt*, ECLI:EU:C:2018:20, 77, 105 (2018), http://curia.europa.eu/juris/document/document.jsf?text=&docid=198532&pageIndex=0&doclang=EN&mode=lst&dir=&occ=first&part=1&cid=997292 (last visited 21 Sep. 2018).

introduction of a distinction between 'new' and 'old' methods of mutagenesis would be a form of judicial redrafting of the directive.[56]

The judgment of the court went in the opposite direction. The court argued that recital 17 justifies a distinction between 'random mutagenesis' and 'directional mutagenesis'. Besides, the court argued that 'new techniques/methods of mutagenesis might prove to be similar to those which result from the production and release of a GMO through transgenesis' and that 'the development of those new techniques/methods makes it possible to produce genetically modified varieties at a rate and in quantities quite unlike those resulting from the application of conventional methods of random mutagenesis'. Eventually, the court ruled that:

Article 2(2) of Directive 2001/18/EC must be interpreted as meaning that organisms obtained by means of techniques/methods of mutagenesis constitute genetically modified organisms within the meaning of that provision. Article 3(1), read in conjunction with point 1 of Annex I B to that directive and in the light of recital 17 thereof, must be interpreted as meaning that only organisms obtained by means of techniques/methods of mutagenesis which have conventionally been used in a number of applications and have a long safety record are excluded from the scope of that directive.

The judgment, and in particular its justification, are not entirely clear (e.g., why is the efficiency of a method mentioned as a risk factor, instead of the volume of change in the genome that a particular method causes), but it is being interpreted as a judgment according to which the products modern mutagenesis (in particular those involving minor genome edits, indistinguishable from naturally occurring mutations) should be subjected to GMO legislation, and hence the costs and red tape related to it. Indeed, such classification of the products might render such products economically unfit for the EU market, since it would be difficult to get them authorised and sold on the common market.[57] There are also calls that the directive should be amended since it does not reflect the scientific progress made in the 20 years from its drafting. Such an amendment could mean a shift in the designation approach, from purely process-based (where the techniques used determine whether an organism is regulated), to a product-based one, (where the features of the organism make the determination).[58] It is still too early to predict the fallout of the judgment and its influence on the adoption of precise genome editing techniques. Should they be treated as leading to the creation of regulated GMOs, the rate of their adoption may fall significantly. Currently, the Council issued a decision requesting the European Commission to perform a study as to the status of novel genomic techniques under Union law, and a proposal for amendment, if appropriate in view of the outcomes of the study.[59]

56. *Ibid.* at 104.
57. Multiple Authors, *Open Letter to Member States on the EU Court Ruling on Mutagenesis* (2019), https://cefs.org/wp-content/uploads/2019/04/Letter-to-Member-States-at-Scopaffs-April-2019.pdf (last visited 9 May 2019).
58. Group of Chief Scientific Advisors, *supra* n. 50 at 6.
59. *Council Decision (EU) 2019/1904 of November 2019 requesting the Commission to submit a study in light of the Court of Justice's judgment in Case C-528/16 regarding the status of novel genomic*

6 CONCLUSIONS

In recent years, the yield progress for the most popular cereals (wheat, rice and maize) was estimated at about 0.9% per year for the first two crops and about 1.6% per year for maize – and it is not certain that this progress can prevent an increase in food prices when combined with the growth of the population.[60] Meanwhile, symptoms of stagnation in the crop yield progress have been observed; however, they are not necessarily attributed to lack of biological progress but rather to environmental factors.[61] The length of the process of developing new plant varieties depends on various factors, such as breeding conditions, the species of plants, etc. Nevertheless, it may even take 20 years to develop a new plant variety in the case of conventional breeding of some more popular agricultural species (e.g., maize), with the length decreasing when more modern biotechnological methods are applied (e.g., five years with genetic engineering methods).[62] The breeding process itself is costly and requires extensive resources, not only in terms of knowledge and experience from highly qualified personnel but also in terms of land for experimentation. This, in turn, requires the breeder to choose their research tools carefully. In particular, as was shown above, choosing a method that would yield products regulated by the GMO legislation in the EU may prove to be economically unjustified, even if such methods were to allow for the process to obtain new products to be shorter. In view of the bureaucratic burdens and the length of the authorisation process, the brevity of the development process of a new variety may be misleading. The administrative barriers create serious difficulty in marketing many plant biotechnology products.

Since the decision about the breeding method is taken at the onset of the breeding process and the process takes years to complete, the breeder needs to be absolutely sure that they will be able to place the product of this process on the market. With the current dubious status of the products of breeding techniques that involve genome editing, breeders might decide not to invest in the development of these methods, or in creating new varieties with their use. The legal uncertainty is present at two levels here. The first has to do with the unclear legal status of the breeding process' products (i.e., whether plants or animals derived through the application of a particular breeding method are going to be regulated as GMOs or not). The second level is connected with the uncertainty as to the outcome of the authorisation process, should such products be classified as GMOs. This is particularly pertinent to plants for cultivation purposes, as they can be banned from the market even if the risk assessment and subsequent authorisation prove them to be safe (*see* above). These uncertainties are yet another

techniques under Union law, and a proposal, if appropriate in view of the outcomes of the study, Official Journal of the European Union L, 2019, no. 293, pp. 103-104.

60. R. A. (Tony) Fischer & Gregory O. Edmeades, *Breeding and Cereal Yield Progress*, 50 Crop Sci. S-85, S-85 (2010); Agnès Ricroch, *The Evolution of Agriculture and Tools for Plant Innovation*, in Plant Biotechnology 13-24, 22 (Agnès Ricroch, Surinder Chopra, & Shelby J. Fleischer eds, 2014), doi: 10.1007/978-3-319-06892-3 (last visited 9 May 2019).
61. Nadine Brisson et al., *Why are wheat yields stagnating in Europe? A comprehensive data analysis for France*, 119 Field Crops Research 201-212 (2010).
62. Ricroch, *supra* n. 60 at 16-17, 20.

obstacle to the marketability of plant biotech products. Estimates show that a six-year delay in the authorisation process may dissuade companies from investing in technology.[63] In the cases described here, not only is the authorisation process lengthy but also treating it with the greatest diligence doesn't guarantee that it will allow for unobstructed access to the market.

As was shown above, the number of patent applications where plants as such are claimed, while rising in recent years, remains at a relatively low level. While European patent law allows for patenting of many kinds of inventions, including DNA sequences, plant cells, plants as such and many processes of their modification and development, it does not seem to be the decisive factor, and less so a driving force when it comes to investments in the development of new plants. There may be many reasons for that, but the obstacles mentioned above seem to be of importance here. A patent for an invention is somewhat useless if there is no possibility to market the patented invention. The apparent length of the authorisation process might also influence the value of a patent in a different way, especially in comparison to a plant variety right. Since the novelty of an invention is examined at the priority date, it is generally advisable to file for a patent at an early stage of development, in order to outrun the competition and avoid a risk of a similar product or process being revealed in the meantime. Unlike in the case of patents, the novelty of a plant variety is estimated based on the date of placing the variety on the market rather than the date of filing or other priority dates (*see* Article 10 of the 2100/94/EC Regulation). It means that while in the case of a patent for a group of plants, the protection period may, to a large extent, be consumed by the duration of the authorisation process, in the case of plant variety protection, the filing for a plant variety right can happen when the product is already authorised to be marketed. This does not necessarily mean that the plant variety protection system is a more suitable system for the protection of innovation in the realm of plant biotechnology. The object, rules and scope of protection in both systems are different, and they exist parallel to each other. Nevertheless, since there is no supplementary protection certificate system for, e.g., transgenic plants that would compensate for the length of the authorisation process, it is not excluded that the protection period of a patented invention may run out before the product becomes profitable on the market.

The abovementioned obstacles seem to make patents for plants not particularly attractive, regardless of which justification for the patent system one would like to adopt (*see* part 2). A patent will not warrant a return on investment if the product is legally or practically unmarketable. It cannot be considered a serious prize for the inventor/investor for similar reasons. It will not facilitate a transfer of technology if there is no demand for such technology (be it for legal or other reasons). A broad patent portfolio may be a factor in increasing the overall value of a company.[64] This does not seem to be the case in the example of patents for plants, given their small numbers. In

63. Stuart J Smyth, Jillian McDonald & Jose Falck-Zepeda, *Investment, regulation, and uncertainty: Managing new plant breeding techniques*, 5 GM Crops Food 44-57, 56 (2014).
64. Alex Coad & Rekha Rao, *Innovation and market value: a quantile regression analysis*, 15 Econ. Bull. 1-10 (2006).

effect, the theoretical value of a plant patent may not be enough to drive the research in this area. After introducing specific rules for the protection of biotechnological inventions, including ones in agriculture, in order to foster their development, the EU introduced a system for authorisation that is ineffective and hamstrings their broad implementation. The current uncertainty about the products of new breeding techniques contributes to this phenomenon.

CHAPTER 9

The Farm-Saved Seed under the Community Plant Variety Rights System in the Light of the "Recommendation Relating to Article 15(2)" of the UPOV Act of 1991 and Article 39(1)(a) TFEU*

*Juan Antonio Vives-Vallés***,***

* An early draft version of this chapter was posted on SSRN on 1 February 2019 as Juan Antonio Vives-Vallés, "*Essay on the Farm-Saved Seed under the CPVR System and Its Sphere of Influence in the Light of the UPOV Act of 1991 and the Contemporary Interpretation of Art. 39(1)(A) TFEU*" (30 January 2019). Forthcoming, Żaneta Pacud and Rafał Sikorski (eds.), *Rethinking Patent Law as an Incentive to Innovation*, 2019. Available at SSRN: https://ssrn.com/abstract=3325972 or http://dx.doi.org/10.2139/ssrn.3325972.

** *Acknowledgments:* To the CPVO and its members, for their excellent training on PVP and the CPVR system, as well as for their kindness during my stays at the institution. To the Office of UPOV and *Naktuinbouw*, for their excellent training on the UPOV system and PVP. To all the experts from the CPVO and the Office of UPOV who have directly or indirectly contributed to improve the analysis here presented. To the MIPLC and the *Max-Planck-Institut für Innovation und Wettbewerb*, for their excellent academic training, and their support during the early stages of its drafting. To the University of the Balearic Islands, most remarkably, to my superiors, friends and colleagues from the Private Law Department and the Faculty of Law, and from the Area of Vegetal Physiology of the Department of Biology of the University as well as the INAGEA.

****Disclaimer:* Research leading to the current chapter was initiated by the author under the framework of the L.L.M. program "Intellectual Property and Competition Law" at the Munich Intellectual Property Law Center (MIPLC), Munich, Germany (October 2017-November 2018) thanks to a scholarship waiver granted by the *Max-Planck-Institut für Innovation und Wettbewerb* (Munich, Germany). The author concluded the current version at the CPVO, thanks to an internship offered by that institution, and revised it at the University of the Balearic Islands. Statements of fact and opinions expressed in this chapter constitute those of the author only and do not represent the views and opinions of the funding/hosting institutions. Permission has been given by UPOV for the reproduction of parts of UPOV publications and documents (including, *inter alia*, part of texts of the Acts of the UPOV Convention, the Records of the Diplomatic Conferences, and other publications and documents available in the UPOV website).

1 INTRODUCTION

1.1 The Community Plant Variety Rights System Within the UPOV System

The European Union (EU) is a UPOV[1] member since July 29, 2005,[2] running "a plant breeders' rights system which covers the territory of its 28 Member States (Member States of the EU: Austria, Belgium, Bulgaria, Croatia, Cyprus, Czech Republic, Denmark, Estonia, Finland, France, Germany, Greece, Hungary, Ireland, Italy, Latvia, Lithuania, Luxembourg, Malta, Netherlands, Poland, Portugal, Romania, Slovakia, Slovenia, Spain, Sweden, United Kingdom)."[3] However, the legal text on which the Community Plant Variety Rights system[4] is based, namely, Council Regulation (EC) no. 2100/94 of July 27, 1994 on Community plant variety rights ("Basic Regulation"[5]),[6] was approved before that date.[7] In spite of this gap, it is generally understood that the CPVR system is adapted to the standards set by the UPOV Act of 1991.[8] This chapter,

1. UPOV stands for "Union for the Protection of New Varieties of Plants". UPOV, "Records of the Diplomatic Conference for the Revision of the International Convention for the Protection of New Varieties of Plants—Geneva 1991 (Publication UPOV N° 346 (E))" (1992) 18 http://www.upov.int/edocs/pubdocs/en/upov_pub_346.pdf accessed May 10, 2019.
2. UPOV, "Members of the International Union for the Protection of New Varieties of Plants: Status on May 2, 2019" (2019) 1 http://www.upov.int/export/sites/upov/members/en/pdf/pub423.pdf accessed July 19, 2019; Gert Würtenberger and others, *European Union Plant Variety Protection* (Oxford University Press 2015) 4, 13; Olga Sánchez Gil, *La Protección de Las Obtenciones Vegetales: El Privilegio Del Agricultor* (Serie ESTU, Ministerio de Medio Ambiente, Medio Rural y Marino 2008) 38; Ángel García Vidal, "El Sistema de Protección de Las Variedades Vegetales" in Ángel García Vidal (ed.), *Derecho de las obtenciones vegetales* (Editorial Tirant lo Blanch SL 2017) 94; José Antonio Gómez Segade, "Diferencias Entre El Sistema de Patentes y El Sistema de Protección de Las Obtenciones Vegetales" in Ángel García Vidal (ed.), *Derecho de las obtenciones vegetales* (Editorial Tirant lo Blanch SL 2017) 116.
3. UPOV, "Members of the International Union for the Protection of New Varieties of Plants: Status on May 2, 2019" (n. 2) 2. *See also* Bart Kiewiet, "Relation between PVP and Patents on Biotechnology" (2003) 3 http://cpvo.europa.eu/sites/default/files/documents/articles/BK Bangkok November 2003.pdf accessed May 30, 2020.
4. The "Community Plant Variety Rights System" (CPVO, "About Us" https://cpvo.europa.eu/en/about-us accessed July 19, 2019), or "CPVR system" (CPVO, "Law & Practice" https://cpvo.europa.eu/en/about-us/law-and-practice accessed July 31, 2019); also known as the "European Union system of plant variety rights" (CPVO, "CPVO Main Page" https://cpvo.europa.eu/en accessed July 19, 2019).
5. Würtenberger and others (n. 2) 4.
6. *Ibid.* 4, 17; García Vidal, "El Sistema de Protección de Las Variedades Vegetales" (n. 2) 95.
7. Würtenberger and others (n. 2) 4.
8. *See ibid.* 4; Sánchez Gil *La protección de las obtenciones vegetales: el privilegio del agricultor* (n. 2) 34, 129; Mrinalini Kochupillai, *Promoting Sustainable Innovations in Plant Varieties*, vol. 5 (1st edn, Springer-Verlag 2016) 25-26, 189 http://link.springer.com/10.1007/978-3-662-52796-2 accessed May 10, 2019; Würtenberger and others (n. 2) 143; Ángel García Vidal, "El material vegetal protegido por una patente o un derecho de obtentor y el empleo del producto de su cosecha con fines de propagación: agotamiento y privilegio del agricultor en Europa y en los EE.UU." (2016) 8 Cuadernos de Derecho Transnacional 76, 77, 91 https://e-revistas.uc3m.es/index.php/CDT/article/view/3020/1726 accessed August 3, 2019; Ángel García Vidal, "Las Relaciones Entre El Sistema de Las Obtenciones Vegetales y El Sistema de Patentes (La Prohibición de Patentar Las Variedades Establecida En Los Derechos Europeo y Español)" in Ángel García Vidal (ed.), *Derecho de las obtenciones vegetales* (Editorial Tirant lo Blanch SL 2017) 143. This link between the CPVR system and the UPOV system is also observed by Sánchez Gil specifically in relation to

although accepting this general idea, contends that, in relation to the FSS, the alignment of the CPVR system to the UPOV system should be further improved.

1.2 The FSS, a Controversial Exception

The "Farm-Saved Seed,"[9] also known as "farmer's privilege,"[10] or "agricultural exemption,"[11] is commonly understood to entail the practice/possibility of "farmers [...] to save seed for sowing on their own farms."[12]

In the UPOV Convention, the FSS is expressly regulated in Article 15(2) of the UPOV Act of 1991:[13]

---

the FSS (*see* Sánchez Gil, *La protección de las obtenciones vegetales: el privilegio del agricultor* (n. 2) 254). Gómez Segade reminds that because of the accession of the EU to UPOV, the UPOV Convention must be taken into account when interpreting the Basic Regulation (*see* Gómez Segade (n. 2) 116). The connection of the CPVR system and national PVR systems in the EU to the UPOV system has led some scholars to analyze them jointly (*see* in this regard, e.g., Ángel García Vidal, "Presentación" in Ángel García Vidal (ed.), *Derecho de las obtenciones vegetales* (Editorial Tirant lo Blanch SL 2017) 40-42; Esperanza Gallego Sánchez, "La Caducidad Del Derecho Del Obtentor" in Ángel García Vidal (ed.), *Derecho de las obtenciones vegetales* (Editorial Tirant lo Blanch SL 2017) 989).

9. Sánchez Gil, *La protección de las obtenciones vegetales: el privilegio del agricultor* (n. 2) 227, 252; Biswajit Dhar, *Sui Generis Systems for Plant Variety Protection* (2002) 15, 21, 22, 24, 25 http://homepages.3-c.coop/tansey/pdfs/sg-col1.pdf accessed 10 May 2019; Kochupillai (n. 8) 66, 67, 179, 198, 307, 309.
10. Ignacio Quintana Carlo, "El Reglamento CE Número 2100/1994 Relativo a La Protección Comunitaria de Las Obtenciones Vegetales" [1994] Actas de derecho industrial y derecho de autor 81 http://vlex.com/vid/relativo-comunitaria-obtenciones-vegetales-262497 accessed 29 February 2020; Ignacio Quintana Carlo, "El Nuevo Régimen Jurídico de Las Obtenciones Vegetales (Comentario de Urgencia a La Ley 3/2000, de 7 de Enero)" [1999] Actas de derecho industrial y derecho de autor 309 http://vlex.com/vid/regimen-juridico-obtenciones-vegetales-262852 accessed 29 February 2020; Würtenberger and others (n. 2) 141; Pablo Amat Llombart, "Concepto, contenido y límites del derecho de obtentor de variedades vegetales según la ley 3/2000 de 7 de enero y el Real Decreto 1261/2005 de 2 de octubre" in Pablo Amat Llombart (ed.), *La propiedad industrial sobre obtenciones vegetales y organismos transgénicos* (Tirant lo Blanch 2007) 222; Olga Sánchez Gil, "El privilegio del agricultor y la excepción en beneficio del agricultor de la ley 3/2000", in Pablo Amat Llombart (ed.), *La propiedad industrial sobre obtenciones vegetales y organismos transgénicos* (Tirant lo Blanch 2007) 337, 338; García Vidal, El material vegetal protegido por una patente o un derecho de obtentor y el empleo del producto de su cosecha con fines de propagación: agotamiento y privilegio del agricultor en Europa y en los EE.UU (n. 8) 91; Manuel Botana Agra, "La Excepción En Beneficio Del Agricultor" in Ángel García Vidal (ed.), *Derecho de las obtenciones vegetales* (Editorial Tirant lo Blanch SL 2017) 611.
11. Würtenberger and others (n. 2) 141; Amat Llombart (n. 10) 222; Sánchez Gil, "El privilegio del agricultor y la excepción en beneficio del agricultor de la ley 3/2000" (n. 2) 338; García Vidal, El material vegetal protegido por una patente o un derecho de obtentor y el empleo del producto de su cosecha con fines de propagación: agotamiento y privilegio del agricultor en Europa y en los EE.UU (n. 8) 91.
12. UPOV, "Records of the Diplomatic Conference for the Revision of the International Convention for the Protection of New Varieties of Plants—Geneva 1991 (Publication UPOV N° 346 (E))" (n. 1) 370. *See also* Dhar (n. 9) 11.
13. Dhar (n. 9) 15; Laurence R Helfer, *FAO Legislative Study 85: Intellectual Property Rights in Plant Varieties: International Legal Regimes and Policy Options for National Governments* (FAO 2004) 29 http://www.fao.org/3/a-y5714e.pdf accessed May 10, 2019; Sánchez Gil, "El privilegio del agricultor y la excepción en beneficio del agricultor de la ley 3/2000" (n. 2) 347; Würtenberger and others (n. 2) 143; Kochupillai (n. 8) 25; García Vidal, El material vegetal protegido por una patente o un derecho de obtentor y el empleo del producto de su cosecha con fines de

> "[Optional exception] Notwithstanding Article 14, each Contracting Party may, within reasonable limits and subject to the safeguarding of the legitimate interests of the breeder, restrict the breeder's right in relation to any variety in order to permit farmers to use for propagating purposes, on their own holdings, the product of the harvest which they have obtained by planting, on their own holdings, the protected variety or a variety covered by Article 14(5)(a)(i) or Article 14(5)(a)(ii)."

With reference to "Article 14(5)(a)(i) or (ii)," Article 15(2) also includes, within the subject matter of the exception, "varieties which are essentially derived from the protected variety, where the protected variety is not itself an essentially derived variety" (Article 14(5)(a)(i) of the UPOV Act of 1991) and "varieties which are not clearly distinguishable in accordance with Article 7 ["Distinctness"] from the protected variety" (Article 14(5)(a)(ii)).[14]

The FSS has been a sensitive issue since the very origin of UPOV,[15] debates focusing to a large extent on its impacts on innovation, with two opposed standpoints: on the one hand, those in favor of a narrow FSS, well represented by the breeders' organizations; [16]on the other hand, those in favor of a broad FSS.[17] Both groups claim to be in favor of innovation, but from two opposite approaches. Those in favor of a narrow FSS ground their position on the role of breeders as innovators,[18] perceiving a

propagación: agotamiento y privilegio del agricultor en Europa y en los EE.UU (n. 8) 89; García Vidal, "El Sistema de Protección de Las Variedades Vegetales" (n. 2) 77; Botana Agra (n. 10) 614, 616. Art 15(2) of the UPOV Act of 1991 has been transcribed from UPOV, "Texts of the Acts of the UPOV Convention" (*UPOV Lex*) https://www.upov.int/upovlex/en/acts.html accessed May 23, 2019.

14. *See also* Botana Agra (n. 10) 615, who refers to these clauses as an "extension" ("*ampliación*") of the FSS.
15. In the Diplomatic Conferences of 1957-1961, the FSS (in its broadest sense) was implicitly contained in the first opening intervention given by the French Secretary of State for Agriculture (UPOV, "Actes Des Conférences Internationales Pour La Protection Des Obtentions Végétales 1957-1961 (Publication UPOV N° 316)" (1974) 21 http://www.upov.int/edocs/pubdocs/fr/upov_pub_316.pdf accessed May 10, 2019). Several statements on the FSS were recorded during that Conference, specifically, from the Committee of Experts (*see* UPOV, "Actes Des Conférences Internationales Pour La Protection Des Obtentions Végétales 1957-1961 (Publication UPOV N° 316)" 44 (adapted from Juan Antonio Vives-Vallés, "The Scope of the Farm-Saved Seed under the UPOV Acts of 1961 and 1978" MIPLC Master Thesis Series (2017/18) 20, 27, 28, 30, 31, 33ff, etc.)), as well as from the Delegations of Switzerland (UPOV, "Actes Des Conférences Internationales Pour La Protection Des Obtentions Végétales 1957-1961 (Publication UPOV N° 316)" 85) and Sweden (*ibid.* 109).
16. *See*, e.g., the interventions of FIS, COMASSO, ASSINSEL and CIOPORA in the Diplomatic Conference of 1991, in UPOV, "Records of the Diplomatic Conference for the Revision of the International Convention for the Protection of New Varieties of Plants—Geneva 1991 (Publication UPOV N° 346 (E))" (n. 1) 357ff. *See also* Administrative and Legal Committee of UPOV, "Revision of the Convention: Position of FIS on the "Farmers Privilege" (CAJ/27/ 7)" (1990) http://www.upov.int/edocs/mdocs/upov/en/caj_27/caj_27_7.pdf accessed July 18, 2019.
17. *See*, e.g., Dhar (n. 9) 5-6, 11, 13, 27; Graham Dutfield, "Food, Biological Diversity and Intellectual Property: The Role of the International Union for the Protection of New Varieties of Plants (UPOV)" (2011) 9 Global Economic Issue Publications, Intellectual Property Issue Paper 4 http://www.quno.org/sites/default/files/resources/UPOV + study + by + QUNO_English.pdf; generally, Kochupillai (n. 8).
18. *See*, e.g., the following excerpt from a position document on the FSS submitted by FIS to the Diplomatic Conference of 1991: "Only an adequate variety protection provides the legal basis and incentive for objective-oriented breeding of plant varieties which meet the particular demands and needs such as yield, quality, adaptability to soil and climate as well as resistance

broad FSS as an abuse of its users (farmers) that deters innovation,[19] while those in favor of a broad FSS generally believe in the role of farmers as innovators.[20] In spite of the crucial interest of the FSS in discussions on innovation,[21] the present chapter does not directly address the impact of the FSS on innovation, nor the foundations of the UPOV system,[22] not even the scope of the FSS.[23] This study analyzes the adjustment of the grounds and scope of the FSS in the CPVR system to the UPOV system, focusing on some aspects in need of scrutiny, most importantly, the grounds of the FSS and their influence on the interpretation of the exception. Many aspects of the FSS, including its

---

[sic.] to plant diseases." Administrative and Legal Committee of UPOV (n. 16) Annex, page 1. An interesting defense of the incentive theory as regards innovation in the breeding sector and in the context of the FSS is made by Sánchez Gil, *La protección de las obtenciones vegetales: el privilegio del agricultor* (n. 2) 151, 246, 259 and García Vidal, "El Sistema de Protección de Las Variedades Vegetales" (n. 2) 79-80. *See also* Helfer (n. 13) 2-3; Kochupillai (n. 8) 23 (in n. 17 of Kochupillai (n. 8) 23); Andre Heitz, "The History of the UPOV Convention and the Rationale for Plant Breeders' Rights", *Seminar on the nature of and reationale for the protection of plant varieties under the UPOV Convention, Budapest, Hungary, September 19 to 21, organized by UPOV in cooperation with the Government of the Republic of Hungary 1990* (UPOV 1991) 27, 36 https://www.upov.int/edocs/pubdocs/en/upov_pub_697.pdf. On the "incentive theory" *see*, e.g., Mikhalien du Bois, "Justificatory Theories for Intellectual Property Viewed through the Constitutional Prism" (2018) 21 Potchefstroom Electronic Law Journal 22 http://www.scielo.org.za/pdf/pelj/v21n1/19.pdf accessed December 16, 2019. On the different theories justifying intellectual property protection *see*, e.g., William Fisher, "Theories of Intellectual Property" in Stephen Munzer (ed.), *New essays in the legal and political theory of property* (Cambridge University Press 2001) https://pdfs.semanticscholar.org/173d/8747f2faaa06805dfd64a556fa2d776431f9.pdf accessed May 12, 2019. On the relation between the incentive theory and the FSS *see* Kochupillai (n. 8) 76, where Kochupillai introduces the antithetic position of her own standpoint.

19. *See*, e.g., Administrative and Legal Committee of UPOV (n. 16): "An extension or abusive use of the so-called farmers' privilege would thus not only prevent innovations within the framework of plant breeding, but also affect an economic area, which guarantees the necessary realization of precisely this breeding progress within agriculture." *Ibid.* Annex, page 1.
20. *See*, e.g., Dhar (n. 9) 5-6, 11, 13, 27; Dutfield (n. 17) 4; generally, Kochupillai (n. 8).
21. *See*, e.g., UPOV, "Actes Des Conférences Internationales Pour La Protection Des Obtentions Végétales 1957-1961 (Publication UPOV N° 316)" (n. 15) 21; Administrative and Legal Committee of UPOV (n. 16) Annex, page 1; Sánchez Gil, O. (2008). *La protección de las obtenciones vegetales: el privilegio del agricultor* (n. 2) 151, 246, 259 and García Vidal, "El Sistema de Protección de Las Variedades Vegetales" (n. 2) 79-80; Dhar (n. 9) 5-6, 11, 13, 27; Dutfield (n. 17) 4; generally Kochupillai (n. 8); nn. 15-20 and text to nn. 15-20.
22. On the foundations of the UPOV system *see*, e.g., Andre Heitz, "The History of the UPOV Convention and the Rationale for Plant Breeders' Rights", *Seminar on the nature of and reationale for the protection of plant varieties under the UPOV Convention, Budapest, Hungary, September 19 to 21, organized by UPOV in cooperation with the Government of the Republic of Hungary 1990* (UPOV 1991) 35ff https://www.upov.int/edocs/pubdocs/en/upov_pub_697.pdf accessed 12 May 2019; Dutfield (n. 17) 5; Vives-Vallés (n. 15) 29-31; Vives-Vallés, *The Scope of the Farm-Saved Seed under the Earliest UPOV Acts* (Aranzadi (in the editorial process)).
23. On the analysis of the scope of the FSS under the earliest UPOV Acts *see*, e.g., generally, Vives-Vallés, *The Scope of the Farm-Saved Seed under the Earliest UPOV Acts* (n. 22). On the key differences of the approach towards the FSS in patent protection and plant variety protection between the EU and the United States of America *see*, e.g., Kiewiet (n. 3); García Vidal, "El material vegetal protegido por una patente o un derecho de obtentor y el empleo del producto de su cosecha con fines de propagación: agotamiento y privilegio del agricultor en Europa y en los EE.UU." (n. 8); Anselmo Martínez Cañellas, "La Protección Dual de La Propiedad Industrial de Las Plantas Transgénicas: Como Invenciones y Como Variedades Vegetales" (2011) 1 Indret: Revista para el Análisis del Derecho http://www.indret.com/pdf/802_es.pdf accessed March 31, 2016.

impact on innovation, are out of the scope of this chapter. However, due to the aforementioned impact of FSS on innovation,[24] the analysis and findings contained in this chapter might be meaningful for innovation.

2 The "Recommendation Relating to Article 15(2)" of the UPOV Act of 1991

Article 15(2) of the UPOV Act of 1991 is not the only provision of that Act referring to the FSS.[25] According to the "Recommendation Relating to Article 15(2)" of the UPOV Act of 1991,[26] "[...] Article 15(2) [...] should not be read so as to be intended to open the possibility of extending the practice commonly called "farmer's privilege" to sectors of agricultural or horticultural production in which such a privilege is not a common practice on the territory of the Contracting Party concerned."[27]

24. *See* UPOV, "Actes Des Conférences Internationales Pour La Protection Des Obtentions Végétales 1957-1961 (Publication UPOV N° 316)" (n. 15) 21; Administrative and Legal Committee of UPOV (n. 16) Annex, page 1; Sánchez Gil, O. (2008). *La protección de las obtenciones vegetales: el privilegio del agricultor* (n. 2) 151, 246, 259 and García Vidal, "El Sistema de Protección de Las Variedades Vegetales" (n. 2) 79-80; Dhar (n. 9) 5-6, 11, 13, 27; Dutfield (n. 17) 4; generally Kochupillai (n. 8); nn. 15-20 and text to nn. 15-20.
25. *See*, e.g., Ángel García Vidal, "El contenido del derecho de "obtentor" de una variedad vegetal (luces y sombras del Convenio de la UPOV)" (2011) 279 Revista de derecho mercantil 99, 127-128.
26. On the "Recommendation Relating to Art. 15(2)" *see*, e.g., Sánchez Gil, *La protección de las obtenciones vegetales: el privilegio del agricultor* (n. 2) 204, 151, 154, 202, 256; Dhar (n. 9) 15; García Vidal, El contenido del derecho de "obtentor" de una variedad vegetal (luces y sombras del Convenio de la UPOV) (n. 25) 127-128; Würtenberger and others (n. 2) 143; Botana Agra (n. 10) 616. Scholars also stress the importance of the "Explanatory Notes on Exceptions to the Breeder's Right under the 1991 Act of the UPOV Convention" (*see*, e.g., García Vidal, El contenido del derecho de "obtentor" de una variedad vegetal (luces y sombras del Convenio de la UPOV) (n. 25) 126-128; Würtenberger and others (n. 2) 143; García Vidal, "El material vegetal protegido por una patente o un derecho de obtentor y el empleo del producto de su cosecha con fines de propagación: agotamiento y privilegio del agricultor en Europa y en los EE.UU." (n. 8) 90-91; García Vidal, "El Sistema de Protección de Las Variedades Vegetales" (n. 2) 92; Botana Agra (n. 10) 615).
27. UPOV, "Records of the Diplomatic Conference for the Revision of the International Convention for the Protection of New Varieties of Plants—Geneva 1991 (Publication UPOV N° 346 (E))" (n. 1) 63. Given its importance in the framework of the present study, the UPOV "Recommendation Relating to Article 15(2)" is transcribed hereinafter:

> "Recommendation Relating to Article 15(2)**
>
> The Diplomatic Conference recommends that the provisions laid down in Article 15 (2) of the International Convention for the Protection of New Varieties of Plants of December 2, 1961, as Revised at Geneva on November 10, 1972, on October 23, 1978, and on March 19, 1991, should not be read so as to be intended to open the possibility of extending the practice commonly called 'farmer's privilege' to sectors of agricultural or horticultural production in which such a privilege is not a common practice on the territory of the Contracting Party concerned.
>
> [...]
>
> ** This Recommendation was published as 'Final Draft' in document DC/91/139." *Ibid.* 63. *See also* Sánchez Gil, *La protección de las obtenciones vegetales: el privilegio del agricultor* (n. 2) 204, 151, 154, 202, 256.

3 THE FSS UNDER THE CPVR SYSTEM

In the CPVR system, the FSS is regulated by Article 14 of the Basic Regulation,[28] by recitals 17 to 19 of the Basic Regulation,[29] as well as by Commission Regulation (EC) no. 1768/95 of July 24, 1995 implementing rules on the agricultural exemption provided for in Article 14(3) of Council Regulation (EC) no. 2100/94 on Community plant variety rights.[30] However, not all of them are equally important as regards the grounds of the FSS.

3.1 "[S]afeguarding Agricultural Production" as the Grounds of the FSS under the CPVR System

Recitals 17 to 19 o the Basic Regulation introduce the FSS as well as its grounds:[31]

> "Whereas, the exercise of Community plant variety rights must be subjected to restrictions laid down in provisions adopted in the public interest;
> Whereas this includes safeguarding agricultural production; whereas that purpose requires an authorization for farmers to use the product of the harvest for propagation under certain conditions;
> Whereas it must be ensured that the conditions are laid down at Community level;"

---

28. For example, Würtenberger and others (n. 2) 143ff; Botana Agra (n. 10) 617. *See also* the case law from the CJEU, e.g., the Judgment of the Court of Justice of the CJEU of October 17, 2019, *Saatgut-Treuhandverwaltungs GmbH v. Freistaat Thüringen*, C-239/18, EU:C:2019:869, paras 6, 23, 25, etc., as well as the Opinion of Advocate General Bobek delivered on May 23, 2019, *Saatgut-Treuhandverwaltungs GmbH v. Freistaat Thüringen*, C-239/18, EU:C:2019:445, paras 5, 24, 51, 67, etc.
29. For example, Sánchez Gil, "El privilegio del agricultor y la excepción en beneficio del agricultor "de la ley 3/2000" (n. 2) 348; Sánchez Gil, *La protección de las obtenciones vegetales: el privilegio del agricultor* (n. 2) 154; Würtenberger and others (n. 2) 142. Sánchez Gil does not seem to include recital 19 Council Regulation (EC) no. 2100/94 of July 27, 1994 ("Whereas it must be ensured that the conditions are laid down at Community level;"), but only the two preceding ones (recitals 17 and 18) (*see* Sánchez Gil, "El privilegio del agricultor y la excepción en beneficio del agricultor "de la ley 3/2000" (n. 2) 348, 358; Sánchez Gil, *La protección de las obtenciones vegetales: el privilegio del agricultor* (n. 2) 154). On the relevance of recitals 17 and 18 Council Regulation (EC) no. 2100/94 of July 27, 1994, *see also* the case law from the CJEU, e.g., the Judgment of the Court of Justice of the CJEU of October 17, 2019, *Saatgut-Treuhandverwaltungs GmbH v. Freistaat Thüringen*, C-239/18, EU:C:2019:869: "23 As the Court has previously pointed out, the provisions of Art. 14 of the basic regulation, which, as is clear from the 17th and 18th recitals thereof, were adopted on the basis of the public interest in safeguarding agricultural production, constitute an exception to that rule (judgments of April 10, 2003, *Schulin*, C-305/00, EU:C:2003:218, paragraph 47, and of October 14, 2004, *Brangewitz*, C-336/02, EU:C:2004:622, paragraph 37)" (para. 23). *See also* para. 3 of the same Judgment, specifically quoting those recitals.
30. For example, Würtenberger and others (n. 2) 144; Botana Agra (n. 10) 617.
31. For example, Sánchez Gil, "El privilegio del agricultor y la excepción en beneficio del agricultor de la ley 3/2000" (n. 2) 347-348, 358; Sánchez Gil, *La protección de las obtenciones vegetales: el privilegio del agricultor* (n. 2) 154; Würtenberger and others (n. 2) 142. On the relevance of recitals 17 and 18 Council Regulation (EC) no. 2100/94 of July 27, 1994, *see also* the case law from the CJEU, e.g., the Judgment of the Court of Justice of the CJEU of October 17, 2019, *Saatgut-Treuhandverwaltungs GmbH v. Freistaat Thüringen*, C-239/18, EU:C:2019:869: paras 3 and 37 (transcribed in n. 29).

It is clear from recital 18 of the Basic Regulation that the basis of the FSS in the CPVR system is "safeguarding agricultural production," a manifestation, according to the same recital, of the "restrictions laid down in provisions adopted in the public interest" mentioned in recital 17.[32]

The same grounds of the FSS ("safeguarding agricultural production") are also mentioned in other provisions of the Basic Regulation and Commission Regulation

32. For example, Sánchez Gil, "El privilegio del agricultor y la excepción en beneficio del agricultor de la ley 3/2000" (n. 2) 347-348, 358; Sánchez Gil, *La protección de las obtenciones vegetales: el privilegio del agricultor* (n. 2) 154; Würtenberger and others (n. 2) 142. On the relevance of recitals 17 and 18 Council Regulation (EC) no. 2100/94 of July 27, 1994, *see also* the case law from the CJEU, e.g., the Judgment of the Court of Justice of the CJEU of October 17, 2019, *Saatgut-Treuhandverwaltungs GmbH v. Freistaat Thüringen*, C-239/18, EU:C:2019:869: paras 3 and 37 (transcribed in n. 29). The literature implicitly or explicitly recognizes the connection between "safeguarding agricultural production" and the FSS with concept of "public interest" (*see*, e.g., Quintana Carlo, "El Reglamento CE Número 2100/1994 Relativo a La Protección Comunitaria de Las Obtenciones Vegetales" (n. 10) 16; Sánchez Gil, "El privilegio del agricultor y la excepción en beneficio del agricultor de la ley 3/2000" (n. 2) 347-348; Sánchez Gil, *La protección de las obtenciones vegetales: el privilegio del agricultor* (n. 2) 126, 129, 151-153, 154, 202, 205, 206, 252-254, 256; Amat Llombart (n. 10) 222-223; Würtenberger and others (n. 2) 142; García Vidal, "El Sistema de Protección de Las Variedades Vegetales" (n. 2) 77; Framiñán Santas, "Biodiversidad y Propiedad Intelectual Sobre Recursos Fitogenéticos" in Ángel García Vidal (ed.), *Derecho de las obtenciones vegetales* (Editorial Tirant lo Blanch SL 2017) 216-217; Botana Agra (n. 10) 612, 614, 617, 634). However, some scholars connect the FSS under UPOV with Art. 9 of the earliest UPOV Acts (Botana Agra (n. 10) 614) or with Art. 17 of the latest Act (Sánchez Gil, "El privilegio del agricultor y la excepción en beneficio del agricultor de la ley 3/2000" (n. 2) 348), not with the preamble of the UPOV Convention from which it seems to emanate (Kochupillai (n. 8) 22ff; Vives-Vallés (n. 15) 29ff). Besides, while the relation between both concepts is clear and explicit under the Basic Regulation, under the UPOV Act of 1991 that connection is only implicit or generic. Furthermore, the alleged relation between such practice and Art. 9 of the earliest UPOV Acts was not even accepted during the Diplomatic Conference of 1991 (*see*, e.g., the reference to "public interest" in Administrative and Legal Committee of UPOV, "Revision of the Convention: Position of FIS on the "Farmer's Privilege" (CAJ/27/ 7)" (1990) Annex, 1 http://www.upov.int/edocs/mdocs/upov/en/caj_27/caj_27_7.pdf accessed July 18, 2019, as well as the intervention of FIS within the Diplomatic Conference of 1991 insisting on its proposal, in UPOV, "Records of the Diplomatic Conference for the Revision of the International Convention for the Protection of New Varieties of Plants—Geneva 1991 (Publication UPOV N° 346 (E))" (n. 1) 357. Adapted from Vives-Vallés (n. 15) 46). It is also worth noting the connection stablished by the CJEU in its Judgment of December 19, 2019, *Club de Variedades Vegetales Protegidas v. Adolfo Juan Martínez Sanchís*, C-176/18, EU:C:2019:1131, para. 34: "In addition, the public interest in safeguarding agricultural production, referred to in the 17th and 18th recitals of Regulation No 2100/94, [...]". However, the Court does not connect recital 18 to the FSS, but to other provisions from the Basic Regulation unrelated with that exception (*see* n. 62). Such connection though, has been repeatedly stablished by the Court in relation to the FSS (*see* the case law from the CJEU, e.g., the Judgment of the Court of Justice of the CJEU of October 17, 2019, *Saatgut-Treuhandverwaltungs GmbH v. Freistaat Thüringen*, C-239/18, EU:C:2019: 869: paras 3 and 37 (transcribed in n. 29)). In fact, by referring to "safeguarding agricultural production" as "that purpose", recital 18 further remarks the nature (or "purpose") of such reference (*see* in this regard the Opinion of Advocate General Bobek delivered on May 23, 2019, *Saatgut-Treuhandverwaltungs GmbH v. Freistaat Thüringen*, C-239/18, EU:C:2019:445, para 51: "The purpose of the agricultural exemption is twofold: to safeguard agricultural production, while ensuring the payment, by the farmer, of an (equitable) remuneration to the holder." Advocate General Bobek not only remarks that "[t]he purpose of the agricultural exemption is [...] safeguard agricultural production [...]", but also "ensuring the payment, by the farmer, of an (equitable) remuneration to the holder.").

(EC) no. 1768/95 of July 24, 1995. In consistency with recital 18, Article 14(1) of the Basic Regulation also refers to "the purposes of safeguarding agricultural production":

> "Article 14
>
> Derogation from Community plant variety right
>
> 1. Notwithstanding Article 13 (2), and for *the purposes of safeguarding agricultural production*, farmers are authorized to use for propagating purposes in the field, on their own holding the product of the harvest which they have obtained by planting, on their own holding, propagating material of a variety other than a hybrid or synthetic variety, which is covered by a Community plant variety right.
>
> [...]"[33]

Furthermore, Article 13(8) of the Basic Regulation establishes that:

> Without prejudice to Article 14 and 29, the exercise of the rights conferred by Community plant variety rights may not violate any provisions adopted on the grounds of [...] *the safeguarding* of competition, of trade or of *agricultural production*.[34]

In fact, Article 13(8) of the Basic Regulation reminds the existent hierarchy between "any provisions adopted on the grounds of certain EU core legal provisions (among which "the safeguarding [...] of agricultural production" is expressly mentioned) and "the exercise of the rights conferred by Community plant variety rights."

Another reference to "safeguarding agricultural production" is also found in recital one of Commission Regulation (EC) no. 1768/95 of July 24, 1995:

> "Whereas Article 14 of the basic Regulation provides for a derogation from Community plant variety right for *the purposes of safeguarding agricultural production (agricultural exemption)*;"[35]
>
> "[T]he monitoring of agricultural production" is mentioned in both, the Basic Regulation (in Art. 14(3) in fine) and Commission Regulation (EC) no. 1768/95 of 24 July 1995 (in Art. 11(2)). However, the context of these references is different and seemingly unrelated to the grounds of the FSS.

33. Emphasis added. E.g., Würtenberger and others (n. 2) 143ff; Botana Agra (n. 10) 617. *Also* the case law from the CJEU, e.g., the Judgment of the Court of Justice of the CJEU of October 17, 2019, *Saatgut-Treuhandverwaltungs GmbH v. Freistaat Thüringen*, C-239/18, EU:C:2019:869, paras 6, 23, 25, etc., as well as the Opinion of Advocate General Bobek delivered on May 23, 2019, *Saatgut-Treuhandverwaltungs GmbH v. Freistaat Thüringen*, C-239/18, EU:C:2019:445, paras 5, 24, 51, 55, 67, etc.
34. Emphasis added. On the analysis of Commission Regulation (EC) no. 1768/95 of July 24, 1995 *see*, e.g., Botana Agra (n. 10) 617ff.
35. Emphasis added. Recital 1 Commission Regulation (EC) no. 1768/95 of July 24, 1995 is expressly quoted by the CJEU in relation to the FSS, in the Judgment of the Court of Justice of the CJEU of October 17, 2019, *Saatgut-Treuhandverwaltungs GmbH v. Freistaat Thüringen*, C-239/18, EU:C:2019:869, para 7. *See also* para. 25 of the same Judgment. On the analysis of Commission Regulation (EC) no. 1768/95 of July 24, 1995 *see*, e.g., Botana Agra (n. 10) 617ff.

3.2 "[S]afeguarding Agricultural Production" as a Limitation of the FSS under the CPVR System

In the context of the FSS within the CPVR system, the grounds of the FSS cannot be seen only in a positive way as the rationale justifying the exception, but they must also be considered a limitation of the exception. In other words, the FSS is only justified and justifiable as long as it serves "the purposes of safeguarding agricultural production" (Article 14(1) Basic Regulation). This is clearly deduced from a historical approach to the provision. Indeed, the reference to "the purposes of safeguarding agricultural production" in Article 14(1) of the Basic Regulation is aligned to a large extent with the Dutch proposal "DC/91/115 " of March 12, 1991 within the Diplomatic Conference of 1991 (i.e., "essential for the food production or the rural economy"[36]), the intent of which was that "member States would be able to introduce the so-called "farmer's privilege," but would have to limit it to those areas in which it was of real importance."[37] The limitative nature of the grounds of the FSS under the CPVR system is also deduced from a contextual interpretation of the reference to "the purposes of safeguarding agricultural production" from Article 14(1) of the Basic Regulation in the context of its recitals 17 to 19. It is clear from these recitals that the reference contained in recital 18 (i.e., "safeguarding agricultural production") is a species of the genus mentioned in recital 17 (i.e., "public interest").[38] In other words, the EU legislature decided that the FSS would be justified by and limited to situations serving "the

36. UPOV, "Records of the Diplomatic Conference for the Revision of the International Convention for the Protection of New Varieties of Plants—Geneva 1991 (Publication UPOV N° 346 (E))" (n. 1). 143. The proposal is transcribed hereinafter:

> "**DC/91/115** March 12, 1991 (Original: English)
>
> Source: Delegation of the Netherlands
>
> **PROPOSAL FOR THE AMENDMENT OF ARTICLE 15(2)**
>
> It is proposed that the following subparagraph (b) be added to Article 15(2):
>
> '(b) A Contracting Party shall apply this provision only to species or groups of species that are essential for the food production or the rural economy of that Contracting Party.'" Ibid. 143.

37. *Ibid*. 366. It is worth noting that the Dutch origin of the "Recommendation Relating to Art. 15(2)" is also mentioned by Sánchez Gil (Sánchez Gil, *La protección de las obtenciones vegetales: el privilegio del agricultor* (n. 2) 204-206) and Botana Agra (Botana Agra (n. 10) 616), but in relation to other proposals, not to proposal "DC/91/115" (*see* n. 43).
38. On the connection between the FSS and "public interest" *see*, e.g., Quintana Carlo, "El Reglamento CE Número 2100/1994 Relativo a La Protección Comunitaria de Las Obtenciones Vegetales" (n. 3) 15; Sánchez Gil, 'El privilegio del agricultor y la excepción en beneficio del agricultor de la ley 3/2000' (n 5) 347-348; Sánchez Gil, *La protección de las obtenciones vegetales: el privilegio del agricultor (n 5)* 126, 129, 151-154, 202, 205, 206, 252-254, 256; Amat Llombart (n. 10) 222-223; Würtenberger and others (n. 2) 9, 142; García Vidal, "El Sistema de Protección de Las Variedades Vegetales" (n. 2) 77; Framiñán Santas (n. 32) 216-217; Botana Agra (n. 10) 612, 614, 617, 634; the case law from the CJEU (e.g., the Judgment of the Court of Justice of the CJEU of October 17, 2019, *Saatgut-Treuhandverwaltungs GmbH v. Freistaat Thüringen*, C-239 /18, EU:C:2019:869: paras 3 and 37 (transcribed in n. 29)); n. 32 and text to n. 32. *See also* the references to the Judgment of the CJEU of December 19, 2019, *Club de Variedades Vegetales Protegidas v. Adolfo Juan Martínez Sanchís*, C-176/18, EU:C:2019:1131 (paras 5, 32, 34) in nn. 32, 62 *in fine*.

purposes of safeguarding agricultural production,"[39] and, therefore, circumscribed the FSS under the CPVR system to some "agricultural plant species."[40]

4 THE GROUNDS OF THE FSS UNDER THE CPVR SYSTEM: BETWEEN THE "RECOMMENDATION RELATING TO ARTICLE 15(2)" OF THE UPOV ACT OF 1991 AND ARTICLE 39(1)(A) TFEU

4.1 The Grounds of the FSS in the CPVR System and the "Recommendation Relating to Article 15(2)" of the UPOV Act of 1991

A mere comparison of the wording of Article 14(1) of the Basic Regulation (i.e., "the purposes of safeguarding agricultural production") and the wording of the "Recommendation Relating to Article 15(2)" (i.e., "to sectors of agricultural or horticultural production in which such a privilege is not a common practice on the territory of the Contracting Party concerned") suffices to evince that the grounds of the restriction of the FSS under both systems differ, at least at first glance. Given this, the possibility of the European Community ignoring the "Recommendation Relating to Article 15(2)" as a possible cause of that divergence must be considered. However, this hypothesis does not withstand a detailed assessment. Indeed, to begin with, it is indisputable that both, Article 14 of the Basic Regulation and the "Recommendation Relating to Article 15(2)" from the UPOV Act of 1991 share the intent to limit the FSS,[41] and, therefore, absolute

39. On the impact of "public interest", "practice" and "policy" on the configuration of the FSS under the CPVR system, including the selection of species within Art. 14(2) of the Basic Regulation, *see* Sánchez Gil, *La protección de las obtenciones vegetales: el privilegio del agricultor* (n. 2) 202, 203-206, 151-154, 256. *See also ibid.* 126, 129, 205, 206, 252-254; Sánchez Gil, "El privilegio del agricultor y la excepción en beneficio del agricultor de la ley 3/2000" (n. 2) 347-348, 358; Quintana Carlo, "El Reglamento CE Número 2100/1994 Relativo a La Protección Comunitaria de Las Obtenciones Vegetales" (n. 3) 15; Amat Llombart (n. 10) 222-223; Würtenberger and others (n. 2) 142; García Vidal, "El material vegetal protegido por una patente o un derecho de obtentor y el empleo del producto de su cosecha con fines de propagación: agotamiento y privilegio del agricultor en Europa y en los EE.UU." (n. 8) 80; nn. 53, 54, 73, 81 and text to nn. 53, 54, 73, 81.
40. Würtenberger and others (n. 2) 144; Opinion of Advocate General Bobek delivered on May 23, 2019, *Saatgut-Treuhandverwaltungs GmbH v. Freistaat Thüringen*, C-239/18, EU:C:2019:445, para. 55. This limitation of the FSS by Art. 14(2) of the Basic Regulation has been also observed by Sánchez Gil, *La protección de las obtenciones vegetales: el privilegio del agricultor* (n. 2) 200-201; García Vidal, El material vegetal protegido por una patente o un derecho de obtentor y el empleo del producto de su cosecha con fines de propagación: agotamiento y privilegio del agricultor en Europa y en los EE.UU (n. 8) 91; Manuel Botana Agra, "La Excepción En Beneficio Del Agricultor" in Ángel García Vidal (ed.), *Derecho de las obtenciones vegetales* (Editorial Tirant lo Blanch SL 2017) 618; Gómez Segade (n. 2) 128; María Victoria Petit Lavall, "Derechos Del Titular de Una Obtención Vegetal" in Ángel García Vidal (ed.), *Derecho de las obtenciones vegetale* (Editorial Tirant lo Blanch SL 2017) 547. *See also* the Opinion of Advocate General Bobek delivered on May 23, 2019, *Saatgut-Treuhandverwaltungs GmbH v. Freistaat Thüringen*, C-239/18, EU:C:2019:445, paras 45, 51, 74; n. 40 and text to n. 40.
41. On the limitation of the FSS under the CPVR system to some species, *see* Würtenberger and others (n. 2) 144; Sánchez Gil, *La protección de las obtenciones vegetales: el privilegio del agricultor* (n. 2) 200-201; García Vidal, El material vegetal protegido por una patente o un derecho de obtentor y el empleo del producto de su cosecha con fines de propagación: agotamiento y privilegio del agricultor en Europa y en los EE.UU (n. 8) 91; Botana Agra (n. 40)

neglect of the "Recommendation Relating to Article 15(2)" by the EU legislature is unlikely. Furthermore, the "Recommendation Relating to Article 15(2)" is the product of the evolution[42] of the Dutch proposal "DC/91/115" of March 12, 1991,[43] which, as it has been already argued in this chapter,[44] may be seen as a precedent of the grounds of the FSS under the CPVR system. Besides, although it is true that the EU acceded to the UPOV Convention only in 2005,[45] many of the participants to the Diplomatic Conference of 1991 were at that time also negotiating the Basic Regulation and in that conference also participated "representatives of the Commission of the European Communities."[46] This circumstance alone suggests that a rejection by the EU legislature of the "Recommendation Relating to Article 15(2)" was implausible,[47] especially

---

618; Petit Lavall (n. 40) 547; the Opinion of Advocate General Bobek delivered on May 23, 2019, *Saatgut-Treuhandverwaltungs GmbH v. Freistaat Thüringen*, C-239/18, EU:C:2019:445, paras 45, 51, 55, 74; n. 40 and text to n. 40. That the UPOV "Recommendation Relating to Article 15(2)" pursues to limit the FSS is also indisputable (*see*, e.g., UPOV, "Records of the Diplomatic Conference for the Revision of the International Convention for the Protection of New Varieties of Plants—Geneva 1991 (Publication UPOV N° 346 (E))" (n. 1) 366ff, 371-372, 396ff; García Vidal, El contenido del derecho de "obtentor" de una variedad vegetal (luces y sombras del Convenio de la UPOV) (n. 25) 127-128).

42. *See* UPOV, "Records of the Diplomatic Conference for the Revision of the International Convention for the Protection of New Varieties of Plants—Geneva 1991 (Publication UPOV N° 346 (E))" (n. 1) 509 and those pages and paras to which it refers.
43. It must be noted that the Dutch origin of the "Recommendation Relating to Article 15(2)" of the UPOV Act of 1991 and its limiting action is also observed by Sánchez Gil, *La protección de las obtenciones vegetales: el privilegio del agricultor* (n. 2) 204 and Botana Agra (n. 10) 616, although seemingly in relation to proposals "DC/91/68" (UPOV, "Records of the Diplomatic Conference for the Revision of the International Convention for the Protection of New Varieties of Plants—Geneva 1991 (Publication UPOV N° 346 (E))" (n. 1) 123, transcribed in n. 76) and "DC/91/119" (*ibid.* 147), respectively, not to proposal "DC/91/115" (*ibid.* 143, transcribed in n. 36). Certainly, the limitation of the species within letter (b) of the Dutch proposal "DC/91/68" (*see ibid.* 123) is connected to Art. 14(2) of the Basic Regulation (Sánchez Gil, *La protección de las obtenciones vegetales: el privilegio del agricultor* (n. 2) 204; text to n. 76), but not so directly to its explicit grounds.
44. *See* text to nn. 36-37.
45. UPOV, "Members of the International Union for the Protection of New Varieties of Plants: Status on May 2, 2019" (n. 2) 1; Würtenberger and others (n. 2) 4, 13; Sánchez Gil, *La protección de las obtenciones vegetales: el privilegio del agricultor* (n. 2) 38; García Vidal, "El Sistema de Protección de Las Variedades Vegetales" (n. 2) 94; Gómez Segade (n. 2) 116.
46. UPOV, "Records of the Diplomatic Conference for the Revision of the International Convention for the Protection of New Varieties of Plants—Geneva 1991 (Publication UPOV N° 346 (E))" (n. 1) 163 (from a communication by a UPOV officer). *See also ibid.* 176 (from a communication by a UPOV officer). It must be noted that 9 of the 19 UPOV member Delegations participating in the Diplomatic Conference of 1991 plus an observer Delegation, Luxembourg (*ibid.* 535-540) were at that time also Member States of the European Communities (European Union, "EUROPA: About the EU: Countries" (*Europa.eu*, 2019) https://europa.eu/european-union/about-eu/countries_en#tab-0-1 accessed July 25, 2019). A similar observation is made by other authors in relation to previous Conferences (*see*, e.g., Heitz (n. 22) 35; Dutfield (n. 17) 7; Würtenberger and others (n. 2) 3; Quintana Carlo, "El Reglamento CE Número 2100/1994 Relativo a La Protección Comunitaria de Las Obtenciones Vegetales" (n. 10) 4). Quintana Carlo also remarks the very significant impact of the UPOV Act of 1991 on the Basic Regulation (*ibid.* 2).
47. This circumstance was remarked by a UPOV officer who was consulted after an early draft of this chapter was posted in SSRN, as Vives-Vallés, "Essay on the Farm-Saved Seed under the CPVR System and Its Sphere of Influence in the Light of the UPOV Act of 1991 and the Contemporary Interpretation of Art. 39(1)(A) TFEU" (30 January 2019).

considering the penultimate recital of the Basic Regulation (stating that "this Regulation takes into account existing international conventions such as the International Convention for the Protection of New Varieties of Plants (UPOV Convention), [...]").[48]

In view of the aforementioned reasons, the hypothesis of the EU legislature willingly departing from the UPOV "Recommendation Relating to Article 15(2)" must be disregarded. Be that as it may, this conclusion does not exhaust the analysis of the apparent mismatch between the grounds of FSS under the CPVR system and the UPOV "Recommendation Relating to Article 15(2)."

4.2 The Grounds of the FSS in the CPVR System as an Implementation in the Secondary EU Law of Article 39(1)(a) TFEU

A possible explanation of the alleged departure of the (formal) grounds of the FSS under the CPVR system from the UPOV "Recommendation Relating to Article 15(2)" might be found in the connection between the grounds of the FSS under the CPVR system and the first Common Agricultural Policy (CAP) objective contained in Article 39(1)(a) TFEU:

> "Article 39
>
> (ex Article 33 TEC)
> 1. The objectives of the common agricultural policy shall be:
>   (a) to increase agricultural productivity by promoting technical progress and by ensuring the rational development of agricultural production and the optimum utilisation of the factors of production, in particular labour;"

Indeed, although nothing has been found in the Basic Regulation nor in Commission Regulation (EC) no. 1768/95 of July 24, 1995 explicitly mentioning this connection, its existence is already hinted at by the reference to "agricultural production" contained in both recital 18 and Article 14(1)[49] of the Basic Regulation and in Article 39(1)(a) TFEU. The general idea of "ensuring the rational development of agricultural production" of Article 39(1)(a) TFEU is also very close if not identical to the idea of "safeguarding agricultural production" contained in the aforementioned provisions of the Basic Regulation. The importance[50] conceded to "agricultural production" by recitals 17-18,

48. The adaptation of the Basic Regulation and the CPVR system to the UPOV Convention is generally accepted by the literature (*see*, e.g., Sánchez Gil, *La protección de las obtenciones vegetales: el privilegio del agricultor* (n. 2) 34, 129, 254; Kochupillai (n. 8) 25-26, 189; Würtenberger and others (n. 2) 4, 143; García Vidal, "El material vegetal protegido por una patente o un derecho de obtentor y el empleo del producto de su cosecha con fines de propagación: agotamiento y privilegio del agricultor en Europa y en los EE.UU." (n. 8) 76, 77, 91; García Vidal, "Las Relaciones Entre El Sistema de Las Obtenciones Vegetales y El Sistema de Patentes (La Prohibición de Patentar Las Variedades Establecida En Los Derechos Europeo y Español)" (n. 8) 143; Gómez Segade (n. 2) 116). *See also* text to n. 8.
49. On "agricultural production" and recital 18 and Art. 14(1) of the Basic Regulation, *see* Sánchez Gil, "El privilegio del agricultor y la excepción en beneficio del agricultor de la ley 3/2000" (n. 2) 347-348, 358; Sánchez Gil, *La protección de las obtenciones vegetales: el privilegio del agricultor* (n. 2) 154; Würtenberger and others (n. 2) 142-143; nn. 31, 33 and text to nn. 31, 33.
50. On the relevance of the preamble of the Basic Regulation, and particularly its recitals 17 to 19, as a justification of the FSS under the CPVR system, *see* Sánchez Gil, "El privilegio del agricultor

Article 14(1) and Article 13(8) of the Basic Regulation reinforces that connection. In fact, Article 13(8) of the Basic Regulation goes even further and establishes a hierarchy between "the exercise of the rights conferred by Community plant variety rights" and "the safeguarding [...] of agricultural production," implicitly reminding (and reinforcing) the connection between the grounds of the FSS under the CPVR system and Article 39(1)(a) TFEU. Interestingly, that hierarchy is also consistent with recitals 17 and 18 of the Basic Regulation portraying "safeguarding agricultural production" as a manifestation of "public interest."[51]

4.3 A Comprehensive Interpretation of the FSS under the CPVR System

It comes from the foregoing that the FSS under the CPVR system must be understood as the result of the combined influence of "the purposes" of the FSS emanating from "public interest" (recital 17),[52] specifically, from the first CAP objective set in Article 39(1)(a) TFEU, on the one hand, and from the limitation of the FSS contained in the UPOV "Recommendation Relating to Article 15(2)" (i.e., the restriction of the FSS "to sectors of agricultural or horticultural production in which such a privilege is not a common practice on the territory of the Contracting Party concerned"),

---

y la excepción en beneficio del agricultor de la ley 3/2000" (n. 2) 347-348; Sánchez Gil, *La protección de las obtenciones vegetales: el privilegio del agricultor* (n. 2) 154; Würtenberger and others (n. 2) 142; the case law from the CJEU, e.g., the Judgment of the Court of Justice of the CJEU of October 17, 2019, *Saatgut-Treuhandverwaltungs GmbH v. Freistaat Thüringen*, C-239/18, EU:C:2019:869: paras 3 and 37 (transcribed in n. 29); n. 31 and text to n. 31. On Article 14(1) *see*, e.g., Würtenberger and others (n. 2) 143 and n. 33 and text to n. 33.

51. On the connection between the FSS and "public interest," *see*, e.g., Quintana Carlo, "El Reglamento CE Número 2100/1994 Relativo a La Protección Comunitaria de Las Obtenciones Vegetales" (n. 3) 15; Sánchez Gil, "El privilegio del agricultor y la excepción en beneficio del agricultor de la ley 3/2000" (n. 2) 347-348; Sánchez Gil, O. (2008). *La protección de las obtenciones vegetales: el privilegio del agricultor* (n. 2) 126, 129, 151-154, 202, 205, 206, 252-254, 256; Amat Llombart (n. 10) 222-223; Würtenberger and others (n. 2) 9, 142; García Vidal, "El Sistema de Protección de Las Variedades Vegetales" (n. 2) 77; Framiñán Santas (n. 32) 216-217; Botana Agra (n. 10) 612, 614, 617, 634; the case law from the CJEU (e.g., the Judgment of the Court of Justice of the CJEU of October 17, 2019, *Saatgut-Treuhandverwaltungs GmbH v. Freistaat Thüringen*, C-239/18, EU:C:2019:869: paras 3 and 37 (transcribed in n. 29)); n. 32 and text to n. 32. *See also* the references to the Judgment of the CJEU of December 19, 2019, *Club de Variedades Vegetales Protegidas v. Adolfo Juan Martínez Sanchís*, C-176/18, EU:C:2019:1131 (paras 5, 32, 34) in nn. 32, 62 *in fine*.
52. On the connection between the FSS and "public interest," *see*, e.g., Quintana Carlo, "El Reglamento CE Número 2100/1994 Relativo a La Protección Comunitaria de Las Obtenciones Vegetales" (n. 3) 15; Sánchez Gil, "El privilegio del agricultor y la excepción en beneficio del agricultor de la ley 3/2000" (n. 2) 347-348; Sánchez Gil, *La protección de las obtenciones vegetales: el privilegio del agricultor* (n. 2) 126, 129, 151-154, 202, 205, 206, 252-254, 256; Amat Llombart (n. 10) 222-223; Würtenberger and others (n. 2) 9, 142; García Vidal, "El Sistema de Protección de Las Variedades Vegetales" (n. 2) 77; Framiñán Santas (n. 32) 216-217; Botana Agra (n. 10) 612, 614, 617, 634; the case law from the CJEU (e.g., the Judgment of the Court of Justice of the CJEU of October 17, 2019, *Saatgut-Treuhandverwaltungs GmbH v. Freistaat Thüringen*, C-239/18, EU:C:2019:869: paras 3 and 37 (transcribed in n. 29); n. 32 and text to n. 32). *See also* the references to the Judgment of the CJEU of December 19, 2019, *Club de Variedades Vegetales Protegidas v. Adolfo Juan Martínez Sanchís*, C-176/18, EU:C:2019:1131 (paras 5, 32, 34) in nn. 32, 62 *in fine*.

on the other hand.[53] The effect of the UPOV "Recommendation Relating to Article 15(2)" on the FSS[54] under the CPVR system is apparently manifested in the limitation of the list within Article 14(2)[55] of the Basic Regulation to some

53. On the combined impact of tradition or "practice" and "public interest" on the configuration of the FSS under the CPVR system, *see*, e.g., Sánchez Gil (n. 1) 151-154, 202, 204, 206, 256. *See also ibid.* 126, 129, 205, 252-254; Sánchez Gil, "El privilegio del agricultor y la excepción en beneficio del agricultor de la ley 3/2000" (n. 2) 347-348; Quintana Carlo, "El Reglamento CE Número 2100/1994 Relativo a La Protección Comunitaria de Las Obtenciones Vegetales" (n. 3) 15; Amat Llombart (n. 10) 222-223; Würtenberger and others (n. 2) 142; García Vidal, "El material vegetal protegido por una patente o un derecho de obtentor y el empleo del producto de su cosecha con fines de propagación: agotamiento y privilegio del agricultor en Europa y en los EE.UU." (n. 8) 80; nn. 39, 54, 73, 81 and text to nn. 39, 54, 73, 81.
54. Sánchez Gil (Sánchez Gil, *La protección de las obtenciones vegetales: el privilegio del agricultor* (n. 2) 202) acknowledges the importance of "practice" ("*costumbre*") in the configuration of Art. 14(2) of the Basic Regulation. However, she gives pre-eminence to "*el interés público y las razones geopolíticas*" (*ibid.* 206). *See also ibid.* 203-206, 151-154, 256; Sánchez Gil, "El privilegio del agricultor y la excepción en beneficio del agricultor de la ley 3/2000" (n. 2) 347-348, 358; Würtenberger and others (n. 2) 142; García Vidal, "El material vegetal protegido por una patente o un derecho de obtentor y el empleo del producto de su cosecha con fines de propagación: agotamiento y privilegio del agricultor en Europa y en los EE.UU." (n. 8) 80; nn. 39, 53, 54, 73, 81 and text to nn. 39, 53, 54, 73, 81.
55. Literally, from Art. 14(2) of the Basic Regulation:

"2. The provisions of paragraph 1 shall only apply to agricultural plant species of:
(a) Fodder plants:

Cicer arietinum L. — Chickpea milkvetch
Lupinus luteus L. — Yellow lupin
Medicago sativa L. — Lucerne
Pisum sativum L. (partim) — Field pea
Trifolium alexandrinum L. — Berseem/Egyptian clover
Trifolium resupinatum L. — Persian clover
Vicia faba — Field bean
Vicia sativa L. — Common vetch
and, in the case of Portugal, Lolium multiflorum lam — Italian ryegrass

(b) Cereals:

Avena sativa — Oats
Hordeum vulgare L. — Barley
Oryza sativa L. — Rice
Phalaris canariensis L. — Canary grass
Secale cereale L. — Rye
X Triticosecale Wittm. — Triticale
Triticium aestivum L. emend. Fiori et Paol. — Wheat
Triticum durum Desf. — Durum wheat
Triticum spelta L. — Spelt wheat

(c) Potatoes:

Solanum tuberosum — Potatoes

(d) Oil and fibre plants:

Brassica napus L. (partim) — Swede rape
Brassica rapa L. (partim) — Turnip rape
Linum usitatissimum — linseed with the exclusion of flax."

species.[56] In other words, the EU legislature seemingly decided that the species listed in Article 14(2) of the Basic Regulation were the only species fulfilling, at the same time, Article 39(1)(a) TFEU, as well as the UPOV "Recommendation Relating to Article 15(2)."[57] Only an interpretation of these higher principles[58] as cumulative criteria in the configuration of the FSS under the CPVR system solves the lack of an explicit reference to the UPOV "Recommendation Relating to Article 15(2)" in the relevant EU statutes (i.e., in the Basic Regulation and in Commission Regulation (EC) no. 1768/95 of July 24, 1995).

The "agricultural" mention in Article 14(1) and recital 18 of the Basic Regulation (i.e., "agricultural production"), as well as the circumscription of the agricultural exemption by Article 14(2) to some species,[59] reinforces the aforementioned interpretation. Sánchez Gil apparently connects the choice made by the EU legislature within

56. On the limitation of the FSS under the CPVR system to some species, *see* Würtenberger and others (n. 2) 144; Sánchez Gil, *La protección de las obtenciones vegetales: el privilegio del agricultor* (n. 2) 200-201; García Vidal, El material vegetal protegido por una patente o un derecho de obtentor y el empleo del producto de su cosecha con fines de propagación: agotamiento y privilegio del agricultor en Europa y en los EE.UU (n. 8) 91; Botana Agra (n. 40) 618; Petit Lavall (n. 40) 547. *See also* the Opinion of Advocate General Bobek delivered on May 23, 2019, *Saatgut-Treuhandverwaltungs GmbH v. Freistaat Thüringen*, C-239/18, EU:C:2019: 445, paras 45, 51, 55, 74; n. 40 and text to n. 40.
57. Regarding the combined impact of tradition or "practice" and "public interest" on the configuration of the FSS under the CPVR system, *see*, e.g., Sánchez Gil (n. 1) 151-154, 202, 204, 206, 256. *See also ibid.* 126, 129, 205, 252-254; Sánchez Gil, "El privilegio del agricultor y la excepción en beneficio del agricultor de la ley 3/2000" (n. 2) 347-348; Quintana Carlo, "El Reglamento CE Número 2100/1994 Relativo a La Protección Comunitaria de Las Obtenciones Vegetales" (n. 3) 15; Amat Llombart (n. 10) 222-223; Würtenberger and others (n. 2) 142; García Vidal, "El material vegetal protegido por una patente o un derecho de obtentor y el empleo del producto de su cosecha con fines de propagación: agotamiento y privilegio del agricultor en Europa y en los EE.UU." (n. 8) 80; nn. 39, 53, 54, 73, 81 and text to nn. 39, 53, 54, 73, 81. On the connection between the concept of "public interest" and "safeguarding agricultural production," *see*, e.g., Quintana Carlo, "El Reglamento CE Número 2100/1994 Relativo a La Protección Comunitaria de Las Obtenciones Vegetales" (n. 3) 15; Sánchez Gil, "El privilegio del agricultor y la excepción en beneficio del agricultor de la ley 3/2000" (n. 2) 347-348; Sánchez Gil, *La protección de las obtenciones vegetales: el privilegio del agricultor* (n. 2) 126, 129, 151-153, 154, 202, 205, 206, 252-254, 256; Amat Llombart (n. 10) 222-223; Würtenberger and others (n. 2) 142; García Vidal, "El Sistema de Protección de Las Variedades Vegetales" (n. 2) 77; Framiñán Santas, "Biodiversidad y Propiedad Intelectual Sobre Recursos Fitogenéticos" in Ángel García Vidal (ed.), *Derecho de las obtenciones vegetales* (Editorial Tirant lo Blanch SL 2017) 216-217; Botana Agra (n. 10) 612, 614, 617, 634; the case law from the CJEU, e.g., the Judgment of the Court of Justice of the CJEU of October 17, 2019, *Saatgut-Treuhandverwaltungs GmbH v. Freistaat Thüringen*, C-239 /18, EU:C:2019:869: paras 3 and 37 (transcribed in n. 29); n. 32 and text to n. 32. What is here highlighted in this chapter is the connection of "safeguarding agricultural production" and Art 39(1)(a) TFEU.
58. That is, those contained in Article 39(1)(a) TFEU as well as the UPOV "Recommendation Relating to Article 15(2)".
59. On recital 18 and Article 14 (1) of the Basic Regulation, *see* Sánchez Gil, "El privilegio del agricultor y la excepción en beneficio del agricultor de la ley 3/2000" (n. 2) 347-348, 358; Sánchez Gil, *La protección de las obtenciones vegetales: el privilegio del agricultor* (n. 2) 154; Würtenberger and others (n. 2) 142-143; the case law from the CJEU, e.g., the Judgment of the Court of Justice of the CJEU of October 17, 2019, *Saatgut-Treuhandverwaltungs GmbH v. Freistaat Thüringen*, C-239/18, EU:C:2019:869: paras 3 and 37 (transcribed in n. 29); nn. 31, 33 and text to nn. 31, 33. On the limitation of the FSS under the CPVR system to some species, *see* Würtenberger and others (n. 2) 144; Sánchez Gil, *La protección de las obtenciones vegetales: el privilegio del agricultor* (n. 2) 200-201; García Vidal, El material vegetal protegido por una

Article 14(2) as regards agricultural species to the name by which the FSS is known at an EU level (i.e., "agricultural exemption,"[60] according to Sánchez Gil).[61] Certainly, an interpretation of this coincidence as a simple accident might find support in the broad use of the term "agricultural," frequently used in contexts broader than agricultural species,[62] but in the EU, in terms of share, agriculture is more about agricultural species than anything else.[63] Therefore, "safeguarding agricultural production" is probably more closely connected to agricultural species than to any other group of species. Furthermore, as pointed out by Sánchez Gil,[64] it is clear that agricultural species, being a staple food, are better suited to serve the purpose of "public interest" (to which the FSS is connected[65]) than other groups of species. This was, in fact, implicitly acknowledged by the European legislature in the Basic Regulation when it narrowed the FSS

patente o un derecho de obtentor y el empleo del producto de su cosecha con fines de propagación: agotamiento y privilegio del agricultor en Europa y en los EE.UU (n. 8) 91; Botana Agra (n. 40) 618; Gómez Segade (n. 2) 128; Petit Lavall (n. 40) 547; the Opinion of Advocate General Bobek delivered on May 23, 2019, *Saatgut-Treuhandverwaltungs GmbH v. Freistaat Thüringen*, C-239/18, EU:C:2019:445, paras 45, 51, 55, 74; n. 40 and text to n. 40.

60. Sánchez Gil, *La protección de las obtenciones vegetales: el privilegio del agricultor* (n. 2) 201.
61. *Ibid.* 201. Sánchez Gil connects the appellation "*Exención de la agricultura*" to "*la salvaguardia de la producción agrícola*" as its "*justificación*" (*ibid.* 203). Afterward, Sánchez Gil points out that the appellation was later changed by "*exención agrícola*" (*ibid.* 203). Far from being a coincidence by chance (as Sánchez Gil apparently suggests out (*see ibid.* 203)), this change or evolution might be also the direct consequence of an attempt of the EU legislature to increase the internal coherency of the FSS provision in the Basic Regulation. The possibility of this being simply the result of the choice by the EU legislature of the appellative commonly used in the English versions of the preparatory documents and in the text finally approved (cf. the references to "*producción agraria*" in: European Commission, "Propuesta Modificada de Reglamento (CEE) Del Consejo Relativo a La Protección Comunitaria de Las Obtenciones Vegetales (COM(93) 104 Final) (93/C 113/09)" https://eur-lex.europa.eu/legal-content/ES/TXT/PDF/?uri=CELEX:51993PC0104&from=EN accessed November 3, 2019, and the references to "*producción agrícola*" (Spanish) or "agricultural production" (English) in the Basic Regulation) cannot be ruled out. But it might have also been the result of the intent to select the appellation (i.e., "agricultural") that better suits the kind of species listed in Art. 14(2) of the Basic Regulation.
62. *See*, e.g., the use of the term "agricultural" in Eurostat, "Statistics Explained: Main Annual Crop Statistics" (2019) https://ec.europa.eu/eurostat/statistics-explained/pdfscache/28946.pdf accessed 27 July 2019. It needs to be further noted that the CJEU, in a recent Judgment on *Citrus*, justified a decision concerning Art. 13(2) and Art. 95 of the Basic Regulation on the basis of "safeguarding agricultural production" in connection to recitals 17 and 18 (*see* the Judgment of the CJEU of December 19, 2019, *Club de Variedades Vegetales Protegidas*, C-176/18, EU:C:2019:1131, paras 5, 32, 34). Therefore, according to the Court, "safeguarding agricultural production" goes beyond the list of species within Art. 14(2) of the Basic Regulation, and even beyond the FSS. However, this interpretation from the CJEU expands the meaning of recital 18 beyond what is allowed by the wording and the context of recital 18, both of them clearly focused on, and restricted to, the FSS. Furthermore, this re-interpretation of recital 18 by the Court does not change its value as historical mean of interpretation.
63. *See* "Figure 1: Main area of crops, EU-28, 2015 (% of total UAA) (Source: Eurostat (apro_acs_a)," in *ibid.* 1.
64. *See* Sánchez Gil, *La protección de las obtenciones vegetales: el privilegio del agricultor* (n. 2) 151-154, 204-205.
65. On the connection between the FSS and "public interest," *see*, e.g., Quintana Carlo, "El Reglamento CE Número 2100/1994 Relativo a La Protección Comunitaria de Las Obtenciones Vegetales" (n. 3) 15; Sánchez Gil, "El privilegio del agricultor y la excepción en beneficio del agricultor de la ley 3/2000" (n. 2) 347-348; Sánchez Gil, *La protección de las obtenciones vegetales: el privilegio del agricultor* (n. 2) 126, 129, 151-154, 202, 205, 206, 252-254, 256; Amat

("the purposes" of which are "safeguarding agricultural production" (Article 14(1) of the Basic Regulation)) to some "agricultural plant species"[66] (Article 14(2)). In other words, if according to Article 14 of the Basic Regulation, "for the purposes of safeguarding agricultural production" only some species ("agricultural plant species"[67]) are essential or really matter, then, under such provision and the Basic Regulation, the notion "agricultural production" must be understood to be constrained to those concrete species.[68] Be that as it may, irrespective of the intent of the drafters of the Basic Regulation, that Article 14(2) of the Basic Regulation narrows the list of species[69] relevant "for the purposes of safeguarding agricultural production" can hardly be disputed. Furthermore, in the Proposal for a Council Regulation (EEC) on Community plant variety rights (COM (90) 347 final) (90/C 244/01) of September 28, 1990, the FSS was foreseen as a rather unlimited provision,[70] and its restriction to some

Llombart (n. 10) 222-223; Würtenberger and others (n. 2) 9, 142; García Vidal, "El Sistema de Protección de Las Variedades Vegetales" (n. 2) 77; Framiñán Santas (n. 32) 216-217; Botana Agra (n. 10) 612, 614, 617, 634; the case law from the CJEU, e.g., the Judgment of the Court of Justice of the CJEU of October 17, 2019, *Saatgut-Treuhandverwaltungs GmbH v. Freistaat Thüringen*, C-239/18, EU:C:2019:869: paras 3 and 37 (transcribed in n. 29); n. 32 and text to n. 32. *See also* the references to the Judgment of the CJEU of December 19, 2019, *Club de Variedades Vegetales Protegidas v. Adolfo Juan Martínez Sanchís*, C-176/18, EU:C:2019:1131 (paras 5, 32, 34) in nn. 32, 62 *in fine*.

66. Würtenberger and others (n. 2) 144; Opinion of Advocate General Bobek delivered on May 23, 2019, *Saatgut-Treuhandverwaltungs GmbH v. Freistaat Thüringen*, C-239/18, EU:C:2019:445, para. 55. On the limitation of the FSS to some species by Art. 14(2) of the Basic Regulation *see also* Sánchez Gil, *La protección de las obtenciones vegetales: el privilegio del agricultor* (n. 2) 200-201; García Vidal, El material vegetal protegido por una patente o un derecho de obtentor y el empleo del producto de su cosecha con fines de propagación: agotamiento y privilegio del agricultor en Europa y en los EE.UU (n. 8) 91; Botana Agra (n. 40) 618; Gómez Segade (n. 2) 128; Petit Lavall (n. 40) 547. *See also* the Opinion of Advocate General Bobek delivered on May 23, 2019, *Saatgut-Treuhandverwaltungs GmbH v. Freistaat Thüringen*, C-239/18, EU:C:2019:445, paras 45, 51, 74; n. 40 and text to n. 40.
67. Würtenberger and others (n. 2) 144; Opinion of Advocate General Bobek delivered on May 23, 2019, *Saatgut-Treuhandverwaltungs GmbH v. Freistaat Thüringen*, C-239/18, EU:C:2019:445, para. 55. *See also* Sánchez Gil, *La protección de las obtenciones vegetales: el privilegio del agricultor* (n. 2) 200-201; García Vidal, El material vegetal protegido por una patente o un derecho de obtentor y el empleo del producto de su cosecha con fines de propagación: agotamiento y privilegio del agricultor en Europa y en los EE.UU (n. 8) 91; Botana Agra (n. 40) 618; Gómez Segade (n. 2) 12; Petit Lavall (n. 40) 547; the Opinion of Advocate General Bobek delivered on May 23, 2019, *Saatgut-Treuhandverwaltungs GmbH v. Freistaat Thüringen*, C-239/18, EU:C:2019:445, paras 45, 51, 74; n. 40 and text to n. 40.
68. The CJEU has recently broadened the meaning of "safeguarding agricultural production" from recital 18 of the Basic Regulation (*see* the Judgment of the CJEU of December 19, 2019, *Club de Variedades Vegetales Protegidas*, C-176/18, EU:C:2019:1131, paras 5, 32, 34 and n. 62 of this chapter), but, in principle, such exercise of interpretation by the CJEU should have no impact on the analysis here made.
69. On the limitation of the FSS to some species by Art. 14(2) of the Basic Regulation, *see*, e.g., Würtenberger and others (n. 2) 144; Sánchez Gil, *La protección de las obtenciones vegetales: el privilegio del agricultor* (n. 2) 200-201; García Vidal, El material vegetal protegido por una patente o un derecho de obtentor y el empleo del producto de su cosecha con fines de propagación: agotamiento y privilegio del agricultor en Europa y en los EE.UU (n. 8) 91; Botana Agra (n. 40) 618; Petit Lavall (n. 40) 547; the Opinion of Advocate General Bobek delivered on May 23, 2019, *Saatgut-Treuhandverwaltungs GmbH v. Freistaat Thüringen*, C-239/18, EU:C:20 19:445, paras 45, 51, 55, 74; n. 40 and text to n. 40.
70. According to Art. 13(4) second subpara. of the Proposal for a Council Regulation (EEC) on Community plant variety rights (COM (90) 347 final) (90/C 244/01) of 28 September 1990: "For

species[71] seems to be strongly connected with the later appearance, in 1991[72] (and therefore, after that proposal), of the UPOV "Recommendation Relating to Article 15(2)." According to the foregoing, it might be concluded that those species that were relevant in the EU "for the purposes of safeguarding agricultural production" were also those species in which seed savings were traditional;[73] or, at least, that the list of species within Article 14(2) of the Basic Regulation is the result of the influence of Article 39(1)(a) TFEU[74] and the UPOV "Recommendation Relating to Article 15(2)."[75]

---

the purpose of safeguarding agricultural production in the case of plant species governed by Community rules on the marketing of seeds or other propagating material, authorization may be given at Community level and in accordance with the procedure laid down in the implementing rules pursuant to Article 109, to permit growers of propagating material of a variety for which a Community plant variety right has been granted to plant on their own holding harvested material obtained therefrom. [...]" European Communities, "Proposal for a Council Regulation (EEC) on Community Plant Variety Rights (COM (90) 347 Final) (90/C 244/01)" 6 <https://eur-lex.europa.eu/legal-content/EN/TXT/PDF/?uri=OJ:C:1990:244:FULL&from=EN> 3 November 2019. Adapted from Sánchez Gil, *La protección de las obtenciones vegetales: el privilegio del agricultor* (n. 2) 203.

71. On the limitation of the FSS by Art. 14(2) of the Basic Regulation, *see* Würtenberger and others (n. 2) 144; Sánchez Gil, *La protección de las obtenciones vegetales: el privilegio del agricultor* (n. 2) 200-201; García Vidal, El material vegetal protegido por una patente o un derecho de obtentor y el empleo del producto de su cosecha con fines de propagación: agotamiento y privilegio del agricultor en Europa y en los EE.UU (n. 8) 91; Botana Agra (n. 40) 618; Gómez Segade (n. 2) 128; Petit Lavall (n. 40) 547; the Opinion of Advocate General Bobek delivered on May 23, 2019, *Saatgut-Treuhandverwaltungs GmbH v. Freistaat Thüringen*, C-239/18, EU:C:2019:445, paras 45, 51, 55, 74; n. 40 and text to n. 40.
72. Approved along as with the revised Convention on 19 March 1991. UPOV, "Records of the Diplomatic Conference for the Revision of the International Convention for the Protection of New Varieties of Plants—Geneva 1991 (Publication UPOV N° 346 (E))" (n. 1) 157; García Vidal, "El contenido del derecho de "obtentor" de una variedad vegetal (luces y sombras del Convenio de la UPOV)" (n. 25) 127.
73. This interpretation is aligned with the findings of Sánchez Gil, who contends that "*las razones que han motivado la selección de las especies de esta lista* [the list within Art. 14(2) of the Basic Regulation] *[...] son [...] la costumbre, el interés público y los criterios de oportunidad política*" (Sánchez Gil, *La protección de las obtenciones vegetales: el privilegio del agricultor* (n. 2) 202). Sánchez Gil indirectly connects the list of species within Art. 14(2) of the Basic Regulation with "*la Recomendación adjunta al CUPOV 91*" (*Ibid.* 204). However, Sánchez Gil gives pre-eminence to other reasons over "practice" and therefore over the UPOV "Recommendation Relating to Article 15(2)", further diluting the grounds of "safeguarding agricultural production" with other grounds (*see ibid.* 206). *See also ibid.* 151-154, 203-206, 256; Sánchez Gil, "El privilegio del agricultor y la excepción en beneficio del agricultor de la ley 3/2000" (n. 2) 347-348, 358; Würtenberger and others (n. 2) 142; García Vidal, "El material vegetal protegido por una patente o un derecho de obtentor y el empleo del producto de su cosecha con fines de propagación: agotamiento y privilegio del agricultor en Europa y en los EE.UU." (n. 8) 80; nn. 54, 81 and text to nn. 54, 81.
74. On the connection between the reference to "safeguarding agricultural production" (within recital 18, Art. 14 of the Basic Regulation, etc.) and Art. 39(1)(a) TFEU, *see* nn. 49-51 and text to nn. 49-51.
75. On the combined impact of tradition or "practice" and "public interest" on the configuration of the FSS under the CPVR system, *see*, e.g., Sánchez Gil, *La protección de las obtenciones vegetales: el privilegio del agricultor* (n. 2) 151-154, 202, 204, 206, 256. *See also ibid.* 126, 129, 205, 206, 252-254; Sánchez Gil, "El privilegio del agricultor y la excepción en beneficio del agricultor de la ley 3/2000" (n. 2) 347-348, 358; Quintana Carlo, "El Reglamento CE Número 2100/1994 Relativo a La Protección Comunitaria de Las Obtenciones Vegetales" (n. 3) 15; Amat Llombart (n. 10) 222-223; Würtenberger and others (n. 2) 142; García Vidal, "El material vegetal protegido por una patente o un derecho de obtentor y el empleo del producto de su cosecha con fines de

In addition to all these elements inherent to the Basic Regulation, further evidence reinforcing this interpretation can be found beyond the CPVR system. The Dutch proposal "DC/91/68" of March 6, 1991 aimed to limit the FSS "to varieties of cereals, peas and potatoes,"[76] i.e., just the species included in Article 14(2) of the Basic Regulation.

It is also worth noting that both, the non-binding nature of the UPOV "Recommendation Relating to Article 15(2)"[77] as well as the CJEU case law on conflicts of law between EU secondary law and international treaties,[78] favor the prevalence of Article 39(1)(a) TFEU over the UPOV "Recommendation Relating to Article 15(2)."[79]

---

propagación: agotamiento y privilegio del agricultor en Europa y en los EE.UU." (n. 8) 80; nn. 39, 53, 54, 73, 81 and text to nn. 39, 53, 54, 73, 81.

76. UPOV, "Records of the Diplomatic Conference for the Revision of the International Convention for the Protection of New Varieties of Plants—Geneva 1991 (Publication UPOV N° 346 (E))" (n. 1) 123 (emphasis deleted). The Dutch proposal is transcribed hereinafter:

> "**DC/91/68** March 6, 1991 (Original: English)
>
> *Source*: Delegation of the Netherlands.
>
> **PROPOSAL FOR THE AMENDMENT OF ARTICLE 15(2)**
>
> It is proposed that Article 15(2) be worded as follows:
>
> '(2) [**Farm-saved seed**] *(a)* Notwithstanding Article 14, each Contracting Party may, within reasonable limits, [and] subject to the safeguarding of the legitimate interests of the breeder *and provided that an equitable remuneration is paid to the breeder*, restrict the breeder's right in relation to any variety in order to permit farmers to use for propagating purposes, on their own holdings, the product of the harvest which they have obtained by planting, on their own holdings, the protected variety or a variety covered by Article 14(2)(a)(i) or (ii).
>
> (b) *This provision shall apply only to varieties of cereals, peas and potatoes.*'" *Ibid.* 123.

See also Sánchez Gil, *La protección de las obtenciones vegetales: el privilegio del agricultor* (n. 2) 204.

77. *See* UPOV, "Records of the Diplomatic Conference for the Revision of the International Convention for the Protection of New Varieties of Plants—Geneva 1991 (Publication UPOV N° 346 (E))" (n. 1) 397.

78. *See*, e.g., the Judgment of the Court (Fourth Chamber) of February 4, 2016, joined *C & J Clark International Ltd* and *Customs and Puma SE*, C-659/13 and C-34/14, EU:C:2016:74, para. 84: "[I]t is apparent from settled case-law that the provisions of an international agreement to which the European Union is a party can be relied upon in support of an action for annulment of a measure of secondary EU legislation, of a plea that such a measure is invalid or of an action for compensation only if, first, the nature and the broad logic of the agreement in question do not preclude this and, secondly, the provisions relied upon appear, as regards their content, to be unconditional and sufficiently precise (*see*, to this effect, judgments in *Intertanko and Others*, C-308/06, EU:C:2008:312, paragraphs 43 and 45, and *FIAMM and Others v. Council and Commission*, C-120/06 P and C-121/06 P, EU:C:2008:476, paragraphs 110 and 120)." *See also* the Judgment of the Court (Second Chamber) of July 16, 2015, case *ClientEarth*, C-612/13 P, EU:C:2015:486, para. 35. Adapted from Laurens Ankersmit and Benedikt Pirker, "Review of EU Legislation under EU International Agreements Revisited: Aarhus Receives Another Blow By' (*European Law Blog: News and comments on EU law*, 2015) https://europeanlawblog.eu/2015/11/17/review-of-eu-legislation-under-eu-international-agreements-revisited-aarhus-receives-another-blow/ accessed August 1, 2019.

79. Aligned, at some extent at least, with the perception on this issue of Sánchez Gil, *La protección de las obtenciones vegetales: el privilegio del agricultor* (n. 2) 206. *See also ibid.* 126, 129, 151-154, 202, 205, 252-254, 256; Sánchez Gil, "El privilegio del agricultor y la excepción en beneficio del agricultor de la ley 3/2000" (n. 2) 347-348; Würtenberger and others (n. 2) 142; García Vidal, "El material vegetal protegido por una patente o un derecho de obtentor y el empleo del producto de

5 FURTHER CONSIDERATIONS ON THE FSS UNDER THE CPVR SYSTEM

As shown in the former section, interpreting the legislative choice of the EU legislature in Article 14 of the Basic Regulation (particularly in relation to the list of species contained in its second paragraph) as the result of the balance between Article 39(1)(a) TFEU and the UPOV "Recommendation Relating to Article 15(2)" is consistent, and coherent with respect to the findings of the literature.[80] However, as it will be shown hereinafter, this interpretation does not settle all the issues concerning the potential mismatch between Article 14 of the Basic Regulation and the UPOV "Recommendation Relating to Article 15(2)." Below, the most remarkable implications arising from this duality are addressed, and some suggestions to solve them are outlined.

5.1 Extension of the Scope of the FSS under the CPVR System Beyond the Limits Set by the "Recommendation Relating to Article 15(2)" and the Logic of the EU Law

Some of the species contained in Article 14(2) of the Basic Regulation might not be traditional in some EU Member States, and even less the practice of the FSS on those species.[81] This seems to be the case of *Trifolium alexandrinum* L., included in Article 14(2) of the Basic Regulation but probably unfamiliar in Northern Europe,[82] the reason

su cosecha con fines de propagación: agotamiento y privilegio del agricultor en Europa y en los EE.UU." (n. 8) 80; nn. 39, 53, 54, 73, 81 and text to nn. 39, 53, 54, 73, 81.

80. *See* particularly Sánchez Gil, *La protección de las obtenciones vegetales: el privilegio del agricultor* (n. 2) 206. *Also ibid.* 126, 129, 151-154, 202, 205, 252-254, 256; Sánchez Gil, "El privilegio del agricultor y la excepción en beneficio del agricultor de la ley 3/2000" (n. 2) 347-348; Würtenberger and others (n. 2) 142; García Vidal, "El material vegetal protegido por una patente o un derecho de obtentor y el empleo del producto de su cosecha con fines de propagación: agotamiento y privilegio del agricultor en Europa y en los EE.UU." (n. 8) 80; nn. 39, 53, 54, 73, 81 and text to nn. 39, 53, 54, 73, 81.
81. Sánchez Gil (Sánchez Gil, *La protección de las obtenciones vegetales: el privilegio del agricultor* (n. 2) 206) gives pre-eminence to other factors (such as "*el interés público y las razones geopolíticas*") over tradition or "practice" in the recourse to the FSS by farmers (literally in Spanish, "*costumbre*") as the main criteria applied by the EU legislature in the conformation of the list of species contained in Art. 14(2) of the Basic Regulation. *See also ibid.* 126, 129, 151-154, 202, 205, 252-254, 256; Sánchez Gil, "El privilegio del agricultor y la excepción en beneficio del agricultor de la ley 3/2000" (n. 2) 347-348, 358; Würtenberger and others (n. 2) 142; García Vidal, "El material vegetal protegido por una patente o un derecho de obtentor y el empleo del producto de su cosecha con fines de propagación: agotamiento y privilegio del agricultor en Europa y en los EE.UU." (n. 8) 80; nn. 39, 53, 54, 73, 80 and text to nn. 39, 53, 54, 73, 80. However, regardless on the influence of policy motives on the final configuration of the list of species within Art. 14(2) of the Basic Regulation pointed out by Sánchez Gil (*see* Sánchez Gil, *La protección de las obtenciones vegetales: el privilegio del agricultor* (n. 2) 206, etc., *supra*), considering the rather uniform nature of the list contained in that precept (with only one singularity breaking that exception, "Lolium multiflorum lam — Italian ryegrass" exclusively applying to Portugal) it seems that the goal of harmonization played the most important role in that regard.
82. *See*, e.g., Muhammad Dost and others, "Egyptian Clover (Trifolium Alexandrinum): King of Forage Crops" (2014) ix, 1, 3, 59, 67, 69 http://www.fao.org/3/a-i3500e.pdf accessed October 2, 2019.

why it was likely excluded from the Lithuanian[83] and Latvian FSS' lists.[84] Other crops listed in Article 14(2) of the Basic Regulation might be in the same situation. It is also rather dubious that a crop like *Trifolium alexandrinum* L., probably not much cultivated in Northern regions and likely with problems to perform well in those latitudes,[85] may be crucial, even interesting, in those regions "for the purposes of safeguarding agricultural production" as justified in Article 14(1) of the Basic Regulation. The fiction created by Article 14(2) of the Basic Regulation seems to be artificially extending the scope of the exception to the Member States without a tradition in the FSS for certain crops, conflicting with the "Recommendation Relating to Article 15(2)" of the UPOV Convention, but also with the justification of the FSS mentioned in Article 14(1) of the Basic Regulation.[86] It needs to be further noted that differences between the CVPR list of species subject to the FSS and its homologous lists at a national level have been claimed to be troublesome.[87] Besides, climate change, by allowing to profitably cultivate certain crops in areas where they were not traditional or even cultivated before,[88] might eventually worsen the negative effects stemming from the aforementioned overextension of the FSS.

To solve this problem, the list within Article 14(2) of the Basic Regulation should be adapted to the national and even regional reality of the FSS in Europe by reducing[89]

83. *See* section 28 of the Lithuanian "Law No. IX–618 of November 22, 2001, on the Protection of Plant Varieties (as amended on April 26, 2012, by Law No. XI-1994) LT080", from UPOV, "UPOV Lex" http://www.upov.int/upovlex/en/ accessed July 30, 2019.
84. *See* section 24 of the Latvian "Plant Varieties Protection Law (as amended up to December 31, 2010)", from *ibid.*
85. *See*, e.g., Dost and others (n. 82) ix, 1, 3, 59, 67, 69.
86. *See* the "Recommendation Relating to Article 15(2)", in UPOV, "Records of the Diplomatic Conference for the Revision of the International Convention for the Protection of New Varieties of Plants—Geneva 1991 (Publication UPOV N° 346 (E))" (n. 1) 63 (transcribed in n. 27). *See also* Sánchez Gil, "El privilegio del agricultor y la excepción en beneficio del agricultor de la ley 3/2000" (n. 2) 347-348, 358; Sánchez Gil, *La protección de las obtenciones vegetales: el privilegio del agricultor* (n. 2) 154; Würtenberger and others (n. 2) 142; the case law from the CJEU, e.g., the Judgment of the Court of Justice of the CJEU of October 17, 2019, *Saatgut-Treuhandverwaltungs GmbH v. Freistaat Thüringen*, C-239/18, EU:C:2019:869: paras 3 and 37 (transcribed in n. 29); n. 29 and text to n. 29. Art. 14(1) of the Basic Regulation is transcribed in text to n. 33. *See also* Sánchez Gil, *La protección de las obtenciones vegetales: el privilegio del agricultor* (n. 2) 204, 151, 154, 202, 256; Dhar (n. 9) 15; García Vidal, El contenido del derecho de "obtentor" de una variedad vegetal (luces y sombras del Convenio de la UPOV) (n. 25) 127-128; Würtenberger and others (n. 2) 143; Botana Agra (n. 10) 616; n. 26 and text to n. 26.
87. Würtenberger and others (n. 2) 144; Amat Llombart (n. 10) 226. Some potential problems stemming from other existent differences between the FSS under the Spanish PVR system and the FSS under the CPVR system have been also reported (*see*, e.g., Sánchez Gil, *La protección de las obtenciones vegetales: el privilegio del agricultor* (n. 2) 183).
88. On the northward expansion of agriculture due to the effect of climate change, *see*, e.g., generally: Myron King and others, "Northward Shift of the Agricultural Climate Zone under 21 St -Century Global Climate Change" (2018) 8 Scientific Reports 1 http://dx.doi.org/10.1038/s41598-018-26321-8; Helder Fraga and others, "Modelling Climate Change Impacts on Viticultural Yield, Phenology and Stress Conditions in Europe" (2016) 22 Global Change Biology 3774 https://doi.org/10.1111/gcb.13382; Bakhtiyor Pulatov and others, "Modeling Climate Change Impact on Potato Crop Phenology, and Risk of Frost Damage and Heat Stress in Northern Europe" (2015) 214–215 Agricultural and Forest Meteorology 281 http://dx.doi.org/10.1016/j.agrformet.2015.08.266.
89. There might be the temptation to take advantage of an eventual revision of Art. 14(2) of the Basic Regulation to include new species not currently listed in it. However, it must not be forgotten

the number of species under the exception depending on whether the requirements stemming from the UPOV "Recommendation Relating to Article 15(2)" (particularly "a common practice on the territory")[90] and Article 14(1) of the Basic Regulation (particularly, "safeguarding agricultural production")[91] are met or not at a national or regional level. As alleged by some experts consulted during the preparation of this chapter,[92] it could be argued that the fragmentation of the exception would automatically end in the fragmentation of the right, against the purpose of full harmonization[93] and the "uniform effect."[94] However, it needs to be remarked that there is already an exception in Article 14(2)(a) of the Basic Regulation (i.e., "and, in the case of Portugal, Lolium multiflorum lam—Italian ryegrass") breaking this principle. Besides, the implementation of the CAP at a national and even at a regional level, as mandated by Article 39(2)(a) TFEU, reinforces and further justifies the need of adapting the FSS to

that the implementation of Art. 15(2) of the UPOV Act of 1991 at a national level is restricted to "the time when the Contracting Party concerned acceded to the Convention" (UPOV, "Records of the Diplomatic Conference for the Revision of the International Convention for the Protection of New Varieties of Plants—Geneva 1991 (Publication UPOV N° 346 (E))" (n. 1) 397). Besides, there are, in principle, no reasons to think that relevant species were forgotten at that time. Furthermore, such move would probably be nonaligned with the purpose of the UPOV Convention (*see*, e.g., UNICE's intervention in the Diplomatic Conference of 1991, in *ibid*. 398) and would affect pre-existing PVR. In other words, the inclusion of new species in the list of Art. 14(2) of the Basic Regulation does not seem legally feasible or convenient.

90. For example, Sánchez Gil, *La protección de las obtenciones vegetales: el privilegio del agricultor* (n. 2) 204, 151, 154, 202, 256; García Vidal, "El contenido del derecho de "obtentor" de una variedad vegetal (luces y sombras del Convenio de la UPOV)" (n. 25) 127-128. *See also* n. 27, 26 and text to n. 27.
91. For example, Sánchez Gil, "El privilegio del agricultor y la excepción en beneficio del agricultor de la ley 3/2000" (n. 2) 347-348, 358; Sánchez Gil, *La protección de las obtenciones vegetales: el privilegio del agricultor* (n. 2) 154; Würtenberger and others (n. 2) 142. *See also* nn. 31, 33 and text to nn. 31, 33.
92. During the preparation of this chapter, several experts from the CPVO were consulted and this observation was made.
93. On the goal of uniformization of the CPVR system, *see* recital 2 of the Basic Regulation: "Whereas industrial property regimes for plant varieties have not been harmonized at Community level and therefore continue to be regulated by the legislation of the Member States, the content of which is not uniform";. *See also* Quintana Carlo, "El Reglamento CE Número 2100/1994 Relativo a La Protección Comunitaria de Las Obtenciones Vegetales" (n. 10) 3; García Vidal, "El Sistema de Protección de Las Variedades Vegetales" (n. 2) 95-96; Würtenberger and others (n. 2) 5. On the alternative nature of the EU and national PVR system, *see* Würtenberger and others (n. 2) 4 (text transcribed in n. 103 *ad initium*); Quintana Carlo, "El Reglamento CE Número 2100/1994 Relativo a La Protección Comunitaria de Las Obtenciones Vegetales" (n. 10) 3; Quintana Carlo, "El Nuevo Régimen Jurídico de Las Obtenciones Vegetales (Comentario de Urgencia a La Ley 3/2000, de 7 de Enero)" (n. 10) 4; Kiewiet (n. 3) 3; García Vidal, "El Sistema de Protección de Las Variedades Vegetales" (n. 2) 104).
94. Art. 2 of the Basic Regulation:

> "Article 2
>
> **Uniform effect of Community plant variety rights**
>
> Community plant variety rights shall have uniform effect within the territory of the Community and may not be granted, transferred or terminated in respect of the abovementioned territory otherwise than on a uniform basis." *See also* Würtenberger and others (n. 2) 5; Quintana Carlo, "El Reglamento CE Número 2100/1994 Relativo a La Protección Comunitaria de Las Obtenciones Vegetales" (n. 10) 3; Kiewiet (n. 3) 3; García Vidal, "El Sistema de Protección de Las Variedades Vegetales" (n. 2) 95.

the national/regional reality of the EU. Furthermore, the need to reform not only the FSS but even "the current EU law implementing [FSS] provisions"[95] has been acknowledged by the European Commission.[96]

5.2 Undue Influence of the List of Species in Article 14(2) of the Basic Regulation on National Lists of Species under the FSS

The United Kingdom's "Plant Breeders' Rights (Farm-saved Seed) (Specification of Species and Groups) Order 1998"[97] contains in its Article 2, a list of "FARM-SAVED SEED-SPECIES AND GROUPS" that, with the exception set by Article 14(2) of the Basic Regulation (i.e., "in the case of Portugal" (i.e., "Lolium multiflorum lam—Italian ryegras")), fully matches the list within that provision. Similarities with the Basic Regulation can also be found in the PVR laws of other EU Member States, like the Lithuanian "Law No. IX–618 of November 22, 2001, on the Protection of Plant Varieties (as amended on April 26, 2012, by Law No. XI-1994) LT080,"[98] the list of which, despite being shorter than the one included in Article 14(2) of the Basic Regulation, is circumscribed to that list.[99] Something similar happens in the case of Latvia.[100] Significant similarities despite some differences are also found in the Spanish list,[101]

95. Opinion of Advocate General Bobek delivered on May 23, 2019, *Saatgut-Treuhandverwaltungs GmbH v. Freistaat Thüringen*, C-239/18, EU:C:2019:445, para. 76. Observation of another expert from the CPVO.
96. *See* the Opinion of Advocate General Bobek delivered on May 23, 2019, *Saatgut-Treuhandverwaltungs GmbH v. Freistaat Thüringen*, C-239/18, EU:C:2019:445, para. 76: "For all these reasons, if the problems outlined in this section do indeed have some basis in reality, it is for the Commission, which seemed to acknowledge at the hearing the somewhat outdated character of the current EU law implementing provisions, to go back to the drawing board and to design a new system.[...] It is somewhat peculiar to attempt to pass that responsibility on to this Court, especially in a legislative context like the present one, where even a well-intended judicial intervention relating to one discrete provision, without altering the overall logic of the system, is likely to generate more problems than solutions."
97. UPOV, "UPOV Lex" (n. 83).
98. *Ibid.*
99. Additionally, Art. 28(2)(3)(1) of the Lithuanian PVR Law seems also to be based to some extent on Art. 14(2)(d) of the Basic Regulation, evinced by some coincidences in the wording, like the reference to "with the exclusion of flax" in relation to "linseed", sharing exactly the same wording. Literally, from Art. 28(2)(3)(1) of the Lithuanian PVR Law:

    > "Article 28. Exceptions to the Breeder's Right
    > [...]
    > 2. Farmers and other land users may use the protected variety without the breeder's authorizsation when: 2. [...]
    > 3. The provisions of paragraph 2 of this Article shall apply to farmers and other land users only in the cases when they:
    >   1) are growing on their own holdings or land plots used by them the following plant species: oats, barley, rye, spelt wheat and durum wheat, triticale, rape, linseed (with the exclusion of flax), peas, beans, vetch, lupine, lucerne, potatoes;" *Ibid.*

100. *See* section 24 of the Latvian "Plant Varieties Protection Law (as amended up to December 31, 2010)," from *ibid.*
101. On the similarities and differences between Art. 14(2) of the Basic Regulation and the list within the Spanish law, *see Sánchez Gil, La protección de las obtenciones vegetales: el privilegio del agricultor* (n. 2) 201; García Vidal, El material vegetal protegido por una patente o un derecho

etc. Therefore, despite the independence between the CPVR system and national PVR systems from the EU Member States,[102] the harmonizing effect of the CPVR system over the legislation of the EU Member States can hardly be denied.[103] Even non-EU countries like Switzerland have apparently converged towards the EU standards.[104] Considering this phenomenon in the context of the aforementioned overextension of the FSS,[105] the revision of the list within Article 14(2) of the Basic Regulation to adjust it to the grounds and purpose of the exemption is all the more necessary. The adaptation to the UPOV "Recommendation Relating to Article 15(2)," of those national lists eventually suffering from that overextension, should also be encouraged.

5.3 The Evolution of the CAP and the FSS under the CPVR System

The interpretation of the CAP has evolved over time.[106] Article 39(1)(a) TFEU is no longer interpreted strictly as a stimulus to boost food production to save Europe from famine, like after the II World War.[107] The latest CAP reform dates back to 2013,[108] but currently, a new reform is underway,[109] and, as it seems, the relevance of "agricultural

de obtentor y el empleo del producto de su cosecha con fines de propagación: agotamiento y privilegio del agricultor en Europa y en los EE.UU (n. 8) 95. Amat Llombart goes even further, by implying that "to achieve the greatest possible harmonization" ("*lograr la mayor armonización posible*") was the goal of the drafters of the Spanish law (Amat Llombart (n. 10) 226).

102. According to Art. 93 of the Basic Regulation. Würtenberger and others (n. 2) xxv, 4. *See also* recital 3 of the Basic Regulation.
103. Würtenberger and others affirm that "[i]t[, the CPVR system,] neither subsitutes nor harmonizes such national systems, but is thought to be an alternative to them" (Würtenberger and others (n. 2) 4). Such statement, coherent with recitals 2 and 3 of the Basic Regulation, seems to be merely descriptive of the law and the written intent of the EU legislature, without referring to, nor explaining, the reality of the interrelation among those systems.
104. According to Art. 7(2) of the Swiss "Federal Law of March 20, 1975, on the Protection of New Plant Varieties (status as of September 1, 2008)" (UPOV, "UPOV Lex" (n. 83)): "The Federal Council shall determine the plant species to which the farmer's privilege shall apply; in so doing, it shall give special consideration to their importance as raw materials for foodstuffs or fodder." Although not using the same wording, the reference "to their importance as raw materials for foodstuffs or fodder" from Art. 7(2) of the Swiss PVR Law closely resembles to "the purposes of safeguarding agricultural production" of Art. 14(1) of the Basic Regulation.
105. *See* the former section of this chapter.
106. On the interpretation of the CAP objectives, *see*, e.g., Ferdinand Kopp, "AEUV Art. 39 (Ex-Art. 33 EGV) [Gemeinsame Agrarpolitik]" (*Streinz, EUV/AEUV 2*, 2012) Rn. 1 https://beck-online.beck.de/?vpath=bibdata/komm/StreinzEUVAEUVKOEuR_2/cont/StreinzEUVAEUVKOEuR.htm accessed August 14, 2017.
107. For example, *ibid.* and Martinez, "AEUV Art. 39 (Ex-Art. 33 EGV) [Ziele Der Gemeinsamen Agrarpolitik]" (*Calliess/Ruffert, EUV/AEUV 5*, 2016) Rn. 5 https://beck-online.beck.de/?vpath=bibdata/komm/CalliesRuffertEUVEGV_5/AEUV/cont/CalliesRuffertEUVEGV.AEUV.a39.glB.glI.htm accessed August 14, 2017.
108. For example, Council of the EU, "Common Agricultural Policy" (2018) https://www.consilium.europa.eu/en/policies/cap-introduction/ accessed August 1, 2019.
109. For example, *ibid.* as well as the "Proposal for a REGULATION OF THE EUROPEAN PARLIAMENT AND OF THE COUNCIL establishing rules on support for strategic plans to be drawn up by Member States under the Common agricultural policy (CAP Strategic Plans) and financed by the European Agricultural Guarantee Fund (EAGF) and by the European Agricultural Fund for Rural Development (EAFRD) and repealing Regulation (EU) No. 1305/2013 of the European Parliament and of the Council and Regulation (EU) No. 1307/2013 of the European Parliament and of the Council (COM/2018/392 final—2018/0216 (COD))."

production" is going to be further relativized,[110] therefore, adding additional pressure to revise the list of species within Article 14(2) of the Basic Regulation in order to adapt it to both, the current relevance of "agricultural production" and the "Recommendation Relating to Article 15(2)" of the UPOV Convention. In fact, in light of the current meaning of Article 39(1)(a) TFEU,[111] it would not be an overstatement to say that the justification, and therefore the very necessity, of the FSS in the current EU context should be seriously discussed by the European legislature.

6 CONCLUSIONS

The scope of the FSS under the CPVR system appears to be out of the limits set by the UPOV "Recommendation Relating to Article 15(2)" and not justified on the basis of "safeguarding agricultural production" either. Even worse, this phenomenon seems to have permeated to national PVR systems of the EU Member States[112] and non-EU countries, that, apparently, in some cases have followed the lead of the EU, and adopted or adapted into their national systems, the list of species from Article 14(2) of the Basic Regulation. Besides, the interpretation of Article 39(1)(a) TFEU and the EU Common Agricultural Policy have evolved,[113] but the regulation of the FSS in the CPVR system has not been revised accordingly. The list of species in Article 14(2) of the Basic Regulation should be amended in order to adapt it to the reality of the FSS at a national and a regional level at the time the CPVR system was created. A similar exercise of adaptation should be carried out on the FSS' lists of species of the EU Member States and other countries influenced in this particular regard by the CVPR system. These adaptations would improve the adjustment of all these PVR systems not only to the UPOV "Recommendation Relating to Article 15(2)" but also to the evolution of the interpretation of Article 39(1)(a) TFEU[114] and the CAP. It is also to be expected that the

110. *See*, e.g., recital 17 of Proposal COM/2018/392 final—2018/0216 (COD): "The CAP should keep ensuring food security, which should be understood as meaning access to sufficient, safe and nutritious food at all times. Moreover, it should help improving the response of Union agriculture to new societal demands on food and health, including sustainable agricultural production, healthier nutrition, food waste and animal welfare. The CAP should continue to promote production with specific and valuable characteristics, while at the same time helping farmers to proactively adjust their production according to market signals and consumers' demands."
111. For example, *ibid.* and José Martinez, "AEUV Art. 39 (Ex-Art. 33 EGV) [Ziele Der Gemeinsamen Agrarpolitik]" (*Calliess/Ruffert, EUV/AEUV 5*, 2016) Rn. 5 https://beck-online.beck.de/?vpath=bibdata/komm/CalliesRuffertEUVEGV_5/AEUV/cont/CalliesRuffertEUVEGV.AEUV.a39.glB.glI.htm accessed August 14, 2017. *See also* text to n. 107.
112. *See* in this regard, *Sánchez Gil, La protección de las obtenciones vegetales: el privilegio del agricultor* (n. 2) 201; García Vidal, El material vegetal protegido por una patente o un derecho de obtentor y el empleo del producto de su cosecha con fines de propagación: agotamiento y privilegio del agricultor en Europa y en los EE.UU (n. 8) 95; Amat Llombart (n. 10) 226; n. 101.
113. On the evolution of the interpretation of Art. 39(1)(a) TFEU *see* Kopp, "AEUV Art. 39 (Ex-Art. 33 EGV) [Gemeinsame Agrarpolitik]" (n. 106); Martinez, "AEUV Art. 39 (Ex-Art. 33 EGV) [Ziele Der Gemeinsamen Agrarpolitik]" (n. 107); nn. 106, 107 and text to nn. 106, 107.
114. On the evolution of the interpretation of Art. 39(1)(a) TFEU *see* Kopp, "AEUV Art. 39 (Ex-Art. 33 EGV) [Gemeinsame Agrarpolitik]" (n. 106); Martinez, "AEUV Art. 39 (Ex-Art. 33 EGV) [Ziele Der Gemeinsamen Agrarpolitik]" (n. 107); nn. 106, 107 and text to nn. 106, 107.

implementation of these proposals by recouping the incentives to the breeders partially lost in the current configuration of the FSS in such systems[115] will also have a significant positive effect on innovation.

115. On this issue, *see* Administrative and Legal Committee of UPOV (n. 16) Annex, p. 1; Sánchez Gil in Sánchez Gil, *La protección de las obtenciones vegetales: el privilegio del agricultor* (n. 2) 151, 246, 259; García Vidal, "El Sistema de Protección de Las Variedades Vegetales" (n. 2) 79-80; Helfer (n. 13) 2-3; Heitz (n. 18) 27, 36; Kochupillai (n. 8) 23 (in n. 17 of Kochupillai (n. 8) 23); n. 18.

PART III Patents and Artificial Intelligence

CHAPTER 10

AI Patents: Is There a Need to Rethink Patent Law?

Iga Bałos

1 INTRODUCTION

Artificial Intelligence (AI) has received a great deal of attention in different industries in recent years. It is worth highlighting that this interest is not limited to AI applications across different sectors, e.g., aviation agriculture, defence industry, financial services, healthcare transportation smart production and many more.[1] Strong emphasis in put upon AI influence not only on economy or employment but also on its social, ethical and legal consequences.

Apart from business and academic communities, disruptive technologies have always been inspirational for mass media and pop culture. In twenty-first century, the Internauts read the latest news about autonomous androids[2] and vehicles. The cinema-goers admire bold visions of the future of humankind[3] dominated by algorithms.

1. WIPO, *WIPO Technology Trends 2019: Artificial Intelligence* (2019 Geneva) www.wipo.int/edocs/pubdocs/en/wipo_pub_1055.pdf accessed 20 August 2020.
2. The most famous seems to be Sophia, a social humanoid robot developed by Hong Kong based company, https://enwikipedia.org/wiki/Sophia_(robot) accessed 20 August 2020. Another humanoid, Erica, is about to become a TV news anchor in Japan: Brandon Specktor, 'Meet Erika, Japan's Next Robot News Anchor' *Live Science* (London, 30 January 2018) www.livescience.com/61575-erica-robot-replace-japanese-news-anchor.html, accessed 20 August 2020. On Erica as an invention, Dylan F. Glas, Takashi Minato, Carlos T. Ishi and Tatsuya Kawahara, 'ERICA: The ERATO Intelligent Conversational Android' (25th IEEE International Symposium on Robot and Human Interactive Communication (RO-MAN), Columbia University, NY, 26-31 August 2016) www.dylanglas.com/research/pdf/glas-roman2016.pdf accessed 20 August 2020.
3. A vision presented in Ridley Scott's 'Blade Runner 2049' is a not-so-distant future. Japanese firm Gatebox offers an artificially intelligent anime character, living in a glass tube and acting as a home assistant: Mark Prigg, *The $1300 holographic AI wife that will 'serve her master' (if you keep*

At least three aspects may be considered when analysing AI in the context of patent law: (a) the aspect of using AI as a tool for improving the process of applying for[4]/granting[5] a patent, e.g., more comprehensive prior art search or translation and classification of patent documentation; (b) the aspect of patent protection for objects of applications filed in the areas of AI; (c) the aspect of AI-generated 'inventions'.[6] Even though this chapter deals solely with patent protection for AI-related applications (inventions), certain assumptions may be useful for further consideration on AI-generated 'inventions'.[7]

AI-related patenting is growing. World Intellectual Property Organization (hereinafter referred to as 'WIPO') informs that the number of AI-related patent applications worldwide rose from 18,995 in 2013 to 55,660 in 2017.[8] The US Patent and Trademark Office (hereinafter referred to as 'USPTO') in 2019 granted 14,838 patents that mentioned AI or Machine Learning (hereinafter referred to as 'ML'), of which 1,275 specifically mentioned AI or ML in their titles or abstracts. This is almost twice as much as in 2018.[9] When it comes to statistics provided by the European Patent Office (hereinafter referred to as 'EPO'), between 2010 and 2018 there were 2,026 patent applications related to AI. As at 2018, fifty-seven were refused, 208 granted and 1,666 were pending.[10]

---

paying her $14 a month 'living expenses'), Daily Mail (London, 17 August 2018) www.dailymail.co.uk/sciencetech/article-6072229/1300-holographic-AI-wife-chat-paying-14-month-living-expenses.html accessed 20 August 2020.

4. AI patent search engines seems to be gaining popularity, *see* 'Patentfield' https://enpatentfield.com; 'Teqmine' https://teqmine.com; 'AIPatents' https://www.aipatents.com all accessed 20 August 2020.
5. The European Patent Office has already been using AI as a helping tool in automatic annotation of patent literature i.e., indexing numerical values or chemical compounds. Another field of AI application is a machine translation through Google's Neural Network based machine. It receives 15,000 request a day covering 32 languages including Chinese, Japanese, Korean and Russian, *see* EPO, 'Artificial Intelligence at the EPO' (Meeting of Intellectual Property Offices (IPOs) on ICT Strategies and Artificial Intelligence (AI) for IP Administration, Geneva, 23-15 May 2018) 3 www.wipo.int/edocs/mdocs/globalinfra/en/wipo_ip_itai_ge_18/wipo_ip_itai_ge_18_p8.pdf accessed 20 August 2020. Using AI during the application procedure may influence the understanding of a person having ordinary skill in the art and the requirement of non-obviousness, *see* Ryan Benjamin Abbott, 'Everything is Obvious' (2018), 66 (2) University of California Law Review 1, https://ssrncom/abstract=3056915 accessed 20 August 2020.
6. I put it in quotation marks since this is a legal term having a particular meaning. At this stage of research, I hesitate to use it in reference to creations of AI systems.
7. Ryan Benjamin Abbott, *I Think, Therefore I Invent: Creative Computers and the Future of Patent Law* (2016), 57 Boston College Law Review, 1079, http://lawdigitalcommons.bc.edu/bclr/vol57/iss4/2 accessed 20 August 2020.
8. WIPO, *WIPO Technology Trends 2019: Artificial Intelligence* (2019, Geneva) www.wipo.int/edocs/pubdocs/en/wipo_pub_1055.pdf accessed 20 August 2020.
9. Al AuYeung, *Who Is Winning the AI Race?* (*IPWatchdog*, 1 February 2020) https://www.ipwatchdog.com/2020/02/01/winning-ai-race accessed 20 August 2020.
10. EPO, *Digitalisation triggers patenting growth*, https://www.epo.org/about-us/annual-reports-statistics/statistics/2019/digitalisation-triggers-patenting-growth.html accessed 20 August 2020; Vítor Sérgio Moreira and Diogo Antunes, *Patents related to Artificial Intelligence in the European Patents Office* (Inventa International, 9 March 2020) https://inventa.com/en/news/article/470/patents-related-to-artificial-intelligence-in-the-european-patents-office accessed 20 August 2020.

Although AI may be defied in many different ways, taking into consideration numerous factors, e.g., field of application or the manner in which data are collected and processed, it does not necessarily help when discussing patent eligibility. The above-mentioned classification do not explicitly refer either to categories listed in patent law acts or to established judicial practice of which matters are is susceptible of patent protection.

For instance, under the United States Patent Classification[11] (hereinafter referred to as 'USPC'), the relevant class no. 706 is named as 'Data Processing – Artificial Intelligence'. The 'General Statement of the Class Subject Matter' provides examples of AI, emphasizing it is not an exhaustive list, such as: knowledge based systems, reasoning systems, and knowledge acquisition systems; and including systems for reasoning with uncertainty (e.g., fuzzy logic systems), adaptive systems, machine learning systems, and artificial neural networks. It also explains that 'this class can accept combinations of data processing arts with artificial intelligence techniques not elsewhere provided for in USPC.'

Under the Cooperative Patent Classification[12] (CPC),[13] so-called Artificial Intelligence belongs to the subclass named as 'Computer Systems Based on Specific Computational Models'. According to general definition statement, the class encompasses 'Computing systems where the computation is not based on a traditional mathematical model of computer'.

It cannot be denied that understanding how a given AI solution operates and awareness of the field of its application is crucial for proper drafting and construction of patent claims. Nonetheless, despite many different categories listed above, AI-related solutions are often classified as sole algorithm or mathematical method, a computer program or a computer-implemented inventions deploying mathematical method. Some authors and activists indicate that AI is just another buzzword for software.[14] They warn against the negative effects of patents for computer programs, whatever their name is.[15]

In order to analyse the question of patent eligibility of AI-related inventions, the first part of the chapter briefs the ongoing discussion on this issue from the US and EPO[16] perspective. It also gives an overview of the existing practice of the EPO and the

11. This classification was superseded by the Cooperative Patent Classification (CPC) in 1 January 2013. It is a bilateral system, developed jointly by the EPO and the USPTO.
12. *See* n. 11.
13. Subclass G06N of the CPC.
14. Roy Schestowitz, *Cloud, AI' and Other Buzzwords as Excuses for Granting Fake Patents on Software* (Techrights, 16 October 2018) http://techrights.org/2018/10/16/buzzwords-facade accessed 20 August 2020; No author identified, *EPO Official Aggressively Promotes Software Patents At CEBIT Fair* (Intellectual Property Watch, 22 March 2017) http://www.ip-watch.org/2017/03/22/epo-official-aggressively-promotes-software-patents-cebit-fair accessed 20 August 2020.
15. Monika Ermert, *European Patent Office Discusses Patenting Artificial Intelligence* (Intellectual Property Watch, 1 June 2018) http://www.ip-watch.org/2018/06/01/european-patent-office-discusses-patenting-artificial-intelligence accessed 20 August 2020.
16. It must be remembered that the legal framework and practice of the EPO does not equal 'European law' or 'EU law'. Such misleading mental shortcuts happen to be repeated by the scholars, especially those originating outside the European continent. Because of political

USPTO. The concept of 'practice' should be understood in a broad sense and not limited solely to an act of granting patents. The second part attempts to answer the question of whether patent protection for AI-related invention is justified on the basis of fostering innovation. The third part discusses public interest in the contest of AI-related patents. The last section provides some possible scenarios on the future of AI patents as well as closing conclusions.

2 AI PATENTS: DETERMINING INVENTION AND ITS PATENT ELIGIBILITY

Although there is no universal patent law system, but it is still possible to have a discussion on legitimacy of AI patents. Despite the differences in various legal orders, the questions of the concept of invention and patent-eligible subject matter raise concerns regarding basic principles of patent law. Some degree of understanding and the interpretation of such concepts as 'invention', 'patent eligibility' or 'patentability' has been reached by signing international treaties.[17] It must be emphasized that it does not mean the uniformity in international patent protection nor on the domestic levels.

The first step in determining an appropriate patent policy with reference to AI solutions is establishing any definition of 'AI invention'. When requesting for comments on patenting AI-related inventions, the USPTO starts with the following question:

> Inventions that utilize AI, as well as inventions that are developed by AI, have commonly been referred to as 'AI inventions.' What are elements of an AI invention? For example: The problem to be addressed (e.g., application of AI); the structure of the database on which the AI will be trained and will act; the training of the algorithm on the data; the algorithm itself; the results of the AI invention through an automated process; the policies/weights to be applied to the data that affects the outcome of the results; and/or other elements.[18]

During the first conference on AI patents organized by the EPO, the panellists indicated three types of AI-related patents:[19] (1) 'core AI' which is usually related to

reasons, the practice of the EPO cannot be omitted. It impacts domestic legal regulations and is taken into consideration by the EU organs. Nonetheless, the unification of law and practice of the EU or particular Member States is not EPO's competence.

17. Art. 27 of the Annex 1C: General Agreement on Trade-Related Aspects of Intellectual Property, TRIPS, 33 I.L.M. 1197; Arts 52-57 of the European Patent Convention, 16th edition (June 2016).
18. United States Patent and Trademark Office, Request for Comments. Docket No. PTO–C–2019–0029 FR 84 (2019) 166, https://www.federalregister.gov/documents/2019/08/27/2019-18443/request-for-comments-on-patenting-artificial-intelligence-inventions accessed 20 August 2020.
19. The above-mentioned classification was presented during the first conference on AI patents organised by the EPO. This simple categorization is recognized by other patent offices, e.g., UK IPO which also acknowledges to follow the EPO's Examination Guidelines. *See* EPO, *EPO hosts first conference on patenting Artificial Intelligence* (European Patent Office, 30 May 2019) www.epo.org/news-issues/news/2018/20180530.html accessed 20 August 2020; EPO, *Patenting Artificial Intelligence, Conference Summary*, 30 May 2018, EPO Munich 5, https://e-courses.epo.org/pluginfile.php/23523/mod_resource/content/2/Summary%20Artificial%20Intelligence%20Conference.pdf accessed 20 August 2020; L. Alexander, *UK IPO Approach to AI*

algorithms being mathematical methods; (2) trained models/machine learning; (3) AI treated as a tool in an applied field, defined by technical effects. The fourth category, not listed above but mentioned several times during the discussions, are patents for software.

Thus far, granting patents for 'core AI' is excluded under the European Patent Convention[20] (EPC) and under many, if not all, domestic provisions on patents. Mathematical methods, as well as computer programs, are not regarded as inventions because of their purely abstract nature and the lack of technical character. Nonetheless, in several domestic acts,[21] the exclusion is usually limited by 'as such' exception by a paragraph resembling Article 52(3) of the EPC.[22] It results in creativity of patent agents while drafting patent claims, trying to convince patent offices and the judges that the patent claims address neither the algorithm nor the computer program 'as such'.

The trend of expanding patent eligibility with regard to AI-related inventions is visible and present not only in the public debates[23] but also in the USPTO and the EPO's practice. Another phase of the process of pushing the AI patentability boundaries in the USA was initiated by the Director of the USPTO Andrei Iancu during the hearing before the Senate Committee on the Judiciary, held on 18 April 2018.[24] Director Iancu was asked directly about AI patents. One of the interlocutors underlined that clear approach towards software patents was crucial for AI systems. In reply to this comment, the

---

Related Patent Applications (Reddie & Grosse, 30 January 2020) https://www.reddie.co.uk/2020/01/30/uk-ipo-approach-to-ai-related-patent-applications accessed 5 August 2020.

20. Convention on the Grant of European Patents of 5 October 1973. The 16th edition of the EPC contains the revised texts of the Convention and its protocols which entered into force on 13 December 2007, and the Implementing Regulations as in force since 1 May 2016; also included is an amendment to those regulations which enters into force on 1 November 2016 www.epo.org/law-practice/legal-texts/epc.html accessed 20 August 2020.
21. For example, para. 1(4) of the German Patent Act (as amended up to Act of 8 October 2017) https://wipolex.wipo.int/en/legislation/details/17611; Art. L611-10 (3) of the French Intellectual Property Code (consolidated version as of 23 December 2018) fr www.legifrance.gouvfr/affichCode.do?cidTexte=LEGITEXT000006069414 en www.legifrance.gouvfr/content/download/1959/13723/version/3/file/Code_35.pdf; Art. 2(3) of the Dutch Patents Act, https://english.rvo.nl/sites/default/files/2013/12/ROW95_ENG_niet_officiele_vertaling_0.pdf all accessed 20 August 2020.
22. 'Paragraph 2 shall exclude the patentability of the subject-matter or activities referred to therein only to the extent to which a European patent application or European patent relates to such subject-matter or activities as such.'
23. During the first EPO conference on patenting AI, *see* n. 19, two panellists, Michelle Holoubek (Sterne, Kessler, Goldstein & Fox, US) and Benjamin Bai (Ant Financial Services Group/Alipay, CN), advocated for changes within patent law enabling granting patents for pure algorithms. Panel discussion 2 Challenges in drafting patent applications for AI-related inventions ('Patenting Artificial Intelligence', Munich, 30 May 2018), *see* recordings of the event, https://e-courses.epo.org/pluginfile.php/23528/mod_resource/content/3/html/page124198.html accessed 20 August 2020.
24. Oversight of the US Patent and Trademark Office, 18 April 2018, recording of the hearing available at www.judiciary.senate.gov/meetings/oversight-of-the-us-patent-and-trademark-office accessed 20 August 2020.

USPTO Director declared that the courts deciding the *Bilski*[25] and *Mayo*[26] cases 'had gone off their initial intent'.[27] According to the USPTO Director, human made algorithms depending on human choices are patentable matters, since they were 'invented as a result of human ingenuity' and hence were different from discoveries and mathematical representations of those discoveries.

The analysis performed by the USPTO Director revealed the upcoming changes in the USPTO patent policy. They materialized in the '2019 Revised Patent Subject Matter Eligibility Guidance' (hereinafter 'the 2019 PEG').[28] According to introductory information, the revision was aimed at clarification of the scope of patent-eligible subject matter. It focused on how to apply the US Supreme Court's framework for evaluating eligibility, known as the *Alice/Mayo* test. In *Alice*,[29] consistent with the earlier *Mayo*, the Court ruled that an abstract idea implemented on a generic computer is patent ineligible subject matter. As the new guidelines explain:

> Properly applying the *Alice/Mayo* test in a consistent manner has proven to be difficult, and has caused uncertainty in this area of law. Among other things, it has become difficult in some cases for inventors, businesses, and other patent stakeholders to reliably and predictably determine what subject matter is patent-eligible. ... In particular, stakeholders have expressed concern with the proper scope and application of the 'abstract idea' exception.[30]

25. *Bilski v. Kappos*, 561 U.S. 593, 611 (2010). The Supreme Court of the United States affirms that the abstract investment strategy set forth in the application is not patentable subject matter. The object of the patent application was a method for managing the consumption risk cost of a commodity sold by a commodity provider at a fixed price.
26. *Mayo Collaborative Servs. v. Prometheus Labs. Inc.*, 566 U.S. 66 (2012). The Supreme Court of the USA holds that a newly discovered law of nature is itself unpatentable and that the application of that newly discovered law is also normally unpatentable if the application merely relies upon elements already known in the art. The object of the patent application: a process embodying researchers' findings that identify correlations between metabolite levels and likely harm or ineffectiveness with precision.
27. The problem of patents for computer algorithms was a subject of legal debate in the USA long before *Bilski* or *Mayo* cases. *See* Pamela Samuelson, *Should Program Algorithms Be Patented?* (1990), 33 (8) Communications of the ACM, 23.
28. Department of Commerce, United States Patent and Trademark Office, *2019 Revised Patent Subject Matter Eligibility Guidance*, Docket No. PTO-P-2018-0053, https://federalregister.gov/d/2018-28282 accessed 20 August 2020. The USPTO issued an update to the 2019 PEG on 17 October 2019. The update is consistent with the 2019 PEG. The update was introduced after receiving public comments on reply to USPTO Requests for Comments (*see* n. 18). The update provides clarification to some of the terms used in the 2019 PEG. *See* October 2019 Patent Eligibility Guidance Update (issued 17 October 2019) https://www.uspto.gov/sites/default/files/documents/peg_oct_2019_update.pdf accessed 20 August 2020.
29. *Alice Corp. v. CLS Bank International*, 573 U.S. 208, 134 S. Ct. 2347 (2014). The object of the patent application: a computer-implemented, electronic escrow service for facilitating financial transactions.
30. *Ibid.* 3.

The revision leaves no doubt as to what 'proper scope' means. Apparently, in relation to the new paragraph 112 guidance on examining computer-implemented invention,[31] it opens patent system for abstract ideas especially related to AI technology.

The 2019 PEG limits 'abstract idea exception' to three groupings of subject matter when recited as such in claims limitations: (1) mathematical concepts – mathematical relationships, mathematical formulas or equations, mathematical calculations; (2) certain methods of organizing human activity – fundamental economic principles or practices (including hedging, insurance, mitigating risk); commercial or legal interactions (including agreements in the form of contracts; legal obligations; advertising, marketing or sales activities or behaviours; business relations); managing personal behaviour or relationships or interactions between people (including social activities, teaching, and following rules or instructions); (3) mental process – concepts performed in the human mind (including an observation, evaluation, judgment, opinion).

The 2019 PEG also provides quite detailed scheme for evaluation. First, the Examiner decides whether the claimed solution constitutes a process, machine, manufacture, or composition of matter (Step 1). If a claim does not cover one out of three categories of abstract ideas listed above, it is eligible of course on the assumption that falling within 'an abstract idea' exception is the only obstacle to patentability. This phase of examination is named Step 2A Prong 1: If a claim does cover one of three categories constructing the concept of 'an abstract idea' according to the 2019 PEG, further examination is required because patent eligibility is not excluded yet. The Examiners are obliged to determine whether the claims are directed to the recited abstract idea (Step 2A Prong 2). They are not if the judicial exception is integrated into a practical application. If it is, then the claim is patent eligible subject matter. If it is not, the claim must be examined under another step (Step 2B), verifying whether the claim is directed to an inventive concept.

The revised guidelines seem to be very favourable to the applicants seeking protection for different kinds of AI patents. In most cases, such claims will not be considered as 'abstract ideas' according to the new understanding of this exception. Due to the amount of the data processed by AI, regardless of the true object of the claims, it will never be classified as 'performed in the human mind'. Such reasoning is applied in the examples recommended to be used in conjunction with the 2019 PEG.[32]

From theory to practice, the USPTO already instructed how to apply its recent guidelines by giving one of its decision, *Ex parte Hannun*,[33] the status of 'informative decision'. It was delivered by the Patent Trial and Appeal Board (PTAB) which is an adjudicative body within the USPTO. It hears appeals from the decisions of patent Examiners, on the condition that the claims have been rejected by the Examiner at least

31. USPTO, *Guidance for Examining Computer-Implemented Functional Claim Limitations for Compliance with 35 U.S.C. § 112*, Federal Register, 7 January 2019, vol. 84, No. 4 www.govinfo.gov/content/pkg/FR-2019-01-07/pdf/2018-28283.pdf accessed 20 August 2020.
32. USPTO, *Subject Matter Eligibility Examples: Abstract Ideas*, 7 January 2019 www.uspto.gov/sites/default/files/documents/101_examples_37to42_20190107.pdf accessed 20 August 2020.
33. Ex Parte HANNUN (2019) US Patent Trial and Appeal Board, Appeal 2018-003323. Decision involves US Application No. 14/735,002 issued as US Patent No. 10,540,957.

twice, and adjudicates the patentability of issued patents challenged by third parties in post-grant proceedings. 'Informative decision' status means that the decision 'provides Board norms on recurring issues, guidance on issues of first impression to the Board, guidance on Board rules and practices, and guidance on issues that may develop through analysis of recurring issues in many cases'.[34]

Facts of the case may be summarized as follows. The patent application related to systems and methods for improving the transcription of speech into text, comprising a computer-implemented method involving trained neural network. The application was rejected twice by the Examiner with regard to all the claims. Although rather little reasoning was provided, the Examiner found the solution unpatentable as directed to an abstract idea. According to the Examiner, claimed invention used the predicted character probabilities (mathematical formula) to decode a transcription of the input audio into words or text data and resembled cases on patent ineligibility of abstract ideas previously decided by the courts. The Examiner also determined that the specification showed that the predicted character probabilities was an algorithm and, consequently, the claimed invention was directed to a mathematical formula. The Examiner summarized the claimed invention into three steps: (1) normalizing the input audio data (manipulating data); (2) generating spectrogram frames based on each audio file (generating information sets based on prior information sets); and (3) using a mathematical formula to convert audio data into text data (Decoding). The Examiner described the abovementioned as the abstract ideas which were categorized under 'Certain Methods of Organizing Human Activity'. According to the Examiner, since human can listen to an audio file and transcribe the audio data into text data which can all be done mentally it falls within judicial exception from patentability. As a result of applying *Alice* test, the Examiner decided the claims did not amount to significantly more than the abstract idea.

On appeal, the PTAB noted that the 2019 PEG identified mental processes as a separate category of abstract ideas from methods of organizing human activity and disagreed with the assessment of the facts provided by the Examiner. According to the appellate body, the claims did not cover either a method of organizing human activity or a mental process. The PTAB stated that:

> While transcription generally can be performed by a human, the claims here are directed to a specific implementation including the steps of normalizing an input file, generating a jitter set of audio files ... and decoding a transcription of the input audio using the predicted character probability outputs. These are not steps that can practically be performed mentally. Nor do we see how the claimed invention recites organizing human activity. For example, the claims do not include fundamental economic principles or practices, commercial or legal interactions, managing personal behaviour or relationships or interactions between people.[35]

The Examiner and the PTAB represented different points of view on the significance of the mathematical formula with regard to invention perceived as a whole. The

34. *See* information provided by the USPTO, https://www.uspto.gov/patents-application-process/patent-trial-and-appeal-board/precedential-informative-decisions accessed 20 August 2020.
35. Ex parte HANNUN (n. 33) 10.

Examiner identified that the specification of the invention disclosed an algorithm to obtain the predicted character probabilities, because the claims did recite using predicted character probabilities to decide a transcription of the input audio, which was using a mathematical formula. According to PTAB, 'the mathematical algorithm or formula, however, is not recited in the claims. As such, under the recent Memorandum,[36] the claims did not recite a mathematical concept.' What is especially important for AI patent eligibility, the PTAB also emphasizes that 'even if the claims were considered to recite a mathematical concept, under prong two of step 2A the claims are not directed to an abstract idea because the alleged judicial exception is integrated into a practical application.' According to the PTAB, as the example of such an application may serve the fact that using DeepSpeech learning, i.e., a trained neural network, along with a language model 'achieves higher performance than traditional methods on hard speech recognition tasks while also being much simpler'.

When analysing other PTAB decisions rendered under the 2019 PEG,[37] certain ways of reasoning and conclusions are worth pointing out. First, reciting AI components in the claims of a patent application does not necessarily exclude patent-eligibility.[38] Second, the more complexity of algorithm is revealed, the lower probability of classifying invention as 'mental processes' category of abstract ideas. The latter is also accurate when reciting 'several different systems' in the claims. Moreover, although not sufficient enough, the fact that a method is performed on a computer may help to overcome the above-mentioned category.[39] Third, it happens that the PTAB applies Step 2B of the PEG providing no convincing reasoning, e.g., that because the claims solve a problem using the abstract idea, they are integrated into a practical application.[40] Since the PTAB's decision is the exact opposite of the decision rendered by the Examiner, it may be expected that the PTAB would specify which and why the additional elements are sufficient to integrate the invention. Fourth, the applicants learn what kind of arguments fit into the 2019 PEG and enable convincing the PTAB that the subject matter is patent eligible, e.g., 'the Examiner over-generalized the claim in characterizing it'.[41]

36. This is a name of the legal act constituting the 2019 PEG.
37. Hector Agdeppa, Conner Hutchisson and Alex Nie, *Machine Learning Patentability in 2019: 5 Cases Analyzed and Lessons Learned Part 1* (JDSUPRA, 6 February 2020) https://www.jdsupra.com/legalnews/machine-learning-patentability-in-2019-25164 accessed 20 August 2020.
38. Ex parte AKLI ADJAOUTE (2018) US Patent Trial and Appeal Board, Appeal 2018-007443. Decision involves US Application No. 14/815,940. The claims were directed to a method for protecting groups of digital electronic appliances used collectively for monitoring the operations of machines and for issuing predictions, warnings and calls for preventative maintenance and equipment failure interventions, The method empanels several different artificial intelligence (AI) classification technologies into a 'jury' uses combinational digital logic to render 'verdicts' about the need for service and impending equipment failures of the machines they monitor.
39. Ex parte JEAN-BAPTISTE TRISTAN et al. (2019) US Patent Trial and Appeal Board, Appeal 018-004459. Decision involves US Application 14/316, 186. The claims were directed to a probabilistic programming compiler that generates data-parallel inference code.
40. Ex parte AKLI ADJAOUTE (n. 38).
41. Ex parte GEOFFREY HYATT et al. (2019) US Patent Trial and Appeal Board, Appeal 2018-004485. Decision involves US Application No. 14/789,857. The claims were directed to maintaining a database of user profiles based, respectively, on user interaction with third-party systems.

The way the 2019 PEG are applied and the USPTO policy may foster questionable transformation of the patent system which is designed not to monopolize abstract ideas. As it is demonstrated above, allowing patents for traditionally excluded matters, yet embodied in different forms of AI-related solutions, does not require any change in subject matter provisions.

The second approach to patent strategy in the AI area seeks protection for trained models and/or machine learning. According to stakeholders who advocate patents for solutions of this kind, it requires considering adopting practices from other areas e.g., industrial chemistry.[42] Therefore, it is emphasized that examples and parameter ranges might be needed for proper disclosure of the invention. During public debate it was also suggested that 'the EPO might be more lenient regarding the technicality conferred by specific datasets and allow the "second use of a model" by analogy to second medical use claims in pharmaceutics. Uses should not be considered equivalent if arrived at by different means.'[43] Since there is no legal definition of 'technical effects', the third option regarding patents for AI-related solutions, which is claiming AI as a tool in an applied field, defined by technical effects, threatens legal certainty. Unfortunately, it allows to adopt double standards during patent granting procedure. Misusing patent system in this way has been apparent, and has a relatively long story, in case of CII (computer-implemented inventions).

The parallel should be no surprise since the first set of recommendations from the EPO on patenting AI expressly referred to the Guidelines for Examination in the EPO particularly the section on patentability of CII.[44] The Guidelines were eventually updated by additional section in relation to patentability of mathematical methods.[45] It is acknowledged at the outset that 'such computational models and algorithms [that artificial intelligence and machine learning are based on] are *per se* of an abstract mathematical nature, irrespective of whether they can be "trained" based on training data.'[46] If the AI or ML method contributes to the technical character of the invention perceived as a whole, patentability may not be excluded. According to the examples provided by the Guidelines, the use of a neural network in a heart-monitoring apparatus for the purpose of identifying irregular heartbeats constitutes the invention's technical contribution to the art. On the contrary, classifying abstract data records or telecommunication network data records without any indication of a technical use being made of the resulting classification is deprived of technical character or technical contribution. The Guidelines, which come down to a text of less than 300 words, declare that there exist some forms of AI or MI unpatentable by definition since they

42. EPO, *Patenting Artificial Intelligence, Conference Summary*, 30 May 2018, EPO Munich 6, https://e-courses.epo.org/pluginfile.php/23523/mod_resource/content/2/Summary%20Artificial%20Intelligence%20Conference.pdf accessed 20 August 2020.
43. *Ibid*. 6.
44. Koen Lievens, *Patenting Artificial Intelligence: Examination practice at the EPO* (Patenting Artificial Intelligence, Munich, 30 May 2018) 18 www.epo.org/learning-events/events/conferences/2018/ai2018.html accessed 20 August 2020.
45. EPO, *Guidelines for Examination 3.3.1 Artificial intelligence and machine learning* applied from 1 November 2018 www.epo.org/law-practice/legal-texts/guidelines.html accessed 20 August 2020.
46. *Ibid*.

represent subcategory of mathematical method or software. At the same time, the Guidelines will not be an obstacle to obtain a patent if the drafter of the patent claims selects cleverly chosen words.[47] It is quite likely that, just like in case of software patents disguised as CII patents, the EPO will put more attention to the buzzwords used in patent application than to the subject matter being claimed.

Both practising lawyers[48] and the EPO's experts[49] provide their own guidelines on overcoming patentability hurdles when applying for European patent for AI-related solutions. A cursory analysis of the titles of the inventions indicates that applicants attempt to direct examiners' attention towards an apparatus of any kind or a method comprising steps performance of which requires using an object (even though its physical character is quite often illusional, e.g., 'file', 'data' or 'bot'). By way of example, in recent years the EPO granted patents for the following inventions: method of controlling electronic apparatus and computer-readable recording medium;[50] provision of physiological data;[51] bot interaction;[52] image transformation for machine learning;[53] system and method of detecting malicious files using a trained machine learning model;[54] and method for detecting freezing conditions for an aircraft by supervised automatic learning.[55]

The Examination Guidelines updated by the EPO[56] provided a list of technical purposes which may be served by a mathematical method. Majority of them may operate as a form of AI/ML. For example, the technical character hurdle was overcome in case of: the identification of arrhythmic patterns based on using an artificial neural network in a cardiac monitoring apparatus; the classification of digital images, videos, audio, or speech signals based on low-level features (e.g., edges or pixel attributes for images); controlling a specific technical system or process, e.g., an X-ray apparatus or a steel cooling process; determining from measurements a required number of passes of a compaction machine to achieve a desired material density; providing a genotype estimate based on an analysis of DNA samples, as well as providing a confidence interval for this estimate so as to quantify its reliability; providing a medical diagnosis by an automated system processing physiological measurements and many more.

47. As one of the IP management companies points out, 'Indeed, we believe that one purpose of the updates to the Guidelines for Examination is to actively advertise to applicants that the EPO is "open for business" for AI patents.' L. Coe, *How to Patent AI Technology at the EPO,* https://www.mewburncom/news-insights/how-to-patent-ai-technology-at-the-epo accessed 6 August 2020.
48. Michael D. Stein, *Patent Drafting for Machine Learning: Structural Claim Limitations, Avoiding Sections 101 or 112 Rejections, Drafting for EPO*, Presented for WSPLA, September 18, 2019, http://wspla.org/wp-content/uploads/2019/08/WSPLA-Sept.-2019-Protecting-Software-Inventions-Including-AI-and-ML-Algorithms.pdf accessed 20 August 2020.
49. Koen Lievens (n. 44).
50. EP3595277B1.
51. EP3477515B1.
52. EP3378204B1.
53. EP3583575B1.
54. EP3474177B1.
55. EP3517442B1.
56. EPO, *Guidelines for Examination 3.3.1 Artificial intelligence and machine learning* applied from 1 November 2018, www.epo.org/law-practice/legal-texts/guidelines.html accessed 20 August 2020.

Thus far, it is difficult to verify how the updated Guidelines are applied by the EPO. The latest case law of the Boards of Appeal[57] does not reveal any new decisions, which would not be previously quoted in the Guidelines, tackling issues on AI patentability.

3 AI PATENTS AND INNOVATION

Answering the question whether patents serve as an incentive to encourage AI-related innovations is difficult, mainly due to the lack of dedicated reports or enquiries regarding this matter. Nevertheless, experience with software patents and CIIs cannot be underestimated in the context of AI patents. Both cases deal with patent eligibility which is doubtful for the same reason, i.e., lacking technical character and its abstract nature. Additionally, as indicated above, the term 'AI patents' may in fact cover software patents. Similarity between those objects of patent applications had been also noted by the EPO in its recommendation for examination of AI-related inventions before dedicated guidelines were drafted.

The report requested by European Commission in 2008[58] provides the findings on patents and software market. It demonstrates that 'ownership of software/CII patents is highly concentrated, with 70% of such patents being held by only 7% of firms in electrical, electronics and computing machinery, industrial and telecommunications equipment, with a similar share of all such patents being held by 13% of firms in software and business services'.[59] It also indicates patents are second least-favourite form of software/CII protection while the most popular way of gaining advantage over competitors is being first to the market. It leads the authors of the report to the conclusion that patents do not serve firms engaged in the software business as an incentive for innovation. Furthermore, software and CII can block innovation. According to the inquiry, 10% of firms declare changing or abandoning software projects due to concerns over possible patent infringement and 11% avoid entire markets for the same reason. Even though report is dated 2008, the conclusions are likely to be accurate also today and, taking into consideration growing number of software/CII patents, can be supported by more data.

In another study prepared for the European Commission in 2016,[60] the conclusions from the above-mentioned report were claimed to be generally valid. After eight years it was once again admitted that:

57. EPO, *Case Law of the Boards of Appeal*, 9th edition, July 2019, https://www.epo.org/law-practice/legal-texts/html/caselaw/2019/e/clr_i.htm accessed 20 August 2020.
58. Reinier Bakels et al., *Study of the Effects of Allowing Patent Claims for Computer-Implemented Inventions Final Report and Recommendations* (2008) https://publications.europa.eu/en/publication-detail/-/publication/90421535-ff72-46f3-b09e-a4bb8e0e711b accessed 20 August 2020.
59. *Ibid* 13.
60. Alain Strowel and Sinan Utku, *The Trends and Current Practices in the Area of Patentability of Computer Implemented Inventions Within the EU and the U.S. Final Report. A Study Prepared for the European Commission* (2016), https://ec.europa.eu/newsroom/document.cfm?doc_id=41192 accessed 20 August 2020.

> allowing the patentability of CI inventions (i) had the potential to stifle innovation by creating a minefield for programmers; (ii) could lead to undue monopolies on interface standards that are magnified by network effects, (iii) could jeopardize open-source software, which it called 'the most innovative development of past decades'; and (iv) could lead to the tragedy of the anti-commons, in which too many patent rights granted to too many actors threaten innovation and the development of technology by bogging down the system with a profusion of patent disputes and litigation.[61]

Another research conducted in the USA in 2011 results in conclusion that software patents 'have not provided a net social benefit in the software industry'.[62] Apart from reasons mentioned above, the authors indicate defensive function of software patents and substantial increase in litigation risk.[63]

The Electronic Frontier Foundation noticed a boom in software innovation,[64] resulting from the famous *Alice*[65] decision. It also gives many examples of businesses which could have gone bankrupt as a result of patent suits without *Alice* ruling. It appears that innovation, measured by R&D, responds positively to weakened patent protection.[66] It is also interesting to learn that large firms undertaking software patenting have lower R&D intensity than their peers.[67]

Software patents were called 'bad for business' almost thirty years ago.[68] Back then only a few programmers and entrepreneurs were convinced that software patents were necessary in conducting their business. There were two other groups interested in such monopoly, the managers of large companies and patent attorneys. The first gained competitive advantage without necessity of improving their product, the other gained new clients. It created barrier to entry for start-ups which cannot afford to pay licence fees or damages for using software or CII they believed were well-known standards.

Many have argued that there is a positive correlation between software patents and innovation. Their arguments are strongly interest driven. In addition, using patent statistics is very convenient when measuring innovation. For example, the innovative activities undertaken by software developers are measured by the quantity of patent

61. *Ibid.* 5.
62. James Bessen, *A generation of software patents* (2011), Boston University School of Law Working Paper No. 11-31, http://ladoc.ffii.fr/BessenJ062111withBeckmanpdf accessed 20 August 2020.
63. *Ibid.* 20.
64. Daniel Nazer, *Happy Birthday Alice: Four Years Busting Software Patents* (*Electronic Frontier Foundation*, 22 June 2018), www.eff.org/pl/deeplinks/2018/06/happy-birthday-alice-four-years-busting-software-patents accessed 20 August 2020.
65. *Alice Corp. v. CLS Bank International*, 573 U.S. 208, 134 S. Ct. 2347 (2014). The Supreme Court of the USA held that that an abstract idea does not become eligible for a patent simply by being implemented on a generic computer.
66. Sridhar Srinivasan, *Do Weaker Patents Induce Greater Research Investments?* (22 December 2018), https://ssrncom/abstract=3185148 or http://dx.doi.org/10.2139/ssrn3185148 accessed 20 August 2020.
67. Michael Webb et al., *Some Facts of High-Tech Patenting* (2018), Harvard Business School Entrepreneurial Management Working Paper No. 19-014, 1, https://ssrncom/abstract=323 3722 accessed 20 August 2020.
68. Simon L. Garfinkel, Richard M. Stallman and Mitchell Kapor, *Why Patents Are Bad for Software* (1991), 8 (1) Issues in Science and Technology 53.

applications.[69] The market value of software patents and the fact that software may support innovative solutions happens to be equated with the positive impact of software patents on innovation. The following opinion is at least questionable: 'Patents play an important role in commercializing software innovation and supporting technology markets. Understanding this commercial role requires a broader view of patents in software innovation than the *all-too-common focus on a small handful of litigated patents and legal questions of patentability and patent quality*.'[70] The positive impact of software patents on innovation is apparent especially to those scholars who are also practising patent attorneys.[71]

It is too early to collect credible data on how AI development may be affected by granting patents. Apart from relative novelty of the phenomenon, at least in the context of reliable research, there are too many types of solutions labelled as AI. It requires any conclusion to be made with reference to particular type of patented AI or its application. Some predictions and possible scenarios are presented in the later section.

Nonetheless, listening to one of the talks delivered during the EPO's conference by Clare Dillon,[72] who advises start-ups and 'helps organisations maximise opportunities presented by the latest trends in technology',[73] is quite informative. According to Dillon, the issue of patent protection form her clients' perspective is of high importance but their awareness is rather low and problem-orientated. The process of acquiring patents is not a stimulant for further or greater work since the programmers' interest in patents is oriented towards the fear of patent infringement threats. They think of patents in a sort of negative way: how far can they go not infringing somebody else's monopoly. It pre-empts considering patent protection for their own benefit. Their needs and expectations are limited to accessibility to patent information so they could avoid patent thickets. What they also find helpful in their work regarding patent protection is creating an effective unblocking mechanisms, e.g., cross-licensing when both parties are patent holders or open-source licensing.

It should be noted that some top AI-developers, including Microsoft, IBM and Google, share their research with open-source community. Certain source codes for machine learning methods are disclosed and free licences in selected fields are

69. Kazuyuki Motohashi, *Software Patent and Its Impact on Software Innovation in Japan* (2009), RIETI Discussion Paper Series 13www.rieti.go.jp/en/publications/summary/09080001.html accessed 20 August 2020.
70. Saurabh Vishnubhakat, *The Commercial Value of Software Patents in the High-Tech Industry* (2015) 3 (emphasis added) https://sls.gmu.edu/cpip/wp-content/uploads/sites/31/2014/04/The-Commercial-Value-of-Software-Patents.pdf accessed 20 August 2020.
71. Richard S. Gruner, *Better Living Through Software: Promoting Information Processing Advances Through Patent Incentives* (2002), 74 (4) St. John's Law Review 977, https://scholarship.law.stjohns.edu/lawreview/vol74/iss4/2 accessed 20 August 2020.
72. *See* n. 19. Keynote 1 AI inventions and the Fourth Industrial Revolution Recordings of the event available at https://e-courses.epo.org/pluginfile.php/23528/mod_resource/content/3/html/index.html accessed 20 August 2020.
73. *See* Claire Dillon's bio at Digital DNA website https://digitaldna.org.uk/speaker/claire-dillon accessed 20 August 2020.

offered.[74] However, it is difficult to assess whether these practices remove any existing barriers to foster innovation or they serve solely as a form of PR.

On the other hand, the big players claim, and it should be reminded that large firms hold the vast majority of software related patents, they need patent protection for AI applications to serve as a defensive strategy. Otherwise, these 'inventions' would be monopolized by patent trolls. It appears that between September and November 2016, DeepMind Technologies, a company acquired in 2014 by Google, was filing patent application with an average frequency of one per week.[75]

According to Google senior patent council, Suzanne Michel, the motivation to build up an impressive software patents portfolio was not stimulated by any great expectations towards patent protection itself. It was, and still is, only about developing a strategy in case of counter lawsuit. She argued that: 'That is the dynamic. It absolutely is the dynamic you have to have it. And Google tried not to and it didn't work. You have to have it. You cannot opt out of the patent system and decide I'm an open source company and anyone can use my stuff. You have to have a massive portfolio of your own and that is really expensive and it is what it is.'[76] These are not proper arguments justifying granting monopolies on AI applications or rethinking the whole system in order to broaden the scope of patentable subject matters.

It may be quite surprising, yet in accordance to the statement cited above, such software and AI giant as Microsoft, Google, and Facebook, signed an amicus brief to the US Supreme Court in 2014, opting for invalidation of most software patents, some of them applied ML and other forms of AI.[77]

Members of the programming community are deeply concerned about practices of the biggest companies, using patents as blocking tools. Developers are worried about monopolization of commonly used techniques.[78] One of the examples is a patent for so-called dropout. The name comes from the act of dropping out units in a neural network.[79] It is a standard technique used by almost everyone training a neural network to avoid overfitting. In 2016 Google was granted a patent on 'System and Method for Addressing Overfitting in a Neural Network'.[80] According to one of the

74. Nathan Calvin and Jade Leung, *Who owns artificial intelligence? A preliminary analysis of corporate intellectual property strategies and why they matter* (2020), Working Paper Centre for the Governance of AI Future of Humanity Institute, University of Oxford 2, https://www.fhi.ox.ac.uk/wp-content/uploads/Patents_-FHI-Working-Paper-Final-.pdf accessed 20 August 2020.
75. Rose Hughes, *DeepMind: First major AI patent filings revealed* (*TheIPKat*, 7 June 2018) http://ipkittenblogspot.com/2018/06/deepmind-first-major-ai-patent-filings.html accessed 20 August 2020.
76. Gene Quinn, *Google: We Don't Sell to Patent Trolls* (*IPWatchdog*, 2 May 2013) https://www.ipwatchdog.com/2013/05/02/google-we-dont-sell-to-patent-trolls/id=39927 accessed 20 August 2020.
77. Nathan Calvin and Jade Leung (n. 74) 3.
78. Jeremy Gillula and Daniel Nazer, *Stupid Patent of the Month: Will Patents Slow Artificial Intelligence?* (*Electronic Frontier Foundation*, 29 September 2017) www.eff.org/pl/deeplinks/2017/09/stupid-patent-month-will-patents-slow-artificial-intelligence accessed 20 August 2020.
79. Nitish Srivastava et al., *Dropout: A Simple Way to Prevent Neural Networks from Overfitting* (2014), 15 Journal of Machine Learning Research 1929 www.jmlr.org/papers/volume15/srivastava14a.old/srivastava14a.pdf accessed 20 August 2020.
80. Geoffrey E. Hinton et al., *System and Method for Addressing Overfitting in a Neural Network*, US Patent No. 9.406,017 issued 2 August 2016, http://patft.uspto.gov/netacgi/nph-Parser?Sect1=

programmers, 'Google needs to clarify the position but even if it does there is no way to make sure it doesn't exercise its patent rights at a later date.'[81] Another alarming problem for AI programmers is weak patents, granting exclusivity over obvious solutions, often paired with very broad patent claims.[82] In most cases they create costs and risk for competitors. Even assuming that patent protection may foster innovation in majority fields of technology, there are exceptions from this rule and patent-quality requirements that must be met. First, in certain fields of technology or due to specific market conditions, there are more efficient incentives, causing lower transactional costs that patents. Second, only high quality patents may have beneficial impact. AI industry, even assuming that it develops many different types of solutions engaging different means, is likely to apply for weak patents. On the basis of experience with software and CII patents, it means poor disclosure, too broadly drafted claims and, quite possibly, monopolizing excluded subject matters.[83]

Another problem is acquiring and executing control over critical large datasets and application-specific algorithms. The concentration of AI patents in a few companies' portfolios, will possibly monopolize research in AI or possibly in any different area[84] and will not stimulate innovation-oriented competition and enhance research productivity. According to some researchers, the latter may be guaranteed only by 'the adoption of policies which encourage transparency and sharing of core datasets across both public and private actors'.[85] They will also contribute to increased level of research productivity.

Special attention should be paid to peculiar patents, which are called 'data-generating patents'. The term was coined by the authors of an article,[86] providing very insightful comments on consequences when trade secrets and patents act as economic complements. The concept of 'data-generating patents' refers to patents on inventions involving technologies that by design generate valuable data through their operation or use. As the authors point out:

PTO1&Sect2 = HITOFF&d = PALL&p = 1&u = %2Fnetahtml%2FPTO%2Fsrchnum.htm&r = 1&f = G&l = 50&s1 = 9,406,017.PN&OS = PN/9,406,017&RS = PN/9,406,017 accessed 20 August 2020.

81. Mike James, *Google Files AI Patents* (*I Programmer*, 8 July 2015) www.i-programmer.info/news/105-artificial-intelligence/8765-google-files-ai-patents.html accessed 20 August 2020.
82. Julie E. Cohen and Mark Lemley, *Patent Scope and Innovation in the Software Industry* (2001) 89 (1) California Law Review 1, https://scholarship.law.georgetownedu/cgi/viewcontent.cgi?article = 1345&context = facpub accessed 20 August 2020.
83. Katya Assaf, *Of Patents and Cobras: Exposing the Problem of Patent Asymmetry* (2017), 35 (1) Cardozo Arts & Entertainment Law Journal, www.cardozoaelj.com/issues/archive/2016-17-archive-volume-35 accessed 20 August 2020.
84. S. Schneegans, *Towards a Monopolization of Research in Artificial Intelligence?* (*UNESCO.org*, 20 July 2018) http://www.unesco.org/new/en/natural-sciences/science-technology/single-view-sc-policy/news/towards_a_monopolization_of_research_in_artificial_intellige accessed 11 August 2020.
85. Ian M. Cockburn, Rebecca Henderson and Scott Stern, *The Impact of Artificial Intelligence on Innovation* (National Bureau of Economic Research Conference on Research Issues in Artificial Intelligence, Toronto, 13-14 September 2017, draft of 16 December 2017) http://www.nber.org/chapters/c14006.pdf accessed 20 August 2020.
86. Brenda M. Simon and Ted Sichelman, *Data-Generating Patents* (2017) 111 Nw. U. L. Rev 377.

> [W]hen data-generating inventions are patented, and the patentee enjoys market power over the invention, by implication, the patentee also effectively enjoys market power over the data generated by the invention. Trade secret law further protects the patentee's market power over the data, even where that data is in a market distinct from the patented invention and especially after the patent expires or is invalidated.[87]

Even though the authors use the expression 'artificial intelligence' only once in their over 60-page-long article, the examples they refer to belong to the realm of machine learning and algorithms. Data generated by the patented inventions may be of at least two kinds. Some of them enable to improve upon the said invention, while others allow to excel in secondary markets. Such data are gathered and processed to create a superior product in the distinct market. One of the examples the authors give to illustrate their concerns is Myriad's data-generating patents over breast cancer diagnostic tests. Myriad's data-generating patents foreclosed other methods of identifying mutations in the BRCA1 and BRCA2 genes for breast and ovarian cancer screening which also foreclosed competitors from generating similar data. As the authors point out:

> [T]he main concern, particularly for data-generating patents, is that innovation and improvements may be thwarted by providing too much protection for this type of data. Although patent holders will often be in the best position to make improvements or extend technology into new areas, they may choose not to do so, particularly where they have invested in a technology that has become the standard in a field and might be superseded by an improvement. ... For example, for over a decade, Myriad failed to adopt comprehensive testing mechanisms to detect mutations that were critical to patient health. Myriad only made improvements to its tests after several studies conducted by nonclinical researchers described the shortcomings of Myriad's offerings.[88]

Another example, provided by B.M. Simon and T. Sichelman, is Google's search engine patents. Information captured throughout the use of the engine allows to improve the algorithms and functionality of the offered product but at the same time allows to develop solutions to be used in the distinct market of targeted online advertising. Such advantage over competitors falls beyond the patent claims describing search engines.

Few conclusions presented by the authors are especially important in the context of rethinking patent law with regard to inventions related to gathering and generating data which, possibly, entail AI application.

First, not all data-generating patents pose policy concerns. The problem is, this far, any credible assessment is possible only ex post i.e., after the patent is granted and, probably, enforced. The authors suggest two criteria to be taken into account while determining social cost of data-generating patents: (1) the extent of expansion into unforeseeable data markets and (2) the strength of pre-empting potential competition in markets for the generated data. The first factor concerns data not directly related to

87. *Ibid.* 377.
88. *Ibid.* 416.

the market covered by the patented invention while the other 'relates to the magnitude of the pre-emptive effect of the data-generating patent on competition in the market regarding the data. The more likely the data-generating patent forecloses competitors from generating similar data, the more likely the invention will be found problematic.'[89]

Second, although there may be some sound reasons for eliminating patent eligibility for data-generating inventions, it is not a recommended solution. Since some of those inventions do not cause any harm for competitiveness, this solution, even if solving ex ante assessment problem, seems to be too radical. Precluding certain patents from enforcement is another idea, yet probably not effective due to trade secrecy option. The authors also consider limiting patent remedies when infringing certain types of patents and the expansion of the independent invention exception to patent infringement for data-generating patents.

The above-mentioned solutions are just a few out of presented range of options. Worth noting, the authors do not recommend rethinking the whole patent system in order to solve problems with one of the categories of patents. They rather indicate the correlation between patent protection and trade secrecy which, combined together, may lead to undesirable effects. One of them is inhibiting innovation.

As it has already been mentioned before, it is too early to gauge the impact of patents on AI development. However, it is possible to anticipate the role of openness in this process. Even though the authors of the research on the impact of AI on innovation[90] describe the results of their work as tentative and preliminary, they are worth taking into consideration. One of the reasons is the authors' awareness that almost everything about AI is uncertain. Paradoxically, this conclusion may be more helpful in planning realistic strategies than sticking to indisputable strategies.

The author of another research[91] distinguishes few aspects of openness. It includes, among others, open-source code, open science, open data, openness about safety techniques and a non-proprietary development regime. The study aims to answer the question whether openness leads to faster development and deployment of AI. The conclusions depend on the time perspective. In case of short-term analysis, the answer is positive, mainly due to the fact that software and knowledge about algorithms are non-rival goods. Free access means more people can benefit from different forms of their application. For the medium and long-term analysis, there are just too many dependencies that have to be taken into consideration so it is impossible to give 'yes or no', or even 'probably yes or probably no', answer. According to Bostrom, some incentives to innovate would remain in a regime of openness and they would not be limited to philanthropic ones. The author underlines that achieving a balance is a must because removing all incentives from monopoly exploitation could lead to the withdrawals from R&D investments. However, he also indicates that:

89. *Ibid*. 382.
90. *See* n. 85.
91. Nick Bostrom, *Strategic Implications of Openness in AI Development* (2017), 8 (2) Global Policy Journal, https://nickbostrom.com/papers/openness.pdf accessed 20 August 2020.

> The patent system involves substantial transaction costs which would be eliminated in a fully open development regime–innovators would then not have to hack their way through 'patent thickets' to get a new product to market. And the relinquishment of trade secrecy and confidentiality would facilitate information flow between researchers who work for different organizations, reducing duplication of effort and other inefficiencies.[92]

4 AI PATENTS AND PUBLIC INTEREST

The legal status of AI patents is uncertain, regardless the latest changes introduced into the practice of the USPTO. Furthermore, it appears that exclusivity granted with a patent may be an obstacle for AI and competitiveness development. The example of Myriad's reluctance to improve their invention, protected by data-generating patent, illustrates that there are sensible markets, e.g., healthcare, where the public interest is not limited to everyday and ordinary consumer issues.

There is also another kind of public interest in not granting certain AI patents. A patent equals control. It is generally accepted on the condition that exclusivity over an invention is limited to profits and undertaking legal acts against patent infringers. When public interest suffers, patent law provides solutions like, e.g., compulsory licences. AI brings new challenges not only for the members of society at the given time but also for the humanity.[93] This issue is brought up by Yuval Noah Harari, who is a historian, philosopher and a bestselling author. Even though he does not refer directly to patent protection, his findings should be taken into consideration while shaping patent policy. In his books, lectures and interviews, he underlines that AI as a human achievement is 'far more potent than steam and a telegraph'.[94] The unique merger of biotech and infotech provided by AI application, enables, for the first time, control of both the world outside the human body as well as what happens inside it. Using AI also implies shifting authority. It is enough to observe the level of trust the average user puts in a GPS system. More and more members of the public prefer to follow algorithm instructions instead of relying on their own knowledge and instincts. Harari also claims technology is not deterministic and it may serve different purposes and create different kind of societies. AI solutions can be a tool used by the governments to invigilate the public or enable the latter the control over those in power. The same may be applied to data collected by the tech giants who offer various services 'for free', i.e., in exchange for raw training material for their algorithms. According to Y.N. Harari, those who own the data, own the future. The statement is still accurate when referring to patent owners. The exclusivity for AI application gives them a special privilege, since these patents often cover an abstract or obvious concepts which are not properly disclosed. Even though Harari does not comment on patent policy, he acknowledges he does not

92. *Ibid.* 3.
93. Alex Hern, *Stephen Hawking: AI will be 'either best or worst thing' for Humanity*, The Guardian (London, 19 October 2016) www.theguardiancom/science/2016/oct/19/stephen-hawking-ai-best-or-worst-thing-for-humanity-cambridge accessed 20 August 2020.
94. Yuval Noah Harari, *Homo Deus: A Brief History of Tomorrow* (1st edn, Harper Collins Publishers, 2017) 275.

trust free market to make best decisions for human kind. Probably the same could be said about patent owners.

The very same conclusion is drawn not by another philosopher but by AI pioneer and AI expert. According to Joshua Bengio, the largest companies increase their customer base and in turn provides access to more and more data: 'All this creates a virtuous cycle, which is good for these companies but unhealthy for society. Such a concentration of power can have a negative impact on both democracy and the economy.'[95] The greater diversity in AI business environment will avoid dangerous monopoly. Granting patents is not a part of this strategy.

Bostrom's research[96] seems to support Bengio's observation but not without a reservation. In the long run, openness of AI may influence the *status quo* powers. Much depends on whether hardware or software turns out to be the bottleneck. It cannot be omitted that:

> If one thinks that it is preferable in expectation that advanced AI be controlled by existing governments, elites, and ordinary people–in proportion to their existing wealth and political power–rather than by some particular group that happens to be successful in the AI field (such as a corporation or an AI lab) then one might favour a scenario in which hardware becomes the principal factor of AI power. Openness in AI development would make such a scenario more likely.[97]

AI, according to Bostrom, may reduce the probability of singleton. The term refers to the model where the decisions are undertaken at the highest level by one coordinated decision-making agency. In the future, the openness must be taken into considerations by policy makers in the context of relevance of AI multiplicity for control problem. The latter results from obtaining a decisive strategic advantage as a consequence of using AI system which got ahead of all the others.

Even though it is emphasized that AI influence over humanity and politics depends on too many known-unknowns and probably some unknown-unknowns, one thing is certain. Despite promises about the least harmful ways the big players are about to exercises their monopolies, patents usually do not favour openness.

5 CONCLUSIONS

The concept of rethinking patent law has been discussed every few decades. Some concussions happened to be quite drastic. The anti-patent movement in the twenty-first century advocated for the total abolition of patents. Articles about controversies that arose over those state-granted monopolies were printed in the daily press. It was

95. Yoshua Bengio, interviewed by Jasmina Šopova, *Countering the monopolization of research* (2018), 3 The UNESCO Courier 18, https://unesdoc.unesco.org/ark:/48223/pf0000265211 accessed 20 August 2020.
96. Nick Bostrom (n. 91) 9.
97. *Ibid*. 6.

an issue of the public interest and not some obscure topic elaborated only by the experts.[98]

Leaving aside challenging the existence of patent protection, also the considerations over the boundaries of the exclusive rights are not the consequence of recent development of disruptive technologies. The rapid technological changes that are witnessed in the twenty-first century, such as AI, bio and nanotechnology, were preceded by other breakthrough inventions. It must be remembered that the telegraph brought similar doubts about the principles of patentability.[99]

Few trends may be distinguished in the context of a general reform of patent law. The need for implementing certain changes is discussed globally without indication of any particular legal order. Most of the requested proposals may influence AI patents.

The first pressing issue is patent eligibility limitation and the definition of an invention. Another urgent problem is the weakness of the patent system regarded as a whole. Some scholars[100] and practitioners indicate it is misused and serves different purposes than it was intended to serve. In some areas it does not promote useful arts and instead of boosting innovation, patents may create entry barriers. It results in diminishing competitiveness instead of fostering diversification.

One of the most frequently raised argument to justify amendments to patent law and patent system is that they do not reflect the state of the art. The provisions and its interpretation are considered to be out of date and neglecting current market trends. The most important question to be answered, and the most difficult at the same time, is whether it is feasible to adapt patent law to technological progress while retaining its basics. In my opinion, not every innovation bringing progress remains in the boundaries of what technology is in the context of patent law even if it is used to called 'technology' by the public. However, many studies have shown that the interest with patent protection and the impact of monopolies over innovation rate vary from industry to industry.[101] This correlation is very important and should be taken into consideration while shaping the policy of granting exclusive rights over intellectual creations. Nonetheless, certain behaviours and business decisions should not result in diversification of the interpretation of the requirements for patent protection. They should not be dedicated to the given industry. This issue has been already elaborated by distinguished scholars but it is difficult to decide if their assumption that 'patent law is technology specific'[102] is a recommendation or a description of the ongoing practice.

Some suggest that AI patents could be specific within their specificity. Therefore, 'Lowering the subject-matter patentability standard for AI inventions relating to areas

98. Fritz Machlup and Edith Penrose, *The Patent Controversy in the Nineteenth Century* (1950), 10 The Journal of Economic History 1, http://c4sif.org/wp-content/uploads/2010/09/Machlup-Penrose-The-Patent-Controversy-in-the-Nineteenth-Century-1950-b.pdf accessed 20 August 2020.
99. Robin Feldman, *Rethinking Patent Law* (1st edn, Harvard University Press, 2012) 3.
100. Assaf (n. 83).
101. Mark A. Lemley and Dan L. Burk, *Policy Levers in Patent Law* (2003), 89 Virginia Law Review 1575, https://ssrncom/abstract=431360 or http://dx.doi.org/10.2139/ssrn431360 accessed 20 August 2020.
102. Dan L. Burk and Mark A. Lemley, *Is Patent Law Technology-Specific* (2002), 17 Berkeley Technology Law Journal 1155.

deemed more socially beneficial, such as healthcare, the environment, criminal justice and education, might be one way to help balance promoting innovation with mitigating ethical concerns.'[103]

In my opinion, such flexibility will not be beneficial for the whole system and market participants. To patent or not to patent is a business choice and probably in some areas the answer is negative. But once the positive decision is made the consequences are felt by competitors, the makers and by the users. The rights conferred on them by the patent, or the limitations imposed by it, should not vary depending on the branch of the industry. In case of state-granted monopolies and exclusive rights, every exception must be subject to intense scrutiny.

Business decisions are driven by many factors. Even though the technological giants made unwritten promise not to monopolize AI solutions, they have already found the excuse why they are 'forced' to fail to keep it.[104] In addition, if the specific character of a given industry imposes changes on the requirements and the scope of patent protection, it demonstrates ineffectiveness of patent protection in those cases. It is more efficient to consider different models of protection than changing the whole system.

For example, taking into consideration the elements of ML models providing competitive advantage, opting out for trade secrecy by non-disclosure seems to be quite sensible. The problem is it does not grant any exclusivity. As a consequence, obtaining patent protection at all cost is so tempting that may lead to the distortion of the basics of the patent system. One of the possible solutions is allowing patents for ML solutions, even those which may appear indefinite, and rely on post-issuance challenges to the validity. It is argued that '[T]he public still has access to the disclosures from the patents and patent applications. In reliance on granted patents, companies may have already invested in growing related businesses, catering to the need of consumers.'[105] The fact that majority of software patent cases (up to thirty-eight out of forty)[106] heard by the courts resulted in invalidation is not a positive sign of self-regulatory system but rather a sign of system pathology. Not to mention the overall costs if such strategy would have been intended.

Nick Bostrom[107] considers scenario in which the hardware turns out to be the bottleneck and determines the impact of openness on the expected degree of control of *status quo* powers. On the other hand, if the interest in claiming protection over inventions, understood as a solution having a technical effect on the physical matter, happens to be almost non-existing, instead of turning the patent system upside down it is about time to create the new one. It imposes on the leaders in AI industry a difficult

103. World Economic Forum, *Artificial Intelligence Collides with Patent Law. White Paper* (2018), 9 www3.weforum.org/docs/WEF_48540_WP_End_of_Innovation_Protecting_Patent_Law.pdf accessed 20 August 2020.

104. Tom Simonite, *Despite Pleading Openness, Companies Rush to Patent AI Tech* (*Wired*, 31 July 2018) www.wired.com/story/despite-pledging-openness-companies-rush-to-patent-ai-tech accessed 20 August 2020; *see* (n. 76).

105. Hyunjong Ryan Jin, *Think Big! The Need for Patent Rights in the Era of Big Data and Machine Learning* (2018) 7 NYU JIPEL 78, 104.

106. *Ibid.* 103.

107. Bostrom (n. 91) 7.

burden to acknowledge their real needs. What they need to succeed is not an exclusivity provided by the patent for claimed solution of a given problem. They need an unlimited access to diversified training data for reasonable price. Collecting and processing data, including proper dimensional reduction and feature extraction generate enormous cost, so the protection of the sole fact of investing is desired. This is also the justification behind the trend of cross-industry collaboration in order to acquire big data for uses different from the original purpose. The question remains whether it is justified within exclusivity model with reference to the invention or data. Having regard to the circumstances, every attempt of changing patent law in the name of promoting progress is simply dishonest and harmful. Instead of rethinking patent law and adjusting it to the needs of some stakeholders, it seems more reasonable now to discuss the problem of using data generated by AI-related solutions to create another product for the distinct market and for the purpose the user of the AI could not have assumed.

Changing patent law in a way enabling protection of the subject matter which requires a total redefinition of the concept of invention or requirements for protection is pointless. It is very convenient at the same time because it allows to fill and prosecute a standard application in the institution everyone accustomed to and according to procedures everyone is familiar with.

Such intangible assets as algorithms must be protected outside the patent system or belong to the public domain. In order to save legal transparency, it is important to admit that many of applications or patents already granted refer to subject matter only described as if it were an invention. Otherwise, AI 'invention' will share the fate of software patents, also named as patents for 'computer implemented inventions'. It will be probably harmful for the development of AI and possibly dangerous for individuals and the humanity.

Finally, treating algorithms as inventions or granting monopolies for obvious solutions only because of deployment of AI will finalize and formalize disruption of the current patent system. The question remains if it solves the alleged problem and, moreover, if it is worth causing the new ones.

CHAPTER 11

Transparency in the Patent System: Artificial Intelligence and the Disclosure Requirement

Alfred Früh[*]

1 INTRODUCTION

The patent system faces fundamental challenges by the recent breakthroughs in Artificial Intelligence (AI). While issues such as patentability and non-obviousness of AI-related inventions – covering both AI-generated output and AI methods *as such* – have already attracted attention,[1] this chapter analyses whether patent law's disclosure requirement is (also) under attack by AI. According to the disclosure requirement, the inventor has a legal obligation to disclose his or her invention in order to acquire an exclusive right. As the functioning of the disclosure requirement is a common justification of the patent system, the issue at hand is highly relevant: If the disclosure

* I owe thanks to AURELIA TAMÒ-LARRIEUX, LUCA FABIÀN, SUZY FRANKEL and DEAN ALDERUCCI for their very helpful comments.

1. Regarding AI-created output, *see* R. ABBOTT, *I Think, Therefore I Invent: Creative Computers and the Future of Patent Law*, Boston College L. Rev. 2016, 1079 et seq.; R. ABBOTT, *Everything Is Obvious*, UCLA L. Rev. 2019, 4 et seq.; P. BLOK, *The Inventor's New Tool: Artificial Intelligence – How Does It Fit in the European Patent System*, E.I.P.R. 2017, 69 et seq.; S. HETMANK/A. LAUBER-RÖNSBERG, *Künstliche Intelligenz – Herausforderungen für das Immaterialgüterrecht*, GRUR 2018, 575 et seq.; R. PEARLMAN, *Recognizing Artificial Intelligence (AI) as Authors and Inventors Under U.S. Intellectual Property Law*, Rich. J. L. & Tech, 2018, issue 2; S. YANISKY RAVID/X. LIU, *When Artificial Intelligence Systems Produce Inventions: An Alternative Model for Patent Law at the 3A Era*, Cardozo L. Rev. 2018, 2215 et seq. Regarding the patentability of AI methods as such K. FIRTH-BUTTERFIELD/Y. CHAE, World Economic Forum, White Paper, *Artificial Intelligence Collides with Patent Law*, April 2018, 8; E. FRASER, *Computers as Inventors – Legal and Policy Implications of Artificial Intelligence on Patent Law*, SCRIPTed., 2016, 311.

requirement were indeed fundamentally challenged by AI, the patent system would run the risk of losing its legitimacy.

This chapter also frames the research question through the lens of transparency. The fact that the disclosure requirement requires patentees to disclose their inventions is crucial for the quality of information in the patent register. Together with the fact that patent registers are open to the public, the disclosure requirement ultimately ensures a certain transparency regarding human inventiveness. With AI entering the picture – which is often scolded for being non-transparent – the question is whether and how this transparency is affected.

We argue that the disclosure requirement indeed is challenged by AI, but that the challenges are less grievous than in other areas of patent law. To be more precise: the use of AI may lead to new disclosure deficits, and some AI-related patents may be considered insufficiently disclosed because they lack reproducibility. However, timely anticipation of these risks allows patent law to adapt, mainly because AI is not only a threat but could also remedy imbalances in the disclosure requirement: addressing these issues properly, AI may lead even to more instead of less transparency.

The argument will unfold in four steps: We first examine the disclosure requirement in patent law (section 2) and the state of the art regarding AI (section 3). We will then combine these parts in order to address the looming challenges of the disclosure requirement confronted with AI (section 4) Lastly, we will also highlight new opportunities brought about by AI (section 5), before concluding (section 6).

2 THE DISCLOSURE REQUIREMENT IN PATENT LAW

The disclosure requirement can be found in most patent laws.[2] While the actual wording of the disclosure requirement may vary, its general mechanism is quite clear to the reasonable onlooker:[3] The inventor discloses his or her invention and, in return, acquires the exclusive right to use it for a limited time. Only (sufficient) disclosure warrants an exclusive right. Lack of disclosure constitutes a ground for annulment.[4]

As will be shown below, the reasonable onlooker could be mistaken. Critics have observed that in real life this mechanism is not working as intended. Some even have doubts whether this should be the way disclosure works at all.[5] As we will see, the disclosure requirement has never been embraced unanimously, and the patent system is not as transparent as the disclosure requirement makes us believe. Even before

2. Be it Art. 5 PCT, Art. 83 EPC (2000) or national provisions such as Art. 50 para. 1 CH-PatG (Switzerland), § 21 para. 2 and § 34 para. 4 DE-PatG (Germany), UK PA 1977, s. 14(3) (United Kingdom) or 35 U.S.C. §112 (USA).
3. Cf. D. Vaver, Sprucing Up Patent Law, Intellectual Property Law Journal 2011, 66 et seq.
4. The legal consequences of insufficient disclosure are invalidity or revocation. The European Patent Convention (EPC) provides three routes to remedy inadequate disclosure: During the patent examination procedure (Art. 94 EPC), during the opposition and limitation procedure (Art. 100 lit. b EPC in connection with Art. 83 EPC) and based on substantive national law, once the patent is granted (Art. 138 para. 1 lit. b EPC). Most national patent laws equally provide remedies for both the pre- and post-grant phase. For the UK: PA 1977, s. 72(1); *see also* L. Bently/B. Sherman, *Intellectual Property Law*, 4th ed., Oxford, 2014, 575.
5. *See infra* s. 2.2.

turning to the new complexities brought about by AI, we face the question of whether and how the disclosure requirement needs to be fixed.

2.1 Historical Background

In 1623-1624, England passed a Statute of Monopolies, prohibiting the crown from granting exclusive rights with the exception of the 'first true inventor of a new product'.[6] But these patents were mainly granted for practicing a useful trade or art rather than technologically innovative information.[7] Accordingly, little attention was given to the disclosure of new technology. While the resulting 'patent letters' were exposed to open view,[8] examinations of the patented products were generally done in secret with no requirement to publish a description of the invention. The actual use of the invention was deemed an adequate disclosure to the public. However, first theories to understand the grant of a patent as a deal in which the patentee exchanged the disclosed information in return for an exclusive entitlement emerged in the 1760s and 1770s and soon became standard.[9] In the late nineteenth century, England attempted to reform its patent law under the pressure of anti-patent thinkers and free traders. They took issue with the fact that patents were state-created privileges and could be used to fend off competition. Interestingly, the proposal included the introduction of stricter rules for the evaluation of the validity of a patent claim. However, the proposal for a patent act revision was withdrawn in 1874.[10]

The North American British colonies and eventually the American states drew on these English foundations, also highlighting the exercise of a publicly useful trade rather than the technology itself.[11] After the Revolution, the idea that information was given to the public as consideration for the exclusive rights of the patentee also became widely accepted. Starting in 1836, the Congress required a patent applicant to submit to the Patent and Trademark Office (PTO) a physical model of the invention, if this was necessary to determine its patentability,[12] and even under today's Patent Act (as amended in 1870), the examiner can require the applicant to provide a model of the invention.[13] However, submitting specifications and thus fully describing the invention in text became more important at the beginning of the nineteenth century, allowing patentees to also submit obscure specifications.[14] Accordingly, for much of the

6. F. Machlup, *Die wirtschaftlichen Grundlagen des Patentrechts*, GRUR Int. 1961, 374.
7. O. Bracha, Owning Ideas, *The Intellectual Origins of American Intellectual Property*, 1790-1909, New York, 2016, 19, 21.
8. A. Mossoff, *Rethinking the Development of Patents: An Intellectual History*, 1550-1800, Hastings L J 2001, 1259.
9. Bracha, *supra* n. 7, 24, 253; *see* A. Mossoff, *supra* n. 8, 1278 et seq. for early case law on the specification of the patent and 1288 for the theoretical (Lockean) foundations of this concept.
10. Machlup. *supra* n. 6, 375.
11. *See* Bracha, *supra* n. 7, 25 et seq. for a detailed account.
12. J.C. Fromer, *Patent Disclosure*, Iowa Law Review 2009, 574.
13. Fromer, *supra* n. 12, 575.
14. Bracha, *supra* n. 7, 24, 297 et seq.

nineteenth century, the notion that the deposited specification fully disclosed the invention to the public had little to do with reality.[15]

Works on the Paris Convention for the Protection of Industrial Property (PC) began in 1873 and led to a first version adopted in 1883. However, the term 'disclosure' did not appear in the Paris Convention until its 1925 reform (The Hague Act), which introduced it in the context of complex patent application examination. Disclosure was used in order to find out whether a patented application covered several inventions and to divisional patents (Article 4 lit. f PC (1925)). In the London Act of 1934, Article 4 of the PC was amended again, inserting the - still valid - provision of Article 4 lit. h that grants priority to claims that were not formulated in the country of origin, 'provided that the application documents as a whole specifically disclose such elements'. While this provision highlights the importance of (sufficient) disclosure, the Paris Convention does not itself entail a definition of the disclosure requirement.

From a European perspective, the first substantive provision explicitly setting forth the disclosure requirement was the Council of Europe's Convention on the Unification of Certain Points of Substantive Law on Patents for Invention, as agreed on in Strasbourg in 1963.[16] Article 8 paragraph 2 of the said Convention reads: 'The description must disclose the invention in a manner sufficiently clear and complete for it to be carried out by a person skilled in the art'. This provision is the predecessor of today's Article 83 of the European Patent Convention (EPC). The wording has remained almost identical.[17]

In the US, a similar description had already been developed roughly twenty years earlier in *Universal Oil Products v. Globe Oil & Refining.*[18] In this decision, the US Supreme Court reasoned:

> As a reward for inventions and to encourage their disclosure, the United States offer a 17-year monopoly to an inventor who refrains from keeping his invention a trade secret. But the *quid pro quo* is disclosure of a process or device in sufficient detail to enable one skilled in the art to practice the invention once the period of the monopoly has expired; and the same precision of disclosure is likewise essential to warn the industry concerned of the precise scope of the monopoly asserted.[19]

It shows that both the European and the US understanding of the disclosure requirement rest on the following assumption: The inventor and the public enter into an agreement in which the inventor discloses secret knowledge in order to benefit from limited protection for commercial use of said knowledge. In turn, the public obtains knowledge that was previously kept secret. Civil law literature calls this the so-called

15. Bracha, *supra* n. 7, 24, 298.
16. A. Briner, *Offenbarung der Erfindung*, in: Schweizer Immaterialgüter- und Wettbewerbsrecht, Band IV, R. von Büren/L. David (eds), Basel 2006, 156.
17. In EPC 2000, the whole 'application' of the patent must disclose the invention, whereas in the Strasbourg Convention it was the 'description'. Moreover, the verb 'must' was replaced with 'shall'.
18. *Universal Oil Products v. Globe Oil & Refining*, 322 U.S. 471 (1944) at 478; *see also* V. Denicolò/L. A. Franzoni, *The Contract Theory of Patents*, International Review of Law and Economics 23 (2004), 365, at 366.
19. *J.E.M. Ag Supply Inc. v. Pioneer Hi-Bred Int'l, Inc.*, 534 U.S. 124, 142 (2001) provides a more recent description of the quid pro quo bargain.

contract theory of patent law,[20] common law jurisdictions usually refer to a quid pro quo bargain.[21] In the following, we will mainly use the term 'contract theory', despite the fact that lawyers trained in common law may find it misleading, as a contract generally implies a consideration.[22]

The contract theory is one of four justifications for the patent system.[23] As all other patent law theories, it was countered by various arguments, particularly by political economists. Two of those arguments merit a closer look. On the one hand, critics point out that firms are not inclined to patent something they can keep secret,[24] implying that there is little or no incentive to patent as long as the invention has to be disclosed.[25] On the other hand, some have argued that inventors often obtain patents despite insufficient disclosure.[26] This is an argument that does not speak against the disclosure requirement per se but addresses its careless enforcement. Incentives to muddy the specifications of one's patent have existed all along. In the eighteenth and nineteenth centuries, disclosing inventions in an unspecific way was a commonly used means to shield off foreign competitors.[27] This may explain why national patent authorities had no interest in tightening the disclosure requirement. Obscure patent disclosures are not only a problem of the nineteenth century alone, but are also commonplace during the twentieth century.[28] As we will see, they persist in the twenty-first century.

2.2 Current Role and Function

Today, the disclosure requirement is part of both US law and the laws of the Member States of the EPC. According to the requirement of 35 USC paragraph 112, the 'specification shall contain a written description of the invention, and of the manner and process of making and using it, in such full, clear, concise, and exact terms as to enable any person skilled in the art to which it pertains, or with which it is most nearly connected, to make and use the same, and shall set forth the best mode contemplated by the inventor or joint inventor of carrying out the invention'. Similarly, yet somewhat shorter, Article 83 EPC (2000) requires that 'the European patent application shall disclose the invention in a manner sufficiently clear and complete for it to be carried

20. Re contract theory, cf. F.-K. Beier, *Die herkömmlichen Patentrechtstheorien und die sozialistische Konzeption des Erfinderrechts*, GRUR Int. 1970, 4 et seq.; Machlup, *supra* n. 6, 377; Denicolò/Franzoni, *supra* n. 18, 365.
21. Vaver, *supra* n. 3, 70; Fromer, *supra* n. 12, 553; A. Devlin, *The Misunderstood Function of Disclosure in Patent Law*, Harvard Journal of Law & Technology, 2010, 408 and 418; D. L. Burk/M. A. Lemley, *Is Patent Law Technology-Specific*, Berkeley Technology Law Journal, 2002, 1186.
22. Suzy Frankel rightly points out that from a common law perspective, the term *social contract theory* would be more fitting; *see also* Mossoff, *supra* n. 8, 1289 et seq.
23. Machlup, *supra* n. 6, 379.
24. M. Boldrin/D. K. Levine, *The Case Against Patents*, J. of Econ. Perspectives, 2013, 9 et seq.; Machlup, *supra* n. 6, 379, 383.
25. For a further critique on the contract theory, *see* Machlup, *supra* n. 6, 383 et seq.
26. For a more detailed account, cf. Machlup, *supra* n. 6, 383.
27. Vaver, *supra* n. 3, 70.
28. Machlup, *supra* n. 6, 383.

out by a person skilled in the art'. These substantive provisions are in line with the above-mentioned contract theory. However, both the contract theory and the disclosure requirement face the same arguments they have faced in the past, two of which have already been introduced in the preceding paragraph.

First, the contract theory (i.e., disclosing the invention) is said not to incentivize innovation and thus may conflict with this primary goal of patent law. Therefore, critics argue that the disclosure requirement is potentially poisonous to broader social goals, particularly when it collides with patent laws' incentive function.[29] They would rather dismiss the disclosure requirement than see it collide with the patent law's primary function of incentivizing innovation. However, whether the presumed conflict between the disclosure requirement and the incentive function indeed exists is controversial. There is at least some economic evidence that the disclosure requirement itself incentivizes innovation.[30] After all, disclosure prevents wasteful duplication of research, allows follow-on innovation, has a signalling function that may attract funding and lets competitors comprehend the boundaries of the invention.[31] Further, information about the inventors, their fields of work, and their geolocalization are also a source of knowledge for research on the technological discovery process.[32] Against this background, the fundamental critique that the disclosure requirement is harmful and should be dismissed is not convincing.

The second argument is that disclosure is ineffective. We are already familiar with this argument,[33] and it hardly evolved during the last century. The public bodies awarding the exclusive rights have to account for the rights they grant by publishing the disclosed invention in their patent registers and thus providing the public with an accurate account of the state of the art. Scholars widely agree on the fact that patentees are not holding their end of the quid pro quo bargain of the contract theory[34] and that disclosure is ineffective. Scholars have come to different conclusions on how to deal with this issue. For some, the appropriate solution is to get rid of the disclosure requirement altogether.[35] Others focus on fixing the problems and restoring the quid pro quo bargain.[36] The latter interpretation is by far more convincing, given the potential benefits of the disclosure requirement: during the term, competitors can use the invention as a source of inspiration, they can invent around and improve upon it, and thus realize and enable the already mentioned economic benefits.

29. Devlin, *supra* n. 21, 403 et seq.
30. Denicolò/Franzoni, *supra* n. 18, 365 et seq.
31. Fromer, *supra* n. 12, 541, 549 et seq.
32. F. Lissoni/G. Cristelli, *Mobility of Research: Patent Data and Inventor Information*, in: Intellectual Property and Digital Trade in the Age of Artificial Intelligence and Big Data, Global Perspectives and Challenges for the Intellectual Property System, X. Seuba/C. Geiger/J. Pénin (eds), CEIPI-ICTSD, June 2018, 145 et seq.
33. *See* 2.1 *supra*.
34. Devlin, *supra* n. 21, 403 et seq.; Fromer, *supra* n. 12, 539 et seq.
35. Devlin, *supra* n. 21, 421.
36. Vaver, *supra* n. 3, 70 et seq.

2.3 Fixing the Disclosure Requirement

How can the flawed quid pro quo mechanism be fixed then? The literature suggests several starting points both on the substantive and procedural[37] level. Not all are equally promising, but two are worth mentioning.

On closer inspection, the disclosure requirement consists of two elements: disclosure and enablement. The patent application must *disclose* the invention in a way that *enables* the person skilled in the art to work the patent. In its wording, the EPC even requires a disclosure that is 'sufficiently clear and complete'[38] – in contrast to provisions of national law (such as the Swiss Patents Act (CH-PatA)[39]). EPC case law interprets these words broadly: it is sufficient that only one way in which the person skilled in the art works the invention is disclosed.[40] Put differently, EPC case law does not require the applicant to disclose the best or most beneficial mode of working the invention.[41] While it is safe to argue that disclosing all possible ways of working an invention would be impossible, this case law generally permits that an applicant discloses the worst way of working the invention, while keeping other modes secret.[42] According to VAVER, it is unclear why this should be allowed: 'One might argue, the invention should be disclosed or not disclosed at all, but a poorly disclosed invention that takes a lot of time and effort to be worked makes no sense'.[43] Deliberately hiding the best way of working an invention duplicates search costs and hampers all other potential benefits of the disclosure requirement. As a consequence, the patent register today is not as useful as it could and should be.[44] This EPC case law is particularly peculiar from a United Kingdom (UK) perspective, as the EPC led to a substantive harmonization of the disclosure requirement, thus overturning the previously established common law principle that the patentee had to disclose the 'most beneficial' mode of working the invention.[45] Of course, even current EPC case law may curb poor disclosure.[46] UK law, for example, requires that the invention can be reproduced

37. US law is an excellent example that procedural rules can have a detrimental effect to the disclosure requirement. In the US, corporate researchers are sometimes advised not to look at patent registers at all. If their employer is sued for patent infringement, the employee's knowledge of the patent may lead to the employer being liable for treble damages, VAVER, *supra* n. 3, 70. *See* FROMER, *supra* n. 12, 589 et seq. for other procedural rules with detrimental effect to disclosure and 547 et seq. for other remedies.
38. Similarly, UK Patents Act 1977, ss 14(3), 72(1)(c): 'The invention be disclosed in a manner that is clear and complete enough for it to be performed by a person skilled in the art.'
39. Art. 50 para. 1 CH-PatA reads: 'The invention must be described in the patent application in such a manner that it can be carried out by a person skilled in the art.'.
40. P. HEINRICH, *PatG/EPÜ Kommentar*, 3rd ed., Berne 2018, PatG 50, nn. 6 and 21, with further references.
41. *Cf. also* AIPPI Resolution Q 69, 3. For Switzerland, BRINER, *supra* n. 16, 159; HEINRICH, *supra* n. 40, PatG 50, n. 50.03, citing EPC Board of Appeal case ECLI:EP:BA:1983:T009482.19830722, consid. 12.4 para. 3.
42. VAVER, *supra* n. 3, 72.
43. VAVER, *supra* n. 3, 73.
44. VAVER, *supra* n. 3, 70.
45. VAVER, *supra* n. 3, 72.
46. HEINRICH, *supra* n. 40, PatG 50, n. 6.

without undue burden, ruling out all activities the courts deem onerous.[47] And Swiss courts would consider disclosure insufficient, if the applicant withheld relevant information.[48] For a potential plaintiff, proving that working the invention is onerous or that the applicant withheld relevant information is an uphill battle. In contrast to the EPC, US law generally contains a best mode requirement.[49] However, the Leahy-Smith America Invents Act (AIA) of 2011 changed 35 U.S.C. 282 to 'provide that the failure to disclose the best mode shall not be a basis on which any claim of a patent may be canceled or held invalid or otherwise unenforceable'.[50] While eliminating best mode as grounds for annulment has certainly weakened the best mode requirement, the USPTO is quick to point out that patent examining practices regarding the best mode requirement remain unaffected.[51] The best mode requirement certainly has its problems such as the temporal issue that an inventor's knowledge and state of mind may change over time, even during the application phase.[52] However, observed from a distance, it is hard to see why patentees should not be forced to put all their cards on the table. Only disclosing the best mode ensures that the patentee holds his end of the quid pro quo bargain of the contract theory. Against this background, introducing the best mode requirement not only seems like a good idea – but also a necessity.

The second issue is related to the fact that the disclosure requirement relies on the hypothetical figure of the person skilled in the art. In a simple world, inventions could be disclosed by simple words and everybody would understand their meaning and would thus be able to work the disclosed invention. However, in the complex world we live in, disclosing an invention to a layperson would be excessive, repetitious and inefficient. Against this background, the hypothetical person skilled in the art has proven to be an effective instrument to truncate disclosure to a reasonable extent. Disclosure of the invention is sufficient if the person skilled in the art is able to work it in the full extent of the claim, without an inventive step.[53] The fictitious person skilled in the art quickly became a critical and universally accepted concept of patent law, as is demonstrated by two AIPPI Resolutions on the subject.[54] The concept is not static; over time it had to adapt to the changes in the inventive process. Because even a person skilled in the art cannot know everything there is to know in the relevant field, the question arose, whether the person skilled in the art could access additional knowledge. In 1978, the person skilled in the art could only resort to the average knowledge required in his or her professional work,[55] whereas 2010 he or she could also include readily available information and perform routine searches.[56] Similarly, in 1978 it was expected that the person skilled in the art had average knowledge in all the relevant

47. Bently/Sherman, *supra* n. 4, 578.
48. Briner, *supra* n. 16, 159.
49. *Benger Labs. Ltd. v. R.K. Laros Co.*, 209 F. Supp. 639, 135 USPQ 11 (E.D. Pa. 1962).
50. USPTO, Manual of Patent Examining Procedure, Chapter 2100, s. 2165.
51. USPTO, Manual of Patent Examining Procedure, Chapter 2100, s. 2165.
52. Heinrich, *supra* n. 40, PatG 50, n. 10.
53. Heinrich, *supra* n. 40, PatG 50, n. 4.
54. AIPPI Resolution to Q 69, Munich 1978 in the context of the disclosure requirement and AIPPI Resolution to Q 213, Paris 2010 in the context of the inventive step.
55. AIPPI Resolution to Q 69, 1.
56. AIPPI Resolution to Q 213, 2; *see also* Bently/Sherman, *supra* n. 4, 578.

technologies.[57] As this assumption became less and less realistic, the 2010 AIPPI Resolution allowed the person skilled in the art to draw on a team of people from different disciplines.[58] Through the lens of society's increasing complexity, these extensions to the concept of the person skilled in the art are very understandable. However, they are also a source of discomfort and a potential threat to the quid pro quo bargain of disclosure. Obscurities in the patent specification may go unnoticed, because defects that would puzzle a layperson can easily be filled in or explained by the vast knowledge of a person skilled in the art.[59] The more knowledge the hypothetical person skilled in the art has, the more difficult it becomes for the public to understand what it gets in return for granting monopoly rights. This imbalance in the quid pro quo bargain of the contract theory is exacerbated by the fact that patent offices not only fulfil a public task but also act in their self-interest. To them, lower standards of disclosure are not an issue. They have the state of the art at their fingertips and subsist on patent fees. Resolving this issue in order to rebalance the quid pro quo bargain of the contract theory is not trivial. It does not seem likely that adjusting the figure of the person skilled in the art could achieve this rebalancing. However, if the public had the knowledge of the person skilled in the art, imbalances would be mitigated. The real issue therefore is one of information asymmetry, which could be remedied by increasing transparency in the patent register. Today, patent registers are freely accessible but hardly usable as tools for the public,[60] a task that is rather technical than normative. We will come back to that.[61]

To conclude this second section, we can summarize that the disclosure requirement is an unchallenged part of substantive law, but the underlying concept of the contract theory and its quid pro quo bargain is both controversial and flawed. Today, there is scant literature on both the importance of a balanced quid pro quo and on options to remedy imbalances. As starting points, this chapter promotes the best mode requirement and demands more transparency for patent registers so that the public understands what it gets in return for granting monopoly rights.

3 ARTIFICIAL INTELLIGENCE

The essence of AI is hard to define.[62] But as indicated by the term 'intelligence', the cognitive capacities of humans are the primary point of reference.[63] Therefore, learning, problem-solving, and decision-making are some of the activities attributed to both human and AI.[64]

57. AIPPI Resolution to Q 69, 1.
58. AIPPI Resolution to Q 213, 2.
59. VAVER, *supra* n. 3, 72.
60. VAVER, *supra* n. 3, 70.
61. *See* s. 5 *infra*.
62. B. WALTL/R. VOGL, *Explainable Artificial Intelligence – The New Frontier in Legal Informatics*, Jusletter IT, 22 February 2018, 1; FIRTH-BUTTERFIELD/CHAE, *supra* n. 1, 5.
63. C. MISSELHORN, *Grundfragen der Maschinenethik*, Ditzingen 2018, 17, with further references.
64. WALTL/VOGL, *supra* n. 62, 1, with further references.

The term 'AI' emerged in the 1950s.[65] After phases of slower development, AI research significantly accelerated in the last two decades.[66] A broad categorization differentiates artificial general intelligence (AGI), which displays a level of intelligence comparable to a human mind, and narrow AI that focuses on solving specific tasks.[67] Regarding the specific AI techniques, further general distinctions can be made between symbolic AI (emphasizing the computational processing of abstract symbols) and sub-symbolic AI such as embodied AI (emphasizing physical engagement of cognitive capacities) or connectionism (emphasizing neural connections that are reproduced in layers and networks).[68] Especially the latter has been driving AI research in recent years,[69] spurring breakthroughs in machine learning (ML), particularly within the categories of artificial neural networks (ANN including deep learning).[70] Besides ANN, genetic programming (GP) is another AI technique that promises to revolutionize the inventive process.[71] It uses computer programs much like a set of genes and adapts them using an evolutionary algorithm, continually increasing its fitness to achieve a certain task.

3.1 AI and Magic

In the literature about AI there are quite some references to magic.[72] AI is compared to a genie, magically fulfilling a wish of the inventor.[73] One might also think about the third of ARTHUR C. CLARKE's famous aphorisms about the future: 'Any sufficiently advanced technology is indistinguishable from magic'.[74]

However, once AI becomes conventional technology, it stops being magical. It even stops being considered AI. IBM's Deep Blue victory over chess champion Garry Kasparov in 1997 was soon belittled by explaining that the machine had used brute force (and not intelligence) to win. AI applications that become commonplace lose their mythical aura. Nowadays, sophisticated pattern recognition is a booming field of AI. However, pattern recognition processes have been used since the mid-1960s, when postal offices introduced automated sorting by using optical character recognition

65. It is credited to JOHN MCCARTHY, having used the term in a proposal related to a scientific conference at Dartmouth College in 1956, FIRTH-BUTTERFIELD/CHAE, *supra* n. 1, 5; MISSELHORN, *supra* n. 63, 17, n. 4.
66. FIRTH-BUTTERFIELD/CHAE, *supra* n. 1, 5.
67. FIRTH-BUTTERFIELD/CHAE, *supra* n. 1, 5.
68. Cf. MISSELHORN, *supra* n. 63, 21 et seqq.
69. This has even led to the fact that sometimes Machine Learning is equated with all of AI, E. ALPAYDIN, *Machine Learning*, Cambridge, MA, 2016, xiii.
70. They have been achieved because of the increased availability of computing power and new adaptations of the backpropagation algorithm that adjusts the weights of the neurons in the network's deep layers during training, *see* J. D. KELLEHER/B. TIERNEY, *Data Science*, Cambridge MA, 2018, 135 et seq.
71. FRASER, *supra* n. 1, 317.
72. WALTL/VOGL, *supra* n. 62, 3.
73. R. PLOTKIN, *The Genie in the Machine: How Computer-automated Inventing is Revolutionizing Law and Business*, Stanford, 2009, 3.
74. A. C. CLARKE, *Profiles of the Future: An Inquiry into the Limits of the Possible*, London 1973, Postscript.

(OCR).[75] No one considers OCR technology to be magical anymore. Against this background, it is easy to predict that current cutting-edge AI applications such as Google Duplex or DeepL will quickly face a similar fate.

What we consider as AI is therefore constantly changing. The scope of AI dynamically expands with each technical development, but is, at the same time, curbed by technology adoption. This fact should remind us to use the term 'AI' carefully – wherever possible, a more precise definition of the actual technology (such as image pattern recognition by deep neural networks) is preferable.

3.2 Explainable AI

The recent successes of ML[76] have uncovered the new issue of explainability. The level of technical development, the complexity of the systems, and their internal structure are such that their inner workings are difficult to understand even for experts.[77] There is a general notion that AI is something opaque and the algorithmic decision-making software are black boxes.[78] Accordingly, the introduction of AI could be an impediment to the patent system, making it less transparent.

However, this view would be too simplistic. Different types of ML techniques have different features regarding explainability. Deep neural networks are among those with particularly poor explainability, but other techniques in the realm of AI are much more transparent.[79] Moreover, some authors suggest, that even if an ML technique has black-box features, explainability may be satisfied by explaining an algorithm's purpose, design, and basic functioning.[80]

3.3 Reproducibility

Modern AI applications and ML require large amounts of data. In general, ML aims to construct a programme that fits the given data.[81] To this end, a data scientist can use different templates and different learning algorithms and use the latter to adjust specific parameters to get the best performance.[82] One of the significant challenges is finding the algorithm whose learning bias is the best match for a given data set.[83]

A data set normally contains a number of instances (*n*, e.g., persons), each having several attributes (*m*, e.g., age, sex, height, weight and so on). The data set is then used to train, validate and test the ML algorithm. The goal is to increase the ML

75. G. Nagy, *Disruptive Developments in Document Recognition*, Pattern Recognition Letters 2016, Vol. 79, 108.
76. Alpaydin, *supra* n. 69, xiii.
77. Waltl/Vogl, *supra* n. 62, 3.
78. Waltl/Vogl, *supra* n. 62, 3.
79. S. B. Kotsiantis, *Supervised Machine Learning: A Review of Classification Techniques*, Informatica 31, 2007, 263.
80. C. Coglianese/D. Lehr, *Transparency and Algorithmic Governance*, U. of Penn. Law School, Public Law and Legal Theory Research Paper Series Research Paper No. #18-38.
81. Alpaydin, *supra* n. 69, 24.
82. Alpaydin, *supra* n. 69, 24.
83. Kelleher/Tierney, *supra* n. 70, 99 et seq.

algorithms performance so far that it applies to any data. ML thus inherently aims for reproducibility. However, as the goal is to get meaningful outputs for varying inputs based on generalizations (and not repetitiously getting the same output for a given input), the results of the process cannot always be reproduced.[84]

First, the data set being used has to have the same attributes as the training data set. This requirement equally applies to the number of attributes (*m*) as well as their type. If *m1* in the training data set is a numeric attribute (such as a person's age), it cannot be substituted with nominal or ordinal attributes (such as old/not old or young/middle aged/old) let alone by an entirely different attribute (e.g., the attitude towards ice cream, dyslexia and so on).

Second, even if the data set has the same structure, the data may contain entirely different biases. As data science extracts patterns in data and the data encodes a prejudicial relationship in society, the algorithm will likely identify this pattern and base its outputs on the pattern.[85] A data set from a middle European population will therefore, for example, not translate to African or Asian contexts without implementing inherent biases – and vice versa. Choosing the data set is therefore of utmost relevance.[86] Applying a given algorithm on a different data set that has other instances and attributes will generally lead to different and unforeseeable outcomes. And even if the data set contains the same instances and attributes as the training data, reproducibility may be an issue depending on the provenance and the preparation of the data set.

4 LOOMING CHALLENGES

While technical obstacles such as computing capacity still limit AI's full potential,[87] patent offices already prepare and adapt to the rise of AI technology,[88] and rightly so. While in 2016, there were (merely) 83 patent applications regarding AI,[89] the average growth rate of AI patent applications at the EPO between 2011 and 2016 was 43 %,[90] with no sign of decline.

84. On the still limited generalization capabilities of neural networks: H. Hosseini/B. Xiao/M. Jaisawal/R. Poovendran, *On the Limitation of Convolutional Neural Networks in Recognizing Negative Images*, 6th IEEE International Conference on Machine Learning and Applications (ICMLA), 2017, 352 et seq.; M. T. Ribeiro/S. Singh/C. Guestrin, *Why should I trust you?: Explaining the Predictions of any Classifier*, Proceedings of the 22nd ACM SIGKDD international conference on knowledge discovery and data mining, 2016, 1135 et seq.
85. Kelleher/Tierney, *supra* n. 70, 191.
86. Kelleher/Tierney, *supra* n. 70, 47.
87. European Patent Office, *Patents and the Fourth Industrial Revolution, The inventions behind digital transformation*, December 2017, 31.
88. Y. Ménière/I. Rudjk, *The Fourth Industrial Revolution Form the European Patent Office Perspective*, in: Intellectual Property and Digital Trade in the Age of Artificial Intelligence and Big Data, Global Perspectives and Challenges for the Intellectual Property System, X. Seuba/C. Geiger/J. Pénin (eds), CEIPI-ICTSD, June 2018, 32.
89. European Patent Office, *supra* n. 87, 31.
90. Y. Ménière/I. Rudjk, *supra* n. 88, 34; European Patent Office, *supra* n. 87, 31.

Involvement of AI in the inventive process can take many forms,[91] ranging from AI merely assisting the inventor[92] to examples of full autonomy such as JOHN R. KOZA's Invention Machine or STEPHEN L. THALER's Creativity Machine.[93] However, rather than making abstract observations regarding this spectrum, we would like to investigate concrete situations in which AI and disclosure meet. We can broadly distinguish five. Of these, the first two (sections 4.1 and 4.2) do not raise new issues, whereas the other three (sections 4.3, 4.4 and 4.5) give rise to intriguing new questions.

4.1 AI-Created Invention, Disclosed

In the first situation, AI partially or fully makes an invention, and the invention is properly and fully disclosed. An example is KOZA's 2005 patent of a PID controller.[94] A PID controller is a technical mechanism to implement a control loop feedback mechanism. It is used almost everywhere in mechanical and technical devices both for industrial applications and end-users. An everyday example is cruise control in a car, that has to react to external inputs, e.g., when driving up a hill. Another example is a now famous patent application regarding the structure of a food or beverage container that was developed autonomously by a machine called DABUS, developed by THALER.[95] The mere fact that these inventions have been made by resorting to AI may be an issue considering inventorship[96] but does not raise any issues regarding the disclosure requirement.

4.2 Inventive AI as the Invention, Disclosed

In the second situation, the enabling teaching itself concerns an AI technique. To use the example of the PID controller: the PID controller mentioned above was 'invented' by AI, and this AI was also patented.[97] Similarly, what now is called DABUS is also patented.[98] This raises the question whether such inventions should be worthy of patent protection at all[99] and could also be discussed in the light of the admissibility of computer-implemented inventions. With regard to the disclosure requirement, however, patenting an AI technique raises no issues.

91. L. VERTINSKY, *Thinking Machines and Patent Law*, in: Research Handbook of Law and Artificial Intelligence, W. Barfield/U. Pagallo (eds), Cheltenham 2018, 490.
92. FRASER, *supra* n. 1.
93. For both, PLOTKIN, *supra* n. 73, 2 and VERTINSKY, *supra* n. 91, 490.
94. Example from PLOTKIN, *supra* n. 73, 1; cf. United States Patent 6,847,851.
95. The UKIPO application no. is GB1816909.4, the publication no. is GB2574909. At the EPO, the application no. is EP3564144. More information can be found on (The Artificial Inventor Project) http://artificialinventor.com/, visited on 16 January 2020.
96. Cf. A. FRÜH, *Inventorship in the Age of AI*, in: C. Godt/M. Lamping (eds), *forthcoming*.
97. United States Patent 7,117,186.
98. United States Patent 10,423,875.
99. Regarding the similar question concerning patents for research tools and scientific building blocks, cf. A. FRÜH/M. LICHTENEGGER, *Schlüsselgegenstände*, in: Europäisches Immaterialgüterrecht, R. M. Hilty/T. Jaeger (eds), 2018, 384, 402 et seq.

4.3 Inventive AI/Working Requires AI, Disclosed, but Unexplainable

Now we look at more interesting situations and consider the case in which an AI technique either *is* the invention (as section 4.2 above) or working the invention requires the application of AI. For the former, imagine that it is unexplainable how DABUS *exactly* conceives its novel output (a fact its inventor would surely contest). For the latter, think of a patented scanner that can detect skin cancer using pattern recognition. Let us assume that in both instances the results can be reproduced but the workings of AI are unexplainable and nobody, not even the software engineers that train or programme the AI know how it operates.

Particularly in the light of the discussion about explainable AI, one might think that this is an issue. For the disclosure requirement, however, it is not. Patent laws are clear that the inventor does not have to know *why* something works. It is sufficient *that* it works.[100] It does not matter whether the inventor errs[101] or the reason the invention works remains completely unknown.[102] Even if the invention relies on a presumed behaviour that does not occur, disclosure can be sufficient.

4.4 Working Requires AI, Concrete Use of AI Undisclosed

Let us next consider a situation, in which working the invention requires the application of AI or an AI technique (such as the fictional skin cancer scanner in section 4.3 above), but this actual AI technique is not disclosed in the patent application. This puts the person skilled in the art in the centre of the attention: He or she has to determine whether the invention can be worked despite its lack of disclosing the exact AI method.[103]

In the context of non-obviousness, there is a heated discussion whether the person skilled in the art may resort to AI or not.[104] The same question is less pressing when assessing the disclosure requirement. The invention is deemed sufficiently disclosed even if the applicant does not explicitly describe certain elements. It is precisely the task of the person skilled in the art to determine whether he or she can fill the missing gaps. While this task is fraught with uncertainty,[105] case law has developed criteria to determine whether and how to fill these gaps. According to German case law, for example, disclosure is sufficient if the person skilled in the art is able to 'read' the

100. For US law, Plotkin, *supra* n. 73, 160 et seq.; for Swiss law, Heinrich, *supra* n. 40, PatG 50, n. 26.
101. Busse Keukenschrijver, PatG Patentgesetz, 8th ed., Berlin, 2016, PatG § 34 N 272.
102. Commercial Court of the Canton of Zurich, 21 September 1990, SMI 1992, 269 consid. 4.4.1; Heinrich, *supra* n. 40, PatG 50, n. 50.11.
103. *See supra* 3, regarding the different methods.
104. Affirmative: C. R. Davies, *An Evolutionary Step in Intellectual Property Rights – Artificial Intelligence and Intellectual Property*, Computer L & Sec Rev 2011, 606; Fraser, *supra* n. 1, 320; cf. *also* W. Samore, *Artificial Intelligence and the Patent System: Can a New Tool Render a Once Patentable Idea Obvious?*, Syracuse J. of Sci. & Tech. L., 2018, 113 et seq., at least after technology adoption; dismissive: Vertinsky, *supra* n. 91, 502.
105. R.A. Rentsch, *Das Europäische Patentrecht und seine Harmonisierungswirkungen in der nationalen Rechtsprechung der Schweiz*, Berne 2016, n. 208.

missing elements 'into the patent' and has to overcome 'certain, but not too big difficulties', all below own inventive capacity.[106] Swiss case law applies similar considerations, and EPC case law influences them.[107] US case law states that the patent must enable the person skilled in the art to work the patent without 'undue experimentation'.[108] In general (and also in the light of the expanding scope of knowledge attributed to him or her[109]), the person skilled in the art will thus - as with any other technology - fill the gaps it can and leave open those it cannot.

However, filling the gaps would be much easier if the person skilled in the art could resort to AI. But resorting to AI has a detrimental effect on disclosure, because the person skilled in the art might be enabled to work an invention even with a very limited patent disclosure.[110] Consequently, there is a risk that use of AI by the person skilled in the art will further increase the disclosure deficits that we already see today.[111] This effect should be kept in mind.

4.5 Working Requires AI, Invention Not Reproducible

To conclude, let us consider the situation in which working the invention requires the application of AI or an AI technique (such as the fictional skin cancer scanner in section 4.3 above), but the AI-related invention cannot be reproduced. This may occur if AI techniques such as ML and deep neural networks are used. Generally, it is the goal of a data scientist that an AI also works on datasets other than the one it was trained on.[112] It is all but clear that these inventions can be reproduced without an appropriate dataset.[113] While basic training data sets are often openly available, specific inventions will regularly work on specific datasets.

Patent law requires that the patent is disclosed in a way that allows a reproduction of the intended technical solution.[114] While isolated failed attempts are accepted, a general inability to reproduce the technical solution must be considered insufficient disclosure.[115] Consequently, some AI-related inventions cannot be considered fully disclosed without additional disclosure of the data set under current patent law and firms are most likely not willing to disclose their data sets, because they often contain valuable business secrets. Neither the - limited scope) of the - European sui generis

106. U. Dreiss, *Der Durchschnittsfachmann als Massstab für ausreichende Offenbarung, Patentfähigkeit und Patentauslegung*, GRUR 1994, 785.
107. One Swiss study suggests that the few existing differences between Swiss and EPC case law are attributable to the individual case rather than to fundamental differences in the interpretation of the EPC, Rentsch, *supra* n. 105, n. 326.
108. In re Wright, 999 F.2d 1557, 1561 (Fed. Cir. 1993).
109. *See supra* s. 2.3.
110. Vertinsky, *supra* n. 91, 503: 'AI-based enablement may thus allow for expanded patent scope for any given disclosure of the invention.'
111. *See supra* s. 2.2.
112. Kelleher/Tierney, *supra* n. 70, 147.
113. *See supra* s. 3.3.
114. Heinrich, *supra* n. 40, PatG 50, n. 9; Beier, *supra* n. 20, 4.
115. Heinrich, *supra* n. 40, PatG 50, n. 16.

regime for database protection[116] nor copyright grants legal protection for data *as such.*[117] In connection with the disclosure requirement this lack of protection may amount to a novel problem that requires some more thought about other legal instruments. One might think about data escrow setups or even tailored legal exclusivity for the data needed to work the invention in order for it to be disclosed.

5 POSSIBLE REMEDIES

The era when the general public understood patents by looking into the patent register is long gone. Nowadays, the knowledge of the person skilled in the art to work an invention is required. We have shown that the knowledge of the person skilled in the art constantly expands,[118] and it seems clear that with AI, this trend will continue. It is a trend that can be visualized on a sliding scale: At first, the patentee – being on one side of the spectrum – had to disclose the invention to the general public on the opposite side of the spectrum. Over time, the disclosure requirements decreased and shifted more and more towards the patentee: Disclosure now no longer had to bridge the information asymmetry between patentee and the public, but between patent holder and the person skilled in the art. Against this background, the observed shortcomings of the quid pro quo mechanism or the contract theory (that still requires the public to be the party on the receiving end of disclosure) are hardly surprising. To really fix the quid pro quo bargain we need to bridge the gap between the person skilled in the art and the public.

Interestingly, the same AI that exacerbates the problem above could just be tool to bridge this gap and thus to remedy this fundamental problem regarding patent disclosure. AI at least has the potential to restore the readability of the patent register. If implemented by patent offices, AI techniques could better explain or visualize the state of the art to the general public, making the disclosed invention more accessible. In doing so, data from patent offices could transform from an unwieldy thicket of technical information into a full human inventiveness repository. Instead of mainly serving the patent offices, as they do today,[119] patent registers would benefit the public again.[120] Such a repository would also allow for much easier identification of disclosure gaps and relevant patents – both of which is practically impossible today.[121] It is essential that patent offices seize this opportunity and quickly address this issue by technical means.

116. Directive 96/9/EC of the European Parliament and of the Council of 11 March 1996 on the legal protection of databases.
117. Regarding the several means of protection for data and rejecting a general 'data ownership' *see* F. Thouvenin/R. H. Weber/A. Früh, *Elemente einer Datenpolitik*, Zurich 2019, *passim*.
118. *See supra* s. 2.3.
119. Fraser, *supra* n. 1, 312, regarding the patent office's disincentive to search for prior art outside the patent register; *see also* Vertinsky, *supra* n. 91, 504.
120. Such research initiatives are already underway. *See* for example Carnegie Mellon's Center for AI and Patent Analysis, which has, *inter alia*, the mission to 'guide the AI research community in solving the largest patent problems collaboratively and incrementally'.
121. Fromer, *supra* n. 12, 585.

6 CONCLUSIONS

To sum up the answer to this chapter's research question: We conclude that patent law's disclosure requirement indeed is under attack by AI, and this may negatively affect the patent system as a whole, particularly its legitimacy that builds on the quid pro quo bargain of the so-called contract theory. While we concede that the challenges may be less fundamental than in other areas of patent law, a closer examination of the disclosure requirement in the context of AI has exposed two particular issues.

First, current patent law requires that a patent is disclosed in a way that allows the intended technical solution to be reproduced. This may be a stumbling block for inventions that require the application of AI or an AI technique. If an AI application is trained on a very specific data set, whose features or configuration are either not known or can neither be duplicated nor achieved by third parties, the invention cannot be reproduced and is thus not sufficiently disclosed. For the time being, it is highly unlikely that specific datasets will either be published or disclosed to the patent office. Nevertheless, both patent offices and applicants cannot disregard this issue: If in these circumstances patents are granted without disclosure of data, the scope of patent law unduly expands. Rather than broadening the scope of protection, other instruments such as tailored legal exclusivity of the data needed to work the invention should be further investigated.

Second, AI has the potential to cause new disclosure deficits if the hypothetical person skilled in the art resorts to AI in order to assess whether an invention is properly disclosed. This chapter has shown that the knowledge attributed to the hypothetical person skilled in the art constantly increased over time. As there are hardly any convincing arguments against such an expansion, the threshold for disclosure subsides, which further increases the already existing imbalance in the quid pro quo bargain of patent law's contract theory. Rebalancing the quid pro quo bargain of patent law is thus a pressing task. The remedies suggested in this chapter to readjust said balance are twofold. Substantive legal remedies such as requiring patentees to disclose the best mode of working their invention[122] should be paired with technical remedies such as a better (AI-powered) use of the patent register to the benefit of the public.[123]

It may come as a surprise, but even through the lens of transparency, the real issues are not the non-transparent character or the unexplainable workings of AI. Instead, the real transparency issues concern balancing the quid pro quo bargain of disclosure. The question is: 'What information does the applicant have to reveal to the patent office in order for the public to understand what it gets in return for granting monopoly rights?.' Adjusting this bargain does not per se require to better understand the workings of the technology, but a policy that ensures that all stakeholders (here: applicants, patent offices and the public) are on equal footing, having equal access to patent information in an equally easy way. Achieving this goal will require both legal and technical efforts.

122. *See supra* s. 2.3.
123. *See supra* s. 5.

CHAPTER 12

Artificial Intelligence, Novelty and Inventive Step: What Is the Impact of AI on Patent Law?*

*Peter R. Slowinski***

1 INTRODUCTION

Artificial intelligence (AI) is a fascinating term and one that is difficult to grasp. It is almost as old as computer science itself, and it was one of the founding fathers of computer science, Allen Turing, who in 1950 offered probably the first AI test.[1] While for decades it was a domain that was almost exclusively of interest to computer scientists, mathematicians, and maybe the science fiction community, it has jumped into the focus of the general public, legislators and lawyers. While the legal focus expands from ethical and constitutional questions to product liability, it does also attract attention with respect to intellectual property law and particularly copyright and patents.[2]

* All online sources have been last visited on 28 August 2020.

** I would like to thank the participants of the conference for very valuable comments that have been incorporated into this chapter.

1. Allen M Turing, *Computing Machinery and Intelligence* (1950) 49 Mind 433-460.
2. Colin R Davis, *An Evolutionary Step in Intellectual Property Rights—Artificial Intelligence and Intellectual Property* (2011) 27 Computer Law and Security Review 601-619; Ben Hattenbach & Joshua Glucoft, *Patents in an Era of Infinite Monkeys and Artificial Intelligence* (2015) 19 Stan. Tech. L. Rev. 32-51, 32; Annemarie Bridy, *Coding Creativity: Copyright and the Artificially Intelligent Author* (2012) 5 Stan. Tech. L. Rev.; Iain M Cockburn, *The Impact of Artificial Intelligence on Innovation; Jenna Burrell, How the Machine "Thinks": Understanding Opacity in Machine Learning Algorithms* (2016) Big Data & Society 1-12; Brian Higgins, *The Role of Explainable Artificial Intelligence in Patent Law* (2019) 31 Intellectual Property & Technology Law Journal 3-8; Tanuja Garde, *Artificial Intelligence and Induced Infringement* (2018) GRUR Int. 1132-1138; Peter Blok, *The Inventor's New Tool: Artificial Intelligence—How Does It Fit in the*

The main goal of this chapter is to demystify the subject of AI by providing an insight into the current most widely used AI technologies. The second goal is to take a closer look at two core patentability requirements, novelty and inventive step, to see how the use of AI in the development of products and processes that may be protected by patents, influences the application of novelty and inventive step. Finally, it is the goal of this chapter to use the disruptive nature that AI may have on patent law to shift the focus of the discussion back to the basics of patent law. It is my belief that the developments, that we can currently observe, should be seen as an opportunity to question and to rethink some of the beliefs that we have cultivated over decades with respect to patents.

This chapter, therefore, follows a very straightforward structure. It takes a look at the technology behind the term "AI," (section 2) and it presents three use cases to demonstrate how AI is influencing patent law already now—and not in 10 or 20 years (section 3). This chapter sheds some light on not only the capabilities but also the limitations of AI to provide a solid understanding of the technology for the purpose of application of patent law. The chapter then outlines the requirements for novelty and inventive step under the European Patent Convention (EPC) and US patent law. It also applies the law to the use cases (section 4). Finally, this chapter broadens the picture and shows how some of the issues brought up by the use of AI in the innovative process may provide us with the opportunity to rethink some of the rationales of patent law (section 5).

In order to focus on the aforementioned points, this chapter has to omit other important issues surrounding AI. Therefore, it does not address the question in what ways AI as such may be protected by patent law. I have addressed this topic elsewhere.[3] It does also not address the question whether or not the AI as such may become an inventor in the sense of patent law or whether this would be desirable. Based on the current case law, it presumes that it cannot be an inventor. Finally, this

European Patent System (2017) 39(2) European Intellectual Property Review 69-73; Ryan Abbott, *Artificial Intelligence, Big Data and Intellectual Property: Protecting Computer-Generated Works in the United Kingdom*; Emily Dorotheou, *Reap the Benefits and Avoid the Legal Uncertainty: Who Owns the Creation of Artificial Intelligence* (2015) 21(4) Computer and Telecommunications Law Review 85-93; Julia Dickenson, Alex Morgan & Birgit Clark, *Creative Machines: Ownership of Copyright in Content Created by Artificial Intelligence Applications* (2017) 39(8) European Intellectual Property Review 457-460; Ralph D. Clifford, *Intellectual Property in the Era of the Creative Computer Program: Will the True Creator Please Stand Up* (1997) 71 Tulane Law Review 1675-1703; Henry T. Greely, *Neuroscience, Artificial Intelligence, CRISPR—And Dogs and Cats* (2018) 51 University of California-Davis Law Review 2303-2330; Ryan Abbott, *I Think, Therefore I Invent: Creative Computers and the Future of Patent Law* (2016) 57 Boston College Law Review 1079-1125; Erica Fraser, *Computers as Inventors—Legal and Policy Implications of Artificial Intelligence on Patent Law* (2016) 13(3) SCRIPTed 305-333; Sven Hetmank & Anne Lauber-Rönsberg, *Künstliche Intelligenz—Herausforderungen für das Immaterialgüterrecht* (2018) GRUR 574-582; Stefan Papastefanou, *Genetic Breeding Algorithms als Form des "Machine Learning" im Urheber- und Patentrecht* (2019) CR 209-215.

3. Peter R. Slowinski, *Rethinking Software Protection in*: Jyh-An Lee, Kung-Chung Liu & Reto M Hilty (eds.), *Artificial Intelligence & Intellectual Property*, Oxford, Oxford University Press, 341-364 (2021).

chapter also does not analyze the complex questions of transparency and disclosure that may substantially influence the patent law applicable to AI.[4]

2 WHAT IS ARTIFICIAL INTELLIGENCE?

AI seems to be a very colorful term. Everyone talks about it but hardly anyone seems to understand the technology behind the term; at least outside the AI-IT-World. Furthermore, there are many aspects such as *deep learning, machine learning* or *neural networks* that are closely linked to the technology incorporated in AI but also terms such *robotics*, *image or speech recognition* and *big data*, that may or may not be specific use cases for AI. Also, many terms used in the discourse and many buzzwords seem to create even more expectations, fears, and half-truths. Therefore, it is important to break down what AI actually is and—maybe more important—what it is not or at least where its current limitations lie.

2.1 Types of AI

The term "AI" is not limited to a specific narrow technology such as machine engineering or pharmacy. Instead, it applies to a wide variety of different technologies that can be applied across various sectors of industry. Some of them have a specific purpose, and some are general-purpose applications. It does not seem to make a lot of sense to discuss the topic of AI without a clear understanding of the technology. While there are many sub-types of AI, this chapter focusses on those types that currently have the largest significance from a practical application point of view, including machine learning (ML), deep learning (DL), artificial neural networks (ANN), and evolutionary or genetic algorithms.

2.1.1 Machine Learning and Deep Learning

When politicians or legal academics or practitioners discuss AI, what they usually mean is the subfield of ML. This does not necessarily mean that ML is the best AI approach to every problem, but it means that it is the area of AI that has seen the fastest development and the broadest application in the last decade.[5] ML is in essence the application of statistical models and pattern recognition to large amounts of data. The concept of ML as such is known since the 1950s without any significant leaps in actual technology development for most of that time. Two factors have influenced the change in this area in the last few years: the now available computing power and, probably

4. For this, *see* Chapter 11 by *Alfred Früh* in this publication.
5. According to studies, publication in the area of ML have been on rise stronger in the last decade when compared to other sub-fields of AI. *See* Iain M Cockburn, Rebecca Henderson & Scott Stern, *The Impact of Artificial Intelligence on Innovation* (the National Bureau of Economic Research, 2018) http://nber.org/papers/w24449 (hereafter Cockburn, Henderson and Stern, *The Impact of Artificial Intelligence on Innovation*).

more important, the availability of large amounts of data that can be used to train the computer.

ML has two main components. The first is the ML-algorithm and the second is the training data. The algorithm is first applied to the training data and thereby taught to recognize patterns. Examples of such pattern recognition can range from picture analysis to vital parts of the control units of self-driving cars.[6] Once the algorithm has been taught, it can be applied to a new data-set where it is able to recognize the patterns autonomously. Deep learning is, simplified, a type of ML with more layers within the software that allow for a more complex analysis of patterns and thus problem solving. DL is implemented in deep neural networks.

2.1.2 Evolutionary/Genetic Algorithms

If ML resembles the process of common human learning and knowledge application, it is not difficult to imagine that in the process of innovation and creativity, such methods may reach limitations pretty fast. After all, it will be difficult, although not entirely impossible, for the AI to go beyond the learned data and patterns and to come up with entirely new concepts. In the area of medical diagnostic applications, ML-based Deep Neural Networks (DNN) have been able to detect skin cancer with high accuracy. However, the quality of the results was highly dependent on the quality of the pictures provided to the AI and, for example, were far less accurate when the application was provided with pictures taken at home or an ordinary hospital instead of perfect IT-lab conditions.[7] Here the human eye-brain-combination and experience still outperforms the AI. Furthermore, an ML-based AI has difficulties to "think" outside the box and present solutions that are way outside of the pool of training data applied to the AI. Particularly when such radically new solutions are desired, a second subfield of AI can be used which may play a key role in patent law in the future. These are evolutionary algorithms that sometimes are also called genetic algorithms.

Instead of mimicking human learning behavior, these AI applications are designed after the way the evolution comes up with new solutions to existing problems.[8] The general concept seems to be rather straightforward. An initial population of potential solutions (e.g., product designs) is created. The AI then tests these first generation solution for fitness to solve the targeted problem (i.e., survive). The best-suited candidates then undergo mutations (i.e., random changes to their parameters) or are mated with each other (i.e., their characteristics are combined into a new potential solution). The new generation is again tested for fitness. This cycle can be repeated either until a predefined fitness value is achieved or for a predefined period of

6. Michael I Jordan & Tom M Mitchell, *Machine Learning: Trends, Perspectives and Prospects* (2015) 349 Science 201, 255.
7. Manu Goyal et al., *Artificial Intelligence-Based Image Classification for Diagnosis of Skin Cancer: Challenges and Opportunities* (2019) arXiv:1911.11872 [eess.IV].
8. *See* for an explanation Stuart J Russel & Peter Norvig, *Artificial Intelligence: A Modern Approach*, 3rd edn, Prentice Hall (2011) 127 ff.

time or a pre-defined number of cycles. Just as in nature, there will hardly ever be a perfect solution, but it is possible to come very close to it.

Based on the working principle of evolutionary algorithms, computer scientists compare them to nature or genes. However, it is also possible to compare them to a certain mindset or method of human thinking. The repeated cycles of designing new solutions, combining or changing them, very much resembles the way a human would brainstorm for solutions. When brainstorming, we do not necessarily rely on learned information from a particular area of expertize, but instead allow our brains to find new solutions to existing problems. In fact, this is the way that engineers and scientists came up with new ideas and products for the last centuries. So evolutionary algorithms seem to be quite close to what we perceive as inventorship. From the perspective of computer science, evolutionary algorithms are classified as search approached, as compared to learning approaches such as ML or DL.[9]

2.1.3 Artificial Neural Networks

ANN or DNN are generally discussed in the context of ML and DL respectively. In fact, particularly DL application rely on DNN. However, ANN/DNN provide a structure for AI application which can be implemented using both ML and EL.[10] The principle behind ANN is that of the human brain. The human brain consists of myriads of neurons that store information and help us process information. Depending on the task at hand different parts of the brain with different neuron structures are involved.

ANN is a software that contains such (artificial) neurons. These neurons are coded mathematical formulas. Each neuron has a certain value, and if information that is fed to the ANN passes through the neuron the value of the information combined with the value stored in the neuron will decide which way the information will take further down the road.[11] A DNN has multiple layers of neurons and thereby is able to provide more fine-tuning to the data that passes through the network since every layer provided multiple possibilities to influence the final output. However, increasing the number of layers does not automatically lead to "better" results. Every DNN has to be designed and adapted to the task at hand. The design of a DNN is at least as much science as it is art and presently involves a lot of try and error to find the optimal system. However, there are studies that show that AI may be better suited for the design of DNN than human developers are.[12]

9. *Ibid.*, 127.
10. Felipe Petroski Such et al., *Deep Neuroevolution: Genetic Algorithms Are a Competitive Alternative for Training Deep Neural Networks for Reinforcement Learning* (2018) arXiv:1712.06567 [cs.NE] (hereafter Salimans et al., "Deep Neuroevolution"), Tim Salimans et al., *Evolutions Strategies as a Scalable Alternative to Reinforcement Learning* (2017) arXiv:1703.03864 [stat.ML].
11. Every input into any AI application including an ANN is a value of some sort. Machines cannot strictly speaking understand words or pictures. They understand numbers. So the input must be translated into numeric values.
12. Hanzhang Hu et al., *Efficient Forward Architecture Search* (2019) arXiv:1905.13360 [cs.LG].

2.2 Summary

So, what can we draw from this? First of all, we can conclude that AI is not thinking in the same way a human being is; at least not yet. Most importantly, it cannot initiate its "thinking" process independently. Right now, it needs humans to decide what task it should address, and the labelling of data and the setting up of the AI system still require many hours of human working time. AI also does not have what we call "intuition". AI needs large amounts of data to learn, while a human being may already learn from only a very small number of examples.[13] On the other hand, AI can find patterns in large amounts of data where humans see only chaos because they cannot process such amounts of information. AI, combined with the world wide web, can connect information from different sources in a very short period of time. Finally, AI can present us with solutions but it still has only limited capabilities to identify problems on its own.

3 THREE USE CASES OF AI AND PATENT LAW

The general understanding of the technology behind the term "AI" is doubtlessly helpful. It provides an insight not only into the general capabilities but also, equally important, into the limits and challenges of the technology. In short, it helps us to demystify the concept of AI to some degree. However, although AI is characterized as a general purpose technology (GPT), this term may be misleading. AI as a general concept is a GPT. But a specific AI is still not capable of solving each and every task that may be suitable for an AI. As of today, AI applications need to be tailored to specific tasks and if based on ML/DL they need to be trained for each task. This is one reason why it is important to look at different use cases of AI to understand its impact on innovation. Another is that concrete examples are always easier to comprehend than abstract concepts. Therefore, in the following paragraphs, this chapter will take a closer look at three particular examples. These examples will finally help with the application of the law.

3.1 Pharmaceuticals

In the last decades, the justification for patent protection has become challenged in various fields of technology, particularly in the IT and mobile communications sector. With respect to pharmaceuticals, however, the common ground seems to be that protection is justified due to the high costs of product development and easy possibilities to come up with generic alternatives.[14] Particularly, with respect to the discovery of new compounds and their use as medicinal products patent protection still seems to be important for technological development. And the current COVID-19 crisis demonstrates once again that research in the field of pharmaceuticals is crucial and that

13. Otherwise it is doubtful that we had survived for such a long time if our ancestors had tried the same poisonous fruit a few thousand times to learn that it is poisonous.
14. This does of course not mean that there is not a lot of debate regarding the limits of the protection and questions of access to affordable medicines.

finding a cure or vaccine for an illness is everything but simple. But there are voices that argue that this may change.

In 2018, the scientific journal *Nature* has published an article on the use of AI in the pharmaceutical sector.[15] This article lists not one or two but numerous companies that let AI search for new compounds that may be suitable for use in the pharmaceutical industry. So basically, AI is now searching for the next blockbuster drug. The advantage, obviously, is that the research investments may be reduced substantially. In the past, only one out of ten compounds that were researched actually made it to the clinical phase. The AI may have the capability to eliminate the nine candidates that are not suitable. The question, however, is whether finding a new compound is actually something worth the patent reward if this is being done—actually or potentially—by an AI.

Furthermore, it is worth noticing, that computer-assisted search for new chemical compounds is not entirely new. Just as the research on and the use of AI is something that has been happening for quite a while. The use of ML and ANN for the discovery of new chemical compounds goes back to the 1990s and has been firmly established in the 2000s.[16] In addition, evolutionary or genetic algorithms have been used for the same purpose for at least a decade.[17] Still, there is no evidence that the time required for the development of new pharmaceuticals has shortened. Currently, we can only speculate on the reasons for this. But it seems fair to say at least that so far, AI has not revolutionized the pharmaceutical industry. Whether it affects the requirements for patenting will be discussed below.

3.2 Product Design and Development

In 2019 and 2020, the European Patent Office (EPO),[18] the UKIPO,[19] and the United States Patent and Trademark Office[20] had to decide whether or not an AI could be named as inventor on a patent application. Steven L. Thaler claimed that a system developed and used by him, DABUS,[21] was the actual inventor behind the patents applications EP 18 275 163, EP 18 275 174, UK, GB 1816909.4, GB 1818161.0, and U.S. Patent Application Number 16/524,350. The patent offices rejected the patent applications on the ground that only a natural person can be an inventor according to

15. Nic Fleming, *How Artificial Intelligence Is Changing Drug Discovery* (2018) Nature 557, S55-S57, DOI: 10.1038/d41586-018-05267-x.
16. Tanja Dimitrov et al., *Autonomous Molecular Design: Then and Now* (2019) ACS Applied Materials & Interfaces 11, 24825-24836, DOI: 10.1021/acsami.9b01226.
17. Tu C Le & David A Winkler, *Discovery and Optimization of Materials Using Evolutionary Approaches*, (2016) Chemical Reviews 116, 6107-6132, DOI: 10.1021/acs.chemrev.5b00691.
18. *See* the published grounds for the decisions at https://register.epo.org/application?documentId = E4B63SD62191498&number = EP18275163&lng = en&npl = false and https://register.epo.org/application?documentId = E4B63OBI2076498&number = EP18275174&lng = en&npl = false.
19. *See* the decision at https://www.ipo.gov.uk/p-challenge-decision-results/o74119.pdf.
20. *See* the decision at https://www.uspto.gov/sites/default/files/documents/16524350_22apr2020.pdf.
21. DABUS is an acronym for Device for the Autonomous Bootstrapping of Useful Information, and its principle has been patented US Patent 7,454,388 in 2008. More information on DABUS is available at http://imagination-engines.com/iei_dabus.php#DABUS%20Patent.

current patent law in the three jurisdictions. The patent applications by Thaler are not the only examples of cases where AI systems have come up with new products. Other examples include a new toothbrush,[22] a controller,[23] or the famous National Aeronautics and Space Administration (NASA) antenna. Both NASA and Thaler claim that the final result of the product design process was something that no expert in the field could have designed and the design process as such took place without human intervention. In simplified terms: the humans turned on the AI, the AI provided a new design, and the humans were able to use this design. I do not want to address the question whether the AI can be an inventor. So the decisions of the patent offices based on the current state of AI technology and the current law seem to be correct. AI is not sufficiently autonomous to grant it the position of an inventor. However, it would be quite interesting to take a closer look at how the AI systems came up with the final "inventions."

As already mentioned, another example of the use of AI in product development is the case of the evolved NASA space antenna.[24] Here the computer systems that were equipped with AI based on evolutionary algorithms required merely ten hours to come up with the unorthodox design that the human team members describe as a bent paperclip. This seems as an extremely fast process of product design. However, the sole focus on the work of the AI ignores the still required human input and its importance for the final product. In fact, approximately three months of work went into the setup of the evolutionary algorithms and the final design of the antenna.[25] When compared, this means that the AI works pretty fast but it currently still requires a lot of human input in terms of time and probably also expertize. The human factor should therefore not be discarded.

A third example from the area of product or process design that is also associated with the aforementioned Steven L. Thaler is a toothbrush.[26] Here, the AI was provided with data on preexisting types of toothbrushes and some information regarding the effectiveness of the cleaning process of those toothbrushes. The AI than went on and combined and changed the original designs until it came up with a new toothbrush that supposedly is better than any previously manufactured. According to the literature, the design was, once again, such that no human designer could have imagined. But here again, the input regarding the prior art and the desired outcome—clean teeth—came from the human.

Also, beyond the examples, the AI does not come up with the idea that an invention is required. It does not initiate the inventive process. This and the input required to start the process of invention may change in the future, but at the moment,

---

22. For a history of this invention, *see* Plotkin, *The Genie in the Machine: How Computer-Automated Inventing Is Revolutionizing Law and Business*, Stanford Law Books, 2009, 51 ff.
23. *See* US patent 7,117,186 B2. The patent claims a method and apparatus for automatic synthesis of controllers.
24. Gregory S Hornby et al., *Automated Antenna Design with Evolutionary Algorithms* (2006) Collection of Technical Papers—Space 2006 Conference https://ti.arc.nasa.gov/m/pub-archive/1244h/1244%20(Hornby).pdf.
25. *Ibid.*
26. *Ibid.* (n. 22).

it is still very much dependent on human beings. The questions that arise with respect to patent law lie elsewhere. Two main requirements for a patent are novelty and inventive step. Novelty meaning that something is totally new and inventive step meaning that coming up with the idea behind the patent requires something more than the ordinary expert in the fields can be expected to come up with. I will address the requirements below. The question now is, if the human controlling the AI would not be able to come up with the resulting design without the AI, can he or she then be an inventor in the sense of the law or how should we determine who the respective expert in the field is.

3.3 Prior Art Search

The EPO is currently researching how AI can be used to support the patent granting procedures.[27] Of course, on a more basic level, we know that the EPO provides us with machine translations of patent documents which are pretty good and which are based on an ANN-type AI system.[28] But AI should be able to do more. It should be able to search prior art more efficiently and on a truly global scale. So, AI may be able to support the examiner in researching prior art and comparing it to the claimed invention. It could search and compare more documents from a much broader source than any examiner or patent attorney ever could.

This automatically leads to the question, whether or not the issue of novelty or the introduction of new prior art will still be an issue in any future post-grant proceedings—either in opposition or litigation. There is a high probability that these issues will still be discussed in the next decades. After all, not all published prior art is available in electronic form that can be researched by and AI and prior art presented on academic conferences or trade shows will probably never be available for analysis by AI. But even with respect to electronically stored information, there are currently doubts regarding the effectiveness and accuracy of AI in the prior art search process. In April 2020 a study by Cardiff University on behalf of the UK PTO has been published regarding the feasibility of AI-assisted prior art search.[29] The results of the study are sobering. The researchers used "a wide range of state-of-the-art supervised and unsupervised machine learning approaches" and suggested a number of areas where AI may be used as a supporting tool in the patent application process but they also concluded that "it was not feasible with current AI tools to provide a fully automated solution as part of the application filing process." So while AI may be helpful in the search of prior art it seems to be far away from identifying each and every available piece of prior art. In some way, this may seem strange because the AI cannot do what

27. *See* the presentation by the EPO *Artificial Intelligence at the EPO* available at: https://www.wipo.int/edocs/mdocs/globalinfra/en/wipo_ip_itai_ge_18/wipo_ip_itai_ge_18_p8.pdf.
28. *See* https://www.epo.org/searching-for-patents/helpful-resources/patent-translate.html#:~:text=The%20EPO%20and%20Google%20have,into%20English%2C%20French%20and%20German.
29. The study is available at https://assets.publishing.service.gov.uk/government/uploads/system/uploads/attachment_data/file/887907/aI-assisted-patent-prior-art-searching-feasibility-study.pdf.

we expect the person skilled in the art to be able to do. This brings us straight to the law on novelty and inventive step.

4 THE LAW ON NOVELTY AND INVENTIVE STEP

If we look at the requirements for patentability, there are four important steps: the question of patentable subject matter, novelty, inventive step, and industrial applicability. Regarding AI as the subject matter of patent protection, the issues lie very much in the details of software protection, and I have discussed them elsewhere.[30] When it comes to the subject matter of products or processes designed by an AI or at least as the result of use of AI, the answers will also very much depend on the specific case and will not differ from general subject matter considerations. In addition, industrial applicability does not seem to be a real issue with respect to the results of AI-based innovation processes. However, novelty and inventive step are patentability requirements that may be strongly influenced by the use of AI and which finally receive more attention.[31] Both requirements are laid down in Article 27 of the Agreement on Trade-Related Aspects of Intellectual Property Rights (TRIPs), which stipulates that "patents shall be available for any inventions, whether products of processes, in all fields of technology, provided they are **new**, involve an **inventive step** and are capable of industrial application."[32] In line with the minimum requirements of TRIPs, the EPC and the US law both contain the respective requirements.

4.1 Novelty

The rationale behind the requirement of novelty is that technology, which is already available to the public (i.e., in the public domain), should not be monopolized through the patent system. The EPC regulates with respect to novelty the following:[33]

> Article 54 EPC:
> (1) An invention shall be considered to be new if *it does not form part of the state of the art.*
> (2) The state of the art shall be held to comprise everything *made available to the public* by means of a written or oral description, by use, or in any other way, before the date of filing of the European patent application.

The requirements in US law are basically the same and laid down in 35 U.S. Code § 102. The important point is that novelty is a one-on-one assessment. The claimed invention is compared to the relevant prior art and only if all features of the patent application can be found in one single piece of prior art, novelty will be declined.

30. Peter R. Slowinski, *Rethinking Software Protection* (n. 3).
31. *See*, for example, Daniele Fabris, *From PHOSITA to the MOSITA: Will "Secondary Considerations" Save Pharmaceutical Patents from Artificial Intelligence?* (2020) 51 IIC 685-708. DOI: 10.1007/s40319-020-00953-8; Ryan Abbott, *Everything Is Obvious*, (2019) 66 UCLA Law Rev 2-52.
32. Emphasis added.
33. Emphasis added.

Although this requirement for patentability is important in light of the reasoning behind patents, it does not play an overly crucial role in practice. Already today, such cases are rare due to the possibilities of prior art search before the application for the patent and also because of the relatively low probability of two inventors coming up with exactly the same idea in the future. Nevertheless, it is important to keep in mind that the state of the art does not only include written descriptions but also oral ones, actual use and any other way, such as display of the technology.

4.2 Inventive Step

While the requirement of novelty aims at excluding identical prior disclosures to be patented, the requirement of inventive step wants to ensure that products or process that are so close to the preexisting knowledge that lie at the fingertips of every expert in the field do not receive a monopoly-like protection. In practice, this is the requirement that is at the heart of every dispute where patentability is actually in question,[34] and it has therefore even been considered to be "The Ultimate Condition for Patentability."[35] For reasons of clarity, it is worth mentioning, that the requirement of inventive step as stipulated by TRIPs and the EPC is in fact called nonobviousness in the US without substantial differences as to the nature of the requirement. According to Article 56 EPC:

> An invention shall be considered as involving an inventive step if, having regard to the state of the art, it is *not obvious to a person skilled in the art.*[36]

The Person Skilled in the Art (POSITA)[37] is not an inventor. It is an expert with average knowledge in his or her field. It may be a team of experts. The POSITA has at her disposal all the tools that are typical in the field. Of course, this is not and never can be an actual person, since no human being and not even a realistically large team of humans, can possess all the knowledge and probably also will not have all the means at their disposal that can be used to get from the prior art to the invention. Instead, it is a legal construct specifically aiming at providing an objective measure for the distance between the available knowledge and the knowledge embedded in the invention. Therefore, while there are some differences between the way how this requirement is established in the US and in Europe,[38] the basic approach is the same: what is the prior art and how can the POSITA/PHOSITA arrive at the teaching of the

---

34. For the US, *see* John R Allison & Mark A Lemley, *Empirical Evidence on the Validity of Litigated Patents*, (1998) 26 AIPLA Q.J. 185, 209 table 2. For the relevance of novelty and inventive step in the assessment of validity of granted patents in Germany, *see* Peter Hess, Tilman Müller-Stoy & Martin Wintermeier, *Are Patents Merely "Paper Tigers"?*, available at https://www.bardehle.com/fileadmin/Webdata/contentdocuments/broschures/Patent_Papiertiger.pdf, originally published in German as Peter Hess, Tilman Müller-Stoy & Martin Wintermeier, *Are Patents Merely "Paper Tigers"?*, Mitt. 2014, 439.
35. *Non-obviousness: The Ultimate Condition of Patentability* (John F. Witherspoon ed., 1980).
36. Emphasis added.
37. In US law the concept is known as PHOSITA—Person Having Ordinary Skill in the Art.
38. For an overview of the differences, *see* Fabris (n. 31) 686 ff.

invention if the prior art is the starting point. For this, other than with novelty, a combination of features is possible.

4.3 Applying the Law to AI in General

The crucial point for the requirements of novelty and inventive step and their assessment is the identification of the prior art. For inventors, patent practitioners, patent offices, and courts, this means (1) access to the prior art and (2) comparison of the prior art with the claimed invention. At least with respect to prior art, that has been stored by electronic means and that can be accessed publicly through the world wide web or other mean of electronic access, AI will have an influence on its availability and therefore can influence the patentability of invention. As mentioned above regarding the study in the UK, the overall usefulness of AI for patent applications is still doubtful.

If AI is used not merely to identify prior art, but to create new inventions, the impact will be mostly seen with respect to inventive step. Since an invention will be usually regarded as obvious if the POSITA would have come up with it by combining features from different pieces of prior art, AI will probably be at an advantage in this respect. An AI system based on ML or DL can combine features much faster and with higher accuracy with respect to the final result than a human can. This may result in a situation where most inventions will become obvious subject to the availability of a suitable AI and the required data.[39] It has therefore been argued by others that the standard of the POSITA should be changed to MOSITA (the Machine of Ordinary Skill in the Art) and that secondary considerations such as the long felt but unsolved needs should become more important than the mere comparison with the prior art.[40] This could in fact prevent a rise of the bar of inventive step to levels that render most inventions obvious. Whether this is required or desirable in light of the ratio behind patents, is a question that I will address in the final part of this chapter.

4.4 Applying the Law to the Use Cases

When we apply the law to the use cases presented earlier, the situation is very similar to that in the abstract application of the law to AI in general. With respect to the use of AI by patent offices such as the EPO or patent applicants and their patent attorneys, the use of AI will with high probability change the patent system over time. Even if the study by Cardiff University shows that a completely autonomous search for prior art is still far away from becoming reality, the same study already hints at possibilities how AI may be applied today to help in the overall process. Therefore, AI may lower the costs for prior art search and therefore for patent applications and thus level the playing field between SMEs and larger players. That is, of course, if the AI-supported search is made available to SMEs. Of course, there will still be cases where the relevant prior art

39. Abbott (n. 31).
40. Fabris (n. 31) 692 and 698 ff.

is based on prior public use or display at a fair but such cases will probably decline in numbers with the continuing digitalization of our society.

In the case of search for new pharmaceuticals or new uses for already discovered compounds, the question remains why the use of AI technologies in the last decades seemingly did not have a substantial effect on the length of product development or the costs of product development. Here additional data would be helpful. It may be that those illnesses that still require treatment or a vaccine are becoming more complex compared to those in the past and therefore AI simply prevents the development cycles from becoming even longer than before. But the question remains, whether the discovery of new uses or new compound by an AI should be rewarded in the same way as it has been in the past. At least as soon as we reach a level where AI will become a tool as common to the pharmaceutical industry as a microscope, new discoveries may remain novel but will very likely become obvious. Denying such inventions the protection through patents may then result in shift away from search for new use and combination of existent compound and knowledge to mere search for completely new compounds. It is quite questionable whether or not this is desired. One way to deal with this development may be an alteration of the requirements for inventive step and a stronger focus on secondary considerations.[41] A different approach may be to question the current absolute compound protection and the protection of secondary uses by means of patents. If no real effort or investment is involved in finding the compound or use, the only rational behind the patent protection for pharmaceuticals remain the high costs of developing a marketable product from the original idea through various stages of clinical and non-clinical trials. However, these trials are not part of the inventive process in the strict sense. Instead, they are the result of regulatory requirements. So we may want to think about alternative ways of compensation for the costs involved in these trials instead of rewarding an automated process that is at the very beginning of the product development.

This leaves us with the third use case, the product development outside of the area of pharmaceuticals. As we have seen, AI in the form of ML/DL and evolutionary algorithms can come up with new products or product designs. This means that the product designer has a new tool at hand. This may of course have an effect if not on novelty then definitely on inventive step if (1) the use of AI is obvious for the task and (2) if the new design is "obvious" for the machine. It is hard to imagine cases where the second requirement will not be present.[42] Here again, just as with pharmaceutical, the solution may be found in changing the standard for inventiveness. But here, even more than with respect to pharmaceuticals, the question is why. If the development of a new product or process can be achieved fairly easy and with fairly low costs, patent protection may not be required. Instead, the market forces of competition combined with the rules against unfair competition and other forms of IP such as design protection may suffice. We may want to think about extending the design protection to technical features in cases where patent protection is not available. So for example in the case of the toothbrush or the NASA antenna a far shorter period for protection may

41. *Ibid.*
42. Fabris (n. 31) 691.

become available and more than adequate with respect to the skill and labor invested in the invention.

5 CONCLUSIONS AND CONSIDERATIONS

AI is definitely a game-changer in many aspects of our lives and with respect to business models and the general economy. However, it is important to assess its impact not only on industry and humanity in a realistic way but also on patent law. Currently, no AI system is able to recognize the need for a new invention by itself and it does not initiate the inventive process by itself. Furthermore, even the feeding of required data, models, and algorithms depends on humans, and in most cases not just one human but whole teams of experts from various fields of technology. So AI is far from becoming an inventor itself. Furthermore, the AI can only access information that is available in electronic form and currently there does not seem to be an AI with the capability of actually researching all electronically available information for use in an invention. However, AI systems keep evolving and their availability and use are becoming more widespread. This may in fact influence the requirements for patentability, namely novelty and most importantly inventive step, in the years to come. It may also mean that the bar for patentability will rise.

This is simply a fact or at least a possibility. It does not tell us whether this is good or bad for innovation and competition as such. Politicians, patent practitioners, and patent offices may see a rise in the bar for patentability and the resulting reduction of patent application and granted patents as negative for innovation. But such a conclusion is far from the truth. We need to remember that patents as such do not provide incentives for innovation per se. It is competition and the pressure to survive in the market that drive innovation. Patents are granted because we know that in some cases the effort put into an innovation may not be sufficiently compensated in the market if imitation follows too easy and too fast after the initial innovation. This free riding can then result in a reduction of incentives to innovate and patents just restore those incentives.

But if the availability and the use of AI should make the process of innovation easier, faster, and cheaper, the costs for innovation drop and the requirement for monopoly prizes based on patents to recoup the costs of innovation are reduced as well. This may mean that in some areas of technology the need for patents as incentives for innovation will vanish. This may also mean that other reasons for the patent system, such as the availability of new knowledge through the patent register or the possibility to trade intangible goods will become more important. In any case, the rise of AI provides us with the opportunity to rethink not only the applicability of some of the patentability requirements as such but also the functioning and set-up of the overall patent system. In light of the fact that patents as drivers or impediments of innovation have now been discussed for some decades, this may be something to be welcomed and not to be feared. After all, technological changes quite often have influenced the law and sharpened the perspective on how it should be shaped to benefit society.

Part IV Patents and ICT Sector

CHAPTER 13

Over-Enforcement Practices by Patent Assertion Entities in Europe: The Practice of National Courts*

Amandine Léonard

The topic of Patent Assertion Entities (hereinafter 'PAEs') in Europe has recently seen an increased interest by the European Commission (EC),[1] the European Patent Office (EPO),[2] industry,[3] as well as academics.[4] Traditionally, it has been argued that the

* This chapter is based on a research conducted for the completion of a PhD Thesis. A. Léonard, *Abuse of Rights in European Patent Law: Reconsidering the principle of the prohibition of abuse of rights as an internal correction mechanism against over-enforcement practices by right holders*, KU Leuven Centre for IT&IP Law (May 2019). The original text is with the author.

1. M. de Heide et al., *Study on the changing role of intellectual Property in the semiconductor industry – including non-practicing entities*, Final Report for the European Commission (April 2015). N. Thumm and G. Gabison (eds) JRC Report, *Patent Assertion Entities in Europe: Their Impact on Innovation and Knowledge Transfer in ICT Markets* (2016), https://ec.europa.eu/digital-single-market/en/news/study-patent-assertion-entities-europe (accessed 10 March 2019).
2. Report from Europe Economics for the EPO. Economic Analysis of the Unitary Patent and the Unified Patent Court (April 2014), https://www.epo.org/about-us/services-and-activities/chief-economist/studies.html (accessed 21 March 2019). ESAB Report for the EPO. Workshops on the unitary patent and the Unified Patent Court (December 2013), https://www.epo.org/news-issues/news/2014/20140430.html (accessed 21 March 2019).
3. IP2Innovate, IP2Innovate calls for UPC judges to receive training to counter abusive patent litigation tactics (13 December 2017), http://www.ip2innovate.eu/advocacy/ (accessed 10 March 2019). IP2Innovate, Supporting Innovation in Europe Through a Balanced Patent System: A Paper Responding to the European Commission's IP Package (June 2018), http://www.ip2innovate.eu (accessed 10 March 2019).
4. B. Love et al., *Patent Assertion Entities in Europe*, in D. Sokol (ed.) *Patent Assertion Entities and Competition Policy*, Cambridge University Press (2017). G. Gabison, *Lessons That Europe Can Learn from the US Patent Assertion Entity Phenomenon*, 24 Info. & Comm. Tech. L., 278 (2015). N. Thumm, *The Good, the Bad and the Ugly – The Future of Patent Assertion Entities in Europe*, 30 Tech. An. & Strat. Mngmnt., 1046 (2018). C. Helmers and L. McDonagh, *Trolls at the High Court?*, LSE Law, Society and Economy Working Paper No. 13/2012 (2012). J. Contreras and P. Picht, *Patent Assertion Entities and Legal Exceptionalism in Europe and the United States: A*

fragmented system of litigation in Europe, the differences in national legal systems, the availability of funding for PAEs as well as cultural differences, have prevented PAEs from entering the European market.[5] However, recent studies show that PAE activities in Europe have grown.[6]

This increase of PAEs activity has created concerns that they may have opportunities to abuse the current (and future) patent litigation system in Europe. In 2017, a Support Study for the evaluation of the intellectual property Enforcement Directive notably mentioned that the presence of Non-Practicing Entities (hereinafter 'NPEs') may suggest that the tools and remedies available to defendants in patent infringement cases may have to be reviewed in order to ensure that an equilibrium between litigants was sustained and that abuses of patent rights were avoided.

This chapter focuses on these concerns vis-à-vis NPEs, and particularly PAEs, and the opportunities they may (or may not) have to abuse the patent litigation system in Europe in the sense of possibilities to engage in over-enforcement practices. The purpose of this chapter is twofold. First, it seeks to assess whether national courts in Europe have taken into consideration the identity of asserters in their evaluation of the case, i.e., whether they have established a distinction between NPEs/PAEs and more conventional patent holders such as operating companies. Second, it also seeks to identify the mechanisms used by these courts to limit the over-enforcement practices of NPEs/PAEs. The case law and other developments discussed in this chapter are up-to-date as of March 2018.

1 GROWING CONCERNS REGARDING OVER-ENFORCEMENT PRACTICES BY PAEs IN EUROPE

In recent years, commentators have argued that the European Directive on the Enforcement of Intellectual Property Rights (hereinafter 'IPRED' or 'Enforcement Directive')[7] may provide for an (overly) strong system of protection in favour of right holders. Undeniably, effective means of enforcing intellectual property rights (hereinafter 'IPRs') are of paramount importance for the success of the internal market as well

Comparative View, Max Planck Institute for Innovation & Competition Research Paper No. 17-11 (2017). K. Larson, *The Exploitation and Enforcement of Patents by Non-practicing Entities: Practices, Developments, and Future Challenges* (Thesis) Haken School of Economics, Economics and Society (2017). D. Krauspenhaar, *Liability Rules in Patent Law – A Legal and Economic Analysis*, Munich Studies on Innovation and Competition, Springer pp. 82 et seq. (2015).

5. A. Mayergoyz, *Lessons from Europe on How to Tame U.S. Patent Trolls*, 42 Cornell Intl. L. J., 241 (2009) p. 265. S. Fusco, *Markets and Patents Enforcement: A Comparative Investigation of Non-Practicing Entities in the U.S. and Europe*, 20 Mich. Telecomm. & Tech. L. Rev., 439 (2014). G. Gabison, *Lessons that Europe Can Learn from the US Patent Assertion Entity Phenomenon*, 24 Info. & Comm. Tech. L., 278 (2015).
6. Darts-IP Report. NPE Litigation in the European Union: Facts and Figures (19 February 2018), https://www.darts-ip.com/npe-litigation-in-the-european-union-facts-and-figures-2/ (accessed 10 March 2019). V. Sterzi, J-P. Rameshkoumar, & J. Van Der Pol, *Non-practicing Entities and Transparency in Patent Ownership in Europe, Bordeaux Economics Working Papers* (2020) BxWP2020-10, https://ideas.repec.org/p/grt/bdxewp/2020-10.html (accessed 17 August 2020).
7. Directive 2004/48/EC of the European Parliament and the Council of 29 April 2004 on the enforcement of intellectual property rights, O.J. L 157/45, 30 March 2004.

as to reach the objectives of substantive intellectual property laws.[8] However, an imbalanced system of litigation offers opportunities for over-enforcement practices which may, in turn, be detrimental to the whole system.[9]

In patent law in particular, US commentators have claimed that patent holders benefit from opportunities to abusively exercise their patent rights[10] or that new uses of patents are inappropriate as they keep pushing the system further away from its intentions.[11] The rise of new actors on the enforcement scene such as NPEs or PAEs (also called patent trolls) has been at the heart of the debate.[12]

8. *Ibid.*, Rec. 3.
9. G. Van Overwalle and E. van Zimmeren, *Functions and Limits of Patent Law* in E. Claes, W. Devroe & B. Keirsbilck (eds) *Facing the Limits of the Law*, Springer (2009). R.M. Hilty, *The Role of Enforcement in Delineating the Scope of IP Rights*, Max Planck Institute for Innovation and Competition Research Paper No. 15-03 (2015), http://ssrn.com/abstract=2602221 (accessed 18 March 2019). T. Dreier, *Balancing Proprietary and Public Domain Interests: Inside or Outside of Proprietary Rights?* in R. Dreyfuss et al. (eds) *Expanding the Boundaries of Intellectual Property: Innovation Policy for the Knowledge Society*, Oxford University Press (2001). D. Krauspenhaar, *Liability Rules in Patent Law – A Legal and Economic Analysis*, Munich Studies on Innovation and Competition, Springer (2015). H.-P. Götting, M. Du Vall, and H. Röder-Hitschke, *Enforcing Intellectual Property Rights: Necessary Instruments Versus Over-enforcement*, Nomos Publishers (2012). R.M. Hilty and K.-C. Liu (eds) *The Enforcement of Patents*, Kluwer Law International (2012). X. Seuba, *The Global Regime for the Enforcement of Intellectual Property Rights*, Cambridge University Press, p. 23 (2017). K. Weatherall, *Safeguards for Defendant Rights and Interests in International Intellectual Property Enforcement Treaties*, 32 Am. U. Int'l. L. Rev. 211 (2016).
10. T. Molino, *Strengthening the Patent System by Ending Patent Abuse*, BSA TechPost (March 2015), https://techpost.bsa.org/2015/03/19/strengthening-the-patent-system-by-ending-patent-abuse/, (accessed 10 March 2019). P. Hall, Patent Law Broken, *Abused to Stifle Innovation*, WIReD (July 2013), https://www.wired.com/insights/2013/07/patent-law-broken-abused-to-stifle-innovation/ (accessed 10 March 2019). T. Worstall, *Is This Apple Abusing The Patent System Or The USPTO Abusing It?*, Forbes (November 2012), https://www.forbes.com/sites/timworstall/2012/11/14/is-this-apple-abusing-the-patent-system-or-the-uspto-abusing-it/#27d56c2c4ce2 (accessed 10 March 2019). R. Bell, *Litigation as an Abuse: European Commission and US Courts Draw a Line under 'Patent Wars' While Adopting a Common Approach on Standard Essential Patents*, Business Law International, 15.3 (2014). M. Street, *Turning the Tide on Patent Abuse: Vermont's New Law Already Inspiring Other States to Act*, 106(2) ABA Banking Journal, (2014). M. Jones, *Application for Central Amendment of a Patent after Revocation at First Instance Does Not of Itself Render an Appeal an Abuse of Process*, 9(7) J.I.P.L.P., 538-540 (2014). J. Mazzone, *Copyfraud and Other Abuses of Intellectual Property Law*, Stanford Law Book (2011).
11. B. Love, *Bad Actors and the Evolution of Patent Law*, 101 Va. L. Rev., 1-13 (2015).
12. M.A. Lemley and R.C. Feldman, *Is Patent Enforcement Efficient?*, 98 B. U. L. Rev., 649 (2018). R.C. Feldman and M.A. Lemley, *The Sound and Fury of Patent Activity*, Olin Stanford Working Paper Series No. 521 (2018). C. Tucker, S. Kiebzak and G. Rafert, *The Effect of Patent Litigation and Patent Assertion Entities on Entrepreneurial Activity*, 45(1) Research Policy, 218-231 (2016). L. Cohen, U.G. Gurun and S.D. Kominers, *Patent Trolls: Evidence from Targeted Firms*, Harvard Business School Finance Working Paper No. 15-002 (2016). D.O. Taylor, *Legislative Responses to Patent Assertion Entities*, 23 Tex. Intel. Prop. L. J., 313 (2015). D.L. Schwartz and J.P. Kesan, *Analysing the Role of Non-practicing Entities in the Patent System*, 99 Cornell L. Rev., 425 (2014). Y. Heled, *Patent Trolls as Parasites*, Ga. St. U. Coll. L., Legal Studies Research Paper No. 2014-33 (2014). M.J. Mazzeo, J.H. Ashtor and S. Zyontz, *Do NPEs Matter? Non-practicing Entities and Patent Litigation Outcomes*, 9 J. Comp. L. & Econ., 879 (2013). A. Hagiu and D.B. Yoffie, *The New Patent Intermediaries: Platforms, Defensive Aggregators and Super-Aggregators*, 27 J. Econ. Persp., 45 (2013). A.W. Wang, *Rise of the Patent Intermediaries*, 25 Berkeley Tech. L.J., 159 (2010). R.P. Merges, *The Trouble with Trolls: Innovation, Rent-Seeking, and Patent Law Reform*, 24 Berkeley Tech. L. J., 1583 (2009).

In 2016, the EC conducted an evaluation of the Enforcement Directive to further improve the application and enforcement of IPRs in Europe. Respondents to the public consultation[13] encouraged that more attention is placed on the risk of abusive litigation by PAEs and that 'a well-balanced approach for injunctive relief in predatory patent assertion cases' should be favoured. Similarly, the authors of the *Support Study for the ex-post evaluation and ex-ante impact analysis of the IPR Enforcement Directive (IPRED)* [14] concluded that there was sufficient evidence indicating a need to further investigate the tools and remedies on the defendant side to assess whether there was a need to re-balance the system of adjudication. A particular issue in this context was the topic of PAEs which may engage in abusive exercises of patent rights and which could develop to sizeable magnitude if enforcement tools happen to be too strong.[15] Following the public consultation and the support study, the Commission published its guidance paper on 'certain aspects of Directive 2004/48/EC on the Enforcement of IPRs'[16] and a communication on 'a balanced IP enforcement system responding to today's societal changes'.[17] In the latter document, the Commission explicitly stated that the communication aimed at ensuring a balanced approach to IPR enforcement *and* to prevent abuse of measures, procedures and remedies set out in the Enforcement Directive.[18]

2 IDENTIFICATION OF THE PRACTICES ADOPTED BY PAEs

Before being able to identify the mechanisms relied upon by national courts to curb over-enforcement practices of PAEs, these practices must be distinguished. A thorough literature review and case law analysis led to the identification of seven categories of practices which are commonly adopted by PAEs. The proposed list is not exhaustive. However, it aspires at being sufficiently flexible to encompass future variations in the practices adopted by PAEs.

First, PAEs can benefit from the fact that they are non-practicing entities, i.e., they are not involved in the manufacturing of products and/or do not provide services to consumers. Strictly speaking, this factor does not necessarily qualify as an element of an enforcement strategy as it is not related to a specific action from a right holder.

13. European Commission – Summary of responses to the public consultation on the evaluation and modernisation of the legal framework for IPR enforcement (14 April 2016), https://ec.europa.eu/digital-single-market/en/news/summary-report-public-consultation-evaluation-and-review-eprivacy-directive (accessed 10 March 2019).
14. Support Study for the ex-post evaluation and ex-ante impact analysis of the IPR enforcement Directive (IPRED). Final Report (2017), https://publications.europa.eu/en/publication-detail/-/publication/1e3b2f41-d4ba-11e7-a5b9-01aa75ed71a1/language-en (accessed 10 March 2019).
15. *Ibid.*, at 139.
16. Communication from the Commission to the European Parliament, the Council and the European Economic and Social Committee – *Guidance on certain aspects of Directive 2004/48/EC of the European Parliament and of the Council on the enforcement of IPRs*. Brussels, 29 November 2017, COM (2017) 708 final.
17. Communication from the Commission to the European Parliament, the Council and the European Economic and Social Committee – *A balanced IP enforcement system responding to today's societal challenges*. Brussels 29 November 2017, COM (2017) 707 final.
18. Communication from the Commission, *supra* n. 16.

However, the type of business model adopted by an asserter may have a particular influence on the overall assessment of over-enforcement practices.[19]

Second, contrary to operating companies which traditionally engage in litigation with their competitors, PAEs target a wide range of potential infringers. In particular, it is argued that PAEs make a business out of suing secondary infringers of a particular technology rather than those who directly manufacture products embodying this technology.[20] They also send multiple demand letters and threats of litigation to end-users, i.e., customers buying off-the-shelf patent products, or retailers.[21]

A third practice common to PAEs relates to the choice they make with regard to the patents they assert. On the one hand, there is a significant body of literature sustaining that the patents enforced by PAEs are of low or dubious quality[22] or that their targets do not infringe the asserted patents.[23] On the other hand, some studies have shown that patents enforced by NPEs were generally similar, in terms of weakness or strength, to other litigated patents by operating companies and therefore refute the theory according to which they only enforce weak patents.[24]

Another common trait of PAEs resides in the fact that they threaten to sue companies but also propose quick settlements at a fraction of the costs of defence in litigation.[25] This technique is referred to as 'nuisance value suits' or 'nuisance value settlements'.[26] As such, the power of courts on nuisance settlements is rather limited as these settlements are concluded outside of the courtrooms. However, to know whether a patent holder engaged in nuisance agreements with alleged infringers can serve as a

---

19. An additional element which could also be considered under this first category is the actual role of PAEs as intermediaries between original inventors and their entitlement in case of infringement. In some studies, it is suggested that transfers from PAEs to original inventors or, more generally, to contributors on the market, are not realized. M. Risch, *Patent Troll Myths*, 42 Seton Hall L. Rev., 457, 493 (2012). Feldman and Lemley, *supra* n. 12, at 92.
20. D.H. Brean, *Ending Unreasonable Royalties: Why Nominal Damages are Adequate to Compensate Patent Assertion Entities for Infringement*, 39 Vt. L. Rev., 867, 881 (2015).
21. Love, *supra* n. 11, at 4. US FTC – *Patent Assertion Entity Activity: An FTC Study*, 63, 78 (2016), https://www.ftc.gov/reports/patent-assertion-entity-activity-ftc-study (accessed 10 March 2019).
22. Cohen, Gurun and Kominers, *supra* n. 12, at 2 and the studies cited. Taylor, *supra* n. 12, at 318. Love *supra* n. 11, at 6. S.P. Miller, *What's the connection between repeat litigation and patent quality? A (partial) defence of the most litigated patents*, 16 Stan. Tech. L. Rev. 313 (2013). B.J. Love, *An Empirical Study of Patent Litigation Timing: Could a Patent Term Reduction Decimate Trolls Without Harming Innovators?*, 161 Univ. Penn. L. Rev., 1309 (2013).
23. Although it is also claimed that better evidence and data is still needed. D.L. Schwartz and J.P. Kesan, *Analysing the role of non-practicing entities in the patent system*, 99 *Cornell L. Rev.*, 425, 451 (2014).
24. Risch, *supra* n. 19, at 480-483, 498. J. Rantanen, *Slaying the Troll: Litigation as an Effective Strategy Against Patent Threats*, 23 Santa Clara Computer & High Tech. L.J., 159 (2006). T. Fischer and J. Henkel, *Patent trolls on markets for technology – An empirical analysis of NPEs' patent acquisitions*, Research Policy, 41(9), 1519-1533 (2012). J.R. Allison, M.A. Lemley and D.L. Schwartz, *How Often Do Non-Practicing Entities Win Patent Suits?*, Stanford Law and Economics Olin Working Paper No. 485 (2016).
25. Brean, *supra* n. 20, at 881. P.R. Gugliuzza, *Regulating Patent Assertions*, B. U. L. Pub. L. Research Paper No. 16-36, 4 (2016).
26. H.O. Chen, *Combating baseless patent suits: Rule 11 sanctions with technology-specific application*, 54 Jurimetrics J., 135, 146 (2014). E. Rogers and Y. Jeon, *Inhibiting Patent Trolling: A New Approach for Applying Rule 11*, 12 Nw. J. Tech. & Intell. Prop., 291 (2014). US FTC Study, *supra* n. 21, at 20.

factor to take into consideration for the assessment of over-enforcement practices. With regard to nuisance suits, PAEs may make frivolous and vexatious claims of infringement in the sense that their claims are vague, overly broad or made without prior investigation and therefore lack substantial ground.

A fifth characteristic of PAEs is that they made a habit of sending vague demand letters to potential infringers threatening litigation.[27] The vagueness of these letters notably comes from the fact that the asserter does not provide sufficient information to the alleged infringer on which patent has been infringed or which technology exploited by the alleged infringer is infringing.

Next to threatening demand letters, PAEs also rely on the threat of injunctive relief. This plays an essential role in the strategy of PAEs as the simple threat of litigation accompanied by the possibility of obtaining an injunction significantly raises their bargaining power in negotiation.[28] This possibility allows PAEs to obtain fairly high settlement fees[29] or licensing fees which may exceed the patent holder's true economic contribution.[30]

Finally, it is argued that some PAEs, by taking a 'wait and sue' approach, engage in hold-up practices.[31] They wait until alleged infringers have made irreversible investments in a particular technology before asserting their claims.[32] The literature on patent hold-up is nonetheless controversial.[33] On the one hand, some argue that PAEs (as well as other patent holders) engage in such practice but that a situation of reverse hold-up (i.e., of hold-out) might be more problematic. Overall a situation of equilibrium should be found between these two extremes position. It remains that, if PAEs do

27. Brean, *supra* n. 20, at 877. V.R. Johnson, *Minimizing the costs of patent trolling*, 18 UCLA J. L. & Tech. 1, 10 (2014).
28. Rantanen, *supra* n. 24. J.L. Contreras, *When a Stranger Calls: Standards Outsiders and Unencumbered Patents*, University of Utah College of Law Research Paper No. 159 (2016). C.B. Seaman, *Permanent Injunctions in Patent Litigation After eBay: An Empirical Study*, 5, 25, 47, 56 (2 June 2015), https://ssrn.com/abstract=2617789 (accessed 24 March 2019). R.T. Holte and C.B. Seaman, *Patent Injunctions on Appeal: An Empirical Study of the Federal Circuit's Application of Ebay*, 92 Wash. L. Rev. 145 (2017).
29. S. Kwon and K. Motohashi, *Effect of Non-practicing Entities on Innovation Society and Policy: An agent-based model and simulation*, IAM Discussion Paper Series #033, 24 (2014).
30. Chen, *supra* n. 26, at 149. M.A. Lemley and C. Shapiro, *Patent Holdup and Royalty Stacking*, 85 Texas L. Rev., 1991 (2007).
31. According to Lemley and Shapiro (2007), a situation of patent hold-up occurs when '*the threat to obtain a permanent injunction greatly enhances the patent holder's negotiating power, leading to royalty rates that exceed a natural benchmark range based on the value of the patented technology and the strength of the patent*'. Lemley and Shapiro, *supra* n. 30, at 1991.
32. J.R. Allison, M.A. Lemley and D.L. Schwartz, *Understanding the Realities of Modern Patent Litigation*, Stanford Public Law Working Paper No. 2442451 (2014). J. Henkel and M. Reitzig, Patent Trolls, *the Sustainability of 'Locking-in-to-extort' Strategies, and Implications for Innovating Firms* (17 December 2010), https://ssrn.com/abstract=985602 (accessed 8 March 2019). K. Osenga, *Formerly Manufacturing Entities: Piercing the 'Patent Troll' Rhetoric*, 47 Connect. L. Rev., 435, 465 (2014). C.V. Chien, *From Arms Race to Marketplace: The New Complex Patent Ecosystem and Its Implications for the Patent System*, 62 Hastings L. J., 297, 319 (2010).
33. N. Siebrasse, *Holdup, Holdout and Royalty Stacking: A Review of the Literature*, in B. Biddle et al. (eds) *Patent Remedies and Complex Products: Toward a Global Consensus*, Cambridge University Press (2019). A. Layne-Farrar and K.M. Schmidt, *Licensing Complementary Patents: 'Patent Trolls', Market Structure, and 'Excessive' Royalties*, 25 Berkeley Tech. L.J., 1121 (2010).

engage in such rent-seeking practices, this may be taken into consideration by courts to assess an overall situation of over-enforcement.

As previously mentioned, this categorisation is not meant to represent an exhaustive list of the practices adopted by PAEs. They nonetheless represent common ways in which PAEs have exercised their patent rights and prerogatives. They will also be useful in the following part of this paper which aims at evaluating how national courts have limited and/or sanctioned over-enforcement practices.

3 THE RESPONSE OF NATIONAL COURTS TO OVER-ENFORCEMENT PRACTICES OF PAEs IN EUROPE

3.1 Methodology

Three sources have been relied upon in order to identify NPEs/PAEs which have been active in Europe. First, the 'Stanford NPE Litigation Dataset and taxonomy'[34] has been used as it provides the largest dataset of patent asserters as well as the most comprehensive categorisation of NPEs to date. Second, a list of NPEs/PAEs active before national European courts and identified in the work of Contreras et al. (2018),[35] Love et al. (2015),[36] Helmers and McDonagh (2012),[37] Pohlmann and Opitz (2010),[38] the JRC Report (2016),[39] as well as the Darts-IP Report (2018)[40] has been drawn. Finally, publicly available information has been used to complete the set of entities studied for this chapter. After this first selection, cases have been collected on the Darts-IP database.[41]

The literature review, as well as the search on the Darts-IP database, led to the identification of 48 entities having litigated in five chosen jurisdictions (i.e., Belgium, France, Germany, the Netherlands and the United Kingdom (UK)). A total of 97 cases (including first instances and appeal decisions) have been studied for this chapter. The majority of these cases took place in Germany (31 instances), followed by the UK (27 instances). Fewer disputes took place in France (19 instances), in the Netherlands (17 instances), and even more rarely in Belgium (3 instances). This result is not particularly surprising as Germany and the UK are the two European jurisdictions where most patent litigation takes place. A selection bias also explains the number of disputes

34. S.P. Miller et al., *Who's Suing Us? Decoding Patent Plaintiffs since 2000 with the Stanford NPE Litigation Dataset*, 21 Stan. Tech. L. Rev., 235 (2018).
35. J. Contreras et al., *Litigation of Standards-Essential Patents in Europe: A Comparative Analysis*, 32(5) Berkeley Technology Law Journal, 1457 (2018).
36. Love et al., *supra* n. 4.
37. C. Helmers and L. McDonagh, *Trolls at the High Court?*, LSE Law, Society and Economy Working Paper No. 13/2012 (2012).
38. T. Pohlmann and M. Opitz, *The Patent Troll Business: An Efficient model to enforce IPR? A typology of patent trolls, using empirical evidence from German case studies*, MPRA Paper No. 27342 (2010).
39. N. Thumm and G. Gabison (eds), JRC Report, Patent Assertion Entities in Europe: Their impact on innovation and knowledge transfer in ICT markets (2016), https://ec.europa.eu/digital-single-market/en/news/study-patent-assertion-entities-europe (accessed 10 March 2019).
40. Darts-IP Report, *supra* n. 6.
41. The case law and other developments discussed in this chapter are up-to-date as of March 2018.

before the courts of these two jurisdictions. So far, the academic studies conducted with regard to the actions of NPEs/PAEs in Europe have been concentrated on the jurisdictions of Germany and the UK. Since these studies served as a starting point for identifying the entities, the number of instances in these countries is necessarily higher than for other jurisdictions.

3.2 Safeguards and Sanctions Imposed by National Courts

The following section examines and describes the actual practices of NPEs/PAEs as well as the approaches adopted by national courts in Europe in order to curb the negative effects of over-enforcement. Notice should be taken that some practices identified in literature (such as nuisance value settlements) are more difficult to study in the context of patent litigation. Moreover, categories of practices may overlap, and a perfect classification of actions associated with specific court decisions was almost an impossible endeavour. Subjective choices have therefore been made in order to provide readable outcomes.

3.2.1 Taking Advantage of Being an NPE

As previously mentioned, PAEs may benefit from the fact that they are NPEs in order to obtain certain advantages which are not readily available to operating companies. One the main elements studied in the case law analysis was to identify whether courts in Europe paid attention to the particular form, or business model, adopted by NPEs/PAEs involved in litigation. Overall, it was found that national courts have not ignored the fact that, first, PAEs do not trade products on the market, second, that PAEs are almost exclusively interested in licensing fees and/or damages, and finally, that PAEs recourse to litigation as a business model.[42] However, the implications of this fact-finding varied.

42. In the UK: *Affymetrix Inc., Affymetrix UK Ltd. v. Multilyte Ltd.* [2004] EWHC 291 (Pat.) at 4: '[Affymetrix is] relatively small, does not trade in products based on its invention, but in the past has looked to the patents in suit as providing it with a stream of income in the form of license fees. Its principle, indeed only business as things stand at the moment, is the protection of its patents by litigation.' *Environmental Recycling Technologies Plc. v. Upcycle Holdings Ltd.* [2013] EWPCC 4, at 120: 'I was also told ... that the defendant does not use the former process (at least at present).'. *Nokia Corp. v. InterDigital Tech. Corp* [2006] EWCA (Civ.) 1618. *Unwired Planet International Ltd. v. Huawei & Samsung* [2016] EWHC 958 (Pat). The High Court observed that Ericsson divided its patent portfolio and assigned part of it to a 'hybrid NPE'. Hybrid because Ericsson retains the right to a substantial share in the licensing revenue and can transfer further (unspecified) patent to Unwired Planet in the future. The High Court also observed that Unwired Planet seeks to monetise patents and therefore has the opportunity and capacity to act aggressively, to threaten to sue and to sue licensees with no adverse consequences, reputational or otherwise. Moreover, the court noted that Unwired Planet had no interest in cross-licensing. *Unwired Planet International Ltd. v. Huawei & Samsung* [2015] EWHC 2097 (Pat.) at 47: 'Unwired Planet is a different kind of undertaking from Ericsson. [It] does not compete on the downstream market ... .' *SanDisk Corp. v. Philips et al.* [2007] EWHC 332 (Ch.), observing that SISVEL is an Italian company which principally carries on the business of licensing patents on behalf of patentees in the domestic electrical equipment field and has no manufacturing interest

First, in the majority of the cases, courts have considered that the fact that an asserter was not involved in the production or marketing of products and/or services, but only focused on litigation and/or licensing activities could not, on its own, be sufficient to claim that, per se, such entity was engaging in over-enforcement practices.

Courts have required that defendants in infringement suits substantially develop and argue how an NPE or PAE may have actually engaged in over-enforcement practices (e.g., anti-competitive practices or other legally reprehensible actions).[43] The case law analysis confirmed the findings of Contreras and Picht (2017) according to which 'courts in Europe seem hesitant to draw patent law or competition law consequences based solely on the fact that a party is a PAE'.[44] Courts have overall found legitimate for right holders (i.e., original owners or inventors as well as subsequent acquirers) to adopt a litigation or licensing business model in order to recoup investments devoted to research and development (R&D).[45] They have held that 'pure patent collecting companies' or 'patent exploitation companies' are entitled to the same measures and orders than operating companies. This seems to be particularly the case in Germany.[46]

---

of its own. In France: TGI Paris (3[e] ch. 2[e] s.) 17 Avril 2015, RG 14/14124. The TGI Paris observed that the business of Core Wireless Licensing Sarl is the monetisation of patents and grants of licences. TGI Paris (3[e] ch. 1[e] s.) 26 May 2016, RG 14/05090. The TGI noted that France Brevets is a company in charge of the monetisation of patents in Europe. T. Comm. Marseille, 20 Sept. 2016, RG 2016F01637, observing that SISVEL is the subsidiary of SISVEL international which ensure a link between manufacturers who wish to obtain an access to technology and the right holders who wish to grant licences to their portfolio. *See also* TGI Paris (3[e] ch. 3[e] s.) 30 October 2015, RG 13/06691. TGI Paris (3[e] ch. 1[e] s.) 17 March 2016, RG 12/12329. TGI Paris (3[e] ch. 3[e] s.) 10 March 2017, RG 14/16022. In Germany: LG Dusseldorf 4b O 140/13 (26 March 2015). LG Dusseldorf 4b O 16/16 (24 May 2016). LG Munchen 7 O 16945/15 (21 April 2016). OLG Munchen 6 U 2888/15 (02 June 2016). LG Mannheim 7 O 38/14 (26 February 2016). OLG Karlsruhe 6 U 29/11 (18 April 2011). LG Mannheim 7 O 20/11 (20 April 2012). LG Mannheim 7 O 255/10 (17 2011). OLG Mannheim 2 O 53/12 (28 February 2014). In Belgium: HvB te Brussel (8[ste] kamer) 03 September 2002, *DSM N.V. et al. v. Rohme Enzyme GmbH et al.* (AR nr. 2000/AR/2557). In the Netherlands: Rechtbank den Haag, 24 October 2014, KG ZA 14-870. Rechtbank den Haag, 6 Juli 2011, HA ZA 10-2069.

43. In the UK, *Vringo Infrastructure Inc. v. ZTE (UK) Ltd.* [2014] EWHC 3924 (Pat): 'although they never say so bluntly, ZTE contend that Vringo are 'patent trolls'. They contend that Vringo have conducted themselves in various inappropriate ways around the world against ZTE. However, ZTE have not alleged or pleaded that any of this conduct amounts to a defence relevant to the issues I have to decide at this trial [i.e. validity and infringement]. For example, no defence in competition law is relied on. Vringo do not accept that ZTE's allegations are correct. Whether ZTE are right or wrong about this is irrelevant and I will ignore these allegations. ... the main issue with ZTE's claim was therefore that it did not substantiate in what way Vringo was mis-behaving or how this could be related to the issues of validity and infringement.' In Germany: LG Dusseldorf 4b O 274/10 (24 April 2012). The LG required that the defendants substantiate their anticompetitive claim.
44. J. Contreras and P. Picht, *supra* n. 4, at 3.
45. In the UK, *Nokia OYJ v. IPCom GmbH & Co. KG* [2012] EWCA Civ 567. In the Netherlands: Rechtbank Den Haag, 24 October 2014, KG ZA 14-870: 'that Vringo does not trade competing products but wants to obtain a license is in itself not a reason to remove the measure. To obtain licensing fees is a 'real business' for which Vringo can rely essentially on its patents' (free translation).
46. *See*, for example, the following instances where German courts, contrary to their other national counterparts, emphasised the role of NPEs/PAEs as licensing companies. LG Dusseldorf 4b O 140/13 (26 March 2015). LG Dusseldorf 4b O 16/16 (24 May 2016). LG Munchen 7 O 16945/15

Second, and despite the fact that courts did not consider that the business model of PAEs was per se reprehensible, the fact that asserters were not engaged in the supply of goods and services, but rather favoured an exploitation based on litigation and licensing practices, nonetheless influenced the approach of certain courts vis-à-vis the measures and orders requested by the parties.

Notwithstanding some differences between national courts, the case law revealed that three fundamental elements of adjudication have been affected by the business model of PAEs. First, in light of the fact that the business model of PAEs relied on enforcement and licensing, courts have been particularly attentive to the validity of the asserted patents. This point is further discussed under '3.2.3. Choice of asserted patents' but one illustration can already be provided here. In 2013 the UK High Court[47] decided to stay the infringement proceedings initiated by an NPE until the EPO would deliver its decision on validity. The court considered that this was, in part, justified by the fact that the 'patentee's whole business is based on the exploitation of its patents. [When this is the case] extended uncertainty over a patent's validity ... is likely to be of significant consequence'.[48] Therefore, a decision on validity by the EPO should have been of primordial importance for the right holder and should have taken place before a decision on infringement by a national court.

The second element which has been affected by the fact that the right holder was a PAE relates to the grant or denial of various measures and orders, such as seizure measures, call-back and destruction orders, or rendering of accounts after findings of infringement. The method of calculation of damages has also been affected by the fact that the successful right holder was a PAE.

With regard to seizure measures, call-back and destruction orders, or the rendering of accounts, courts in all five jurisdictions have, on few occasions, taken into consideration the nature of the right holder in a broader proportionality exercise.[49] Once again, however, the fact that PAEs may have been non-producing companies did

(21 April 2016). OLG Munchen 6 U 2888/15 (02 June 2016). LG Mannheim 7 O 38/14 (26 February 2016). LG Dusseldorf 4b O 120/14 (19 January 2016). LG Mannheim 7 O 20/11 (20 April 2012). The court observed that (at 40): 'insofar as the defendants point out that the plaintiff is a pure collecting society and no producing competitor of the defendant, in the Chamber's view this is not likely to undermine the creditor's interest in enforcing injunctions' (free translation). OLG Karlsruhe 6 U 38/09 (11 May 2009). The defendant claimed that the applicant's interests as a patent licensing company in the enforcement of injunctive relief may not be equally worthy of protection as a participant in the market. On the other hand, the court considered that without enforcement, the right holder may suffer exceptionally high losses for which compensation may be difficult to obtain *ex post*. LG Dusseldorf 4b O 274/10 (24 April 2012) at 81: 'Even a pure "patent collecting society" is in principle entitled to injunctive relief. If it enforces [this remedy] to convince infringers to take a licence, that is fundamentally neither annoying nor unlawful. Rather, it is based on the permissible behaviour inherent in the current legal and economic order' (free translation).

47. *IPCom v. HTC* [2013] EWHC 2880 (Ch.) at 24: 'The commercial circumstances of the parties, including the fact that IPCom is not engaged in the supply of goods affected by the Patent, are [not] irrelevant. I do regard it as a pertinent factor.'
48. *Ibid.*, at 31.
49. In Germany, LG Dusseldorf 4b O 157/14 (19 January 2016).

not, in itself, suffice to argue that a measure was disproportionate.[50] It only served as one element to be taken into consideration in the balancing exercise which is conducted by national courts before granting these measures or orders.

As for the method of calculation of damages, French courts have been particularly clear on the fact that NPEs/PAEs are generally only entitled to obtain reasonable royalties.[51] The other two methods traditionally available to right holders for the determination of damages (i.e., lost profits or the infringer's profits) were not available to NPEs/PAEs. This has been justified on the ground that, first, NPEs/PAEs could not have suffered from a loss of sales since they did not exploit a patented invention on the market, and, second, the sales made by infringers could not be considered sales that right holders would have made but for the acts of infringement.[52]

Finally, the business model of PAEs has also affected the decision of courts with regard to the grant, or the refusal to grant, injunctive relief. This point is, nonetheless, discussed further under section 3.2.6. Threat of Injunction.

Notice should be taken that, in some instances, national courts have emphasised the role of right holders as licensing companies[53] and the importance of ensuring a functioning enforcement system in order to effectively recoup the heavy investments which may have been made with regard to R&D activities.[54] Courts have however not sought to know whether licensing companies were actually engaging in any kind of transfer which would foster further innovative developments. They also have not

50. In Germany with regard to the request of a destruction order. LG Dusseldorf 4b O 274/10 (24 April 2012).
51. In France: TGI Paris (3e ch. 4e s.) 22 November 2012, RG 10/18196, at 33-34: 'CARREFOUR provided the Court with sufficiently detailed evidence on the number of infringing products that have been sold. There is no need to grant a measure to the right holders to obtain more information. However, *since SISVEL and Institut [...] do not exploit the patent, the amount of damages cannot be based on the amount of benefits CARREFOUR made on the sale of the infringing products.* Their economic activities based on the patent, before its expiration, was only to collect royalties. They cannot have suffered an economical harm based on lost sales of the products because of the commercialisation of infringing products. The negative economic consequences correspond to *the loss of royalties that should have been collected for the commercialisation of the infringing products*' (free translation – emphasis added). CA Paris, 5-2, 9 December 2016, RG 16/02891. The Paris Court of Appeal overturned a decision of the TGI which awarded damages to an NPE because the damages had solely been based on the actual profits made by the infringer. The court considered that this was contrary to the principle according to which victims of infringement must justify their actual losses in order to be fully compensated. In light of the circumstances of the case and the fact that the patent holder was not exploiting the patent at stake, it could not obtain the profits made by the infringer without actual proof of negative economic consequences for the patent holder. *See also*: TGI Paris (3e ch. 2e s.) 17 November 2005, RG 02/05119. TGI Paris (3e ch. 4e s.) 22 November 2012, RG 10/18196. TGI Paris (3e ch. 4e s.) 02 July 2015, RG 12/11488.
52. In France: CA Paris, 5-2, 9 December 2016, RG 16/02891.
53. In Germany: OLG Berlin 5 U 149/14 (20 February 2015). in France: TGI Paris (3e ch. 3e s.) 07 June 2013, RG 10/08326. In the Netherlands: Rechtbank Den Haag, 24 October 2014, KG ZA 14-870.
54. In the UK: *Unwired Planet International Ltd. v. Huawei & Samsung* [2015] EWHC 2097 (Pat). *SanDisk Corp. v. Philips et al.* [2007] EWHC 332 (Ch.). *Nokia OYJ v. IPCom GmbH & co. KG* [2012] EWCA Civ 567.

sought to know whether the original investor in R&D was actually rewarded for its investments. This was sometimes simply assumed.[55]

3.2.2 Choice of Targeted Company

In the literature, a particular element of concern is that PAEs sue market participants which are active on the downstream market, such as final resellers, instead of addressing their infringement claims towards manufacturers who are implementing the technology and are in a better position to defend themselves in courts. One particular instance in France has evoked the choice of right holders to sue not only manufacturers but also participants on the downstream market. The defendant, who was essentially a reseller, argued that the right holder should have sued a manufacturer. However, this claim was unsuccessful.[56]

Courts in all five jurisdictions have considered that, as long as an asserter (including NPEs/PAEs) meets the procedural requirements requested under national law to engage in litigation, i.e., that it has the necessary legal standing to sue a proper defendant, and a proper cause of action, the asserter may choose to sue direct and/or indirect infringers.[57] There is no requirement that an asserter must always start an action against a manufacturer or another direct infringer.

Nevertheless, the cases studied revealed that some courts have been particularly attentive to this question of legal standing or legal capacity to sue. As previously mentioned, PAEs are rarely the initial inventors or patent applicants. A large portion of PAEs obtains patent rights and prerogatives through transfers. If these transfers are not registered by the time these PAEs engage in litigation, they technically cannot claim to have proper standing to sue.[58] Courts have recognised that defendants need to be protected against assertion from entities which they cannot identify beforehand.

In France, for example, it has been found illegitimate to engage in litigation (or even to send a notice of infringement) when the claimant knew (or should have known) that it lacked legal standing due to the fact that a transfer of rights in his favour had not been registered at the French *Institut National de la Propriété Industrielle* (INPI).[59]

Next to the question of legal standing, courts have also examined whether defendants could, legally, be considered as infringers or if they could benefit from an exception under patent law. This was particularly the case in instances where defendants could successfully argue a patent exhaustion defence. For example, on the basis of a chain of licences for which the PAE (or previous owners) had given the

55. *Unwired Planet International Ltd. v. Huawei & Samsung* [2015] EWHC 2097 (Pat).
56. TGI Paris (3[e] ch. 4[e] s.) 22 November 2012, RG 10/18196. TGI Paris (3[e] ch. 1[e] s.) 17 March 2016, RG 12/12329.
57. In Germany: LG Dusseldorf 4a O 54/12 (11 December 2012).
58. In France, Arts L. 613-9 and L. 614-11 CPI. In the UK, ss 33 and 68 of the Patents Act. In the Netherlands, Arts 65(3) and 70(5) Dutch Patent Act 1995. In Germany, para. 30 PatG.
59. In France: CA Paris (4[e] ch. s. A) 29 May 2005, RG 2001/05850. CA Paris, 5-1, 25 November 2009, RG 08/07235. CA Paris, 1-3, 28 January 2014, RG 13/08128. TGI Paris (3[e] ch. 3[e] s.) 10 March 2017, RG 14/16022.

authorisation to exploit. The main issue with such a defence has nonetheless been to collect sufficient evidence of the chain of licences. Courts have granted discovery measures in favour of defendants to obtain additional information from right holders. However, these measures have been granted with caution as they hold the risk of being used by alleged infringers as fishing expeditions.[60]

Therefore, if PAEs, like any other right holders, are allowed to sue direct and/or indirect infringers, these alleged infringers must be capable of being liable for infringement. PAEs have to carefully select which infringer(s) to sue, as courts in Europe may dismiss infringement actions (and therefore allocate the costs of litigation to defendants) on the ground that defendants could not have been considered as infringers.

3.2.3 Choice of Asserted Patents

Literature is split on the question of the quality of patents enforced by PAEs. While some argue that PAEs enforce weak and vague patents, others have shown that the quality of asserted patents by PAEs does not differ much from those asserted by operating companies. Without weighing too much on the question of 'weak or strong' patents, the case law analysis revealed that national courts have nonetheless, on some occasions, emphasised the importance of asserting a 'valid and infringed' patent.

In particular in the UK, some courts have contended that if PAEs are in the business of litigation, they may have, compared to operating companies, more time and resources to devote to investigate[61] whether the patents they are trying to enforce are actually valid and infringed. In one instance, the High Court observed that a PAE abandoned reliance on some of its patents, right before a decision from the court on validity. The court expressed some scepticism with regard to a patentee who is engaged in the enforcement and licensing business but seems too eager to avoid having its patents tried and tested.[62]

More generally, and without specifically attaching a particular knowledge to the identity of certain types of right holders, courts in France and the UK have held that, to pursue an infringement action on the basis of a patent known (or should have been known) to be either invalid and/or non-infringed, could turn the right to engage in litigation into an abusive exercise of such prerogative.[63] This type of exercise relates not only to the quality of the asserted patents but also to the frivolousness of certain claims. The two categories overlap (*infra* 3.2.4).

With regard to claims of infringement, certain courts, particularly in France, have been fairly strict vis-à-vis broad and vague assertion of a patent portfolio. This was predominately the case with regard to Standard Essential Patents (hereinafter 'SEP')

60. As claimed but nonetheless rejected in LG Dusseldorf 4a O 154/15 (13 July 2017).
61. *Sandvik IP AB v. Kennametal UK Ltd., Kennametal Europe GmbH* [2011] EWHC 3311 (Pat.) at 193.
62. *Vringo Infrastructure Inc. v. ZTE (UK) Ltd.* [2014] EWHC 3924 (Pat.) at 115.
63. In France: CA Paris (4ᵉ ch. s. A) 23 October 2002, RG 1996/20620. In the UK: *SanDisk Corp. v. Philips et al.* [2007] EWHC 332 (Ch.). *Rovi Solutions Corp. & United Video Properties, Inc. v. Virgin Media Ltd. et al.* [2015] EWHC 646 (Pat.).

which had been promised to be licensed under Fair, Reasonable and Non-Discriminatory (hereinafter 'FRAND') terms.[64] Courts have required that right holders clearly substantiate their claims of infringement instead of proceedings via broad assertion. Outside of the SEP/FRAND context, and in light of certain specific circumstances, to proceed via assertion instead of substantiating infringement claims, has notably been considered by a court in Belgium as constitutive of acts of unfair competition.[65]

In a similar manner, in one instance in France, and in the context of SEPs and promise to license on FRAND terms, the court has requested that right holders provide some evidence of essentiality of the asserted patents before being able to rely on an assumption of infringement. Traditionally, there might be an assumption that, due to the fact that a patent is declared essential to a standard, compliance of third party's products or processes with the standard necessarily involves an act of infringement (if the compliance is not covered by a licensing agreement).[66] The Paris District Court proceeded with caution with regard to this assumption and required further evidence of essentiality and compliance before engaging in an infringement analysis. It held that, if a right holder wishes to proceed on the assumption basis, it could not proceed by assertion but should substantiate its claims.[67]

64. In Germany: LG Dusseldorf 4a O 154/15 (13 July 2017). OLG Dusseldorf 2 U 16/11 (09 August 2012). In France: CA Paris (3^{e} ch.) 28 January 2014, RG 13/08128. TGI Paris (3^{e} ch. 3^{e} s.) 30 October 2015, RG 13/06691. TGI Paris (3^{e} ch. 1^{e} s.) 17 March 2016, RG 12/12354. CA Paris (4^{e} ch. s. A) 06 Dec. 2006, RG 05/15570. In the UK: *Sandvik IP AB v. Kennametal UK Ltd., Kennametal Europe GmbH* [2011] EWHC 3311 (Pat). *Starsight Telecast, Inc. & United Video Properties, Inc. v. Virgin Media Ltd. et al.* [2014] EWHC 828 (Pat.) at 9 and 10.

65. Voorz. Kh. Antwerpen, 03 April 2012, *United Video Properties Inc. (UVP) v. NV Telenet* (A/11/05443). Despite multiple requests from the defendant to obtain more information on the potentially infringed patents, the right holder refused to provide such information. It also refused to provide information regarding the actual acts of infringement. It only provided a list of more than 100 patents and patent applications and argued that it was for the defendant to identify the relevant patents for its defence in court. The defendant repeatedly asked for more information and indicated to the right holder its intention to advance the matter amicably. The right holder only responded that it would be more expensive for the defendant to contract individual licences for the said-infringed patents than to opt for a general licence on the right holder's portfolio. In light of these circumstances, the President of the Antwerp District Court held that the right holder engaged in unfair commercial practices and violated the general standard of good faith. The President concluded that, if the right had an exclusive right to exclude third parties, this right came with responsibilities and had to be exercised with caution. To merely refer to various patents without specifying which patents were actually infringed and which actions were constitutive of patent infringement, especially when the alleged infringer sought clarification on this point, amounted to an abuse and therefore an act of unfair competition. In its notice letter, the right holder referred to patents which had been either invalidated in a foreign jurisdiction (i.e., in the UK), revoked at the EPO, or not even in force in Belgium and which were irrelevant for the case at hand. It also relied on patents which were subsequently not invoked in the infringement action.

66. *IPCom GmbH & Co. KG v. HTC Europe co. Ltd., Ingram Micro (UK) Ltd.*, HTC Corp [2017] EWCA (Civ.) 90, at 8.

67. TGI Paris (3^{e} ch. 2^{e} s.) 17 April 2015, RG 14/14124. TGI Paris (3^{e} ch. 3^{e} s.) 30 November 2015, RG 13/06691. For a similar case on the Netherlands, *see*: Rechtbank's-Gravenhage, 26 May 2009, KG-ZA 09-157.

3.2.4 *Frivolous Litigation*

The fourth category of practices adopted by PAEs and identified in the literature review refers to multiple actions which can be included under the general terms of 'frivolous' or 'vexatious' litigation. This formulation comprises a.o. the assertion of vague or overly broad claims, but also the assertion of claims without substantial ground. This category of practices overlaps with the practice of asserting invalid and/or non-infringed patents (as presented under 3.2.3).

In the instances studied, defendants in infringement actions have raised multiple arguments which were claimed to fall within the scope of a defence based on frivolousness. This was particularly the case before the French and UK courts.[68] These claims have nonetheless been generally unsuccessful. Once again, courts have been reluctant to find that an action (e.g., to initiate an infringement action) or the request for a specific measure, was frivolous simply because the right holder was an NPE or a PAE. Substantive claims of frivolousness have been required. The burden of proof, which relied on defendants, was however fairly heavy.

Regarding the right to initiate an infringement claim, in one instance before the Paris District Court,[69] a defendant argued that it was abusive (and therefore frivolous) for a PAE to choose to engage in accelerated proceedings on the merits instead of regular proceedings on the merits. The court held that such choice of proceedings could only be considered abusive if the PAE had acted with malicious intent, bad faith or gross negligence. Since the defendant did not bring forward any evidence of an intention to harm or some 'blameworthy thoughtlessness' (*légèreté blâmable*) in the part of the right holder, the court could not rule that the action was frivolous.

As previously mentioned, to engage in litigation while knowing that a patent is invalid and/or non-infringed has been considered abusive by some courts. Alternatively, to engage in litigation with such knowledge may also mean that right holders assert claims without substantial ground, since they know they cannot be successful, and therefore act frivolously. Here again, the burden of proof of such knowledge, which relies on defendants, is particularly heavy.[70] Courts have, on multiple occasions, found that right holders could have misinterpreted the scope of their rights and

68. *SanDisk Corp. v. Philips et al.* [2007] EWHC 332 (Ch.).
69. TGI Paris (3e ch. 2e s.) 17 April 2015, RG 14/14124.
70. TGI Paris (3e ch. 3e s.) 07 June 2013, RG 10/08326. The defendant argued that the right holder could not have ignored that its patents were, first, invalid due to EPO reports and national decisions in the UK and the Netherlands, and, second, non-infringed in light of a German decision. It was argued that, due to the infringement proceedings, the defendant was in moral and financial distress. The ongoing action made it more difficult to have bargaining power vis-à-vis banks and other financial institutions. The Paris District Court rejected this argument on the basis of the fact that the EPO ultimately granted the patents, the UK decision related to different rights, the Dutch decision had been issued after the introduction of this action and that the German decision did not touch upon the question of validity. The Court also observed that the right holder did not illegally forced or pressured the defendant into a licensing agreement. Ultimately, the Court held the patent invalid but did not sanction the right holder for any type of misconduct.

therefore did not act frivolously when initiating an infringement action even if it was later found that their patents were invalid.[71]

With regard to specific requests or execution of measures such as seizure measures, as well as multiplication of (unnecessary) requests or actions, national courts have also been strict in admitting claims of frivolousness. Excessiveness has been insufficient to sustain a claim of frivolousness or abuse. Without clear oppression, intention to harm, bad faith, or malicious intent, these requests have rarely been denied or sanctioned on the ground that they were frivolous or vexatious.[72]

However, some national courts have refused to grant disproportionate, unsubstantiated, or unreasonable measures or requests.[73] The room of manoeuvre left to national courts vis-à-vis these provisional and evidentiary measures allowed them to deny certain requests without having to enter into a strict assessment of frivolousness.

In the UK for example, courts have followed the general principle according to which the objectives of measures and orders granted by a court are to achieve the balance of justice between the parties having regard to all the relevant circumstances of the particular case.[74] In one instance, the High Court held that the particular form adopted by a litigant could be taken into account before authorising the right holders to inspect confidential licensing documents disclosed in a parallel action.[75] In France, to proceed by assertion instead of developing a substantial argument which would legally justify the grant or enforcement of a measure has been considered insufficient by certain courts to grant or authorise the enforcement of a requested measure.[76]

71. TGI Paris (3e ch. 3e s.) 10 March 2017, RG 14/16022.
72. In France: TGI Paris (3e ch. 3e s.) 24 May 2013, RG 11/09609. In the UK: *Nokia Corporation v. Interdigital Technology Corp.* [2004] EWHC 2920 (Pat.).
73. In France: TGI Paris (3e ch. 3e s.) 08 April 2011, RG 11/02062. TGI Paris (3e ch. 1e s.) 16 April 2015, RG 12/12329. TGI Paris (ord. ref.) 28 June 2011, RG 11/55030, at 12. The Paris District Court held that it would be disproportionate and premature to order the publication of an interim relief decision. The successful party should await a decision on the merits before requesting such measure.
74. On proportionality vis-à-vis the ordering of evidence in the UK, *see Shire Pharmaceutical Contracts Ltd. v. Mount Sinai School of Medicine of New York University* [2011] EWHC 3492 (Pat.).
75. *IPCom GmBH & Co KG v. HTC Europe Co. Ltd. et al.* [2013] EWHC 52 (Pat.). IPCom requested to have access to documents from the defendants in order to determine the level of royalty to be paid as well as FRAND terms for a licence. The court noted that only two individuals were actually running IPCom and that its main commercial endeavour was the licensing of the Bosch patent portfolio. The court found that these two individuals would be able to understand certain documents or make contributions to the case based on these documents, but that to authorise them to have access to these documents would contribute to the risk that it will give IPCom an unfair advantage in the marketplace.
76. CA Paris, 1-3, 28 January 2014, RG 13/08128. The court observed that, since an ex parte seizure measure may be of an exceptional severity for an alleged infringer and can give access to restricted documents of a competitor, the request could not be based on simple allegations. The court affirmed the first instance decision withdrawing the seizure measures which had been provisionally granted. In first instance, the Paris District Court held that the right holder lacked loyalty in handling the proceedings since it refrained from informing the court of existing licences which could have been taken into consideration before granting invasive measures such as a seizure measure. By withholding information, the right holder misled and contravened to the mission of the judge in charge of ordering the seizure.

However, in two instances in the Netherlands, courts have been giving overriding importance to the interests of right holders (i.e., NPEs) over the interests of alleged infringers. In one instance, the court deemed that the enforcement business of the right holder was a factor to take into account to justify the grant of a physical seizure which could be conducted during a public fair over the grant of a descriptive seizure.[77] In the other instance, it is the licensing business of right holders which was regarded as a particularly important factor in the balance of interests.[78]

When measures and requests have nonetheless been considered unreasonable by courts, without necessarily reaching the threshold of frivolousness, this unreasonableness has sometimes been reflected in the allocation of costs. This was particularly the case in the UK, where courts benefit from some discretionary powers vis-à-vis the allocation of litigation costs,[79] but also in jurisdictions where the apportionment of costs is made on an issue-by-issue or claim-by-claim basis such as in the Netherlands.[80] Overall, the case law confirmed that the fee-shifting rule combined with an additional recovery of costs generated by unnecessary or disproportionate requests might serve as a deterrent mechanism against some litigation strategies adopted by PAEs and might protect alleged infringers against frivolous lawsuits or vexatious claims.[81]

On the other hand, the burden of proof required to demonstrate that an action or a claim is frivolous or vexatious may hamper the actual effectiveness of such defence. The focus on subjective elements, such as the bad faith or the intention to harm of a right holder represents a serious hurdle for defendants.

3.2.5 Vague Demand Letters

In all jurisdictions, courts have scrutinised demand letters which have been communicated to either alleged infringers or third parties before initiating an infringement action. Under certain conditions, these letters have either fell within the scope of the law of unfair competition (in Belgium, France,[82] the Netherlands[83] and Germany) or

77. Court of Amsterdam, 12 September 2008, KG ZA OS 1721 WT/MB.
78. Rechtbank Den Haag, 09 November 2005, KG 05/1175.
79. *Rambus Inc. v. Hynix Semiconductor UK Ltd. and Rambus Inc. v. Micron Europe Ltd.* [2004] EWHC 2313 (Pat.). *Unwired Planet International Ltd. v. Huawei & Samsung et al.* [2015] EWHC 1029 (Pat.). *Research in Motion UK Ltd. v. Visto Corporation* [2008] EWHC 819 (Pat.). *Rovi Solutions Corp. & United Video Properties, Inc. v. Virgin Media Ltd. et al.* [2015] EWHC 646 (Pat.).
80. Rechtbank's-Gravenhage, 26 May 2009, KG-ZA 09-157. Rechtbank Den Haag, 06 July 2011, HA ZA 10-2069.
81. F. Fischmann, *Patent litigation and cost shifting in Europe: critical appraisal and proposal of alternative solutions*, J.I.P.L.P., 10(2), 98-108, 105 (2014). C. Helmers et al., *The Effect of Fee-Shifting on Litigation: Evidence from a Court Reform in the UK*, Toulouse School of Economics (TSE) Working Papers No. 16-740 (2017).
82. CA Versailles (14^{e} ch.) 06 November 2013, RG 12/08367, confirmed by C. Cass (Comm.) 27 May 2015, D14-10.800. The court observed that; the letter focused exclusively on the licensing programme offered by the right holders, the terms used were threatening, and that there was no explanation on the allegedly infringing acts. *A contrario*: T. Comm Marseille, 20 September 2016, RG 2016F01637.
83. Rechtbank Den Haag, 10 October 2007, KG ZA 07-1000.

specific patent law provisions (in the UK[84]). Courts have assessed whether the content of those demand letters amounted to acts of disparagement or denigration (under the different laws of unfair competition) or qualified as unjustified threats (under the UK Patents Act).

Overall, the case law analysis revealed that right holders who proceed with broad assertions in their demand letters have been perceived quite negatively by courts. This was especially the case when the letters were sent to third parties such as the customers or the resellers of alleged infringers. To be successful on the claim that letters sent to third parties were actually damaging to alleged infringers, the latter nonetheless had to demonstrate that the letters harmed the commercial relationship established between the receiver of the letters and the alleged infringers.

Noticeably, many instances in which a claim of threatening demand letters has been raised took place in the specific context of SEP litigation. According to the decision of the Court of Justice of the European Union (hereinafter 'CJEU') in *Huawei v. ZTE* (C-170/13),[85] SEP holders which have promised to license their patents under FRAND terms have to communicate with alleged infringers before requesting an injunction. To discuss the exact content of these communications would go beyond the scope of this paper. However, they do fall within the scope of the general assessment of FRAND negotiations and also have to respect the general principle of pre-contractual good faith which is common to the contract laws of many European Member States. Moreover, beside the specific framework established by the CJEU decision, the national rules concerning acts of disparagement under the laws of unfair competition or specific patent law provisions, are equally applicable to demand letters issued within the context of SEP litigation.

3.2.6 Threat of Injunction

As previously mentioned, PAEs are said to heavily rely on the threat of injunction (provisional and permanent) as a way to heighten their bargaining power against alleged infringers. In continental Europe, courts grant permanent injunctions on a quasi-automatic basis. Findings of validity and infringement are necessary and sufficient conditions for their grant. In Germany, due to the system of bifurcation, infringement is even sufficient.[86] On the other hand, courts in Europe benefit from some leeway vis-à-vis the grant or denial of preliminary injunctions. Courts regularly assess all the circumstances of a case and engage in a balancing exercise between the interests of the parties before issuing these measures. In the UK, injunctive relief is an

84. Intellectual Property (Unjustified Threats) Act of 2017. Entered into force on 1 October 2017, http://www.legislation.gov.uk/ukpga/2017/14/contents/enacted (accessed 17 March 2019). *See also Cintec International Ltd. v. John. H. Parkes (t/a Dell explosives) and Martin Frost* (2003] EWHC 2328 (Ch.), at 6.
85. Judgment of 16 July 2015, *Huawei Technologies Co. Ltd. v. ZTE Corp. and ZTE Deutschland GmbH*, C-170/13, EU:C:2015:477.
86. In Germany, claims of infringement and validity are decided by different courts. Regional courts and higher regional courts decide exclusively on infringement while the Federal Patent Court (*Bundespatentgericht' – BpatG*) decides exclusively on validity.

equitable remedy, and courts hold discretionary powers to grant or refuse an injunction (preliminary and permanent).[87]

3.2.6.1 Preliminary Injunction

With regard to preliminary injunctions, the identity of the right holder (i.e., whether it was an NPE or not) and its business model (i.e., to be essentially engaged in licensing activities instead of traditional exploitation of patents on the market) has sometimes, although fairly rarely, been taken into consideration by national courts before granting, tailoring, or refusing a preliminary injunction.[88]

Regardless of the identity of the right holder, national courts have also been attentive to the fact that mandatory, and essentially procedural, requirements for the adjudication of patents were met before granting preliminary injunctions. In particular, courts require that claimants provide any reasonably available evidence in order to satisfy the courts with a sufficient degree of certainty that they are the right holders, that their rights are prima facie valid, as well as being infringed, or that such infringement is imminent.[89] Additionally, courts also commonly require that a situation of urgency, or of timeliness, justify the requests for preliminary injunctions. In particular in the case of ex parte proceedings. Urgency is not only evaluated in terms of time but also in light of the material circumstances of a case.[90] In other words, once the right holders become aware of potential acts of infringement, they have to act promptly.

It has been argued in the literature that some PAEs adopt a 'wait and sue' strategy. Under this approach, PAEs wait until alleged infringers make irreversible investments in a certain technology before asserting their claims. If this approach has traditionally led to issues in terms of competition law (i.e., patent ambush and lock-in), it is important to note that, in some instances, courts have denied the grant of preliminary injunctions on the basis of lack of urgency or lack of timely request.[91]

For example, in one instance in Germany, the Dusseldorf Regional Court[92] observed that:

> *The plaintiff has long known the defendants as a market participant ... in some communication the defendants had already been mentioned [and] the group of the*

87. *Stretchline IP Ltd. v. H&M Hennes & Mauritz UK Ltd.* [2016] EWHC 162 (Pat.) at 9. *Unwired Planet International Ltd. v. Huawei & Samsung et al.* [2015] EWHC 1029 (Pat.).
88. In France: TGI Paris (3e ch. 3e s.) 15 April 2016, RG 15/01377.
89. Contrary to the two other conditions, the condition of prima facie validity is not explicitly mentioned in Art. 9(3) of the Enforcement Directive. However, it is required by the national patent laws of the jurisdictions studied here.
90. In Germany: OLG Berlin 5 U 149/14 (20 February 2015).
91. Rechtbank Den Haag, 06 January 2017, KG ZA 16-906. Although ultimately rejected in this instance, the court observed that, under certain circumstances, the inaction of the plaintiff can result in the fact that there is no more urgency. This would notably be the case if the inaction lasted for a long period and where no new set of facts or circumstances could justify delaying the introduction of the proceedings. This was also evoked, but ultimately rejected, in *Rechtbank's-Gravenhage*, 26 May 2009, KG-ZA 09-157.
92. LG Dusseldorf 4b O 16/16 (24 May 2016). OLG Berlin 5 U 149/14 (20 February 2015).

> *defendant is one of the biggest in the world, [therefore] professional circles should have known of its existence. The fact that the right holder withdrew its first application for a preliminary injunction and decided to wait for the decision on validity before the Federal Patent Court is a sign that there is no urgency* (Free translation).

The court ultimately held that the right holder adopted a hesitant and negligent behaviour in terms of legal action and did not meet the legal requirements to obtain a preliminary injunction. Such instance is nonetheless a quite isolated case.

Under such analysis, a wait and sue strategy adopted by PAEs may be rather unsuccessful as the threat generally associated with the availability of injunctive relief is less realistic. German courts have, however, clearly specified that right holders are not under a duty to monitor the market. They have indicated that in the event right holders have tangible indications of infringement by a third party they should act promptly if they wish to obtain a preliminary injunction. If they fail to do so in such a way that their inaction, objectively suggests an indifference in the pursuit of their own legal interest, then, the urgency in obtaining the measure is lost.[93] Additionally, in some instances, the lack of urgency has also been analysed in combination with the commitment made by right holders to license their patents under FRAND terms. These two factors have affected the decisions of courts to grant, tailor, or deny injunctive relief.[94]

3.2.6.2 Permanent Injunction

As for permanent injunctions, only a few instances have led to findings of validity and infringement.[95] It was, therefore, difficult to observe whether courts would also consider the fact that the successful right holder was an NPE or PAE. Some courts, particularly in the UK and in Germany, have sporadically evoked the possibility of moderating or tailoring the conditions of enforcement of injunctions granted in the first instance pending appeal or pending a decision on validity. This was notably the case in the context of SEP litigation, but not exclusively.[96] These national courts have suggested that, under certain circumstances, the enforcement of an injunction could be stayed for a certain period (e.g., until appeal, until a design-around solution could be found or because of reasons of public interest). In these cases, whether to grant or deny a stay has been partially evaluated in light of the fact that the successful party was an NPE/PAE.[97]

German courts have nonetheless been fairly strict on the conditions justifying a stay. They have recognised that a balance of interests may be conducted when deciding on whether to provisionally stay the enforcement of an infringement decision. On the

93. OLG Berlin 5 U 149/14 (20 February 2015). OLG Dusseldorf I-2 U 23/17 (18 July 2017).
94. LG Dusseldorf 4a O 154/15 (13 July 2017). OLG Dusseldorf I-2 U 23/17 (18 July 2017).
95. Out of the 97 decisions studied, permanent injunctions have only been granted in 19 cases. By a large majority, German courts have been the most incline to grant this remedy (i.e., in 11 cases).
96. *Unwired Planet International Ltd. v. Huawei & Samsung* [2017] EWHC 711 (Pat.).
97. OLG Karlsruhe 6 U 38/09 (11 May 2009). LG Dusseldorf 4b O 274/10 (24 April 2012).

one hand, they have accepted to take into account whether there was an imminent risk of harm for defendants if a sentence was enforced. They have also recognised that the possibility of designing around may be a factor to take into consideration. However, German courts have strongly emphasised that, in principle, the interests of the creditor (i.e., the successful right holder) supersede those of the debtor (i.e., the infringer) and therefore have priority. Only exceptional circumstances could justify a stay, such as a high likelihood that the patent will be invalidated before the Federal Patent Court.[98]

Overall, and despite a timid evolution vis-à-vis the tailoring of injunctive relief in the event of SEP litigation and FRAND commitments,[99] German courts have adopted a particularly strong view on the fact that there can be little to no reason for treating NPEs or PAEs differently than OCs.[100] They also have been more reluctant than other European courts to deny or tailor injunctive relief in general.

3.2.7 Patent Hold Up

The last category of practices identified in the literature review refers to the possibility for PAEs to engage in patent hold-up and rent-seeking behaviour. In the cases studied, courts have occasionally referred to the possibility for right holders, and not specifically for PAEs, to engage in hold-up[101] or rent-seeking behaviour. They have resorted to the rules of competition law to assess these situations.[102]

What has also been emphasised by national courts, in particular in SEP litigation, is the role that may be played by competition law in limiting excessive enforcement practices by right holders. Since an in-depth analysis of a defence based on competition law falls outside the scope of this paper, it will only be mentioned that, in the instances studied, defendants have widely argued that right holders should be held liable on the ground that they would have abused their dominant position by either, initiating an infringement action, or requesting specific measures such as preliminary injunctions.[103]

This defence is particularly burdensome as it requires defendants to demonstrate not only that right holders hold a dominant position on a defined market, but also that

98. LG Mannheim 7 O 182/08 (18 December 2009). OLG Karlsruhe 6 U 29/11 (18 April 2011). LG Dusseldorf 4b O 176/11 (18 December 2012).
99. In Germany: LG Dusseldorf 4b O 157/14 (19 January 2016). LG Dusseldorf 4a O 154/15 (13 July 2017). In the UK: *Unwired Planet International Ltd. v. Huawei & Samsung* [2016] EWHC 958 (Pat.). *Unwired Planet International Ltd. v. Huawei & Samsung* [2017] EWHC 711 (Pat.).
100. LG Mannheim 7 O 94/08 (27 February 2009).
101. In Germany, the Dusseldorf Regional Court has nonetheless evoked the risks associated with the practice of hold-out from implementers. LG Dusseldorf 4b O 157/14 (19 January 2016). LG Dusseldorf 4b O 120/14 (19 January 2016).
102. In Germany: LG Dusseldorf 4b O 274/10 (24 April 2012). LG Dusseldorf 4a O 54/12 (11 December 2012). In the UK: *Unwired Planet International Ltd. v. Huawei & Samsung* [2017] EWHC 711 (Pat.). *SanDisk Corp. v. Philips et al.* [2007] EWHC 332 (Ch.).
103. In France: TGI Paris (3[e] ch. 2[e] s.) 17 April 2015, RG 14/14124. In the UK: *SanDisk Corp. v. Philips et al.* [2007] EWHC 332 (Ch.). In Germany: LG Dusseldorf 4b O 140/13 (26 March 2015).

they have abused this dominance.[104] Additionally, in all jurisdictions studied, and in particular in Germany, courts have frequently emphasised that patents are protected rights under Article 17(2) of the EU Charter of Fundamental Rights and that the right to access to court under Article 47 of the EU Charter is extremely important. Therefore, to be successful on a competition law defence, alleged infringers must identify and specify anti-competitive harm justifying the limitation of the protection offered by IPRs.[105]

4 CONCLUSION

4.1 Mechanisms in Place

As summarised in Table 13.1, national courts in Europe benefit and have resorted to multiple mechanisms in order to assess, and sometimes sanction, the (over-)enforcement practices of NPEs/PAEs. In particular, three bodies of rules have been relied upon.

First and foremost, the rules of competition law have been heavily relied upon. This holds particularly true in the context of SEP litigation but not exclusively. Arguably, the assessment framework elaborated by the CJEU in *Huawei v. ZTE* (C-170/13) has offered the most elaborate set of guiding principles to courts. Defendants in infringement actions have primarily argued that to engage in litigation, or to request specific measures, amounted to an abuse of dominant position and therefore should be considered an over-enforcement practice. *Second*, the rules of unfair competition law in continental jurisdictions or the specific provision under UK patent law have provided some comfort to litigants vis-à-vis the practice of PAEs sending overly vague demand letters or which proceed with broad assertions of claims. *Finally*, courts have resorted to national conceptions of the principle of the prohibition of abuse of rights or the principle of bad faith, under the general terms of 'frivolous and vexatious' litigation, when required by exceptional circumstances.

Next to these three bodies of rules, courts have been attentive to the fact that mandatory, and essentially procedural, requirements for the adjudication of patents were met. Such as in the case where an NPE/PAE had not registered a transfer of rights before asserting its patents or where it did not meet the condition of urgency or timeliness to obtain a preliminary injunction.

Finally, national courts have made use of the room of manoeuvre left in national patent laws to refuse to grant unreasonable or disproportionate measures requested from right holders. These requests have overwhelmingly concerned evidentiary measures (i.e., seizure measures or search orders), recall and destruction orders, publication orders, and to a certain extent, preliminary injunctions. Courts have taken into account all the circumstances of a case and have engaged in a balancing exercise

104. This could be the case if the conditions envisaged under Case C-170/13 of 16 July 2015, *Huawei Technologies Co. Ltd. v. ZTE Corp.*, *supra* n. 85, or those elaborated in Judgment of 17 July 1998, *ITT Promedia NV v. Commission of the European Communities*, Case T-111/96, EU:T:1998:183.
105. LG Dusseldorf 4b O 140/13 (26 March 2015).

between the interests of the parties involved in litigation, before granting these measures.

Overall, and despite the fact that courts were indeed 'hesitant to draw patent law or competition law consequences based solely on the fact that a party is a PAE',[106] they did provide some responses to over-enforcement practices as practices that could either be classified as anti-competitive or reprehensible under other sets of legal rules such as unfair competition law, the prohibition of abuse of rights, the principle of good faith, and procedural rules governing the adjudication of patents.

Table 13.1 Practices of PAEs Identified in Literature and the Response from Courts in Europe

Categories of Practices	*Responses from National Courts in Europe*
1. Take advantage of being an NPE	No direct consequences of being an NPE – same treatment as OCs Consider chain of ownership and transfers (UK, FR) Publication orders to re-assure the market (UK, FR)
2. Choice of targeted companies	Can sue upstream and downstream BUT legal standing (register transfer, FR) and proper defendants (patent exhaustion defence, FR) ! Knowledge + consequences
3. Choice of asserted patents	Valid and infringed in light of reasonably available evidence SEP: essential and part of a standard (FR, ~ UK and NL) Broad and vague assertion – unfair competition (BE) ! Knowledge + consequences
4. Nuisance suits and frivolous claims	Need malicious intent, bad faith, gross negligence (FR, DE) BUT provisional/evidentiary assessed in light of 'all the circumstances of the case' – balance of interests Unreasonable/unsubstantiated or disproportionate claims rejected (FR, UK) Interests of right holders more valuable (NL, DE) Sanction: costs of litigation
5. Vague demand letters	Laws of unfair competition (FR, NL, DE, BE) or Unjustified Threat Act (2017) (UK) – Actionable threats No pure 'cease and desist' – No false statements Need 'moderate terms' in particular vis-à-vis third parties not involved in litigation Specific framework: SEP litigation – Huawei *v.* ZTE

106. Contreras and Picht, *supra* n. 4, at 3.

Categories of Practices	*Responses from National Courts in Europe*
6. Threat of injunction	Permanent: quasi automatic – need exceptional circumstances First instances injunctions: Stay enforcement until appeal or design-around (+ proportionality UK, exceptional circumstances, ~ DE) Damages in lieu of injunction (~ UK) Safeguard: Bank guarantee for enforcement (DE, ~ NL) Preliminary: 'All circumstances of the case' and 'balance of interests' (~ DE) Urgency (DE) and timeliness – patent expiry (FR) – FRAND commitment
7. Hold-up and rent seeking	Unclear from the case law General: Competition law applicable

Source: Author's own work.

4.2 Potential Drawbacks

Notwithstanding the positive outcome of the case law analysis, three drawbacks have been identified. *First*, the reliance on three distinct bodies of legal rules in addition to mandatory procedural requirements and more traditional principles of patent law, did not make the analysis of the cases a straightforward endeavour. The disparities between national courts in their interpretation of the different rules have also acted as a barrier to a common interpretation of the specific issues brought by PAEs litigation. It appeared clearly that, despite the adoption and implementation of the Enforcement Directive in all jurisdictions studied, the provisions of the Directive, and in particular Article 3 of the Directive,[107] have rarely, if ever, been explicitly relied upon by the national courts.

Second, the burden of proof which lied on defendants to either prove that a right holder engaged in anti-competitive practices or frivolous and vexatious litigation, was particularly burdensome. To require defendants to demonstrate that right holders acted with bad faith, or malicious intent was especially demanding. It is not argued here that these defences should be successful on a lower burden of proof. However, it is argued that there might be over-enforcement practices which do not necessarily fall within the scope of these defences, because they do not reach the level of harmfulness required, but which could nonetheless be subjected to a proportionality test. For example, the

107. Art. 3 of the Enforcement Directive stipulates that:

(1) Member States shall provide for the measures, procedures and remedies necessary to ensure the enforcement of the intellectual property rights covered by this Directive. Those measures, procedures and remedies shall be fair and equitable and shall not be unnecessarily complicated or costly, or entail unreasonable time-limits or unwarranted delays.
(2) Those measures, procedures and remedies shall also be effective, proportionate and dissuasive and shall be applied in such a manner as to avoid the creation of barriers to legitimate trade and to provide for safeguards against their abuse.

approach adopted by certain courts to assess unreasonableness in the exercise of patent prerogatives, a lack of proportionality, as well as acts of unfair competition, appear to provide some positive results in terms of limiting over-enforcement claims.

Third, one of the main concerns identified in the literature regarding the enforcement practices of PAEs was that PAEs can heavily rely on the threat of injunctive relief. The case law analysis has been semi-conclusive regarding this opportunity in Europe as only a few instances led to the conclusion that a patent was valid and infringed.

Some implications may nonetheless be drawn from the cases. A distinction must be made between preliminary and permanent injunctions. With regard to permanent injunctions, the quasi-automatism with which national courts grant injunctive relief may naturally feed into the identified concerns. The few instances in which courts have granted a stay on enforcement during a certain period (i.e., until appeal, for design-around purposes, or during FRAND negotiations) have been too sporadic to draw strong conclusions. They nonetheless point in the direction of more tailored responses to specific circumstances and should be encouraged. Alternatively, the practice of German courts to condition the enforcement of an injunction obtained in the first instance, to the provision of a security, should also be encouraged as they protect the defendant's interests. On the other hand, the rules and practices adopted by the courts vis-à-vis preliminary injunctive relief seem to already provide for some safeguards against overly broad requests, claims which are not justified on a timely basis, or which seriously disadvantage the interests of the defendants.

CHAPTER 14

Standard Essential Patents: Between Open Access and Rewarding Innovation

Dietrich Kamlah

1 INTRODUCTION

Modern telecommunication with fast access to data from almost anywhere has changed the world. It heavily depends on common standards ensuring interoperability between different devices. These standards work on the basis of complex technology being covered by numerous patents. The balance between open standards and the fair reward for the inventors shall be guaranteed by licenses under FRAND (Fair, Reasonable and Non-Discriminatory) terms. What FRAND really means and how it can be implemented in practice, however, is the subject of intense legal battles in courts all over the world. Despite years of litigation, there is still no commonly accepted solution. With the rise of industry 4.0 and connected cars, the concept of FRAND terms for access to patented standards will become even more important and a necessity for virtually every industry. The issue is further complicated by the international implementation of the FRAND concept. While courts in various jurisdictions all use the term "FRAND," the underlying legal principles are not harmonized and can vary substantially in different jurisdictions.

In its landmark decision *Huawei v. ZTE*, the Court of Justice of the European Union (CJEU) laid out a procedural framework for negotiating FRAND terms applicable within the European Union.[1] Generally the patentee has to notify the defendant of the patent, and in case the defendant expresses his willingness to take a FRAND license make a license offer to the defendant under FRAND terms, before a standard essential patent can be enforced by injunctive relief. If the patentee's initial offer appears unacceptable, the defendant has to react in a timely and constructive manner and make

1. CJEU Case C 170/13—*Huawei v. ZTE*, judgment of July 16, 2015.

a counteroffer. Moreover, the defendant has to render accounts for past sales and provide a financial security to the patentee, which covers the royalties accrued until the dispute over the FRAND royalty rates is resolved.[2]

With regard to setting the FRAND royalty rate, however, the CJEU provided no guidance, because it was simply not part of the questions referred to the CJEU in *Huawei v. ZTE*.[3] This issue was left to the national courts entirely.

In subsequent patent cases national courts within the European Union applied *Huawei v. ZTE* in very different ways. The following contribution will therefore give an overview of the legal framework of the FRAND undertaking and its legal effects in patent litigation. Moreover, the development of the case law in Germany and the application of the underlying principles of European law by the German courts will be discussed.

2 THE LEGAL FRAMEWORK OF THE FRAND DECLARATION

2.1 FRAND Declarations for Standardization

The FRAND declarations are issued by participants in standardization projects to ensure compliance with competition law. The standardization of technology by the industry is generally beneficial to the society. Complex systems like mobile communication cannot work without standardized methods and protocols for the transmission of speech and data. Moreover, standardization can improve market access for small and medium companies (SMEs), who would not be able to compete with their own proprietary technology against major market players. However, standardization also limits competition. Instead of bringing competing technical solutions to the market and offering customers a choice, major industry players agree on one solution, which has to be adopted by everyone. For this reason, standardization falls within the scope of Article 101 TFEU and is admissible only if the conditions for an exception laid down in Article 101(3) TFEU are met.

In this context, the European Commission has laid down the principles for admissible standardization projects in its Guidelines on Horizontal Co-operation Agreements.[4] In a nutshell these Guidelines require that standards are open in two ways. On the one hand, the standardization process must be open to participation by all interested parties. On the other hand, the use of the resulting standard must be open to all implementers. To secure the latter, participants who propose the inclusion of patented technology into the standard must provide a FRAND declaration. The FRAND declaration shall secure access to the standard for everyone under fair, reasonable and nondiscriminatory—i.e., competition law compliant—terms. At the same time, a

2. C-170/13—*Huawei v. ZTE*, paras. 61 to 67.
3. *See* referral by the Düsseldorf Regional Court (Landgericht) of March 21, 2013 as cited in C-170/13, para. 39.
4. Guidelines on the applicability of Art. 101 of the Treaty on the Functioning of the European Union to Horizontal Co-operation Agreements of January 14, 2011, 2011/C 11/101, OJ 2014, C11/1, Chapter 7., Standardization Agreements.

participant in the standardization is not forced to give away proprietary technology for free, but may ask for a fair reward, if the proprietary technology is used as part of the standard.

2.2 The Direct Contractual Effect of the FRAND Declaration

The FRAND declaration is usually addressed to the standard setting organization (SSO), which organizes the standard setting process on a technical level. Still, the SSO is not the beneficiary of the FRAND declaration. The beneficiaries shall be all members of the SSO and the general public, who are interested in using the standard. Whether the members of the public as the intended beneficiaries of this FRAND declaration can rely directly on the FRAND declaration as a license to all or merely claim a right to the grant of a license by the intellectual property right (IPR) holder depends on the wording of the FRAND declaration and the applicable law.

One frequently discussed example is the FRAND declaration issued in the standardization of mobile communications such as UMTS and LTE under the framework provided by ETSI. Under the ETSI IPR Policy, a standard text for FRAND declarations is proposed to the participants in ETSI projects.[5] Since ETSI is organized as an association under the French law, the ETSI FRAND declaration is explicitly governed by French law. Under the French law, the prevailing view is that the FRAND declaration is a binding legal promise to everyone to grant a license under FRAND terms upon request ("stipulation pour autrui").[6] Consequently, every implementer of ETSI standards using patents held by a contributor to the standard can assert a direct contractual right to a FRAND license under national French law.

2.3 The Effect of the FRAND Declaration under EU Competition Law

In addition to its direct contractual effect, the FRAND declaration also has two distinct effects under European competition law.

First of all, FRAND declarations by the participants of a standardization project secure that the entire standardization agreement complies with Article 101 TFEU. Creating a standard based on patented technology of the contributors, which is not available for use by the public, has the potential to close the relevant markets to outsiders who need to use the standardized technology to offer competitive products and services. This effect to outsiders can render the entire standardization agreement illegal under Article 101 TFEU and therefore has to be prevented by binding FRAND declarations of the contributors to the standard.[7]

Moreover, the FRAND declaration has a secondary effect in competition law under the CJEU decision *Huawei v. ZTE*. In a long line of precedents such as Magill,

5. The ETSI IPR Policy is published under https://www.etsi.org/intellectual-property-rights (downloaded on July 18, 2019).
6. *See* McGuire, *Die FRAND-Erklärung*, GRUR 2018, 128.
7. Guidelines on Horizontal Co-operation Agreements, OJ 2014, C11/1, example in para. 327.

Bronner and IMS Health,[8] the CJEU has established that the owner of IPR, which are needed to compete in a downstream market for products or services, holds a market dominant position. Blocking the access of competitors to the downstream products or services market by refusing to grant a license to the required (essential) IPR can therefore constitute the abuse of dominant position under Article 102 TFEU. The IPR are seen in this context as essential facilities similar to railway networks, harbors or airports.

However, the owner of an essential facility is not always obliged to grant licenses to competitors and certainly not unconditionally. In its landmark case *IMS Health*, which concerned a de facto standard for the format of certain sales data in Germany, the CJEU decided that the right to a license under Article 102 TFEU requires an individual balancing of the interests of the holder of the essential IPR and the competitor interested in competing in a downstream market. The competitor's interests in a license can prevail over the interests of the right holder, for example, if the competitor is not just copying the products of the owner of the essential IPR, but brings new and improved products to the market.[9]

When the CJEU in *Huawei v. ZTE* applied the essential facilities doctrine to a declared standard relying on essential patents covered by a FRAND declaration, it came to a modified conclusion for the balancing of interests between the right holder and its competitor requesting the license. The FRAND declarations by the contributors to the standard create trust by the public that the standard will be open to everyone. This trust is the basis for the general adoption of the standard by the market participants. Consequently, the public trust in the availability of the standard impacts the balancing of interests in favor of the standard users.[10] A balancing of the competing interests of the right holder and the implementer in the individual case is not required. The owner of the patent, which is included in the FRAND declaration, profits from the public trust, because the patent will be widely used as part of the standard and generates royalties. In return, the patent owner cannot refuse a license to other implementers of the standard under FRAND terms.

The FRAND declaration therefore creates not only a potential contractual claim to a license but also sets the ground for a right to a license under the essential facilities doctrine in the framework of Article 102 TFEU. This competition law right to a license is based on factual circumstances, i.e., the dominant position of the patent owner in the upstream technology market, which was due also to the trust of the market in the availability of the patent, and therefore independent of the national contract law, which was chosen in the FRAND declaration.

Given the factual basis of the FRAND declaration's competition law effect, it is arguably not affected by later assignments of the FRAND-encumbered patent to third parties. Even if the new owner of the FRAND-encumbered essential patent does not issue a renewed FRAND undertaking or adopt the contractual obligations of the

8. Cases C241/91—*Magill*; C-7/97—*Bronner*; C-418/01—*IMS Health*.
9. Case C-418/01—*IMS Health*, reply to the second question.
10. Case C 170/13—*Huawei v. ZTE*, paras. 53-55.

previous owner under the original FRAND undertaking, the right to a license under FRAND terms under EU competition law will apply.[11]

2.4 Result: Two Ways to a FRAND License

With the dual effect of the FRAND declaration as a contractual undertaking and its impact on the balancing of interests in competition law, it provides the users of a standard essential patent with two separate claims to a FRAND license. The implementer of a standard interested in using the standard essential patent can either bring a contractual claim based on the direct effect of the FRAND declaration or rely on Article 102 TFEU and assert his right to use the patent as essential facility under competition law.

In the case of standard essential patents relevant to UMTS or LTE, one option would be a claim under French law. In this context, not only French law would have to be observed but also the wording of the FRAND declaration and whether it is binding on the current owner of the standard essential patent. This can become an issue in cases where the patent was assigned and the new owner refuses to acknowledge the effect of the original owner's FRAND declaration.[12]

If the right to a FRAND license is claimed under Article 102 TFEU, details of French law do not matter and the right to a license can be directed against the current owner of the standard essential patent regardless of whether the FRAND declaration was assigned with the patent or not.

These two legal grounds for claiming a FRAND license are legally distinct and the requirements of the application of each have to be reviewed on their own. At least from a German law perspective, the two grounds cannot be mixed when arguing for the right to a FRAND license. If a right to a FRAND license is asserted under French law, the contents of the FRAND undertaking will also have to be assessed under the same law. In this case, fairness and reasonableness of the royalty rate as well as the absence of discrimination will have to be assessed under French law principles. If the claim to a FRAND license is based on Article 102 TFEU, fairness and reasonableness as well as nondiscrimination will have to be reviewed under European competition law. In this case, the implementer seeking a license also has to show that the patent actually creates a market dominant position, because it gives its owner control over access to a relevant downstream product or services market.[13] Moreover, if the right to a FRAND license is based on Article 102 TFEU, the implementer needs to comply with the criteria for a willing licensee established by the CJEU in *Huawei v. ZTE*. Therefore, it is not correct to rely on the binding effect of the FRAND declaration as stipulation pour autrui under French contract law, assess whether the implementer is a willing licensee under

11. The Düsseldorf Higher Regional Court has now even argued that the FRAND undertaking is automatically linked to the patent, *see* judgment of March 22, 2019 in Case I-2 U 31/16—*Unwired Planet v. Huawei*.
12. *See* McGuire, *Die FRAND-Erklärung*, GRUR 2018, 128.
13. Established case law in Germany, *see* Federal Court of Justice, case KZR 36/17—*Sisvel v. Haier; also* Düsseldorf Higher Regional Court, case I-2 U 31/16—*Unwired Planet v. Huawei*; Karlsruhe Higher Regional Court, case 6 U 183/16—*Philips v. Wiko*.

the criteria defined by the CJEU in *Huawei v. ZTE* and then determine the FRAND royalty rate under English common law as this was done by the UK High Court in *Unwired Planet v. Huawei*. Once French contract law is chosen as basis for the FRAND license, French contract law will have to be applied all the way, including the determination of the FRAND royalty rates.

Of course, if the FRAND declaration is used for its direct contractual effect and construed under French law, European competition law can still become relevant in case the disputed IP right creates a market dominant position. European competition law defines the binding minimum requirements for market access and is directly applicable in all EU Member States. Therefore, even if the FRAND declaration is taken as a directly applicable French contractual stipulation, it will have to be construed in accordance with European competition law principles.

3 THE FRAND DEFENSE UNDER *HUAWEI V. ZTE* IN GERMANY

3.1 Limited Guidance from the CJEU

So far, the German courts have opted for the competition law approach under Article 102 TFEU when deciding over a FRAND defense. Contractual effects of a FRAND undertaking under the ETSI IPR Policy did not play a role and arguments on this basis were dismissed by the courts for various reasons. The German preference for the competition law approach is already highlighted by the fact that the CJEU decision *Huawei v. ZTE* followed a referral from the Düsseldorf Regional Court. However, since the underlying questions to the CJEU were limited to procedural issues of raising the FRAND defense and were not concerned with the substance of the FRAND determination, the guidance provided by the CJEU is equally limited. Consequently, while the CJEU has provided some guidance on the formal requirements and the timeframe for the FRAND defense, the determination of the FRAND royalty and other terms and conditions of a FRAND license were fully left to the national courts.

In the decisions following *Huawei v. ZTE*, the German courts had a strong focus on the formalities of the FRAND defense. In several early cases, a FRAND defense was denied, because the defendant had made its FRAND offer too late or did not provide a sufficient financial security.[14] In other early cases, the courts focused on the defendant's counteroffer, instead of the plaintiff's initial FRAND offer. The Düsseldorf Regional Court and the second chamber in the Mannheim Regional Court, for example, took the view that the defendant is always obliged to make a proper FRAND counteroffer as soon as the plaintiff has made an offer, regardless of whether it is FRAND or not.[15] The courts then started with a review of the plaintiff's counteroffer, which was held to be insufficient for various reasons in almost all published cases.

14. *See*, e.g., Düsseldorf Regional Court, Case 4a O 144/14—*Sisvel v. Haier*.
15. Düsseldorf Regional Court, Case 4a O 144/14—*Sisvel v. Haier*; Mannheim Regional Court, Case 2 O 106/14—*Saint Lawrence v. Deutsche Telekom*.

These decisions highlight that the burden of proof has significant impact on the FRAND determination. In cases where the court started with a review of the defendant's counteroffer, the FRAND defense did not succeed, because defendants naturally first tried to submit offers limited to the patents in dispute and to the country, where these patents are actually litigated (Germany). Such counteroffers were dismissed, because in the German courts' view the plaintiff is entitled to a worldwide license to the entire portfolio of patents, which are essential to the given standard.

Moreover, once a court accepts that there is a range of various royalty rates, which can be considered FRAND and from which the patentee can chose freely,[16] the defendant's counteroffer in the view of the German courts needs to be so high that the patentee cannot refuse it because a higher royalty would be abusive under Article 102 TFEU. It is obvious, however, that a defendant would not enter into negotiations with a counteroffer based on the highest conceivable royalty rate for the entire worldwide portfolio. At last, it is very difficult for the defendant to make a proper counteroffer, because at the time when defendants had to make their counteroffers in the earlier German cases, they did not have any information about other license agreements concluded by the patentee.

This early approach by the lower German courts was effectively the continuation of the courts' approach under the previous Orange Book decision by the Federal Court of Justice,[17] which was dismissed by the CJEU in *Huawei v. ZTE*. The approach of the lower German courts changed only after several landmark decisions by the Higher Regional Courts in Düsseldorf and Karlsruhe. With the first decision of the Federal Court of Justice in *Sisvel v. Haier*[18] of May 5, 2020, important concepts of the lower courts' decisions are confirmed, while in some aspects the standards applied in the lower courts have to be readjusted. However, even after the Federal Court of Justice has spoken, we still have no guidance from the German legal system as to which royalty rate is actually FRAND.

3.2 The *Sisvel v. Haier* Case in the Federal Court of Justice

3.2.1 The Decision of the Düsseldorf Higher Regional Court in Sisvel v. Haier

The case *Sisvel v. Haier*[19] concerned patents, which are declared essential to standards relevant for UMTS. This case first got international attention, when the Düsseldorf Higher Regional Court in second instance for the first time put the focus on the plaintiff's obligations in a FRAND determination in Germany.

16. For this concept of FRAND, *see* Düsseldorf Higher Regional Court, Case I-2 U 31/16—*Unwired Planet v. Huawei.*
17. Federal Court of Justice, Case KZR 39/06—*Orange Book*, decision of May 6, 2009. The Federal Court of Justice required a license offer by the defendant, which the plaintiff cannot refuse without behaving in a discriminating or abusive manner.
18. Federal Court of Justice, Case KZR 36/17—*Sisvel v. Haier,* judgment of May 5, 2020.
19. Düsseldorf Higher Regional Court, Case I-15 U 65/15—*Sisvel v. Haier,* judgment of March 30, 2017.

In the first instance, the Düsseldorf Regional Court had not assessed the plaintiff's initial offer but was content that the plaintiff had made a license offer after the defendant had shown some interest in negotiating a license before the litigation started.[20] The defendant's assertions that the plaintiff's offer might be inadequately high or that the defendant could be discriminated against compared to other licensees were dismissed without any review of the plaintiff's other license agreements. The court in first instance had focused only on the defendant's counteroffer, accounting and security, which was regarded as too late. Accordingly, the defendant was injuncted from selling smartphones with UMTS functionality in Germany.

Upon the defendant's application in the course of appeal proceedings, the Higher Regional Court of Düsseldorf suspended the injunction against the defendant in an interim decision[21] and held that the Düsseldorf Regional Court in first instance had failed to properly review the plaintiff's license offer. According to the Düsseldorf Higher Regional Court, the CJEU required not just any offer by the plaintiff, but specifically a FRAND offer. Moreover, the duties of the plaintiff and the defendant under the CJEU decision in *Huawei v. ZTE* are conditional upon each other. In the Düsseldorf Higher Regional Court's view, the defendant is under no duty to make a counteroffer until the plaintiff has made a proper FRAND offer. Therefore, the Düsseldorf Regional Court was obliged to review whether the plaintiff's offer is actually FRAND. If this is not the case, the defendant is not even obliged to make any counteroffer.

In the ongoing litigation between Sisvel and Haier at the appeal stage, the Düsseldorf Higher Regional Court then issued a detailed guidance order to the parties instructing them how the court sees the burden of proof.[22] In this order, the Düsseldorf Higher Regional Court advised the parties that it sees an obligation of the plaintiff to show that the initial offer is not only fair and reasonable but also not discriminatory. In the view of the court, this requires information about the patentee's prior license agreements so that the defendant as well as the court can review the plaintiff's offer for the absence of discrimination. As far as these prior license agreements are under NDAs with third parties, they have to be disclosed to the defendant only after the defendant has signed a reasonable NDA.[23] Access of the defendant's personnel to the license agreements may be restricted, but is mandatory since there is no such thing as "attorneys eyes only" limitations in Germany. This makes sense, since the in-house legal departments of the parties are usually most experienced in negotiating license agreements and have knowledge of usual royalty rates in their technology market. Only when the plaintiff has provided sufficient information on its prior license agreements, the court is able to decide whether the plaintiff's offer is actually FRAND. If the

---

20. Case 4a 144/14, decision of November 3, 2015.
21. Case I-15 U 65/15, order of January 13, 2016.
22. Case I-15 U 65/15, order of November 17, 2016.
23. Case I-2 U 31/16—*Unwired Planet v. Huawei*, orders of December 14, 2016 and of January 17, 2017; even though these orders were issued by a different division of the Higher Regional Court, the underlying principles were apparently also followed in the case between *Sisvel v. Haier*, where the plaintiff disclosed license agreements with third parties.

defendant refuses this required disclosure, the court cannot confirm that the plaintiff made a FRAND offer and will have to dismiss the motion for an injunction.

In its appeal judgment the Düsseldorf Higher Regional Court dismissed the plaintiff's motion for an injunction after the plaintiff had disclosed its prior license agreements to the court. Even though substantial parts of the judgment are redacted, it is clear that the plaintiff had entered into at least one other license with a competitor of the defendant in the defendants home market. The terms of this other license were in the court's view substantially more favorable for the licensee than the terms offered to the defendant. The plaintiff's explanation that it was under pressure from government authorities in the defendant's home market and therefore had no choice but to accept very low royalty rates in one case was dismissed as insufficient justification of discrimination. The Düsseldorf Higher Regional Court therefore concluded that the plaintiff discriminated against the defendant. With this decision, the Düsseldorf Higher Regional Court confirmed that just one license agreement with a significantly lower royalty rate, which cannot be justified by objective reasons, can give rise to discrimination.

3.2.2 **Sisvel v. Haier *Before the Federal Court of Justice***

Following the appeal judgment, both Sisvel and Haier filed a further legal appeal to the Federal Court of Justice. While Haiers' appeal directed against the finding of infringement failed, Sisvel's appeal directed against the dismissal of its motions for an injunction, recall and destruction succeeded.

In its review of the Higher Regional Court's decision, the Federal Court of Justice confirmed important concepts applied by the lower courts. First of all, the Federal Court of Justice confirmed that the FRAND defense is based on Article 102 TFEU and the legal standards of European competition law apply for assessing FRAND compliance, e.g., when it comes to assessing discrimination.

The Federal Court of Justice also allowed the patentee to offer a license to the asserted patent only as a worldwide portfolio license as long as the patents in the portfolio are selected in compliance with the applicable European competition law rules for bundling. This usually means that the offered portfolio needs to be limited to patents, which are essential for the same standard.

Moreover, the Federal Court of Justice agreed with the Düsseldorf Higher Regional Court that the patentee is under an obligation to explain why he considers the offered royalty rate as FRAND. This requires not only a transparent royalty calculation but also the opportunity for the defendant to review the patentee's license offer for discrimination. Usually the defendant has to be granted access to the plaintiff's existing licenses to the same portfolio with third parties to enable the review for nondiscrimination.

However, Federal Court of Justice disagreed with the Düsseldorf Higher Regional Court when it came to the defendant's obligation to express willingness to take a license. The Düsseldorf Higher Regional Court, in line with virtually all other German courts in the lower instances, had applied a generous approach when assessing whether the defendant, after being notified about the patent, expressed his willingness to take a license. Even unspecific statements hinting at a willingness to negotiate where considered sufficient. According to the Federal Court of Justice, however, willingness to negotiate is not enough. Rather the defendant has to express the willingness to conclude a license at actual FRAND terms without reservations regarding the amount of the royalties. In this context the Federal Court of Justice cited the UK High Court, which expects a willingness to accept "whatever rate the court decides is FRAND."[24] The Federal Court of Justice will not look for an explicit statement, but rather review the defendant's overall conduct and whether the defendant acted as a willing licensee or applied delaying tactics and did not really engage in serious negotiations.

In the case at hand, Haier had reacted only one year after Sisvel first made contact and had merely asked Sisvel whether discounts are available. During the court proceedings, Haier did not engage in any real negotiations either. Only at a very late stage in the first instance proceedings, Haier made an obviously insufficient counter-offer, which was limited to the asserted patents and the territory of Germany and other EPC Member States where the asserted patents are validated. During the appeal stage, Haier stated that it is willing to take a license, but only under the condition that the patents asserted in Germany are actually found valid and infringed. These statements during the proceedings were dismissed as insufficient, because the defendant has to make an unconditional counteroffer. In the view of the Federal Court of Justice, Haier did not show genuine willingness to come to a FRAND license, but applied typical delaying tactics until at least one of the two asserted patents was expired in Germany.

Given that Haier was not a willing licensee in the first place, the Federal Court of Justice dismissed the FRAND defense without further review of the plaintiff's license offer. However, it remarked that the finding of discrimination by the Düsseldorf Higher Regional Court is questionable in its view. Pressure by government authorities—assuming the plaintiff's statements were correct—can be a justification to grant lower royalty rates to one licensee without applying these low rates also to other licensees. In the view of the Federal Court of Justice, nondiscrimination does not mean that the patentee has to apply a "one size fits all" approach to licensing, but can apply different royalty rates as long as the differences are justified under Article 102 TFEU and applicable competition law rules.

With this decision the Federal Court of Justice has shifted the balance of rights duties in FRAND negotiations significantly in favor of the plaintiff after the Düsseldorf Higher Regional Court had first put the burden of making an actual FRAND offer on the plaintiff.

The Federal Court of Justice provided no guidance on the proper calculation of a FRAND royalty. This is due to the German procedural system. German courts will generally not determine FRAND rates independently of the parties, but merely review the parties' offers as arbiters and either accept them as compliant with FRAND requirements or as insufficient. Therefore, once it is established that either the plaintiff or the defendant has not complied with one of the mandatory consecutive steps in the

24. UK High Court, Case (2017) EWHC 711 (Pat)—*Unwired Planet v. Huawei*.

FRAND negotiations under *Huawei v. ZTE*, the plaintiff's motion for an injunction will either be granted or dismissed on this basis and there is not necessarily a determination of the actual FRAND rate.[25]

3.2.3 *Parallel Case Between Sisvel and ZTE*

In a slightly later case brought by Sisvel against ZTE[26] in which infringement of the same patents was asserted, the plaintiff refused to disclose its license agreements in the Düsseldorf Regional Court due to disputes about the terms required for an NDA to protect the plaintiff's license agreements from unauthorized disclosure. Following the guidance by the Düsseldorf Higher Regional Court in *Sisvel v. Haier*, the Düsseldorf Regional Court decided that it would have been the plaintiff's burden to show that it does not discriminate against the defendant when compared to other previous licensees, as it was now confirmed by the Federal Court of Justice in *Sisvel v. Haier*. It is therefore the plaintiff's obligation to enable the submission of its prior license agreements to the court under an appropriate NDA. Even though the parties disagreed on the terms of the required NDA, according to the Düsseldorf Regional Court the plaintiff could nevertheless have provided more specific information about its prior license agreements in a redacted form without disclosing the identity of the respective licensees. Because the plaintiff had not taken any such steps, the court concluded that the plaintiff had not cooperated in a sufficient manner to enable the review of its license agreements by the court and therefore had not acted in compliance with FRAND requirements. Accordingly, the plaintiff's motion for an injunction was dismissed in this case.

3.3 Case Law of the Düsseldorf Higher Regional Court and Regional Court

3.3.1 *Düsseldorf Higher Regional Court*—Unwired Planet v. Huawei

In the German litigation between Unwired Planet and Huawei, the Düsseldorf Higher Regional Court had another opportunity to explain its views on the FRAND defense.[27] In this case, which is based on the more or less identical facts as the UK High Court case, the Düsseldorf Higher Regional Court also dismissed the plaintiff's motion for an

25. With the motion for an injunction, the motions for recall and destruction of the attacked products were also dismissed by the Higher Regional Court. This is established practice also in other German courts (*see*, e.g., Mannheim Regional Court, Case 7 O 209/15—*Philips v. Archos*). Moreover, in the Düsseldorf courts the claim for information about past infringement does not include information about the defendant's costs and profits, because damages for a plaintiff, who is not FRAND compliant are limited to an adequate royalty, which can be calculated without knowledge of the defendant's profit margins (different in Mannheim, *see*, e.g., Mannheim Regional Court, Case 7 O 28/16—*Philips v. Asus* with detailed reasons).
26. Düsseldorf Regional Court, Case 4a O 16/16—*Sisvel v. ZTE*, decision of July 13, 2017.
27. Case I-2 U 31/16, decision of March 22, 2019.

injunction, which had been successful in first instance.[28] Following the principles of the previous *Sisvel v. Haier* decision, the plaintiff apparently disclosed its license agreements with third parties to the court. However, it refused to disclose license agreements concluded by the prior owner of the asserted patents.

The Düsseldorf Higher Regional Court ruled that for the review of discrimination all license agreements to the asserted patents are relevant, whether they are concluded by the plaintiff as current owner or by any previous owner of the patents. The limitations, which apply to FRAND-encumbered patents in the enforcement of claims for injunctive relief, are passed on from the first owner of the patents, who issued the FRAND declaration and concluded initial license agreements, to any later owner of the patent. Later owners are not only bound by the FRAND undertaking as such but also by the standards the previous owners had established for the licensing of the patents. The absence of discrimination has to be assessed taking into account all license agreements concluded for the asserted patents as far as those license agreements are still in force. Only expired license agreements, which have become truly obsolete, do not have to be taken into account when assessing discrimination. Since Unwired Planet had not submitted license agreements to the asserted patents concluded by the previous owners, the Düsseldorf Higher Regional Court was not able to assess the absence of discrimination and dismissed Unwired Planet's action for an injunction. Again, the actual FRAND rate did not have to be determined by the court, because it could decide the case based on Huawei's failure to prove the absence of discrimination.

Since the German courts focus on the effect of the license agreement in the market, it is likely that individual circumstances of the case such as temporary financial distress of a licensor may not be sufficient to justify different royalty rates for different licensees.[29] Moreover, the Düsseldorf Higher Regional Court did not justify the effect of a FRAND undertaking on every future owner of the patent by relying just on the considerations under Article 102 TFEU, but went even further and held that the patents themselves become FRAND encumbered and any limitations arising from a FRAND declaration or the patentee's licensing practice would be linked to the patents like a right in rem and automatically follow the patents in any later assignment or other transfer in the same way a license under a patent is effective against any patent owner under section 15(3) German Patent Act. This is a deviation from the decision in the first instance where the Düsseldorf Regional Court had decided that a new owner of a patent portfolio is not bound by the previous owner's royalty rates, but may raise the rates as long as this does not severely distort competition between the different licensees.[30]

28. Düsseldorf Regional Court, Case 4b O 49/14, decision of January 19, 2019.
29. Other than the High Court in *Unwired Planet v. Huawei*, decision of April 5, 2017, (2017) EWHC 711 (Pat), which disregarded agreements concluded under special individual circumstances such as financial distress in its FRAND royalty setting.
30. *See* Düsseldorf Regional Court, Case 4b O 49/14.

3.3.2 Düsseldorf Regional Court—MPEG LA v. Huawei *and* MPEG LA v. ZTE

Even though in *Sisvel v. Haier* and *Unwired Planet v. Huawei* decisions, the Düsseldorf Higher Regional Court established strict requirements for the plaintiff's conduct before a claim for injunctive relief may be asserted, patentees still have very substantial discretion in selecting the terms under which they license their standard essential patents. This is highlighted by two recent decisions in cases brought by licensors of the MPEG LA AVC patent pool against Huawei and ZTE.[31] This litigation intended to put pressure on Huawei and ZTE to sign the MPEG LA AVC patent portfolio license. Therefore, the plaintiffs who held certain patents, which were contributed to the MPEG LA AVC patent pool, did not submit FRAND offers of their own, but merely referred the defendants to the MPEG LA AVC pool license, which would include a license to the plaintiffs' patents. ZTE was prepared to sign the MPEG LA AVC patent portfolio license, but only for the defendant in the German case, i.e., ZTE's local German subsidiary. Huawei rejected the MPEG LA AVC patent portfolio license, because in Huawei's view it was not FRAND.

As a matter of principle, Huawei argued that it should be entitled to a license offer from the plaintiff in the case at hand and not just from a patent pool, which includes not only the plaintiff's patents but also numerous other patents not asserted in the pending litigation. This argument was rejected by the Düsseldorf Regional Court. According to the court, patentees who make their standard essential patents available via a patent pool are not obliged to offer individual licenses independently of the pool. While the patent pool may not request patentees to give up their right to grant nonexclusive licenses outside the pool, patentees are not obliged to grant these individual licenses actually in the view of the Düsseldorf Regional Court. The court stated that as long as the use of the standard requires the patents from all participants in the patent pool, the defendant does not have a legitimate right to request a license from just one pool member. An exception could be made, if there is a meaningful use case, which involves only the patents of one patentee, but not the others. This, however, may not be a very relevant exception for standards created by large working groups with multiple contributors.

In this context, Huawei alleged that not all patents in the MPEG LA AVC patent pool are actually essential for the AVC video coding standard with some patents being relevant only for certain AVC profiles, which are not used in every application and other patents not being truly essential at all. The Düsseldorf Regional Court accepted that the pool license is compliant with FRAND principles as long as the composition of the patents in the pool is reasonable and non-essential patents are not included intentionally. Since MPEG LA performs essentiality checks for each patent via an independent agency, before the patent is accepted into the pool, the court was satisfied that the selection of the patents in the MPEG LA AVC pool is reasonable. Consequently,

31. Düsseldorf Regional Court decisions of November 9, 2018 in Case 4a O 63/17 against Huawei and in Case 4a O 15/17 against ZTE.

Huawei's argument that the MPEG LA AVC patent pool constitutes anticompetitive bundling of essential and nonessential patents failed.

When it came to the royalty rates requested by MPEG LA, the court was satisfied with the plaintiff's explanation that its royalty rates had been widely accepted in the industry. The plaintiff stated that the MPEG LA patent portfolio license had been signed more than 2,000 times with over 1,400 license agreements currently in force. The licensees named in the proceedings included a number of larger participants in the market. The court accepted that the overall amount of the royalty is fair and reasonable without requiring further explanations or justifications relating to the value of the licensed patents and the calculation of the exact amounts payable to the MPEG LA AVC pool. In the court's view MPEG LA was also free to grant volume discounts and apply royalty caps to other licensees. As long as such discounts and royalty caps are not designed to benefit individual licensees but are achievable for all licensees in the same way, the court saw no discrimination in volume discounts and royalty caps.

Another argument by Huawei concerned a differentiation of royalty rates for different regions of the world. The MPEG LA AVC pool applies the same rates worldwide. Huawei rejected this and requested a reduced rate for China. According to Huawei, the number of MPEG LA AVC licensees in China is still rather limited. This argument corresponds to the UK High Court's decision in the case *Unwired Planet v. Huawei* where the UK High Court accepted that significantly reduced royalty rates apply to China and certain other regions. The Düsseldorf Regional Court did not accept this argument. Based on the evidence before the court, China could not be regarded as a low-price market for smartphones and tablets and therefore there was no justification for reduced royalty rates compared to the rates applicable to the US and Europe.

In the parallel case against ZTE, one major issue was whether the parent company of ZTE would have to sign the MPEG LA patent portfolio license even though it was not even sued in the German case. The defendant wanted to limit the acceptance of the MPEG LA AVC patent portfolio license to itself as the German subsidiary, which was sued in the case in Düsseldorf. The defendant in the Düsseldorf case was prepared to sign the license proposed by MPEG LA with worldwide effect. Even though this counteroffer by the defendant is in line with the guidance given by the CJEU in *Huawei v. ZTE* in that the defendant has to make a counteroffer, the argument was rejected by the Düsseldorf Regional Court. The German subsidiary is not in charge of sales in other parts of the world, and consequently a worldwide license signed by the German subsidiary would not cover the worldwide sales of the ZTE group. In the court's view this is not the truly worldwide license the patentee can expect. Since German courts had decided in many previous cases that the owner of a standard essential patent can ask for a worldwide license, the patentee does not have to accept license offers by defendants who are part of a global organization, but whose own sales territory is limited to Germany. Even though the defendant's parent company was not even a party to the German case, a FRAND defense by the German defendant would have required the acceptance of the MPEG LA AVC patent portfolio license also by the defendant's parent company to make it a truly global license in the court's view.

These two decisions on the MPEG LA AVC patent portfolio license show the wide discretion German courts grant to the patentee in selecting between various licensing options and in setting the terms of the license agreement. This discretion is in line with the assumption that FRAND does not define one specific rate or one specific set of contract terms, but merely a wide range in which the patentee can choose between different, equally acceptable options. This of course means that once the plaintiff has made an offer, which can be seen as FRAND, and provided sufficient explanations and information for the defendant to review this offer, it will be very hard for defendants to challenge the FRAND compliance of the offer. As long as the patentee's license terms are not discriminatory or abusive, German courts will likely accept them as FRAND.

3.4 The Case Law of the Karlsruhe Higher Regional Court and Mannheim Regional Court

3.4.1 Mannheim Regional Court and Karlsruhe Higher Regional Court—Pioneer v. Acer

In the early FRAND cases following the CJEU decision *Huawei v. ZTE*, the Mannheim Regional Court was very focused on maintaining the efficiency of patent enforcement in Germany. There was a considerable concern that proceedings over infringement of standard essential patents could become an unbearable burden to the court, if the court had to undertake a FRAND determination in each single case.[32] With the high number of patent infringement cases in Mannheim, a lengthy FRAND trial with economic experts would slow the court down and also delay decisions in other more straightforward cases, because the judicial capacities would be blocked by FRAND trials. Therefore, in the first series of cases, including *Pioneer v. Acer*, the Mannheim Regional Court held that while the plaintiff has to make an initial FRAND offer, the court will not fully review whether this offer is actually FRAND, but merely conduct a high level preliminary check.[33] Unless the plaintiff's offer is prima facie in clear breach of FRAND principles, the court would always turn to the defendant's counteroffer and security bond and assess whether the defendant has fulfilled its obligations under the CJEU decision *Huawei v. ZTE*. This review of the defendant's offer would be a full review and in all the published cases, the defendants failed the test, because they typically did not want to commit to substantial worldwide royalty payments before the court has even decided whether the asserted patents are valid and infringed.

The Karlsruhe Higher Regional Court interfered with this handling of FRAND cases by the Mannheim Regional Court and partially suspended the enforcement of the injunction granted by the Mannheim Regional Court in *Pioneer v. Acer* until the final decision on appeal.[34] In the interim decision, the Karlsruhe Higher Regional Court held that the plaintiff has to make a FRAND offer and that it is the court's obligation to

32. *See*, e.g., Case 2 O 106/14—*Saint Lawrence v. Deutsche Telekom* or Case 7 O 99/14—*Pioneer v. Acer*.
33. Mannheim Regional Court, Case 7 O 96/14—*Pioneer v. Acer*. The court defended this view in an obiter also in later cases such as 7 O 209/15 and 7 O 238/15 despite the different view of the Karlsruhe Higher Regional Court in Case 6 U 55/16.
34. Case 6 U 55/16, decision of May 31, 2016. The enforcement was suspended as far as recall and destruction of the accused products were concerned. With regard to the injunction, the

review whether the plaintiff's offer is actually FRAND. This is in line with the general principles of German procedural law, which require the court to review all the relevant arguments and the evidence presented by a party, if it may affect the outcome of the case. Concerns regarding the overall efficiency of patent enforcement in Germany do not justify a deviation from these legal principles for civil procedures in the German Civil Procedural Code (ZPO). While this was a victory for the defendants, the Karlsruhe Higher Regional Court also stated that patentees had a significant discretion in selecting the terms under which they want to license their standard essential patents. Due to a change in the panel of judges at the Karlsruhe Higher Regional Court, there was no final decision, which confirmed and further expanded upon the principles set forth in this interim decision.

3.4.2 Mannheim Regional Court—Philips v. Archos

Following the interim decision of the Karlsruhe Higher Regional Court, the Mannheim Regional Court changed its approach in subsequent cases such as *Philips v. Archos*[35] and *Philips v. Asus*.[36] In these cases, the court put a strong focus on the information a plaintiff has to provide to enable the court to perform a FRAND review. As in the courts in Düsseldorf, the Mannheim Regional Court required plaintiffs to provide information as to how they arrived at the royalty rate they are offering and why they regard this royalty rate as FRAND.[37]

An important issue is the timing of this explanation by the plaintiff. Other than the Düsseldorf Regional Court and Higher Regional Court, the Mannheim Regional Court required all the information from the plaintiff, before the action for an injunction is filed. Once the action for an injunction is filed, the plaintiff cannot remedy an insufficient explanation of the royalty rate by submitting additional information during the trial. According to the Mannheim Regional Court, the CJEU in *Huawei v. ZTE* intended to give the defendant a chance to review and negotiate the plaintiff's FRAND offer without being under the pressure of an action for an injunction. Therefore, the FRAND offer and the information required for its review and a proper counteroffer have to be available to the defendant before the action for an injunction puts the defendant under pressure. If the action for an injunction is already pending, when the plaintiff first submits a proper license offer to the defendant, the plaintiff can either withdraw the action (with costs) or apply for a suspension of the infringement case, to give the defendant a chance to review the license offer without undue pressure.

defendant had failed to show the danger of severe damage from the enforcement, because it had stopped the distribution of the accused products for commercial reasons anyway.

35. Case 7 O 209/15.
36. Case 7 O 238/15.
37. This is correct at least for the seventh division. The second division did not require any information on the calculation underlying the royalty setting in several cases, e.g., Case 2 O 106/14—*Saint Lawrence v. Deutsche Telekom* and Case 2 O 157/16—*Saint Lawrence v. ZTE*, decision of January 13, 2017.

Otherwise the motions for an injunction will be dismissed as currently unfounded by the court.[38]

With this strict requirement as to the timing of the information to be provided to the defendant, plaintiffs, who had already filed their actions in reliance on the previous case law in Mannheim failed in obtaining injunctions even without a full FRAND review by the court. Accordingly, Philips' motions for an injunction in the cases against Archos and Asus were dismissed. However, the court explicitly maintained its position that a full review of the plaintiff's license offer for FRAND compliance should not be required despite the opposite view of the Karlsruhe Higher Regional Court. Because this did not matter for the outcome of the cases due to the strong focus on the timing of the required information from the plaintiff, the court stated this in a detailed obiter dictum.

3.4.3 Mannheim Regional Court—**Philips v. Asus** ***and*** **IP Bridge v. HTC**

Following a change on the judges' panel in the Mannheim, the court modified its position again in two later cases. First of all, the court held in a case *Philips v. Asus*[39] that the plaintiff has to provide information on prior license agreements with other licensees, if there are doubts about the plaintiff's FRAND compliance. In this case plaintiff's description of its licensing practice was obviously incomplete so that potential discrimination against the defendant seemed a real issue and not just a purely hypothetical possibility. Since the plaintiff refused to provide additional information to enable a review whether its licensing practice is actually discriminating or not, the motion for an injunction was dismissed.

This position was further developed by the Mannheim Regional Court in the decision *IP Bridge v. HTC*,[40] where the Mannheim Regional Court (seventh division) explicitly adopted the approach of the Düsseldorf Higher Regional Court as set forth in *Sisvel v. Haier*. Consequently, plaintiffs who enforce FRAND-encumbered standard essential patents in Mannheim will now generally have to disclose their prior license agreements with third parties to enable FRAND review by the defendant. This disclosure has to take place sufficiently long before the action for an injunction is filed to give the defendant a fair chance to review the offer and formulate a counteroffer without the pressure of a pending action for an injunction. In this context, the court indicated that the minimum time period, which should be available for the defendant after receiving the plaintiff's offer and explanations, is about two months.

In this context, it is worth noting that plaintiffs in Germany often start FRAND cases by first filing a patent infringement action with limited motions directed at information and damages for the past use of the patent and merely a declaratory ruling instead of an enforceable injunction regarding the future use of the patent. The motions

38. If the motion for an injunction is dismissed as 'currently unfounded' the dismissal is not final and the plaintiff can sue for an injunction again as soon as the missing requirement, i.e., the proper FRAND offer, is completed.
39. Case 7 O 28/16—*Philips v. Asus*, decision of November 10, 2017.
40. Case 7 O 165/16—*IP Bridge v. HTC*, decision of September 28, 2018.

can then be amended to include also a motion for an injunction at short notice during the already ongoing trial. The decisive time limit for making the FRAND offer in this constellation is the date when the motion for an injunction order is brought into the already ongoing case, because in the view of the German courts this is the time of "bringing the action for an injunction" according to the CJEU decision *Huawei v. ZTE*.[41]

3.4.4 Karlsruhe Higher Regional Court—Philips v. Wiko

The Karlsruhe Higher Regional Court rendered its first full decision in a FRAND case in October 2019 in a dispute between Philips and Wiko,[42] which is a parallel case to the cases *Philips v. Archos* and *Philips v. Asus*. In this decision, the Karlsruhe Higher Regional Court confirmed the concepts developed in more recent case law of the Mannheim Regional Court such as *IP Bridge v. HTC*. If certain steps in the FRAND negotiation process are omitted or delayed by a party, later compliance with these steps can remedy the situation even after the infringement action was filed. However, if the defendant expressed is willingness to take a license in a sufficient manner before the proceedings, the plaintiff has to agree to a temporary suspension of the infringement proceedings, if the first FRAND offer is made only after filing the action. The defendant shall have the opportunity to review the plaintiff's FRAND offer without the pressure of a pending injunction action. If the defendant expressed its willingness to conclude a FRAND license only after being sued, the plaintiff still has to make a FRAND offer, but the proceedings will not be suspended or delayed due to the defendant's late compliance with FRAND obligations.

When it came to the review of the plaintiff's actual FRAND offer, the Karlsruhe Higher Regional Court stressed the importance of a transparent offer. This requires the disclosure of existing third party licenses by the plaintiff at least in cases where third parties were granted different conditions by the plaintiff. Since the plaintiff refused this disclosure, the motion for an injunction was dismissed by the Karlsruhe Higher Regional Court.

4 SUMMARY OF THE CURRENT PRACTICE IN FRAND CASES IN GERMANY

Even though the German FRAND cases so far did not deal with the actual royalty calculation itself, they already cover a lot of relevant issues. Since at least some of the decisions are still subject to appeal to the Federal Court of Justice, which has decided only over very few aspects in *Sisvel v. Haier*, the German case law still might change. Nevertheless, the published decisions provide a good insight into the German courts' view on dealing with FRAND royalties and for some issues there seems to be a relatively broad consensus.

41. *See* CJEU Case C-170/13—*Huawei v. ZTE*, para. 60. This practice is accepted by the German courts, *see*, e.g., Mannheim Regional Court, Case 7 O 165/16—*IP Bridge v. HTC*.
42. Karlsruhe Higher Regional Court, Case 6 U 183/16—*Philips v. Wiko*.

4.1 Transparency Requirement for FRAND Offers

Because German procedural law does not provide for pretrial discovery, the courts in Düsseldorf and Mannheim have developed a transparency requirement as a necessary element of a FRAND offer, which was approved by the Federal Court of Justice in general terms in *Sisvel v. Haier*. The plaintiff has to provide sufficient information to enable a review of its FRAND offer in order to fulfill its obligations under the FRAND declaration and Article 102 TFEU. This puts the defendant in a reasonable negotiating position because without this information the defendant could not really assess the FRAND quality of the plaintiff's offer. It is not foreseen that the defendant also provides information on its prior licensee agreements. From a German perspective, this makes sense because it is first the plaintiff's task to make a reasonable offer and avoid discrimination. The plaintiff—holding a dominant position—is not free to negotiate royalty rates in the same way the defendant is.

With this transparency requirement, the German courts have ensured that they can perform a meaningful FRAND review and will not be tricked by alleged standard license agreements, which are presented to the courts, but not really used in actual negotiations in many cases.

4.2 Royalty Review, Not Royalty Setting

While the German courts fully review the royalty rates presented by the parties, they do not engage in active royalty setting. This is due to the procedural context of the FRAND defense, which is raised by the defendant in a case concerning an infringement action with a motion for an injunction. As a result of the FRAND review a German court will make a decision whether to grant or deny an injunction requested by the plaintiff. In this context, the court will decide whether a plaintiff's offer is FRAND or not. If this decision can be made based on a review for discrimination, the court will not go all the way and determine the royalty rate, which it believes should be agreed. If the plaintiff's royalty rate is not discriminatory, the court will proceed and review whether it is beyond the threshold of abuse under Article 102 TFEU. Below this threshold, the courts grant plaintiffs wide discretion in setting the royalty rate. Finding exactly the right royalty rate is not part of the courts' review when performing a FRAND assessment under Article 102 TFEU and is left entirely to the parties. Under the German Civil Procedural Code, the German courts have no means to set royalty rates instead of the parties and to order the conclusion of a license agreement at these rates in a regular patent infringement trial.

Determining the fair value for the use of the asserted patents would only be part of a damages trial, which under German procedural law is typically a separate trial following the initial infringement trial. In this separate damages trial, the court could set a fair royalty rate as damages for the past use of the asserted patent upon a corresponding application of the plaintiff. The damages case, however, would be limited to the patents actually asserted in court and not extend to the plaintiff's entire worldwide portfolio. Therefore it would be limited to Germany and typically one or two patents and the result would be a rather insignificant damages amount for Germany compared to a royalty for the use of an entire worldwide portfolio. For this reason plaintiffs asserting standard essential patents in Germany usually focus on getting an injunction in the initial trial as leverage for a worldwide royalty negotiation, but do not follow up to initiate a German damages trial.

4.3 FRAND Defines a Range

Since the entire FRAND discussion in Germany is based on competition law, FRAND merely defines a range of possible royalty rates. The plaintiff is free to choose a suitable royalty rate as long as it is not abusive or discriminatory under Article 102 TFEU. This gives plaintiffs a broad range in which a royalty rate can be selected. From the plaintiff's perspective the ideal royalty rate is just below the amount, which would be regarded as excessive and therefore abuse of a dominant position. Even though this issue was not yet decided explicitly, it appears that plaintiffs are under no obligation to accept a lower royalty rate, which would be in the middle of the FRAND range or even at its lower end.[43]

The plaintiff's room for maneuver in royalty setting becomes narrower as soon as the plaintiff has already concluded license agreements with third parties. As the Düsseldorf Higher Regional Court elaborated in the case *Unwired Planet v. Huawei*, once the royalty rate is fixed in initial license agreements, the plaintiff cannot deviate from this rate substantially to the detriment of later licensees without a sound justification. Therefore, in a scenario where the plaintiff has already concluded a number of license agreements, the courts' FRAND review will primarily focus on the issue of discrimination and only in a second step on the reasonableness and fairness of the absolute royalty amount.

4.4 Formalities of the FRAND Negotiation

When it comes to the formalities of the FRAND negotiation, the German courts are not too strict. The plaintiff's initial infringement notice to the defendant can be rather short. Claim charts are definitely sufficient, but may not even be required.[44] It could be sufficient to point the defendant merely to the relevant patents and the sections in the standard, which give rise to an infringement allegation. The defendant's indication of willingness to take a license should not be taken too lightly as illustrated by the Federal Court of Justice in *Sisvel v. Haier*. It is still not a major hurdle, provided the defendant expresses the willingness to conclude a license at the actual FRAND rate.

43. In Case I-2 U 31/16—*Unwired Planet v. Huawei*, the Düsseldorf Higher Regional Court mentions that the absolute amount of the royalty rate initially chosen by the plaintiff needs to be free of exploitation (*ausbeutungsfrei*) and states that plaintiffs may chose the upper end of the range, which is possible under the aspect of exploitation.
44. *See*, e.g., Mannheim Regional Court, Case 7O 96/14—*Pioneer v. Acer* or Düsseldorf Regional Court, Case 4a O 73/14—*Saint Lawrence v. Vodafone*.

The formal requirements for the initial license offer by the plaintiff are also not too high. The offer can be communicated in an informal way, e.g., via e-mail, and needs to contain only the essential terms of a later license agreement. At this stage it does not have to be a formally executed contract, which can be directly accepted by the defendant's signature. Moreover, it is not required that the license offer is directed at the legal entity, which is the defendant in the German case. If license agreements are usually negotiated on a company group level, it is sufficient to direct license offers to the parent company of the defendant or another affiliate, which is in charge of licensing negotiations for the group.[45] The focus of the German courts therefore lies primarily on the substance of the plaintiff's offer and the information about the calculation of the royalty rate.

4.5 Open Issues

Since the case law on FRAND in Germany following the CJEU decision *Huawei v. ZTE* is still developing, there are of course still a number of open issues. These include frequently discussed topics in the international context, which were not yet addressed by the German courts.

For example, the German courts have not expressed a final view on the definition of the royalty base and specifically whether this should be the Smallest Salable Patent-Practicing Unit (SSPPU) as postulated in the IEEE Standards Board Bylaws.[46] While there is case law in Germany on the royalty base, e.g., in the context of remuneration for employed inventors or damages calculations, the courts would likely follow the actual industry practice in license agreements when it comes to defining the royalty base and rate for a FRAND license. So far, however, this issue has not really become relevant in any of the published cases.

The question whether everybody is entitled to a license ("license to all") or whether the patentee can choose to grant licenses only on selected levels of the supply/distribution chain has not been addressed in German courts either. In one case, the Karlsruhe Higher Regional Court said that a license offer made by defendant's supplier cannot simply be ignored, because it is not from the defendant itself. In this case, the plaintiff sued one of the major German network operators as retailer of smartphones from various manufacturers in its shops. In its action, the plaintiff had already carved out smartphones from those manufacturers who had taken a license. The action therefore focused on the smartphones of unlicensed manufacturers, which were available in the defendant's shops. One of these manufacturers made a license offer to the plaintiff, but this was ignored by the plaintiff and the court in first instance, arguing that the license offer has to come from the defendant in the case. As such licenses are usually concluded on the level of the manufacturers, however, in the view of the Karlsruhe Higher Regional Court a reasonable plaintiff would first make a

45. *See*, e.g., Düsseldorf Regional Court, Case 4a O 15/17—*MPEG LA v. ZTE*, where a copy of a standard license agreement was sent to the defendant's parent company.
46. IEEE-SA Standards Boards Bylaws, s. 6.1 Definitions '*Reasonable Rate*', published under https://standards.ieee.org/about/policies/bylaws/sect6-7.html (downloaded on July 18, 2019).

licensing offer to the manufacturer and not the retailer.[47] Beyond that, however, German courts have not expressed a view whether suppliers on certain levels in the supply chain are entitled to a license by virtue of competition law, even if patentees do not usually grant licenses on this level.

5 FINAL CONCLUSION

The published decisions of German courts on FRAND already cover a large number of highly relevant aspects, which are intensely debated in the worldwide battle for the proper definition of FRAND. While German courts have taken decisive action to protect implementers against discrimination by patent owners, they have not yet provided real guidance how the fair value of standard essential patents should be determined. The decisions published so far suggest that German courts would rather grant the patentee wide discretion in setting royalty rates and other license terms and only interfere in cases of abuse under Article 102 TFEU. It remains to be seen whether this approach is enough to ensure fair market access in fields like telecommunications where every manufacturer or service provider has to use of multiple essential patents to third parties to participate.

47. Karlsruhe Higher Regional Court, Case 6 U 44/15, decision of April 23, 2015.

CHAPTER 15

Should Standard Essential Patents Be Licensed to Makers of Components or Manufacturers of Final Products? *A View from Competition Law Perspective*

Rafał Sikorski

1 INTRODUCTION

Technical standards are widely applied in multiple sectors of modern economy. They allow for interoperability of devices manufactured by multiple independent producers.[1] Some of the most widely used standards – such as 3G, LTE, Wi-Fi or Bluetooth – enable connectivity with telecommunication networks or communication between various devices. Soon, especially with the roll-out of the 5G standard, it will be hard to imagine a device that would not be connected to global networks.[2] Technical standards are developed within standard setting organizations (SSOs). They are highly complex and are frequently protected by multiple patents held by numerous rights holders.[3] Patents protecting such standards are referred to as standard essential patents (SEPs). Implementing a patent-protected standard requires a licence. SSOs, in order to ensure that standards may be widely adopted, require participants of the standard-setting process to commit themselves to license the use of their inventions on terms that would on the one hand ensure proper remuneration to the patentees and on the other allow for wide implementation of such standards by market participants. Thus, SSOs

1. Jorge Contreras, *Introduction* in Jorge Contreras (ed.) *The Cambridge Handbook of Technical Standardization* (Cambridge University Press 2018), 1.
2. David J. Teece, *5G and The Global Economy: How Static Policy Frameworks Can Defeat Open Innovation*, 3(2) CPI Antitrust Chronicle 13 (2019).
3. Tim Pohlmann, Knut Blind, *Landscaping Study on Standard Essential Patents* (2016), 10-52.

typically require patentees to grant licences to all willing potential licensees on fair, reasonable and non-discriminatory (FRAND) terms.[4]

Though FRAND commitments have become ubiquitous and are required by all major SSOs, what FRAND terms precisely mean is often disputed by both patentees and potential licensees. Such disputes have concentrated around reasonableness of royalties or the meaning of the non-discrimination. Currently, one of the most hotly debated issues by standards implementers as well as by numerous practitioners and academics is whether SEP holders are free to decide whether to licence manufacturers of final products or manufacturers of components. The nature of these disputes can be best illustrated by examples from automotive and smartphone industries.[5] Both cars and mobile phones communicate with telecommunications networks. They do so because they implement telecommunication standards, such as 3G and 4G. The connectivity with networks is enabled by so-called chips, that are special components where the relevant patent-protected technical standard technologies are implemented. SEP holders decide whether to license the maker of the communication enabling components or manufacturer of an end product – a car or a smartphone. Some SEP holders have decided to license final product manufacturers rather than component makers. It seems that they have been motivated by the desire to expand the base for calculating royalties due for the use of their patented technologies. Indeed, in many cases by licensing final manufacturers they have been able to obtain higher royalties from their licensees.

Component makers have complained about licensing practices of those SEP holders who license producers of final products only. They claim that refusal to license SEPs to component makers who are willing to conclude a licence on FRAND terms not only violates FRAND commitments made to SSOs during the standard-setting process but that such refusal also violates competition laws. Thus, component makers in such cases may try to hold SEP holders liable on two separate grounds. First, they may claim that such refusal constitutes a breach of a commitment to license on FRAND terms. This, in essence, leads to a contractual dispute, the resolution of which largely rests on interpretation of a particular FRAND pledge made to the SSO. Second, they may also resort to liability for breach of competition rules. Such liability largely depends on whether a refusal to license harms competition. Generally, it is widely accepted in competition law that a refusal to deal, including refusal to license, only exceptionally may result in liability for breach of competition law.

In this chapter the author will concentrate on the competition law aspect of refusals to license producers of components. Since FRAND commitments are in the very centre of the disputes concerning SEP licensing, therefore before introducing the contents of this chapter, the author would like to take a brief look at FRAND origins. Interestingly, the obligation to license willing licensees on FRAND terms has both competition and contract law origins. First, the US courts ordered patentees to license on FRAND terms in antitrust disputes initiated in the first half of the twentieth century

4. *Id.*, at 36-39.
5. Brief of Amici Curiae Continental Automotive Systems, Inc. and Denso Corporation in Support of Appellee Federal Trade Commission, *Federal Trade Commission v. Qualcomm Incorporated*, US Court of Appeals for the 9th Circuit, Case No. 19016122, 2-6 (29 November 2019).

as a reaction to numerous anticompetitive agreements entered into in major industries such as oil, fuels, metal, gypsum and glass.[6] Pooling and cross-licensing arrangements were used as a cover for hardcore violations of competition laws such as price fixing and market sharing agreements. Patentees, holding large patent portfolios, through various forms of cross-licensing and technology pooling agreements were capable of foreclosing access to various key markets and significantly affect the competitive process on those markets. The courts ordered FRAND licensing as a remedy for anticompetitive practices by patent holders. Second, at roughly the same time SSOs in the US were also interested in setting standards even though some of the technologies had already been patented.[7] The concept of FRAND licensing was also invoked to ensure that patents would not be used to hinder the development, spread and use of such standards.

The idea of licensing on FRAND terms was reintroduced towards the end of the twentieth century.[8] At that time, in consumer electronics and telecommunications sectors, technologies such as 2G, 3G, MPEG 2, MPEG 4 or CD and DVD were developed. Since numerous patents held by multiple patentees read on those technologies, a number of patent pools were formed to enable cost-effective licensing of large patent portfolios. In order to clear such arrangements entered into by competitors before competition authorities, the licensors proposed that patent portfolios would be licensed on FRAND terms to all interested parties. The principle of FRAND licensing is also widely accepted by SSOs all over the world. Standard-setting bodies such as European Telecommunications Standards Institute (ETSI), Institute of Electrical and Electronics Engineers (IEEE) or International Standards Organization (ISO) require that those participating in the standard-setting process, pledge to license their patent portfolios on (F)RAND terms, prior to accepting standard specifications covered by patents.[9]

Though the concept of licensing on FRAND terms has been so widely applied and accepted by patentees, licensees as well as competition authorities, still many issues related to FRAND licensing remain unclear. The question whether component makers should be entitled to a SEP licence is one of such issues. In this chapter the author focuses particularly on the hotly debated issue whether SEP holders may be liable for breach of competition laws if they decide to license final product manufacturers only rather than producers of components in which such technical standards are in fact implemented. The chapter is divided into four sections. Following this introductory section, in section 2, the issue of licensing at different levels of the supply chain will be

6. Jorge Contreras, *Origins of FRAND Licensing Commitments in the United States and Europe* in Jorge Contreras (ed.) *The Cambridge Handbook of Technical Standardization*, 150-157 (Cambridge University Press 2018); Jorge Contreras, *A Brief History of FRAND: Analyzing Current Debates in Standard Setting and Antitrust Through a Historical Lens*, 80 Antitrust Law Journal 40 (2015), 46-55; Rafał Sikorski, *Funkcjonowanie Zasobów Patentowych w Prawie Konkurencji Unii Europejskiej*, 54-70 (C.H. Beck 2013).
7. Contreras, *supra* n. 6, at 162-163; Contreras, *supra* n. 6, at 43-46.
8. Robert P. Merges, *Institutions for Intellectual Property Transactions* in Rochelle C. Dreyfuss, Diane L. Zimmerman, Henry First (ed.) Expanding the Boundaries of Intellectual Property, (Oxford University Press 2001).
9. *See* Art. 6.1 ETSI Intellectual Property Rights Policy; Art. 6.2 IEEE Standards Board By-Laws; Art. 2.2 ISO/IEC/ITU Common Patent Policy.

presented from the perspective of market participants, namely manufacturers of final products and components as well SEP licensors. In section 3, various approaches of courts and competition authorities to licensing of component makers will be analysed. In section 4, the author will briefly discuss the likely developments in the field and possible solutions, as well as insert concluding remarks.

2 LICENSING SEPs TO MANUFACTURERS OF COMPONENTS VERSUS LICENSING SEPs TO MANUFACTURERS OF FINAL PRODUCTS: INDUSTRY PERSPECTIVES

The practice of licensing end product manufacturers rather than component makers is not entirely new. The licensing programmes already available on various technology markets have envisaged licensing to end product manufacturers for quite some time. Such programmes have been made available in various sectors such as consumer electronics, telecommunications or with respect to lighting products.[10] Many such licensing programmes are made available by organizations administering various patent pools. Generally, such practices have not been challenged in the past. Particularly, market participants have not pointed to the anticompetitive potential of such licensing schemes. However, this has changed once Qualcomm adopted its strategy of licensing final product manufacturers only. Qualcomm insisted on licensing its SEP portfolio to mobile devices (such as smartphones) manufacturers rather than manufacturers of chip components which ensure network connectivity in such devices. A similar licensing pattern can now be observed in the automotive industry where holders of SEP portfolios prefer to license car makers rather than component manufacturers who develop components that actually implement SEP-protected technologies responsible for ensuring connectivity with telecommunication networks.

2.1 Qualcomm's 'No License, No Chips' Licensing Model

Qualcomm's practices with respect to SEP licensing have in the past few years attracted a substantial degree of attention and have been subject of proceedings in numerous Asian jurisdictions (China, Japan, South Korea and Taiwan)[11] and in the US (particularly *FTC v. Qualcomm*[12]). Qualcomm's licensing model deserves to be presented in greater detail. Qualcomm used to license its SEP portfolio to component manufacturers such as chip makers.[13] Later, it changed its long-established practice however, and

10. *See* licensing programmes offered by leading licensors such as: MPEG LA (www.mpegla.com) or Koninklijke Philips NV (https://www.ip.philips.com/licensing/program/100/led-based-luminaires-and-retrofit-bulbs).
11. The proceedings against Qualcomm in Asia were briefly discussed by Judge Lucy Koh in: *Federal Trade Commission v. Qualcomm Incorporated*, Case No. 17-CV-00220-LHK US District Court Northern District of California, 10-12.
12. The decision by US District Court Northern District of California in *FTC v. Qualcomm* was appealed to the US Court of Appeals for the 9th Circuit. The US Court of Appeals for the 9th Circuit in *FTC v. Qualcomm*, Case No. 19-1612 reversed the decision of the District Court.
13. *FTC v. Qualcomm*, US District Court Northern District Court, 6-7.

instead of providing licences to manufacturers of components who implement its SEPs, Qualcomm decided that it would rather license manufacturers of end products who use components which implement SEPs from its patent portfolio.[14]

It is noteworthy that Qualcomm is known as one of the industry leaders. It participated in the development of CDMA and LTE standards, and it has a sizeable portfolio of SEPs covering CDMA (3G) and LTE (4G) communication standards. Qualcomm's portfolio, though significant, is not the largest.[15] As a participant in the standard-setting process, it is committed to license its SEP portfolio on FRAND terms.[16] Qualcomm is not only an industry leader on technology markets. Additionally, Qualcomm has a very strong position on the market for chips, where it holds a dominant market position.[17] Although there are other chip makers, manufacturers of mobile devices are dependent on Qualcomm for the supply of Qualcomm's connectivity enabling chips. In fact, manufacturers of mobile devices have no choice but to obtain the supply of component chips from Qualcomm as the remaining chip suppliers do not have the potential necessary to satisfy the demand.[18]

The inventions protected by Qualcomm's SEPs are implemented in communication enabling chips. These chips are later used in end products such as mobile devices, smart home appliances or cars. With the roll-out of next generation communication technologies such as 5G and the rise of IoT, such chips will be used by producers of numerous other devices which will also become connected to global communication networks. The rise of IoT only shows that the number of potential licensees will significantly increase if the practice of licensing final product makers continues. There is a concern that such practice will only raise transactions costs of licensing.

Qualcomm stopped licensing component manufacturers and adopted a licensing policy known as 'no license, no chips'. According to Qualcomm's novel business strategy, final product manufacturers would not be able to buy chips produced by Qualcomm unless they enter into a licensing agreement with Qualcomm.[19] For many key players on the mobile devices market losing Qualcomm as a chip supplier would mean that they would not able to produce any of their final products. After all, a smartphone without a connectivity module is worthless.

Qualcomm however did not require its customers to obtain their chip supplies exclusively from Qualcomm. In fact, customers would pay the same royalty whether they bought Qualcomm's chips or chips from third-party suppliers. The royalty rate offered by Qualcomm was disputed. Component suppliers claimed that the royalty rates were not reasonable.[20] From Qualcomm's perspective, the royalty rates could not discourage customers from buying Qualcomm's chips. Qualcomm could always lower the chip price. Its overall income would likely remain the same. The only question was the source from which Qualcomm's income would come. However, by raising the

14. *Id.*, at 7, 127-128.
15. *Id.*, at 165-167.
16. *Id.*, at 5.
17. *Id.*, at 24-33 (CDMA chips), 34-41 (LTE chips).
18. *Id.*, at 44.
19. *Id.*, at 113.
20. *Id.*, at 162-194.

royalty rates beyond what is reasonable, Qualcomm could easily discourage its customers from buying chips from other producers. Higher royalty rates would mean that Qualcomm's competitors on the chip market would have to cut their chip prices to remain competitive vis-à-vis chip customers.[21] The royalty rates were not the only tool which Qualcomm employed to discourage its customers from buying chips from its competitors. It also offered bonuses in the form of payments; however, these payments would be available only to those who bought Qualcomm's chips.[22] These practices had a noticeable effect on the market. There is evidence which shows that the introduction of new chips was delayed, and that numerous market participant had to leave the market, while others were less likely to enter because they believed it was no longer profitable.[23]

Qualcomm has not sued component manufacturers, neither for damages nor in order to get an injunction. It was not interested in doing so. This is not surprising. It knew well that having pledged to the SSO to grant licences on FRAND terms to willing licensees it would not be able to obtain an injunction. Qualcomm must have also been aware that it would be unlikely for it to obtain excessive royalties from the manufacturers of such components. Thus, by choosing to license manufacturers of final products, who were dependant on the supply of Qualcomm's chips, Qualcomm has avoided disputes over its licensing terms.

2.2 Licensing in the Automotive Industry

Car manufacturers ensure that cars, just like other devices, are connected to telecommunication networks. Such connectivity allows for emergency communication, access to maps, travel information and various forms of entertainment as well as vehicle diagnostics.[24] In order to provide customers with access to cellular networks car manufacturers equip their cars with Telematic Control Units (TCUs).[25] These are provided to car manufacturers by Tier 1 manufacturers. TCUs allow for communication with cellular networks because there are equipped with special modules which are supplied by Tier 2 suppliers.[26] Module producers ensure network connectivity using special chips which are made by Tier 3 suppliers.[27] In fact, it is the chips which implement the technology ultimately responsible for communication with communication networks. Thus, it is at the chip level where technologies protected by SEPs – such as 3G or LTE – are implemented.[28]

21. *Id.*, at 187.
22. *Id.*, at 187-190.
23. *Id.*, at 194-200.
24. Brief of Amici Curiae Continental Automotive Systems, *supra* 5, at 3.
25. *Id.*, at 2.
26. *Id.*, at 3.
27. *Id.*
28. *Id.*, at 4.

In the automobile sector, it is normal for the car makers to source components from multiple suppliers.[29] Naturally, car manufacturers require the suppliers to indemnify them in case there are any IP infringement claims related to the components supplied. Car makers do not bother themselves with concluding licensing agreements for the use of IP used in those components. In the case of components which ensure connectivity, it would be natural for patentees who hold SEPs reading on the various communication standards implemented in those components to license chip makers. The market practice of numerous SEP holders however has shifted.[30] Many SEP holders prefer to license final product makers - in this case, the car producers - rather than manufacturers of components.[31] The reasons for such a shift are quite straightforwardly put by the patent holders. The strategy allows them to maximize profit from licensing their patent portfolios because the royalties are calculated as a fraction of the final product rather than the component.[32]

2.3 Industry Responses to Component Level Licensing

Various market participants have voiced their concerns over licensing final product manufacturers rather than those who implement patent-protected technologies. Basically, many market players underline that licensing at the component level is the most efficient mode of licensing and one that brings maximum certainty to the market.

When patent licensing occurs at component level, the subsequent first sale of the component leads to patent exhaustion. In the car industry, that would mean that neither Tier 2 and 1, nor car manufacturers need to worry about patent infringement. Exhaustion ensures that the product which implements patent-protected technology may circulate freely. Suppliers up in the supply chain would not have to worry about negotiations of licensing agreements for the use of technologies they know very little about.

Licensing at component manufacturer level is also the most efficient form of licensing because it is the actual implementers at component level who know the most about patent-protected technologies implemented in their products.[33] They are in the best position to assess the validity of such patents and assess whether these patents are indeed essential, that is necessary for the practice of a given standard.[34] They, as actual implementers, are also in the best position to assess what value such patented technologies contribute to the product.[35]

---

29. Brief of Association of Global Automakers and Alliance of Automobile Manufacturers as Amici Curiae Supporting Appellee, *Federal Trade Commission v. Qualcomm Incorporated*, US Court of Appeals for the 9th Circuit, Case No. 19016122, 2-6 (29 November 2019), 5.
30. Brief of Amici Curiae Continental Automotive Systems, *supra* 5, at 6.
31. Brief of Amicus Curiae Nokia Technologies Oy in Support of Neither Party, *Federal Trade Commission v. Qualcomm Incorporated*, US Court of Appeals for the 9th Circuit, Case No. 19016122, 2-6 (30 August 2019), 15-17.
32. Brief of Amici Curiae Continental Automotive Systems, *supra* 5, at 24.
33. Brief of Amici Curiae Continental Automotive Systems, *supra* 5, at 19.
34. *Id.*
35. *Id.*

Licensing manufacturers of final products generally results in higher prices. Royalty rates tend to be higher when they are calculated on the basis of the value of the final product rather than the price of the components.[36] This may result in a situation when the royalty base used for the calculation of the royalty reflects not only the value of the licensed inventions but also various other technologies implemented in a final product.[37] In such a case the SEP licensor may end up being overcompensated, while the consumers will likely face higher prices.[38]

3 APPROACHES TOWARDS REFUSAL TO LICENSE COMPONENT MAKERS IN SELECTED JURISDICTIONS

The practice of refusing to license SEPs to component makers has already been examined in numerous jurisdictions around the world. Both courts and competition authorities have assessed the practices of licensing only at the final product level in light of competition law. Particularly, the authorities analysed such practices as possible abuses of dominant position held on the market for components and SEP-protected technologies. Interestingly, in Asia (China, South Korea, Taiwan) competition authorities have quite unanimously found Qualcomm in breach of competition rules, imposing significant monetary sanctions.[39] In the US, in the court battle between Federal Trade Commission (FTC) and Qualcomm, on appeal the 9th Circuit ruled in Qualcomm's favour upholding the practice of licensing only to end product manufacturers as compliant with US antitrust and competition laws. Additionally, the Department of Justice (DOJ) has quite recently cleared the practice of granting licences to final product makers when assessing the impact of Avanci patent pool on competition.[40] In the EU, although the practice was drawn to the attention of the Commission it has not so far led to the Commission formally initiating proceedings against SEP holders.[41] That the matter goes to the Court of Justice of the European Union (CJEU) was initially strongly suggested by the German *Bundeskartelsamt* in the context of one of the patent disputes in Germany between an SEP holder – Nokia and a German automaker –

36. *Id.*, at 20.
37. *Id.*, at 22.
38. *Id.*, at 23.
39. *See* the decisions by the following competition authorities and courts: Korea Fair Trade Commission Decision from 21 December 2016 imposing remedial orders against Qualcomm Inc. and two of its affiliates. The decision was upheld on 4 December 2019 by the Seoul High Court; Taiwan Fair Trade Commission Decision from 11 October 2017 imposing, among others, a monetary fine on Qualcomm Inc. The case was later settled between the Taiwan Fair Trade Commission and Qualcomm Inc.; National Development and Reform Commission decision from 10 February 2015 imposing administrative penalty against Qualcomm Inc.
40. Department of Justice, Antitrust Division, Business Review Letter for Avanci LLC, 28 July 2020.
41. Kushita Vassant, *EU's Daimler v. Nokia SEP probe moves forward with round of questions*, 25 June 2020, available at: https://mlexmarketinsight.com/insights-center/editors-picks/area-of-expertise/antitrust/eus-daimler-nokia-sep-probe-moves-forward-with-third-round-of-questions. Kushita Vassant reports on the state of informal actions taken by the EU Commission which is currently gathering information from the interested parties on the market situation concerning the licensing of SEPs to component and final product makers.

Daimler.[42] Finally, the decision to refer the case of component/final product licensing to the CJEU was taken by the court in Düsseldorf.[43]

3.1 Recent Developments in the US

3.1.1 FTC v. Qualcomm

Qualcomm's licensing model described above was challenged in *FTC v. Qualcomm*. FTC sued Qualcomm and demanded an injunction alleging that Qualcomm's licensing policies and practices excluded competitors and harmed competition in the modem chip markets and therefore violated *inter alia* §§ 1 and 2 of the Sherman Act and § 5(a) of the FTC Act. The District Court ordered a permanent, worldwide injunction which prohibited Qualcomm from continuing its business practices.

The District Court found that: (1) Qualcomm's refusal to license rival chip makers violated both the FRAND commitments and constituted violation of an antitrust duty to deal under § 2 Sherman Act; (2) Qualcomm's royalty rates were 'unreasonably high' because they were based on its market share and the handset price rather than on the value of its patents; (3) Qualcomm's royalties together with the 'no license, no chip' policy imposed an artificial and anticompetitive surcharge on rivals' chips and increased their price resulting in anticompetitive exclusivity; (4) Qualcomm's 'no license, no chips' policy amounted to anticompetitive conduct against Original Equipment Manufacturers (OEMs); (5) Qualcomm's exclusive deals with Apple foreclosed substantial share of the modem chip market in violation of both Sherman Act provisions. The District Court found that collectively Qualcomm's practices and licensing policy created insurmountable and artificial barriers for Qualcomm's competitors. Qualcomm appealed and the Court of Appeals for the 9th Circuit reversed the District Court's ruling.

3.1.1.1 Duty to Deal

The Court of Appeals examined whether Qualcomm was under a duty to deal with its competitors. The Court referred to well-established precedent and stated that generally under the Sherman Act a trader or a manufacturer was free to decide with whom he deals and on what terms.[44] The Court stated that the exception to the general rule of no duty to deal was narrowly defined by the Supreme Court in *Aspen Skiing Co. v. Aspen*

---

42. Florian Muller, *Federal Cartel Office of Germany asks regional courts to refer component-level standard essential patent licensing questions to CJEU, disagrees with Nokia* (22 June 2020), available at: http://www.fosspatents.com/2020/06/breaking-news-federal-cartel-office-of.html. Florian Muller reports about a letter from high ranking official in the German Cartel Office urging the courts in Mannheim and Dusseldorf to stay the patent infringement proceedings and refer questions concerning refusals to license the use of SEP-protected technology to manufacturers of components.
43. Landesgericht Düsseldorf, 4c O 17/19.
44. The Court referred to the well-established precedents on the right of every business to exercise discretion and make its own decision as to the parties with whom he wishes to deal citing

Highlands Skiing Corp.[45] There the Supreme Court specified the conditions which had to be met to establish the existence of such a duty. Refusal to deal would be anticompetitive if: (1) a company unilaterally terminates a voluntary and profitable course of business; (2) the only rational explanation for such behaviour is sacrificing short-term profits for long-term gains resulting from exclusion of a rival; (3) the refusal to deal already involves products that the defendant sells in the existing market to other similarly situated customers. The Court found that the requirements for establishing a duty to deal under § 2 had not been met. First, the Court found that there was no evidence that Qualcomm, after having obtained monopolistic position on the relevant chip market, licensed other component manufacturers. Thus, the prior course of dealing was missing.[46] Second, the Court also found that there was no proof that Qualcomm intended to sacrifice short-term profits. Rather, as the Court observed, the purpose was to maximize both short- and long-term profits. Qualcomm only followed into the footsteps of other SEP licensors, in order to adopt a more lucrative licensing model.[47] Third, the Court stated that this case was different because, unlike in *Aspen Skiing*, Qualcomm did not single out any of its competitors in order to put him out business, rather Qualcomm treated all of its competitors on the chip market in a similar manner. The Court stressed that Qualcomm declined to enforce its patents against any of the competitors.[48]

To those familiar with EU competition law the approach taken by the Court of Appeals towards what constitutes an abusive practice might seem both narrow and rather formalistic. The Court observes that refusal to deal may be abusive only within the very narrow limits defined in the *Aspen Skiing*. The principle that in a market economy anyone may freely decide whether one wishes to deal with others is recognized both in the US, the EU and other jurisdictions. Generally, it is also accepted that a duty to deal may arise under competition law in limited set of circumstances. The CJEU for example has consistently treated refusal to deal as an abuse of dominant position only in exceptional cases. The analysis of CJEU case law suggests that indeed the CJEU is cautious in recognizing such a duty. However, the approach of the US antitrust law seems to be unnecessarily cautious.

The CJEU case law shows that refusals to deal may harm competition not only in the narrow circumstances found in the US Supreme Court's decision in *Alpen Skiing*. The Supreme Court found that there was no violation of §2 Sherman Act because there was no prior course of dealing. Indeed, in duty to deal cases it is often the case that the parties had business relations prior to one of the parties deciding to terminate them. In *Microsoft*,[49] for example, the Court of First Instance clearly established that Microsoft – prior to deciding that it would no longer make the information allowing for ensuring interoperability of its operating system with server operating systems offered by third

Supreme Court's decisions in *United States v. Colgate & Co.*, 250 U.S. 300 (1919) and *Verizon Communications Inc. v. Law Offices of Curtis V. Trinko*, LLP, 540 U.S. 398 (2004).

45. *Aspen Skiing Co. v. Aspen Highlands Skiing Corp.*, 472 U.S. 585 (1985).
46. *FTC v. Qualcomm Inc.*, US Court of Appeals for the 9th Cir., Case No. 19016122, 33-34.
47. *Id.*, at 34.
48. *Id.*, at 35.
49. T-201/04, *Microsoft v. Commission*, EU:T:2007:289.

parties - in fact provided its competitors with such information. Microsoft stopped to share the information necessary to ensure interoperability when it saw that it would allow it to eliminate its competitors on the market for server operating systems. In *Magill*[50] the CJEU however found abuse of dominant position even though there was no prior course of dealing between the television stations that refused to make available the weekly TV programmes thus hindering the appearance of a new product on the market, namely a comprehensive weekly TV guide comprising of information on the planned broadcasts by each of the respective TV stations. The CJEU found that as a result of the refusal to license, new products for which there was consumer demand could not be put on the market. Finally, in *Huawei v. ZTE*[51] prior course of dealing between the parties - the SEP owner and the SEP implementer - was not a factor at all. Rather the court was concerned with foreclosure on the downstream markets where the standard technology was implemented. Its concerns seem to have centred over harm that might arise for consumers as a result of the foreclosure and a less intensive price competition.

Courts, being cautious in recognizing a duty to deal under competition law, have a tendency to adhere very closely, sometimes too closely, to previously decided cases and particular sets of circumstances. They become overly cautious and reluctant to recognize that abusive behaviour may also occur in other circumstances. Requiring prior course of dealing would for example exclude the possibility of applying antitrust laws in cases when newcomers are denied access to SEPs. A newcomer, by definition, would have no prior course of dealing with an SEP holder. Similarly, if we were to stick to the new product requirement resulting from the *Magill* decision, it would not be possible for the CJEU to reach the conclusion reached in *Huawei v. ZTE*, since access to patent-protected standard technologies does not necessarily result in the implementer introducing a new product to the market. Often, access to standards merely results in greater price competition, rather than satisfying new consumer needs.

3.1.1.2 Qualcomm's Royalties as an Artificial Surcharge

The Court of Appeals also rejected the idea that violations of § 2 Sherman Act resulted from breaches of FRAND commitments made by Qualcomm to the SSOs during the standardization process, in particular breach of a commitment to license SEPs on reasonable licensing terms. FTC claimed that breaches of commitments to license on FRAND terms allowed Qualcomm to collect a surcharge from its customers. The Court stated that if indeed there was a surcharge it had an impact on Qualcomm's customers, not rivals.[52] It also stressed that the licensing policy was chip-supplier neutral, since Qualcomm collected the same royalties from all OEMs irrespective of the chips that they used.[53] The Court added that FRAND commitments should be enforced rather via

50. C-241/91 P and C-242/91 P, *RTE and ITP v. Commission*, EU:C:1995:98.
51. C-170/13, *Huawei v. ZTE Corp.*, EU:C:2015:477.
52. *FTC v. Qualcomm Inc.*, US Court of Appeals for the 9th Cir., Case No. 19016122, 36.
53. *Id.*

patent and contract laws than antitrust law, as contract and patent laws are better equipped to resolve commercial disputes.[54]

The Court rejected the idea that calculating royalties on the basis of price for the whole handset rather than prices of the smallest saleable patent practicing unit (SSPPU) made the royalties unreasonable. The SSPPU in the Court's opinion was not a per se rule for establishing royalties. Rather it was a useful tool that could be used to establish reasonable level of royalties in jury cases.[55] Therefore, the SSPPU test, though helpful in establishing the level of reasonable royalties, could not be considered part of patent substantive damages law. Consequently, referring to the price of the cellphone as a benchmark for establishing reasonable royalties was acceptable. The Court also rejected the idea that royalties automatically become anticompetitive if they are not in line with current, intrinsic value of the patent portfolio nor the rates charged by other patent holders with respect to their portfolios.[56]

The Court – when rejecting the idea that the royalties charged constituted an artificial surcharge on Qualcomm's competitors – differentiated Qualcomm's practices from the practices described in *Caldera Inc. v. Microsoft Corp.*[57] where Microsoft charged royalties on all equipment produced by OEM manufacturers, irrespective of whether the OEM manufacturers used Microsoft's MS-DOS or software made by other software producers. Microsoft's practices resulted in OEM manufacturers having to pay royalties twice even though Microsoft's software was not installed. In *FTC v. Qualcomm* the facts were different, cellphone manufacturers needed access to Qualcomm's SEP portfolio, and they were granted such access on the same licensing terms regardless of the source for the chips implementing Qualcomm's SEPs. Therefore, the Court rejected the idea that Qualcomm's licensing practice resulted in exclusivity of chips supply.

The FTC alleged that Qualcomm's anticompetitive royalties imposed a surcharge on its rivals because they allowed Qualcomm to charge ultralow prices for its chips. This enabled Qualcomm to exclude its competitors from the chip market by squeezing their margins on the chip sales. FTC also alleged that Qualcomm could transfer the artificial surcharge obtained from cellphone manufacturers to subsidize its chips' sales. The Court rejected these claims as well, establishing that for the margin squeeze to lead to antitrust liability, there would have to be either a duty to deal or predatory pricing. In the Court's opinion there was no evidence neither for the existence of such duty nor of predatory pricing.[58]

3.1.1.3 Qualcomm's 'No License, No Chips' Policy

When assessing the novel licensing model adopted by Qualcomm, the Court found no anticompetitive harm for Qualcomm's competitors. The Court underlined that the fact

54. *Id.*, at 39-40.
55. *Id.*, at 42-43.
56. *Id.*, at 43-44.
57. *Caldera, Inc. v. Microsoft Corp.*, 72 F. Supp. 2d 1295 (D. Utah 1999).
58. *FTC v. Qualcomm Inc.*, US Court of Appeals for the 9th Cir., Case No. 19016122, 47.

that Qualcomm demanded royalties for the use of its SEP-protected technologies regardless whether OEM manufacturers obtained their chips from Qualcomm or other producers by nature could not have had a negative impact on competition.[59] The level of royalties, the Court admitted, could impact the overall price that the OEM manufacturers would have to pay for the SEP-implementing chips, but not the competition on the chip market.[60] The Court also stressed that whether the royalties were reasonable was an issue that should be dealt with in patent and not antitrust law.[61] Finally, the Court stated that the competing chip manufacturers could have had antitrust claims if Qualcomm instead of adopting 'no license, no chips' policy adopted a 'no chips, no license' policy. Then, the licence would be contingent on sourcing chips from Qualcomm. Such tying could indeed foreclose access to the markets for chip manufacturers. However, the policy adopted by Qualcomm, as chip source-neutral, did not have such anticompetitive effect.[62]

Consequently, the Court of Appeals reversed the decision of the District Court on all grounds. It adopted the view that there was no need to apply antitrust laws to Qualcomm's licensing practices. The Court was of the opinion that FRAND disputes could satisfactorily be resolved just on the basis contract and patent law.

3.1.1.4 Critique of the Court of Appeals' Decision

The Court of Appeals seems to have adopted a very formalistic approach to assessment of the effects that Qualcomm's licensing policy had on competition. First, the Court strongly insisted that Qualcomm could not have hurt competition because its licensing policy applied irrespective of the source from which OEM manufacturers bought components implementing Qualcomm's SEP-protected technologies. Second, the Court also stressed that FRAND disputes would be better resolved in contract and patent law than through competition law. Thus, claims that royalties demanded by Qualcomm were exceeding what is reasonable should have been resolved not by applying antitrust laws.

Indeed, it is true that FRAND disputes concerning SEPs may be resolved under contract and patent laws and indeed they are often successfully resolved without making reference to competition law. However, when assessing licensing practices of an SEP holder, the connection between FRAND licensing terms and standardization is one that can hardly be overrated. In its Guidelines on horizontal agreements,[63] the Commission rightly sees both procompetitive[64] and anticompetitive potential of standard setting.[65] In particular, the Commission rightly recognizes that standardization

59. *Id.*, at 48.
60. *Id.*, at 49.
61. *Id.*
62. *Id.*, at 50.
63. Communication from the Commission – Guidelines on the applicability of Art. 101 of the Treaty on the Functioning of the European Union to horizontal co-operation agreements (Guidelines on horizontal agreements), 2011/C 11/01.
64. *Id.*, at 263.
65. *Id.*, at 264.

may result in foreclosure of competitors, if they are to be excluded from accessing the standard.[66] If there was foreclosure, the assessment of standardization under EU competition law would have to be negative. However, when SEP-protected standards are made available to all willing licensees on FRAND basis then the anticompetitive potential of standardization will not be realized.[67] If in addition to commitment to FRAND licensing, the standardization process is transparent and access to standard setting is not restricted – than the Commission will assume that there is no restriction of competition within the meaning of Article 101(1) TFEU.[68] Thus, whether FRAND commitments are observed by SEP holders or not is crucial when conducting competitive law assessment of the practices of patentees holding SEPs.

To claim that SEP holders should be free to set the royalties in order to maximize their profits and that competition law should not intervene in such cases because that would undermine incentives for innovation misses the point. And while it is generally true that competition authorities should not get involved in price setting and becoming price regulators, in the standard-setting context it is only when patentees voluntarily limit themselves to royalties that are reasonable that the benefits of standardization can be realized. So, though SEP holders are limited with respect to the amount of royalties that they can demand, they are instead obtaining a much wider potential market for their patent-protected technologies.

Raising the royalties above the FRAND level may have significant anticompetitive effects. This is especially the case when the SEP holder is actively competing with potential licensees on the product market. In such cases the SEP holder may decide whether his profit should come from royalties or from the downstream product market. Raising royalties beyond what is reasonable would raise the costs of the competitors, reduce their margins and potentially drive them out of the downstream product markets. The Court of Appeals in *FTC v. Qualcomm* seems to underestimate these potential risks resulting from violating FRAND commitments by SEP holders. Thus, the fact that Qualcomm charges the same royalties to each end product maker irrespective of the source of components might be of little assistance from competition point of view. Higher royalties allow the SEP holder to lower the price of its own products, while still retaining satisfactory profit levels. For competitors however that would mean the necessity of reducing profit margins on the sale of their SEP-implementing components.

So, while keeping royalties at reasonable level is essential for the SEP holders in order to maintain incentives for innovation into the patent-protected technologies, royalties that exceed reasonable level might lead to foreclosure. A policy of licensing only at the end product level, as the patentee acknowledges, enables the SEP holder to charge higher royalties. Additionally, it – to a greater degree, though not absolutely – insulates the SEP holder's rates from legal challenges in the courts. Whereas generally the royalties' levels are disputed when SEP holders initiate infringement proceedings, here the SEP holder does not initiate such litigation. End product manufacturers are

66. *Id.*, at 268.
67. *Id.*, at 285.
68. *Id.*, at 280.

generally in a worse position to challenge the level of royalties, as they often do not specialize in the technologies adopted by component makers. In such cases, if a component maker would like a license, he would have to initiate lawsuits alleging the duty to license arising under competition law. Burden of proof of the conditions justifying the grant of such a licence would be on such a willing licensee.

The Court's piecemeal approach towards Qualcomm's practice does not help in comprehensive assessment of its anticompetitive effects. Recognizing the effects on competition of the 'no license, no chips' policy requires looking at the practice as a whole.

3.1.2 DOJ Business Review Letter Concerning Avanci Patent Pool[69]

Patent pools have generally been perceived positively by the DOJ as well as by competition authorities and courts around the world.[70] In a number of Business Review Letters in the past years, the DOJ recognized procompetitive effects of patent pools.[71] They have generally been cleared as enabling transfer of technology by providing a one-stop shop and thus reducing transaction costs. The Avanci pool is interesting, because the DOJ dealt with a pool that envisaged licensing to manufacturers of final products, rather than manufacturers of components.

Avanci operated patent pools aggregating patents essential to the practice of cellular standards such as 2G, 3G and 4G in vehicles and smart meters.[72] This time Avanci sought from the DOJ a Business Review Letter of its proposed patent licensing pool designed for the licensing of 5G standard essential patents to the automotive industry and the distribution of royalties among patent holders.[73] The pool is open to all those who hold at least one patent that reads on the relevant cellular standard.[74]

Patent holders are not allowed to join other competing pools for the same products for which Avanci pool was established, unless a patentee had already participated in such a pool prior to joining Avanci pool or a patentee withdraws from Avanci pool.[75] The pool participants are however free to license their patents for the

---

69. Department of Justice, Antitrust Division, Business Review Letter for Avanci LLC, 28 July 2020.
70. Communication from the Commission – Guidelines on the applicability of Art. 101 of the Treaty on the Functioning of the European Union to technology transfer agreements, 2014/C 89/03, para. 245.
71. *See*, in particular, Letter from Joel I. Klein, Acting Assistant Attorney Gen., U.S. Dep't of Justice, to G.R. Beeney, Esq. (16 December 1998), available at: http://www.usdoj.gov/atr/public/busreview/2121.pdf (3C DVD Business Review Letter); Letter from Joel I. Klein, Acting Assistant Attorney Gen., U.S. Dep't of Justice, to Carey R. Ramos, Esq. (10 June 1999), available at: http://www.usdoj.gov/atr/public/busreview/2485.pdf (6C DVD Business Review Letter); Letter from Joel I. Klein, Acting Assistant Attorney Gen., U.S. Dep't of Justice, to G.R. Beeney, Esq. (26 June 1997), available at: http://www.usdoj.gov/atr/public/busreview/215742.pdf (MPEG-2 Business Review Letter); Letter from Charles A. James, Acting Assistant Attorney Gen., U.S. Dep't of Justice, to Ky P. Ewing, Esq. (12 November 2002), available at: http://www.usdoj.gov/atr/public/busreview/200455.pdf (3G Business Review Letter).
72. Business Review Letter for Avanci LLC, *supra* 68, at 3.
73. *Id.*, at 1.
74. *Id.*, at 3.
75. *Id.*, at 4.

use in products other than the ones for which the Avanci pool was established. With respect to such products they are free to join other pools or license their patents independently.[76] They are also free to license independently component manufacturers.[77]

The Review Letter also refers to the *Antitrust Guidelines for the Licensing of Intellectual Property*[78] and states the field-of-use limitations, such as being limited to connected vehicles rather than components such as telematic units, allow the licensor to effectively exploit its patents by increasing the licensor's incentive to further license its invention and so on.[79] Additionally, the Review Letter points to the fact that limiting field of use to connected cars results in numerous licensing efficiencies, as it simplifies the scope, pricing and licensee collection.[80] Avanci also underlines that vehicle manufacturer base is smaller and more consistent and stable over time than the component manufacturers.[81] Avanci claims that it would be more difficult for it to track component manufacturers at Tier 1, 2 or 3.[82]

The DOJ adds that end-level licensing also ensures that licensors are properly compensated for their innovation. The DOJ accepts the fact that the pool sets the royalty rates at the level of the value of technology to vehicle manufacturers.[83] This – according to the DOJ – allows to recoup the investment in the development of the patented technology. This may also encourage greater licensor participation and allow to further reduce the costs of licensing as more licensors join the Avanci licensing programme.[84]

3.2 Developments in the EU

In the EU, the unwillingness of some of the SEP holders to license willing component makers has already been brought to the attention of the EU Commission by car maker Daimler and component part manufacturers such as Continental, BURY, Valeo and Gemalto. The practice of the SEP holders to deny licences to component manufacturers has also been challenged in the German courts in numerous proceedings that the SEP holders initiated against car makers.

---

76. *Id.*, at 16.
77. *Id.*, at 17.
78. Department of Justice and the Federal Trade Commission, *Antitrust Guidelines for the Licensing of Intellectual Property,* 12 January 2017.
79. Business Review Letter for Avanci LLC, *supra* 69, at 18.
80. *Id.*, at 18.
81. *Id.*, at 18-19.
82. *Id.*, at 19.
83. *Id.*, at 20.
84. *Id.*, at 21.

3.2.1 **Nokia v. Daimler** ***(Mannheim Regional Court)***[85]

In the course of the patent infringement proceedings initiated by Nokia against Daimler in the Mannheim Court, the German *Bundeskartelsamt* sent a letter to the court in which it suggested that the court stays infringement proceedings and seeks a preliminary ruling from the CJEU on a number of issues related to the interpretation of Article 102 TFEU. First, the *Bundeskartelsamt* suggested that the Mannheim Court asked the CJEU whether an SEP holder, who sought injunctive relief against an end product manufacturer while at the same time refusing to provide a comprehensive licence to its suppliers, abused dominant position held on the market for standard technologies. Second, the *Bundeskartelsamt* also suggested to ask the CJEU whether an SEP holder was free in deciding against whom the infringement proceedings should be initiated. The third question related to specific circumstances when the supplier would be entitled to obtaining a licence. Finally, the *Bundeskartelsamt* proposed to ask the CJEU if the SEP holder was free to license only to a particular supplier in the supply chain.

Unfortunately, the Mannheim Court decided not to refer the questions concerning the interpretation of Article 102 TFEU to the CJEU. The court decided not to stay the proceedings because of the relatively short remainder of the term of protection of the patent-in-suit. Interestingly, the short remaining period was considered to be weighing in favour of the patentee rather than the SEP implementer.

3.2.2 **Nokia v. Daimler** ***(Dusseldorf Regional Court)***[86]

Although, the Mannheim Regional Court decided not to refer questions concerning the interpretation of Article 102 TFEU to the CJEU, similar issues have also been raised in proceedings in the court in Dusseldorf and Munich.[87] The Dusseldorf Regional Court again plays a key role in providing the CJEU with a possibility of developing the EU law with respect to licensing activities of SEP holders, by referring questions on the legality of the practice of refusing to license SEPs to component manufacturers.

A number of questions referred to the CJEU concern issues important from the perspective of this chapter.[88] First, the Dusseldorf Regional Court asks if refusal to license willing suppliers of components which implement SEP-protected technologies and subsequently initiating infringement proceedings in order to obtain injunctive relief against manufacturers of final products can be considered an abuse of dominance within the meaning of Article 102 TFEU. The referring court also asks whether the fact that it is a customary practice of downstream producers to require suppliers of components to clear all relevant IP rights and to obtain necessary licences matters when assessing the activities of the SEP holders. The referring court also asks if there is any preference for licensing SEPs at a particular level of the supply chain, particularly

85. Landgericht Mannheim, Case No. 2 O 34/19 *Nokia v. Daimler*.
86. Landgericht Dusseldorf, Case No. 4c O 17/19.
87. Florian Muller discusses extensively the cases against auto makers at www.fosspatents.com.
88. For an English translation of the questions referred to the CJEU, *see* for example: https://www.lexology.com/library/detail.aspx?g=3d71ae13-dae7-4dc8-ad6f-7db25782a636.

to the immediate suppliers of components to final producers, or whether suppliers at all levels of the supply chain are entitled to a licence. Second, the Dusseldorf Court asks whether the licence for upstream suppliers should be for all relevant uses of standard technology so that manufacturers of final products no longer require an independent licence from an SEP holder. Finally, if the CJEU decides that initiating infringement proceedings against a manufacturer of final products does not constitute abuse within the meaning of Article 102 TFEU, the referring court seeks to know what criteria would be relevant to assess whether seeking an injunction against upstream component manufacturers at other levels in the supply chain could constitute such abuse.

3.2.3 **Huawei v. Nokia** ***(Dusseldorf Regional Court)***[89]

Huawei, a Chinese manufacturer of components ensuring network connectivity, decided to sue Nokia, alleging that Nokia's refusal to license its SEPs to Huawei constituted abuse of dominant position within the meaning of Article 102 TFEU. Huawei stated that it was entitled to a license to practice certain SEPs held by Nokia. Interestingly, breach of competition law was used by Huawei as the basis for attacking Nokia, rather than as a defence in patent infringement proceedings.

If Huawei were successful, the Court would require Nokia to provide Huawei with a licensing offer on FRAND terms. This would initiate the procedure established by the CJEU in *Huawei v. ZTE*. It would also most likely, sooner or later, lead to Huawei – a connectivity module supplier to automobile industry – obtaining a FRAND licence to practice Nokia's SEPs. Such a licence would be a licence to make and have made products compliant with the relevant standards. Thus, the licence would cover not only Huawei but also its immediate suppliers. In effect, if Huawei put such products on the market the relevant SEP would be exhausted. Car makers would no longer be bothered with possible patent infringement claims from SEP holders such as Nokia because they would obtain supplies of standard-compliant components from properly licensed component maker.

3.2.4 ***Licensing Between SEP Holders and Component Makers***

Interestingly, some of the patentees who hold substantial portfolios of SEPs reading on telecommunication standards have decided to license component makers directly. First, Sharp – a Japanese SEP holder – has recently granted an exhaustive licence to Huawei.[90] This allowed Huawei to produce chipsets, telecommunications modules and telematics control units supplied later to car makers, without infringing Sharp's patents. As a result of the licensing agreement concluded with Huawei, Sharp's

89. *See* the comment on *Huawei v. Nokia* by Florian Muller, *Game changer in automotive patent wars? Huawei brought antitrust complaint against Nokia in German court to get exhaustive module-level SEP license*, available at www.fosspatents.com (30 October 2019).
90. Florian Muller, *Sharp grants automotive component-level SEP license to Huawei, partially withdraws patent infringement suits against Daimler*, www.fosspatents.com (13 July 2020).

disputes with a German car manufacturer Daimler have become meritless in so far as Daimler implements components sourced from Huawei.

Similar settlement agreement has recently been concluded by Sisvel with a Swiss IoT component maker U-blox, a company that supplies components not only for the automotive market.[91] U-blox was successful in obtaining such licences in the past with other SEP holders. Once U-blox places its components on the market, patents will be exhausted. Those who buy such component will no longer be threatened by patent infringement litigation.

4 FUTURE DEVELOPMENTS: POSSIBLE SOLUTIONS – CONCLUSIONS

4.1 Future Developments

The policy of licensing end product manufacturers rather than component makers is likely to be further challenged in the courts on both sides of the Atlantic and more generally in jurisdictions around the world. In the EU, absent SEP holders abandoning their policy of licensing only end products manufacturers, the role of CJEU in resolving disputes over competition law implications of such licensing practices will be crucial. The practice of licensing end product makers may in the future also become the subject of proceedings before the EU Commission. In the US, although in *FTC v. Qualcomm* the Court of Appeals for the 9th Circuit denied the petition for rehearing *en banc*[92], the disputes over licensing component makers might come before the courts on other grounds than antitrust.

4.2 Licensing Makers of Final Products Does Not Always Raise Competition Concerns

Licensing end product manufacturers rather than component makers does not always raise antitrust concerns. If an SEP licensor grants licences on genuinely FRAND terms to end product makers than indeed there could be no harm to competition.[93] This is much more likely with an SEP licensor who is not present on the downstream product market where the technology is implemented. Such a purely technological licensor has little or no interest to foreclose other market participants from competing with him on the downstream product markets. However, when an SEP holder is present on the downstream product market where his SEPs are implemented, he has a greater incentive to eliminate others from that market, especially when the downstream

91. Florian Muller, *Component-level SEP licensing gains ground as Avanci member and notorious patent troll Sisvel settles litigation with Switzerland's U-blox*, www.fosspatents.com (26 September 2020).
92. For the decision denying the petition to rehear *en banc, see* https://www.docketalarm.com/cases/US_Court_of_Appeals_Ninth_Circuit/19-16122/FTC_v._Qualcomm_Inc/270/.
93. Jorge Padilla, Koren Wong-Ervin, *Portfolio Licensing at the End-User Device Level: Analyzing Refusals to License FRAND-Assured Standard-Essential Patents at the Component Level* (2016), text available at: https://ssrn.com/abstract=2806688, 18-20.

product business is profitable. In particular, such an SEP holder may raise the royalties beyond what is fair and reasonable thus causing greater costs for other market participants and reducing margins on the implementer's products, consequently making such an implementer less competitive on the downstream product market.

4.3 Setting-up a Dedicated Licensing Company

Vertically integrated SEP holders may also try to avoid potential claims that their licensing practices violate competition laws by setting-up licensing companies that would be organizationally independent from them. Such companies, if run by truly independent experts, could guarantee that their licensing policies would not harm competition on the downstream product markets. Such experts could not only independently assess the value of patent-protected technologies and consequently set royalties at levels complying with FRAND commitments but could also be helpful in ensuring that only essential patents are licensed, that is, patents that are valid and necessarily infringed when a given standard technology is implemented.

If such organizational steps were taken, the independence of the licensing company from the initial vertically integrated SEP owner was ensured and if the licences were indeed granted on FRAND basis, than it would be possible not to license at all possible levels of the supply chain and concentrate on licensing only the final product makers without running the risk of infringing competition laws. Whether such a licensing practice would comply with commitments made to an SSO during the standard-setting process is another issue but at least antitrust risks could be eliminated.

4.4 Room for Competition Law in Enforcing FRAND Commitments

Competition law has an important role in policing SEP licensing and FRAND commitments. Though indeed on many occasions the implementer will be able to defend himself against an SEP owner eager to impose un-FRAND licensing conditions, the law of patent remedies or contract law may not always be sufficient. First, some jurisdictions still are hesitant to resort to proportionality when deciding upon remedies. Second, sometimes these instruments will be of little use. This is precisely the case when a willing licensee, including a manufacturer of components, would like to obtain a licence that the SEP owner denies him, though he had earlier – during the standard-setting process – committed himself to license anyone willing to conclude such an agreement. Third, competition law takes broader interests into account, ones which transcend the interests of individual implementers. Thus, when a healthy competition is at stake, as was the case in the *FTC v. Qualcomm*, competition law is the right tool to apply.

www.ingramcontent.com/pod-product-compliance
Ingram Content Group UK Ltd.
Pitfield, Milton Keynes, MK11 3LW, UK
UKHW020234290926
15470UKWH00002B/546

9 789403 524139